**Preventive
Psychology
(PGPS-122)**

# Pergamon Titles of Related Interest

**Catalano** HEALTH, BEHAVIOR AND THE COMMUNITY:
An Ecological Perspective
**Farber** STRESS AND BURNOUT IN THE HUMAN
SERVICE PROFESSIONS
**Geller/Winett/Everett** PRESERVING THE ENVIRONMENT:
New Strategies for Behavior Change
**Krasner** ENVIRONMENTAL DESIGN AND HUMAN BEHAVIOR:
A Psychology of the Individual in Society

# Related Journals*

CLINICAL PSYCHOLOGY REVIEW
EVALUATION AND PROGRAM PLANNING
NEW IDEAS IN PSYCHOLOGY
PERSONALITY AND INDIVIDUAL DIFFERENCES

**\*Free specimen copies available upon request.**

PERGAMON GENERAL PSYCHOLOGY SERIES
EDITORS
Arnold P. Goldstein, *Syracuse University*
Leonard Krasner, *SUNY at Stony Brook*

# Preventive Psychology
## Theory, Research and Practice

Edited by

### Robert D. Felner
*Auburn University*

### Leonard A. Jason
*DePaul University*

### John N. Moritsugu
*Pacific Lutheran University*

### Stephanie S. Farber
*Yale University*

**Pergamon Press**
**New York  Oxford  Toronto  Sydney  Paris  Frankfurt**

Pergamon Press Offices:

| | |
|---|---|
| **U.S.A.** | Pergamon Press Inc., Maxwell House, Fairview Park, Elmsford, New York 10523, U.S.A. |
| **U.K.** | Pergamon Press Ltd., Headington Hill Hall, Oxford OX3 0BW, England |
| **CANADA** | Pergamon Press Canada Ltd., Suite 104, 150 Consumers Road, Willowdale, Ontario M2J 1P9, Canada |
| **AUSTRALIA** | Pergamon Press (Aust.) Pty. Ltd., P.O. Box 544, Potts Point, NSW 2011, Australia |
| **FRANCE** | Pergamon Press SARL, 24 rue des Ecoles, 75240 Paris, Cedex 05, France |
| **FEDERAL REPUBLIC OF GERMANY** | Pergamon Press GmbH, Hammerweg 6, D-6242 Kronberg-Taunus, Federal Republic of Germany |

**Copyright © 1983 Pergamon Press Inc.**

**Library of Congress Cataloging in Publication Data**

Main entry under title:

Preventive psychology.

    (Pergamon general psychology series ; 122)
    Includes bibliographies and index.
    1. Community mental health services. 2. Mental
illness--Prevention. 3. Community mental health
services--United States. I. Felner, Robert D.
(Robert David), 1950-   . II. Series. [DNLM:
1. Community mental health services. 2. Mental
disorders--Prevention and control. WM 30 P944]
RA790.P7736   1983    362.2′0425   82-24542
ISBN 0-08-026340-2

*Printed in the United States of America*

With love and gratitude to:

Joseph and Roslyn Felner,
Jay and Lynn Jason,
Richard and Hisayo Nisikawa Moritsugu,
Leonard, Lauren and Paul Farber.

# CONTENTS

# FOREWORD

## George W. Albee

Back in 1959, as director of the Task Force on Manpower of the Joint Commission on Mental Illness and Health, I spent a year surveying the nation's needs and resources in the field called mental health. In writing the book *Mental health manpower trends* (Albee, 1959) I came face to face with a very real problem. The number and distribution of persons with serious emotional problems in our society were far beyond what our resources, in terms of both personnel and institutions, could deal with on a one-to-one basis. The gap was so wide as to be impossible ever to bridge. This reality forced me to look for alternatives to the "early treatment" that was the basic message of the final report of that commission, *Action for mental health* (1960). The answer I found was primary prevention. I became convinced of the logic of the public health dictum that holds that no mass disorder afflicting humankind is ever eliminated or brought under control by attempting to treat affected individuals, or by attempting to train individual practitioners in larger numbers. My insight was not widely shared, and the 1960s saw the enthusiastic development of community mental health centers that focused on early treatment. This early treatment, combined with a widespread program of wholesale deinstitutionalization of the severely damaged, was hailed as a revolution in mental health care. Now, with the per-spective of the intervening couple of decades, it is clear that these Bold New Approaches are not working.

Every assessment of the distribution of disturbance in the society arrives at an estimate of approximately 15 percent of the population. In addition to this number of "hard-core cases," each year there is a much larger number of people experiencing intense life crises. And when we realize that in any given year only about 7 million separate persons are seen throughout the entire mental health system, both public and private, we can begin to appreciate the hopelessness of our present efforts. And when we learn that more than 70 percent of all money spent in the mental health field still goes to support mental cases in state institutions and nursing homes, and less than 5 percent is spent on community mental health center inter-ventions, we begin to appreciate where the power lies, and the mismatch between rhetoric and reality.

Clearly the logistics of the situation demand in-creased efforts at primary prevention. But logic and good sense do not always guide the formulation and development of social policy. Too many vested interests depend heavily on an ideology that finds mental ill-nesses inside each individual who displays problems and insists on one-to-one therapy, including the use of psychotropic drugs and other organic forms of treat-ment. We are witnessing the "medicalization of psychiatry" and strong, growing opposition to efforts at social change aimed at alleviating the stresses that many of us believe to be responsible for the higher rate of emotional disturbance among the poor, the powerless, the disenfranchised, and the exploited. The medical model of mental illness is defended vigorously, and proposals favoring social change as critical to primary prevention are attacked with equal vigor (see Lamb and Zusman, 1980; Joffe & Albee, 1981).

Since the authors of the current volume invited me to write the foreword I have been mulling over ways of identifying and crystallizing the sources of the widespread strenuous opposition to primary prevention, to community psychology, and to efforts at positive social change. Recently I have written a long essay on "The politics of nature and nurture" (Albee, 1982). I confessed my growing conviction that:

> Instead of facts being useful as the objective building blocks of theories, rather it is more accurate to say that people, and especially social scientists, select theories that are consistent with their personal values, attitudes, and prejudices and then go out into the world, or into the laboratory, to seek facts that validate their beliefs about the world and about human nature, neglecting or denying observations that contradict their personal prejudices . . . [p. 5].

If social scientists' values influence their perceptions of the world, despite training in the dangers of error and bias, then we should not be surprised to discover that those citizens with the fiercest objections to community improvement programs, to community psychology's efforts, are not making judgments based on unbiased values and perceptions. Pastore (1949) long ago demonstrated the relationship between political values and the preference for nature or nurture explanations of human behavior.

I regard community psychology, of all the psychological specialties, as the most humanistic in its orientation because its primary goal is to improve the human condition, to achieve a more just and fair society and world. And, in the words of a recent street philosopher, those who are not part of the solution are part of the problem.

At the heart of the disagreement over such matters as the usefulness of community mental health programs and social interventions is the larger question of human and societal perfectibility. Those with a humanistic view take the position that human beings can act to save themselves and that human society is perfectible

or improvable. The conservatives, and especially the religious fundamentalists, are convinced that the fall from grace following the disobedience in the Garden of Eden has doomed humankind (they say "man") to eternal damnation except for those who are saved through rebirth and redemption.

The humanistic view of human nature began, according to most historians of philosophy, during the Renaissance in Italy. The early humanistic philosophers emphasized the importance of human freedom and heterodoxy, in opposition to the authoritarian and orthodox intellectual regimentation of the Middle Ages. A new intoxification with freedom, particularly freedom to think forbidden thoughts, often led to intellectual rebellion and consequently to attempts at repression by church authority.

Renaissance humanism stressed the importance of the liberal arts in education, and in particular sought to foster the intellectual independence that had existed in the Greek and Latin cultures before the Middle Ages imposed the authoritarian control of church and state and the rigid class structure of feudalism. The emerging humanistic movement in Italy sought to overthrow those fundamentalist institutions that stressed hierarchy and the determination of social class by the accident of birth. One of the most important Italian humanistic philosophers was Pico della Mirandola (1463–94), a contemporary of Christopher Columbus. Pico published a widely quoted essay entitled "Oration on the dignity of man." He imagined that God's instructions to Adam were as follows:

> I have given you, Adam, neither a predetermined place for a particular aspect nor any special prerogatives in order that you may take and possess these through your own decision and choice. The limitations on the nature of other creatures are contained within my prescribed laws. You shall determine your own nature without constraint from any barrier, by means of the freedom to use power I have entrusted you. I have placed you at the center of the world so that from that point you might see better what is in the world. I have made you neither heavenly nor earthly, neither mortal nor immortal, so that, like a free and sovereign artificer, you might mold and fashion yourself into that form you yourself shall have chosen [see Abbagnano, 1967].

Humanists continue to stress the importance of human freedom, especially the freedom to mold and change people and society, and they emphasize the interrelationship of human beings and nature. This includes the naturalness of the human body. Humanists reject repression and asceticism and they value pleasure, and the value of giving others pleasure, including especially sexual pleasure. Indeed, some of the early Italian humanists argued that the pursuit of pleasure was the sole purpose of human existence. In part, this view was a revolt against the monasticism and aestheticism that had prevailed during the Middle Ages. The early humanists rejected the passive religious life in favor of the active political life, leading, for example, to the message of Machiavelli—that a redistribution and realignment of power was possible through social and political action. It even has been argued (see Abbagnano, 1967) that the Renaissance brought about an awareness of historical perspective, leading eventually to an awareness of the uniqueness and individuality of human personality.

In the field of religion, the humanists emphasized the importance of tolerance for all religions and religious views. Their position was that the different theological beliefs all had a common religious origin, and so they urged mutual respect among various religious views.

Finally, they laid the goundwork for the development of empirical science by questioning the authority of Aristotle and of the Church and insisting on the freedom to investigate questions already regarded as settled by ecclesiastical authority. Among their philosophers of science were Occam and Buridan.

Contemporary humanists include persons embracing diverse economic and political positions. Humanism is a term often applied to Marxism, to Freudianism, to liberalism, to feminism, and to existentialist philosophy. And the pointed hostility expressed by creationist fundamentalists to Darwinian evolution and the social sciences put these in the humanist camp ("if your enemy is my enemy, then we are friends").

Humanists are inclined to focus their attention and interest on the human condition and to believe in its improvability, even perfectibility. It is this view that most angers the fundamentalists. This faith in the malleability of people and of societies poses a serious threat to the theology of the Calvinists, the creationists, the authoritarians, and to conservatives in general, who believe in and yearn for a more rigidly structured society impervious to significant change and inhabited by people forced by their sinful nature to compete for scarce resources—a world of winners and losers, the saved and the damned.

The 19th century witnessed an enormous shift in the direction of more humanistic views of the ultimate fate of humankind. Three thinkers advanced ideas of such power that they changed the course of human thought. The three, of course, were Marx, Darwin and Freud. All three are at the top of the "enemies list" of the fundamentalists.

Marx saw clearly that alienation and dehumanization accompanied the capitalistic industrial society in which the mass of workers had no choice but to sell their labor to perform meaningless tasks for long hours and low pay under the most degrading and unhealthy working conditions. Unwilling to accept such human exploitation as the natural order of things, and seeing religion as the opiate of the masses, Marx had a vision of a future, more perfect world where people would enjoy the products of their own labor, where power was redistributed and decentralized, and where human freedom was enjoyed by all. As yet, no truly Marxist society has appeared.

Marx, of course, was a materialist whose view of the human conditions starts and ends with the physical world. He emphasized the importance of work directed to humanizing nature in order to make the world more hospitable. Humans, through work, can transform their environment, and in a sense create a new world. He emphasized the importance of the social context in forming human consciousness, a phenomenon that is mediated through language, itself learned in a social context. For Marx, alienation develops when people are forced, out of economic necessity, to produce things that do not belong to the worker-producer, who, in the process, becomes alienated from his or her own peers. Workers are nonfulfilled when work is meaningless and they become robotlike. But people can actually choose to change the situation by reaching class consciousness, and injustice can be corrected through societal revolutionary change, when conditions are favorable, according to Marx.

Fromm (1962, pp. 30–31) quotes Marx as saying, "The whole of what is called human history is nothing but the creation of man by human labor, and the emergence of nature for man; he therefore has the evident and irrefutable proof of his *self-creation* and his own *origins*."

Darwin's work was also a dangerous threat to the rigid status quo. At the core of his description of evolution was a doctrine of endless change. Humankind, according to this new view, was not a separate and fixed creation, the result of divine intervention some six thousand years ago, when life was alleged to have been breathed into godlike creatures just a little lower than the angels, creatures who proceeded to disobey God and incur his wrath, thereby earning permanent disfavor and an immutable sentence endlessly to do sweaty toil. Rather the human species, according to Darwin, evolved over millions of years, just like other species. The implications shook religion to its foundations and undermined the traditions on which religious authority was based. The new idea had the power, if accepted, to overturn the doctrine of original sin and of religious pessimism about human nature.

Was Freud a humanist? There is some disagreement. Erich Fromm in *Beyond the chains of illusion* (1962, p. 37) is not sure of his evaluation of Freud as a humanist. Fromm sees the thinking of both Marx and Freud as growing out of a common soil, the humanistic tradition. Fromm argues that Freud's defense of human reason as a source of social control is also in the best tradition of humanism.

Calvin Hall, a serious student of Freud's writings, defines Freud as a true humanist. Hall (1979) suggests that Freud decided on a career in science after listening to a public reading of an essay on nature by Goethe, one of the heroes of humanism. Freud, says Hall,

> always insisted that love and reason could prevail over hate and irrationality. Moreover, he was a humanist through and through; not the kind of humanist who sermonizes about the goodness of people; but rather a humanist who is concerned enough about his fellow men and women to devote his long adult life to treating people, observing and analyzing them, and formulating systematic theories to explain their behavior. The 23 volumes of his writings are an enduring testament to his humanism [p. ii].

After reviewing the similarities and differences between the work of Marx and Freud, Fromm summarizes his own related personal credo. He sees human beings as the product of natural evolution, being part of nature and yet transcending it because of reason and self-awareness. Among other beliefs, Fromm argues that the most important developmental influence is the social structure, the values of the society in which persons are born. He argues for the "perfectibility of man" through reason, in a context of hope and belief, and he concludes that there is ultimately only "One main concern: the question of war and peace," the question of human survival as a race.

A view of human nature almost diametrically opposite to humanism is represented most importantly by the theology of John Calvin and Martin Luther. A number of other Protestant reformers also contributed similar views, but let us call this position "Calvinism," recognizing that its origins include many other sources.

Rotenberg, a professor at Hebrew University, has written extensively on the influence of Calvinism on our views of human nature and especially of human deviance (Rotenberg, 1975, 1978).

Calvin and Luther were theologians who spoke for the growing number of aspirants to middle-class status. They also have been described as being among the greatest haters in history. There were only two ways to escape from the peasantry into the middle class. The first was through relentless dedication to work, so that one could accumulate enough modest capital to become a small entrepreneur. The second was through acquiring an education in reading, writing, and arithmetic, so that one could become a scribe or clerk in the growing commercial world. Both of these routes to middle-class respectability required postponement of marriage and parenthood for long years. Religions that pronounced sex to be sinful and hard work to be righteous helped the necessary process of repression and renunciation.

Calvin insisted on the doctrine of *predestination*: that each person's fate was determined from before his or her birth. The outcome was fixed—eternity in hell or heaven—and nothing one did during one's lifetime could have the slightest effect on the predetermined outcome. This theology stressed rigid determinism and obviously reduced opportunities for human freedom and effective social change to near zero. The doctrine of predestination leads to stigmatic labels (the *good-elect* and the *wicked-damned*) and to the position that human beings are unchangeable. In the Calvinistic tradition, no human intervention can save a person who is damned or hurt a person who is saved. This Calvinist view was the spiritual and historical forerunner of Puritanism and of modern industrial capitalism as well as of the coldly rational scientific approach to the world and to nature. Max Weber, in one of the most famous essays of all time, "The Protestant ethic and the spirit of capitalism," argued that the Protestant ethic provided the spirit of restraint of pleasure, and devotion to work, required by capitalism. One was saved when one was successful in one's calling, and one was damned if one was an economic or moral failure.

It is clear that the possibility of compromise between the Calvinists and the humanists is small. The differences in belief and world view are profound. The most important difference, of course, is the question of individual and social perfectibility. The humanists think perfection may be strived for, and the Calvinists know it is not only impossible but a subversive idea. For Calvin, economic success was a favorable sign of ultimate salvation; moral looseness, sloth, and pleasure-seeking all pointed to damnation. (And so the two positions still hold today.)

In the field of psychopathology, the Calvinistic position was well represented by Herbert Spencer's views on social Darwinism, the economic survival of the fittest, and by Lombroso's view that criminals showed physical defects that identified them as born criminal types, which led to his proposal that natural-born murderers be put to death as a way of helping the process of natural selection. Both Rotenberg and Fromm concluded that Calvinism denies the modifiabilty of human beings once born, and supports the general disbelief in the possibility of change. If a person is either mad or bad, he or she cannot be saved.

It should not surprise us to find a close association between authoritarian Calvinistic political and religious beliefs and the view that "mental illness" is due to personal defect arising out of constitutional inferiority and genetic and/or biochemical weakness. Closely associated with this view of mental illness as reflecting a personal internal defect are treatment philosophies that stress organic intervention—shock therapies, lobotomies, and other physiological kinds of intervention, including massive doses of heavy tranquilizing drugs. (I am *not* arguing that everyone who does physiological or genetic or biochemical research on psychopathology is, ipso facto, a Calvinist or an authoritarian. But I *am* saying that extremists who insist with certainty and without firm data that biological causes are responsible for mental disorders, racial differences, sexual inequality, and the natural superiority or inferiority of any group of human beings are Calvinists under the skin.)

Persons holding *humanistic* views are much more likely to see psychopathology as resulting from normal learning processes occurring in pathological social environments. Sincere persons listening to the debate between the organicists and the environmentalists might sometimes ask, "What difference does it make? The behavior is identical, whether the person's disturbance is caused by bad genes or by a bad infancy or early childhood." The answer to this question is also fairly simple: The *Calvinistic* view holds out no hope for any kind of efforts at social and community change, while the *humanistic* view leaves open the possibility of effective approaches to primary prevention.

Again we come face to face with the question of human perfectibility. The Calvinists deny any possibility of improving the human condition and the humanists insist that it is possible.

There are several misunderstandings frequently associated with the humanistic view of mental disturbance. Some of these may be deliberate distortions invented by the opposition, but others may be honest misunderstandings.

First of all, the organicists often attack the humanists by calling them *dualists*, and ridicule any explanation of human behavior that is alleged to arise from the operations of an ethereal "mind." They argue that all true scientists must come to the defense of the biological origins of behavior, and that the humanists are unscientific in suggesting that "mental illness" can occur in the absence of organic pathology. Let us make clear that the humanistic view does not need, nor depend on, the concept of *mind*. Rather it argues that it is the concept of mental *illness* that is unnecessary (except in the case of a few specific organic conditions). The humanists do not disagree with the view that all behavior can be understood as resulting from underlying *biological* activity, from measurable physical processes. Similarly, all mental events, they agree, can also be understood as resulting from biological changes. The critical point is that the humanistic view does not require that these underlying processes be pathological or abnormal. Certainly both the Freudians and the behaviorists would agree that all behavior can be traced to underlying biological and chemical "causes." Those who argue against the concept of mental "illness" do not deny the existence of behavior that can be called abnormal or pathological. They simply hold that abnormal behavior can be learned through perfectly normal processes—and what can be learned can be unlearned, or prevented.

I am pleased to line up with the community psychologists, and those other humanists, who believe in social change, the effectiveness of consultation and education, the primary prevention of human physical and emotional misery, and the maximization of individual competence.

## References

Abbagnano, N. Humanism. In P. Edwards (Ed.), *The encyclopedia of philosophy*. Vol. 3. New York: Macmillan & Free Press, 1972.

*Action for mental health*. Final Report of the Joint Commission on Mental Illness and Health. New York: Basic Books, 1960.

Albee, G. W. *Mental health manpower trends*. New York: Basic Books, 1959.

Albee, G. W. The politics of nature and nurture. *American Journal of Community Psychology*, 1982.

Fromm, E. *Beyond the chains of illusion: My encounter with Marx and Freud*. New York: Simon and Schuster, 1962.

Hall, C. A *primer of Freudian psychology*. Cleveland: World Publishing Company, 1954; New American Library, Inc., 1979.

Joffe, J. & Albee, G. (Eds.) *Primary prevention of psycho-pathology*. Vol. 5. *Prevention through political action and social change*. Hanover, N.H.: University Press of New England, 1981.

Lamb, H. & Zusman, J. Primary prevention in perspective. *American Journal of Psychiatry*, 1979, **136**, 12–17.

Pastore, N. The nature-nurture controversy. New York: Columbia University Press, 1949.

Rotenberg, M. The Protestant ethic against the spirit of psychiatry: The other side of Weber's thesis. *The British Journal of Sociology*, 1975, **26**(1), 52–65.

Rotenberg, M. *Damnation and deviance*. New York: Free Press, 1978.

# PREFACE

The decision to undertake this volume was influenced by several factors. Perhaps the most overriding was our concern with how, if prevention is to best continue to grow and thrive within psychology, it should relate to existing specialties such as clinical, developmental or social. In its infancy, prevention was safely and almost exclusively housed in community psychology. As prevention grew, parallel shifts occurred in the orientations of other specialties to include applied concerns in addition to basic research. Work that was either directly or indirectly relevant to or identifiable as prevention began to appear with increasing frequency outside the confines of community psychology. However, due to the traditional separations between those in the subdisciplines of psychology, as well as those regularities that support and foster these distinctions (e.g., separate journals, etc.) there was often insufficient cross-fertilization, although parallel bodies of knowledge bearing on prevention were being developed. Issues of "turf," however unintentionally, have inhibited the growth of an integrated body of knowledge to inform prevention. Along with many others, the editors of this volume have spent long hours trying to answer the troubling questions of what a community psychologist does and how it differs from what a pediatric/applied, social/applied, developmental/health or clinical psychologist does. That such distinctions often serve useful purposes

is unquestionable; it is also clear that individuals may become "cathected" to their identities. Anyone who doubts this should call a clinician a developmentalist or vice versa. More often than not, the offender will at the very least find himself being quickly corrected. However, at least for us, what has gradually emerged from the long debates is that when it comes to prevention's future in psychology, such traditional distinctions may be as detrimental to its growth as they are facilitative. One of the strengths of prevention is the breadth and diversity of perspectives that contribute to current paradigms. We have now reached a point where an identifiable "core" body of knowledge is emerging which may inform both the conceptualization and implementation of prevention efforts. If this process is to continue, it is important that those concerned with prevention transcend traditional specialty boundaries and labels, recognize the commonality of their concerns, and increase the level of intraspecialty interchange. It is our hope that this text, by presenting graduate students and professionals with a critical examination of work from each of the contributing specialties, will facilitate the attainment of these goals and, hence, advance the growth of preventive psychology.

As a second goal, we hope to stimulate the education of a next generation of preventive psychologists, from diverse specialties, by providing a single volume that is appropriate for a course with that goal and constituency. Current volumes on community psychology have much to contribute to prevention; indeed, the area of prevention owes more than a little of its current ascendancy to its community psychology roots. As we have noted, however, the two are no longer one and the same. Similarly, while volumes on applied developmental, applied social, or environmental psychology may have as much or more to offer preventive psychologists on the particular issues covered in some of the chapters in this book, they neither seek to present nor provide an overview of the broad range of prevention's concerns. This volume was designed to sample the wide range of prevention's conceptual empirical base and provide a broader context for more specialty-focused efforts that may follow.

We hope that by making the tasty smorgasbord of issues and challenges that prevention offers accessible to students in one volume, it will stimulate interest in such efforts by those who might otherwise have focused their efforts elsewhere. As students who went to school when a different Zeitgeist was present in the land, we are all too aware of how current conditions, while making prevention an appealing idea, may lead students to turn to more secure, clearly defined, and financially rewarding alternatives. Prevention is a difficult enough endeavor to engage in for professionals. The additional obstacle of having to draw together a broad and often scattered knowledge base may lead some who might otherwise have become involved in "doing" to falter early in their efforts. We hope that this volume may make the way just a little bit smoother.

We owe a debt of gratitude to many people who contributed directly or indirectly to this book. Our special thanks to Emory L. Cowen and Seymour B. Sarason whose ideas, caring, and friendship have helped to mold not only this book but our lives. No words can fully express the gratitude and affection we feel toward them. A number of good friends, among them N. Dickon Reppucci, Julian Rappaport, Edward Seidman, Raymond Lorion, Louis Heifetz, Richard Price, LaRue Allen, David Britt, and Edwin Zolik have added to our thinking about prevention over the years and have been important sources of support. David Stenmark and the bright and stimulating University of South Florida graduate students hosted the Tampa Conference where the initial idea for this volume was born. To them we are sincerely grateful.

We would also like to extend thanks to the following individuals who read parts of this volume and offered valuable constructive feedback: Mark Mathews, Susan Shorr-Zaline, David Glenwick, Thomas Rose, and Leonard Krasner. Expert editing of several sections of the book by Pamela Woll and the assistance of Nancy Rospenda in the preparation of parts of the manuscript are also deeply appreciated.

Throughout the long journey this volume has followed from idea to finished product, Jerry Frank, senior editor at Pergamon, has been there to encourage, prod, "nudge," and in whatever other way possible provide aid in moving the project to completion. We thank him for his commitment to excellence, his belief in us, and his patience.

To exercise my "right" as senior editor, I would like also to make some special acknowledgments. Completing this work while dealing with other "transitional tasks" might have proven impossible without the intellectual climate and emotional support provided by Peter Harzem and Phillip Lewis. I thank them for their forbearance, friendship, and support. Mark Aber, Janet Gillespie, Annette Stanton, and Leonard Doerfler provided sympathetic ears, critical comments, and boosts for my flagging spirits when they were sorely needed.

Much of this book belongs to one who is not listed among the authors or contributors. She saw me through long hours of revisions, editing, and frustration. Her critical comments, hard work, and commitment to the project have contributed immeasurably to making this a better manuscript. Only she knows what it meant for her to be there at its end. Without her warmth, good humor, and companionship, my experience with this project and my life would both be much the poorer. For what she has given me, I give her my love and affection.

This volume arose out of the joint effort of friends and valued colleagues, and, as anyone who has undertaken a similar task knows, it is a tribute to that friendship that those bonds are all the stronger for our shared experiences. While each of us was responsible for different aspects of the book, our ideas and thoughts, both on prevention and on this volume, are so intertwined that it would be impossible to trace the beginning and ending of either.

R. D. F.
January, 1983

# Preventive Psychology
# (PGPS-122)

# PART I
# PERSPECTIVES ON PREVENTION

# 1 PREVENTIVE PSYCHOLOGY: EVOLUTION AND CURRENT STATUS

Robert D. Felner,
Leonard A. Jason,
John Moritsugu, and
Stephanie S. Farber

A concern with the application of the knowledge base and conceptual frameworks of psychology and psychiatry to the prevention of emotional and physical disorder is now well established as having a central place in the mental health field. Indeed, in discussing primary prevention in mental health, Cowen (1982) states, "For diverse reasons (primary prevention) is an 'in' term and a valued term—an appealing movement that many people would like to join [p. 240]." Excellent discussions of the evolution of primary prevention as a focus of mental health professionals, the paradigm shifts required, and the controversies which have surrounded such shifts have been offered in a number of volumes (e.g., Bloom, 1975; Caplan, 1964; Cowen & Zax, 1967; Glenwick & Jason, 1980; Iscoe & Spielberger, 1970; Rappaport, 1977; Sarason, Levine, Goldenberg, Cherlin & Bennett, 1966). While we shall provide a brief overview below of some of the key factors which have shaped the evolution of preventive psychology and serve as a context for understanding its current status, the reader is encouraged to consult these works for more detailed treatments of the historical background of psychology and psychiatry's concern with prevention.

Given this background of established interest and scholarly activity we were quite unprepared for the comments we received on the title of this volume as we discussed its progress with colleagues. Statements ranged from "What are you going to do—prevent psychology?" to "It's about time we used the term 'preventive psychology'—psychiatry and social work have been recognizing a distinct specialty in prevention within their disciplines for years." This latter comment came from a member of the staff of the Prevention Office of the National Institute of Mental Health. It should be noted that the former comment, or ones similar to it, came from a number of sources, generally in fun, but often, it seemed, accompanied by genuine puzzlement. The reasons for such puzzlement as well as for the development of this volume, and why we feel that the time has come for psychology to recognize the field of preventive psychology (a term which reflects the broad-based conceptual, programmatic, and empirical efforts which characterize current preventive efforts in mental health) can perhaps be best understood in the context of a brief overview of the birth and evolution of a focus on prevention by psychology.

## Historical Factors and Evolution of Prevention

Sarason (1981) has eloquently underscored the role of federal legislative priorities and funding patterns in shaping the mental health establishment's definition of psychological problems as well as the appropriate strategies for dealing with them. As a key example he points to the ways in which the federal government's identification of the psychological needs of discharged and returning veterans at the end of World War II as a matter of national priority, and the consequent appropriation of large sums of money to the Veterans Administration, served to shape the development of clinical psychology. Government funding patterns and statements of priorities may also be seen to have both provided the impetus for preventive psychology and shaped its evolution. Much, although certainly not all, of the research which played a central role in leading to a focus on prevention as an important and viable alternative model for mental health (Cowen, 1980) may be seen to be directly attributable to legislative actions. Let us now briefly provide an overview of the key historical occurrences which may help to illuminate this process.

The Joint Commission on Mental Health and Mental Illness was established by Congress in 1955 by the passage of the Mental Health Study Act. The mandate of the Joint Commission was heavily weighted toward the development of preventive programs (Caplan, 1964). Caplan notes that part of the commission's directive was "to carry out a nationwide analysis and reevaluation of the human and economic problems of mental illness and of the resources, methods and practices currently utilized . . . as may lead to the development of comprehensive and realistic recommendations . . . as give promise of resulting in a marked reduction in the incidence or duration of mental illness, and, in consequence, a lessening of the appalling emotional and financial drain on those affected or on the economic resources of the States and of the Nation [Joint Commission Report, 1961, p. 303]." While the final report gave relatively less emphasis to prevention than to strategies for treating individuals who already were displaying dysfunction (Caplan, 1964; Iscoe & Spielberger, 1970), it nonetheless still had considerable significance for the development of an increased emphasis on prevention in mental health. Under the sponsorship of the Joint Commission, a number of studies of the distribution of mental health services, the magnitude of mental health problems, the adequacy of mental health resources, and the limitations of what, at that time, were the accepted forms of mental health practice were carried out (Cowen & Zax, 1967; Iscoe & Spielberger, 1970). One such study by Robinson, DeMarche, and Wagle (1960) found that available mental health resources were woefully inadequate and inequitably distributed. Mental health services to ethnic and racial minority groups were found to be almost totally lacking, with the exception of state hospitals, and less than a quarter of the nation's counties were found to have mental health clinics. Gurin, Veroff,

and Field (1960) demonstrated that the utilization of mental health resources was in large part determined by socioeconomic factors, with mental health services generally being unavailable to the lower classes. Finally, in what has now become a landmark work, Albee (1959) documented the shortage of mental health manpower which would result from the continued reliance on a rehabilitative, one-to-one model of mental health service delivery. In arguing for the expansion of preventive efforts and research he stated:

> What we need are techniques and methods enabling far more people to be reached per professional person. If we do not at present have such techniques then we should spend time looking for them. . . . Just as typhoid fever was never brought under control by treating individual cases of the disease, but rather by discovering and taking steps to remove the source of the disease, so may we find that time might be spent more effectively in prevention, in research, or in public health approaches to mental disorder [p. 254].

These studies and others were integrated into the final report of the Joint Commission, and its recommendations were reflected in President Kennedy's Message on Mental Health and Mental Retardation to the U.S. Congress in February 1963. In this message the president called for an approach to mental health which emphasized that the prevention and treatment of mental illness was a community responsibility and not a private problem (Caplan, 1964). Consistent with this emphasis and the findings of the Joint Commission, he proposed the establishment of comprehensive community mental health centers. In response, Congress passed the Mental Retardation Facilities and Community Mental Health Centers Construction Act of 1963 (Public Law #88-164), which provided for the establishment of comprehensive community mental health centers across the country. Iscoe and Spielberger (1970) point out that as a result of this act and the services it mandated centers to provide, "For the first time in the history of the mental health movement the focus of treatment was ostensibly to be in the community as contrasted to the mental hospital [p. 9]."

The findings of the Joint Commission studies and the resultant legislation were not the only factors leading to the search for alternative strategies for dealing with mental health problems in the 1950s and 1960s. Concerns about the efficacy and limitations of psychotherapy were also serving to focus attention on the potential of preventive approaches. For example, after discussing the promise and problems of psychotherapy Cowen and Zax (1967) stated, "Our hopes for the future should reside as much, or more, in cutting down the flow of disorder as in developing more effective technologies for undoing damage [p. 18]." In a similar vein, psychology more generally was recognizing the need for a shift in the emphasis of mental health programs. A position paper on comprehensive mental health centers adopted by the Council of Representatives of the American Psychological Association in 1966 underscored the need for approaches to community mental health problems which were quite different from the more traditional clinical approaches. A focus on social systems and social processes in the community was emphasized, as well as the prevention of disorder and the promotion of mental health (Iscoe & Spielberger, 1970).

Parallel developments in psychiatry and public health further fueled the evolution of an emphasis on prevention in mental health. Caplan (1964) has documented the central place mental health holds in public health professionals' views of what the essential facets of preventive efforts are. Similarly, psychiatry draws heavily on Erich Lindemann's (1944) studies of the bereavement reactions of the survivors of those killed in the Coconut Grove nightclub fire, and his development of the fundamentals of crisis theory, for the early development of conceptual frameworks for prevention (Caplan, 1964). Given the sentiments of Sarason (1981), noted above, about the central role of funding availability in shaping the direction taken by mental health, it is also worth noting that Caplan (1964) points to the key role of the financial support provided by the W. T. Grant Foundation in supporting the early studies in preventive psychiatry by Lindemann and others (Leighton, 1959; Ojemann, Levitt, Lyle, & Whitesie, 1955; Prescott, 1957). Assuredly, such private support was also invaluable in maintaining the growth of preventive approaches before they were widely accorded a central place in mental health.

The confluence of these factors led to the recognition of the need for appropriate training of psychologists in community mental health, consultation, community-oriented program development, and prevention (Iscoe & Spielberger, 1970). In response, a conference on the "Education of Psychologists for Community Mental Health" was held in Swampscott, Massachusetts, in the spring of 1965. Here the term "community psychology" was coined to indicate that the role of psychologists in community affairs was broader than merely community mental health. Further, the latter was viewed as but a subspeciality of community psychology, with clinical psychology seen

as a variant of community mental health (Iscoe & Spielberger, 1970). Particularly emphasized as primary concerns for community psychology were prevention and the need to examine social institutions, systems, and settings as determinants of the emotional well-being of individuals. By contrast, the role of more traditional clinical services was downplayed. These positions have been reiterated and expanded upon in later conferences on the nature and evolution of community psychology (Iscoe, Bloom, & Spielberger, 1977; Rosenblum, 1971).

The model of prevention adopted by psychology was in large part borrowed from the field of public health. Here the term "prevention" is an all-embracing one, having three separate levels: primary, secondary, and tertiary (Goldston, 1977). Tertiary prevention closely parallels traditional approaches. The focus is on the individual who has established disorder, and the goals are to reduce the residual effects of it and to rehabilitate the individual to a level where he or she may readjust to community life. Secondary prevention efforts are characterized by attempts at early identification and intervention with individuals who are displaying initial signs of disorder, but for whom it is not yet ingrained. Zax and Spector (1974) caution that it may be argued that early detection and effective treatment of mental disorder in an individual may be little more than what has long been viewed as good mental health care.

Finally, primary prevention has been an elusive term. A number of alternative goals and strategies have been proposed (Bloom, 1979; Cowen, 1982; Goldston, 1977). However, the goals of primary prevention may be broadly subsumed under the heading of either (1) the reduction of new cases of disorders or (2) the promotion of health and building of competencies as protection against dysfunction (Felner & Aber, 1983).

Ironically, even a clear focus on prevention may to some extent systematically focus our attention on some of primary prevention's goals at the expense of others. That is, by emphasizing "prevention" our focus may, however unintentionally, remain on the avoidance of disorder, at the expense of focusing on factors which may produce positive outcomes. Illustratively, Cowen (1982) has pointed out that the extent of efforts focused on the latter concern are relatively insignificant when compared to the field's investment in pathology.

Taking this argument several steps further, Rappaport (1981), in discussing preventive approaches, suggests that they may be incorrect interventions insofar as they portray the interventionists as experts who provide remedial skills or competencies to individuals.

As a response to this one-sided solution, Rappaport proposes an empowerment model in which efforts are made to allow natural helpers and other citizens to solve their own problems, with the psychologist acting as a resource provider. In this collaborative model the psychologist is working not to "tag" individuals and help them avoid uncomfortable life patterns, but to help citizens become empowered by providing resources and support to enable them to activate self-corrective capacities. We believe this position is a valuable caveat for professionals working within an alternative delivery style such as prevention. However, we also feel that this model is not incompatable with a "preventive" model which is focused on the enhancement of competencies and the facilitation of optimal development unimpeded by environmental hazards as well as the avoidance of the development of disorders. Skills and competencies may be provided to individuals and aspects of the environment modified to meet these goals in ways which do not imply unequal power between those impacted by the intervention and those who design it. Preventive mental health professionals may negotiate with individuals and/or settings to establish contracts to reach prevention goals in collaborative fashion, rather than "placing" the program "on" them. And certainly it would be difficult to conceive of intervention efforts which modify environments in ways which are complementary to the coping skills and abilities of the individual in them, or which remove hazards such as stress-exacerbating conditions, as placing the "target" in a "one down" position. To further insure this does not occur, preventive psychologists, consistent with the empowerment model (Rappaport, 1981), need to be sensitive to the culture and traditions of the individuals or settings they work with. Toward this end, two-way communication in designing preventive interventions is an essential ingredient. As can be seen, within the context of preventive psychology many (although perhaps not all) of the activities and goals may be congruent with, or at the least not contradictory to, those of empowerment. Indeed, it should be noted that the basic goals of preventive psychology—optimal development, reduction of environmental hazards, avoidance of maladaptation, and enhancement of coping skills and ability—are precisely those conditions which empower persons in their daily lives.

It should be recognized that while a great deal of conceptual rhetoric and debate about primary prevention has been generated since the early 1960s, the actual accomplishments have been far less (Cowen, 1982). Certainly far more of the preventive efforts undertaken in the name of prevention or community psychology, at least to date, would be better categorized as focused on secondary prevention and/or pathology than can be legitimately viewed as concerned with positive adaptive outcomes. Given the difference between rhetoric and action, it may be justifiably asked what factors have systematically contributed to this gap. As is discussed in more detail in several of the chapters which follow (for example, Chapter 2 and Chapter 12), some of the blame can be attributed to the lack of conceptual clarity which has characterized efforts to delineate the domain of prevention. However, it is also important to understand the nature and historical regularities of the mental health field, and particularly psychology, in order to understand the evolutionary path prevention has followed. Prevention did not emerge full-blown as a distinct alternative to more traditional approaches, represented by a set of advocates who were immersed in its traditions and educated in its conceptual, empirical, and programmatic knowledge base. For the most part, neither such traditions nor such knowledge existed. Instead, prevention as a focus for psychology grew out of the context of the field as it existed at the time of the Joint Commission Report and the Swampscott Conference. While wishing to evolve new and revolutionary alternatives to traditional mental health services, the early proponents of prevention were at the same time constrained by their own training and professional socialization experiences. Although they spoke about the need to consider social settings and institutions and emphasize prevention, the fact was that the participants in the Swampscott Conference had been trained in a tradition, that of clinical psychology, that focused on the individual as the source of his or her own difficulties and which emphasized symptoms over competencies (Sarason, 1981). This point is graphically brought home by Iscoe and Speilberger (1970), who point out that a large proportion of the charter members of the Division of Community Psychology were not only trained in clinical psychology but were senior persons in the field, many with ABEPP diplomas in clinical psychology.

The point in psychology's history at which prevention came to the fore not only limited the vision of those who were involved in its early development, it also limited who was "legitimately" involved. Although there were notable exceptions, social, developmental, and other "nonclinical" psychologists of that time were generally not primarily concerned with direct application and development of intervention programs. Practical applications, and particularly interventions with or for the emotionally disturbed, were the province of the clinical psychologist and the newly born community psychologist, with the laboratory generally the private preserve of the experimental social psychologist or developmentalist.

Given this backdrop it is not surprising that many of community psychology's early preventive efforts, while certainly innovative for the time, appear upon careful examination suspiciously like clinical interventions. For example, the use of nonprofessionals to work with schoolchildren identified as displaying early signs of maladjustment was certainly a radical departure from much of what had gone before. The use of nonprofessionals, the timing of the interventions, and the setting in which they took place were all innovative and important steps forward in mental health delivery and the path to prevention. Nonetheless, it needs to be recognized that these early efforts still reflected a model that was built upon one-to-one or small group intervention between "helpers" and a child who demonstrated some clearly identifiable maladaptive behavior (Zax & Spector, 1974). It is not our intent to imply that current secondary prevention models, or those which preceded them, are not vital elements of the mental health field. Rather, our intent is to illustrate that although the rhetoric of mental health has changed rapidly toward prevention, the necessary conceptual frameworks, knowledge bases, and program models have been slower in developing. Indeed, Cowen (1982) has noted that serious substantive differences continue to exist between primary prevention's content and methodology and that of most mental health training programs, and these differences continue to constrain the development of effective preventive efforts.

While Cowen (1982) is certainly correct, at least to some extent, in his contention that the gaps between mental health training generally, the knowledge base it may draw on, and primary prevention are still quite large, significant changes in the field of psychology since the Swampscott Conference have narrowed these gaps and give promise of continued progress. Within clinical psychology, many of the ideas and intervention strategies which seemed so new and innovative when initially raised by community psychology as a reaction to traditional clinical psychology are now widely accepted as part of the latter's standard knowledge base. Crisis intervention and crisis centers using nonprofessionals, consultation with regard to social settings and institutions, and a concern with prevention are but a few of the ideas and practices which have gone from innovative to mainstream status in clinical/community psychology training programs. One only has to examine the recent guidelines of the National Institute of Mental Health on defining priority areas for funding through Clinical Psychology Training grants to see just how far this integration has gone. Prevention was one of four priority areas enumerated; a second related to the serving of underserved settings. Clearly, even if prevention is not always a welcome guest in clinical psychology's house, it is at least now a generally accepted one.

Another important evolutionary development in psychology in the almost two decades since Swampscott is in the orientation of the "nonclinical" areas. Developmental, social, and other nonclinical psychologists have become involved in intervention program development and direct provision of mental health services at ever-increasing levels. Preventive efforts such as Head Start, infant stimulation programs, projects for high-risk infants (Jason, 1977), and enhancement of problem-solving in children (see Chapter 3 of the present volume), as well as the increasingly prominent preventive role of psychologists in pediatric settings (Felner, 1982), well illustrate the range of involvement by developmentalists in prevention. Preventive activities of social psychologists range from efforts to understand and modify the effects of physical and social environments on human adaptation (Krasner, 1980; see also Chapter 5 of this volume) to concern with psychological factors which relate to physical health maintenance and promotion (for example, Janis & Rodin, 1979). The increasingly central place such activities occupy for social and developmental psychologists is also reflected in the recent emergence of such scholarly journals as the *Journal of Applied Social Psychology, The Journal of Applied Developmental Psychology,* and *The Journal of Social and Clinical Psychology.*

The importance of these developments for the continued evolution of successful prevention strategies cannot be underestimated. Cowen (1982) has pointed out that a key factor underlying the shortage of innovative and effective program paradigms for primary prevention may be that the knowledge base required for such programming extends across many of the areas of psychology, as well as beyond it, to related disciplines such as sociology and political science.

In developing this volume, our particular concern in defining a field of preventive psychology was to recognize, encourage, and facilitate the increasing involvement of psychologists from many different specialties in preventive activities. It was our hope that by avoiding labels such as "community" or "applied" psychology, and instead employing one which reflected the transcendence of specialty boundaries that is reflected in successful preventive efforts, we may contribute to the evolution of an integrated and shared knowledge base for preventive psychologists, whatever their background specialty. We are accustomed to thinking of prevention programs being mounted primarily under the banner of community psychology. However, by recognizing a field of preventive psychology we may acknowledge the broader domain from which may be drawn the essential conceptual and empirical knowledge base that can inform successful interventions. Community psychology, developmental psychology, health psychology, social psychology, and environmental psychology are distinct basic specialties, as is preventive psychology. The domains of these specialties, compared to one another, are broader in focus in some aspects and narrower in focus in others. None of the other specialties are part of preventive psychology or superordinate to it. However, the concerns of each of the other specialties do overlap those of preventive psychology to some extent, and this may provide theory and empirical data which may be integrated to help inform the essential core concerns of preventive psychology. That is, the nature of those abilities, skills, and characteristics of individuals and those aspects of the social and physical environment which relate to an individual's or a population's differential vulnerability and resistance to the development of somatic or psychological dysfunction and which facilitate positive adaptive outcomes, competency, and well-being.

Preventive psychology owes much to its roots in community psychology and to the contribution of the other specialties within psychology, as well as such related fields as social policy analysis and law, which fostered its growth in their home soil until it was strong enough to stand on its own. We feel that because of what has been learned to date, as well as the demands which will be placed on prevention in the future, the time has come for the field of preventive psychology to begin to clearly establish its own identity and, by so doing, facilitate the growth and integration of theory and empirical evidence which may lead to successful prevention efforts.

## Overview of the Volume

The volume is organized into six major sections, with brief overviews of the rationale for the contents of each and the chapters they encompass provided at the outset of all but this the introductory section. The principal aims of the present chapter are to explore those forces which have shaped the evolution of preventive psychology, to define its place within the specialties of psychology, and to elaborate the theoretical perspectives and concerns which have guided the development of this volume. The second chapter provides a more detailed examination of the background and current guiding frameworks and concerns of primary prevention, particularly in mental health. Taken

together they serve to define the scope of this volume and provide a context for viewing the contents of the chapters which follow.

The second, third, and fourth sections provide perspectives on some of the central conceptual and empirical issues which have served as the principal foci around which theory and practice in prevention have been organized to date. It was our intent in choosing this approach—as opposed to one which, for example, organized discussions around populations targeted or settings involved—to highlight the theoretical and empirical bases which underlie preventive efforts across a wide array of settings and populations and, in so doing, to facilitate both their refinement and application in as yet untried ways. Thus contributors in these sections, as well as later ones, were asked to focus their discussions wherever possible in such a way as to cut across applications and specific problems, and to emphasize overriding conceptual issues.

The chapters in the second section of the volume have as their focus perspectives on prevention which emphasize enhancing development of the individual through promoting social competence, particularly problem-solving abilities and social skills. Whether to include a chapter on general coping skills and abilities was a question which we also confronted. Certainly the relevance of such material for our concerns is undeniable. However, as the volume evolved it became clear that due to the nature of coping and its interaction with the particular concerns of the chapters in this section and the two which follow it, each chapter would, in fact, be discussing a set of factors which contribute to an individual's coping abilities or interact with them to shape their adaptive functioning. Thus we elected to focus on such concerns as they specifically related to the theoretical issues and data in an area, rather than providing a more global discussion. Indeed, given the focus of prevention on the enhancement of functioning and reduction of vulnerability to disorder, it may be said that all of the specific content areas which contribute to preventive efforts comprise elements of the coping process.

The third section is devoted to elaborating characteristics of social systems and the physical environment which impact on the adjustment of individuals and which may be utilized in preventing disorder and/or facilitating development. The section begins with a discussion of the impact of the social environment on human adaptation and elaborates current conceptual and empirical literature relating to efforts to assess and change social environments. A second chapter examines the nature of social support systems and explores their links to adaptive functioning and well-being. The third chapter elaborates current work and thought concerning the dimensions of the physical environment which influence adjustment and health. The final chapter of the section discusses behavioral contingencies which exist in the environment and ways of perceiving settings which allow for the modification of such contingencies to prevent somatic and psychological dysfunction.

The fourth major section of the book also deals with environmental influences on an individual's adjustment. However, rather than focusing on environmental variables which may be modified to facilitate adaptation, this section focuses on environmental factors which are hazardous to an individual's functioning, such as stressful life circumstances and life changes around which preventive efforts may be organized. The chapters in this section draw heavily on the theory and evidence discussed in the preceding ones and illustrate the utility of this knowledge, when integrated, for conceptualizing and attacking specific risk-predisposing factors. The first three chapters in this section concentrate on the effects of lower socioeconomic group status, chronic minority status, and economic stress more generally. The fourth chapter, somewhat different in focus, centers upon the implications of stressful life events and transitions for preventive efforts and elaborates how such events and changes may be conceptualized to aid in the development of efforts to produce positive adaptive outcomes as well as forestall dysfunction.

The fifth section of this book deals with some of the broad concerns which confront the preventive psychologist in moving from theory and data to action. The first chapter confronts what is the often critical distinction between preventive efforts in mental health and those where psychological processes interact with physical well-being, toward the goal of developing fuller and better-integrated knowledge bases for both areas. The overlap among some of the core concerns of each area is elaborated and the differences discussed. In the next chapter issues involved in interdisciplinary collaboration are presented and illustrated. The third chapter examines the reasons for the differences between psychology's efforts in the social policy arena and its actual impact, as a way of cautioning and informing future ventures in this area by preventive psychologists. Finally, the fourth chapter considers the place of evaluation in preventive intervention and offers a framework for understanding the need for and guiding of implementation.

The final section of the volume offers two chapters on the problems and prospects for training preventive psychologists. The first of these examines how training in prevention has been incorporated into traditional training settings and offers suggestions for future efforts in this vein. The second chapter confronts some of the broad issues in the education of psychologists who must deal with the range of issues encompassed by the domain of prevention.

Finally, we are fortunate to have the contributions of Dr. George Albee and Dr. John Glidewell, whose unique experiences with and perspectives on prevention in psychology and its evolution have been brought to bear in the discussions which frame this volume, in their Foreword and Afterword, respectively.

Though many of the theoretical frameworks, lines of inquiry, and strategies for application and training discussed in this volume are still in an early stage of development, they are nonetheless important, as they are among the first clear-cut paradigms to emerge for informing preventive psychology. If this volume facilitates the further elaboration and refinement of these developments and serves as a stimulus to further integration and innovation in developing prevention's knowledge base, then it will have achieved its goals.

## References

Albee, G. W. *Mental health manpower trends.* New York: Basic Books, 1959.

Bloom, B. L. *Community mental health: A general introduction.* Monterey, Calif.: Brooks/Cole, 1975.

Bloom, B. L. Prevention of mental disorders: Recent advances in theory and practice. *Community Mental Health Journal,* 1979, **15,** 179–191.

Caplan, G. *Principles of preventive psychiatry.* New York: Basic Books, 1964.

Cowen, E. L. The wooing of primary prevention. *American Journal of Community Psychology,* 1980, 8, 258–284.

Cowen, E. L. The special number: A complete roadmap. *American Journal of Community Psychology,* 1982, 10, 239–250.

Cowen, E. L., Gardner, E. A., & Zax, M. (Eds.) *Emergent approaches to mental health problems.* New York: Appleton-Century-Crofts, 1967.

Cowen, E. L., & Zax, M. The mental health fields today: Issues and problems. In E. L. Cowen, E. A. Gardner, & M. Zax (Eds.), *Emergent approaches to mental health problems.* New York: Appleton-Century-Crofts, 1967.

Felner, R. D. Primary prevention in pediatric settings: Enhancing coping in vulnerable children. Presentation to the 90th Annual Meeting of the American Psychological Association, Washington, D.C., August 1982.

Felner, R. D., & Aber, M. S. Primary prevention for children: A framework for the assessment of need. *Prevention in Human Services,* 1983, in press.

Glenwick, D. S., & Jason, L. A. *Behavioral community psychology: Progress and prospects.* New York: Praeger, 1980.

Goldston, S. E. Defining primary prevention. In G. W. Albee & J. M. Joffee (Eds.), *Primary prevention of psychopathology.* Vol. 1. *The issues.* Hanover, N.H.: University Press of New England, 1977.

Gurin, G., Veroff, J., & Field, S. *Americans view their mental health.* New York: Basic Books, 1960.

Iscoe, I., & Spielberger, C. D. The emerging field of community psychology. In I. Iscoe & C. D. Speilberger (Eds.), *Community psychology: Perspectives in training and research*. New York: Appleton-Century-Crofts, 1970.

Iscoe, I., Bloom, B. L., & Spielberger, C. D. (Eds.). *Community psychology in transition*. New York: Halstead Press, 1977.

Janis, I. L., & Rodin, J. Attribution, control, and decision making: Social psychology and health care. In G. C. Stone, F. Cohen, & N. E. Adler (Eds.), *Health psychology*. New York: Jossey-Bass, 1979.

Jason, L. A. A behavioral approach in enhancing disadvantaged children's academic abilities. *American Journal of Community Psychology*, 1977, 5, 413–422.

Joint Commission on Mental Illness and Health. *Action for mental health*. New York: Basic Books, 1961.

Krasner, L. Environmental design in perspective: Theoretical model, general principles, and historical context. In L. Krasner (Ed.), *Environmental design and human behavior: A psychology of the individual in society*. New York: Pergamon Press, 1980.

Leighton, A. H. *My name is legion*. New York: Basic Books, 1959.

Lindemann, E. Symptomatology and management of acute grief. *American Journal of Psychiatry*, 1944, 101, 141–148.

Ojemann, R. H., Levitt, E. E., Lyle, W. H., & Whitesie, M. F. The effects of the "casual" teacher-training program and certain curricular changes on grade school children. *Journal of Experimental Education*, 1955, 24, 97–114.

Prescott, D. A. *The child in the education process*. New York: McGraw-Hill, 1957.

Rappaport, J. *Community psychology: Values research and action*. New York: Holt, Rinehart & Winston, 1977.

Rappaport, J. In praise of paradox: A social policy of empowerment over prevention. *American Journal of Community Psychology*, 1981, 9, 1–27.

Robinson, R., DeMarche, D. F., & Wagle, M. *Community resources in mental health*. New York: Basic Books, 1960.

Rosenblum, G. *Issues in community psychology and preventive mental health*. New York: Behavioral Publications, 1970.

Sarason, S. B., Levine, M., Goldenberg, I., Cherlin, D. L., & Bennett, E. M. *Psychology in community settings*. New York: Wiley, 1966.

Sarason, S. B. *Psychology misdirected*. New York: Free Press, 1981.

Zax, M., & Spector, G. A. *An introduction to community psychology*. New York: Wiley, 1974.

# 2 PRIMARY PREVENTION IN MENTAL HEALTH: PAST, PRESENT, AND FUTURE

## Emory L. Cowen

### Prevention Terminology

Although the terms "prevention," "prevention in mental health," "primary prevention," and "primary prevention in mental health" are often used interchangeably, they mean different things. Failure to understand or respect basic distinctions among them creates confusion that inhibits the development of primary prevention in mental health—the focus of this chapter.

"Prevention" is the most inclusive of the four terms—so inclusive, in fact, that it is virtually without specific meaning. The term's infinite elasticity manifests itself in two key ways: with respect to program *goals* and *methods*. It can be applied with equal appropriateness to the goal of forestalling a limitless array of adverse outcomes—cancer, schizophrenia, Down syndrome, damage from vehicular accident, venereal disease, heartburn, and athlete's foot. Although several of those conditions, and others that could be added, pertain to mental health, most do not.

The narrower term "prevention in mental health" directs attention to target variables or conditions relevant to mental health's purview—be they complex syndromes such as schizophrenia and depression or lesser states such as anxiety, tension, and feelings of insecurity or interpersonal ineffectiveness. But even to use that

narrower term falls far short of resolving the terminological problem; it does not yet come to grips with the vexing issues of *methods* of prevention. In everyday usage the term is a catchall, sufficiently global to embrace three *qualitatively* different strategies: primary, secondary, and tertiary prevention (Caplan, 1964; Zax & Cowen, 1976). Those strategies bear further comment.

Tertiary prevention seeks to reduce the residual effects and adverse consequences of rooted disorder. It is for the seriously disturbed. For someone who experiences major mental illness, appropriate (tertiary) prevention goals are to establish at least minimal interpersonal and job effectiveness. Such goals are neither unworthy nor unneeded; they are simply *not* prevention, leastwise not if that term is to have discriminative meaning.

Secondary prevention, by contrast, seeks to keep less severe psychological disorders from becoming prolonged and debilitating, that is, to shorten the duration and lessen the negative consequences of early-identified dysfunction. There are two distinct pathways to secondary prevention: (1) identify prodromal signs of serious disorder early, so that prompt effective steps can be taken to avert dire psychological consequences, and (2) identify signs of dysfunction as soon as possible in a person's (child's) life history and use the best available tools to short-circuit later, more serious problems. A common element in all secondary prevention work, however, is that it addresses already evident dysfunction, albeit less crystallized dysfunction than in tertiary prevention.

Primary prevention differs markedly from all other forms of prevention. It has two aspects: actions designed to prevent the development (rate of occurrence) of psychological disorder, and interventions to promote well-being as an inoculant against dysfunction. It is directed to the as yet unaffected, not the already sick. Its terrain, aims, and methodologies are qualitatively different from those of other types of so-called prevention.

Although little in what has been thus far said is new, there are still important reasons for saying it. The most important is to underscore the fact that the terms "prevention" and "prevention in mental health," as used, are far from unitary concepts. Specific programs and practices that people label "prevention" are strikingly dissimilar in terms of the types of people to whom they are directed, the point in time they occur, their basic objectives, and what they actually do. To lump such diversity under a unified banner of "prevention" is sheer sleight of hand. We already have ample vocabulary to describe the "operations" of tertiary and (most of) secondary prevention: words and concepts such as deinstitutionalization, psychodiagnostic evaluation, psychotherapy, day hospital, halfway house, behavior modification, each addressed to people already experiencing problems. Calling such things prevention (each prevention modified by the adjective secondary or tertiary) only dilutes and obscures a set of conceptually attractive alternatives to past ineffectual mental health ways. It perpetuates what we always have done, in a slightly altered terminological guise. For that reason, I would count it a major blessing and a catalyzing force in the development of primary prevention in mental health for amorphous, overinclusive terms such as "prevention" and "prevention in mental health" literally to be stricken from the vocabulary. Right now, they do more harm than good.

With that argument as a backdrop, we can consider the last two (more useful) concepts: "primary prevention" and "primary prevention in mental health." The term "primary prevention" describes a family of procedures designed to promote many different kinds of wellness and forestall diverse dysfunctions. Primary prevention in mental health is a narrower case of primary prevention, with the same general goals but more specific objectives: to strengthen *psychological* wellness and to prevent *psychological* dysfunction (i.e., maladjustment). That difference is critical. Primary prevention includes, but does not focus primarily on,

mental health outcomes. Properly, it embraces activities such as water fluoridation to prevent dental caries, the use of vehicular safety devices to minimize the occurrence, and consequences, of accidents, promulgation of diet and exercise patterns to improve physical health, and programs to curtail smoking to reduce instances of lung cancer and coronary heart disease. By contrast, primary prevention in mental health addresses exclusively psychological variables and outcomes. There are, to be sure, certain reciprocities between the two approaches, if only because people are intrinsic wholes—an intervention designed to promote physical well-being can have beneficial fallout for psychological well-being. Thus people may come to feel less anxious and more secure, as well as to be healthier physically, if they cease to share an apartment with rats and vermin. Similarly, an effective diet or smoking-cessation program can enhance people's psychological as well as physical well-being. Within this framework, note that the backbone of primary prevention research (and research on primary prevention in mental health) is the specific evaluation of the effectiveness of programs designed to build (psychological) health or to avert (psychological) dysfunction.

Primary prevention and primary prevention in mental health are conceptually yoked, useful, definable terms that describe *qualitatively* different ways (i.e., *bona fide* alternatives) for addressing ancient refractory problems. Both are important and needed. This chapter, however, focuses exclusively on primary prevention in mental health, not only to be consistent with the volume's purposes, but because primary prevention is so broad and complex and includes so many fields of specialization and activity that to address its full range is far beyond the ken and competencies of this merely mortal observer.

## The Place of Primary Prevention in Mental Health

Current problems, phenomena, and dilemmas are not well understood (and hence errors are repeated and ineffective ways are perpetuated) when considered apart from their historical roots (Rappaport, 1977; Sarason, 1974, 1981). Accordingly, neither the need for primary prevention nor its proper place in mental health can be well grasped without considering how and why the mental health field evolved as it did.

In the beginning, humankind was not concerned with matters psychological. Other problems (for example, survival) were far more pressing. The earliest interest in behavior was in florid deviations from established norms (Zax & Cowen, 1976). Such deviations were not well understood; indeed, they were frightening and threatening. The goal of overcoming, or at least minimizing, them became face-valid. It is far easier to see why this was the wellspring for humankind's first concerns about behavior than it is to understand why such concerns have played the predominant role— even in the face of failure—in shaping mental health's course right up to the present day.

To be sure, our sophistication in understanding and perhaps even in dealing with such problems has grown. Demoniac, spiritistic, theological explanations of deviance have yielded to biological and environmental explanations, and with those changes new ways have developed to engage psychological aberrance. Yet those advances have failed to produce either fully satisfactory understandings or reliable cures. More restrictively, there have been dogged constancies in how, structurally, we perceive and strive to overcome such problems.

What has changed (broadened) over time, reflecting slow, evolutionary processes, is society's definition of psychological problems. Many more (and more subtle) conditions than ever before are now accepted as part of mental health's proper purview: symptom and character neuroses, antisocial behavior, psychosomatic dysfunction, and existential turmoil, and, short of such entities, everyday conditions such as unhappiness, ineffective personal relationships, and waste of talent. Gradual social changes, such as the resolution of basic problems of human survival, improved living conditions, technological and scientific advance, and emergence of social philosophies that place greater value on the social well-being of humankind (Rieff, 1959; Zax & Cowen, 1976) are significant factors underlying society's broadening concept of psychological problems.

The expansion of mental health's horizons made new problems apparent. Searches for cause and cure for "victims" of those problems overtaxed the finite resources of the mental health system, and stimulated interest in the influential people in an individual's life space and in the social institutions that shape human development.

At a certain point in that unfolding process, a formal mental health discipline came into being. Constrained by history's heavy imprint, its mandate, stated or implied, was to do something about the mess of human psychological aberration: a mandate that said more about *what* was to be done than *how*. One can readily see, in retrospect, that many "how" scenarios could have been written, but only one was: a conception that reflected prior history, the beliefs and pressure points of the time, and the then-current practices and successes of the field of medicine from which mental health was spawned. Physical medicine was responsible for sick bodies; mental health was to be responsible for sick minds. That charge has endured as the prime shaping force in how we think about human psychological problems and how we deal with them in day-to-day practice. Our overarching goals have been, and remain, to chart the dark, winding labyrinths of psychological dysfunction and to do our heroic best to undo vexing disorders.

It is said that mental health has gone through major revolutions or "paradigm shifts" (Kuhn, 1970; Rappaport, 1977), that is, periods of heightened churning and ferment, and consequent changes in practice, which come about when regnant concepts and approaches are seen as insufficient to solve known problems or problems as redefined. I come more and more to question whether any true revolutions have occurred. A factor that starkly limits all of them is that none has basically challenged mental health's unswerving restorative thrust. For me, the powerful appelative "revolution" implies new assumptions and qualitatively different derivative practices. That has not yet happened to any appreciable extent in mental health.

The point can be made more concrete by looking at the essences of mental health's three most widely recognized revolutions. The first, inaugurated by Philippe Pinel in the late 18th century and later joined by figures such as Dorothea Dix and Clifford Beers, was born of shock and revulsion over the inhumane treatment of the mentally ill. It sought to bring about urgently needed and sweeping humanitarian reform in hospital care and treatment. However laudable that goal, the movement neither reconceptualized disordered behavior nor involved significant theoretical advance. Extreme deviance remained the target. The short-term goal was to bring about more humane care, with a longer-term objective of improved recovery rates.

Sigmund Freud was the giant of the second, so-called psychodynamic revolution. His genius turned attention to a vast range of more subtle psychological disorders, heretofore of greater interest to faith healers, physicians, neurologists, and charlatans than to mental health. His brilliant efforts to chart the nature and treatment of conditions we now call the neuroses significantly shaped the course of mental health's thinking and practices for a century. Though incontestably the quantum leaps of the second "revolution" vastly expanded mental health's horizons and scope, they did not significantly alter its basic thrust—to rescue damaged psyches. And, indeed, with the cumulation of field experience and trial-and-error wisdom we came to perceive many problems that were *not* solved—or, indeed, even raised—by that revolution.

Those concerns have been reviewed in detail elsewhere (Cowen & Zax, 1967; Zax & Cowen, 1976; Cowen, 1981a). Common denominators that cut through them include: (1) a growing awareness of the field's past singular emphasis on rooted dysfunction, and its limited success with such conditions (Bergin & Lambert, 1978; Bergin & Suinn, 1975; Paul, 1969) spotlighted the question of whether psychological damage could really be undone once it had passed a certain point (Scheff, 1966); and (2) the costly, time-consuming, culture-bound nature of mental health's pivotal services, and their unavailability to, or inappropriateness for, major segments of society-in-need (Cowen, 1973; Hollingshead & Redlich, 1958; Lorion, 1973; President's Commission, 1978; Reiff, 1967; Ryan, 1969; Sanua, 1966; Srole, Langner, Michael, Opler, & Rennie, 1962) created pressures to find more flexible, effective new approaches.

Those gathering storm clouds were noted in the reports of three recent presidential commissions (Joint Commission on Mental Health, 1961; Joint Commission on the Mental Health of Children, 1969; President's Commission, 1978). The second revolution had run its course. Society had changed. People's problems had changed. Once again mental health's technology could not satisfactorily resolve problems that were being encountered. Another paradigm shift, a third mental health revolution, was called for. And, indeed, the dawn of such a revolution was heralded by Hobbs (1964)—the community mental health revolution, at its core an active, systematic search for more effective ways to reach many more people in need.

The community mental health (CMH) movement has witnessed significant developments in early detection and screening; mental health consultation; crisis intervention; new settings and service delivery patterns presumably more "in synch" with the needs and lifestyles of their intended service recipients; and an expansion of the number and types of help agents accepted as appropriate service providers. Viewed absolutely, those developments can be called good, useful, significant, and liberalizing. No doubt because of them, we have a somewhat more effective, farther-reaching mental health service delivery system today than we did 25 years ago. However beneficial those changes, they do not overcome many serious problems cognized as fallout from the second revolution. At its core, the CMH thrust does less to challenge past core assumptions than it does to question whether specific practices derived from them are the only, or the best, ways to give expression to those assumptions.

Future historians (leastwise those who are more impressed than I am with the view that there *have* been major mental health revolutions) may thus come to see what is now called the third revolution as little more than a late twist in the second.

The CMH thrust, if nothing else, has been a multipronged protest against the identified biases, narrowness, and ineffectuality of mental health's past ways. A second, qualitatively different, and more basic set of alternatives, now gathering force, may ultimately come better to epitomize a true mental health revolution. These new alternatives significantly challenge mental health's pivotal assumptions, just as, years before, epidemiology and public health medicine shaped attractive, preventive alternatives to medicine's previously dominant disease-containment approaches. Both developments reflect the realization that no disordered condition—physical *or* psychological—can be overcome by treating its victims (Bloom, 1979; Goldston, 1977a). An attractive alternative is to recognize that it is more sensible, humane, pragmatic, and cost-effective to build psychological health and prevent maladjustment than to struggle, however valiantly and compassionately, to stay its awesome tide.

The preceding is the quintessential kernel of primary prevention in mental health. Its concepts, practices, requisite training, and skills all differ qualitatively from mental health's rutted ways. It is a fresh new approach to ancient, refractory problems. Its paramount goals are to promote psychological health and to prevent dysfunction from occurring in the first place, not to counterattack after things have already gone sour. With the wisdom of hindsight, one can see that primary prevention *might* have been one way for the mental health field to have construed its original mandate. But that was, at best, only a latent possibility in a hypothetical "universe of alternatives" (Sarason, 1971). History favored another course and shaped another destiny. Yet as we look at mental health's current needs and pressure points through the spectacles of a long and well-documented history of accomplishments (and nonaccomplishments), primary prevention approaches appear both to be sorely needed and to offer the field the most attractive set of genuine alternatives it has ever had.

## Primary Prevention in Mental Health: A Closer Look

Mounting dissatisfaction with past insufficient ways and the logical appeal of primary prevention in mental health combine to make the latter a rising star. Its ascent can be seen in several forms: (1) The concept is cited ever more often in talks, in journal articles (indeed, several new journals are devoted exclusively to the topic), on convention programs, and in the reports and recommendations of influential policy groups; (2) it has been identified as a priority area for new program development and it has started slowly to infiltrate graduate training; (3) new primary prevention offices and study groups have been established at the federal, state, and municipal levels, and based on their efforts, programs that are at least called primary prevention in mental health have started to develop, and additional support is being contemplated.

Readiness for primary prevention in mental health is thus growing. A supporting rhetoric is there. The challenge is to harness those ingredients to maximize productive achievement. Fuzzy notions of primary prevention in mental health will only hamper such a development. It may therefore help to consider the specifics of several widely cited definitions of the concept.

Caplan (1964) defined primary prevention in mental health as follows:

> . . . lowering the rate of occurrence of new cases of mental disorder in a population . . . by counteracting harmful circumstances before they have had a chance to produce illness. It does not seek to prevent a specific person from becoming sick. Instead it seeks to reduce the risk for the whole population so that although some may become ill, their numbers will be reduced [p. 26].

Bower's (1969) definition is:

> Any social or psychological intervention that promotes or enhances emotional functioning, or reduces the incidence and prevalence of emotional maladjustment in the general population [p. 498].

Goldston (1977b) uses the following definition:

> . . . activities directed to specifically identified vulnerable high risk groups who have not been labelled psychiatrically ill and for whom measures can be undertaken to avoid the onset of emotional disturbance and/or to enhance their level of positive mental health [p. 27].

And Cowen (1980) describes it this way:

> Programs that engineer structures, processes, situations and events that maximally benefit in scope and temporal stability, the psychological

adjustment, effectiveness, happiness and coping skills of many (as yet unaffected) individuals [p. 264].

Although those definitions are not identical, they are consistent and present no major contradictions. They all emphasize the broad twinned goals of enhancing people's psychological health and forestalling the development of psychological problems. They imply that the backbone of the approach lies in the development of programs (interventions) designed to advance those goals and they point to several essential (before-the-fact) qualities that programs must have: (a) they must be mass- or group-oriented, not targeted to individuals; (b) directed to essentially "well" people, not to the already affected, though targets can appropriately include those who, by virtue of life circumstances or recent experiences are known (epidemiologically) to be at risk for adverse psychological outcomes; (c) "intentional," that is, rest on a knowledge base which suggests that a program's operations hold promise for strengthening psychological health or reducing psychological maladjustment.

Although those structural requirements are extremely important, it is just as important to emphasize that they do *not* restrict a program's basic substance or content; its underlying methodology (for example, mental health education, social system modification, competence training); or the key characteristics (age, sociodemographic status) of its target groups. That observation is not intended to blur the fact that the structural restrictions are very tough. To the contrary, to meet them adequately calls for soundly grounded, complex programs and major commitments of time, energy, and resources. But that is what's needed for a stern test of primary prevention's distinctive potential in mental health.

Many, even most programs that purport to be primary prevention in mental health fail to meet one or more of the preceding exacting requirements; for instance, they are for individuals already experiencing significant psychological problems or they are not primarily concerned with mental health variables. Within the definitional framework established above, they are, in other words, "primary prevention" or simply "prevention"—*not* "primary prevention in mental health." But when definitional distinctions are as hazy as they now are, failures of such programs in mental health are chalked up as failures of primary prevention in mental health. The danger of that situation is that primary prevention in mental health can be cast aside before it is fairly evaluated.

To date, lack of understanding of, or respect for, exacting definitional requirements for primary prevention in mental health has probably been the foremost deterrent to that field's development (Cowen, 1977a, 1977b, 1980). But there is a second as well. Interventions which, before the fact, meet those demanding standards are still only *aspiring* programs. In order to *be* a primary prevention program in mental health, positive outcomes (improved psychological health or diminished maladjustment on criterion measures appropriate to a program's purposes) must be shown. And in the long pull, more than that; as several authors (Kelly, 1977; Cowen, 1977a) have suggested, short-term positive findings must be ultimately shown to endure over time.

A program that does not pass muster on taut, before-the-fact definition criteria cannot be a primary prevention program and there can be no primary prevention research based on it. If it does meet those standards but is either not evaluated or fails to show positive effects, it remains an aspiring primary prevention program, one that might have failed for any of a number of reasons: an inadequate underlying conception, weak translation from concept to program elements, improper adaptation to the qualities (for example, age or sociodemographic attributes) of the target group or inadequate research evaluation. In such instances, it's back to the drawing boards.

If the concerns I've thus far expressed seem too abstract or remote, they can perhaps be vivified through concrete examples.

1. Several years ago, during a presidential address on primary prevention (Cowen, 1977a) that I gave to the APA Division of Community Psychology, I had the people in the audience identify, on a form provided, what they considered to be the single "most important contribution to primary prevention in mental health." Of the more than 200 responses from that presumably knowledgeable group, I could at best relate 30 percent (most of them citing books or thought pieces) to a very loose definition of the topic; no more than 2 percent to research in that area.

2. A recent mental health journal number, with 16 papers, was devoted exclusively to the topic of primary prevention. Measured against this chapter's harsh standards, only 3 of the 16 qualified as being about primary prevention programs in mental health.

3. A new primary prevention journal included a section called the Primary Prevention Program Clearinghouse. Its (worthy) stated purpose was to enhance communication about primary prevention by publishing brief 50-word abstracts of programs in primary prevention mental health. The process by which programs were so classified was not made clear. Bearing in mind the profound limit imposed by a 50-word description, I compared all 30 published abstracts to the present definitional criteria for primary prevention in mental health. All 30 submittals, of course, related to mental health; fewer than half (many of which lacked evaluation components), however, met the before-the-fact standards for primary prevention in mental health; and at most one *might* have been a research demonstration of such effects. Insofar as I could judge, the prime factor governing the inclusion of an abstract as an example of primary prevention in mental health was the author's decision to so label it.

The point of these examples is clear. What is called primary prevention in mental health and what *is*, are vastly different things. The first category may exceed the second a hundredfold. Otherwise put, the rhetoric of primary prevention in mental health is many leagues ahead of its documented accomplishments. A major source of that unfortunate discrepancy is the chronic failure to pay heed to a taut, exacting definition of the concept. The field will profit less from the sheer number of contributions that carry that honorific label, and more from a finite number of quality-controlled, research-documented, successful models of the approach.

## Primary Prevention Programs in Mental Health: Sources and Substance

### Source

Sound primary prevention programs in mental health will come from a nourishing soil elsewhere called its "generative" base (Cowen, 1980)—a substrate formed by systematic observations and/or empirical (e.g., correlational, epidemiological) demonstrations of relationships between situations, experiences, characteristics, or qualities and positive (or negative) psychological outcomes. The full primary prevention "cycle" in mental health can be thought of as having two key components: a generative strand that establishes a need and rationale for a program, and an executive strand, conducting and evaluating the program that derives from that generative base (Cowen, 1980).

Several examples illustrate the point. (1) Epidemiological data show clearly that adults with disrupted marriages, as compared to those with stable ones, experience greater maladjustment and higher rates of occurrence of diverse pathologies (Bloom, Asher, & White, 1978). That knowledge provides the generative base for building primary prevention programs for newly divorcing adults not yet experiencing maladjustment, designed to build strengths in them and to avert otherwise anticipable unfortunate psychological outcomes. (2) A long line of research studies (Spivack, Platt, & Shure, 1976) shows that clinical and maladjusted groups are deficient in a family of interpersonal cognitive problem-solving skills (ICPS), such as alternative-solution, consequential, and means-end thinking, leading to the view that such skills may actively mediate positive adjustment. That generative base justifies developing, implementing, and evaluating ICPS training programs (executive primary prevention programs in mental health) to impart those skills to young children, as a way of strengthening their adjustment.

Generative knowledge to power primary prevention programs in mental health comes about in two ways (Cowen, 1980): (1) *intentionally*, that is, investigators undertake such work purposively to establish a groundwork for primary prevention programming (for example, a study is done to show relationships between specific qualities of the social environment of classrooms and adjustment in children, with the specific later goal of engineering class environments that can strengthen children's adjustment), or (2) *serendipitously*, that is, in studying relationships between parent-child communication patterns and children's reading skills, elliptic communication is found to relate both to the study's prime outcome criteria, reading problems, and to measures of insecurity and low self-esteem in the child, which were included secondarily because of their possible relationship to reading problems.

Only a relatively minor fraction of the knowledge comprising the current generative base for primary prevention in mental health comes from intentionally generative studies; most of that base is to be found in work undertaken for very different purposes. Thus generative knowledge for primary prevention in mental health can be seen as ore to be mined by aspiring program developers. But the ore must first be discovered. That will take some doing, since it is currently well scattered not only within psychological but, more importantly, in diverse other fields such as sociology, education, family relationships, child development, political science, social work, economics, architecture, and environmental engineering. Although the preceding list may strike those imbued in mental health's orthodoxy as "strange bedfellows," it realistically reflects a new pattern of inputs needed to shape a strong generative base for primary prevention in mental health. That view has significant implications for preparing and training people for such work. Mental health's past classic training is simply not enough.

Forming a solid generative base for primary prevention in mental health is important in its own right. Such work is different from (*not* better or worse, *not* more or less important than) true (executive) primary prevention work. Indeed, the two go hand in glove.

The current base exists more through happenstance than through focused, planful, intentional development—understandably so, given the field's evolving status, conceptual fuzziness, and relaxed definitional standards.

A sound generative base is surely essential for effective future programming and research in primary prevention in mental health. Although it is quite appropriate to gather and use serendipitously available pieces, focused, intentional studies are needed to catalyze the development of such a base. Even though the task of building a truly solid generative base remains as a significant, long-term challenge, we have enough anchor points to justify undertaking a number of promising programs right now.

### Substance

Two molar strategies can be followed to advance primary prevention in mental health's major goals of promoting psychological well-being and preventing maladjustment: (a) strengthening people's competencies, resources and coping skills by direct training or through environmental engineering, and (b) reducing sources of stress. Those, however, are indeed global strategies which can be implemented in many different ways. The next sections identify some half dozen of those ways—substantive areas that account for most currently known programs of primary prevention in mental health.

Mental health education (MHE) is a deeply rooted, theoretically attractive, health-building option. Its goal is to promote mental health by helping people to acquire knowledge, attitudes, and behavior patterns that foster and maintain psychological well-being. The approach is especially appealing both because it lends itself readily to proactive, mass-oriented programs and because it is very flexible in terms of topical foci, target groups, formats, and timing. Although some MHE programs have indeed shown positive primary prevention effects in mental health (Hereford, 1963; Johnson & Breckenridge, 1982; Ojemann, 1961, 1969), the approach has basically failed to realize its enormous potential (Bloom, 1980). One problem is that the term is so broad and projective that virtually any kind of activity can be "licensed" under that banner. In practice, the generative base for many programs called MHE is weak, and the programs are conducted more in the name of an "amorphous good" than for justifiable reasons of primary prevention. When Davis (1965) suggested that the main reason for MHE's poor performance was that we do not yet have useful, practical bodies of knowledge to communicate to the public, he was indicting weaknesses in MHE's generative base.

Another factor that restricts MHE's contributions is that many programs of that type are either not evaluated at all or improperly evaluated. Improper evaluation often stems from the fact that many MHE programs are taught to intermediaries such as parents or teachers, even though their ultimate goal is to strengthen the adjustment of the children affected by those intermediaries. Of course if a program is not evaluated, primary prevention effects cannot be shown. And if, as most often happens, the evaluation focuses on the direct recipients (the intermediaries), the easiest and most obvious variables to study are how much they enjoyed and profited from the program, grew in knowledge, and experienced positive attitude change. But however interesting or even "reinforcing" such changes are in their own right, they in no way insure adjustment gain in the program's ultimate intended targets. The latter is what evaluation of primary prevention in mental health *should* be all about.

To realize MHE's enormous potential for primary prevention in mental health, future programs will need to be built on much stronger generative bases, and their evaluations will need to focus more on adjustive gain in ultimate intended targets.

Skill or competence training is another conceptually attractive pathway to primary prevention in mental health (Prevention Task Panel Report, 1978), one that is narrower and more focused than broad gauge MHE. The approach rests on the view that certain core competencies, different no doubt for different age groups, mediate positive adjustment. Programs to impart such cognitive and interpersonal skills, especially to young children, can provide tools both to enhance adjustment and to ward off the development of problems.

This basic approach is exemplified through Ojemann's (1961, 1969) early work developing curricula to teach youngsters to think causally, efforts by the Hahnemann group (Shure & Spivack, 1978; Spivack & Shure, 1974; Spivack, Platt, & Shure, 1976) and others (Allen, Chinsky, Larcen, Lochman, & Selinger, 1976; Elardo & Caldwell, 1979; Gesten, Flores de Apodaca, Rains, Weissberg, & Cowen, 1979; Weissberg, Gesten, Rapkin, Cowen, Davidson, Flores de Apodaca, & McKim, 1981) to create programs that teach children interpersonal (or social) cognitive problem-solving skills, and conceptually kindred programs to teach skills such as realistic goal-setting (Stamps, 1975) and relationship enhancement (Vogelsong, Most, & Yanchko, 1978). The common denominators that link these diverse competence training programs are that they: (1) meet stringent

definitional requirements for primary prevention in mental health; (2) present evidence that focal skills can be acquired by appropriate target groups; (3) demonstrate that skill acquisition is paralleled by adjustive gain. Parenthetically, the same generalized approach has also been shown to be useful for those experiencing relatively mild early problems, for example, specific social skill training and "coaching" programs for young children (Furman, Rahe, & Hartup, 1979; Hartup, 1980; La Greca & Santagrossi, 1980; Oden, 1980; Oden & Asher, 1977).

The key questions that power an attractive, maximally general competence training approach are: (1) Which core competencies mediate adjustment for different groups? (2) Can programs be developed to teach those skills successfully? (3) Does skill acquisition lead to improved adjustment? (Cowen, 1977a).

Both life stress in general and specific adverse events have been shown to relate strongly to a variety of unfortunate psychological outcomes (Dohrenwend & Dohrenwend, 1974; Felner, Farber, & Primavera, 1980; Felner, Stolberg, & Cowen, 1975; Holmes & Masuda, 1974; Holmes & Rahe, 1967). Such events include marital disruption (Bloom et al., 1978), bereavement (Silverman, 1969, 1976), sudden infant death (Goldston, 1977b), and job loss (Dooley & Catalano, 1980). Stressful situations and crises have been viewed as times of both danger and opportunity. Improperly handled, they leave serious psychological scars; well handled, they can fortify adjustment and strengthen future coping skills (Caplan, 1964). If that is so, it structures an intriguing challenge for primary prevention in mental health: to build programs that short-circuit known negative psychological consequences of life crises and stressful events. Such an approach, as Bloom (1979) points out, implies an important paradigm-shift for mental health: (1) identify, epidemiologically, stressful events or experiences that have adverse psychological effects on many people; (2) assess comparatively those who are and are not currently experiencing such events and chart their specific adverse consequences; (3) mount and evaluate programs designed to enhance people's strengths and resources and/or to forestall otherwise anticipable adverse outcomes.

We are just beginning to see demonstrations of the workability and effectiveness of such a model in action. One example is the program for divorcing adults recently reported by Bloom, Hodges, and Caldwell (1982). Those investigators describe a systematic intervention, based on mental health education and support system approaches, for newly divorcing adults that reduced anticipable maladjustment in that group. In like manner, Felner, Ginter, and Primavera's

(1982) program, based on environmental change and strengthening social supports during students' transition to high school, reduced anticipable decrements in self-concept and performance and strengthened students' views of the school environment. Another example: Each year thousands of children go through anxiety-producing dental, medical, and surgical procedures, which has been shown to have both short- and long-term negative psychological consequences. A growing body of data suggests that the use of expressive and modeling procedures at peak crisis points helps young children to cope more effectively with, and adjust better to, such unavoidable crises (Graziano, DeGiovanni, & Garcia, 1979; Melamed & Siegel, 1975; Thelen, Fry, Fehrenbach, & Frautschi, 1979). Graziano et al. (1979) suggest that stress inoculation training in coping and mastering techniques have much potential for advancing primary prevention in mental health.

Social systems analysis and change are another important area for primary prevention in mental health. At a macrosocietal level, clear, compelling associations (generative base) have been shown between poor living conditions, the lack of food, education, job, and life opportunities, social isolation, and demeaning attitudes on the one side, and maladaptation on the other, so much so, in fact, that some observers (e.g., Rappaport, 1977; Reiff, 1968) see that as community psychology's (primary prevention in mental health's) greatest challenge. Meeting that challenge, however, requires more wisdom, resources, power, and technology and better access lines than are available to the mental health fields. Even so, attempts have been made to address limited aspects of that problem, with implications for primary prevention in mental health. Iscoe (1974), for example, developed the concept of the competent community and suggested ways to further that goal. And, efforts to build programs based on enhancing community competencies have in fact been modeled (e.g., Hodgson, 1979; Rappaport, Davidson, Wilson, & Mitchell, 1975).

Progress toward the goal of system change has been made in work with specific institutional structures such as schools, churches, and new communities. One characteristic of such high-impact environments is their nonneutrality—they are likely to affect people's psychological well-being for better or for worse. The question posed by that reality is how to engineer environments to maximize people's development and psychological well-being—a clear objective of primary prevention in mental health. That question implies a complex but intriguing three-stage process—two generative and one executive.

Take schools (classrooms) as a case in point, since such settings exercise a powerful formative influence on children's psychological development. The first challenge is to develop reliable, sensitive ways to assess high-impact dimensions of the class environment. Important contributions to such understandings have come from extensive methodological work reported by people such as Moos (1974, 1979a, 1979b) and Stallings (1975). The availability of such measures makes a second key step possible: charting relationships between environment qualities and relevant psychological (and educational) outcomes. Illustratively, Trickett and Moos (1974) found that student satisfaction and positive mood were highest in classes that were seen as high in involvement and as having close student-teacher relationships. Similarly, pupils in elementary classes who were seen as high in order and organization, involvement, and affiliation, compared to their opposites, have more positive moods, greater peer acceptance, and higher teacher-rated adjustment (Wright & Cowen, 1982), as well as better self-control (Humphrey, 1981). Those are essential generative leads. They pave the way for engineering class environments, through consultation, structural change, new teaching formats, etc., that can produce more positive adjustive outcomes in children (e.g., Aronson, Blaney, Stephan, Sykes, & Snapp, 1978). When such outcomes are shown empirically to have occurred, we have a demonstration of true primary prevention effects in mental health.

Support systems are yet another area that has attracted the attention and activity of people with interest in primary prevention in mental health (President's Commission, 1978). A strong generative base suggests that: (a) many maladjusted people lack significant psychological support; (b) many upset individuals, for a variety of reasons, use natural, accessible support sources, sooner and far more often, than formal professional helping outlets (Gottlieb, 1976; Gurin, Veroff & Feld, 1960); and (c) in some sectors of society, natural support systems are the prime, if not only, de facto source of help available to distressed people (Collins & Pancoast, 1976).

Several types of primary prevention programs in mental health can be built on that knowledge base: for example, (a) forming support groups for divorce, bereavement, moving to a new community, chronic infertility, school transfer, child abuse, and many other problems; (b) engineering situations to promote the natural development of support and mutual help groups in communities or neighborhoods characterized by isolation, fragmentation, and anomic reactions, both to strengthen residents' resources, self-image, and day-to-day functioning and to avert feelings of anxiety, loneliness, and depression. When such planned support mechanisms are shown to produce those outcomes, primary prevention in mental health is demonstrated.

The so-called helper-therapy principle (Riessman, 1965), an intriguing variant of the generalized support group approach, also has direct implications for primary prevention in mental health. That principle rests on the awareness that certain low-status, disenfranchised social groupings such as inner-city residents, retired adults, and tuned-out high school students are susceptible to various maladjustments. The question is: Are there ways to avert such maladjustment? As one aspect of an innovative mental health program established for inner-city residents, Riessman (1967) used such individuals as direct service providers for peers in neighborhood storefronts. He noted that that unique kind of pairing not only brought meaningful help to poor inner-city residents in a very realistic way, but also that such involvements had beneficial effects for the helpers themselves. Thus active participation in the process of helping others in genuine need enhanced the mental health of those who provided the help. A similar point is made by Staub (1979) in the very different context of the development of children's prosocial behavior.

Harnessing the helper-therapy principle through a before-the-fact intentionality has important implications for primary prevention in mental health. And indeed, studies have been reported showing adjustive gain in help agents following programmatic helping activities with target persons in genuine need. Programs in which retirees (Cowen, Leibowitz, & Leibowitz, 1968), and tuned-out high school students (Tefft & Kloba, 1982) served as help agents with young maladapting primary graders in the schools and one in which indigenous retirees served as community facilitators and resource people for fellow retirees (Gatz, Barbarin, Tyler, Hurley, Mitchell, Moran, Wirzbicki, Crawford, & Engelmann, 1982) each reported gains, both for help agents and target persons. Hence it appears that support programs based on the helper-therapy principle can help to identify mutually supportive solutions to pressing human problems, by yoking primary prevention approaches for help agents with secondary prevention approaches for program targets.

## Current Problems and Future Needs

Primary prevention in mental health today remains an exciting promise that has not yet been fulfilled. The field is still struggling to establish a clear identity and to chart optimal ways of contributing to the solution of vexing and still unresolved major mental health problems. As the new field crystallizes and searches for its place in the mental health order, it has understandably been concerned with obstacles to its own development (Prevention Task Panel, 1978). Among the important deterrents cited in that report: (1) We live in a crisis-oriented society that emphasizes visible, pressing, here-and-now problems. Primary prevention in mental health is largely future-oriented and conveys the "illusion" of postponability; it thus has a weak constituency. (2) The approach's defining goals and methods are not always warmly received because they differ so much from mental health's established repairing emphases and from the practices best known to mental health professionals. It also threatens some professionals' (understandable) needs for status, economic gain, and the gratification of seeing one's personal efforts directly help a distressed other. (3) The approach is threatening to others because it raises sensitive issues about social and environmental change. (4) Primary prevention competes with better-rooted traditional approaches for limited mental health monies during a time of scarce resources. (5) Primary prevention activities in mental health do not well fit the support mechanisms that undergird current mental health activities (for example, funds for third party reimbursement, treatment staffs, hospital beds, and the construction of classic mental health facilities).

Although those concerns are real and I do not wish to discount their importance, they focus on "enemies from without." One thesis of this chapter is that there are equally real and important "enemies from within." The difference between the two is that the *second* cluster points to specific, achievable goals that can be addressed now by actions under our control. Convincing documentation of viable, effective program models of primary prevention in mental health might be the best of all antidotes to resistance from without.

One serious internal deterrent to the development of primary prevention in mental health, stressed throughout this chapter, has been overly elasticized, imprecise use of terminology; in effect, that has meant that most things so labeled are *not* legitimate examples of the approach. And as a result we only think we are, but are not in fact, getting a fair and reasonable test of needed new alternatives in mental health. That serious problem is compounded by widespread deficits in the *documentation* of effective primary prevention programs in mental health. By definition there can be no true research on primary prevention in mental health without true primary prevention programs. If (as has been the case) most programs that bear that label are false pretenders, and the few legitimate contenders are not evaluated, or fail to produce positive primary prevention effects, the development of effective models of primary prevention in mental health will be slow enough to discourage interest in the field, if not to lose it altogether.

Some of the drawbacks to research on primary prevention in mental health (Cowen, 1981b) are well known in other contexts; others are particular to that field. For one thing, the amount of work involved in running such programs can be enormous, involving as it does time-consuming and sometimes delicate activities such as negotiating and planning for a program with a host system; writing often elaborate curricula and training and supervising relevant personnel in their use; and conducting the program conscientiously. If, as often happens, people in the host system, despite genuine interest in the program, feel overwhelmed by its demands and/or have no interest in research, then research can readily be seen as an unnecessary, indeed burdensome "add-on" to an already oppressive set of demands. Too, primary prevention programs typically unfold in natural community contexts, and are subject to the research-weakening vicissitudes of such contexts, such as antagonism, real or perceived, between program and research needs, difficulties in finding appropriate control groups, setting changes and subject attrition while the program is going on— all factors that detract from the clarity and purity of research evaluations (Cowen, 1978; Cowen & Gesten, 1980; Cowen, Lorion, & Dorr, 1974).

Diversity is another quality of primary prevention programming and research in mental health. Relevant knowledge bases and skills needed for program work and research in environmental engineering, training young children in interpersonal problem-solving, and helping adolescents to cope with the demands of school transition not only differ from each other, but as a group differ from the things that mental health professionals are trained to do, know best, and are most comfortable with. It is not that such skills differ absolutely from ones already known to psychology and other social sciences; rather, they require significant recombinations of existing patterns of training, knowledge, and technology.

Good, tautly defined primary prevention programs in mental health are scarce; such programs with supporting research documentation are even scarcer. They are urgently needed, less to satisfy the illusory fantasy of "once and forever" definitive demonstrations, but rather for their potentially heuristic, pump-priming effects. A fuzzy, loosely used concept must be made more precise, and excellence within that more restrictive, demanding framework must be modeled if the field is to have a genuine contrast to mental health's past established ways. One recent effort in that direction bears special mention—a single complete journal number devoted exclusively to research on primary prevention programs in mental health (Cowen, 1982). Each contribution to that special number: (a) was judged, before the fact, to meet primary prevention in mental health's exacting definitional standard; (b) included a program evaluation component, and (c) demonstrated *some* positive primary prevention effects (that is, adjustive gain or reduction in maladjustment). No single study had perfect results, and searching critics could no doubt raise legitimate questions about each. Hence the number's prime value does not come from the "ultimate validation" it provides for primary prevention in mental health, but rather from how it illustrates and models that approach within the confines of harsh definitional criteria that contrast sharply with orthodox mental health ways. The number thus lights a pathway, spotlighting approaches that can be pursued with greater exactness, rigor, and sophistication in the future. A skid has been greased. Especially noteworthy is the fact that the component programs differ sharply in the knowledge-bases on which they rest, the target groups they address, the specific conditions (adjustment-related dependent variables) they seek to affect, and the basic "change" methodologies they use. They well illustrate the potential diversity of primary prevention approaches in mental health, even within the straitjacket of a restricting definitional concept.

It is clear from all that has been said that primary prevention programs and research in mental health can go astray in many ways, most of which are readily found. Demonstrating primary prevention effects in mental health requires that many complex pieces fall exactly into place. That will not happen without tenacious effort, and many failures en route. But the stakes are high, if only because history tells us that unless we give this new way the full, clear trial it merits, mental health generations hence will face the same dilemmas it has faced for many centuries and still faces today.

## Summary and Overview

The family of approaches called primary prevention in mental health offer the mental health field the most far-reaching, attractive set of alternatives it has had since its inception. Its goals—promoting psychological adjustment and preventing the occurrence of maladjustment—contrast sharply with mental health's past narrow emphasis on containing or minimizing psychological dysfunction. Right now that appealing concept is far ahead of its documented effectiveness base. Although some have stressed that powerful external barriers (such as competition for scarce funds, vested interests) are the prime factors that retard development of primary prevention in mental health, and those factors should not be discounted, this chapter argues that intrinsic deficiencies in the field's early unfolding have also significantly retarded its development. The latter view identifies ways in which the situation can be improved by actions under our immediate control.

The first, very important addressable problem is that the concept's exacting definitional essence (that which sets it apart from, and maximizes its contrast with, mental health's past rutted ways) has been neither sufficiently cognized nor respected. As a result, most things that have been labeled, and cited as, primary prevention in mental health are not that at all—a circumstance that delays and confuses evaluation of the approach's special potential. A second pervasive problem is that primary prevention programs have been underresearched and inadequately researched. The end result is that there are woefully few "true" primary prevention programs in mental health with supporting research documentation. Models of such accomplishment are urgently needed to catalyze the field's development.

The following steps, each within our control, can be taken now to accelerate the development of primary prevention in mental health. Since a sound generative knowledge base is the source for all such programming, it is essential that that base be solidified. That can happen in two ways: (1) through systematic identification of existing bodies of knowledge, including new recombinations, showing relationships between life circumstances, settings, qualities, characteristics of people, events, and circumstances, and positive or negative psychological outcomes, and by (2) developing new, highly intentional generative knowledge that will provide rationales and objectives for new programs. A second basic need is to adhere closely to an exacting differential set of definitional guidelines for primary prevention in mental health to facilitate discriminative assessment of the power of that conceptually attractive family of approaches. Taken properly, that step will mean fewer but better and more informative programs that are so labeled in the future.

Third, interventions must be evaluated carefully and positive adjustment effects must be shown before programs can be called primary prevention in mental health. A relatively few programs of excellence in the coming years would do more to advance the field than a plethora that fail to pass muster on quality control standards. Modeling excellence and the clear illumination of pathways are our current most important needs. If in that process diverse models and pathways (program substance and methodology) are identified, so much the better.

One can debate *ad infinitum* the theoretical beauty of primary prevention in mental health and the many alleged deterrents to its development, but the ultimate battle will be won or lost in terms of what the highest usage of the approach can show. With positive demonstrations of efficacy, tenacious enemies and skeptics can be transformed into supporters—perhaps even into doers.

Much remains to be done in developing primary prevention programming and research in mental health. At the very best it will be a difficult, frustrating uphill climb. But that may well be an intrinsic cost of a *bona fide* mental health revolution. Primary prevention seems to have that potential. The concrete steps proposed in this chapter seek to harness that potential and thus to build toward a more robust, credible, socially contributory tomorrow in mental health.

## References

Allen, G. J., Chinsky, J. M., Larcen, S. W., Lochman, J. E., & Selinger, H. V. *Community psychology and the schools: A behaviorally oriented multi-level preventive approach.* Hillsdale, N.J.: Lawrence Erlbaum Associates, 1976.

Aronson, E., Blaney, N., Stephan, C., Sykes, J., & Snapp, M. *The jigsaw classroom.* Beverly Hills: Sage Publications, 1978.

Bergin, A. E., & Lambert, M. J. The evaluation of therapeutic outcomes. In S. L. Garfield & A. E. Bergin (Eds.), *Handbook of psychotherapy and behavior change: An empirical analysis.* (2nd ed.) New York: Wiley, 1978.

Bergin, A. E., & Suinn, R. M. Individual psychotherapy and behavior therapy. In M. R. Rosenzweig & L. C. Porter (Eds.), *Annual Review of Psychology,* 1975, **26,** 509–556.

Bloom, B. L. Prevention of mental disorders: Recent advances in theory and practice. *Community Mental Health Journal,* 1979, **15,** 179–191.

Bloom, B. L., Asher, S. J., & White, S. W. Marital disruption as a stressor: A review and analysis. *Psychological Bulletin,* 1978, **85,** 867–894.

Bloom, B. L., Hodges, W. F., & Caldwell, R. A. A preventive intervention program for the newly separated: Initial evaluation. *American Journal of Community Psychology,* 1982, **10,** 251–264.

Bower, E. M. Slicing the mystique of prevention with Occam's razor. *American Journal of Public Health,* 1969, **59,** 478–484.

Caplan, G. *Principles of preventive psychiatry.* New York: Basic Books, 1964.

Collins, A. H., & Pancoast, D. L. *Natural helping networks: A strategy for prevention.* Washington, D.C.: National Association of Social Workers, 1976.

Cowen, E. L. Social and community interventions. *Annual Review of Psychology,* 1973, **24,** 423–472.

Cowen, E. L. Baby-steps toward primary prevention. *American Journal of Community Psychology*, 1977, **5**, 1–22. (a)

Cowen, E. L. Psychologists and primary prevention: Blowing the cover story. *American Journal of Community Psychology*, 1977, **5**, 481–489. (b)

Cowen, E. L. Some problems in community program evaluation research. *Journal of Consulting and Clinical Psychology*, 1978, **46**, 792–805.

Cowen, E. L. The wooing of primary prevention. *American Journal of Community Psychology*, 1980, **8**, 258–284.

Cowen, E. L. Choices and alternatives for primary prevention in mental health. In M. P. Goldstein (Ed.), *Preventive intervention in schizophrenia*. NIMH Primary Prevention Series. Washington, D.C.: Government Printing Office, 1981. (a)

Cowen, E. L. Primary prevention research: Barriers, needs and opportunities. *Journal of Prevention*, 1981, **2**, 131–137. (b)

Cowen, E. L. (Ed.). Research on primary prevention in mental health. *American Journal of Community Psychology*, 1982, **10**, Whole No. 3, 239–367.

Cowen, E. L., & Gesten, E. L. Evaluating community programs: Tough and tender perspectives. In M. Gibbs, J. R. Lachemneyer, & J. Sigal (Eds.), *Community psychology: Theoretical and empirical approaches*. New York: Gardner Press, 1980.

Cowen, E. L., Leibowitz, E., & Leibowitz, G. The utilization of retired people as mental health aides in the schools. *American Journal of Orthopsychiatry*, 1968, **38**, 900–909.

Cowen, E. L., Lorion, R. P., & Dorr, D. Research in the community cauldron: A case report. *Canadian Psychologist*, 1974, **15**, 313–325.

Cowen, E. L., & Zax, M. The mental health fields today: Issues and problems. In E. L. Cowen, E. A. Gardner, & M. Zax (Eds.), *Emergent approaches to mental health problems*. New York: Appleton-Century-Crofts, 1967.

Davis, J. A. *Education for positive mental health*. Chicago: Aldine, 1965.

Dohrenwend, B. S., & Dohrenwend, B. S. (Eds.). *Stressful life events: Their nature and effects*. New York: Wiley, 1974.

Dooley, D., & Catalano, R. Economic change as a cause of psychological disorder. *Psychological Bulletin*, 1980, **87**, 450–468.

Elardo, P. T., & Caldwell, B. M. The effects of an experimental social development program on children in the middle childhood period. *Psychology in the Schools*, 1979, **16**, 93–100.

Felner, R. D., Farber, S. S., & Primavera, J. Children of divorce, stressful life events, and transitions: A framework for preventive efforts. In R. H. Price, R. F. Ketterer, B. C. Bader, & J. Monahan (Eds.), *Prevention in mental health: Research, policy and practice*. Beverly Hills: Sage Publications, 1980.

Felner, R. D., Ginter, M., & Primavera, J. Primary prevention during school transitions: Social support and environmental structure. *American Journal of Community Psychology*, 1982, **10**, 277–290.

Felner, R. D., Stolberg, A. L., & Cowen, E. L. Crisis events and school mental health referral patterns of young children. *Journal of Consulting and Clinical Psychology*, 1975, **43**, 305–310.

Furman, W., Rahe, D., & Hartup, W. W. Social rehabilitation of low interactive preschool children by peer intervention. *Child Development*, 1979, **50**, 915–922.

Gatz, M., Barbarin, O. A., Tyler, F. B., Hurley, D. J., Mitchell, R. B., Moran, J. A., Wirzbicki, P. J., Crawford, J., & Engelmann, A. Enhancement of individual and community competence: The older adult as community worker. *American Journal of Community Psychology*, 1982, **10**, 291–304.

Gesten, E. L., Flores de Apodaca, R., Rains, M. H., Weissberg, R. P., & Cowen, E. L. Promoting peer related social competence in schools. In M. W. Kent & J. E. Rolf (Eds.), *The primary prevention of psychopathology*. Vol. 3. *Social competence in children*. Hanover, N.H.: University Press of New England, 1979.

Goldston, S. E. Defining primary prevention. In G. W. Albee & J. M. Joffe (Eds.), *Primary prevention of psychopathology*. Vol. 1: *The issues*. Hanover, N.H.: University Press of New England, 1977. (a)

Goldston, S. E. An overview of primary prevention programming. In D. C. Kline & S. E. Goldston (Eds.), *Primary prevention: An idea whose time has come*. DHEW Publication No. [ADM] 77-447. Washington, D.C.: Government Printing Office, 1977. (b)

Gottlieb, B. H. Lay influences on the utilization and provision of health services: A review. *Canadian Psychological Review*, 1976, **17**, 126–136.

Graziano, A. M., DeGiovanni, I. S., & Garcia, K. A. Behavioral treatment of children's fears: A review. *Psychological Bulletin*, 1979, **86**, 804–830.

Gurin, G., Veroff, J., & Feld, S. *Americans view their mental health: A nationwide interview survey*. New York: Basic Books, 1960.

Hartup, W. W. Peer relations and the growth of social competence. In M. W. Kent & J. E. Rolf (Eds.), *Primary prevention of psychopathology*. Vol. 3. *Social competence in children*. Hanover, N.H.: University Press of New England, 1979.

Hereford, C. F. *Changing parental attitudes through group discussion*. Austin: University of Texas Press, 1963.

Hobbs, N. Mental health's third revolution. *American Journal of Orthopsychiatry*, 1964, **34**, 822–833.

Hodgson, S. *Intervening to support parents in high-risk populations*. Toronto: University of Toronto Press, 1979.

Hollingshead, A. B., & Redlich, F. C. *Social class and mental illness: A community study*. New York: Wiley, 1958.

Holmes, T. H., & Masuda, M. Life changes and illness susceptibility. In B. S. Dohrenwend & B. P. Dohrenwend (Eds.), *Stressful life events: Their nature and effects*. New York: Wiley, 1974.

Holmes, T. H., & Rahe, R. H. The Social Readjustment Rating Scale. *Journal of Psychosomatic Research*, 1967, **11**, 213–218.

Humphrey, L. L. Children's self-control in relation to perceived social environment: A naturalistic investigation. Unpublished Ph.D. dissertation, University of Rochester, 1981.

Iscoe, I. Community psychology and the competent community. *American Psychologist*, 1974, **29**, 607–613.

Joint Commission on Mental Illness and Health. *Action for mental health*. New York: Basic Books, 1961.

Joint Commission on the Mental Health of Children. *Crisis in child mental health: Challenge for the 1970's*. New York: Harper & Row, 1969.

Johnson, D. L., & Breckenridge, J. N. The Houston Parent-Child Development Center and the primary prevention of behavior disorders in young children. *American Journal of Community Psychology*, 1982, **10**, 305–316.

Kelly, J. The search for ideas and deeds that work. In G. W. Albee & J. M. Joffe (Eds.), *Primary prevention of psychopathology*. Vol. 1. *The issues*. Hanover, N.H.: University Press of New England, 1977.

Kuhn, T. S. *The structure of scientific revolutions*. (2nd ed.) Chicago: University of Chicago Press, 1970.

La Greca, A. M., & Santagrossi, D. A. Social skills training with elementary school students: A behavioral group approach. *Journal of Consulting and Clinical Psychology*, 1980, **48**, 220–227.

Lorion, R. P. Patient and therapist variables in the treatment of low-income patients. *Psychological Bulletin*, 1973, **79**, 263–270.

Melamed, B. G., & Siegel, L. J. Reduction of anxiety on children facing hospitalization and surgery, by use of filmed modeling. *Journal of Consulting and Clinical Psychology*, 1975, **43**, 511–521.

Moos, R. H. *Evaluating treatment environments: A social ecological approach*. New York: Wiley, 1974.

Moos, R. H. *Evaluating educational environments*. San Francisco: Jossey-Bass, 1979. (a)

Moos, R. H. Improving social settings by social climate measurement and feedback. In R. F. Muñoz, L. R. Snowden, & J. G. Kelly (Eds.), *Social and psychological research in community settings*. San Francisco: Jossey-Bass, 1979. (b)

Oden, S. L. A child's social isolation: Origins, prevention, intervention. In G. Cartledge & J. F. Milburn (Eds.), *Teaching social skills to children*. New York: Pergamon Press, 1980.

Oden, S. L., & Asher, S. R. Coaching low-accepted children in social skills: A follow-up sociometric assessment. *Child Development*, 1977, **48**, 496–506.

Ojemann, R. H. Investigations on the effects of teacher understanding and appreciation of behavior dynamics. In G. Caplan (Ed.), *Prevention of mental disorders in children*. New York: Basic Books, 1961.

Ojemann, R. H. Incorporating psychological concepts in the school curriculum. In H. P. Clarizio (Ed.), *Mental health and the educative process*. Chicago: Rand-McNally, 1969.

Paul, G. L. Chronic mental patient: Current status—future direction. *Psychological Bulletin*, 1969, **71**, 81–94.

President's Commission on Mental Health. *Report to the president*. Vol. 1. Stock No. 040-000-00390-8. Washington, D.C.: Government Printing Office, 1978.

Prevention Task Panel Report. *Task Panel reports submitted to the President's Commission on Mental Health*. Vol. 4. Stock No. 040-000-00393-2. Washington, D.C.: Government Printing Office, 1978.

Rappaport, J. *Community psychology: Values, research, and action*. New York: Holt, Rinehart & Winston, 1977.

Rappaport, J., Davidson, W. S., Wilson, M. N., & Mitchell, A. Alternatives to blaming the victim or the environment: Our places to stand have not moved the earth. *American Psychologist*, 1975, **30**, 525–528.

Reiff, R. Mental health manpower and institutional change. In E. L. Cowen, E. A. Gardner, & M. Zax (Eds.), *Emergent approaches to mental health problems*. New York: Appleton-Century-Crofts, 1967.

Reiff, R. Social interventions and the problem of psychological analysis. *American Psychologist*, 1968, **23**, 534–541.

Rieff, P. *Freud: The mind of the moralist*. New York: Viking Press, 1959.

Riessman, F. The "helper" therapy principle. *Social Work*, 1965, **10**, 27–32.

Riessman, F. A neighborhood-based mental health approach. In E. L. Cowen, E. A. Gardner, & M. Zax (Eds.), *Emergent approaches to mental health problems*. New York: Appleton-Century-Crofts, 1967.

Ryan, W. (Ed.) *Distress in the city: Essays on the design and administration of urban mental health services*. Cleveland: Case-Western Reserve University Press, 1969.

Sanua, V. D. Sociocultural aspects of psychotherapy and treatment: A review of the literature. In L. E. Abt & L. Bellak (Eds.), *Progress in clinical psychology*. Vol. 8. New York: Grune & Stratton, 1966.

Sarason, S. B. *The culture of the school and the problem of change*. Boston: Allyn & Bacon, 1971.

Sarason, S. B. *The psychological sense of community: Prospects for a community psychology*. San Francisco: Jossey-Bass, 1974.

Sarason, S. B. *Psychology misdirected*. New York: Free Press, 1981.

Scheff, T. J. *Being mentally ill: A sociological survey*. Chicago: Aldine, 1966.

Shure, M. B., & Spivack, G. *Problem-solving techniques in childrearing*. San Francisco: Jossey-Bass, 1978.

Silverman, P. R. The widow-to-widow program: An experiment in preventive intervention. *Mental Hygiene*, 1969, **53**, 333–337.

Silverman, P. R. The widow as a caregiver in a program of preventive intervention with other widows. In G. Caplan & M. Killilea (Eds.), *Support systems and mutual help: Multidisciplinary explorations*. New York: Grune & Stratton, 1976.

Spivack, G., Platt, J. J., & Shure, M. B. *The problem solving approach to adjustment*. San Francisco: Jossey-Bass, 1976.

Spivack, G., & Shure, M. B. *Social adjustment of young children*. San Francisco: Jossey-Bass, 1974.

Srole, L., Langner, T. S., Michael, S. T., Opler, M. K., & Rennie, T. A. C. *Mental health in the metropolis*. New York: McGraw-Hill, 1962.

Stallings, J. Implementation and child effects of teaching practices on follow-through classrooms. *Monographs of the Society for Research on Child Development*, 1975, **40**, (serial no. 163).

Stamps, L. W. Enhancing success in school for deprived children by teaching realistic goal setting. Paper presented to the Society for Research in Child Development, Denver, 1975.

Staub, E. *Positive social behavior and morality*. Vol. 2. *Socialization and development*. New York: Academic Press, 1979.

Tefft, B. M., & Kloba, J. A. Underachieving high school students as mental health aides with maladapting primary grade children. *American Journal of Community Psychology*, 1981, **9**, 303–320.

Thelen, M. H., Fry, R. A., Fehrenbach, P. A., & Frautschi, N. M. Therapeutic videotape modeling: A review. *Psychological Bulletin*, 1979, **86**, 701–720.

Trickett, E. J., & Moos, R. H. Personal correlates of contrasting environments: Student satisfaction in high school classrooms. *American Journal of Community Psychology*, 1974, **2**, 1–12.

Vogelsong, E. L., Most, R. K., & Yanchko, A. Relationship enhancement training for preadolescents in public schools. *Journal of Clinical Child Psychology*, 1979, **8**, 97–100.

Weissberg, R. P., Gesten, E. L., Rapkin, B. D., Cowen, E. L., Davidson, E., Flores de Apodaca, R., & McKim, B. J. The evaluation of a social problem-solving training program for suburban and inner-city third grade children. *Journal of Consulting and Clinical Psychology*, 1981, **49**, 251–261.

Wright, S., & Cowen, E. L. Student perception of school environment and its relationship to mood, achievement, popularity and adjustment. (Submitted.)

Zax, M., & Cowen, E. L. *Abnormal psychology: Changing conceptions*. (2nd ed.) New York: Holt, Rinehart & Winston, 1976.

# PART II
# COMPETENCE-BASED PERSPECTIVES

# INTRODUCTION TO PART II

Preventive psychology has, among its defining characteristics, an overarching concern with competency and the enhancement of development. A full discussion of the range of programs aimed at enhancing human competence and the knowledge base which inform them is well beyond the scope of this or any other single volume. In this work we have chosen to focus on those aspects of such work which have to date been most heavily represented in preventive efforts. In later sections of this volume discussions are offered of ways elements of the social and physical environment may facilitate or be hazardous to optimal development. By contrast, this section's two chapters focus on efforts to develop frameworks and empirical evidence to guide programs targeted toward enhancing the coping skills and social competencies of individuals more directly. The strong contributions of developmental psychology to those efforts is clear. These concerns underlie programs ranging from those for high-risk infants, to educationally based, competence-focused ones such as Head Start, to those aimed at facilitating the development of skills in older adults for adapting to retirement.

The first chapter by Joseph Durlak examines theory and data pertaining to social problem-solving approaches to prevention. A discussion of the relationship of social problem-solving abilities to social competence

and social skills more generally is presented. Social problem-solving abilities are seen as but one of a set of social skills broadly defined, with social competence a general supraordinate concept reflecting effective adaptive functioning. Four areas of particular concern are examined: the nature of problem-solving abilities and their relation to adjustment, the viability of programs for enhancing problem-solving ability, the long-term effects of such programs, and the association between skill enhancement and adjustment. In his discussion and elaboration of these concerns Durlak proposes a framework for distinguishing among three theoretical approaches to understanding and enhancing social problem-solving. Distinctions are drawn between approaches which are primarily focused on social problem-solving abilities as cognitive processes, as key aspects of social-cognitive development, and as task-specific skills. The evidence for each is evaluated and their implications for preventive programming elucidated.

In the second chapter Steven Danish, Nancy Galambos, and Idamarie Laquerta argue that competency building is a reasonable preventive activity, but that the preventive capacity of this kind of training is best viewed in the context of a life development perspective. Competency is seen to be addressable via skill building in specific areas, with social skills defined as sets of behaviors that can be modeled, shaped, and reinforced. While Danish et. al. note that cognitive assessment for internalization of these skills is still in need of refinement, the observational assessment techniques available currently do allow for measurement of learning.

The training of competencies is believed to be important for dealing with developmental changes since the skill set so acquired, if sufficiently generalizable, can be used over and over for future life changes. Given that changes in people's lives are inevitable, such skills are seen as central in preventing or reducing stress and the consequent onset of disturbance. For the sake of giving substance to the theory, examples of programs attempting such interventions are provided.

A particular issue Danish and his colleagues raise from this review relates to the "building" or "enrichment" perspective of skill programs. The "building" orientation focuses on stress and attempts to prevent disorder. The "enrichment" orientation attempts to encourage growth and increase health. The authors point out that one perspective has had as its target prevention of illness and the other, the promotion of health. While both activities presently come under the heading of preventive activity, the basic differences in such goals are seen as potentially confusing for a preventive model.

These chapters provide two different but complementary perspectives on competency building. They review a range of examples as well as two different frameworks for building programs. The number of questions and issues posed by both chapters give pause, but they also give hope for the development of competency enhancing programs. A careful assessment of time and place for a skill as well as the cognitive, affective, and behavioral components of a skill is imperative for successful developmental competency building programs. Interventions require careful monitoring and a knowledge of environmental contingencies, if the enhancement efforts are to have generalizable effects.

# 3 SOCIAL PROBLEM-SOLVING AS A PRIMARY PREVENTION STRATEGY

## Joseph A. Durlak

Problem-solving training is enjoying increasing interest in the field of clinical psychology, and this type of intervention has become one of the most frequently cited aproaches to primary prevention. Social problem-solving (or interpersonal problem-solving) refers to the ability to resolve successfully and appropriately conflicts or problems that arise in real-life interpersonal situations. The intent of this chapter is to provide both an overview and an analysis of the current status of this burgeoning field. Rather than offer a comprehensive research review, it will present and discuss representative studies in different areas. The intent is to highlight the advantages and limitations of problem-solving interventions and to offer recommendations designed to improve future research and practice.

In order to place social problem-solving into its appropriate context, it is necessary to distinguish among such terms: "social competence," "social skills," and "social problem-solving." Whether social competence is viewed as a general trait or a summation of task-specific skills depends on one's theoretical orientation. However, as noted by McFall (1982), social competence is best viewed as a general evaluative term referring to the quality of a person's behavior in social situations. Among the many factors that contribute to social competence are general intelligence, physical capabilities, environmental advantages, and social skills. Recently the latter concept has been emphasized as a major source of the variance in social competence.

Placing the above concepts in context, problem-solving abilities are one set of social skills broadly defined; social skills are one important contributory factor toward social competence; and social competence is a supraordinate concept reflecting effective interpersonal functioning. Therefore, problem-solving programs are competency-building primary prevention interventions that attempt to prevent negative outcomes by training individuals in what are believed to be important social skills, namely, interpersonal problem-solving skills. Whereas the present chapter discusses social problem-solving, Chapter 4 evaluates other social skills interventions.

It is easy to accept the potential value of effective problem-solving abilities. Good problem-solvers, it would seem, are flexible and adaptable in different social circumstances, able to deal effectively with stress, and able to develop suitable methods to attain personal goals and satisfy their needs. Moreover, repeated success in problem-solving would be expected to heighten self-confidence, motivation, and perseverance, thus facilitating future task performance.

Regardless of how logical this seems, effective theory and research is needed to confirm the value of interpersonal problem-solving skills. For example, Cowen (1977) has noted that four important questions must be answered by primary prevention programmers who seek to promote social competence. With respect to interpersonal problem-solving, these questions are: (1) are problem-solving skills important factors in adjustment? (2) can programs be developed to teach effective problem-solving? (3) are program effects enduring? and finally, (4) is there a relationship between skill-enhancement and adjustment? The remainder of this chapter discusses the extent to which current problem-solving interventions have answered these questions.

## Theoretical Approaches to Problem-Solving

Tables 3.1, 3.2, and 3.3 summarize the characteristics and outcomes of representative problem-solving programs. The studies are divided into three categories for conceptual reasons. Although distinctions across categories are not always clear-cut, and there are exceptions, each group of studies is related to a different theoretical position regarding problem-solving skills. Before discussing particular studies, it is helpful to summarize these three theoretical approaches.

### TABLE 3.1: COGNITIVE PROGRAMS

Studies in Table 3.1 view problem-solving as a series of cognitive processes that are generalizable to many situations. The problem-solving process is broken down into its component features, and these components become the object of intervention, generally to the exclusion of any other skills or competencies. A major hypothesis is that a central core of cognitive problem-solving processes mediate adjustment: improving these cognitive processes should lead directly to improved behavioral adjustment. This theoretical approach has been most strongly influenced by research conducted by the staff at the Hahnemann Medical College in Philadelphia (Spivack, Platt, & Shure, 1976; Spivack & Shure, 1974).

Spivack and Shure (1974) theorize that certain cognitive skills determine problem-solving ability. The most important skills include alternative thinking (the ability to develop alternative solutions to problems), consequential thinking (the ability to anticipate the consequences of one's actions upon others), and means-end thinking (the ability to develop a step-by-step problem-solving approach and modify this approach as the situation dictates). Spivack and Shure have concentrated their attention on interventions for young

schoolchildren. They believe that all schoolchildren can benefit from training directed at improving these three problem-solving skills.

### TABLE 3.2: DEVELOPMENTAL PROGRAMS

This approach also emphasizes the acquisition of core skills with important implications for adjustment, but cognitive problem-solving skills are considered to be of secondary importance to more primary skills. These primary skills are social-cognitive abilities emphasized in the developmental literature such as social sensitivity, social cognition, and role-taking skills (perspective-taking). Therefore, studies in this category are identified as developmental studies. It is assumed that before individuals can act effectively in social situations, they must be able to understand and interpret what is expected and appropriate in each setting. To do so successfully, they must be skilled in social perception, social sensitivity, or role-taking skills so that they can understand and interpret the communications and behaviors of others, particularly the emotions and intentions guiding others' behaviors. Therefore, to behave effectively in interpersonal situations, individuals must possess certain primary social cognitive abilities. These primary social-cognitive abilities become the main focus of training. The major hypothesis is that improvement in such abilities as role-taking will improve interpersonal functioning, including problem-solving skills. Cognitive developmental theory (Flavell, 1963) has stimulated this research orientation.

### TABLE 3.3: TASK-SPECIFIC PROGRAMS

The third approach differs from the first two in that problem-solving is viewed in task-specific terms. Different tasks require different skills. Typically, skills targeted for training are based upon a careful task analysis or review of prior research comparing skilled to unskilled individuals. Usually, discrete overt responses (assertiveness, communication skills) receive equal or greater weight in training compared to cognitive problem-solving skills. Therefore, the third approach does not assume the existence of a common set of problem-solving skills that mediate adjustment; problem-solving skills are dependent most of all on situational demands. Different skills are required in different situations to accomplish different tasks.

The work of D'Zurilla and Goldfried (D'Zurilla & Goldfried, 1971; Goldfried & D'Zurilla, 1969) is most relevant to this approach. D'Zurilla and Goldfried assert that cognitive processes are important in problem-solving and identify a core set of five cognitive processes that are applicable across situations; however, they also maintain that cognitive factors interact with affective and behavioral factors to influence problem-solving in each situation. Moreover, these affective and behavioral factors are situation-specific.

For example, fear and anxiety may inhibit problem-solving on particular tasks, whereas feelings of self-confidence and high expectations of success may facilitate performance. The behavioral skills needed to resolve each problem situation vary depending on the task. Individuals may be skilled to perform some tasks but not others. D'Zurilla and Goldfried's approach demands a multidimensional needs-assessment prior to intervention. Affective states, cognitive problem-solving skills, and task-specific behavioral skills must be assessed so that subsequent intervention can be directed appropriately at individuals' problem-solving deficits.

In effect, whereas the first two theoretical approaches are individually oriented and general in nature (what general abilities must an individual possess to solve problems effectively?), the third approach is interactional and specific (what specific abilities are demanded by each situation and is the individual able cognitively, behaviorally, and affectively to meet these task demands?).

## Representative Problem-Solving Programs

### TABLE 3.1: COGNITIVE PROGRAMS

Table 3.1 presents representative programs emphasizing the cognitive approach to problem-solving training. Since these programs have been described at length elsewhere (Kirschenbaum & Ordman, 1982; Urbain & Kendall, 1980), only a prototypical example is presented here.

Spivak and Shure (1974) have developed methods to assess various cognitive problem-solving skills such as alternative thinking, consequential thinking, and means-end thinking and have also developed a curriculum to teach these skills to young schoolchildren. Basically, their program involves a series of structured group meetings in which one trainer sees six to eight children in daily 20- to 30-minute sessions for two to four months. Training for preschool and kindergarten children is divided into three parts. The children are first taught prerequisite cognitive and linguistic concepts such as same-different and if-then, and the identification of different emotions such as happy, sad, and angry. Children are then trained in generating alternative solutions to problems, understanding the consequences of proposed behaviors, and then pairing these problem-solving skills together. Group discus-

sions, visual aids, puppet play, and role-playing are used during training following a carefully prepared program manual. Older schoolchildren are also trained in means-end thinking using the same training format and procedures.

Other studies listed in Table 3.1 illustrate alternative types of school-based problem-solving training for children. The goal is similar across these programs— to train children in cognitive problem-solving skills— but there are several differences in terms of program implementation. For example, researchers have targeted three (Poitras-Martin & Stone, 1977; Press et al., 1981), five (Allen et al., 1976) seven (Russell & Roberts, 1979) or eight (Weissberg, Gesten, Carnrike et al., 1981; Weissberg, Gesten, Rapkin et al., 1981) specific problem-solving processes for training. For the most part, teachers have implemented the programs either alone or with the assistance of trained undergraduates, but graduate students and unidentified experimenters (Poitras-Martin & Stone, 1977; Russell & Roberts, 1979; Stone et al., 1975) have also served as trainers. Children have usually been taught problem-solving skills using videotaped modeling alone or in combination with discussion and role-playing exercises (Allen et al., 1976; McClure et al., 1978; Stone et al., 1975; Weissberg, Gesten, Carnrike et al., 1981; Weissberg, Gesten, Rapkin et al., 1981); specially prepared student workbooks have been used as the primary training vehicle in some programs (Houtz & Feldhussen, 1976; Russell & Roberts, 1979). Programs have varied in length from only a few sessions (Russell & Roberts, 1979; Stone et al., 1975) to over fifty (Weissberg, Gesten, Rapkin et al., 1981).

Not all the studies in this category are directed at children. The approach of Briscoe, Hoffman, and Bailey (1977) in training nine lower-socioeconomic adults in problem-solving skills deserves special attention. The effects of training were assessed as the trainees participated in group meetings as policy board members of a federally funded community self-help project. A well-controlled multiple baseline design across subjects and skills indicated success in training the board members in the successive skills of (a) identifying a problem, (b) stating and evaluating alternative problem solutions, and (c) implementing a course of action for each problem. Training effects were still apparent at two-month follow-up. Moreover, four judges independently rated videotapes of board meetings during baseline and training conditions. Judges' ratings confirmed the social validity of the intervention in terms of producing clinically significant changes in the trainees' problem-solving ability. The study by Briscoe et al. (1977) illustrates that problem-solving

## Table 3.1. Characteristics and Outcomes of Representative Cognitive Problem-Solving Programs

| STUDY | SAMPLE | GENERAL DESIGN[a] | OUTCOME MEASURES | RESULTS[b] | LENGTH OF FOLLOW-UP AND RESULTS |
|---|---|---|---|---|---|
| Allen, Chinsky, Larcen, Lochman, & Selinger (1976) | 150 3rd & 4th graders | E = trained<br>C = controls | (a) Problem-solving skills<br>(b) Simulated problem situation<br>(c) Locus of control<br>(d) Teacher ratings<br>(e) Sociometric<br>(f) Self-esteem<br>(g) Level of aspiration | (a) $E>C$<br>(b) $E>C$<br>(c) $E>C$<br>(d) $E=C$<br>(e) $E=C$<br>(f) $E=C$<br>(g) $E=C$ | (a) 4 months,[c] $E = C$ |
| Briscoe, Hoffman, & Bailey (1977) | 9 lower-SES adults | Multiple Baseline | (a) Problem-solving skills<br>(b) Social validity of skill change | (a) Positive<br>(b) Positive | (a) 2 months, positive |
| Dixon, Heppner, Petersen, & Ronning (1979) | 50 college students | E = trained<br>C = controls | (a) Problem-solving skills | (a) $E>C$ | None |
| Houtz & Feldhusen (1976) | 240 4th graders | $E_1$ = trained & rewarded<br>$E_2$ = trained only<br>C = controls | (a) Problem-solving skills | (a) $E_2>E_1>C$ | None |
| McClure, Chinsky, & Larcen (1978) | 178 3rd & 4th graders | $E_1$ = video training<br>$E_2$ = video & discussion<br>$E_3$ = video & role-playing<br>C = Controls | (a) Problem-solving skills<br>(b) Simulated problem-situation<br>(c) Locus of control | (a) $E_2>E_1,E_3,C$<br>(b) $E_1,E_2,E_3>C$<br>(c) $E_1,E_2,E_3>C$ | None |
| Poitras-Martin & Stone (1977) | 36 6th graders | E = trained<br>$C_1$ = attention controls<br>$C_2$ = untreated controls | (a) Problem-solving skills | (a) $E=C_1=C_2$ | (a) 2 weeks, $E=C_1=C_2$ |
| Press, Alvarez, Cotler, & Jason (1981) | 24 4th graders | E = trained<br>C = controls | (a) Problem-solving skills<br>(b) Simulated problem situation<br>(c) Teacher ratings<br>(d) Behavioral observations<br>(e) Sociometric<br>(f) Self-esteem | (a) $E>C$<br>(b) $E=C$<br>(c) $E=C$<br>(d) $E=C$<br>(e) $E=C$<br>(f) $E=C$ | 4 months:[d]<br>(a) Positive<br>(b) Negative<br>(c) Negative<br>(d) Negative<br>(e) Negative<br>(f) Negative |

| Study | N / Sample | Treatment conditions | Outcome measures | Results[b] | Follow-up |
|---|---|---|---|---|---|
| Russell & Roberts (1979) | 34 4th graders | E = trained<br>C = controls | (a) Problem-solving skills | (a) E>C | None |
| Shure & Spivack (1978) | 40 preschoolers | E = trained mothers<br>C = control mothers | (a) Problem-solving skills<br>(b) Teacher ratings | (a) E>C<br>(b) E>C | None |
| Shure & Spivack (1979) | 131 nursery & kindergarten children | $E_1$ = trained yrs. 1 & 2<br>$E_2$ = trained yr. 1 only<br>$E_3$ = trained yr. 2 only<br>C = controls | (a) Problem-solving skills<br>(b) Teacher ratings | (a) $E_1>E_2,E_3>$C<br>(b) $E_1,E_2,E_3>$C | (a) 1 yr., $E_2>$C[c] |
| Spivack & Shure (1974) | 219 preschoolers | E = trained<br>C = controls | (a) Problem-solving skills<br>(b) Teacher ratings | (a) E>C<br>(b) E>C | (a) 6 months, E>C<br>(b) 6 months, E>C |
| Stone, Hinds & Schmidt (1975) | 144 3rd–5th graders | E = trained<br>C = controls | (a) Problem-solving skills | (a) E>C | None |
| Weissberg, Gesten, Carnrike, Toro, Rapkin, Davidson, & Cowen (1981) | 563 2nd–4th graders | E = trained<br>C = controls | (a) Problem-solving skills<br>(b) Simulated problem situation<br>(c) Teacher ratings<br>(d) Sociometric | (a) E>C<br>(b) E>C<br>(c) E>C<br>(d) E=C | None |
| Weissberg, Gesten, Rapkin, Cowen, Davidson, de-Apodaca, & McKim (1981) | 243 3rd graders | E = trained<br>C = controls | (a) Problem-solving skills<br>(b) Simulated problem situation<br>(c) Teacher ratings<br>(d) Role-taking skills<br>(e) Sociometric<br>(f) State-trait anxiety<br>(g) Self-concept | (a) E>C<br>(b) E>C<br>(c) E>C<br>(d) E=C<br>(e) E=C<br>(f) E=C<br>(g) E=C | None[d] |

[a] Unless otherwise indicated, C = untreated controls.

[b] An > indicates significant differences between treatment conditions.

[c] These follow-up results were reported in McClure, Chinsky, & Larcen, 1978.

[d] Controls were given training during follow-up; results reported as a function of change from pre to follow-up for E group.

35

training can be effectively introduced into complex and potentially important community settings.

EVALUATION OF COGNITIVE PROGRAMS

There are too few programs for adults to reach any conclusions, but programs for children have generally yielded discouraging results. Studies clearly indicate that it is possible to improve children's problem-solving abilities through training, but whether this improvement has any effect on their overt behavioral adjustment is questionable.

With one exception (Poitras-Martin & Stone, 1977) all the child-oriented programs have obtained positive training effects on problem-solving outcome measures. However, only the Hahnemann group, using teacher ratings, has consistently demonstrated effects on children's adjustment status (Shure & Spivack, 1978, 1979; Spivack & Shure, 1974). Other investigators either did not measure the effects of problem-solving training on general adjustment (Houtz & Feldhusen, 1976; Poitras-Martin & Stone, 1977; Russell & Roberts, 1979; Stone et al., 1975), failed to obtain positive changes on various adjustment measures (Allen et al., 1976; McClure et al., 1978; Press et al., 1981), or noted that children's improvement in interpersonal functioning was generally uncorrelated with gains in problem-solving ability (Weissberg, Gesten, Carnrike et al., 1981; Weissberg, Gesten, Rapkin et al., 1981). These latter findings suggest that factors other than cognitive problem-solving skills are operating to effect change.

Moreover, additional studies have failed to find significant relationships between young children's problem-solving skills and other indices of adjustment that have included naturalistic observations of classroom and play behavior, teacher ratings, and sociometric status (Butler, 1978; Gillespie, Durlak, & Sherman, 1982; Rickel & Burgio, 1982; Winer, Hilpert, Gesten, Cowen & Schubin, 1982). In general, current data fail to support the fundamental assumption that cognitive problem-solving skills are important to adjustment.

In addition to these discouraging findings, methodological problems characterize many current programs. There is a need for attention-placebo control groups, more adequate follow-up, and more objective outcome data. For example, only four studies have collected follow-up data, and two of these (Allen et al., 1976; Poitras-Martin & Stone, 1977) obtained negative results. The latter study is apparently the only investigation to include attention control groups, an important design element when evaluating interventions for young children. The unpublished study

by Press et al. (1981) has been the only one to collect independent behavioral observations assessing treatment effects, and negative results were obtained on this measure.

Moreover, investigators never seem to question the assumption that all children need and can benefit from problem-solving training. It is important to investigate whether some children already possess adequate problem-solving skills but need other skills training, or alternatively, whether other skills are more important than problem-solving for effective interpersonal functioning.

Therefore, comparative studies of problem-solving and non-problem-solving interventions are definitely needed. For example, children receiving problem-solving training can be compared to those receiving training in academic skills or other social skills. Studies comparing role-taking and problem-solving training are also needed (see below).

Notwithstanding the above considerations, there is the possibility that cognitive problem-solving has not received an adequate test. For example, Shure[*] has argued that "dialoguing" is essential in insuring generalization of problem-solving training. "Dialoguing" involves teacher interventions throughout the school day to assist children in the application of a problem-solving orientation in their social interactions. In effect, it is an effort to program generalization of newly acquired skills. It has become axiomatic in the behavioral literature that for maximum success investigators should program generalization into their training rather than expecting it to occur naturally. Unfortunately, it is difficult to discern from published reports whether dialoguing was implemented. Furthermore, the dialogue process is difficult to standardize as a programmatic component, making evaluations across studies difficult.

With regard to program implementation, Weissberg and Gesten (1982) have raised some additional issues. These investigators note that problem-solving interventions "are complex undertakings, and much battleline program experience and trial-and-error work is needed to develop an age-appropriate curriculum and effective training procedures [p. 61]." They report that successive modifications over a three-year period were made in order to strengthen their problem-solving program. The third-year effort, which was most successful (Weissberg, Gesten, Carnrike et al., 1981), differed in several fundamental ways from their first

[*] Shure, M. B. Promoting social competence: A cognitive strategy. In Rolf, J. E. (Chair), Progress in identifying and promoting social competence in vulnerable children. Symposium presented at the American Psychological Association, New York, September 1979.

attempt (Weissberg, Gesten, Rapkin et al., 1981), which had limited impact.

For problem-solving programs in general, the question then arises: Which program changes are needed because of inexperience on the part of program developers and front-line change agents (teachers), which are necessary to suit the situational parameters of a community setting, and which are essential in maintaining the integrity of the problem-solving model? Sensitivity is needed in disentangling these issues. Carefully controlled comparative studies are needed to assess which training procedures are more effective and which programmatic features generalize successfully to other settings.

### TABLE 3.2: DEVELOPMENTAL PROGRAMS

The four studies in Table 3.2 illustrate the range of attempts to train children in role-taking skills and measure the effects of this training on problem-solving ability and other indices of adjustment. Role-taking involves the ability to recognize and understand the internal states of others. These studies have been reviewed elsewhere (Urbain & Kendall, 1980) and are only summarized here.

Findings have not been altogether consistent. Elardo and Caldwell (1979) evaluated the impact of the Project Aware training program, which emphasizes both perspective-taking and problem-solving training. Teachers implemented the program in their fourth and fifth grade classrooms; 25-minute sessions were held twice a week over a seven-month period. Teachers followed a carefully prepared curriculum plan that included activities designed to promote children's understanding of the thoughts and feelings of others. Activities also allowed children the opportunity to generate alternative solutions to problem situations and to evaluate the relative consequences of different problem solutions. Project Aware training significantly improved children's classroom adjustment as measured by teacher ratings. However, improvement was obtained on only one of six stories assessing problem-solving skills, and there were no significant changes in role-taking skills over time. Such data make it difficult to say which aspects of training were responsible for the children's apparent classroom improvement.

Iannotti (1978) investigated two types of role-taking training with six- and nine-year-old boys. In a role-taking condition, each child assumed the perspective of one character in a story; in a role-switching condition, the boys switched roles frequently during the enactment of the story. There were no outcome differences between the two training conditions. Role-taking training significantly improved kindergarten children's altruism, but not their empathic behaviors or problem-solving abilities. Marsh et al. (1980) evaluated the effects of role-taking training on eighth grade students' problem-solving skills. Training involved role-playing exercises specifically designed to help the students articulate the thoughts and feelings of characters involved in problematic situations. The role-playing was videotaped and played back to participants for discussion purposes. Training failed to affect students' means-end problem-solving abilities but did result in gains on a specially designed measure of problem analysis. Finally, Enright et al. (1977) supervised sixth graders who served as discussion group leaders for first graders. The supervisory procedures, which were designed to affect the older children's role-taking skills, did increase their level of moral development but not their means-end thinking.

### EVALUATION OF DEVELOPMENTAL PROGRAMS

It is difficult to reconcile the above results. There is the suggestion, but no more than that, that role-taking training may influence the development of problem-solving skills and affect other aspects of interpersonal functioning. However, this conclusion is clouded by the disparate subject samples, training procedures, and outcome measures used across studies.

Nevertheless, the above findings have implications for future research. Both role-taking and problem-solving skills should be assessed in future programs in which either or both of these skills are trained. Role-taking and problem-solving skills are competing theoretical explanations for the development of social competence. As noted previously, whereas some investigators believe that problem-solving skills are necessary and sufficient for effective interpersonal functioning, others believe role-taking skills are the more primary and important factor. Designs permitting analysis of the relative importance of these skills would be elucidating. It may be that either or neither of the above skills is causally related to adjustment, or that both are.

### TABLE 3.3: TASK-SPECIFIC PROGRAMS

Table 3.3 presents representative task-specific problem-solving training programs. The studies in Table 3.3 are discussed in detail here *precisely because these investigations are often overlooked as problem-solving programs.* Invariably, reviewers attend exclusively to cognitive programs for children. But as the following discussion illustrates, several problem-solving interventions for adolescents and adults have been implemented.

## Table 3.2. Characteristics and Outcomes of Representative Developmental Problem-Solving Programs

| STUDY | SAMPLE | GENERAL DESIGN[a] | OUTCOME MEASURES | RESULTS[b] | LENGTH OF FOLLOW-UP AND RESULTS |
|---|---|---|---|---|---|
| Elardo & Caldwell (1979) | 68 4th & 5th graders | E = trained<br>C = controls | (a) Problem-solving skills<br>(b) Role-taking skills<br>(c) Teacher ratings | (a) E = C<br>(b) E = C<br>(c) E > C | None |
| Enright, Colby, & McMullin (1977) | 24 6th graders | E = trained<br>C = controls | (a) Problem-solving skills<br>(b) Referential communication<br>(c) Moral development | (a) E = C<br>(b) E = C<br>(c) E > C | None |
| Iannotti (1978) | 60 kindergarten & 3rd graders | $E_1$ = role-switching training<br>$E_2$ = role-taking training<br>C = controls | (a) Role-taking skills<br>(b) Empathy<br>(c) Problem-solving skills<br>(d) Altruism | (a) $E_1, E_2 > C$<br>(b) $E_1 = E_2 = C$<br>(c) $E_1 = E_2 = C$<br>(d) $E_1, E_2 > C$ | None |
| Marsh, Serafica, & Barenboim (1980) | 64 8th graders | E = trained<br>C = controls | (a) Problem-solving skills<br>(b) Problem analytic skills<br>(c) Social role-taking<br>(d) Affective role-taking | (a) E = C<br>(b) E > C<br>(c) E = C<br>(d) E = C | None |

[a] Unless otherwise indicated, C = untreated controls.
[b] An > indicates significant differences between treatment conditions.

Table 3.3. Characteristics and Outcomes of Representative Task-Specific Problem-Solving Programs

| STUDY | SAMPLE | GENERAL DESIGN[a] | OUTCOME MEASURES | RESULTS[b] | LENGTH OF FOLLOW-UP AND RESULTS |
|---|---|---|---|---|---|
| Avery, Ridley, Leslie, & Milholland (1980) | 37 marital couples | E = REP<br>C = attention controls | (a) Communication skills | (a) E > C | (a) 6 months, E > C |
| Azrin, Flores, & Kaplan (1975) | 120 unemployed adults | E = Job Club<br>C = Controls | (a) Employment<br>(b) Starting salary | (a) E > C<br>(b) E > C | None |
| Guerney, Coufal, & Vogelsong (1981) | 61 mothers & daughters | E = REP<br>$C_1$ = attention controls<br>$C_2$ = untreated controls | (a) Communication skills<br>(b) Quality of dyadic relationship | (a) E > $C_1$, $C_2$<br>(b) E > $C_1$ > $C_2$ | None |
| Haynes, Wise, Sherman, Jensen, & Stein (1979) | newly married couples | E = behavioral training<br>C = controls | (a) Marital adjustment<br>(b) Child problems<br>(c) Communication skills | In progress | |
| Hurd, Johnson, Pechacek, Bast, Jacobs, & Luepker (1980) | 1,245 7th graders | $E_1$ = Social pressure<br>$E_2$ = $E_1$ + personalization<br>$E_3$ = $E_1$ + $E_2$ + commitment<br>C = controls | (a) Smoking rate | (a) $E_1$ + $E_2$ + $E_3$ > C | None |
| Jessee & Guerney (1981) | 52 marital couples | $E_1$ = REP<br>$E_2$ = Gestalt therapy | (a) Marital adjustment<br>(b) Communication inventory<br>(c) Quality of relationship | (a) $E_1$ = $E_2$<br>(b) $E_1$ > $E_2$<br>(c) $E_1$ > $E_2$ | None |
| Kim (1981b) | 14,117 5th–12th graders | E = ombudsman<br>C = controls | (a) Drug use | (a) E > C | None |
| Markman & Floyd (1980) | 8 couples | E = behavioral training<br>C = controls | (a) Communication skills<br>(b) Marital problems<br>(c) Marital adjustment | (a) C > E<br>(b) E = C<br>(c) E = C | None |
| Pinsker & Geoffroy (1981) | 40 parents | $E_1$ = PET<br>$E_2$ = behavioral training<br>C = controls | (a) Family conflict<br>(b) Self-concept<br>(c) Child problem behavior | (a) $E_1$ > $E_2$, C<br>(b) $E_1$ = $E_2$ = C<br>(c) $E_2$ > C | None |
| Schinke, Blythe, & Gilchrist (1981) | 36 adolescents | E = trained<br>C = controls | (a) Problem-solving skills<br>(b) Sexual knowledge<br>(c) Assertiveness<br>(d) Birth control practices | (a) E > C<br>(b) E > C<br>(c) E > C | (d) 6 months, E > C |
| Schinke, Gilchrist, Smith, & Wong (1978) | 26 adolescent mothers | E = behavioral training<br>C = attention controls | (a) Employment application<br>(b) Simulated job interview<br>(c) Social validity of performance in (b) | (a) E > C<br>(b) E > C<br>(c) E > C | None |

## DRUG PREVENTION PROGRAMS

The prevention of drug abuse has posed a continuous challenge to investigators. Historically, programs in these areas have assumed that accurate information about drugs would influence subsequent attitude and behavioral change. Previous programs, therefore, have been didactically oriented, using fear-arousal techniques which emphasize the hazardous effects of drugs. Unfortunately, there is general agreement that such programs have not been effective (Kinder, Pape, & Walfish, 1980; Schaps, Churgin, Palley, Takata, & Cohen, 1980).

Guided by empirical findings, a consensus is building among independent investigators that a variety of psychosocial factors influence youthful drug taking. Considered among the most important are adult and peer modeling effects, personal and social reinforcement regarding drug use, ineffective decision-making skills, and lack of assertiveness in withstanding peer pressure (Huba, Wingard, & Bentler, 1979; Jalali, Jalali, Crocetti, & Turner, 1981; Kim, 1981a, 1981b).

These findings suggest that in order to prevent drug taking, youths should be trained in decision-making and assertiveness skills and provided with opportunities to interact with appropriate models (meaning those who do not advocate drug taking). These programmatic features have been successfully incorporated into several recent studies, two of which are presented in Table 3.3 and discussed below.

Kim (1981a, 1981b) has reported on the success of the most comprehensive program to date, developed by the staff of the North Carolina Charlotte Drug Education Center. The core of the intervention is a three-phase program (Ombudsman) developed for elementary and high school students. The first phase focuses upon self-awareness and teaches students how to examine and understand their feelings, attitudes, and values. The second phase, group skills, trains students in communication skills, decision-making, and problem-solving by practicing these skills in a small group context and then extending their application to other interpersonal situations involving peers and family. In the final phase of the program, students again actively apply their previously acquired knowledge and skills by developing and conducting relevant new projects in their schools and communities. In some investigations the core Ombudsman program has been supplemented by specialized support and training services for participating teachers, school administrators, parents, and adult volunteers. Several thousand students have been involved in the Ombudsman program and, as a group, show a reduction in drug usage compared to nonparticipant controls.

Unfortunately, current evaluations of Ombudsman have relied upon self-report measures. Nevertheless, this comprehensive effort at drug prevention is impressive in scope and execution, and future research may help elucidate the most effective programmatic elements.

Another study focused specifically upon the prevention of cigarette smoking in junior high schoolers (Hurd et al., 1980). Over 1,500 seventh grade students at four schools were assigned to a control condition or to treatment conditions involving one, two, or three program elements, identified as social pressures curriculum, personalization, and commitment.

In the intervention involving the social pressures curriculum, college student group leaders presented didactic information designed to increase sensitivity to the social pressures favoring smoking and then monitored students during role-playing exercises so that the students could practice resisting social pressures to smoke. In the personalization component, students at one of the program schools who previously had been nominated by their peers as individuals whose "opinions were respected" were brought to the university and coached as they made an antismoking videotape film. This film was shown and discussed in the relevant school. In the final treatment component, commitment, students were asked to declare publicly that they would not smoke and to offer reasons for their decision. Each student's commitment was videotaped in front of the class and then replayed for all the students. Overall, the intervention appeared to reduce the onset of smoking; students exposed to all three aspects of the intervention appeared to show more change than those exposed to only one component. Self-report outcome data indicated that fewer students in the program schools than in the control schools became regular smokers at the end of the school year; there were also more students in the program schools who quit smoking entirely and fewer who were considered to be experimental smokers. Furthermore, thiocyanate analysis of saliva samples provided confirmatory evidence of the effects of the intervention.

## PREVENTION OF UNWANTED PREGNANCY

Schinke and his colleagues have developed an impressive programmatic research effort directed at preventing unwanted teenage pregnancy, currently occurring at epidemic proportions throughout the country (Schinke et al., 1981; Schinke, Gilchrist, & Blythe, 1980; Schinke, Gilchrist, & Small, 1979).

Reviewing contemporary research findings including some of their own investigations, Schinke et al. concluded that developmental and interpersonal factors interacted to influence adolescent sexual activities. Many adolescents are unable to master the critical tasks required by their developing sexuality. For example, adolescents must not only understand what physical and affective changes are occuring during their sexual maturation but also must integrate these changes into their self-concepts and interpersonal behavior. Moreover, adolescents must be sensitive to similar changes occuring among their peers. These developmental tasks are made more difficult if, as data suggest, adolescents process inadequate knowledge concerning sexuality and contraceptive methods. Research also indicates that individuals who have an unplanned pregnancy cannot communicate their feelings effectively and/or cannot assert themselves in sexual situations.

In effect, sexual maturation is a critical life transition which many adolescents attempt to negotiate with poor communication skills, lack of assertiveness, gross misinformation about sexuality and contraception, and inadequate decision-making skills. The result is high risk of pregnancy, over one million adolescent pregnancies annually.

Accordingly, an intervention was developed to train adolescents in effective decision-making, communication skills, interpersonal problem-solving, and assertiveness. Training takes place in small groups using social learning principles: adolescents are shown and then reinforced for such sex-related behaviors as refusing unreasonable demands, making appropriate requests of others, and expressing themselves positively and specifically.

This cognitive-behavioral approach to pregnancy prevention has yielded several promising findings. A recent study (Schinke et al., 1981) demonstrated that compared to untrained controls, trained adolescents displayed more accurate sexual information and were better problem-solvers immediately following intervention; they also practiced more effective contraception at six-month follow-up.

#### JOB PROGRAMS

Two studies, one directed at adolescents and the other at adults, addressed an important problem with far-reaching personal, social, and economic consequences—unemployment.

Azrin, Flores, and Kaplan (1975) developed a Job-Finding Club for unemployed adults from a small rural town. In terms of the problem-solving process, the intervention conceived of certain factors as important in the employment process. These included obtaining social and emotional support from others, effective information-seeking behaviors, interpersonal behavior during the interview process, and resource sharing and mutual cooperation among job-seekers. The Job Club was a daily group meeting that addressed these issues. Participants were taught how to seek and share information about job leads, contact potential employers over the phone, obtain good letters of recommendation, prepare an effective résumé, and obtain more support and help from family and friends. Supervised role-playing of simulated job interviews was also conducted. In two months' time, 90 percent of the Job Club members (54 of 60) had obtained employment at an average starting salary approximately one-third higher than 55 percent of the controls (38 of 60) who started working during the same time period. Extensions of similar interventions for the handicapped (Azrin & Philip, in press) and for welfare recipients (Azrin, Philip, Thienes-Hontas, & Bassalel, 1980) have also been successful. Moreover, the strategy exemplified by the Job Club has been adopted by the Department of Labor as a standard component of the Work Incentive Program (see Stolz, 1981).

Since many unwed mothers are from minority groups and have left school because of pregnancy, their employment prospects are even bleaker than those for teenagers in general. Schinke et al. used social-learning techniques that emphasized instructions, modeling, role-playing, and performance feedback to teach mothers such behaviors as how to answer questions clearly and concisely and how to highlight personal strengths and decrease negative self-statements during the interview process. Before and after training, mothers completed employment applications and participated in a simulated, videotaped personal job interview. Trained mothers showed significant improvement on both outcome indices over time compared to those in an attention-placebo control group. Hiring recommendations offered by an independent personnel specialist who viewed the taped job interview supported the social validity of the performance change attained by the experimental group. Unfortunately, no data were obtained on the mothers' ability to obtain actual jobs following training.

#### PARENT AND FAMILY PROGRAMS

Parent Effectiveness Training (PET) is a parent training program that incorporates a problem-solving component. PET is a humanistically oriented approach that trains parents in active listening, communication skills, and conflict resolution skills. PET workshops typically are conducted for eight weekly three-hour sessions, require a fee, and are led by a trained group leader. Sessions include lectures, discussions, readings, role-playing, demonstrations, and homework assignments. Outcome evaluations of PET have been discouraging. Rinn and Markle's (1977) analysis of PET outcome studies failed to support its effectiveness as a preventive or intervention strategy; there were few unequivocal indications that PET produces consistent positive changes in participating parents and even less data suggesting that children are affected.

A recent multioutcome study included in Table 3.1 (Pinsker & Geoffroy, 1981) has compared the effectiveness of PET and behavior modification parent training. Differential treatment effects were found. The PET group displayed significantly more family cohesion and less family conflict following training than the behavior modification group. However, children of those parents in the behavioral group showed a significant reduction in their problem behaviors at home as reflected by behavioral observations, whereas PET training failed to produce such changes in children over time. No follow-up was conducted. Groups were not assigned randomly in the Pinsker and Geoffroy study and there are some questions regarding their statistical analyses; however, the use of multioutcome measures including independent observations of children's behavior stands as a definite improvement over prior PET outcome studies. Nevertheless, it is disconcerting that so little evidence exists for the effectiveness of PET when one considers that as of 1976 over 250,000 parents had participated in PET programs (Gordon, 1976).

The Relationship Enhancement Program (REP) developed by Guerney (1977) attempts to help individuals deal with future interpersonal conflicts and crises by training participants in communication skills considered necessary in developing satisfying interpersonal relationships. These skills relate to client-centered principles concerning the clear and specific expression of feelings; understanding and accepting another's feelings, attitudes, and values; and empathy. Effective communication skills are not only problem-oriented. In the absence of conflict, good communication skills can be used to enhance the quality and satisfaction of interpersonal relationships. REP has wide applicability. Programs have been implemented for young children (Vogelsong, 1978), mother–adolescent daughter dyads (Guerney et al., 1981), father-son dyads (Ginsberg, 1977), and premarital and marital couples (Jessee & Guerney, 1981; Ginsberg & Vogelsong, 1977). Only a few of these programs are listed in Table 3.3.

Positive outcome data are accumulating for REP. For example, REP has consistently improved participants' communication skills and these changes go beyond those manifested by attention-placebo controls (Guerney et al., 1981); moreover, short-term follow-up (six months) suggests that training effects are durable (Avery et al., 1980).

An important issue concerns whether or not REP participants' problem-solving skills also improve with training. Ridley et al. (1981) specifically addressed this question. Premarital couples attending an attention-placebo control discussion group and REP were compared on their mutual problem-solving behavior, assessed during role-playing interactions conducted before and after intervention. REP participants significantly improved their problem-solving skills relative to controls.

MARITAL PROGRAMS

There has been a tremendous proliferation of preventively oriented marital programs. By 1975, 180,000 couples had participated in various marriage enrichment programs (Otto, 1975), and by 1977 over 400,000 had been involved in Catholic Marriage Encounters (Demarest, Sexton, & Sexton, 1977). These programs are designed to improve satisfactory marriages; most programs emphasize instruction and training in communication and conflict resolution skills in order to increase interpersonal intimacy and marital satisfaction. Unfortunately, serious methodological shortcomings preclude reaching any definite conclusions regarding the impact of these programs (Gurman & Kniskern, 1977). The same can be said for preventive programs directed at premarital couples (Bagarozzi & Rauen, 1981).

Two behaviorally oriented research groups have recently described a similar approach to the prevention of marital dissatisfaction (Haynes et al., 1979). Previous findings had indicated that compared to satisfied couples, dissatisfied couples can be characterized by poor communication patterns, excessive use of aversive control methods, inadequate knowledge of spouses' attitudes and feelings, lack of enjoyment in the expression of affection and physical intimacy, and finally, inability to negotiate conflicts and achieve mutually satisfying solutions to problems. The programs by Markman and Floyd (1980) and Haynes et al. (1979) are similar in their attempts to affect participants' status on these variables by a combination of cognitive-behavioral and social learning techniques. Communication and problem-solving training are emphasized within multicomponent interventions that also include such elements as direct instruction regarding marital adjustment and sexual functioning, cognitive restructuring, and behavioral contracting.

Rather unexpectedly, Markman and Floyd (1980) reported that the short-term results from their program indicated that untreated controls improved more than participating couples in their response to their spouses' communications. However, the authors noted that a ceiling effect may have contributed to this finding and that long-term treatment effects are the more important criteria. The Haynes group's research effort is designed to collect follow-up measures for up to five years on the program's effects on such negative outcomes as communication difficulties, marital dissatisfaction, child and spouse abuse, child behavior problems, sexual dysfunction, and separation and divorce. Long-term follow-up is the only certain way of assuring a program's true preventive impact.

Nevertheless, both of the above marital programs have high expectations, in that treatment is quite brief: eight 1½-hour sessions (Haynes et al., 1979) and six 3-hour sessions (Markman & Floyd, 1980). It may be very naive to believe that such a brief intervention can provide couples with the skills needed to resolve the many problems that may appear within the entire course of a marriage.

EVALUATION OF TASK-SPECIFIC PROGRAMS

It is difficult to offer broad conclusions concerning the studies in Table 3.3 because investigations differ widely in execution and purpose. In addition to basic methodological considerations, studies that include objective outcome data, conduct follow-up assessment, and control for nonspecified therapeutic effects inspire the most confidence. On that basis, the Relationship Enhancement Program appears very promising, and the programs to prevent drug taking and adolescent pregnancy also have merit. Programs relating to job-seeking also deserve attention. Since work possesses such potentially strong economic, social, and psychological effects, programs to assist individuals in gaining satisfactory employment may ultimately have the strongest preventive consequences. Interventions for parents and premarital and marital couples have not been subject to sufficient scrutiny to permit conclusions regarding program impact.

As a group, the above programs offer some convergent validity to Goldfried and D'Zurilla's (1969) conceptualizations. That is, researchers working in different settings and attempting to achieve different goals have independently come to the conclusion that multicomponent problem-solving programs are necessary. Goldfried and D'Zurilla (1969) maintain that cognitive, behavioral and affective factors interact to produce effective problem-solving. Each of these elements is present in current task-specific programs.

Across the programs reviewed here, behavioral skills training has received the greatest emphasis, followed by training in cognitive problem-solving processes. Affective factors have received the least amount of attention, but have not been overlooked. For instance, personal inhibitions and anxieties interfering with task performance have often been dealt with during the course of communication and assertiveness skills training. In summary, current data offer tentative support to D'Zurilla and Goldfried's theory regarding interpersonal problem-solving.

Admittedly, the first stage of research on preventively oriented change techniques is usually the easiest: namely, to demonstrate that programs "work"—produce some positive effects. Subsequent evaluations become more demanding. Investigators must achieve greater specificity and control over experimental variables and demonstrate that program effects are durable over time and have preventive implications.

It must be emphasized that current task-specific programs are complex multicomponent interventions and it is not possible to evaluate the relative contributions of each programmatic element. Nevertheless, we eventually need to know how each element of an intervention contributes to behavioral change in order to eliminate unnecessary procedures, improve ineffective ones, and capitalize upon the most potent change mechanisms. A few suggestions regarding future research can be offered.

First of all, it is important to assess potential participants to see if they possess deficiencies in the skills to be taught. Ideally, interventions should match the complexity and intensity of a program to individuals' needs. Therefore, multidimensional assessment of problem-solving skills should be accomplished prior to intervention to identify participants' assets and liabilities in each relevant area of problem-solving. Some individuals may need training in several areas, whereas others may need assistance in only one.

Following a needs assessment for training in problem-solving skills, the value of different components in a complex intervention package can be assessed using a dismantling treatment strategy. In such an approach a complex treatment is divided into its separate components. Outcome comparisons are then made among groups who receive different parts of the treatment. Group A may receive the total program, which involves three components; Group B may receive only one component; and Group C may receive two of the three components. Over time, successive research studies following this design can begin to clarify how to provide different forms of problem-solving training effectively and efficiently.

## Assessment of Problem-Solving Skills

The adequate measurement of relevant constructs is fundamental to theoretical and empirical progress. Therefore, it is important to offer some remarks regarding the measurement of problem-solving skills according to each theoretical perspective.

### Cognitive Programs

For the most part, standardized measures developed by the Hahnemann group have been used or modified for use in cognitive problem-solving programs for children. The most frequently used measures are the Preschool Interpersonal Problem-Solving Test (PIPS), the What Happens Next Game, and the Means-End Problem-Solving Test. Butler and Meichenbaum (1981) provide an excellent critique of these and similar measures. Depending on the specific measure, there may be problems involving test reliability, internal consistency, and content validity; for problem-solving measures in general, there are the failures to develop measures that distinguish between ability and performance and that assess problem-solving in qualitative as well as quantitative terms. (Typically, current assessment procedures only use quantitative scoring.)

Others have also expressed reservations concerning the nonevaluative aspect of problem-solving assessments (Camp, Blom, Hebert, & van Doorninck, 1977). Camp et al.'s work with aggressive children led them to suggest that aggressive problem solutions are well within the repertoire of such children and that it would be helpful to these children to actively discourage aggressive solutions and direct them to develop more socially appropriate nonaggressive responses. Furthermore, current cognitive theories fail to specify critical levels of problem-solving ability; the implicit assumption is that "more is better." Yet it is likely that while a minimum level of ability is critical, an asympotote is eventually reached such that a further increase in skills is unlikely to be of much benefit.

A brief discussion of the PIPS, one of the most widely used measures, will illustrate several of these points. On the PIPS, the child is presented with a problem involving a peer or mother figure and asked to generate as many different solutions to the problem as possible. In the peer problem, a child wants to play with a toy that another child has; in the mother problem, a child has damaged some property that could make his or her mother angry and the child must think of ways to avoid her anger. Minor details involving the toy, damaged property, and name of the child character are changed during the test, but basically the same peer or mother problem is presented repeatedly until the child's ability to produce a new

type of solution is exhausted. Each different solution receives one point credit and a total PIPS score is calculated. Higher scores are interpreted to reflect better problem-solving ability.

Several important issues emerge with respect to the PIPS as a reliable and valid measure of problem-solving. First, test-retest reliabilities have been as low as .6 for a four-month period (Spivack & Shure, 1974); as a result, a child's score may fluctuate rather substantially over time as a function of measurement error. Second, there is the question of whether or not test items are an adequate representation of problem situations for children. As noted above, only two types of problems are presented. Furthermore, many cognitive problem-solving programs are school-based interventions and the PIPS does not seem to adequately sample children's problem-solving ability vis-à-vis the school setting. Third, scoring procedures give equal credit to aggressive and prosocial problem solutions; two children can thus earn the same PIPS score by generating qualitatively different types of responses. Fourth, total PIPS scores do not necessarily reflect children's actual preferences for solving real-life problems. Child A with a PIPS score of 7 may consistently display only aggressive or dependent solutions to real-life problems, whereas Child B, who earns a PIPS score of 4, may demonstrate more socially appropriate attempts at real-life problem solutions. Under such circumstances, many observers would consider Child B to be better adjusted socially than Child A, regardless of PIPS scores. Finally, perhaps both Child A and B would not actually attempt more than one or two different solutions to any interpersonal problems they encountered, leaving at issue the practical significance of total PIPS scores. Each of the above issues needs to be resolved, particularly since current data fail to support the theory that children's problem-solving skills, as these are currently measured, are directly related to their interpersonal adjustment.

Standardized problem-solving measures for adults are virtually nonexistent. The psychometric properties of the recently developed problem-solving inventory by Heppner and Petersen (1982) appear promising enough to warrant further investigation.

### Developmental Programs

Problems also emerge with respect to the measurement of social cognitive abilities such as perspective-taking. For example, no theoretical consensus exists regarding the developmental progression of this skill or its measurement. As a result, different assessment methods with varying psychometric properties have been developed. For example, there are measures of perceptual, social-cognitive, and affective role-taking, depending on whether the child is asked to understand the literal visual perspective of another; to identify others' thoughts, motives, or social behaviors; or to intuit others' feelings or emotions. Typically, such measures do not correlate very highly with each other, raising the question of which types of measures should be used in which circumstances for what purposes. Moreover, definitive evidence is lacking that cognitive abilities such as role-taking are causally related to interpersonal functioning. Group comparisons between adapting and maladapting children do not always uncover significant differences on various social-cognitive abilities. Kendall, Pellegrini, and Urbain (1981) and Underwood and Moore (1982) provide an excellent discussion of these issues.

### Task-specific Programs

If problem-solving is viewed in task-specific terms, then a careful task analysis is needed. The problem must be broken down into its component parts and behaviors needed to perform each component successfully must be described. Comparing the performance of skilled and unskilled individuals often provides invaluable data in this regard. This assessment approach is tedious, but a careful task analysis increases the validity of the targeted skills. The drawback is that the development of standardized measures is unlikely, since situational demands argue against discovering a general set of problem-solving abilities applicable across divergent types of problems.

### Other Issues

Butler and Meichenbaum (1981) have proposed that self-appraisal may successfully predict effective problem-solving behavior. If so, it is important to assess individuals' perceptions of their personal problem-solving abilities. Three investigators offer relevant methodologies. Bandura (1978) has assigned self-efficacy a central role in performance and motivation. In brief, self-efficacy is the conviction that one can effectively perform a required behavior. Self-efficacy is believed to strongly influence which behaviors are initiated and the persistence and effort that is expended in relation to these behaviors in the face of obstacles. Measurement of self-efficacy has been used successfully in several treatment studies (see Condiotte & Lichtenstein, 1981). Harter (1982) has recently developed a "personal sense of competence" scale for use with third to ninth grade children. This instrument assesses children's sense of competence on cognitive, social, and physical tasks and also yields a measure of general self-worth. The Personal Problem-Solving Inventory

developed by Heppner and Petersen (1982) can be used with adults and yields a measure of self-confidence in problem-solving. It is possible that dimensions such as self-efficacy, sense of competence, and problem-solving confidence strongly influence the execution of problem-solving behaviors. It is also possible that such self-appraisals are enhanced by rather than precede successful task performance. These alternate possibilities should be examined in future studies.

### Current Status of Social Problem-Solving

In evaluating current programs, it is necessary to emphasize two serious limitations. First, there is the noticeable lack of a clearly documented long-term causal relationship between problem-solving and mental health. Invariably, the value of various problem-solving skills has been suggested on the basis of correlational findings. For example, comparative studies indicate differences in problem-solving abilities between maladapting and well-adapting groups, or follow-up research suggests a relationship between measures of problem-solving at time 1 and measure of adjustment at time 2. In neither case, however, are causal factors necessarily implicated. To say that a maladapting group differs from their well-adapting peers on variable $a$, $b$, and $c$ in no way implies that any or all of these variables are causally responsible for the differential adjustment of these two groups. Similarly, correlations existing between early measures of problem-solving and later indices of adjustment do not permit one to assume that improving problem-solving at time 1 will necessarily prevent the appearance of subsequent problems.

A second major problem is that current programs cannot claim success in terms of primary prevention. To be successful, preventive programs must first demonstrate that some important negative outcome has indeed been prevented, and then that the effects of intervention are relatively long-lasting. Whereas some programs have achieved the former goal, none has effectively met the latter criterion. Problem-solving programs seek to promote adaptive behaviors in target groups, but the crucial determinant of primary prevention lies in the extent to which success at mental health-promotion reduces the subsequent appearance of new problems. The functional relationship between positive behaviors that were increased or enhanced and negative behaviors/problems that were subsequently reduced must be shown before the claim of prevention can be accepted (Poser & Hartman, 1979). Otherwise, the question "Prevention of what?" goes unanswered.

In summary, the tenuous empirical underpinnings of problem-solving programs restrict the discussion to merely the promise and not the fact of primary prevention. Furthermore, evaluations must be offered cautiously. There is so much enthusiasm surrounding social problem-solving that the field's data base is likely to double or triple within the next few years, making current assessments obsolete or misleading. Nevertheless, it is helpful to appraise what has happened to date.

Many approaches to primary prevention have been criticized because empirical investigations are seldom grounded in theory. Such is not the case for problem-solving programs. As this chapter has made evident, there are three competing theories regarding the nature of problem-solving skills. Each theory offers an alternative view regarding the assessment, implementation, and evaluation of problem-solving interventions. This theoretical backdrop is a definite plus for future research and practice. The availability of current problem-solving theories will serve to help organize and interpret obtained data, launch investigations to evaluate rival hypotheses, and modify subsequent conceptualizations and interventions accordingly. The current theoretical underpinnings for problem-solving approaches to primary prevention thus assure an active and rich life for the area in the coming years.

Which theory related to problem-solving appears to be the most promising? Current data offer greatest support to the task-specific approach, compared to the cognitive and developmental approaches. For example, there is little data to support the theoretical position that cognitive problem-solving skills mediate adjustment. Outcome data from developmental programs offer the suggestion, but no more than that, that certain developmental abilities such as role-taking having important influences on interpersonal functioning and problem-solving skills.

In contrast, the task-specific strategy has yielded several positive results across a broad spectrum of settings and problems. Programs have been successfully launched to affect preadolescent drug taking, teenage pregnancy, parent-child relations, marital conflict, and unemployment. Task specific approaches are interactional in nature. Each situation (problem to be prevented) is analyzed into its component parts so that the skills needed to master the situation can be identified. Then multicomponent interventions are implemented to help individuals deal cognitively, affectively, and behaviorally with the presenting problem or situation.

Although we still have much to learn, a broad spectrum approach toward problem-solving has merit. The causes of adjustment (and maladjustment) are multiple and interactive and it is unlikely that a "magic bullet," a single causative agent that explains most of the variance of either positive or negative outcomes, will ever be discovered. As missing elements of the total picture regarding mental health are clarified, it is more likely that different skills assume differential importance at different development periods, and that at each point in time they interact with a host of familial, social, and environmental factors. Therefore, strategies that conceive of problems in multidimensional terms and mount corresponding interventions probably have the greatest likelihood of success. Once complex interventions are found to be effective, subsequent research can assess how each treatment component helps different individuals master different tasks.

In closing, it must be emphasized that social problem-solving cannot be viewed as a panacea. Interpersonal problem-solving skills may play only a small role in the prevention of many adjustment problems. Recognizing the limited applicability of problem-solving skills is just as important as recognizing their relevance in terms of reaching conclusions regarding the value of problem-solving interventions in preventive programs. Problem-solving may be of enormous value to some individuals at certain times, and in certain situations. To date, however, the who, when, and what in this interpersonal equation have yet to be satisfactorily clarified and explained.

# References

Allen, G. J., Chinsky, J. M., Larcen, S. W., Lochman, J. E., & Selinger, H. V. *Community psychology and the schools: A behaviorally oriented multilevel prevention approach.* Hillsdale, N.J.: Lawrence Erlbaum Associates. 1976.

Avery, A. W., Ridley, C. A., Leslie, L. A., & Milholland, T. Relationship enhancement with premarital dyads: A six-month follow-up. *American Journal of Family Therapy*, 1980, **8**, 23–30.

Azrin, N. H., Flores, T., & Kaplan, S. J. Job-finding club: A group-assisted program for obtaining employment. *Behavior Research and Therapy*, 1975, **13**, 17–27.

Azrin, N. H., & Philip, R. A. The Job Club method for the job-handicapped: A comparative outcome study. *Rehabilitation Counseling Bulletin*, in press.

Azrin, N. H., Philip, R. A., Thienes-Hontas, P., & Basalel, V. A. Comparative evaluation of the Job Club program with welfare recipients. *Journal of Vocational Behavior*, 1980, **16**, 133–145.

Bagarozzi, D. A. & Rauen, P. Premarital counseling: Appraisal and status. *American Journal of Family Therapy*, 1981, **9**, 13–30.

Bandura, A. Self-efficacy: Toward a unifying theory of behavioral change. *Psychological Review*, 1977, **84**, 191–215.

Briscoe, R. V., Hoffman, D. B., & Bailey, J. S. Behavioral community psychology: Training a community board to problem solve. *Journal of Applied Behavior Analysis,* 1977, **8,** 157–168.

Butler, L., & Meichenbaum, D. The assessment of interpersonal problem-solving skills. In P. C. Kendall & S. D. Hollon (Eds.), *Assessment strategies for cognitive-behavioral interventions.* New York: Academic Press, 1981.

Butler, L. J. The relationship between interpersonal problem-solving skills and peer relations and behavior. Paper presented at the meeting of the Canadian Psychological Association, June 1978.

Camp, B. W., Blom, G. E., Hebert, F., & van Doorninck, W. J. "Think aloud": A program for developing self-control in young aggressive boys. *Journal of Abnormal Child Psychology,* 1977, **5,** 157–169.

Condiotte, M. M., & Lichtenstein, E. Self-efficacy and relapse in smoking cessation programs. *Journal of Consulting and Clinical Psychology,* 1981, **49,** 659–667.

Cowen, E. L. Baby-steps toward primary prevention. *American Journal of Community Psychology,* 1977, **5,** 1–22.

Demarest, D., Sexton, J., & Sexton, M. *Marriage encounter.* St. Paul, Minn.: Carillon Books, 1977.

Dixon, D. N., Heppner, P. P., Petersen, C. H., & Ronning, R. R. Problem-solving workshop training. *Journal of Counseling Psychology,* 1979, **26,** 133–139.

D'Zurilla, T. J., & Goldfried, M. R. Problem-solving and behavior modification. *Journal of Abnormal Psychology,* 1971, **78,** 107–126.

Elardo, P. T., & Caldwell, B. M. The effects of an experimental social development in program on children in the middle childhood period. *Psychology in the Schools,* 1979, **16,** 93–100.

Enright, R. D., Colby, S., & McMullin, I. A social-cognitive developmental intervention with sixth and first graders. *Counseling Psychologist,* 1977, **6,** 10–12.

Flavell, J. H. *The developmental psychology of Jean Piaget.* Princeton: Van Nostrand, 1963.

Gillespie, J. F., Durlak, J. A., & Sherman, D. Relationship between kindergarten children's interpersonal problem-solving skills and other indices of school adjustment: A cautionary note. *American Journal of Community Psychology,* 1982, **10,** 149–153.

Ginsberg, B. G. Parent-adolescent relationship development program. In. B. G. Guerney, Jr. (Ed.), *Relationship enhancement: Skill-training programs for therapy, problem prevention, and enrichment.* San Francisco: Jossey-Bass, 1977.

Ginsberg, B. G., & Vogelsong, E. Premarital relationship improvement by maximizing empathy and self-disclosure: The PRIMES program. In B. G. Guerney, Jr. (Ed.), *Relationship enhancement: Skill-training programs for therapy, problem-prevention, and enrichment.* San Francisco: Jossey-Bass, 1977.

Goldfried, M. R., & D'Zurilla, T. J. A behavioral-analytic model for assessing competence. In C. D. Spielberger (Ed.), *Current topics in clinical and community psychology.* Vol. 1. New York: Academic Press, 1969.

Gordon, T. *P.E.T. in action.* New York: Wyden Books, 1976.

Guerney, B. G., Jr. (Ed.) *Relationship enhancement: Skill-training programs for therapy, problem prevention, and enrichment.* San Francisco, Jossey-Bass, 1977.

Guerney, B. G., Jr., Coufal, J., & Vogelsong, E. Relationship enhancement versus a traditional approach to therapeutic preventative enrichment parent-adolescent programs.

*Journal of Consulting and Clinical Psychology,* 1981, **49,** 927–939.

Gurman, A. S., & Kniskern, D. P. Enriching research on marital enrichment programs. *Journal of Marriage and Family Counseling,* 1977, **3,** 3–11.

Harter, S. The perceived competence scale for children. *Child Development,* 1982, **53,** 87–97.

Haynes, S. N., Wise, E., Sherman, D., Jensen, B., & Stein, M. Primary prevention of marital dissatisfaction: Issues and a model. Paper presented at the meeting of the American Psychological Association, New York, September 1979.

Heppner, P. P., & Petersen, C. H. The development and implications of a personal problem-solving inventory. *Journal of Counseling Psychology,* 1982, **29,** 66–75.

Houtz, J. C., & Feldhusen, J. F. The modification of fourth graders' problem solving abilities. *Journal of Psychology,* 1976, **93,** 229–237.

Huba, G. J., Wingard, J. A., & Bentler, P. M. Applications of a theory of drug use to prevention programs. *Journal of Drug Education,* 1980, **10,** 25–38.

Hurd, P. D., Johnson, C. A., Pechacek, T., Bast, L. P., Jacobs, D. R., & Luepker, R. V. Prevention of cigarette smoking in seventh grade students. *Journal of Behavioral Medicine,* 1980, **3,** 15–28.

Iannotti, R. J. Effect of role-taking experiences on role taking, empathy, altruism, and aggression. *Developmental Psychology,* 1978, **14,** 119–124.

Jalali, B., Jalali, M., Crocetti, G., & Turner, F. Adolescents and drug use: Toward a more comprehensive aproach. *American Journal of Orthopsychiatry,* 1981, **51,** 120–130.

Jessee, R. E., & Guerney, B. G., Jr. A comparison of gestalt and relationship enhancement treatments with married couples. *American Journal of Family Therapy,* 1981, **9,** 31–41.

Kendall, P. C., Pellegrini, D. S., & Urbain, E. S. Approaches to assessment for cognitive-behavioral interventions with children. In P. C. Kendall & S. D. Hollon (Eds.), *Assessment strategies for congnitive-behavioral interventions.* New York: Academic Press, 1981.

Kim, S. An evaluation of ombudsman primary prevention program on student drug abuse. *Journal of Drug Education,* 1981, **11,** 27–36. (a)

Kim, S. How do we know whether a primary prevention program on drug abuse works or does not work? *International Journal of the Addictions,* 1981, **16,** 359–365. (b)

Kinder, B. N., Pape, N. E., & Walfish, S. Drug and alcohol education programs: A review of outcome studies. *International Journal of the Addictions,* 1980, **15,** 1035–1054.

Kirschenbaum, D. S., & Ordman, A. M. Preventive interventions for children: Cognitive behavioral perspectives. In A. W. Meyers & W. E. Craighead (Eds.), *Cognitive behavior therapy for children.* New York: Plenum Press, 1982.

Markman, H. J., & Floyd, F. Possibilities for the prevention of marital discord: A behavioral perspective. *American Journal of Family Therapy,* 1980, **8,** 29–48.

Marsh, D. T., Serafica, F. C., & Barenboim, C. Effect of perspective-taking training on interpersonal problem solving. *Child Development,* 1980, **51,** 140–145.

McClure, L. F., Chinsky, J. M., & Larcen, S. W. Enhancing social problem-solving performance in an elementary school setting. *Journal of Educational Psychology*, 1978, 70, 504–513.

McFall, R. M. A review and reformulation of the concept of social skills. *Behavioral Assessment*, 1982, 4, 1–33.

Otto, H. Marriage and family enrichment programs in North America—report and analysis. *Family Coordinator*, 1975, 24, 137–142.

Pinsker, M., & Geoffroy, K. A comparison of parent effectiveness training and behavior modification parent training. *Family Relations*, 1981, 30, 61–68.

Poitras-Martin, D., & Stone, G. L. Psychological education: A skill-oriented approach. *Journal of Counseling Psychology*, 1977, 24, 153–157.

Poser, E. G., & Hartman, L. M. Issues in behavioral prevention: Empirical findings. *Advances in Behavior Research and Therapy*, 1979, 2, 1–25.

Press, S., Alvarez, J., Cotler, S., & Jason, L. A. Developing a problem-solving program in a school setting. Paper presented at the meeting of the Midwestern Psychological Association, Detroit, 1981.

Rickel, A. U., & Burgio, J. C. Assessing social competencies in lower income preschool children. *American Journal of Community Psychology*, 1982, 10(6), 635–647.

Ridley, C. A., Avery, A. W., Harrell, J. E., Leslie, L. A., & Dent, J. Conflict management: A premarital training program in mutual problem solving. *American Journal of Family Therapy*, 1981, 9, 23–32.

Rinn, R. C., & Markle, A. Parent effectiveness training: A review. *Psychological Reports*, 1977, 41, 95–109.

Russell, M. L., & Roberts, M. S. Behaviorally-based decision-making training for children. *Journal of School Psychology*, 1979, 17, 264–269.

Schaps, E., Churgin, S., Palley, C. S., Takata, B., & Cohen, A. Y. Primary prevention research: A preliminary review of program outcome studies. *International Journal of the Addictions*, 1980, 15, 657–676.

Schinke, S. P., Blythe, B. J., & Gilchrist, L. D. Cognitive-behavioral prevention of adolescent pregnancy. *Journal of Counseling Psychology*, 1981, 28, 451–454.

Schinke, S. P., Gilchrist, L. D., & Blythe, B. J. Role of communication in the prevention of teenage pregnancy. *Health and Social Work*, 1980, 5, 54–59.

Schinke, S. P., Gilchrist, L. D., & Small, R. W. Preventing unwanted adolescent pregnancy: A cognitive-behavioral approach. *American Journal of Orthopsychiatry*, 1979, 49, 81–88.

Schinke, S. P., Gilchrist, L. D., Smith, T. E., & Wong, S. E. Improving teenage mothers' ability to compete for jobs. *Social Work Research and Abstracts*, 1978, 14, 25–29.

Shure, M. B., & Spivack, G. *Problem-solving techniques in childrearing*. San Francisco: Jossey-Bass, 1978.

Shure, M. B., & Spivack, G. Interpersonal cognitive problem solving and primary prevention: Programming for preschool and kindergarten children. *Journal of Clinical Child Psychology*, 1979, 8, 89–94.

Spivack, G., Platt, J. J., & Shure, M. B. *The problem-solving approach to adjustment*. San Francisco: Jossey-Bass, 1976.

Spivack, G., & Shure, M. B. *Social adjustment of young children: A cognitive approach to solving real-life problems*. San Francisco: Jossey-Bass, 1974.

Stolz, S. B. Adoption of innovations from applied behavioral research: Does anybody care? *Journal of Applied Behavior Analysis*, 1981, 14, 491–505.

Stone, G. L., Hinds, W. C., & Schmidt, G. W. Teaching mental health behaviors to elementary school children. *Professional Psychology*, 1975, 6, 34–40.

Underwood, B., & Moore, B. Perspective-taking and altruism. *Psychological Bulletin*, 1977, 41, 95–109.

Urbain, E. S., & Kendall, P. C. Review of social-cognitive problem-solving interventions with children. *Psychological Bulletin*, 1980, 88, 109–143.

Vogelsong, E. L. Relationship enhancement training for children. *Elementary School Guidance and Counseling*, 1978, 12, 272–279.

Weissberg, R. P., & Gesten, E. L. Considerations for developing effective school-based problem-solving (SPS) training programs. *School Psychology Review*, 1982, 11, 56–63.

Weissberg, R. P., Gesten, E. L., Carnrike, C. L., Toro, P. A., Rapkin, B. D., Davidson, E., & Cowen, E. L. Social problem-solving skills training: A competence building intervention with 2nd–4th grade children. *American Journal of Community Psychology*, 1981, 9, 411–424.

Weissberg, R. P., Gesten, E. L., Rapkin, B. D., Cowen, E. L., Davidson, E., de Apodaca, R. F., & McKim, B. J. The evaluation of a social problem-solving training program for suburban and inner-city third grade children. *Journal of Consulting and Clinical Psychology*, 1981, 49, 251–261.

Winer, J. I., Hilpert, P. L., Gesten, E. L., Cowen, E. L., & Schubin, W. E. The evaluation of a kindergarten social problem-solving program. *Journal of Prevention*, 1982, 205–216.

# 4 LIFE DEVELOPMENT INTERVENTION: SKILL TRAINING FOR PERSONAL COMPETENCE

Steven J. Danish,*
Nancy L. Galambos, and
Idamarie Laquatra

Over the last decade psychologists, especially community psychologists, have written extensively trying to convince other psychologists and the public of the importance and value of primary prevention. It has not been a particularly successful struggle. Although there have been social and political forces which have sought to "prevent prevention" (Albee, 1979, 1981), several other problems have impeded the adoption of the concept and its acceptance as a viable intervention modality. The first problem may be labeled "definitional difficulties." Primary prevention has been defined as both the elimination of illness *and* the promotion of health (Goldston, 1977). Problems arise regarding the expected outcomes of the intervention when the definitions are so different. While it is beyond the focus of this chapter to examine the conceptual confusion surrounding the definition of primary prevention, some of the issues will be briefly considered in a later section. Interested readers are referred to previous work by the senior author for a more detailed consideration of the topic (Danish,

1977, 1980; Danish & D'Augelli, 1980; Danish, Smyer, & Nowak, 1980).

A second problem has been the inability to delimit what constitutes primary prevention. Kessler and Albee's (1975) review of primary prevention activities is often cited because of the enormous and amorphous scope of the activities considered. Cowen (1977, 1978) has sought to provide some organization to the extensive range of activities. He grouped the activities into two categories: (1) those concerned with the analysis and modification of social systems; and (2) those concerned with promoting competence. It is the latter category with which this chapter is concerned.

A third problem has been the lack of an established intervention technology. With the delineation of activities which constitute primary prevention, efforts to identify specific intervention methods have begun. The Vermont Conference on Primary Prevention devoted its second issue to environmental influences on primary prevention (Forgays, 1978) and its third and fourth issues to the study of competence in children (Kent & Rolf, 1979), and adults (Bond & Rosen, 1980). A number of specific interventions were identified in each. In the volumes on competence, several chapters focused specifically on skill training.

In many ways it seems very appropriate to identify skill training as a major intervention modality for primary prevention. The assumption that skills can

* This chapter was completed while the senior author was on sabbatical leave at the University of Connecticut. He would like to thank the faculty and staff of the School of Allied Health Professions, and especially Dean Polly Fitz, for their support and suggestions during this period. The assistance and comments of Anthony R. D'Augelli are also appreciated.

49

be taught as a means of eliminating interpersonal deficits or teaching new behaviors is consistent with a behavioral rather than disease orientation toward service delivery (Rappaport, 1977). From a behavioral orientation, personal competence is seen as a series of skills which an individual either possesses or can learn through training. The acquisition of certain skills may generalize to facilitate the development of competence in other aspects of one's life. Thus while it appears as if skill training may be an ideal intervention modality in developing personal competence, a number of questions persist: What are the range of skills related to developing personal competence? Who determines what skills are to be taught? How can the skills be best taught to optimize learning, transfer, and generalization? How may the skills be best evaluated? Is the promotion of competence by teaching individuals new skills the same as the elimination of skill deficits? These questions form the basis of this chapter. The first task is to define what constitutes the skills of personal competence.

## The Domain of Skill Training

Skills have been divided into social, cognitive, and physical skills. All three domains of behavior contribute to the development of personal competence. Although a discussion of the contributions of the intellectual-functioning aspects of cognitive skills and a consideration of physical skills is beyond the scope of this chapter, it is important to note that adults can be taught to develop and maintain their intellectual functioning throughout the life span (Baltes & Schaie, 1976) and that physical fitness training can lead to improved personal competence (Folkins & Sime, 1981). Training in cognitive skills (Baltes & Willis, 1983) and physical skills (Allsen, Harrison, & Vance, 1980; Cooper, 1968; Folkins & Sime, 1981; Whiting, 1971) has been developed and found effective.

Most of the skill training related to personal competence comes under the general rubric of social skills. The term "social skills" has been used to denote a wide range of behaviors. It has been used to refer to a set of skills involved in *initiating* personal relationships, including such surface contacts as greetings and introductions. The term has often been used interchangeably with "interpersonal skills" or "communication skills" to refer to the process of *developing* and *maintaining* personal relationships, especially intimate ones. Behaviors involved in developing and maintaining intimate relationships include being self-disclosing, communicating feelings accurately and unambiguously, being supportive, and being able to resolve conflicts and relationship problems constructively (Johnson, 1981). Guerney (1977) has referred to training in these skills as "relationship enhancement" training, and Gordon (1970) has referred to such training as "parent effectiveness training" when used between parents and children. Different terms, then, have been used to describe the same skill. However, a more difficult problem is that the same term has been used to mean very different behaviors. Self-disclosing and solving interpersonal conflicts require a different repertoire of behaviors. Considering both as "social skills" may be confusing. Resolving interpersonal conflicts would seem to require a much more cognitive problem-solving dimension than would self-disclosure. Because of the potential confusion involved in labeling various skill dimensions, we have chosen to identify the skills related to personal competence as life development skills.

Life development skills include the *cognitive* and *physical* skills mentioned earlier: *interpersonal* skills such as initiating, developing, and maintaining relationships; and *interpersonal* skills such as developing self-control, mastering tension management and relaxation, setting goals, and taking risks. The latter skills are often overlooked by skill trainers interested in personal competence. Prior to expanding on the perspective of life development skills, it seem appropriate to review some of the recent skill training literature. Most of the literature available is on interpersonal skills. Consequently, our review will focus on these skills as an example of the present status of skill training.

## 'State of the Art' of Interpersonal Skills Training

In recent years the skills literature has abounded with descriptions of research focused on improving the interpersonal effectiveness of a variety of populations. Maladapted children (Rinn & Markel, 1979), adults with heterosocial skills deficits (Galassi & Galassi, 1979), psychiatric patients (Hersen, 1979), couples with communication problems (Birchler, 1979), and unassertive adults and children (Bornstein, Bellack, & Hersen, 1977; Linehan & Egan, 1979) have been among the major targets of this surge of skill training. The work of Zigler and his colleagues (e.g., Levine & Zigler, 1973; Phillips & Zigler, 1964; Zigler & Phillips, 1961, 1962), which first demonstrated an inverse relationship between social competence and various psychiatric disorders, was instrumental in the proliferation of interst in interpersonal skill training. One of the most important findings to emerge from this series of studies was that posthospital adjustment of psychiatric patients was positively correlated with their levels of social competence or skill prior to hospitalization. Thus if clinical and high-risk populations were trained to be more interpersonally skillful, perhaps the incidence and severity of psychopathology in the general population could be reduced, and its occurrence in individual cases prevented.

The assumption of a causal relationship between interpersonal skills and psychopathology served as the guiding hypothesis for investigators and practitioners from the traditional approaches within psychiatry and psychotherapy as well as behavior therapy (e.g., Frank, 1974; Gladwin, 1967). Researchers from the field of behavior therapy, however, have contributed most to the systematic study of socially deficient behaviors. From their work identification and assessment of social skills and procedures for training to overcome skills deficits have emerged (Hersen, 1979). While there has not been a single widely accepted definition of "social and interpersonal skills," Bellack (1979) outlined four principles that underlie most conceptions: (1) behavior in social situations is composed of specific verbal and nonverbal response component (Trower, Bryant, & Argyle, 1978); (2) appropriate behavior varies according to the social context (Eisler, Hersen, Miller, & Blanchard, 1975); (3) various response components are *learned* skills; and (4) specific skills can be taught to individuals with skill deficits.

### Assessment of Interpersonal Skills

One of the hallmarks of the behavioral approach to interpersonal skills training is the importance placed on the assessment of interpersonal skills, both prior and subsequent to training. Recommended strategies for assessing skills in both college student and psychiatric populations consist of the measurement of multiple response channels (Hersen & Bellack, 1977). For example, Hersen (1973) and Lang (1971) recommended that motoric, physiological, and cognitive measures of social responses be included in assessment. Most of the research to date, however, has focused on evaluation on the motoric and cognitive responses only (Hersen & Bellack, 1977). Assessment has primarily consisted of administering self-report inventories and making behavioral observations of role-played social encounters; interviewing, self-monitoring, sociometric ratings, and physiological measures have been used much less (Bellack, 1979).

#### SELF-REPORT INVENTORIES

There are several self-report inventories which attempt to tap specific behavioral deficits as well as cognitive aspects (for example, anxiety) associated with performance in a social situation. Examples of inventories are the Social Anxiety and Distress Scale (SAD) developed by Watson and Friend (1969) to measure negative feelings in social situations, the College Self-Expression Scale (CSES) that attempts to measure degree of assertiveness in college students (Galassi, DeLo, Galassi, & Bastein, 1974), and the Interpersonal Situation Inventory (ISI), which measures the ability of psychiatric patients to deal with problematic interpersonal situations (Goldsmith & McFall, 1975). These and other inventories have been developed with research purposes in mind—to broadly categorize individuals on a particular skill and to be used as outcome measures in studies. Their usefulness to trainers and therapists has been limited, however, because most existing inventories are not psychometrically sound and do not assess interpersonal skills with enough precision to assist in labeling specific deficits (Bellack, 1979).

#### BEHAVIORAL OBSERVATION

While there are three major types of behavior observation—*in vivo*, naturalistic, and role-play tests—the naturalistic and role-play tests have been the primary methods used in interpersonal skills assessment (Bellack, 1979). *In vivo* observation, which entails observation of social behavior in actual situations, is not often used because interpersonal skills assessment usually requires quick, efficient, and accurate measures of behaviors that may occur very infrequently. Naturalistic observation, in which social interactions are staged (often using a confederate) to simulate actual situations, is useful for observing particular instances of social behavior. For example, Arkowitz, Lichtenstein, McGovern, and Hines (1975) asked subjects to "pretend" they were interested in a female whom they had just met, while trained observers rated the interaction for level of interpersonal skill. Naturalistic interactions can be arranged so that the subject is not aware that a confederate is employed (Bellack, 1979). The third type of behavioral observation, the role-play test, requires the subject to respond to another person or an audiotape of a social vignette. Rehm and Marston (1968) developed the Situation Test (ST), consisting of ten situations calling for heterosexual interaction. Situations were presented orally on tapes to which the subject responded as in a real life conversation. The latter two methods of behavior observation often pose difficulties in generalization because of the artificial conditions that are created (Bellack, 1979).

#### INTERVIEWS

The interviewing technique, while the least empirically sound of assessment strategies, yields important information about the nature of an individual's social behavior (Bellack, 1979). The interviewer can inquire into the history of the individual's interpersonal behavior, including specific feelings associated with various social situations, and can informally observe the individual's style of interaction (Bellack & Hersen, 1978). All of this information helps to identify those areas of skill that the individual sees as important (Bellack, 1979). Bellack (1979) argues that the interview is a potentially useful tool for assessment, provided that empirical techniques are used to establish reliability and validity. He suggests that standardized interview schedules be designed such that an individual's responses can be compared to derived norms, a practice that would reduce the subjective quality of interviews.

In his critique of interpersonal skills assessment, Bellack (1979) concluded that current strategies of assessment are in need of more careful development, refinement, and empirical evaluation. Without means of adequately identifying specific skills deficits, knowledge of what deficits to treat and how to treat them suffers. Furthermore, outcome research may be invalid as a result of inadequate measuring instruments.

## Methods for Training Skills

Methods for training skills have been largely influenced by the behavioral orientation of the researchers. The basic pattern of training begins with specific instructions about performance of a particular skill followed by modeling of that skill, behavioral rehearsal by the trainee, and feedback on the trainee's performance (Hersen & Eisler, 1976). In some cases it is sufficient to simply give instructions to the individual on how to improve his interpersonal effectiveness; for example, the trainer, after careful observation of the individual's social behavior, might say, "Be sure to look directly at a person when you are speaking to him, rather than staring at the floor." In many difficult cases, however, it is necessary to model appropriate social behavior, *in vivo* or on videotape, after which the individual rehearses the target behaviors (Hersen & Eisler, 1976). Furthermore, specific feedback on the individual's social performance and its effects on others is given in order to reinforce behaviors that have reached an acceptable level, and to criticize constructively those that have not (Eisler, Hersen, Miller, & Blanchard, 1975). Some studies have also included such cognitive techniques as covert modeling (e.g., Kazdin, 1974) and training in perceptions of self and others (e.g., Trower et al., 1978).

Interpersonal skills training thus consists of a general treatment package that varies somewhat with the se-

verity of the skill deficit. Curran (1979) urged researchers to isolate those components (for instance, modeling, instructions) or combination of components that account for the effects of a particular training package. While several studies have evaluated different training procedures, the success of various components has not been clearly established. This appears to be the result of problems with design, measurement, and internal validity of the studies that have been conducted (Trower et al., 1978).

## The "Preventive Approach" to Social Problem-Solving

The interpersonal skills literature is replete with studies based on behavior conception-waiting mode approaches (Rappaport, 1977). The basic objectives of these approaches are to identify specific skills deficits in individuals and to rebuild their behavioral repertoire. Until recently, skill training has been less widely used for "prevention" purposes. In a preventive focus it is assumed that individuals can be taught specific skills such that ineffective social functioning will not occur or that socially effective behaviors, such as a problem-solving orientation, can be learned. Thus the focus is on prevention rather than remediation.

Researchers working in the area of social problem-solving skills have used the preventive approach to teach problem-solving skills to children, adolescents, and adults (Gesten, Flores de Apodaca, Rains, Weissberg, & Cowen, 1979; Spivack, Platt, & Shure, 1976). While the same general methods of training described in the previous section are used to teach social problem-solving skills (for example, instructions, modeling, behavioral rehearsal, and feedback), the training is carried out in group settings, often in the classroom. In addition, group discussions are employed, and in the training of children competitive games are frequently used as a training procedure. More often than not the subjects have not been identified as having skills deficits. One of the underlying assumptions of this type of approach is that interpersonal social skills are just one more set of skills to be learned, similar to reading or driving a car.

Assessment of social problem-solving skills has consisted of both paper-and-pencil tests measuring the ability to solve problems and naturalistic observation of behavior in contrived situations requiring problem-solving skills (e.g., Weissberg, Gesten, Rapkin, Cowen, Davidson, Flores de Apodaca, & McKim, 1981). Measures of personality and social adjustment have also been widely employed in this particular area of research. The functions of assessment are different in the clinical as opposed to the preventive approaches.

While assessment from the clinical perspective is conducted to identify specific deficits in individuals and to measure the change in skill over time, researchers taking the preventive approach are more interested in using the measures in outcome studies to determine the effectiveness of skills training for the total group of individuals.

### The Enrichment Approach to Marital Communication

The clinical approach to training married couples in communication skills can be contrasted with the enrichment approach. While the clinical approach targets couples who are distressed and dissatisfied with their relationship, the enrichment approach is for nondistressed couples who feel that their marriage relationship could simply be enhanced via better communication skills. Again, the focus is on building competencies in "normal" individuals rather than remediating skills deficits. The use of a group format for teaching is also encouraged. Both approaches use instructions, feedback, live or videotape modeling, and behavioral rehearsal. The enrichment approach is increasingly adopting skills taught by behavior therapists (such as conflict resolution, negotiation, and contingency contracting) and the behavior therapists are teaching skills previously taught in enhancement programs (expression of feelings, support) (Birchler, 1979).

Conjugal Relationship Enhancement (CRE), developed by Bernard Guerney (Guerney, 1977), is one example of the enhancement approach to marital communication skills. While the enhancement approach has not been empirically studied as much as has the clinical approach (Birchler, 1979), CRE has been evaluated and empirically supported (Collins, 1971; Ely, Guerney, & Stover, 1973). Assessment measures have included self-report inventories of communication behavior, marital adjustment questionnaires, and role-play tests of conflict situations. Again, in contrast to the clinical approach, assessment is not used to identify specific areas of skill deficits but performs the function of evaluating outcomes of training programs.

## Skill Training as a Developmental Intervention

### Values, Mental Health, and Skill Training

As our exploration of the "state of the art" of interpersonal skills training has demonstrated, a variety of populations have been targeted for training in interpersonal skills, and a number of methods of training and assessment have been developed. The implications of this approach for individuals, families, and society are significant and potentially far-reaching. Although further research is needed to develop more effective training programs and assessment procedures and more sophisticated outcome studies, the basis for an effective intervention modality exists. With the possible exception of the social problem-solving training and the marital enrichment programs described previously, the bulk of the social skill literature is governed by the concept of "social skill deficits." Assessment procedures are developed with the purpose of identifying and labeling those skills that the individual lacks or cannot perform effectively. Even much problem-solving skill training seems to be oriented toward secondary versus primary prevention, since many of the individuals trained have been identified as "interpersonal or academic risks" (Cowen, 1977).

Delineating skill training as a means of increasing personal competence epitomizes the dilemma faced by advocates of primary prevention. Is the focus of primary prevention as it relates to skill training to eliminate "illness" by reducing skill deficits, or is it to promote health by teaching behaviors associated with "wellness"? More specifically, what is the goal of skill training, and who determines this goal? In light of these questions, even the term "skills training" becomes confusing—skills for whom? For example, to put it perhaps too simplistically, one person's social skill may be another person's antisocial behavior. While assertiveness in women is presently seen as a valued skill among the middle class, evidenced by the number of skill training groups currently teaching women assertiveness, this has not always been the case. Historically, assertiveness in women was not a virtue. Consequently, several generations of women have been made to feel that they are deficient in the way they relate to others and have been encouraged to learn how to become more assertive. As many older women, in particular, have learned to be more assertive they have often experienced more conflicts with husbands and family members, who may view this new assertiveness as a threat.

It is the confusion and misinterpretation associated with the term "social and interpersonal skills" that makes relating the term to mental health and prevention so difficult. If prevention is defined as the elimination of illness or the promotion of mental health, problems arise regarding the expected outcomes of the intervention. For example, "mental health" is usually defined as the absence of "mental illness." How does one know, then, that an intervention has promoted health, except by the inference that there is an absence of illness? When one attempts to evaluate the success of the intervention and finds no incidence of disease, should one conclude that the primary prevention intervention has succeeded, or that there was no danger of illness to begin with? If the intervention does not succeed in preventing illness, should one conclude that the intervention has failed and that health has not been promoted? Either conclusion seems indefensible (Danish, 1980).

### The Characteristics of Developmental Interventions

The problems associated with considering skill training within a mental health context have led us to search for an alternative model within which to place such training. We have chosen a life span human development perspective. This framework presupposes continuous growth and change. As originally characterized by Baltes (1973), Danish (1977), and Danish and D'Augelli (1980), this model: (1) incorporates statements about desirable goals or endstates of behavior; (2) focuses on sequential changes; (3) emphasizes techniques of optimization; (4) considers the individual or system as an integrative biopsychosocial unit (Ford, 1974) and, therefore, amenable to multidisciplinary focus; and (5) looks at the individuals or systems as developing in a changing biocultural context.

This framework is oriented toward a multidisciplinary view of the individual throughout the life span. It presupposes an upward progression. While behavior is ordered, the progression is not smooth, since it takes place within an ever-changing social context. Riegel (1975) has stated that

> developmental leaps are brought about by discordance, asynchrony, or conflict between these (inner-biological, individual-psychological, cultural-sociological, outer-physical) planes of progression. But rather than regarding these critical episodes in a negative manner or from a fatalistic point of view, they provide the very basis which makes the development of the individual and of society possible [p. 100].

Thus contrary to the view that critical episodes are destructive events, they in fact may serve to intensify a restructuring process and marshal resources toward further growth.

A developmentally oriented model of intervention has the following attributes: (1) a central focus on life events; (2) a developmental as opposed to disease conception; and (3) a belief that past life events help one prepare for future life events. The framework is summarized here. A more complete description of such a model has been presented elsewhere (Danish & D'Augelli, 1980; Danish, Smyer, & Nowak, 1980).

LIFE EVENTS

Although life events has become a popular topic of conversation and study, no single view of life events has emerged as universally accepted. The Dohrenwends (1974) and Holmes and Rahe (1967), for example, envision life events as crises which lead to physical and emotional illness. Costa and McCrae (1980) also see them as crises, ones which are especially difficult for people with somewhat nonadaptive personality styles. Others acknowledge the importance of life events for personal growth, but choose to focus on single events (e.g., Lopata, 1973, on widowhood; Parkes, 1964, on the death of a spouse; Rossi, 1968, on parenthood). Still others view life events as antecedents to behavioral change (Baltes & Willis, 1979; Hultsch & Plemons, 1979). What is striking across these different perspectives is the unanimity that life events play a pivotal role in individual development.

Events have been viewed in two ways: as markers and as processes. When events have been viewed as markers, they are seen as milestones or transition points which provide direction to a person's life (Neugarten & Hagestad, 1976). "For example, becoming pregnant is a marker in the course of one's family development. It signifies to a couple and to those interacting with them, that a specific course of events is beginning to unfold, namely, the birth of a child, child rearing, child launching, and so on [Danish, Smyer, & Nowak, p. 342]." Events are processes as well as markers. They have histories of their own from the time they are anticipated, through their occurrences, until their aftermaths have been determined and assessed. It is this process that the marker signifies but does not describe. If events are viewed only as markers the importance of the *context* of events is underestimated. Events do not occur in a vacuum; they are part of the total life space of the individual, including competing demands from a variety of areas (such as work, family life, physical development) and people significant to the individual. For example, pregnancy is not merely a marker event in the family life cycle. For many individuals it is the result of a conscious decision-making process which includes the effects of a child on the couple's marital relationship, work roles, physical health, and economic well-being (Elder & Rockwell, 1976).

Viewing events as markers only also ignores the importance of the individual's experience of the event. For social scientists, events are viewed in the larger perspective of life cycle development. For the individual the event and its current impact assume an importance of their own. For the pregnant women pregnancy may be more the morning sickness than the anticipation of the child's sex or future occupation (Danish, Smyer, & Nowak, 1980).

Events can be viewed as the substance of life. If we were able to envision our lives over their entire course, we would be confronted with tens of thousands of life events. Some would be "caused" by our growth as an organism, others by our relations with people, and still others by our relationships with a physical environment we are unable to control. Life events, their properties and structures and our reactions to them are essential to understand. Brim and Ryff (1980), Danish, Smyer, and Nowak (1980), and Reese and Smyer (1982) have defined and described some of the properties and structures of events, especially as they are seen as processes. Cohn (1982) has provided a vivid example of how these properties and structures can be used to understand the process of divorce.

RELATING PAST, PRESENT,<br>AND FUTURE EVENTS

Since most people do not have an active orientation toward self-development, experiencing these life events is often problematic, because they may signify great change in an individual's life. However, as noted by Riegel (1975), Caplan (1964), and others, the results of change may either be positive or negative. In Figure 4.1 we depict the potential outcomes an individual may experience following the occurrence of a life event.

We believe that our lives are comprised of literally tens of thousands of life events and that each serves as a marker for development. It is not only the present experience of the event which influences our reactions, it is the interaction of the event with our past history. The effect of the same critical life event will not be the same on every individual, nor is the effect of different life events necessarily the same for any one

individual. Lawton and Nahemow (1973), for example, have proposed that an individual's response to an external stress is in part dependent on the individual's past history with similar phenomena. They suggest that experiences with similar events increase one's competence, thus providing the capacity to cope successfully with a wider range of environmental demands.

The ability to respond effectively to events because of past successes can be explained as the development of an expanded repertoire of behaviors. Caplan (1964) has labeled these behaviors "resources." While this explanation can account for the behavior once the individual encounters the event, it does not fully explain the individual's initial appraisal of the situation. Part of the reason why individuals with a history of effective responses to events are able to respond to present events effectively is their ability to recognize the similarity among past, present, and future events. Individuals who respond effectively understand that they have experienced similar situations. At a cognitive level, they know they *can* deal with the event. At the behavioral level, they employ a behavioral sequence successful in the past. Therefore the psychological uniqueness of the event becomes deemphasized and similarities are highlighted (Danish, Smyer, & Nowak, 1980). Thus individual interventions for each life event are not necessary. The goal of an effective life development intervention program is to teach those skills that are most helpful across situations.

### Skills to Enhance Personal Competence

The developmental intervention model we've proposed implies growth; it recognizes that people have both competencies and deficits (Kahn, 1975), and can be active problem-solvers and participants in their own growth. *The development of personal competency, a goal of the intervention, is defined as the ability to be self-reliant and to do life planning.* Personal competence is in great part dependent on the individual's level of resources. The more resources individuals

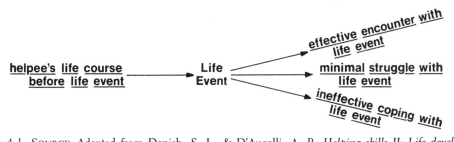

Figure 4.1. SOURCE: Adapted from Danish, S. J., & D'Augelli, A. R. *Helping skills II: Life development intervention*. New York: Human Sciences Press, 1982.

have, the better able they are to deal with an event and grow from the encounter with it. Thus resources are not only *interpersonal skills*, such as the ability to relate effectively to others, but also *intrapersonal skills*, such as competence in setting goals, acquiring knowledge, making decisions, taking risks, developing self-control, and understanding oneself; and having a network of *social support* (caring friends and family).

While we may not have control over all our resources, we do have control over many of them. Resources are, to borrow from a popular advertisement, "a piece of the rock" for critical life events (Danish & D'Augelli, 1982). As mentioned earlier, the first step in successfully encountering an event is the ability to recognize the similarity between the present event and both past and future events. What an individual did to encounter successfully a past event must be recalled. The past success experience can help in the present if the individual is able to make the connection between one event and another. Lazarus (1979) called this "anticipatory coping." If the individual's past experience with the event was not successful, he or she should be encouraged to consider what might have been done to make it more successful, and then the connection should be made. In other words, while the *content* or *knowledge* one needs to encounter the events differ, the *skills*, *risks*, and *attitudes* necessary for a successful outcome generally overlap. For example, the life events of beginning a new job and marriage differ in the content of events, but require related skills—decision-making, risk-taking, and so on (Danish, Smyer, & Nowak, 1980).

It is our perspective that there are a limited number of generic skills which may be learned and applied in coping effectively with a variety of events. The events serve as markers for which one can prepare, and the intervention is explicitly anticipatory socialization. As one becomes more skilled in encountering each event, new events are experienced with renewed confidence and are seen as opportunities for growth and challenge rather than periods of stress and anxiety. Our endstate, then, is not a particular outcome of a particular event but the ability to be planful in confronting each event (Danish & D'Augelli, 1980).

### Life Development Intervention

As the skills began to be identified, a program was designed to teach these skills. The program, *Helping skills II: Life development intervention* (Danish & D'Augelli, 1982), was developed to be taught to intervention agents; these agents could in turn use the skills in the program to counsel and teach others. The program consists of six individual skills: (1) goal assessment, (2) knowledge acquisition, (3) decision-making, (4) risk assessment, (5) creation of social support, and (6) planning of skill development. The focal point of the program is the goal-setting component. While descriptions of interpersonal skills training have emphasized the uniqueness of different behaviors (for example, separate assessment instruments that tap specific motoric, cognitive, or physiological responses), the uniqueness of the *individual* has been ignored. The individual's motivations, desires, needs, and personal goals have not been included in such skill training and assessment. Explicit in the assessment literature is the belief that there will be variation among individuals with respect to degree of skill. It is assumed that if the source of the variation can be pinpointed, then the skill training can be implemented in order to reduce variation about the mean. Thus in most other training programs while there is a highly individualistic nature to diagnosis and treatment, it is not the individual who decides what is important to learn, what goals to attain, or how to attain them. The training that the individual receives is controlled by scores on self-report inventories and observations of professionals—by the experts. Even the interview, which by nature usually allows persons to freely express their desires, has been identified as needing greater structure and less subjectivity (Bellack, 1979).

The underlying issue that we are addressing is one of empowerment (Rappaport, 1981). What skills, if any, do the individuals want to learn? How would they like to cope with a specific event; what are their life goals? Helping individuals identify their goals and develop plans to attain them is an empowering act. It makes intervention a collaborative process.

The process of setting goals is difficult. While the energy involved in attaining the goal is considerable, all the energy expended is useless if the goal is not identified clearly and in a form which makes achievement possible. Goal assessment involves three parts: goal identification, goal importance, and delineation of the barriers to achieving the goal. Goals must involve the identification of a specific, positive behavior. When goals involve "nots" so much attention is focused on the behavior to avoid that this may lead to anxiety or inaction. The determination of a specific, positive behavior provides an opportunity for individuals to initiate action and then to evaluate whether these actions are related to how they wish to behave. In addition to setting positive and behaviorally stated goals, the importance of the goal must be determined. Goals which are more important to significant others or to the intervenor are less likely to be attained than ones important to the goal-setter.

Once the goal has been set and its importance determined, the process of goal attainment can begin. To understand what is required to attain the goal, it is necessary to recognize what barriers and roadblocks exist to goal achievement. In other words, what is preventing the individual from achieving the goal? Four roadblocks have been identified—a lack of knowledge, a lack of skill, an inability to assess the risks involved in changing behavior, and a lack of social support. A lack of knowledge refers to information or facts which are needed if the goal is to be achieved; for example, an overweight person wishing to lose weight may not know how many calories are in different foods. When individuals lack skills they know *what* to do but not *how* to do it. For example, indecisive people lack decision-making skills. Some individuals know what their goals are and how to achieve them but are *afraid* to initiate the necessary actions because of the risk involved. Risks are the benefits of an action minus the costs. When the costs outweigh the benefits the risk is too great and actions are rarely taken. Thus individuals may want to make new friends and may know how, but fear rejection and do not take the risk. The final roadblock has to do with the lack of social support. Even when individuals know how and are willing to change, the lack of support from important people in their lives may inhibit action. For example, the individual wishing to make new friends may even be willing to risk rejection; however, the lack of support from present friends may impede goal achievement. Social support is especially crucial in maintaining a new behavior.

Each of these roadblocks has been developed into specific skills taught in the Life Development Intervention program. One last skill has been included in the program: planning skill development. This skill is really an example of "giving psychology away." It is process designed to help individuals learn how to design and implement their own skill programs.

As noted earlier, the program was developed to teach intervention agents how to use this program with others. However, because the program format is conducive to being taught directly to individuals wishing to increase their skills, it has recently been adapted for this purpose. The goal-assessment and planning-skill-development stages have been adapted and taught to individuals interested in losing weight (Leonard-Perez, 1982), changing diet and exercise behaviors (Lang, 1981), or changing eating patterns (Mazzeo, 1981). In addition, these two skills have formed the basis of a program developed to teach sport psychology skills directly to athletes and coaches (Danish & Hale, 1982).

Lang (1981) compared the life development intervention model to a prescriptive program for diet and exercise. Twelve obese women were divided into two groups and various body weight and heart rate measures were taken. The prescribed group was instructed to attend at least three activity sessions weekly. Members of the life development group were taught and practiced a goal-setting model for diet and exercise. They were free to attend the activity sessions or to choose other methods for obtaining their goals. Following the 12-week program there were no differences in body weight, body fat, and submaximal heart rate. However, participation in the life development group resulted in greater gains in the $V_{0_2}$ max. Additionally, members of the group that had been taught goal-setting felt significantly more confident in continuing their exercise plans and experienced a greater feeling of independence from the group and the counselors.

## Issues in Skill Dissemination and Evaluation

### Skills Training and the Educational Model

In our review we noted that, in general, skill dissemination efforts have followed a general instructional format (Gagne, 1970). This format includes being provided a conceptual understanding of the components of the skill, viewing others demonstrate aspects of the skill, and practicing the skill while receiving feedback. More specifically, the process of skill training consists of the following steps: (1) the skill is defined in behavioral terms; (2) the rationale for the skill is presented and discussed; (3) a skill attainment criterion is specified; (4) a model of effective and ineffective skills is presented; (5) the skills are practiced under intensive supervision; (6) outside practice emphasizing continued behavioral rehearsal is assigned; and (7) during the subsequent session an evaluation of skill levels is conducted using behavioral checklists and other evaluation tools (Danish, 1977).

In implementing life development intervention skills, we have used an educational model of service delivery. This approach uses the school as its model and instruction as the means for enhancement. The intervenor becomes a teacher rather than a therapist. Adopting such a model allows the intervenor to be a skill trainer who teaches the life skills previously proposed and facilitates the retention of skills through the life span. What is important here is not the context of the intervention as much as the role of the helper. In other words, not only is a medical-disease orientation rejected for a learning one, but a mass teaching model is used instead of a clinical treatment model (Danish & D'Augelli, 1981).

As the mass teaching model becomes the model of choice for skill dissemination, skill training becomes a more do-it-yourself treatment process. While we believe this to be an admirable goal, at present it is just that—a goal. Although the self-help movement has exploded, most self-help materials, especially self-help books, do not teach skills, they disseminate knowledge. As was stated previously, knowing *what* to do is not the same as knowing *how* to do it. More effective models of implementation must be developed before skill training becomes a do-it-yourself enterprise. Readers interested in learning more about the problems of self-help materials are referred to Glasgow and Rosen (1978) and Rosen (1979).

### Problems of Transfer and Maintenance

In any type of skill training programs, a salient issue is whether individuals use the skills taught in the natural environment. Transfer of training from the teaching to the nontraining environment and the maintenance of the skills once training is discontinued do not occur naturally (Kazdin & Bootzin, 1973; Kuenthe, 1968; Stokes & Baer, 1977). Despite the provision of sufficient practice during training, transfer and maintenance may fail to occur (Hanna & Owen, 1977). Obstacles in the nontraining environment are thought to be the cause (Sundel & Sundel, 1975). These include (1) inadequate reinforcement for desired responses; (2) reinforcement for inappropriate responses; and (3) the presence of elements dissimilar to the training environment. Specific efforts, therefore, must be made to ensure skill use across settings and over time. Most research on transfer and maintenance has concluded that when reinforcement for responding appropriately and pressure to use the skills in the natural environment are lacking, these phenomena do not occur.

An alternative explanation involves the different motivational processes within the trainee. Kelman (1958) identifies these as compliance, identification, and internalization. Compliance occurs when an individual participates in the training program to gain rewards or avoid punishment. The trainee performs the required behaviors to achieve favorable reactions from the trainer rather than due to a belief in the rationale. When skills are performed as a result of compliance, transfer and maintenance are not likely to occur. A higher-level process is identification. Trainees learn the skills in an effort to establish or maintain a satisfying relationship with the trainer. Satisfaction is derived from conforming. Problems

occur with transfer and maintenance because trainees fail to exhibit the skills when the trainer can no longer exert influence, that is, when trainees move out of the training to the natural environment. The highest level of the motivational processes is internalization. This occurs when trainees learn the skills because the rationale for learning agrees with their value system. Because performance of the skills is intrinsically rewarding, trainees are more likely to maintain use of the skills in diverse environments. Internalization can be facilitated if the relevance of skill use outside of the training situation is perceived. This requires that significant others in the natural environment model effective use of the skills and reinforce the trainee for responding appropriately.

Descriptions of compliance problems are commonplace in the literature, especially the health literature. It has been estimated that one-third to one-half of all patients fail to follow the treatment prescribed for them (Davis, 1969; Stone, 1979). Given the definition of compliance and the lack of inherent rewards, it is not difficult to understand why levels of compliance are so low. Only when skills to be learned fit into the values of the learner will learning for generalization and transfer likely occur. At a minimum, then, the learner should be involved in every level of decision with regard to what skills are to be learned and how they will be taught. For example, Stuart and Davis (1972) in their book on weight loss provide readers with a list of possibly helpful techniques and encourage readers to choose from among them.

An alternative process for enhancing internalization is one we have suggested—teaching the learner a personal goal-setting process. The effects of goal-setting upon performance were initially recognized through repeated experimental task studies demonstrating that the more difficult the goal established, the higher the level of performance observed (Bryan & Locke, 1967; Locke, 1965, 1967; Locke & Bryan, 1967). Goal-setting in industry has been found to produce a significant increase in productivity by individuals as well as groups (Latham & Baldes, 1975; Latham & Kinne, 1974; Terborg, 1976). Development of specific goals has also resulted in a more positive attitude toward the task, as well as the use of more creative tactics to achieve the goal. Teaching goal-setting and life development intervention should lead to a higher level of commitment, allow for individualized strategy development and increased self attribution, and encourage the transfer and maintenance of these new skills to other areas of the individual's life.

### Summary

Skill training is increasingly being recognized as an important means for developing personal competence.

It is perhaps one of the most well established individual interventions under the general rubric of primary prevention. While the methods of skill training are based on learning theory, it has lacked a conceptual base. Without a clear theoretical basis for intervention we are left asking the question, "Intervention: Why, how and for what purpose?" Our use of a life span human development perspective gives an answer to these questions. We believe that intervention must involve an alignment with a theoretical knowledge base. It is not our intention to ignore values and norms. Although we have not identified specific end-states (such as particular social skills), we do believe in the value of life planning, in setting goals, and developing feelings of self-efficacy. Our skill program seeks to teach such values and behaviors. By itself, the adoption of a life development philosophy may serve as an important intervention and as a deterrent to the "mental health–mental illness" orientation which permeates much of the work of today's primary prevention specialists.

## References

Albee, G. W. The prevention of prevention. *Physician East*, 1979, 4, 28–30.

Albee, G. W. Politics, power, prevention and social change. In J. M. Joffe & G. W. Albee (Eds.), *Prevention through political action and social change*. Hanover, N.H.: University Press of New England, 1981.

Allsen, P. E., Harrison, J. M., & Vance, B. *Fitness for life: An individualized approach*. (2nd ed.) Dubuque, Iowa: W. C. Brown, 1980.

Arkowitz, H., Lichtenstein, E., McGovern, K., & Hines, P. The behavioral assessment of social competence in males. *Behavioral Therapy*, 1975, 6, 3–13.

Authier, J., Gustafson, K., Guerney, B. G., & Kasdorf, J. A. The psychological practitioner as a teacher: A theoretical-historical and practical review. *Counseling Psychologist*, 1975, 5, 31–50.

Baltes, P. B. Prototypical paradigms and questions in life-span research on development and aging. *Gerontologist*, 1973, 13, 458–467.

Baltes, P. B., & Schaie, K. W. On the plasticity of intelligence in adulthood and old age: Where Horn and Donaldson fail. *American Psychologist*, 1976, 31, 720–725.

Baltes, P. B., & Willis, S. L. Life-span developmental psychology, cognitive functioning, and social policy. In M. W. Riley (Ed.), *Aging from birth to death*. Boulder, Colo.: Westview Press, 1979.

Baltes, P. B., & Willis, S. L. Enhancement (plasticity) of intellectual functioning in old age: Penn State Adult Development and Enrichment Project (ADEPT). In F. I. M. Craik & S. E. Trehub (Eds.), *Aging and cognitive processes*. New York: Plenum Press, 1983, in press.

Bellack, A. S. Behavioral assessment of social skills. In A. S. Bellack & M. Hersen (Eds.), *Research and practice in social skills training*. New York: Plenum Press, 1979.

Bellack, A. S., & Hersen, M. Chronic psychiatric patients: Social skills training. In M. Hersen & A. S. Bellack

(Eds.), *Behavior therapy in the psychiatric setting*. Baltimore: Williams & Wilkins, 1978.

Birchler, G. R. Communication skills in married couples. In A. S. Bellack & M. Hersen (Eds.), *Research and practice in social skills training*. New York: Plenum Press, 1979.

Bond, L. A., & Rosen, J. C. (Eds.), *Competence and coping during adulthood*. Hanover, N.H.: University Press of New England, 1980.

Bornstein, M. R., Bellack, A. S., & Hersen, M. Social skills training for unassertive children: A multiple-baseline analysis. *Journal of Applied Behavior Analysis*, 1977, 10, 183–195.

Brim, O. G., Jr., & Ryff, C. D. On the properties of life events. In P. B. Baltes & O. G. Brim, Jr. (Eds.), *Life-span development and behavior*. Vol. 3. New York: Academic Press, 1980.

Bryan, J. F., & Locke, E. A. Goal setting as a means of increasing motivation. *Journal of Applied Psychology*, 1967, 510, 274–277.

Caplan, G. *Principles of preventive psychology*. New York: Basic Books, 1964.

Cohn, M. D. The structure of stressful life events: The case of mid-life divorce. Unpublished doctoral dissertation, Pennsylvania State University, 1982.

Collins, J. D. The effects of the conjugal relationship modification method on marital communication and adjustment. Unpublished doctoral dissertation, Pennsylvania State University, 1971.

Cooper, K. W. *Aerobics*. New York: Bantam Books, 1968.

Costa, P., & McCrae, R. Still stable after all these years: Personality as a key to some issues in aging. In P. S. Baltes & O. G. Brim, Jr. (Eds.), *Life-span development and behavior*. Vol. 3. New York: Academic Press, 1980.

Cowen, E. L. Baby-steps toward primary prevention. *American Journal of Community Psychology*, 1977, 5, 1–22.

Cowen, E. L. Demystifying primary prevention. In D. G. Forgays (Eds.), *Primary prevention of psychopathology*. Vol. 2. Hanover, N.H.: University Press of New England, 1978.

Curran, J. P. Social skills: Methodological issues and future directions. In A. S. Bellack & M. Hersen (Eds.), *Research and practice in social skills training*. New York: Plenum Press, 1979.

Danish, S. J. Human development and human services: A marriage proposal. In I. Iscoe, B. L. Bloom, & C. C. Spielberger (Eds.), *Community psychology in transition*. New York: Halsted, 1977.

Danish, S. J. Making sense of prevention. In C. H. Adams (Ed.), *Symposium proceedings of Prevention equals good health*. Storrs, Conn.: School of Applied Health Professions, 1980.

Danish, S. J., & D'Augelli, A. R. Promoting competence and enhancing development through life development intervention. In L. A. Bond & J. C. Rosen (Eds.), *Competence and coping during adulthood*. Hanover, N.H.: University Press of New England, 1980.

Danish, S. J., & D'Augelli, A. R. *Helping skills II: Life development intervention*. New York: Human Sciences Press, 1982.

Danish, S. J., & Hale, B. D. Sport psychology: Teaching skills to athletes and coaches. *Journal of Physical Education, Recreation and Dance*, 1982.

Danish, S. J., Smyer, M. S., & Nowak, C. A. Developmental intervention: Enhancing life-events processes. In P. B.

Baltes & O. G. Brim, Jr. (Eds.), *Life-span development and behavior*. Vol. 3. New York: Academic Press, 1981.

Davis, M. S. Variations in patients' compliance with doctors' advice: An empirical analysis of patterns of communication. *American Journal of Public Health*, 1968, **58**, 274–288.

Dohrenwend, B. S., & Dohrenwend, B. P. (Eds.), *Stressful life events: Their nature and effects*. New York: Wiley, 1974.

Eisler, R. M., Hersen, M., Miller, P. M., & Blanchard, E. B. Situational determinants of assertive behaviors. *Journal of Consulting and Clinical Psychology*, 1975, **43**, 330–340.

Elder, G. H., Jr., & Rockwell, R. Marital timing in women's life patterns. *Journal of Family History*, 1976, **1**, 34–53.

Ely, A. L., Guerney, B. G., Jr., & Stover, L. Efficacy of the training phase of conjugal therapy. *Psychotherapy: Theory, Research and Practice*, 1973, **10**, 201–207.

Folkins, C. H., & Sime, W. E. Physical fitness training and mental health. *American Psychologist*, 1981, **36**, 373–389.

Ford, D. H. Mental health and human development: An analysis of a dilemma. In D. Harshbarger & R. Maley (Eds.), *Behavior analysis and systems analysis: An integrative approach to mental health programs*. Kalamazoo, Mich.: Behaviordelia, 1974.

Forgays, D. G. (Ed.), *Primary prevention of psychopathology*. Vol. 2. Hanover, N.H.: University Press of New England, 1978.

Frank, J. D. Therapeutic components of psychotherapy: A 25-year progress report of research. *Journal of Nervous and Mental Disease*, 1974, **159**, 325–342.

Gagne, R. *The conditions of learning*. New York: Holt, Rinehart & Winston, 1970.

Galassi, J. P., DeLo, J. S., Galassi, M. D., & Bastein, S. The college self-expression scale: A measure of assertiveness. *Behavior Therapy*, 1974, **5**, 165–171.

Galassi, J. P., & Galassi, M. D. Modification of heterosocial skills deficits. In A. S. Bellack & M. Hersen (Eds.), *Research and practice in social skills training*. New York: Plenum Press, 1979.

Gesten, E. L., Flores de Apodaca, R., Rains, M., Weissberg, R. P., & Cowen, E. L. Promoting peer-related social competence in schools. In M. W. Kent & J. E. Rolf (Eds.), *The primary prevention of psychopathology*. Vol. 3. *Social competence in children*. Hanover, N.H.: University Press of New England, 1979.

Glasgow, R. E., & Rosen, G. M. Behavioral bibliotherapy: A review of self-help behavior therapy. *Psychological Bulletin*, 1978, **85**, 1–23.

Gladwin, T. Social competence and clinical practice. *Psychiatry*, 1967, **30**, 30–43.

Goldsmith, J. B., & McFall, R. M. Development and evaluation of an interpersonal skill-training program for psychiatric inpatients. *Journal of Abnormal Psychology*, 1975, **84**, 51–58.

Goldston, S. E. Defining primary prevention. In G. W. Albee & J. M. Joffe (Eds.), *Primary prevention of psychopathology*. Vol. 1. Hanover, N.H.: University Press of New England, 1977.

Gordon, T. *Parent effectiveness training*. New York: Peter H. Wyden, 1970.

Guerney, B. G., Jr. *Relationship enhancement*. San Francisco: Jossey-Bass, 1977.

Hanna, R., & Owen, N. Facilitating transfer and maintenance of fluency in stuttering therapy. *Journal of Speech and Hearing Disorders*, 1977, **42**, 65–76.

Hersen, M. Self-assessment of fear. *Behavior Therapy*, 1973, **4**, 241–257.

Hersen, M. Modification of skill deficits in psychiatric patients. In A. S. Bellack & M. Hersen (Eds.), *Research and practice in social skills training*. New York: Plenum Press, 1979.

Hersen, M., & Belleck, A. S. Assessment of social skills. In A. R. Ciminero, K. S. Calhoun, & H. E. Adams (Eds.), *Handbook of behavioral assessment*. New York: Wiley, 1977.

Hersen, M., & Eisler, R. M. Social skills training. In W. E. Craighead, A. E. Kazdin, & M. J. Mahoney (Eds.), *Behavior modification: Principles, issues, and applications*. Boston: Houghton Mifflin, 1976.

Holmes, T. H., & Rahe, R. H. The social readjustment rating scale. *Journal of Psychosomatic Research*, 1967, **11**, 213–218.

Hultsch, D., & Plemons, J. Life events and life-span development. In P. B. Baltes & O. G. Brim, Jr. (Eds.), *Life-span development and behavior*. Vol. 2. New York: Academic Press, 1979.

Johnson, D. W. *Reaching out*. (2nd ed.) Englewood Cliffs, N.J.: Prentice-Hall, 1981.

Kahn, R. L. The mental health system and the future aged. *Gerontologist*, 1975, **15**, 24–31.

Kazdin, A. E. Effects of covert modeling and model reinforcement on assertive behavior. *Journal of Abnormal Psychology*, 1974, **83**, 240–252.

Kazdin, A. E., & Bootzin, R. R. The token economy: An examination of issues. In R. D. Rubin, J. P. Brady, & J. D. Henderson (Eds.), *Advances in Behavior Therapy*, 1973, **4**, 169–176.

Kelman, H. C. Compliance, identification and internalization: Three processes of opinion change. *Journal of Conflict Resolution*, 1958, **2**, 51–60.

Kent, M. W., & Rolf, J. E. *Primary prevention of psychopathology*. Vol. 3. Hanover, N.H.: University Press of New England, 1979.

Kessler, M., & Albee, G. W. Primary prevention. *Annual Review of Psychology*, 1975, **26**, 557–591.

Kuenthe, J. L. *The teaching-learning process*. Chicago: Scott, Foresman, 1968.

Lang, P. J. The application of psychological methods to the study of psychotherapy and behavior modification. In A. E. Bergin & S. L. Garfield (Eds.), *Handbook of psychotherapy and behavior change*. New York: Wiley, 1971.

Lang, D. A. Goal assessment as an alternative to traditional prescriptions for diet and exercise in treating obesity. Unpublished thesis, Pennsylvania State University, 1981.

Latham, G. P., & Baldes, J. The "practical significance" of Locke's theory of goal setting. *Journal of Applied Psychology*, 1975, **60**, 122–124.

Latham, G. P., & Kinne, S. B. Improving job performance through training in goal setting. *Journal of Applied Psychology*, 1974, **59**, 187–191.

Lawton, M. P., & Nahemow, L. Ecology and the aging process. In C. Eisdorfer & M. P. Lawton (Eds.), *The psychology of adult development and aging*. Washington, D.C.: American Psychological Association, 1973.

Lazarus, R. S. Shaping up the coping concept. In L. A. Bond & J. C. Rosen (Eds.), *Primary prevention of psy-*

*chopathology*. Vol. 4. Hanover, N.H.: University Press of New England, 1979.

Leonard-Perez, J. E. Goal assessment as a strategy for weight control in self-help weight-reduction groups. Unpublished master's thesis, Pennsylvania State University, 1982.

Levine, J., & Zigler, E. The essential-reactive distinction in alcoholism: A developmental approach. *Journal of Abnormal Psychology*, 1973, **81**, 242–249.

Linehan, M. M., & Egan, K. J. Assertion training for women. In A. S. Bellack & M. Hersen (Eds.), *Research and practice in social skills training*. New York: Plenum Press, 1979.

Locke, E. A. The relationship of task success to task liking and satisfaction. *Journal of Applied Psychology*, 1965, **49**, 379–385.

Locke, E. A. Toward a theory of task motivation and incentives. *Organizational and Human Performance*, 1968, **3**, 157–189.

Locke, E. A., & Bryan, J. Performance goals as determinants of level of performance and boredom. *Journal of Applied Psychology*, 1967, **51**, 120–130.

Lopata, H. Z. *Widowhood in an American city*. Cambridge, Mass.: Schenkman, 1973.

Mazzeo, S. E. The effect of a self-directed versus diet-directed treatment on following the U.S. Dietary Goals and Guidelines. Unpublished master's thesis, Pennsylvania State University, 1981.

Neugarten, B., & Hagestad, G. Age and the life course. In R. H. Binstock & E. Shanas (Eds.), *Handbook of aging and the social sciences*. New York: Van Nostrand Reinhold, 1976.

Parkes, C. M. Effects of bereavement on physical and mental health: A study of the medical records of widows. *British Medical Journal*, 1964, **2**, 274–279.

Phillips, L., & Zigler, E. Role orientation, the action-thought dimension and outcome in psychiatric disorder. *Journal of Abnormal and Social Psychology*, 1964, **68**, 381–389.

Rappaport, J. *Community psychology: Values, research and action*. New York: Holt, Rinehart & Winston, 1977.

Rappaport, J. In praise of paradox: A social policy of empowerment over prevention. *American Journal of Community Psychology*, 1981, **9**, 1–25.

Reese, H. A., & Smyer, M. A. The dimensionalization of life events. In E. J. Callahan & K. McClusky (Eds.), *Life-span developmental psychology: Normative life events*. New York: Academic Press, 1982.

Rehm, L. P., & Marston, A. R. Reduction of social anxiety through modification of self-reinforcement: An instigation

therapy technique. *Journal of Consulting and Clinical Psychology*, 1968, **32**, 565–574.

Riegel, K. Adult life crises: A dialectic interpretation of development. In N. Datan & L. Ginsberg (Eds.), *Life-span developmental psychology: Normative life crises*. New York: Academic Press, 1975.

Rinn, R. C., & Markel, A. Modification of social skill deficits in children. In A. S. Bellack & M. Hersen (Eds.), *Research and practice in social skills training*. New York: Plenum Press, 1979.

Rosen, G. M. Guidelines for the review of do-it-yourself treatment books. *Contemporary Psychology*, 1981, **26**, 189–191.

Rossi, A. Transition to parenthood. *Journal of Marriage and the Family*, 1968, **30**, 26–39.

Spivack, G., Platt, J. J., & Shure, M. B. *The problem-solving approach to adjustment*. San Francisco: Jossey-Bass, 1976.

Stokes, T. F., & Baer, D. M. An implicit technology of generalization. *Journal of Applied Behavior Analysis*, 1977, **10**, 349–367.

Stone, G. C. Patient compliance and the role of the expert. *Journal of Social Issues*, 1979.

Stuart, R. B., & Davis, B. *Slim chance in a fat world: Behavioral control of obesity*. Champaign, Ill.: Research Press, 1972.

Sundel, M., & Sundel, S. S. *Behavior modification in the human services: A systematic introduction to concepts and applications*. New York: Wiley, 1975.

Terborg, J. The motivational components of goal setting. *Journal of Applied Psychology*, 1976, **61**, 613–621.

Trower, P., Bryant, B., & Argyle, M. *Social skills and mental health*. London: Methuen, 1978.

Watson, D., & Friend, R. Measurement of social-evaluative anxiety. *Journal of Consulting and Clinical Psychology*, 1969, **33**, 448–457.

Weissberg, R. P., Gesten, E. L., Rapkin, B. D., Cowen, E. L., Davidson, E., Flores de Apodaca, & McKim, B. J. The evaluation of a social problem-solving training program for suburban and inner city third grade children. *Journal of Consulting and Clinical Psychology*, 1981, **49**, 251–261.

Whiting, H. T. A. *Acquiring ball skills*. Philadelphia: Lea & Felinger, 1971.

Zigler, E., & Phillips, L. Social competence and outcome in psychiatric disorder. *Journal of Abnormal and Social Psychology*, 1961, **63**, 264–271.

Zigler, E., & Phillips, L. Social competence and the process-reactive distinction in psychopathology. *Journal of Abnormal and Social Psychology*, 1962, **65**, 215–222.

# PART III
# ECOLOGICAL AND ENVIRONMENTAL PERSPECTIVES

# INTRODUCTION TO PART III

Preventive approaches have consistently emphasized the need to develop conceptual frameworks and empirical methods for understanding and appraising elements of the ecological context which influence the adaptive functioning of individuals and populations. Drawing heavily from the traditions of behavioral, social, community, and environmental psychology, in this section there are four chapters devoted to examining those social and physical characteristics of the environment which impact on the adjustment of individuals and which have been utilized in the development of preventive efforts. Because most practitioners have been trained to deliver services using individually oriented approaches, the shift to an environmental focus is a particularly important development. The section begins with a chapter by Trudy Vincent and Edison Trickett, who use an ecological perspective to understand the impact of the social environment on human adaptation. Kelly's ecological analogy is first described and shown to be an excellent model for generating and testing complex questions about social environments. Questions raised from this perspective heighten our awareness of the research relationships and existing resources in settings. Moos's social ecological approach is then discussed, providing a view that new assessment devices which indicate that social environments, like people, can

be systematically assessed and categorized. The case is made for the importance of preventive practitioners to become adept at assessing environments and their influence on human development. At least part of the interest in an environmental focus is that considerable research has indicated that many social environments tend to discourage autonomy, independence, and creativity: many prisons, schools, and rehabilitation centers exert pernicious influences on their inhabitants, and merely teaching social skills or competencies probably would not alter the social system influences predisposing to pathology. Attempting to understand those factors which affect the social climate is a critical undertaking, one which is necessary in order to intervene to ultimately create more healthy, satisfying, and growth-producing settings. In addition, Vincent and Trickett illustrate the need for preventive professionals to become skillful in determining which individuals, with which specific competencies, are most compatible with which particular social climates.

The next chapter, by Kenneth Heller and Ralph Swindle, explores the nature and functions of social support systems. The authors review the social-support-stress-buffering hypothesis, which predicts that those individuals exposed to high stress and provided adequate support resources should develop significantly less symptomatology than those exposed to high stress but having few social supports. While some research has supported this hypothesis, Heller and Swindle point out that many of the studies examining this topic have been marred by conceptual and methodological flaws. In recent years a growing number of investigators have been attracted to examining the influences of social supports in moderating life stresses. This chapter provides a healthy dose of caution in interpreting the findings which have so far appeared in professional journals. The authors suggest that future research might profitably be directed toward exploring questions such as how supports change over time and how individuals select and determine the types of supports they receive. One problem with the term "social support" is that it implies a positive bias. However, we all know that ties with other individuals are not always supportive. A more useful construct, explicitly defined by Heller and Swindle, is "perceived social supports," the subjective impact of social connections on the individual. By using more accurate and precise terms to describe the connections people experience with others, much conceptual and practical ambiguity will be avoided. The chapter also examines how a variety of factors, including ecological factors, social connections, stressful life events, and personal characteristics, influence perceived social supports. The importance of these concepts is partly due to the fact that many child and clinical practitioners and researchers are extremely interested in these influences on adjustment. It may be profitable to have more collaboration and dialogue between preventive and clinical professionals on these ideas.

While the first two chapters in this section deal with an environment's social climate and social connections, Chapter 7 by Abraham Wandersman and his colleagues focuses on current work and thought concerning the physical environment, and particularly those aspects which influence adaptation. A lucid model is first presented indicating how the physical environment (environmental stressors and the built environment) and individual differences affect perceptions of the environment and the ability to cope. There are several implications for prevention, which the authors discuss based on their model. For example, preventive psychologists might work toward either eliminating environmental stresses or reducing stress in high-density situations. The former strategy could be achieved by consulting with school systems and advising them not to build schools near airports, for instance, which are extremely noisy, a factor that does impair the ability to learn. Stress could be reduced in high-density settings by constructing housing which emphasized territoriality, thereby increasing inhabitants' sense of ownership and possibly as a consequence

reducing stress. Central to these interventions is the goal of facilitating a sense of control and effective coping, since individuals with these attributes are more likely to be mentally healthy and able to deal with life stresses and crises. More often than not, the individuals responsible for constructing the built environment are either not interested in these concepts or not aware of them. As a consequence buildings are constructed, hospitals renovated, and schools redesigned without much, if any, input from preventive-oriented social scientists. This is a regrettable state of affairs, particularly given the robust effects, so well documented in this chapter, of the physical environment on adjustment. Besides the need for more input from mental health professionals, there is an urgent need for more collaborative citizen participation in environmental projects, for this represents another way to enhance coping and maximize control by those groups most directly affected by the constructed buildings.

In the last chapter of this section, Leonard Jason and Anne Bogat discuss the relevance of behavioral principles for environmental interventions. They note that behavioral practitioners have tended to embrace a traditional medical model in the delivery of mental health services, whereas preventive-oriented mental health professionals have generally adopted nonbehavioral intervention approaches. Jason and Bogat maintain that this is an unfortunate state of affairs because the two approaches have much to offer each other. The behavioral approach is based on a rigorous, empirical foundation and has been able to document stable, behavioral changes following interventions in a wide variety of clinical problems. Community and preventive theorists, on the other hand, have been more visionary in suggesting higher-level interventions focusing on systems of socialization and institutional change. Research cited in this chapter indicates that dialogue and collaboration has begun to occur between behavioral and preventive-oriented psychologists. The authors describe the basic contributions and principles of both the behavioral and the preventive approaches, and then present examples of preventive-behavioral interventions. Perhaps the most significant developments in the 1970s in this regard were the increasing interest in and development of the fields of prevention and behavioral treatment. Jason and Bogat suggest there are limitless possibilities in merging the best features of these approaches. Explicitly articulating possible benefits of both approaches might function to encourage more investigators to utilize preventive and behavioral principles when conceptualizing and mounting interventions.

# 5 PREVENTIVE INTERVENTIONS AND THE HUMAN CONTEXT: ECOLOGICAL APPROACHES TO ENVIRONMENTAL ASSESSMENT AND CHANGE*

## Trudy A. Vincent and Edison J. Trickett

P reventive activity is designed to increase the resilience and resourcefulness of persons and settings. The human contexts where persons develop, learn, work, and receive service thus constitute important sites for preventive activity, for it is through these various settings—the family, the school, the job, the hospital or clinic—that persons develop, or fail to develop, successful adaptations as they progress through the life cycle. Because these contexts are important mediators of experience, it is central to a psychology of preventive interventions to develop ways of understanding these contexts and their effects on people. Regardless of whether or not the preventive activity involves community consultation and community development, development of programs such as Head Start to provide young children with core skills, attempts to influence social policy, or community research, the social contexts where these interventions occur define the nature of the intervention, provide the resources which ensure that the intervention will endure, and, over time, become the primary vehicle for promoting the resilience and resourcefulness of individuals and settings.

Our focus on the centrality of social contexts for a psychology of preventive interventions stems from several sources. First, settings such as the school, the job, and the psychiatric ward have significant influences on the experience and development of individuals. What kind of school one attends does make a difference in one's adaptive ability and their future options. The quality of the work environment does affect productivity and feelings about the job and about oneself. Psychiatric hospitals do differ in the nature of their therapeutic environment, resulting in different patient experiences and outcome.

Second, such settings are often stable over a long period of time, giving their impact an increasingly cumulative quality. The traditions of institutions, including their norms, resource networks, support systems, and linkages with external groups, endure and influence cohorts of persons for decades. The inevitable fact of their longevity thus provides incentive to understand their nature and impact, for to the degree that they can be resources for cohorts of individuals over time, they provide the conditions for a truly useful preventive intervention with long-range impact.

Third, these kinds of contexts are those which process large numbers of persons, thus fulfilling one canon of preventive activities—namely, that they be addressed to populations rather than discrete individ-

* The authors wish to thank John Buckner, Sara Corse, Harold Perl, Katy Tracy, and Rod Watts for their comments on the manuscript, and Ellie Lehan for help in its preparation.

uals. Some approaches to preventive interventions with populations are primarily person-centered, in that the emphasis is on developing skills in groups of individuals which will aid their adaptive capacity over time. The development of interpersonal problem-solving skills in cohorts of children falls within this general orientation. Our emphasis, however, is on the impact of the settings which provide the experiences for individuals; thus accessible settings which deal with large numbers of persons become the figure, not the ground.

The focus of this chapter is on one general orientation to the understanding of social contexts which we believe provides a particularly useful approach, namely, an ecological perspective. Most basically, the study of ecology as applied to human systems focuses on the study of person-environment interdependence in determining human adaptation. However, the general term "ecology" has taken on multiple and contrasting meanings in recent years. Environmental psychology, for example, has stressed the importance of the physical environment as a shaper of human interaction and development (see Proshansky, Ittleson, and Rivlin, 1976, for an overview of work within this general perspective). Thus psychologists with this orientation have been interested in preventive interventions dealing with the design of new environments or the restructuring of existing settings such as college dormitories and psychiatric wards (Holahan, 1979; Holahan & Wilcox, 1978).

The term "ecological psychology" has long been used by Roger Barker and his colleagues (Barker, 1968; Barker & Gump, 1964). They have developed an ecological psychology which defines the environment in terms of behavior settings which exert directional influence over the behavior of the individuals in them. Barker asserts that one of the best ways to predict the behavior of individuals is to know what setting the individuals are in. "When in church, people behave 'church'" captures the primary importance Barker places on the setting as a shaper of behavior. Barker and his colleagues have also developed a theory of how behavior settings and people are interrelated based on the fit between the demands of the setting and the persons available to fulfill those demands (see Price, 1976; Stokols, 1977; and Willems, 1977, for overviews of Barker's ecological psychology and recent developments in "manning theory"). Though Barker's perspective may have direct implications for the design of preventive interventions (see Willems, 1977), its primary purpose has thus far been descriptive and taxonomic. However, as a perspective which focuses unequivocally on the importance of understanding the ecological environment, Barker's work is unique in its impact on the field of psychology.

More recently the term "ecology" has found a niche in the area of child development. In an influential book called *The ecology of human development*, Bronfenbrenner (1979) has used the term as an organizing principle for understanding the behavior of children in their natural settings. In Bronfenbrenner's view, individuals' behavior is mediated through a variety of broader social and cultural contexts, such as the roles played in varied social settings, the kind of family interaction in the home, and the cultures and subcultures in which they are raised. However, this perspective does not emphasize the nature of the broader environment per se as an object of study and is just beginning to explore the influence of these environments on individual behavior.

In terms of a psychology of preventive interventions, the development of more ecologically valid knowledge would vastly improve decisions about how to construct programs and policies affecting children. Unless and until such knowledge is generated, Bronfenbrenner's perspective stands as a cautionary beacon against prematurely generalizing findings across varied populations occupying different ecological niches. Like the environmental psychologists and Barker, Bronfenbrenner has offered a compelling paradigm for illuminating the relationship between persons and their environmental contexts.

### Community Psychology and the Ecological Metaphor

The issue of understanding social contexts as a site for and object of preventive interventions has also been a central conceptual thrust for the field of community psychology, with its dual commitment to understanding and action. It too has been developing the metaphor of ecology as a general heuristic for studying and intervening in social environments. As programs for specific groups are developed, as mental health facilities decide how to design their services and relate to other agencies, as the spirit of community development becomes of increasing concern, the need to develop heuristics for understanding social contexts increases.

From within the emerging tradition of community psychology, we have selected two contrasting approaches to the assessment of social environments which have direct implications for the design of preventive interventions—the ecological analogy developed primarily by James Kelly and the social ecological approach primarily attributable to Rudolf Moos.

The ecological analogy is a heuristic originally drawn from field biology which is applicable to the assessment of human communities and social settings. Here the effort has been to derive ways of looking at human environments which can both generate research into the nature of the environment *and* be used to stimulate the positive development of the environment. As such, it is an explicit orientation toward environmental assessment which focuses on preventive intervention through community development. The social ecological approach of Moos and his colleagues (e.g., Moos, 1974a, 1974b, 1976, 1979a, 1979b) represents a taxonomic approach to describing a wide variety of social environments. It is perhaps the most extensive empirical attempt to illuminate the nature of environments and their impact on people. In addition, the information about the environment has—in the spirit of community development—been used in a series of feedback studies to influence the positive development of the setting.

The present chapter first discusses the ecological analogy and its implications for both research and preventive interventions. Next, the social ecological perspective is presented, with an emphasis on the role of environmental assessment and change in preventive interventions.

## The Ecological Analogy

The ecological analogy is an evolving set of ideas designed to aid our understanding of human communities and social environments. It is an analogy, a heuristic, which has guided a way of thinking about

a wide range of problems relevant to the design of preventive interventions, including the relationships among service-delivering agencies (Kelly, 1966), the definition of maladaptation (Kelly, 1966), the role of the psychological consultant in contrasting environments (Kelly, Note 1), the possibilities of administrative leadership for the enhancement of a school (Trickett & Ochberg, Note 2), and research on adolescent adaptation to high school (Kelly, 1979). The tone for the analogy is set by its originator, James Kelly, and focuses on the dual need for community psychologists to create knowledge that is simultaneously *pragmatic and valid*. Thus the ecological analogy assumes the dual mandate of conducting community research which serves as a resource for the community and of creating valid knowledge about the social context. Doing so requires both attention to assessing the nature of the social context and concern about how the research investigator is contributing to or detracting from the research site.

### Four Basic Ecological Principles: Interdependence, Cycling of Resources, Adaptation, and Succession

In its earlier statements (Kelly, 1966; Trickett, Kelly, & Todd, 1972; Trickett & Todd, 1972), the ecological analogy revolved around four ecological principles

### Table 5.1. The Ecological Analogy

A. *Four Principles for an Ecological Paradigm*
1. The *interdependence* principle focuses on the interactive nature of the system and the manner in which its component parts are coupled.
2. The *cycling of resources* principle alerts the investigator to the manner in which resources in the setting are defined, distributed, and developed. It focuses on the evolutionary, the proactive, and the potential of social settings.
3. The *succession* principle orients the researcher to the time dimension of settings, including both historical events and persons relevant to the earlier development of the setting and the anticipatory mechanisms and processes which may be useful in promoting its future development.
4. The *adaptation* principle addresses the "substance" of the environment—those norms, values, processes, and demand characteristics which constrain some kinds of behavior while facilitating others.

B. *Ten Corollaries Embodying the Spirit of Ecological Inquiry*

*Cycling of Resources*
1. The ecological paradigm advocates the conservation, management, and creation of resources.
2. Persons, settings, and events are resources for the development of the community and the research relationship.
3. The activating qualities of persons, settings, and events are emphasized.

*Adaptation*
4. Coping and adaptation are the dominant means of growth and change.
5. The search for systemic events illuminates the process of adaptation.

*Interdependence*
6. Persons and settings are in dynamic interaction.

*Succession*
7. Persons, settings, and events are assessed over time.

*Research Relationship*
8. Community research and the research relationship are designed to be coupled with the host environment.
9. Attending to the side effects of community research is a priority.
10. Ecological inquiry is a flexible, improvisational process.

and their implications for assessing social contexts and communities. The four basic principles (found in Table 5.1A) are interdependence, cycling of resources, adaptation, and succession.

### THE INTERDEPENDENCE PRINCIPLE

The principle of interdependence focuses on the interactive nature of various aspects of the social environment. Viewing the social environment as an interrelated system orients the investigator or intervenor to look at how component parts of a setting (such as the norms governing teacher behavior toward children and the kinds of behaviors children are permitted in classrooms) are coupled. Such a perspective helps focus both research questions and questions related to how change in the environment might occur. In terms of research, it suggests such questions as: How does the implementation of a new policy affect persons occupying different roles in the social setting? How does a teacher's relationship to the principal relate to his or her in-class treatment of children? How does the service delivery pattern of a mental health center change when a new crisis hotline springs up in the neighborhood?

The implications for preventive interventions stem from the implication that alterations made in one part of the social context will have effects throughout the system. Thus any planned change will not only affect those persons or policies directly involved with the effort but also have effects throughout the entire system. It is these so-called unanticipated consequences of interventions which highlight the usefulness of the interdependence principle for designing preventive interventions. An example of the way in which the interdependence principle can operate in the area of service delivery is provided by Kelly (1966) in reference to the relationship between mental health services and other community services. Kelly points out that "any change in the operation of one service unit will affect the operation of all other service units. An increase in admissions to one local mental health facility, for example, can be attributed to a decrease in service opportunities at another facility or may indicate changes in stress tolerance for the social structure of the local population [p. 535]."

### THE CYCLING OF RESOURCES PRINCIPLE

The cycling of resources principle alerts the investigator to the manner in which resources in the setting are defined, distributed, and developed. Resources can be human, as in the unique competencies or community connections of members; they can be technological, involving everything from pencils to in-

formation retrieval computer software; and they can involve the nature of the existing social context, as when the focus is on those settings and events in the larger environment that promote positive adaptation of the community or promote the competencies of members. A resource perspective orients the researcher to assess what qualities in the setting are available for use in the setting's own development. What persons have latent leadership skills which the environment is not tapping? What technologies can ease the paperwork and free up time for organizational planning? What settings generate energy and enthusiasm for the community which can be harnessed to develop the community and work toward shared goals?

The implications for preventive interventions focus on the potential and the proactive qualities of the setting rather than its deficits. Where in the social environment are persons with the necessary competencies to carry out an intervention program? What resources does the setting need if the planned intervention is to succeed?

### THE SUCCESSION PRINCIPLE

The succession principle emphasizes the dynamic properties of social environments by advocating attention to their time dimension. Social environments, like people, have histories, and like people, have been shaped by the persons, traditions, structures, and events that they have experienced. The importance of a historical perspective is perhaps best highlighted by such writers as Sarason (1972) and Goldenberg (1971), who discuss the creation of settings. Sarason, in *The creation of settings and the future societies* (1972), describes in detail how the way we create programs and social environments profoundly affect their evolution, and Goldenberg, in *Build me a mountain* (1971), presents a compelling example of how attention to the ideas behind creating a setting can illuminate the process and help make predictable the issues that arise. Both argue for the importance of understanding institutional history as a prelude to trying to change institutions. The implications of the succession principle for preventive interventions into the social environment become evident as an orientation for the investigator. For example, why does school have a policy which implicitly rewards students for missing school rather than coming late? How did the policy evolve, and is it still serving the function for which it was originally designed? Can the attempt to introduce a particular intervention to the community be informed by similar past experiences?

### THE ADAPTATION PRINCIPLE

The adaptation principle draws attention to the current dynamic equilibrium of the setting by asserting that there is a continual process of accommodation between persons and their environment as individuals revise their coping behavior in response to environmental constraints and opportunities. By focusing on the "substance" of the environment and how persons cope with it, the adaptation principle frames the task of understanding not only individual adaptation or mal-adaptation to social settings but also how norms, values, and demand characteristics of the social setting constrain and promote certain behaviors. As has been stated elsewhere (Trickett, Kelly, & Todd, 1972), "To the extent that this analogy from biological ecology can generate operational methods for assessing person-environment relations it may contribute to a view of coping behavior as a sequence of multivariate behaviors tied to specific social settings [p. 385]."

By focusing on the nature of the current environment the adaptation principle orients the investigator to an explicit search for the rules—implicit and explicit—by which the environment operates, the values which are core and those which are peripheral, and the range of tolerance the setting has for deviant behavior, external intrusion, and innovation. This is not only useful in generating valid data about the nature of social environments; it is of prime importance in the design of preventive interventions, for interventions in the social environment which are not responsive to local norms and conditions are likely to be viewed as intrusive and suspect.

Taken together, these four orienting principles form the basis for an ecological mindset that can inform the nature of the research questions, the manner in which the researcher relates in the host community, and the more general goal of designing and implementing preventive interventions. The following section expands on what the ecological analogy considers to be the key vehicle for maximizing the changes of successfully achieving that goal—the relationship between the researcher(s) and the host community.

## The Research Relationship
## as a Preventive Intervention

Research has often been viewed as an activity which is primarily designed to generate knowledge about a particular phenomenon rather than an activity which has an immediate impact on the setting where it occurs. Elsewhere we have presented data on research efforts in the public schools which suggest that researchers generally pay little attention to the impact of their work on the community setting (Billington, Washington, & Trickett, 1981). At best, the intent is to gather data while minimizing the negative impact on the setting where the data is gathered. At worst, varied reports in the published literature cite instances where citizens, incensed over some research project, have forced researchers to abandon their work (e.g., Eron & Walder, 1961; Nettler, 1959; Voss, 1966) because of the harm which they felt the research was doing.

The ecological analogy adopts a radically different viewpoint toward research in community settings, namely, that *research in a community setting represents an intervention in that setting,* and that the research relationship between the researcher and the community setting is *a vehicle for making that intervention a preventive intervention.* Three important assertions are involved in this perspective. First is the belief that all research in community settings, regardless of whether the content is "basic" or "applied," will have an impact on the environment where it occurs. Taking children out of class for testing, deciding whether or not feedback will be provided to participating teachers and the parents of children who served as subjects, all of the seemingly small details of the research process have incremental impact on individuals and the setting. Of course, where research projects involve large numbers of persons, long time periods, or sensitive topics the probability of impact greatly increases.

The second assumption is that a primary vehicle for making the research into a useful preventive intervention is the research relationship between the external researcher and the setting where the research occurs. The ecological analogy takes a broad view of preventive activities under the assumption that activities which strengthen the resourcefulness of a setting to deal with its problems, plans its own future, and develop a sense of community all constitute preventive goals. In this vein, the research relationship constitutes an instance of how an outsider (or team of outsiders) can work toward aiding the setting which serves as the site for research.

Finally, within the ecological analogy it is not possible to disentangle the substance of the research (what the research problems are) from the nature of the research relationship, for one aspect of the research relationship in the service of preventive interventions is to develop a dialogue with the host community about its definition of what research questions are salient.

Regardless of the specific research project per se, the ecological analogy provides a heuristic for viewing the research relationship as a preventive intervention. (This is not intended to imply that the content of research is trivial—rather, that special attention be paid to the definition of the research relationship in its own right.) The value orientation for this task is found in a later elaboration of the ecological analogy (see Trickett, Kelly, & Vincent, in press). The first principle (see Table 5.1B) in this elaboration states that "the ecological paradigm advocates the conservation, management, and creation of resources," an explicit assertion that the researcher be alert for possible ways of using the research to contribute to the resources of the setting. This could mean a variety of activities, including offering minicourses to school faculty and students, responding to a need from the setting to generate information on a local problem, or hiring members of the setting to help link the research project and the site more effectively. Basically, however, it is a mindset for the researcher which involves an intelligent and informed caring about how the research impacts on the setting and how to maximize its resource value.

Fundamental to the ability of the researcher to develop a research relationship which can have preventive impact on the setting is the ability to understand what the setting is like. All too often researchers unfamiliar with the local norms and traditions of research sites betray their ignorance in ways which are harmful both to the research project and the research relationship (Billington, Washington, & Trickett, 1981). The next six corollaries, numbers 2 through 7, are designed as further heuristics for understanding both what the particular setting is like and how that information can aid in settling development. For example, Corollary 2 and Corollary 3 underscore the importance for the prevention-oriented researcher of doing *environmental reconnaissance* to discover *who* in the setting is a source of ideas, energy, and commitment; *where* in the research site are the settings, the groups, the structures which promote positive community values; and *which* events celebrate and stand for important community values.

Principles 8 through 10 address directly the notion that ecological research is designed to empower citizens in the process of community development. Principle 8 states a superordinate goal: that "community research and the research relationship are designed to be coupled with the host environment." Coupling with the host environment implies designing a research process which empowers the research site with respect to the way in which the research project is conducted. Its goal is to integrate the needs of the research project with the research site. Only by promoting local investment in the research and the research process can the research relationship become a useful preventive intervention, for unless it is integrated into the ongoing life of the setting it will be viewed as an irritant to be extruded as soon as possible.

One anticipated effect of any research project in a social environment is that it will affect many aspects of the social system of that setting; indeed, this is the assumption behind the interdependence principle. Thus, to the degree to which the researcher can anticipate and attend to the so-called side effects of the research project, the better able he or she will be to serve in a preventive role. This is the intent of Principle 9. Side effects of research can, of course, be positive or negative. For example, teachers whose classes have participated in research projects involving the Classroom Environment Scale (Trickett & Moos, 1973) often have become more interested in altering classroom dynamics as a consequence of discussing data on their classroom with the researcher. On the other hand, negative side effects can accrue if the research project involves gathering knowledge in sensitive areas from children whose parents have not been fully informed about the nature of the project.

The tenth and final principle, "Ecological inquiry is a flexible, improvisational process," suggests the spirit with which the research relationship is carried out. By advocating a flexible process as opposed to a more rigidly defined, technology-oriented approach to conducting community research, the ecological analogy is designed to encourage the researcher, in the quest to have positive impact on the research setting, to be willing to negotiate the style of the working relationship, to be responsive to emerging needs in the setting, and to evolve over time a relationship which serves as a resource for the setting. Unless the researcher is willing to adapt this flexible stance, the preventive potential for the research relationship will be limited.

The ecological analogy, then, views the research relationship between researcher and research site as an opportunity to develop a preventive intervention. Doing so implies not only a commitment on the part of the researcher to spend time getting to know the setting and vice versa, but also a commitment to work over a period of time developing projects and working toward becoming a useful resource for the site. This emphasis makes the ecological analogy a distinctive paradigm for preventive interventions.

### Research and Intervention Examples of the Ecological Analogy

The foregoing has outlined a paradigm for thinking ecologically about the social context and for viewing the research relationship as a vehicle for preventive interventions. The flavor of this work may be conveyed concretely by examining research and intervention examples.

## RESEARCH WITHIN THE ECOLOGICAL FRAMEWORK: BOYS' ADAPTATION TO HIGH SCHOOL

The ecological analogy has chosen the high school as the main focus thus far for empirical work conducted explicitly within the ecological framework. The rationale is that the high school is a prime setting for preventive interventions, as it is the one *controllable* force in the socialization of adolescents. As Kelly (1967) has pointed out, high schools were chosen with the belief that school life has pronounced, encompassing effects on adolescents' behavior even when they are not physically in the school.

Kelly and his colleagues designed a longitudinal study to examine the ecological constraints on the adaptation of male students in two constrasting high school environments. As summarized by Kelly (1979):

> The specific aim of the study was to examine how boys with different needs to explore the school environment adapted to two contrasting schools. We have also assessed the two schools and evaluated how the social interactions and personal satisfactions of students and faculty changed over time. Observed differences in the ways the cultures of the schools developed and the way boys with different levels of social exploration responded to their school environment provide evidence of how socialization processes functioned in the two high schools [p. 5].

To say that this research was conducted from an ecological perspective is not to say that a particular technology was used. Instead, the paradigm was used as an assumptive structure for considering how to go about the process of inquiry. The basic premise of this particular research project is one taken directly from the ecological analogy: the paramount importance of assessing the interdependence of person and environmental variables in order to understand the adaptation of individuals to their settings.

Kelly (personal communication, 1982) provides insight into the way in which the paradigm generated the framework for choosing the individual variable which would be examined in the study. Congruent with the paradigm, it was necessary that the variable (1) assess a competence rather than a deficit; (2) show effects over time; and (3) interact with social system variables to illustrate social system effects. Exploratory behavior, a coping style defined as preference for trying out alternative behaviors and sampling diverse social situations, was chosen because it satisfied all of these criteria.

With regard to the social setting, the variable of population exchange, or turnover rates of students during the academic year, was used to guide the selection of schools. It was hypothesized that differences in turnover rate would produce different qualities or climates in the schools, with a high turnover school characterized by a more changing and diverse environment and a low turnover school characterized by a more stable, "steady state," unchanging environment. It was felt that this basic school environment difference would interact with the personal variable of coping style *and* impact on two aspects of the informal social structure of the schools: (1) the development of student "cliques" or groups, and (2) the nature of the informal interactions between students and staff.

With respect to the person variable of social exploration, it was anticipated that persons high in social exploration would express more satisfaction with the diverse and changing environment of the high turnover school than they would in a more stable and predictable low turnover environment, while the reverse would be true of low explorers. The high turnover school was viewed as yielding a variety of diverse student groups formed in response to the more chaotic environment and serving to support student adaptation to change, while in the stable school the formation of student cliques was predicted to center around in-groups and out-groups as judged by the dominant social norms of the student-faculty culture. In the stable school, tolerance for diversity among students would be less. Faculty-student interaction was also viewed as differing in these contrasting environments, with greater informality and wider norms around what could be discussed to be found in the high turnover school. Thus, the basic intent of the research was to develop dynamic portraits of how the ecological variable of turnover rate would affect varied aspects of the school environment and, by creating different kinds of environments, show that the personal qualities of students which were helpful in adapting to School A were less helpful when confronted with School B.

In addition to generating the content of this investigation and the variables of interest, the ecological perspective guided the process of the research as well. The study was longitudinal, following boys from eighth grade through twelfth grade. Much initial time was spent in a careful reconnaissance of the environment, which informed the development of the assessment methodology. The assessment of both individuals and the environment was multilevel and multimodal, relying in large part on naturalistic observation rather than experimental manipulation.

Most importantly, the coupling of the research project with the host environment was conducted in such a way that both the investigators and the setting members benefited. This successful coupling, a hallmark of the ecological analogy, seemed to be due in large part to the inclusion of school staff members as collaborators with the research staff. One of the principals felt that the unusually active teacher interest in the project had to do with the role of the staff member who served as "field coordinator," who had the respect and trust of faculty and students and who could reassure teachers that " 'research' does not mean espionage [Kelly, 1979, p. 223]." This principal also commented that "this study is one of the few efforts that has seriously tried to understand the natural setting of the school before designing treatment programs and curriculum reform [p. 222]."

With respect to the findings of the study, the complex multimodal methods make a thorough reporting prohibitive (for a detailed description of both methodology and results, the reader is referred to Kelly, 1979, and Edwards & Kelly, 1980). While population exchange rate did yield two schools with quite different social climates, as the research unfolded it became clear that other factors besides population exchange were influential in creating two quite different school environments. Thus in one school a principal with a participatory leadership style developed a decision-making process which was more open to student and faculty influence than was the case in the other school. In addition, the two communities in which the schools were located differed in the average educational level of parents and in their involvement in the school. Neither of these influences could easily be attributable to the variable of population exchange per se, though according to the research both influenced the nature of the environments in the two schools.

Though the environmental variable (exchange rates) could not be unconfounded from a number of other factors, some main effects for the schools did emerge, such as a difference in the degree of extracurricular activity that students engaged in and the degree of involvement and amount of satisfaction students felt. In addition, the student coping style of exploration preference was found to be related to the development of several competencies. High levels of exploration preference were related to increased initiative, less depression, fewer social problems, higher levels of role performance, participation in extracurricular activities, and increased class involvement. Thus the results of the study affirm that the quality and diversity of the social environment has a definite impact on the way in which the student learns to cope with environmental demands.

The overriding implication of this research for preventive interventions is that the design of any intervention depends upon linking the technology of the change program to the specific requirements of the local setting. As succeeding efforts continue to establish the empirical properties of contrasting settings, a knowledge base can be evolved for change programs that meet local requirements.

Over ten years ago Trickett, Kelly, and Todd (1972) set forth some ideas about specific areas where empirical work needed to be established to understand the high school setting. While Kelly and his colleagues (1979) began to address some of these areas, the need for more extensive data gathering remains:

> We must learn about organizational functioning if we are to anticipate organizational side effects of our interventions. We must learn more about the links of the high school to surrounding environments if we are to assess the alternative costs and benefits of contrasting programs for change. Because of these gaps in knowledge and relevant training, we must learn how to learn about how environments vary. We need to know more about: (1) the structural aspects of the school environment itself—how ecological variables, such as size and racial composition, affect styles of adaptations and the opportunity structures of high schools; (2) populations at risk—how individuals and groups of students emerge as candidates for service in different social environments; (3) the adaptation process—how personal values and coping styles are affected over time by the high school environment, and how opportunity structures of the high school absorb students and differentially socialize them as a function of their varying coping styles; and (4) changes in the functions of environments over time—how the organizational history of the environment provides constraints on generating the change process. . . . Finally, we must cultivate the ability to tolerate the fact that effective change in a school environment is a long-term proposition. It is our belief that successful intervention in and redevelopment of the high school lies in an adequate conceptualization and understanding of the forces impinging on it [Trickett, Kelly, & Todd, 1972, p. 400].

## CLINICAL INTERVENTIONS AS A VEHICLE FOR PREVENTIVE ACTIVITY

Just as research can be a vehicle for preventive interventions, so clinical interventions, when embedded in an ecological framework, also may serve the goal of preventive activity. By clinical interventions we mean those efforts designed to help individuals identified as maladaptive in particular settings. Here, while the overt, identified problem involves a particular individual, the strategy for intervention involves the use of the broader ecological context in both diagnostic assessment and the intervention process. Embedding the intervention in the natural context is intended to strengthen local resources by involving them in the assessment and intervention process, thus wedding the notion of community development to the clinical intervention.

Let us return to the four basic principles and give an example of how they can transform clinical interventions into resource-enhancing activities, using the area of psychological testing in the schools as an example.* Basically, the consultant working from an ecological perspective must conceptualize the assessment task as an understanding of the way characteristics of a given individual interact with a particular environment. From this initial premise, the consultant can work from the four basic ecological principles to carry out an interactive assessment and plan a clinical intervention.

For the tester, the principle of Interdependence asserts that one must take into account the social context in which the behavior labeled deviant occurs. When considering test results, this principle suggests that those characteristics of the child which interact with the specific environment in adaptive or maladaptive ways are most relevant to the inquiry. For example, if on inquiry it appears that a child has difficulty with nonstructured tasks or in nonstructured settings, and the only classroom setting available to the child is highly unstructured, this is important information.

The adaptation principle turns the attention of the tester to the way in which the environment labels behavior as adaptive or maladaptive. The tester must attend to the boundaries of flexibility beyond which the individual cannot bring himself to meet the requirements of a given setting and beyond which a setting will not bend to incorporate a particular individual. Whether or not the subsequent intervention is personological, environmental, or some interaction of the two depends on the assessor's perception of the problem. In some cases the consultant may be aware of alternative classrooms which provide a better "fit" for the student; in other cases those behavioral styles which may be more adaptive in the available classroom setting can be reinforced in the student.

* For the most part, this section is derived from an unpublished paper by O'Neill and Trickett called "Ecological considerations in psychological testing" (Note 3).

While the principles of interdependence and adaptation provide a perspective from which to assess behavior, the cycling-of-resources and succession principles are important in considering what changes could and should take place. The cycling-of-resources principle turns the tester's attention to the way the environment defines and distributes resources. The testing process itself is one of those resources, and the psychologist can learn a good deal by observing how his or her own services are used. Who is recommended for testing, and by whom? What prompted the referral? Is the assessment procedure used for early identification, or as the last step before discipline or expulsion? The tester should assess not only the personality and roles of the labeled person but also his or her resources in the environment, and the potential resources in the environment to better meet the individual's needs. Succession, for the tester, implies that the traditions of a setting will constrain the kinds of interventions that can be planned and carried forward in meeting a particular problem. Thus a setting-appropriate intervention can only be made if the tester has some appreciation for the history and tradition of the school.

The foregoing suggests a broad design for the dimensions along which individuals and environments can be assessed. The actual operationalization of this design in a particular setting where the tester is an "outsider" is no small order. The following is a summary of a successful attempt made to accomplish this task by a consultant working in a high school setting. As a consultant on specific cases he was not in a position to make any systematic evaluation of the environment. In order to operate within an ecological framework, he had to have some means of probing the environment as it expressed itself toward a particular student. For that purpose, the test referral procedure was a prime source of information.

A new referral form was developed which was intended to provide every opportunity for differences of opinion about the student's behavior in different settings to come to light. Whenever a student was referred by a particular teacher, it was sent to each staff member who had classroom contact with the student, asking whether he or she would have referred the student for assessment, on what basis, and to gain what type of information. The form asked not only for behavior ratings but also invited subjective comments to explore the possibilities for development of resources for that particular student.

In addition, an interview and a standard battery constituted an assessment of the individual. However, the interpretation of test data continued to refer to individual qualities as they interacted with the school environment, within the heuristic framework of the ecological principles previously described.

The interactional assessment method which was developed proved to be very valuable for the treatment of the individuals being assessed. However, the implications for preventive intervention can be even more far-reaching. Understanding how different behaviors come to be labeled deviant, what the resources available to deal with problems are, and what factors in the social environment may be contributing to individual behavior problems are important first steps in developing programs and settings to reduce the occurrence of behaviors labeled maladaptive.

In addition, the processes set in motion by such an ecological orientation to assessment augment the involvement of school personnel in these issues. Finding out that a particular student was a severe problem in one classroom but functioned adequately in another aided teachers in discussions of classroom dynamics and increased their connectedness with each other. Involving them as resource locators and, in select circumstances, as resources for working with individual students increased their sense of contribution and altered the way they thought of students. Indeed, the ideas of referral took on a different, more ecologically oriented meaning.

The preceding examples of research and service illuminate the potential of the ecological analogy to serve as a heuristic for the design and implementation of a wide variety of preventive interventions. For the following section, the social ecological perspective illustrates another way of thinking about the influence of social environments on adaptation. The prime empirical emphasis of this perspective is the assessment and redesign of social environments.

## Social Ecology

While many psychologists have contributed to the methodologies and rationale behind the social ecological perspective (e.g., Pace and Stern, 1958; Stern, 1970), the orientation is predominantly associated with the work of Rudolf Moos (1974a,b; 1976; 1979a,b). The social ecological approach shares many basic assumptions with the ecological analogy, including a belief in the fundamental importance of the environment as a shaper of behavior, an applied orientation, and a value stance emphasizing empowerment of individuals in controlling their environments. In clarifying the social ecological perspective, Moos (1976) cites several points of special emphasis.

First, the social ecological approach attempts to understand the impact of the environment from the perspective of the individual, for it is the individual who must come to grips with, adapt to, or try to change his or her social context. Thus a social ecological approach, like the ecological analogy, emphasizes individual coping and adaptation in response to the environment. To understand these responses it is first important to understand the many ways in which the environment constrains some forms of coping and adaptation and facilitates others. Second, the social ecological approach attempts to synthesize the study of the physical and social environment, since the two are inextricably related. Thus while environmental psychology highlights the importance of the physical environment's impact on individuals, the social ecological approach is likely to consider a variety of possible contributions to the individual's experience of the environment, *including*, when appropriate, its physical characteristics.

Finally, like the ecological analogy, the social ecological approach has an avowed applied orientation based on a value premise—the attempt to discover means of organizing environments so that inhabitants can maximize personal growth. The approach for doing this, to be described more fully later, involves strategies for providing more complete information about the nature of existing environments and environmental choices. With respect to the value premise, Moos states that

> a social ecological approach has an explicit value orientation; it is not simply an approach for science. It is also a humanistic approach by which to benefit mankind. A social ecological approach is dedicated to increasing the amount of control individuals have over their environments, and to the question of how environmental planners can plan environments and still avoid acting as agents of social control. It is dedicated to increasing individual freedom of choice in selecting environments [1976, p. 31].

### Conception of the Environment

In the social ecological approach, the environment of social settings is conceptualized as including three general domains experienced by individuals: the relationship domain, the personal growth or goal orientation domain, and the system maintenance and system change domain. Briefly, they are defined as follows:

1. *The relationship domain* involves the extent to which people are involved in their environment, the extent to which they support and help one another, and the degree of spontaneity and free and open expression among the participants in the environment.

2. *The personal growth or goal orientation domain* assesses those aspects of the environment which become salient as a function of the goals of the setting. Because the underlying goals of different types of environments tend to differ, this domain varies more than the other two domains from setting to setting. For example, on a psychiatric ward the goal orientation domain would include an emphasis on the development of *insight* on the part of patients, whereas a classroom might emphasize *competition* among students in the service of the classroom goal of learning. Because of its emphasis on human service or educational environments, the social ecological approach has often equated personal development with goal orientation, since in these types of settings the goals usually center on the personal development of members. In settings less oriented toward human development per se (for example a factory or an airport) this is not as frequently the case.

3. *The system maintenance and system change domain* assesses the extent to which the environment is orderly and clear in its expectations, maintains control via rules and regulations, and, in terms of system changes, initiates variety in procedures and innovations in its everyday life. Thus, system maintenance primarily involves the authority relationships in the environment and the regulations governing behavior, while system change primarily involves the degree to which the environment itself changes from time to time. It is important not to confuse this latter meaning of system change with the broader use of the term as implying intervention and alteration of a particular social system.

Moos notes that other investigators have described conceptually similar sets of social environment variables in assessing environments, suggesting that these three domains are generalizable and applicable in a variety of settings.

### Translation of the Conceptualization of the Environment into Perceived Environment Scales

The basic translation of the social ecological perspective into operational terms has involved the creation of a set of social climate scales designed to measure the three general domains of the environment as perceived by their inhabitants. The idea of "perceived environment" is central to this approach, and is based on the premise that the impact the environment has on the individual is mediated by how the individual perceives the environment. To arrive at a general idea about what the environment is like, it is thus necessary to pool the perceptions of members of the environment

into an "averaged perception." While individuals and groups do, of course, differ in how they view the environment (e.g., Brown, Note 4), the environment, in the social ecological approach, is defined by these pooled perceptions.

The tradition of this perspective on "perceived environment" has been traced by Moos from Henry Murray (1938) and the notion of "environmental press" through George Stern (1970), who characterized "press" as a "taxonomic classification of characteristic behaviors manifested by aggregates of individuals in their mutual, interpersonal transactions." In this tradition, Moos states that environmental press tends to define what the individual must adapt to and cope with and indicates the way he or she must behave to be adequately satisfied with the environment.

Thus far, Moos and his colleagues have developed scales to measure the social environments of eleven types of social settings. Moos (1979) describes two of these as educational settings (high school classrooms and college student living groups), three as primary settings in which most people function (families, work settings, and social- and task-oriented groups), three as treatment-oriented settings (hospital-based programs, community-based programs, and sheltered care settings), and two as total institutions (correctional institutions and military basic training companies). In addition, a new set of scales (Moos & Lemke, Note 5) assesses the environment of a number of sheltered care settings for the elderly.*

### The Classroom Environment Scale: An Example of the Social Climate of the Classroom

To clarify the specifics of these perceived environmental scales, let us briefly describe one such scale, the Classroom Environment Scale (Trickett & Moos, 1973). As is true of the other perceived environment scales, the Classroom Environment Scale (CES) assesses three general domains of the classroom. Within each of these three general domains are several specific dimensions of the social climate. Table 5.2 describes the general domains and the specific dimensions with these domains. Each of the nine dimensions contains ten items which students are supposed to respond to as being true or false in their classroom. For example, under the dimension of Involvement is the item "students put a lot of energy into what they do around

---

* Other work has been carried out toward developing perceived environment scales using a basically similar methodology (e.g., Manderscheid, Koenig, & Silbergeld, 1977; Pace & Stern, 1958; and Walberg & Anderson, 1968) with emphasis on educational institutions.

### Table 5.2. Brief CES Subscale Descriptions

Relationship Dimensions

| | |
|---|---|
| 1. Involvement | Measures the extent to which students have attentive interest in class activities and participate in discussions. The extent to which students do additional work on their own and enjoy the class is considered. |
| 2. Affiliation | Assesses the level of friendship students feel for each other, i.e., the extent to which they help each other with homework, get to know each other easily, and enjoy working together. |
| 3. Teacher Support | Measures the amount of help, concern, and friendship the teacher directs toward the students. The extent to which the teacher talks openly with students, trusts them, and is interested in their ideas is considered. |

Personal Development Dimensions

| | |
|---|---|
| 4. Task Orientation | Measures the extent to which it is important to complete the activities that have been planned. The emphasis the teacher places on staying on the subject matter is assessed. |
| 5. Competition | Assesses the emphasis placed on student competition for grades and recognition. An assessment of the difficulty of achieving good grades is included. |

System Maintenance Dimensions

| | |
|---|---|
| 6. Order and Organization | Assesses the emphasis on students behaving in an orderly and polite manner and on the overall organization of assignments and classroom activities. The degree to which students tend to remain calm and quiet is considered. |
| 7. Rule Clarity | Assesses the emphasis on establishing and following a clear set of rules, and on students knowing what the consequences will be if they do not follow them. An important focus of this subscale is the extent to which the teacher is consistent in dealing with students who break rules. |
| 8. Teacher Control | Measures how strict the teacher is in enforcing the rules, and the severity of the punishment for rule infractions. The number of rules and the ease of students getting in trouble is considered. |

System Change Dimension

| | |
|---|---|
| 9. Innovation | Measures how much students contribute to planning classroom activities, and the amount of unusual and varying activities and assignments planned by the teacher. The extent to which the teacher attempts to use new techniques and encourages creative thinking by the students is considered. |

Source: Moos & Trickett, *Classroom Environment Scale Manual*, Consulting Psychologist Press, Palo Alto, 1974.

here." If a student answers "true" to this item, it counts as positive indication of the emphasis, or environmental press, for involvement in the classroom. To find out the classroom score on each dimension, individual student scores on each dimension are averaged and compared to a larger normative sample of classrooms to see how they compare.

Figure 5.1 shows how this data is presented and how it allows a portrait of the classroom to emerge. Two English classes are compared, one in a public alternative high school and one in a traditional high school. One can see from the figure that these two classes differ considerably in their perceived environment. Consistent with the broader ideology of the school, the alternative school English class is perceived by students as very involving (Dimension 1), supportive (Dimension 3), and innovative (Dimension 9). Indeed, all these dimensions are above the 80th percentile compared to a national sample of classrooms. On the other hand, the degree of competition in the classroom (Dimension 5) is near the 10th percentile, indicating an extremely noncompetitive atmosphere in the classroom. This alternative school English class is also above the 70th percentile in the emphasis on

order and organization in the classroom (Dimension 6), and slightly below the 30th percentile on teacher control (Dimension 8). From these varied dimensions emerges a picture of a classroom which is student-oriented and involving, organized yet not strict in rules, and very noncompetitive. The traditional school classroom profile is much more "flat," with few dimensions extremely high or low. Several aspects of the classroom, such as involvement and order and organization, are average nationally, and task orientation, slightly over the 70th percentile, is stressed considerably. Compared to the alternative school class, the traditional high school class is less involving, less innovative, has a less supportive teacher, and has significantly more competition among students. It is these kinds of comparative differences that the CES is designed to capture.

With this image in mind, let us briefly discuss the kinds of research generated by this approach and its use as a technique for changing environments. Because of the large volume of research involving these scales, it is useful to restrict our selective review to the Classroom Environment Scale (see Moos 1974a, 1976, 1979a, for a summary of research on many of the

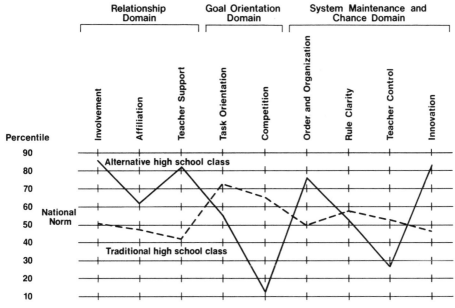

Figure 5.1. CES Dimensions.

social climate scales). Since the previous approach, the ecological analogy, also emphasizes the high school setting, such a choice should allow the reader a better sense of the differences and similarities between these approaches.

### Social Ecological Research, the High School Classroom, and Preventive Interventions

Various kinds of research on classrooms have generated information useful to the design of preventive interventions. The selective review of this research is designed to highlight some main themes in this area and their relevance to preventive interventions in the social environment.

#### STUDENT CORRELATES OF CONTRASTING CLASSROOMS

Perceived environment scales are based on the assertion that environments differ from each other and that these differences make a difference in the experience of persons in them. One theme in this research, then, is the impact of these differences in environments on persons. The implications for the design of preventive interventions are clear—if we can predict the effects of creating certain kinds of environments on persons, *and* we know what kinds of environments create those effects, then our task is to design environments to maximize positive effects and minimize negative con-

sequences. For example, various dimensions of the psychosocial environment of the high school classroom have been found to relate systematically to several different student outcomes, including student satisfaction and mood (Trickett & Moos, 1974), and student absenteeism (Moos & Moos, 1978). In addition, Kaye, Trickett, and Quinlan (1976) found that student perceptions of Teacher Support and Teacher Control in the classroom correlated with certain aspects of teacher-student verbal interaction and with ratings of outside observers of the classroom.

A few of the findings from these studies highlight the difficulty in viewing this kind of research as easily translatable into a preventive intervention, however. For example, Trickett and Moos (1974) found that different aspects of the classroom environment predicted different outcomes for students. Thus affiliation was correlated with student satisfaction about classmates, but not with satisfaction about how much students were learning in class. Competition among students in the classroom was positively correlated with student satisfaction with how much they were learning but not with general satisfaction with the class. It quickly becomes clear that the kind of environment one wishes to create depends on the specific goals one has, and that these goals reflect a variety of values about which people differ. Thus this line of research immediately suggests that preventive interventions in the social environment necessitate much thought in advance about the goals of such an intervention, and the need to evaluate interventions across a wide variety of outcomes to pick up both positive and negative impacts.

The picture of preventive interventions in the social environment becomes more complex when we examine the data showing that individual differences affect the student experience in different kinds of classes. The message here is that there is a fit between certain personal qualities of students and the kinds of classroom environments they find most satisfying. In designing and evaluating preventive interventions in the classroom, therefore, it is important to consider how the same intervention will affect different students in different ways, or to consider the possibility that different interventions may be necessary with different types of students.

A sample of the research in this area highlights what some of these person-environment interactions might involve. Harpin and Sandler (1979) studied the relationship of the student personality variable Locus of Control in classrooms which differed in their emphasis on Teacher Control. They found an interaction between student Locus of Control and Teacher Control in the classroom for male students. Externally oriented males reported more adjustment problems in low- than in high-control classrooms, while internal males received poorer grades in high- than in low-control classrooms. The fact that there were no significant effects for the female students also speaks to the need to examine environmental impact on subgroups within classrooms. Nielsen and Moos (1978) divided classrooms into those high in exploration climate (that is, encouraging diversity and novelty for students) and low in exploration climate. They found that, in general, students in high exploration climates were more satisfied and better adjusted than students in low exploration classrooms. They also found that there was a match between high exploration classroom climates and students who were high in exploration preference, a coping style variable (Edwards & Kelly, 1980). In high exploration classrooms, students who were high explorers were more satisfied and better adjusted than were low explorers in those same classrooms. In low exploration climates, few significant differences were found between high and low explorers.

Brown (Note 4) presents data on another aspect of this interaction by showing that poorly behaved and well-behaved students not only (by definition) behave differently in the classroom, but actually perceive the classroom environment very differently. Not surprisingly, the direction of these differences in almost all instances shows that the poorly behaved students view the classroom in less "positive" terms than the well-behaved.

The findings of these types of studies provide strong evidence of the need to examine subgroups of students within classrooms to understand best the impact of environments on people. It further complicates the problem posed by preventive interventions in the social environment, suggesting that one central assessment task for preventive interventions is anticipating whether or not an intervention designed for a whole environment can be made responsive to individual differences in its impact. Designing or redesigning the social environment is still a primary goal, but with the understanding—more often preached than practiced—that it will affect different individuals differently.

## Normative Classroom Environments and Their Determinants

The previous sections have discussed some implications of preventive interventions in the classroom for students as a whole and for subgroups of students. The following section examines additional issues which broaden our understanding of social environments and have further implications for how to think about preventive interventions, such as how classrooms fit into the larger context of the school and what determines the classroom environment.

### NORMATIVE CLASSROOM ENVIRONMENTS

Student experience is shaped not only by the classroom environment but also by the characteristics of the larger school environment. Such ecological variables as size of school (Barker & Gump, 1964), racial composition of the student body (Gottlieb & Tenhouten, 1965), and turnover rate of students (Kelly, 1967, 1979) have been shown to influence student experience. With respect to normative classroom environments, Trickett (1978) points out that "while the average classroom of any school is not presumed to capture the rich environmental press of the school as a whole, it is reasonable to view the classroom as a reflection of the broader school culture [p. 409]."

To address the normative differences among some types of schools, Trickett (1978) examined normative data from classrooms in five kinds of public schools—urban, suburban, rural, alternative and vocational. While each of these types of schools differed from the others, alternative and vocational schools provided the greatest contrast. Alternative schools emphasized interpersonal aspects of classroom experience, while vocational schools stressed rules and regulations. In general, the differences between the classroom environments in these two types of schools seemed to reflect their differing underlying ideologies and goals. Specific comparisons between alternative and urban public school classrooms were reported by Trickett, McConahay, and Gruber (Note 6), again reflecting the ideological differences between the two types. Finally, Trickett, Pendry, and Trickett (Note 7) found consistent differences between the normative environments of single-sex (female) and coed private schools, with single-sex school classrooms ranking higher in such aspects of academic climate as task orientation, order and organization, and competition.

These normative differences represent important understandings not only in their own right but in terms of the design and evaluation of preventive interventions. As was repeatedly stressed in the section on the ecological analogy, the notion of environmental reconnaissance is central to designing useful interventions, and such normative data aids in this diagnostic process. For example, if one is interested in changing a particular classroom, it is important to know whether or not the proposed changes are congruent or incongruent with the broader norms of the school.

### MULTIPLE DETERMINANTS OF STUDENT OUTCOME AND CLASSROOM ENVIRONMENT

One of the central aspects of preventive interventions involves the diagnosis of the problem or issue, and a central aspect of this diagnosis involves the selection of a theoretical perspective or level of analysis from which to investigate the problem or issue. Mitchell and Trickett (Note 8) cite Caplan and Nelson (1973) as providing an articulate argument for the potency with which one's theoretical frame of reference tends to guide one's research and intervention. Their examination of *Psychological Abstracts* for a six-month period revealed that most studies on black Americans and social problems tended to focus on person-centered characteristics, to the exclusion of more environmental-centered variables. Mitchell and Trickett point out, "The cumulative effect of such person-centered research is to imply that the characteristics of persons are primarily responsible for behavioral outcomes. . . . One can easily attribute an inordinate amount of causality to whatever level of variable one is studying."

The implications for the design of preventive interventions in the schools are critical. Classroom environments are multidetermined, and the most salient determinants of classroom environment and student outcome must be understood before deciding what kind of preventive intervention to implement. If, for example, organizational characteristics of the school predict certain student outcomes better than do the characteristics of the teacher, it would suggest that preventive interventions may usefully be directed at the organizational-structure level. If classroom environment is primarily determined by teacher characteristics, and certain environments are, for whatever reason, valued, then teacher selection would be a prime target for preventive interventions. We currently lack an empirically based model which can account for the multiple determinants. However, some initial work has been carried out to develop such a model, and the data has proved complex and interesting.

### DETERMINANTS OF STUDENT OUTCOME

Moos (1979a) has begun to piece together the puzzle of determinants of student outcome, using five predictor variables to explain five indices of student reaction in the classroom. The five student classroom reactions were students' self-report of friendship formation, sense of well-being, satisfaction with learning, satisfaction with the teacher, and alienation in the classroom. One predictor domain consisted of student perceptions of classroom environment types formed by cluster analysis of CES scores. Six types emerged from this analysis: innovation oriented, structured relationship oriented, supportive task and supportive competition oriented, unstructured competition-oriented, and control oriented. The other four classes of predictor variables were school and subject matter type (e.g., investigative classes, realistic and conventional classes); organizational characteristics (e.g., class size and grade level); aggregate student characteristics (e.g., percent female, internal control, and social exploration); and aggregate teacher characteristics (e.g., years of experience, ability to inculcate love of learning).

Moos found that the total variance accounted for in different student outcomes by the five predictive domains ranged from 46 to 59 percent. Most interesting for the development of theories of environments was the finding that *different* predictive domains were most influential in predicting *different* indices of student reaction. For example, the classroom climate variable uniquely explained about half the predictable variance in students' satisfaction with the teacher and feelings of alienation, and 20 to 25 percent of the variance in their sense of well-being and satisfaction with learning. However, it only explained about 3 percent of the predictable variance in friendship formation, where aggregate student characteristics uniquely accounted for the largest proportion of the predictable variance.*

### DETERMINANTS OF CLASSROOM ENVIRONMENT

Similar analyses were done by Moos and Trickett (in Moos, 1979a) in attempting to predict the determinants of classroom environment. They developed a conceptual model of the determinants of classroom social climate based on five sets of classroom characteristics: (a) overall context (e.g., type of school, educational program, and class subject matter); (b) organizational characteristics; (c) architectural characteristics (e.g., open classrooms); (d) teacher characteristics; and (e) aggregate student characteristics. The general model was tested using a sample of 241 classrooms grouped by cluster analysis into the same classroom types mentioned in the preceding model. Four of the five sets of determinants specified by the model were used to predict to these classroom orientations (architectural characteristics were excluded).

The four sets of determinants, taken together, accounted for a significant proportion of the variance in each of the six student-perceived classroom climate types. As was true in the determinants of the student outcomes, each of the four sets of variables uniquely account for some of the predictable variance in each of the six climates, but the amount of that variance differs greatly between climate types. For example, control-oriented climates, according to Moos, were found to be mainly determined by organizational characteristics (primarily grade level) and aggregate student characteristics (primarily a higher proportion of males and a lower social exploration orientation), although teacher characteristics (primarily male teachers, and orientation to prepare students for work, and a wish to be seen as competent by administrators) also are important. Innovation-oriented climates, on the other hand, were most heavily influenced by type of school and subject matter and by teacher characteristics.

The two studies outlined above serve to underscore the multiple determinants of the classroom environment. The implication for the planning of preventive interventions is that there are many levels at which an intervention can occur. Depending upon the level (or levels) the investigator chooses, there may be greatly different implications with regard to effect on both

classroom climate and the individuals within that classroom.

### Social Climate Scales as Instruments for Environmental Change

The foregoing suggest that both the process of instituting environmental change and the assessment of its impact involve a complex series of assessments, value decisions about how and where to intervene, and the need to develop multiple measures of impact to account for the various positive and negative changes experienced by different individuals in the environment undergoing change.*

Generally, preventive interventions in the social environment using the social climate scales have not reached a very high level of complexity. However, several efforts have been made to use feedback from the scales to facilitate and monitor environmental change. The social ecological approach advocates a specific framework to be followed regardless of the type of environment in which the intervention is being conducted. It involves a basic survey-feedback methodology, and includes the following steps:

1. The particular perceived environment scale is administered to different individuals in the environment. Two forms of the scale are given—the "real," to assess the actual environment, and the "ideal," to assess the preferred environment.

2. Feedback to participating groups is provided, with emphasis on the discrepancies between the perception of the "real" and the "ideal." This process highlights those dimensions of the environment which particular groups of individuals feel are discrepant from the way they would prefer them to be.

---

* There were a number of other findings, including second, third, and fourth order shared effects (combinations of variables) regarding student outcomes. The reader is referred to Moos (1979a) for further details.

---

* Recently, Moos and his colleagues have developed a set of instruments which provide a much more comprehensive evaluation of the social environment of one type of setting. The Multiphasic Environmental Assessment Procedure (MEAP) (Moos & Lemke, Note 5) is designed to assess the environmental resources of sheltered care settings for the elderly. This procedure consists of five instruments which can be used separately or together: the *Physical and Architectural Features Checklist*, which assesses nine dimensions of the physical and architectural resources of a facility; the *Policy and Program Information Form*, which covers financial and entrance arrangements of the facility, the types of rooms or apartments available, the way in which the facility is organized, and the services provided for residents; the *Resident and Staff Information Form*, which covers the residents' social backgrounds and functional abilities, the types of activities in which residents participate, and the characteristics of staff and volunteers; the *Rating Scale*, which taps outside observers' impressions concerning the physical environment and resident and staff functioning; and the *Sheltered Care Environment Scale*, which assesses seven characteristics of a facility's social environment as perceived by residents and staff.

3. On the basis of a discussion of this feedback, participants develop concrete plans about specific ways the environment of the setting might be changed. These plans are then implemented.

4. After a period of time following the implementation of the plans, reassessment of the environment is made to see if people perceive it differently. Hopefully, the discrepancy between the "real" and "ideal" profiles will have been decreased as a result of the changes instituted. It is important to consider this step not as an end to the process, but as one component of an ongoing cycle of an assessment-feedback-change-reassessment cycle.

Though a number of studies using this methodology have appeared in the literature, only one study has been reported which has attempted to change classroom environments on the basis of feedback from the CES. DeYoung (1977) administered a short form of the CES to a college undergraduate social science class. Real-ideal discrepancies from his class indicated that students wanted more involvement, greater stress on innovative teaching methods, and clearer notions about the organization and direction of the class. He used this data to restructure his approach in the next semester's class, including seeing students individually, clarifying grading policies, and encouraging innovative projects and classroom participation.

After implementing these changes, the CES was administered to students in the revised class the following semester. While the "ideal" social climate in both classes was virtually identical, there were large differences in the way students in the two classes perceived the actual environments. The major differences were on those dimensions of the CES which the investigator had attempted to change as a result of the feedback. Also, the differences were linked to greater student interest and participation and a higher student attendance rate.

Though this is the only reported attempt to facilitate change in classroom environments, there have been other change studies in broader educational environments. Daher, Corazzine, and McKinnon (1977) developed a program designed to enable students to enhance the match between their needs and their residence hall environment. This program included gathering data on the real and ideal forms of the University Residence Environment Scale (URES), discussing the implications of these results with students, and planning an environmental intervention based on these results. The Group Environment Scale has been used to help residence hall staff focus on milieu management and design better social settings (Schroeder, 1979).

Moos (1979b) cites other settings in which social climate scales have been used to facilitate change. The Ward Atmosphere Scale (WAS) has been used to facilitate change in psychiatric hospital wards (Pierce, Trickett, & Moos, 1972) and to plan humanistically oriented changes in an ongoing behaviorally oriented program that patients and staff were dissatisfied with (Curtiss, 1976). The Community-Oriented Programs Environment Scale (COPES) has been used to facilitate change in two alcoholism treatment programs (Bliss, Moos, & Bromet, 1976) and to evaluate change and stability in a community-based residential treatment program for acute schizophrenic patients (Mosher, Menn, & Matthews, 1975).

Moos (1979b) provides a list of benefits beyond a more positive environment for individuals in the setting that may occur in the process of planning and facilitating change. Some of these benefits are: (1) participants can untangle and analyze the multiple dimensions of setting functioning; (2) important characteristics that are often overlooked are systematically called into awareness, such as the clarity of expectations regarding policies and procedures; (3) in some settings issues surrounding the utilization of social climate feedback can provide relevant discussion topics, such as an analysis of patient versus staff roles or of institutional sanctions and sources of resistance to change; (4) supervisors may subtly change their perceptions of their own role—for example, they may begin to emphasize their role as facilitators of learning in addition to their administrative role; and (5) involvement may be increased, simply because people are engaged in the common task of changing their own social environment.

## Conclusions

Preventive interventions in the social environment are predicated on an understanding of what the social environment is like. In this chapter we have sketched a rationale for preventive interventions which focuses on the social environment, and have presented two alternative frameworks for environmental assessment and intervention. Kelly's ecological analogy and Moos's social ecology approach were selected because of their heuristic value, empirical base, and concern with the blending of understanding and action. Concluding comments focus on a brief comparison of their dominant features and limitations, and the challenges they frame for the area of preventive interventions.

The ecological analogy rests on a heuristic with broad application to the understanding of social contexts and the ways in which the research relationship can serve as a vehicle for preventive interventions. It is a dynamic perspective which locates the search for environmental understanding in the structures, processes, relationships, norms, and events which—interactively—give settings their unique character. As such, it provides a useful superordinate framework for thinking about the nature of social contexts and intervention in them.

The ecological analogy constitutes an unusually stimulating set of concepts of a psychology of preventive interventions. Yet thus far vivid examples of integrated research-intervention work within this perspective are sparse. Part of this current lack is probably due to the complicated conceptual problem of linking research and the research relationship to work which is simultaneously designed to generate valid data *and* serve as a resource for the host environment. Indeed, the intellectual and energy demands of such an effort are considerable. Still, the ecological principles contained in the analogy provide a rich source of research questions. How do environments define resources, and when do hidden talents of individuals emerge? When thinking about the nature of institutional history, as suggested by the succession principle, how do we account for the probability that different groups in a setting may view history differently, and how do these differing perspectives relate to the design of interventions? These kinds of questions are waiting to be examined. Until such inquiry occurs, they should serve as both a challenge and a caution to those involved in preventive interventions in the social environment. The challenge stems from the potential usefulness of the ideas, the orientation, provided by the paradigm; the caution involves recognition of the fact that such terms as "resource" and "institutional history" are exceedingly complex and multifaceted in their particulars. For example, while we have stressed the notion of environmental reconnaissance as a primary task, it should be noted that there is no readily available set of procedures, nor a clearly defined sequencing of steps, for that goal.

Moos's social ecological approach does provide one technology which may aid in this task: its taxonomy of varied small social environments generated from the perception of members of the setting. Its empirical emphasis has added substantially both to our thinking about the nature of social environments and the experience of individuals. Evidence thus far provides the contours of a very complicated set of factors which influence the nature of the social context, including the qualities of individuals, the particular goals of the setting, and the larger organizational context within which the smaller setting is embedded.

Yet the social ecological approach has thus far concentrated more on clearly bounded environments and on taxonomies of settings than on the dynamic properties of settings. These properties would include such things as the influence of the setting's history on its current function or the interaction of the environment with surrounding institutions or settings. In addition, the work using these perceived environment measures as a way of intervening in the social environment has thus far been limited to a particular technology—survey feedback—and has concentrated on environmental changes per se without specification of the effects of that change on individuals over time. The subtle and differentiated effects of environments documented in the empirical literature has not been included in those studies assessing change in the social environment.

It is clear that both the ecological analogy and the social ecological approach provide useful, though quite different, heuristics for developing preventive interventions in the social environment. While they focus on the social context in different ways, highlight different aspects of the social context, and involve differing methodologies of environmental assessment and change, they can perform complementary roles in the study of social contexts and the design of preventive interventions. The predominantly conceptual heuristic of the ecological analogy may benefit from the social ecological assessment methodology to generate valid data, and the social ecological approach can use the ecological analogy to generate and test more complex questions about the nature of social environments than has thus far been the case. In addition, the differing emphasis each perspective brings to the task of designing and evaluating preventive interventions can serve a complementary function, with the ecological analogy heightening awareness of the research relationship and the indigenous resources in the setting, and the social ecological approach providing one among several potential strategies for gathering empirical data, generating discussion about the setting and possible changes in it, and providing solid methods for assessing the impact of the intervention.

In sum, both perspectives highlight the complexity of the social context and the challenge of designing preventive interventions in it. Such work requires a high energy level, a long-range time perspective, and a strong supportive structure to cope with the uncertainties involved. Most of all, however, it is work which derives its value from a richness of ideas and the mindset of putting those ideas into enlightened practice. Within this perspective, the ecological approaches already discussed are, and will be, increasingly influential in shaping a psychology of preventive interventions in the social context.

## Reference Notes

1. Kelly, J. G. The socialization of competence as an eco-logical problem. Paper presented at an American Psychological Association Convention, Symposium on Social Competence, Washington, D.C., September 6, 1971.
2. Trickett, E. J., & Ochberg, F. Student activism and administrative coping: Toward an ecological conception of student leadership. Unpublished manuscript, University of Maryland, 1979.
3. O'Neill, P., & Trickett, E. J. Ecological considerations in psychological testing. Unpublished manuscript, Yale University, 1973.
4. Brown, E. The climates within classrooms: A partial function of informal roles. Unpublished dissertation, University of Maryland, 1981.
5. Moos, R. H., & Lemke, S. *Multiphasic Environmental Assessment Procedure (MEAP) Preliminary Manual.* Palo Alto, Ca.: Social Ecology Laboratory, Veterans Administration, and Stanford University Medical Center, 1979.
6. Trickett, E. J., Gruber, J. E., & McConahay, J. M. Evaluation of high school in the community. Educational Research Service, New Haven, Connecticut, 1974.
7. Trickett, P. K., Pendry, C., & Trickett, E. J. A study of women's secondary education: The experience and effects of attending independent secondary schools. Final Report, Rockefeller Bros. Fund, 1976.
8. Mitchell, R. E., & Trickett, E. J. Perceived learning environments: Conceptual implications for theories of environments. Paper presented at the 35th annual meeting of the American Psychological Association, Toronto, August 1978.

## References

Barker, R. G. *Ecological psychology: Concepts and methods for studying the environment of human behavior.* Stanford: Stanford University Press, 1968.

Barker, R. G., & Gump, P. V. *Big school, small school.* Stanford: Stanford University Press, 1964.

Billington, F. J., Washington, L. A., & Trickett, E. J. The research relationship in community research: An inside view from public school principals. *American Journal of Community Psychology,* 1981, 9(4), 461–479.

Bliss, F., Moos, R., & Bromet, E. Monitoring change in community-oriented treatment programs. *Journal of Community Psychology,* 1976, 4, 315–326.

Bronfenbrenner, U. *The ecology of human development: Experiments by nature and design.* Cambridge: Harvard University Press, 1979.

Caplan, N., & Nelson, S. D. On being useful: The nature and consequences of psychological research on social problems. *American Psychologist,* 1973, 28, 199–211.

Curtiss, S. The compatibility of humanistic and behavioristic approaches in a state mental hospital. In A. Wandersman, P. Poppen, & D. Ricks (Eds.), *Humanism and behaviorism: Dialogue and growth.* New York: Pergamon Press, 1976.

Daher, D. M., Corazzini, J. D., & McKinnon, R. D. An environmental residential redesign program for residence halls. *Journal of College Student Personnel,* 1977, 18, 11–15.

DeYoung, A. Classroom climate and class success: A case study at the university level. *Journal of Educational Research,* 1977, 70, 252–257.

Edwards, D. W., & Kelly, J. G. Coping and adaptation: A longitudinal study. *American Journal of Community Psychology,* 1980, 8(2), 203–215.

Eron, L., & Walder, L. Test-burning II. *American Psychologist,* 1961, 16, 237–244.

Goldenberg, I. I. *Build me a mountain.* Cambridge: MIT Press, 1971.

Gottlieb, D., & Tenhouten, W. Racial composition and the social system of three high schools. *Journal of Marriage and the Family,* 1965, 27, 204–212.

Harpin, P., & Sandler, I. Interaction of sex, locus of control, and teacher control: Towards a student-classroom match. *American Journal of Community Psychology,* 7, 621–632.

Holahan, C. Redesigning physical environments to enhance social interactions. In R. Munoz, L. Snowden, & J. Kelly, (Eds.), *Social and psychological research in community settings.* San Francisco: Jossey-Bass, 1979.

Holahan, C., & Wilcox, B. Residential satisfaction and friendship formation in high and low rise student housing: An interactional analysis. *Journal of Educational Psychology,* 1978, 70, 237–241.

Kaye, S., Trickett, E. J., & Quinlan, D. M. Alternate methods of environmental assessment: An example. *American Journal of Community Psychology,* 1976, 4, 367–377.

Kelly, J. G. Ecological constraints on mental health services. *American Psychologist,* 1966, 21, 435–439.

Kelly, J. G. Naturalistic observations and theory confirmation: An example. *Human Development,* 1967, 10, 212–222.

Kelly, J. G. Toward an ecological conception of preventive interventions. In J. W. Carter, Jr. (Ed.), *Research contributions from psychology to community mental health.* New York: Behavioral Publications, 1968.

Kelly, J. G. Qualities for the community psychologist. *American Psychologist,* 1971, 26, 897–903.

Kelly, J. G. (Ed.) *Adolescent boys in high school: A psychological study of coping and adaptation.* New Jersey: Lawrence Erlbaum Association, 1979.

Manderscheid, R. W., Koenig, G. R., & Silbergeld, S. Dimensions of classroom psychosocial environment. *American Journal of Community Psychology,* 1977, 5, 299–306.

Moos, R. H. *The social climate scales: An overview.* Palo Alto, Ca.: Consulting Psychologists Press, 1974. (a)

Moos, R. H. Systems for the assessment and classification of human environments: An overview. In Moos, R., & Insel, P. (Eds.), *Issue in human ecology.* Palo Alto, Ca.: National Press Books, 1974. (b)

Moos, R. H. *The human context: Environmental determinants of behavior.* New York: Wiley, 1976.

Moos, R. H. *Evaluating educational environments.* San Francisco: Jossey-Bass, 1979. (a)

Moos, R. H. Social climate measurement and feedback. In Munoz, R., Snowden, L., & Kelly, J. (Eds.), *Social and psychological research in community settings.* San Francisco: Jossey-Bass, 1979. (b)

Moos, R. H., & Moos, B. Classroom social climate and student absences and grades. *Journal of Educational Psychology.* 1978, 70, 263–269.

Mosher, L., Menn, A., & Mathews, S. Soteria: Evaluation of a home-based treatment for schizophrenia. *American Journal of Orthopsychiatry,* 1975, 45, 455–467.

Murray, H. *Explorations in personality.* New York: Oxford University Press, 1938.

Nettler, G. Test burning in Texas. *American Psychologist*, 1959, **14**, 682–683.

Nielsen, H., & Moos, R. Exploration and adjustment in high school classrooms: A study of person-environment situations. *Journal of Educational Research*, 1978, **72**, 52–57.

Pace, C., & Stern, G. An approach to the measurement of psychological characteristics of college environment. *Journal of Educational Psychology*, 1958, **49**, 269–277.

Pierce, W., Trickett, E. J., & Moos, R. Changing ward atmosphere through staff discussion of the perceived ward environment. *Archives of General Psychiatry*, January 1972, **26**, 35–41.

Price, R. The behavior setting. In Moos, R. H., *The human context*. New York: Wiley, 1976.

Proshansky, H. M., Ittelson, W. H. & Rivlin, L. G. (Eds.), Environmental Psychology: Man and his physical setting. (2nd ed.) New York: Holt, Rinehart & Winston, 1976.

Sarason, S. B. *The creation of settings and the future societies*. San Francisco: Jossey-Bass, 1972.

Schroeder, C. Designing ideal staff environment through milieu management. *Journal of College Student Personnel*, 1979.

Stern, G. *People in context*. New York: Wiley, 1970.

Stokols, D. (Ed.) *Perspectives on environment and behavior*. New York: Plenum Press, 1977.

Trickett, E. J. Toward a social ecological conception of adolescent socialization: Normative data on contrasting types of public school classrooms. *Child Development*. 1978, **49**, 408–414.

Trickett, E. J., Kelly, J. G., & Todd, D. M. The social environment of the high school: Guidelines for individual change and organizational redevelopment. In S. G. Golann & C. Eisdorfer (Eds.), *Handbook of community mental health*. New York: Appleton-Century-Crofts, 1972.

Trickett, E. J., Kelly, J. G., & Vincent, T. The spirit of ecological inquiry in community research. In Klein, D., & Susskind, E. (Eds.), *Knowledge in building in community psychology*, in press.

Trickett, E. J., & Moos, R. H. Assessment of the psychosocial environment of the high school classroom. *Journal of Educational Psychology*, 1973, **65**, 93–102.

Trickett, E. J., & Moos, R. H. Personal correlates of contrasting environments: Student satisfaction in high school classrooms. *American Journal of Community Psychology*, 1974, **2**, 1–12.

Trickett, E. J., & Todd, D. M. The assessment of the high school culture: An ecological perspective. *Theory into Practice*, 1972, **11**, 28–37.

Voss, H. Pitfalls in social research: A case study. *American Sociologist*, 1966, **1**, 136–140.

Walberg, H. J., & Anderson, G. Classroom climate and individual learning. *Journal of Educational Psychology*, 1968, **59**, 414–419.

Willems, E. Behavioral ecology. In D. Stokols (Ed.), *Perspectives on environment and behavior*. New York: Plenum Press, 1977.

# 6 SOCIAL NETWORKS, PERCEIVED SOCIAL SUPPORT, AND COPING WITH STRESS*

## Kenneth Heller and Ralph W. Swindle

T he main goal of this paper is to present a model that links the different aspects of social support to effective coping with stress. We start by tracing some historical antecedents to social support that can be found in the social psychological literature. We next consider why the social support and stress buffering literature has produced such ambiguous results, and we conclude with the presentation of a model that distinguishes between support networks, perceived social support, and support-seeking. Throughout, our aim is to make social support constructs more precise in order to increase the likelihood of producing meaningful and useful research findings.

## Social Psychological Antecedents to Social Support

Over the last several decades, social psychologists and sociologists have studied the impact of the group on

* Portions of this paper were presented as an invited address at the Seventeenth Interamerican Congress of Psychology, Santo Domingo, Dominican Republic, June 25, 1981. Unpublished data reported in this paper come from research conducted by Jae Cho, Mark Fondacaro, Mary Procidano, and Ralph Swindle.

individual attitudes and behavior. Some of this work focused on solving real-life problems, particularly during and after World War II, when Kurt Lewin and his disciples developed an applied social psychology whose goal was to "improve democracy" (Zander, 1979, p. 419). The development of community psychology in the 1960s was in part inspired by similar ideals and interests. Indeed, at the present time the distinction between community and applied social psychology is often blurred by mutual concern for the effects on behavior of environmental variables at community, organizational, and group levels.

Many community psychologists may be unaware of the fact that their current interest in the effects of "social support" and "support networks" was shared by social psychologists and sociologists in previous decades. A case in point is the work on *reference group theory* which flourished in the 1940s and '50s, and which Sherif at the time warned was in danger of becoming "a magic term to explain anything and everything concerning group relations [Sherif, 1968, p. 85]." The goal of reference group theory was to determine how an individual "takes the values and standards of other individuals and groups as a comparative frame of reference" around which attitudes and behaviors are shaped (Merton & Rossi, 1968, p. 35). Research was conducted on the manner in which group norms influenced behavior and set the standards against which actions were judged. To cite a few examples, the "reference group" concept was used to explain the action of soldiers in combat, the reaction of blacks to the perception of social inequity, and the changes in attitudes of college students from freshman to senior year. (See Hyman & Singer, 1968, for a summary of reference group theory and research.) The point is that even before the language of social support was utilized, the influence of the group on the development and maintenance of attitudes and behaviors was well known.

The work on reference group theory antedated and set the stage for the development of Festinger's (1954) social comparison theory, whose basic tenet was that individuals have a drive to evaluate their opinions and attitudes through comparison with either objective standards or the behavior of others. Since most of the time the social world is confusing and ambiguous and objective standards for behavior are not available, the theory states, individuals have little choice but to employ the behavior of others as the standard of comparison.

Festinger's work on social comparison has been described as "a theory about how persons gain self-knowledge and discover reality about themselves [Mettec & Smith, 1977, p. 96]." Its relevance for social support is in its elaboration of the motivation for affiliation under conditions of uncertainty or stress. People affiliate with others to obtain a better idea of how they themselves should act. Thus the theory postulates that people will choose similar others for comparison since information from similar others will be more useful to the self.

By the late 1950s Festinger's attention had shifted from social comparison to cognitive dissonance, and the reference group and social comparison tradition was carried on by others. The contributions of greatest relevance to social support came from Schachter's (1959) theory of affiliation and Zajonc's (1965) work on social facilitation. The relevance of these ideas for social support has been reviewed elsewhere (Heller, 1979), but some important highlights will be presented here. Schachter demonstrated that a preference for being with others occurred among emotionally aroused individuals. The desire to affiliate was present for those exposed to fear stimuli (Sarnoff & Zimbardo, 1961), and was strongest when others were described as similar in personality to the subject (Miller & Zimbardo, 1966), confirming a central postulate of Festinger's social comparison theory.

While the original work on Schachter's theory was concerned with attitudinal preferences for affiliation, later work demonstrated that affiliation improved performance under stress and reduced physiological reactivity (Amoroso & Walters, 1969; Angermeier, Phelps, & Reynolds, 1967; Kissel, 1965). Perhaps most intriguing were studies demonstrating when affiliation would be *avoided*. Isolation was preferred to affiliation when subjects were made to feel embarrassed and when subjects with tendencies toward avoiding fear-arousing stimuli experienced an intense, emotionally arousing accident (Latané & Wheeler, 1966). Thus the social comparison literature suggests two conditions under which affiliation under stress is *not* likely to occur—when the individual anticipates being devalued by the affiliation experience, and when the individual's response style is to avoid arousing events. Furthermore, the work on both affiliation and social facilitation indicates that the mere presence of others is not sufficient to produce reduced anxiety or improved performance under stress (Epley, 1974). The expectation that others will be a source of negative evaluation has been found to *increase* anxiety while experiencing stressful events with companions (Geen & Gange, 1977). Decreased anxiety in the presence of companions typically has been found to occur only when previous associations with the companion have been positive (Geen & Gange, 1977) or when the companion behaves in a calm and sympathetic manner (Epley, 1974).

There are some important differences between the current interest in social support and the social psychological concepts of social comparison and affiliation developed earlier. In the social psychological experiments, the dependent variables typically were attitudinal in nature, while in the social support literature interest has been more general. Attitudes and self-concept variables are considered important, but so too are performance and health-related outcomes. Perhaps a more significant difference is that social support generally is considered as an environmental variable. In the 1960s social psychological theories were becoming increasingly more cognitive and the focus of interest became not social structures but how the individual used social input for self-enhancement. As we shall note shortly, social support does have a cognitive component. However, the major reason for the current popularity of social support is because of its preventive and therapeutic promise through environmental change. The shift in emphasis does not detract from the previous social psychological work but broadens its focus.

## The Social-Support–Stress-Buffering Hypothesis

The current wave of interest in social support was sparked by claims that social support operated as a stress buffer moderating the relationship between stressful life events and symptomatology. The possibility of developing new forms of intervention (support networks) was quickly noted, and social support soon became the latest mental health fad. As was once true for the reference group concept, social support currently is in danger of becoming "a magic term to explain anything and everything" about helping behavior. The problem is that, as is often the case in the development of new concepts in psychology, the research base for social support has lagged considerably behind the enthusiasm of those convinced that they had discovered a new helping modality with enormous treatment and prevention possibilities. In social support psychologists rediscovered the value of family and friendship ties. This clearly was a positive development, because previous generations of clinical theorists had seen family members as responsible for the "traumatic experiences" reported by patients; many therapists, particularly those of a psychodynamic orientation, had concluded that patients must be freed totally from family influences. In the eyes of many clinicians close interpersonal ties, particularly with family members, were merely a source of stress. Now, with the rediscovery of social support, close ties came to be seen as a source of strength. Obviously, family members had not changed that much. What had changed was how they were viewed.

The importance of the social-support–stress-buffering hypothesis lies in the implication that characteristics of interpersonal relationships could in some way mitigate health-related responses to stressful life events (Cohen & McKay, 1979). Perhaps by studying social support we can learn more about the effective ingredients in helpful interpersonal relationships. Thus clarifying the manner in which social support operates could be of great value in explicating helping behavior more generally.

Unfortunately, close examination of the existing social support literature quickly leads to disappointment. While the area of social support has received very optimistic reviews (Cobb, 1976; Dean & Lin, 1977; Gottlieb, 1979), we believe that the case for the buffering effects of support has been overstated. We fear that without a more realistic reappraisal, future research will remain unfocused, repeating the mistakes of past research. Furthermore, disenchantment with uncritical plaudits eventually will lead to total rejection of the field—even though positive benefits of support indeed may be present.

The "buffering" role of social support builds upon the life events literature that generated great interest in the 1970s (Dohrenwend & Dohrenwend, 1974). The research on life events was concerned with the role of undesirable life events in the onset of psychological and physical illnesses. What was consistently demonstrated was that life events had a significant but small role in the development of symptomatology. It was suggested that life events were a weak predictor only because other variables (such as social support) moderate and obscure the events-symptoms relationship.

The buffering hypothesis states that individuals experiencing significant life stress, but with strong social support, will be protected from developing symptomatology associated with stress. The expectation is that individuals experiencing high stress but with good support resources should develop significantly less symptomatology than individuals experiencing high stress but with little social support.

We have located fifteen studies pertinent to the buffering hypothesis. Some of these are widely cited (Brown, Bhrolchain, & Harris, 1975; Gore, 1973; Nuckolls, Cassel, & Kaplan, 1972). Others are similar in design though less well-known (Andrews, Tennant, Hewson, & Valliant, 1978; Barrera, 1981; de Araujo, van Arsdel, Holmes, & Dudley, 1973; Eaton, 1978; Holahan & Moos, 1981; LaRocco, House, & French, 1980; Lieberman & Mullan, 1978; Liem & Liem, 1976; Lin, Simeone, Ensel, & Keo, 1979; Miller & Ingham, 1976; Sandler, 1980; Wilcox, 1981).

While most reviewers believe that a buffering role for social support has been demonstrated in at least fourteen of the fifteen studies, our analysis would suggest that a tentative role for social support as a stress buffer can be found in at most six. The other studies are marred by such conceptual and methodological deficiencies that few firm conclusions can be drawn from them.

One major problem is the vagueness of the social support construct itself. Investigators have been somewhat laissez faire in dealing with the question of what social support is and how it should be assessed. Definitions of support have varied considerably, the concept has been confused with other related terms, and scales have been constructed with questionable psychometric properties. Two examples will illustrate the problem.

The most widely quoted study in past reviews of the role of social support in buffering stress, by Nuckolls, Cassel, and Kaplan (1972), really was a study of "psychosocial assets" rather than social support. Nuckolls et al. found that women with high levels of stress but good "assets" had fewer pregnancy complications than women experiencing high stress with low "assets." It is now generally recognized that a major problem with this study was the confounding of assets and support. Included among assets were items tapping variables such as ego strength, self-perception of health, adaptability, crying, marriage duration, relationship to in-laws, religious similarity of husband and wife, and friendship patterns. These items were summed into a unidimensional scale which earlier uncritical reviewers seemed willing to accept as a measure of support.

In another widely cited study (Gore, 1973, 1978) support was assessed by a 13-item self-report measure covering the subjects' perceptions of friend and relative support, frequency of activities, opportunities to talk about problems, and opportunities to engage in satisfying social activity. In order to derive a single index of support with which to designate the lowest third as unsupported, Gore chose to weight the items in the scale "in an atheoretical manner, based on the results of a stepwise multiple regression using a measure of Depression as the criterion [1973, p. 108]." Unfortunately, then, Gore contaminated her independent and dependent variables. It is little wonder that a relationship between low support and depression in

unemployed men was one of the strongest findings in this study.

The studies just cited indicate two of the problems in the literature—confounding of support with measures of other personal characteristics, and confounding of independent and dependent measures. Other methodological problems present in several studies are a failure to adequately deal with and test the interaction between stress and support, using scales of untested psychometric properties, and the use of inappropriate and arbitrary cutting points to constitute comparison groups.[1] Still, we believe that the major problem in the field is conceptual, not methodological. If the social support construct could be more clearly defined, crisper measurement would be more likely to follow. Different modes of support (for example, support-seeking, network characteristics, and perceived support) have been discussed as if they were equivalent. Yet the role of social support in mediating stress probably is in part a function of the type of support presented and how it is perceived. Therefore in the next section of this paper a model of the role of social support in the coping process is presented.

## A Model of Social Support and Coping

Our view of the relationship between support and coping is presented in Figure 6.1. As can be seen

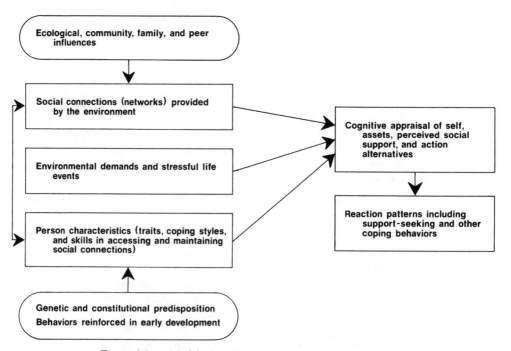

Figure 6.1. A Model of Social Support and the Coping Process.

from examination of the figure, a distinction can be made between social networks; the environmental and ecological variables that encourage their formation; the personal attributes of individuals that make it likely that social connections will be accessed and maintained; the cognitive appraisal that support is available or that further help is needed; and finally, support-seeking behavior that results from the appraisal process. We believe that the equivocal results of past studies of stress buffering is due, in part, to a failure to explicate the relationship between the various facets of support and other aspects of the coping process. Specifically, whether an individual uses support effectively during stressful events depends upon support availability, personal competencies in accessing supportive others, and the reaction patterns developed over time in which seeking support from others becomes part of an effective coping strategy.

There are a number of conceptual distinctions that flow from the model. The first involves the time dimension. The facets of the support domain are not static in time, but are developmental in nature. Not only is one's current support a function of one's previous support, but one's current support can change under the impact of stressful events and the development of symptomatology. Also, support may play different roles in the anticipation of a stressful life event, concurrent with that event or following the event. Failure to recognize these distinctions probably will lead to research ambiguity.

A second distinction implicit in the model is that support does not simply affect individuals unidirectionally, but persons also select and determine the amount and type of support they receive. Individuals play an active role in determining their friends and associates. Not only is it important to study the effects of environments on individuals, but it is also important to study how individuals select supportive or non-supportive environments. The individual is an active "transacting" agent in the development and use of a network. There are multiple networks in most environments that could be joined and accessed to deal with different kinds of stressors. It is important to look developmentally at the factors and learning history leading to an individual's decision to "select" friends, networks, and so on, and which sources are chosen for "supportive transactions" in times of stress (if they are chosen at all). The assets and skills necessary to enter many networks are perhaps as important in understanding the "potency" of that network as are the network's activities and functions.

Another conceptual issue that must not be overlooked is that social support all too often has been considered in isolation when studying its relationships to stress and symptomatology. The influences of support are only one factor in the coping process. In coping with stress, an individual utilizes a variety of coping strategies such as intrapsychic mechanisms and direct actions. Just as most personality researchers should not have made the mistake of overlooking variables in the support domain, social support researchers should not make the mistake of overlooking the important roles of other coping modes. To do so is to overlook potentially important interrelationships between coping and social support.

In summary, then, our model suggests that social support is most profitably viewed in terms of an interaction between environment and person variables occurring across time. More concretely, support levels achieved by an individual are a function of the availability of supportive structures in the environment interacting with individual skills and competencies in accessing and maintaining supportive relationships that present themselves in the environment. Support received at any point in time depends not only on support currently available, but also on the individual's prior history of support availability, accessing and maintenance skills in interpersonal relationships, and past support-seeking behavior.

Each of the major factors in Figure 6.1 now will be discussed in turn.

### Social Connections Provided by the Environment

As an aid in clarifying the ambiguity surrounding the concept "social support," it would be useful to distinguish the terms "social connections" (or "social networks") and "social support." Wellman (1981) argues that studying only "support" oversimplifies the nature of social ties and networks because ties are not always supportive and support often is transmitted in ambiguous ways. Hammer (1981) agrees and suggests that the term "social support" already is associated with a positive bias that confounds independent behaviors or actions with their effects. For example, it might be considered support if a child took the advice of a parent who suggested alternative actions to help the child resolve a dilemma with his or her peers. But would that action be labeled support if the child, resenting the parent's interference, decided to leave home? Occasionally, the confounding of events in the environment and their effects can be seen explicitly in social support definitions. For example, Caplan, Robinson, French, Caldwell and Shinn (1976), define social support as "any input directly provided by another person (or group) which moves the receiving person toward goals which the receiver desires [p. 39]." Similarly, Tolsdorf (1976) defines social support as "any action or behavior that functions to assist the focal person in meeting his personal goals or in dealing with the demands of any particular situation [p. 407]." However, we agree with Hammer (1981) that the concept would be clearer and easier to work with in research if behaviors and their effects were separated. To emphasize this distinction we will use the term "social connections" or "social networks" to refer to behaviors provided by the environment and the term "perceived social support" when describing the subjective impact of that behavior on the individual.

If networks are assessed only from the perspective of a single subject, social connections and perceived support are not totally independent. The same biases that lead to the perception of high or low support also can lead to expansive or constricted network descriptions. For example, Frame (1981) found that former schizophrenics and manic depressives reported lower perceived support than did normals, and also reported smaller networks. A remedy for this problem would be to assess networks from the perspective of more than one network participant. For example, the typical method of obtaining information about support reciprocity in a network is to ask the subject to indicate for each individual in his or her network the extent to which support is given and received. A more accurate measure of reciprocity would be to contact network members nominated by the subject to discover their view of the support exchanged with the subject. Thus, Procidano and Heller (1983) asked subjects to participate with either a close friend or sibling. Information about emotional support reciprocity was obtained by asking all participants to indicate the extent of their general willingness to confide in their companions during the experimental session. Results indicated that friends and sibs were equally willing to confide in one another in general, but that disclosure reciprocity in this specific experiment was higher for sibs than for friends. In other words, subjects willing to confide in their sibs had sibs who were willing to reciprocate. However, the same degree of reciprocity was not found for friends. The authors concluded that because sibs know one another longer than do friends, they are more certain of how much they can say about themselves to one another in a novel experimental situation.

Marsella and Snyder (1981) suggest that social networks can be characterized by four dimensions, each of which can consist of several related variables. Distinguishing among network dimensions is important because doing so provides a way to facilitate research on specific components of the support phenomenon.

Marsella and Snyder's categories of network characteristics are as follows:

1. *Structure.* This dimension includes morphological variables such as size, density, frequency of interaction, and the individual's position within a network.

2. *Interaction.* This dimension consists of variables that describe the relationship between various network actors. Thus reciprocity, symmetry, and directionality are interaction characteristics. So too are the number of content linkages (for example, uniplex or multiplex linkages) that individuals provide for one another.

3. *Quality.* Included here are variables that describe the affective quality of the linkages. Networks can be described in terms such as level of friendliness, intimacy, or affection.

4. *Function.* This dimension describes the specific function served by network members. Networks can provide information and feedback, comfort and cheer, material aid, advice, help in constructive problem solving, and so forth.

The research that has been accumulating on each of these network dimensions reinforces the view that each of them is related in independent ways to perceived support, coping, and eventual adjustment. The more traditional global social support construct simply would not suffice to explain the diversity of research findings.

There is some research on the structure, quality, function, and interaction dimensions of support networks, but these variables usually have not been studied systematically. Also generally absent in the literature are studies of the interaction between network and person characteristics as these affect cognitions, behaviors, or various mental health outcomes.

Since Hammer (1981) and Mitchell and Trickett (1980) provide excellent reviews of the social network literature, a detailed review need not be repeated here. In general, however, the social network literature leaves one with the distinct impression that closer networks are not always better. The value of specific network characteristics depends upon the task to be performed. For example, in a family crisis involving sickness or death of a young parent with children, a high-density, close network might provide the least disruptive help for the children (Hammer; 1981). In instances of mobility, relocation, or similar life transitions, a low-density extensive network might be desirable. Granovetter (1973), in discussing the "strength of weak ties," points out that strong ties tend to concentrate interactions *within* particular groups, while weak ties are more likely to link members of different groups. Thus in tasks in which linking outside of the primary group is facilitative (such as job seeking or relocating), weak ties are more facilitative. Extending his analysis to the community level, Granovetter further suggests that community organization will be more effective in neighborhoods in which weak ties predominate. It can be difficult to encourage individuals to work together when they rarely interact outside of their immediate family circle, particularly if they are suspicious of others who are not members of that circle.

The value of less dense, multidimensional networks can be seen in a study by Hirsch (1980), who investigated the adjustment of recent young-to-middle-age widows and mature women returning to college. For both groups, a dense boundary linking nuclear family members and personal friends (as when family members and friends know one another) was significantly related to greater symptomatology, poorer mood, and lower self-esteem. One might expect that for both groups of women experiencing a significant life transition, adjustment would be facilitated by the establishment of new contacts. Thus it is not surprising that those women who were able to develop new ties outside of their existing family networks were better adjusted.

There is now a small body of studies on the network characteristics of schizophrenics (Cohen & Sokolovsky, 1978; Frame, 1981; Sokolovsky, Cohen, Berger, & Geiger, 1978; Tolsdorf, 1976). The results of these studies tend to be similar. Compared with normals, the networks of schizophrenics were found to be asymmetrical, uniplex, and with a lower ratio of friends to family in the network. The picture that emerges is that while schizophrenics may receive as much support from others as do normals, particularly from family members, they tend not to give support to others and are unable to maintain the reciprocity necessary for friendship formation. The primary deficit in their relationships is not in receiving support but in giving it. Of course, it can be argued that the reason schizophrenics have withdrawn from reciprocal relationships is because the *quality* of support given them by family members leaves much to be desired. Leff (1976) and Vaughn and Leff (1981) reported that independent of the patient's behavioral disturbance or work impairment, highly critical or involved family members were more likely to be associated with patient relapse and the return of florid symptoms. As Leff hypothesizes, the social withdrawal exhibited by many schizophrenic patients and the nongiving, asymmetrical nature of their relationships with others may function as a protection against excessive and disturbing social stimulation.

For those interested in providing social support networks to schizophrenics as a therapeutic and rehabilitative strategy, the question these results pose is whether schizophrenics would use the networks to which they might be linked. One clear possibility suggested by Leff's research is that they would withdraw from attempts to involve them with others. A second possibility is that they would withdraw only if threatened by critical others or by individuals who attempted excessively close or intimate relationships. Vaughn and Leff (1981) suggest that the best outcomes occur when family members are nonintrusive, tolerant of symptom behaviors, "cool" and "controlled" (that is, not overly emotional). A third possibility is that schizophrenics need to learn better ways to modulate the intensity of relationships initiated by others and that a social skills strategy would be the most appropriate way to help such patients deal with the demands made in interpersonal relationships. The approach to community living for schizophrenics adopted by Test and Stein (1977) combines these strategies. Patients are encouraged to live in the community independent of their families. They are linked to outreach workers who are helpful but who insist on responsible adult behavior. The workers are not overly emotionally involved with the patients, and they teach skills important for managing day-to-day chores in the community. However, we should add that at this point we know of no program in community living for schizophrenics that teaches patients how to modulate the emotional intensity of relationships with others.

In addition to the research already cited, we can point to a study by Frame (1981), who found that recovered former schizophrenics or manic depressives living in the community had smaller social networks than normal controls. Members of the recovered schizophrenics' group reported fewer reciprocal relationships than normals, while former manic depressives reported networks in which family members predominated more than did normals or recovered schizophrenics. This is one of the few studies assessing network characteristics of patient groups other than schizophrenics. Its importance is as an illustration that network impairment for patient groups is not limited to the stage of florid symptomatology or to schizophrenic disorders exclusively.

There are more unanswered questions about the role personal networks play in moderating adjustment than there is firm knowledge that can be used as a basis for planning preventive or therapeutic interventions. In part this is because of the correlational nature of the evidence cited earlier, and in part because of the still poorly articulated specification of crucial support elements. For example, intimacy and the presence of a single confiding relationship (Lowenthal & Haven, 1968) or confidante (Brown et al., 1975) seem important. However, still unknown is whether confidants only are needed, whether specific functions or types of help must be provided, or whether the role relationships among network members are crucial. Our hunch is that networks function in more specific ways than have been operationalized thus far. For example, Wellman (1981) suggests that future research might find that emotional-aid ties are most effective if they are reciprocal and egalitarian, but that material-aid ties are more likely to be asymmetric and hierarchical. It is this level of specification that should be examined in future research.

### Ecological and Community Influences on the Development of Social Networks

Some settings are more network-enhancing than others in terms of the opportunities they offer for interaction, their role requirements, their physical structure, and their norms. The literature pertinent to these factors includes research on urban settings, manning and social climates.

The social norms that determine how networks are perceived, accessed, and utilized obviously vary from culture to culture. Major influences include ethnic values (for instance, the extent to which altruism is culturally reinforced), population density, and degree of urbanization. For many early sociologists the village community with close personal ties to neighbors and kin represented an ideal of helpful reciprocity. They feared that the Industrial Revolution and the subsequent growth of large cities would irreparably harm social life (Fischer, 1975). Isolation and anomie were seen as the inevitable consequences of city life, with its highly compartmentalized and fragmented social roles. This view suggested that degree of urbanization should have a negative impact on network support characteristics.

One line of research on the physical environment seemed to confirm these negative expectations. Overall, research evidence indicated that with increased urbanization, helpfulness and friendliness toward others decreased (see Korte, 1978, and Michelson, 1970, for reviews of the literature on urban environments, helping behavior, and friendship networks). Typical of this literature were findings that helpfulness decreased in noisy and crowded environments, and that attentiveness to ordinary social cues decreased under conditions of stimulus overload. Similarly, residents of high-rise apartments were found to be less likely to develop friendships among coresidents and neighbors compared with residents of low-rise or single family homes. While a differential selection into environments may play a role, in that less helpful people may be attracted to urban environments or less gregarious individuals may be attracted to high-rise apartments (Korte, 1978), there is sufficient experimental literature to confirm that environmental characteristics (noise, density, ambiguous stimulus cues, the presence of unknown others, and so on) do influence helpfulness toward others.

The conclusion that urbanization is associated with decreased altruism also is concordant with research on the size and manning of behavior settings. Following the research tradition originally developed by Roger Barker, several studies have found that participation and satisfaction are lessened considerably in overmanned settings (see Wicker, 1979, for a review of the manning literature). In both high schools and churches, smaller organizations have been found to encourage their members to take on more positions of responsibility, participate in a greater variety of settings within the organization, and experience a higher level of obligation to the organization and to other members within it.

The variety of impacts that manning might have on the development of supportive relationships needs to be considered in a social support model. For example, a student transferring to an overmanned school is likely to have fewer opportunities to develop a network than in an undermanned setting. An overmanned setting places a premium on individual skills and competencies as the "entrance requirement" into a role and network. A student whose social skills and assets just suffice to gain him access to a variety of social roles and networks in a more undermanned school may find himself isolated, with fewer social connections, in a more overmanned school. A corollary which follows from this ecological perspective on support is that in a more overmanned setting there will be a stronger relationship of social skills and assets to having well-developed social connections than in a more undermanned setting. One therefore would expect the relationship between support and accessing competencies to vary from sample to sample depending on ecological factors such as manning.

Although large organizations (and cities) may encourage a decreased sense of obligation and helpfulness to others, it does not follow that in the long run there is a general lessening of social ties. While social patterns do change with increases in size, social disintegration does not follow as a necessary concomitant of urbanization. Despite the fears of isolation and anomie in the city, research also shows that social ties in the city remain strong. Ties to kin and friends, while sometimes neighborhood-based (Fried & Gleicher, 1970), are more likely to be maintained at some distance by communication and transportation aids—

telephones, automobiles, and so on (Craven & Wellman, 1974). Compared to villagers, city dwellers are likely to have a wider and more compartmentalized array of helping options. Urban networks have been described as sparsely knit, multiple, overlapping, and varied (Wellman, 1981), quite different from the dense networks with tight boundaries characteristic of village ties. Helping in village communities is based on proximity, kinship, and ethnic homogeneity. Where ethnic "villages" exist in urban neighborhoods (Gans, 1962; Suttles, 1968), these same factors are important. However, a more frequent pattern in the city is for neighbors to be accessed less frequently and only for specialized functions. Urban networks, while including friends and kin, also include membership in formal and informal associations (Smith, 1975; Tomeh, 1974). These tend to be based on similarity of interests; shared ethnic, religious, and cultural values; and occupationally based subcultures (Fischer, 1976).

If social ties and social participation are maintained in cities, albeit in specialized networks, why does the literature on the urban environment consistently report decreased altruism and helpfulness as a function of urban conditions? One answer to this question lies in the polarization between public and private activity that occurs in urban settings (Bahrdt, 1973). The urbanite lives in a world of strangers (Fischer, 1976). Constantly alert for dangerous or compromising situations, the urbanite learns to maintain distance and to avoid involvement in situations that could lead unpredictably to negative personal consequences. For self-protection, the urbanite is less helpful in public settings. However, in private and familiar settings social obligation flourishes, as do altruism, courtesy, and concern. The distinction between public wariness and private friendliness and support can be seen graphically in Suttles's example of the reaction to strangers in some stores and business establishments in an ethnically isolated neighborhood in Chicago.

Many business establishments are so thoroughly acknowledged the property of a single minority group that customers outside the group seem like intruders. When I first went into the Addams area, I entered several places where I was asked, "Whatta you want?" as if I were lost. At the time I thought them inhospitable or 'prejudiced.' What I did not know was that these places are almost never confronted by someone they have not known for years and that they are thoroughly tailored to the needs and personal peculiarities of a small network of friends within a single minority group. To them my presence was

totally inexplicable. At worst, I could be a policeman, some sort of city inspector, or a troublemaker. At best, I might have got there by accident, not knowing any better. . . .

All the ethnic groups in the area have such establishments, and the general public seldom enters them. When someone from outside the area or from another ethnic group enters, the proprietor and regular customers view them with great suspicion and, in some cases, use *ad hoc* measures to insure their safety. Sometimes they will simply wait for the intruder to get his bearings and leave. If that fails, the proprietor may eventually get around to asking what he wants. In the meantime, everyone in the store stops and stares.

The treatment of regular customers, of course, is exactly the opposite. Commercial relations with these people are intimate, and all economic transactions are buried in the guise of friendship and sentiment. In large part this is the reason they cannot tolerate the presence of strangers from another ethnic group. Among themselves the customers set aside their public face and disclose much of their private life to one another. Their conversations, their exchanges, and their understandings are simply too intimate to be carried out before the general public [Suttles, 1968, pp. 47–49].

A final area of research that has bearing on the role of ecological factors are the studies by Moos and his colleagues on the assessment of social climates (Moos, 1974, 1975). Among the dimensions which Moos has found that consistently characterize settings and environments is their perceived degree of supportiveness. It is important to note that the perceived supportiveness of some settings is relatively independent of the individuals perceiving the setting. Moos reports that for settings such as psychiatric hospital wards and correctional settings, the social climate of a setting can remain highly stable despite a complete turnover of the members comprising that setting. Moos also has found social climate to be related to numerous other environmental factors such as population size and architecture. The average social climate of a setting therefore appears to be another environmental influence on the development of social networks, and an influence relatively independent of the particular individual perceiving the setting.

Our goal in this section has been to highlight the importance of social structure and environmental factors in the development of social networks. We have concentrated on variables in the ecological environment because of our belief that the pervasive role of the social environment too often is overlooked by psychologists studying coping and adaptation. We agree with Mechanic (1974) that "man's abilities to cope with the environment depend on the efficacy of the solutions that his culture provides . . . and the adequacy of the preparatory institutions to which he has been exposed [p. 33]."

### Person Characteristics Associated with the Likelihood of Accessing and Maintaining Social Connections

Correlational studies claiming to have found that social support buffers individuals against the effects of stress are subject to a serious uncontrolled rival hypothesis. The reported buffering effect may be due not to social support but to social competence. As one of us stated in a previous review:

> . . . The often repeated finding in naturalistic studies that persons with established support networks are in better mental and physical health than are the unsupported may be due to variables other than social support. . . . It is possible that competent persons, wo are more immune to the adverse effects of stress, are also more likely to have well developed social networks as a direct result of their more general social competence [Heller, 1979, p. 361].

In our model, Figure 6.1, person characteristics, like social competence, contribute to the individual's perception of self and the level of support received. We choose the most general term, "person characteristics," to include assets such as attractiveness, athletic skill, gregariousness, and relational skills, all of which can serve as "entrance tickets" to many roles and relationships. Thus the level of support enjoyed by the individual depends not only upon environmental structures and the actions of others, but also on the individual's abilities and predilections to link to others and elicit support from them. Our favorite example to highlight this interaction comes from the literature on adolescent drinking practices. While a drinking peer culture is an important predictor of alcohol use, there is evidence to suggest that attitudes toward alcohol use are already established by the late teens, and that individuals subsequently choose their friends and associates to match these values. Britt and Campbell (1977) surveyed students on two occasions—just before high school graduation and then again one year later at college. They found that the norms established in high school exerted a considerable influence on social

relations and drinking behavior in college. If students drank in high school, they were more likely to drink in college, choose friends who also drank, and participate in settings in which drinking was expected. We use this example to illustrate that while networks influence behaviors, individuals also choose networks to reinforce behaviors and values to which they already are committed.

What skills are important in the ability to access and maintain social networks? Since there is little research on this question, we must turn to the general literature on social competence for clues as to relevant component skills. Here we find numerous distinct definitions of social competence available in the literature. Procidano (1981), who has reviewed this work, suggests a number of broad classes of abilities of direct relevance to the maintenance of social relations. These are sociability or extraversion, assertiveness, comfort in intimacy, lack of social anxiety, conversational skill, role-taking skill (that is, the ability to take the role of another or see things from another's perspective), and social problem-solving skills (the capacity to generate alternative solutions to difficult social problems). While the ability to perform competently in each of these areas depends upon predispositional variables and prior training in childhood, evidence is accumulating that social competence in adults can be improved with training (Bond & Rosen, 1980), even for those with severe skill deficiencies (Goldsmith & McFall, 1975; Goldstein, Sprafkin, & Gershaw, 1976).

Trower (1980) argues that the socially unskilled are lacking not only in specific component abilities, such as the ability to talk about their behavior and feelings, but also in process skills that allow them to modulate their behavior according to the social cues provided by others. Using an experimentally controlled encounter with two strangers, Trower found that skilled patients performed more component skills than did unskilled patients (for example, speaking, looking, smiling, gesturing, and varying posture). Skilled patients also showed process skills that allowed them to vary their behavior according to situational demands, whereas unskilled patients showed *less* variability across situations. Trower uses these results to argue that social skills training programs need to do more than teach component skills (starting a conversation, listening, saying no to an unreasonable request, and so forth) but also need to teach cue-reading and monitoring skills that would help the unskilled grasp the rules of social interactions.

It is our impression that for the most part the social skills literature has concentrated more on accessing skills than on maintenance skills. The skills needed to start a conversation with an individual whose friendship one seeks are undoubtedly quite different from the skills that help an individual keep friends once initial contact has been established. Friendships are maintained not only on the basis of shared interests and values but also by specific social skills, such as comfort in intimacy and the ability to take the role of others, engage in reciprocal sharing, and manage conflict. When deficits in these skills occur it is unlikely that support networks, even if provided, can be maintained without prior programs emphasizing training in friendship maintenance skills (Heller, 1979).

### Perceived Support, Support-Seeking, and the Appraisal Process

The classical paradigm in stress research has been the reiterative appraisal model set forth by Magda Arnold (1960) and elaborated by Richard S. Lazarus (1966, 1968; Lazarus, Averill, & Opton, 1970, 1974). The basic element of this model is that an individual's emotional reactions to a situation depend upon his appraisals of that situation as threatening. Each emotional reaction is a function of the primary appraisal of threat or harm in a situation. Secondary appraisal refers to the perception of coping alternatives through which the threat can be mastered. As an individual completes the coping alternatives implicit in secondary appraisal, reappraisal of threat recurs in response to a change in the internal or external conditions implied by that threat.

Central to this and related models (Schachter, 1966) is the role of the perceived meaning of the stressor and the response alternatives available to the individual. According to Lazarus et al. (1974), "All coping and emotion flow from these mediating appraisals, and it has been our position that we must understand the appraisal process and the conditions that influence it in order to understand coping and emotion [p. 260]."

Within this framework, social support can play a role in the coping process in two ways. First, perceived support resources may become a salient focus during secondary appraisal. This suggests that it is social support *as perceived* that mediates the utilization of support in coping. When threat is appraised, perceived social support may function to bolster self-esteem and self-concept in secondary appraisal, or may lead the individual to initiate supportive transactions with the relevant members of his or her support network. As conceptualized this way, perceived social support is a coping resource that can be classified alongside other more widely studied modes, such as direct action on the self or environment, and intrapsychic processes (Lazarus et al., 1974).

The second role social support can play in coping with stress is through the unsolicited actions of significant others. If a strong helping norm exists within the individual's helping network(s), someone can act to help the individual cope with a stressor by providing information about action alternatives or resources, or by initiating direct action on the environment. Thus even if perceived support is not a salient element in an individual's secondary appraisal, it may be a relevant component in the empathic appraisals of significant others who can potentially augment individual coping alternatives.

A recent updating of the appraisal model (Averill, 1979) points to some interesting directions for investigations of the role of social support in the coping process. Averill focuses on the potential importance of information in the regulation of stress. He suggests that there are no adequate simple models of stress and coping: "Because the nature of stress is complex, the regulation of stress is necessarily also complex [p. 368]." Averill emphasizes the role of information because of considerable evidence that information is extremely important in coping and because information frequently can be varied when little else can, with potent effects in terms of stress regulation. Furthermore, he argues against the simplistic assumption that all information given to an individual helps reduce stress, citing evidence that "information can sometimes increase rather than decrease stress." This is important to the role of perceived support and supportive transactions, because it raises the possibility that the type of information one individual receives from another is not always stress-reducing. It suggests that an important aspect of the appraisal process may be whether the individual feels he or she needs additional information, what type of information, and from whom that information may be available. Thus the implication is that support-seeking results from appraisals that there is indeed a "threat," that more information is needed, and that it is likely to be available within one's support network(s). If an individual fails to make all three of these appraisals, support-seeking is less likely to occur.

One implication of this view is that support-seeking ouside of one's normal network occurs when an individual appraises his or her current resources for problem resolution as inadequate, because either personal coping alternatives or help from indigenous others is insufficient or unavailable. For this reason, support-seeking can represent a failure of normal adaptation that is associated with an increase in symptoms of distress (Brown, 1978). Thus we see another reason for the contradictory findings in the stress-buffering literature. Support-seeking within an indigenous network can be an integral part of normal adaptation. However, support-seeking also can indicate inadequate coping or a breakdown in network resources.

### Research on Perceived Social Support

If, as our model suggests, the perception of support is part of the appraisal process, it should be considered distinct from social connections and cannot be assessed using network measures. Recognizing this distinction, Procidano and Heller (1983) developed a Perceived Social Support inventory which was designed to measure the extent to which an individual perceives that his or her needs for support are fulfilled by friends (PSS-Fr) or family members (PSS-Fa). The distinction between friend and family support parallels the distinction in role theory between "ascribed" and "achieved" networks. There is little one needs to do to join an ascribed network such as a family—membership is ours by birth. However, an achieved network of friends and intimates requires greater skill for network entry and maintenance. Data collected by our research group at Indiana bear out the importance of this distinction. For Indiana college students, PSS-Fr was found to be correlated significantly with social competence (both dating and assertion skills), as measured by the Levenson and Gottman (1978) Social Competence Scale, and with the Sociability, Social Presence, and Good Impression scales of the California Personality Inventory (Gough, 1957). The correlations between PSS-Fa and the above measures of social competence were considerably smaller. On the other hand, PSS-Fa was significantly related to the Cohesion subscale of the Family Environment Scale developed by Moos (1975); rated intimacy with both mother and father; and the rated proportion of emotional support provided by family members. Furthermore, low support perceived from family members was related to elevations on MMPI D, Pt, and Sc. Overall, these correlations indicate that while PSS-Fr is related to social skills, PSS-Fa is related more to other measures of the family environment and to measures of symptoms and distress (Procidano and Heller, 1983).

For example, in a study investigating the adjustment of adult daughters of alcoholic, mentally ill, and normal fathers, Benson (1980) found that daughters of alcoholics and mental patients perceived less family support during their teen years than did daughters of normal fathers. Furthermore the best predictors of the current positive adjustment of daughters of alcoholic fathers did not include the father's reported drinking level. Rather, daughters' adjustment was related to the absence of conflict in the home, the ability to relate to the alcoholic parent, and the level of perceived family support.

That perceived support and network measures of support are relatively independent constructs was verified by separate factor analyses performed by Swindle (1981) and by Cho (1981), and by a study in which Corty and Young (1980) found that perceived social support was not related to the amount of social contact with others but *was* negatively correlated with feelings of loneliness. The Corty and Young result also is congruent with our assertion that perceived support should be considered part of the appraisal process.

That perceived support should be viewed as depending upon the appraisal of both personal networks and social competence also can be seen in work by Fondacaro (1981), who found that while intimacy levels, emotional support, and dating skills each correlate with PSS-Fr at between .32 and .37, the multiple $r$ predicting Pss-Fr from these network and skill measures was .52. Thus while network measures of support, perceived support, and social competence are relatively independent measures, together network support and competence account for a significant share of the variance in perceived support.

Finally, in an experiment designed to validate the perceived support scales by studying interaction rates with companions, Procidano and Heller (1983) found that individuals who reported high levels of perceived support from their friends spoke longer in interactions with friends or sibs and spoke more about themselves than did individuals of low perceived friend support. Individuals with high perceived support from friends were more open and disclosing to both friends and sibs. Perceived support from family members affected interaction rates with companions in a more specific manner. Perceived family support only affected interactions with sibs, in that individuals who reported low family support when interacting with their sibs showed a marked verbal inhibition compared with members of the other groups. [2]

## Future Directions for Research

Perhaps in reaction to the difficulties of ameliorating stress-producing conditions in the environment directly, by the end of the 1970s a widespread and enthusiastic lobby had developed espousing the value of social support as a stress buffer. However, contrary to the conclusions reached in earlier reviews (Cobb, 1976; Dean & Lin, 1977; Gottlieb, 1979), this enthusiasm was not well grounded empirically. With the notable exception of research by Brown, Bhrolchain, and Harris (1975), early studies suffered severe conceptual and methodological problems which rendered their conclusions uninterpretable with regard to the buffering hypothesis.

Fortunately for those who climbed onto the bandwagon early, recent buffering studies are much stronger, both conceptually and methodologically. As far as they are able, they tend to support a buffering role for social support variables in the stress-illness relationship (Barrera, 1981; Eaton, 1978; LaRocco et al., 1980; Sandler, 1980; Wilcox, 1981). However, this recent research evidence still must be qualified in one important respect. Although the interaction of support and stressful life events has been demonstrated in this recent work using multiple regression techniques, the methods involved still are correlational, and there is little data available pertinent to the *causal* hypothesis involved. The major rival hypothesis of social competence or skill still remains a plausible possibility to account for the "buffering" effect found in correlational studies.

We believe that current approaches to buffering have taken the literature as far as they can, and future research should move away from the well-trodden ground of the classical cross-sectional correlational buffering study. The first step in future research should involve a clearer conceptualization of what is meant by support, linking the different types of support to other aspects of adaptation and coping (such as environmental and person characteristics and cognitive appraisal). This first step is descriptive and is intended to answer questions concerning who uses support, what behaviors are considered supportive, and when supportive transactions are most likely. For example, it is likely that there are important sex, age, social class, and ethnic group differences in support usage which up till now have been largely ignored.

There are three types of research designs that should be used in future studies of social support. The first is exploratory rather than confirmatory of causal hypotheses and involves intensive N-of-1 research with individuals at risk for stress. Much is yet to be learned about how various types of support relate to each other over time. Many fruitful hypotheses for more rigorous designs can be uncovered by studying coping in a few individuals prior to, during, and subsequent to a major life event.

The second involves short-term longitudinal (panel) design studies in which groups are followed over time to examine the sequential effects of stressful events, social support, symptoms, and coping. Assessment at each time period should include relevant coping and support measures (network variables, perceived support, support-seeking, etc.) as well as important life events and demographic variables. Such a design much more powerfully permits causal inferences and explorations

of confounding, but also involves a much greater level of data complexity and expense, and requires greater conceptual and methodological sophistication. Researchers would be required to deal with problems of subject attrition biases, disentangling measurement unreliability and change (Cronbach & Furby, 1971; Wiley & Wiley, 1970), and choosing among a variety of data analysis strategies (Duncan, 1975; Jöreskog, 1973; Kenny, 1975).

A third class of designs permitting causal inferences are "hybrid" questionnaire-laboratory studies that combine cross-sectional data with randomized experiments. Ecological validity or generalizability, generally recognized as a major problem in laboratory research (Heller, 1971; Kazdin, 1978), can be improved by combining questionnaire studies assessing subject behavior in naturalistic settings with the study of these same individuals in specific laboratory stress situations. Subjects can be stratified for levels of skill or coping style and randomly assigned to various support interventions. Important factors that can be studied in hybrid laboratory studies are male-female differences in support transactions (for example, are women more disclosing and emotionally supportive than men? Do men tend to problem-solve more than women?), differences in interactions with friends versus strangers, and the relative importance of supportive relationships as compared to other variables such as accessing skills. Useful experimental studies have been Janis's (1975) randomized design assigning companions to individuals attempting to stop smoking, and Procidano and Heller's (1983) work studying the social interaction of sibs and friends in high and low perceived support dyads.

## Conclusion

We began this chapter with a brief review of social psychological concepts of relevance to social support. The work in social psychology on reference groups, social facilitation, and affiliation demonstrated how individuals use others as standards of comparison to shape their own attitudes and behavior. Similar processes may be operating in social support. The research on facilitation and affiliation also suggested some limiting conditions. Affiliation with others in anticipation or during a stressful event was found to reduce anxiety, except that the mere presence of any companion was not sufficient to produce the effect. Negative expectations concerning companions, derived from past negative associations with them, could increase anxiety when the individual experienced stress in their presence. Thus we are reminded that interactions with indigenous others can have either positive or negative effects, and that support from others is not an un-qualified "good."

In order to increase the precision of thinking about social support, a model was presented that links social support and coping. In the model, a distinction is made between social networks, perceived social support, and support-seeking. *Social networks* describe the social connections available in the environment that vary in terms of structure and function. *Perceived social support* (the appraisal that one is supported) is in part a function of the availability of social networks, but also depends upon interpersonal skills in accessing and maintaining supportive relationships. *Support-seeking* occurs in response to threat and results from an appraisal that more help or information is needed. Support seeking can be part of normal adaptation, but also can be a sign of inadequate coping or a breakdown in network resources, particularly when it occurs outside of an indigenous network. Our call for greater conceptual and research specificity, which parallels similar conclusions of other recent reviewers (see Gottlieb, 1981), reflects a growing appreciation for the complexity of the social support phenomenon.

Most of us probably would accept as a truism that individuals feel more satisfied and fulfilled working and living with others than alone. Since man is a social animal, there is an intuitive appeal to the social support construct. Perhaps this is why it is hard to believe that the literature concerning the role of social support in buffering stress still has so many unanswered questions.

With regard to the existing literature, positive effects for the role of support in buffering stress among adults has been fairly well established for support defined as the presence of confidants (Brown, Bhrolchain, & Harris, 1975) and as not living alone (Eaton, 1978). Positive effects with children also have been found for support defined as the presence of older sibs, and two- as opposed to one-parent families (Sandler, 1980). For other aspects of networks, perceived support, or support-seeking the evidence is of poor quality.

Current approaches to the buffering hypothesis involving cross-sectional correlational studies have taken the literature as far as they can. The resulting ambiguity is both conceptual and methodological and leads us to call for a moratorium on classical buffering studies until more careful work can be done explicating the different aspects of social support. The structure, function, and quality of relationships with others in one's network, individual competency levels, the nature of environmental demands and whether they can be modified, and how these variables are perceived and appraised all contribute to eventual coping and adjustment, and should be studied.

Research in social support is improving and we are now beginning to see the development of psychometrically reliable and valid assessment devices for different aspects of the support construct (Barrera, Sandler, & Ramsey, 1980; Procidano & Heller, 1983; Sarason, Levine, Bashem & Sarason, 1981). We expect that as the field becomes more sophisticated the claims for social support will become more modest, but also more realistic. We further expect that as research on social support develops, we will move beyond the demonstration phase (Does social support have an effect?) to a more careful explication of the processes underlying the support phenomenon. When this occurs, we expect that the processes involved will be ones with which we already may be familiar (such as social comparison, affiliation, modeling, intimacy and disclosure reciprocity, and the role of anticipation and rehearsal in stress reduction) but that our study of support and coping will enable us to understand these factors with a new richness.

## Notes

[1] The use of arbitrary cutpoints, and failing to test for stress x support interactions are especially severe problems plaguing the support literature. In far too many buffering studies, stress x support interactions are either inappropriately treated using cutpoint-based strategies, or interaction terms are left out of multiple regression tests of the buffering hypothesis.

The data analysis practice of using mean or median splits is a major unrecognized shortcoming in the literature that too often results in the confounding of independent variables (Andrews et al., 1978; Gore, 1973, 1978; Liem & Liem, 1976; Lin et al., 1979; Nuckolls et al., 1973). It is common practice to convert continuous, interval-level measures of life events, social support, and social competence into ordinal categories—for example, to designate "high" and "low" stress subjects and "high" and "low" support subjects. The search for interaction effects then follows an ANOVA-like strategy as if subjects had been randomly assigned to these levels of the independent variables. Subjects above some arbitrary cutpoint on stress and support are compared with subjects above the cutpoint on stress but below it on support.

This strategy has major drawbacks. In addition to the fact that the cutpoints are usually completely arbitrary, this practice assumes the independence of stress and support throughout the distributions of both variables. The difficulty with this assumption is that support and stress are frequently correlated such that subjects with high stress have low support. When a high-stress, high-support group is compared with a high-stress, low-support group, it is possible that the groups will *not* be equated for levels of stress due to the correlations of support and stress in this portion of their joint distribution. This potential confound is clearly illustrated in the study by de Araujo et al. (1973). They report a highly significant effect for a high-stress, low-assets group using a cutpoint approach. Their data reveals, however, that due to the cutpoint approach the high-stress, high-assets group had an average stress score (LCU) of 685, whereas the high-stress, low-assets group had an average LCU of 738—a 53-point LCU difference between groups supposedly equated for amounts of stress. It is therefore not possible to determine if the high-stress, low-assets group is worse off because of its lower level of assets or its higher stress level, or both.

In most cases the use of cutpoints is an arbitrary and unreliable way of reducing interval level data for use with ordinal statistical methods (Namboodiri, Carter, & Blalock, 1975, p. 579). The research designs that result from this practice are usually nonorthogonal and confounded. Data analysis results capitalize on chance, the number of categories used, and the potential effects of extreme cases in skewed marginal distributions. The problems resulting from the use of cutpoints could be largely avoided by the use of multiple regression analyses and/or structural equation approaches (Duncan, 1975).

Researchers who do utilize a multiple regression approach should be wary, however, of falling into the other pitfall, sometimes noted in the literature, which is to fail to test the stress x support interaction term for significance in the multiple regression equation. All too often only simple main effects are reported in evidence of the buffering hypothesis (Holahan & Moos, 1981; Liem & Liem, 1976; Lin et al., 1979; Miller & Ingham, 1976; Miller, Ingham, & Davidson, 1976). It is encouraging, however, that five of the more recent buffering studies (all of which find support for the buffering effect) utilize multiple regression approaches *and* test for the stress x support interactions (Barrera, 1981; Eaton, 1978; LaRocco et al., 1980; Sandler, 1980; and Wilcox, 1981).

[2] Research by Barrera (1981) provides data on "support satisfaction" which conceptually bears some resemblance to Procidano and Heller's perceived social support measures, although the method of measurement is quite different in the two scales. Procidano and Heller ask about perceived support from friends and family viewed globally, while Barrera asks about support satisfaction with specific individuals who provide six distinct types of help (material aid, physical assistance, intimacy, guidance, feedback, and social partic-ipation). Still, despite differences in methodology, findings were similar. Barrera found that support satisfaction and network support were independent constructs, and that for pregnant adolescents support satisfaction was a better predictor of reported symptomatology than were network measures. Barrera concludes that "knowledge of people's subjective appraisals of the adequacy of support is more critical to the prediction of their well-being than simply collecting infor-mation about the number of supporters or the quantity of supportive behaviors to which they have access [p. 85]." However, as we have already stated, the reporting of support satisfaction and of symptomatology can be confounded, since both are part of subjective approval. Thus it is important to anchor perceived support either in objective behavior or in confirmation by the report of significant others concerning subject well-being.

# References

Amoroso, D. M., & Walters, R. H. Effects of anxiety and socially mediated anxiety reduction on paired-associate learning. *Journal of Personality and Social Psychology*, 1969, 11, 388–396.

Andrews, G., Tennant, C., Hewson, D. M., & Valliant, G. E. Life events stress, social support, coping style and risk of psychological impairment. *Journal of Nervous and Mental Disease*, 1978, 166, 307–316.

Angermeier, W. F., Phelps, J. B., & Reynolds, H. H. Verbal stress and heart-rate in humans exposed in groups. *Psychonomic Science*, 1967, 8, 515–516.

Arnold, M. *Emotion and personality.* New York: Columbia University Press, 1960.

Averill, J. R. A selective review of cognitive and behavioral factors involved in the regulation of stress. In R. A. Depue (Ed.), *The psychobiology of the depressive disorders: Implications for the effects of stress.* New York: Academic Press, 1979.

Bahrdt, H. P. Public activity and private activity as basic forms of city association. In R. L. Warren (Ed.), *Perspectives on the American community.* Chicago: Rand McNally, 1973.

Barrera, M. Social support in the adjustment of pregnant adolescents: Assessment issues. In B. H. Gottlieb (Ed.), *Social networks and social support.* Beverly Hills: Sage, 1981.

Barrera, M., Sandler, I. N., & Ramsay, T. B. Preliminary development of a scale of social support: Studies on college students. *American Journal of Community Psychology*, 1981, 9, 435–447.

Benson, C. Coping and support among daughters of al-coholics. Unpublished doctoral dissertation, Indiana University, 1980.

Bond, L. A., & Rosen, J. C. (Eds.) *Competence and coping during adulthood.* Hanover, N.H.: University Press of New England, 1980.

Britt, D. W., & Campbell, E. Q. A longitudinal analysis of alcohol use, environmental conduciveness and nor-mative structure. *Journal of Studies on Alcohol*, 1977, 38, 1640–1647.

Brown, B. B. Social and psychological correlates of help-seeking behavior among urban adults. *American Journal of Community Psychology*, 1978, 6, 425–439.

Brown, G. W., Bhrolchain, M. H., & Harris, T. Social class and psychiatric disturbance among women in an urban population. *Sociology*, 1975, 9, 225–254.

Caplan, R. D., Robinson, E. A. R., French; J. R. P., Jr., Caldwell, J. R., & Shinn, M. *Adhering to medical reg-imens: Pilot experiments in patient education and social support.* Ann Arbor: Institute for Social Research, Uni-versity of Michigan, 1976.

Cho, J. Unpublished research, Indiana University.

Cobb, S. Social support as a moderator of life stress. *Psy-chosomatic Medicine*, 1976, 38, 300–314.

Cohen, C., & Sokolovsky, J. Schizophrenia and social net-works: Expatients in the inner city. *Schizophrenia Bulletin*, 1978, 4, 546–560.

Cohen, S., & McKay, G. Social support, stress and the buffer hypothesis: Theoretical and empirical issues. Un-published manuscript, 1979.

Corty, E., & Young, R. D. Social contact and loneliness in a university population. Paper presented at the meeting of the Midwestern Psychological Association, St. Louis, 1980.

Cottrell, N. B. Social facilitation. In C. G. McClintock (Ed.), *Experimental social psychology.* New York: Holt, Rinehart & Winston, 1972.

Cottrell, N. B., & Epley, S. W. Affiliation, social comparison and socially mediated stress reduction. In J. M. Suls & R. L. Miller (Eds.), *Social comparison processes: The-oretical and empirical perspectives.* Washington: Hem-isphere, 1977.

Craven, P., & Wellman, B. The network city. In M. P. Effrat (Ed.), *The community: Approaches and applications.* New York: Free Press, 1974.

Cronbach, L. J., & Furby, L. How we should measure "change"—or should we? *Psychological Bulletin*, 1970, **74**, 68–80.

Dean, A., & Lin, N. The stress buffering role of social support: Problems and prospects for systematic investigation. *Journal of Nervous and Mental Disease*, 1977, **165**, 403–417.

de Araujo, G., vanArsdel, P. P., Holmes, T. H., & Dudley, D. L. Life change, coping ability and chronic intrinsic asthma. *Journal of Psychosomatic Research*, 1973, **17**, 359–363.

Dohrenwend, B. S., & Dohrenwend, B. P. *Stressful Life events: Their nature and effects.* New York: Wiley, 1974.

Duncan, O. D. *Introduction to structural equation models.* New York: Academic Press, 1975.

Eaton, W. W. Life events, social supports, and psychiatric symptoms: A reanalysis of the New Haven data. *Journal of Health and Social Behavior*, 1978, **19**, 230–234.

Epley, S. W. Reduction of the behavioral effects of aversive stimulation by the presence of companions. *Psychological Bulletin*, 1974, 271–283.

Festinger, L. A theory of social comparison processes. *Human Relations*, 1954, **7**, 117–140.

Fischer, C. S. The study of urban community and personality. *Annual Review of Sociology*, 1975, **1**, 67–89.

Fischer, C. S. *The urban experience.* New York: Harcourt Brace Jovanovich, 1976.

Fondacaro, M. Unpub. research, Indiana University, 1981.

Frame, C. L. Cognitive and social functioning in schizophrenic and manic-depressive outpatients: A descriptive study. Unpublished doctoral dissertation, Indiana University, 1981.

Fried, M., & Gleicher, P. Some sources of residential satisfaction in an urban slum. In H. M. Proshansky, W. H. Ittelson, & L. G. Rivlin (Eds.), *Environmental psychology: Man and his physical setting.* New York: Holt, Rinehart & Winston, 1970.

Gans, H. J. *The urban villagers: Group and class in the life of Italian-Americans.* New York: Free Press, 1962.

Geen, R. G., & Gange, J. J. Drive theory of social facilitation: Twelve years of theory and research. *Psychological Bulletin*, 1977, **84**, 1267–1288.

Goldsmith, J. B., & McFall, R. M. Development and evaluation of an interpersonal skill-training program for psychiatric inpatients. *Journal of Abnormal Psychology*, 1975, **84**, 51–58.

Goldstein, A. P., Sprafkin, R. P., & Gershaw, N. J. *Skill training for community living: Applying structured learning therapy.* New York: Pergamon Press, 1976.

Gore, S. The influence of social support and related variables in ameliorating the consequences of job loss. Unpublished doctoral dissertation, University of Pennsylvania, 1973.

Gore, S. The effect of social support in moderating the health consequences of unemployment. *Journal of Health and Social Behavior*, 1978, **19**, 157–165.

Gottlieb, B. H. The primary group as supportive milieu: Applications to community psychology. *American Journal of Community Psychology*, 1979, **7**, 469–480.

Gottlieb, B. H. (Ed.) *Social networks and social support.* Beverly Hills: Sage, 1981.

Gough, H. *Manual for the California Personality Inventory.* Palo Alto, Calif.: Consulting Psychologists Press, 1957.

Granovetter, M. S. The strength of weak ties. *American Journal of Sociology*, 1973, **78**, 1360–1380.

Hammer, M. Social supports, social networks and schizophrenia. *Schizophrenia Bulletin*, 1981, **7**, 45–57.

Heller, K. Laboratory interview research as analogue to treatment. In A. E. Bergin & S. L. Garfield (Eds.), *Handbook of psychotherapy and behavior change.* New York: Wiley, 1971.

Heller, K. The effects of social support: Prevention and treatment implications. In A. P. Goldstein & F. H. Kanfer (Eds.), *Maximizing treatment gains: Transfer enhancement in psychotherapy.* New York: Academic Press, 1979.

Hirsch, B. J. Natural support systems and coping with major life changes. *American Journal of Community Psychology*, 1980, **8**, 159–172.

Holahan, C. J., & Moos, R. H. Social support and psychological distress: A longitudinal analysis. *Journal of Abnormal Psychology*, 1981, **90**, 365–370.

Hyman, H. H., & Singer, E. (Eds.) *Readings in reference group theory and research.* New York: Free Press, 1968.

Janis, I. L. Effectiveness of social support for stressful decisions. In M. Deutsch & H. Hornstein (Eds.), *Applying social psychology: Implications for research, practice and training.* Hillsdale, N.J.: LEA Associates, 1975.

Jöreskog, K. G. A general method for estimating a linear structural equation system. In A. S. Goldberger & O. D. Duncan (Eds.), *Structural equation models in the social sciences.* New York: Seminar Press, 1973.

Kazdin, A. E. Evaluating the generality of findings in analogue therapy research. *Journal of Consulting and Clinical Psychology*, 1978, **46**, 673–686.

Kenny, D. A. Cross-lagged panel correlation: A test for spuriousness. *Psychological Bulletin*, 1975, **82**, 887–903.

Kissel, S. Stress-reducing properties of social stimuli. *Journal of Personality and Social Psychology*, 1965, **2**, 378–384.

Korte, C. Helpfulness in the urban environment. In A. Baum, J. E. Singer, & S. Valins (Eds.), *Advances in environmental psychology.* Vol. 1. *The urban environment.* Hillsdale, N.J.: Lawrence Erlbaum, 1978.

LaRocco, J. M., House, J. S., & French, J. R. P., Jr. Social support, occupational stress and health. *Journal of Health and Social Behavior*, 1980, **21**, 202–218.

Latané, B., & Wheeler, L. Emotionality and reactions to disaster. *Journal of Experimental Social Psychology*, supplement, 1966, **1**, 95–102.

Lazarus, R. S. *Psychological stress and the coping process.* New York: McGraw-Hill, 1966.

Lazarus, R. S. Emotions and adaptation: Conceptual and empirical relations. In W. J. Arnold (Ed.), *Nebraska Symposium on Motivation.* Lincoln: University of Nebraska Press, 1968.

Lazarus, R. S., Averill, J. R., & Opton, E. M., Jr. Toward a cognitive theory of emotion. In M. Arnold (Ed.), *Feelings and emotions.* New York: Academic Press, 1970.

Lazarus, R. S., Averill, J. R., & Opton, E. M., Jr. The psychology of coping: Issues of research and assessment. In G. V. Coelho, D. A. Hamburg, & J. E. Adams (Eds.), *Coping and adaptation.* New York: Basic Books, 1974.

Leff, J. P. Schizophrenia and sensitivity to the family environment. *Schizophrenia Bulletin*, 1976, **2**, 566–574.

Levenson, R. W., & Gottman, J. M. Toward the assessment of social competence. *Journal of Consulting and Clinical Psychology*, 1978, **46**, 453–462.

Lieberman, M. A., & Mullan, J. T. Does help help? The adaptive consequences of obtaining help from professionals and social networks. *American Journal of Community Psychology*, 1978, **6**, 499–517.

Liem, J. H., & Liem, R. Life events, social supports and physical and psychological well-being. Paper presented at the meeting of the American Psychological Association, Washington, D.C., September 1976.

Lin, N., Simeone, R. S., Ensel, W. M., & Keo, W. Social support, stressful life events and illness: A model and an empirical test. *Journal of Health and Social Behavior*, 1979, **20**, 108–119.

Lowenthal, M. F., & Haven, C. Interaction and adaptation: Intimacy as a critical variable. *American Sociological Review*, 1968, **33**, 20–30.

Marsella, A. J., & Snyder, K. K. Stress, social supports and schizophrenic disorders: Toward an interactional model. *Schizophrenia Bulletin*, 1981, 7, 152–163.

Mechanic, D. Social structure and personal adaptation: Some neglected dimensions. In G. V. Coelho, D. A. Hamburg, & J. E. Adams (Eds.), *Coping and adaptation*. New York: Basic Books, 1974.

Merton, R. K., & Rossi, A. K. Contributions to the theory of reference group behavior. In H. H. Hyman & E. Singer (Eds.), *Readings in reference group theory and research*. New York: Free Press, 1968.

Mettec, D. R., & Smith, G. Social comparison and interpersonal attraction: The case for dissimilarity. In J. M. Suls & R. L. Miller (Eds.), *Social comparison processes: Theoretical and empirical perspectives*. Washington, D.C.: Hemisphere, 1977.

Michelson, W. *Man and his urban environment: A sociological approach*. Reading, Mass.: Addison-Wesley, 1970.

Miller, N., & Zimbardo, P. G. Motives for fear-induced affiliation: Emotional comparison or interpersonal similarity. *Journal of Personality*, 1966, **34**, 481–503.

Miller, P. McC., & Ingham, J. G. Friends, confidants and symptoms. *Social Psychiatry*, 1976, 11, 51–58.

Miller, P. McC., Ingham, J. G., & Davidson, S. Life events, symptoms, and social support. *Journal of Psychosomatic Research*, 1976, **20**, 515–522.

Mitchell, R. E., & Trickett, E. J. Social networks as mediators of social support: An analysis of the effects and determinants of social networks. *Community Mental Health Journal*, 1980, 16, 27–44.

Moos, R. H. *Evaluating treatment environments*. New York: Wiley-Interscience, 1974.

Moos, R. H. *Evaluating correctional and community settings*. New York: Wiley, 1975.

Namboodiri, N. K., Carter, L. F., & Blalock, H. M. *Applied multivariate analysis and experimental designs*. New York: McGraw-Hill, 1975.

Nuckolls, K. B., Cassel, J., & Kaplan, B. H. Psychosocial assets, life crisis and the prognosis of pregnancy. *American Journal of Epidemiology*, 1972, **95**, 431–441.

Procidano, M. E. An analysis of social competence in schizotypic, subclinically depressed, and subclinically psychopathic individuals. Unpublished doctoral dissertation, Indiana University, 1981.

Procidano, M. E., & Heller, K. Measures of perceived social support from friends and from family: Three validation studies. *American Journal of Community Psychology*, 1983, 11, 1–24.

Sandler, I. N. Social support resources, stress and maladjustment of poor children. *American Journal of Community Psychology*, 1980, 8, 41–52.

Sarason, I. G., Levine, H. M., Bashem, R. B., & Sarason, B. R. Assessing social support: The social support questionnaire. Unpublished manuscript, Office of Naval Research, Arlington, Va., 1981.

Sarnoff, I., & Zimbardo, P. G. Anxiety, fear and social affiliation. *Journal of Abnormal and Social Psychology*, 1961, **62**, 356–363.

Schachter, S. *The psychology of affiliation: Experimental studies of the sources of gregariousness*. Stanford: Stanford University Press, 1959.

Schachter, S. The interaction of cognitive and physiological determinants of emotional state. In C. D. Spielberger (Ed.), *Anxiety and behavior*. New York: Academic Press, 1966.

Sherif, M. The concept of reference groups in human relations. In H. H. Hyman & E. Singer (Eds.), *Readings in reference group theory and research*. New York: Free Press, 1968.

Smith, D. H. Voluntary action and voluntary groups. *Annual Review of Sociology*, 1975, 1, 247–270.

Sokolovsky, J., Cohen, C., Berger, D., & Geiger, J. Personal networks of ex-mental patients in a Manhattan S.R.O. hotel. *Human Organization*, 1978, 37, 5–15.

Suttles, G. D. *The social order of the slum: Ethnicity and territory in the inner city*. Chicago: University of Chicago Press, 1968.

Swindle, R. W. Unpublished research, Indiana University.

Test, M. A., & Stein, L. I. A community approach to the chronically disabled patient. *Social Policy*, 1977, 8, 8–16.

Tolsdorf, C. C. Social networks, support and coping: An exploratory study. *Family Process*, 1976, 15, 407–417.

Tomeh, A. K. Formal voluntary organizations: Participation, correlates and interrelationships. In M. P. Effrat (Ed.), *The community: Approaches and applications*. New York: Free Press, 1974.

Trower, P. Situational analysis of the components and processes of behavior of socially skilled and unskilled patients. *Journal of Consulting and Clinical Psychology*, 1980, **48**, 327–339.

Vaughn, C. E., & Leff, J. P. Patterns of emotional response in relatives of schizophrenic patients. *Schizophrenia Bulletin*, 1981, 7, 43–44.

Wellman, B. Applying network analysis to the study of support. In B. H. Gottlieb (Ed.), *Social networks and social support*. Beverly Hills: Sage, 1981.

Wicker, A. W. *An introduction to ecological psychology*. Monterey, Calif.: Brooks/Cole, 1979.

Wilcox, B. L. Social support, life stress, and psychological adjustment: A test of the buffering hypothesis. *American Journal of Community Psychology*, 1981, 9, 371–386.

Wiley, D. E., & Wiley, J. A. The estimation of measurement error in panel data. In H. A. Blalock (Ed.), *Causal models in the social sciences*. Chicago: Aldine Atherton, 1971.

Zajonc, R. B. Social facilitation. *Science*, 1965, **149**, 269–274.

Zander, A. The psychology of group processes. *Annual Review of Psychology*, 1979, **30**, 417–451.

# 7 ENVIRONMENTAL PSYCHOLOGY AND PREVENTION*

## Abraham Wandersman, Arlene Andrews, David Riddle, and Carrie Fancett

Michelle Dooley, a 25 year old New Jersey housewife, suffered a miscarriage last January. She was not alone. Shortly before or after Mrs. Dooley's miscarriage, six out of nine of her pregnant friends living in Cape May County also suffered miscarriages. "When only one healthy baby was born out of those nine pregnancies," Mrs. Dooley said, "we began to suspect something must be wrong."

suspect that pesticides sprayed in heavily agricultural Cape May County may have contributed to their miscarriages. So last April they formed an organization called the Concerned Parents Association, which now involves about 60 people who operate a telephone hotline for women in the area with any kind of pregnancy problems. Mrs. Dooley said the Concerned Parents are collecting local birth defect statistics and are pressuring state health officials to do extensive testing of the local water supplies. (Initial tests of 16 wells showed that eight had high levels of nitrates, she said.)

"It is important to remember that mothers and fathers and other concerned people are the only ones who can get something like this started," Mrs. Dooley said. "In our case, it started with only six of us sitting around talking. Sometimes when we walk down the street, people say, 'Oh, those crazy women again,' but I lost a baby. . . . If there's anything I can do to keep another man or woman from having to go through that, I'll do it" [Klemesrud, 1980, p. 6-B].

That story illustrates several of this chapter's important themes:

1. Our everyday physical environments can affect coping and cause physical and psychological damage.
2. The physical environment affects many people who generally remain outside the community mental health system as it presently operates.
3. Interventions can be attempted to prevent problems by working with individuals affected by the environment (for instance, through telephone counseling) or by attempting to change or eliminate the noxious environmental condition.

Most clinical mental health interventions are aimed toward changing the person rather than the environment.

* We would like to thank Irwin Altman, Andrew Baum, Elizabeth Nelson, Lois Pall Wandersman, and Alan Wicker for their helpful comments and suggestions.

There is an increasing recognition that the prevention professional must go beyond interventions focused on strengthening the host to those involving systems change. . . . Through the application of current knowledge about such stressors as noise, crowding, economic fluctuations, cultural and linguistic alienation and social isolation, the community mental health professional can be instrumental in preventing negative outcomes and promoting healthy environments for persons who will otherwise remain outside the community mental health system [Swift, 1980, p. 226].

In order to accomplish this goal, we need to understand how the environment is related to stress and to positive and negative outcomes and to search for fruitful points of intervention including how to change the environment. In the present chapter, we discuss how the physical environment is related to important effects and suggest potential points of intervention, including changing the environment as well as changing the individual.

Our major purpose in this chapter is to bring together concepts and research from environmental psychology, community psychology, and clinical psychology on the topic of the physical environment and prevention. Since this is largely an unexplored area, this is a large undertaking and there may be sizable gaps. Also, we expect that many readers will be somewhat unfamiliar with environmental psychology. Therefore, we approach the chapter first by outlining a framework focusing on the relationship between the physical environment, stress, coping, and outcomes, and potential points of preventive interventions. Second, we discuss the major components of the framework in more detail, describing concepts and research in a selective fashion. Due to space limitations, we take an illustrative approach, rather than attempting a comprehensive literature review. More detailed reviews of environmental psychology are available in sources such as Bell, Fisher, and Loomis (1978), Stokols (1978), and Russell and Ward (1982). Then we discuss implications of the concepts and research discussed in the framework for prevention. This section is followed by some suggestions for collaboration between environmental, community, and clinical psychologists.

## A Framework of Environmental Psychology and Prevention

In this chapter we develop a framework to (1) relate the physical environment to perception of the environment, coping, and effects; and (2) suggest points for preventive interventions. The framework takes a stress approach and assumes stress-producing environmental conditions will be associated with attempts to cope, that the coping attempts may be successful or unsuccessful, and that positive or negative outcomes may result. In this section we will briefly describe the framework and fill in additional details in the following sections (see Figure 7.1).

Our framework is influenced by Lazarus's (1966) stress model, Baum, Singer, and Baum's (1981) approach to stress and the environment, and Bell, Fisher, and Loomis's (1978) model relating the physical environment to psychological effects. The first aspect of the framework deals with physical environmental conditions or features. We will discuss two major types of environmental conditions: environmental stressors, and the built environment. Individual differences such as developmental experiences and personality influence the perception of the environment as acceptable (with resulting homeostasis) or not acceptable. (This perception process is analogous to primary appraisal in Lazarus's model.) The concept of control over the environment plays an important role in appraising an environment as acceptable or not acceptable. If an environment is perceived as not acceptable, the framework suggests that stress and/or arousal is produced. In response to the stress the individual attempts to cope. If coping is successful, there may or may not be harmful effects on the individual. On the other hand, if coping is not successful, there is continued arousal and/or stress, which results in probable negative effects. Since most of the actual research on the effects of the physical environment focuses on negative effects and since most prevention efforts are aimed at reducing or eliminating negative effects, the emphasis in this chapter is on potential negative effects of environments and the prevention or reduction of negative effects. We do wish to recognize, however, that environments can facilitate positive, competence-enhancing effects, and we hope that future research and practice will focus on these aspects of the environment.

The framework suggests that there are different points in the process where prevention efforts can be directed. Catalano and Dooley (1980) distinguish between two types of *primary* prevention. Proactive primary prevention attempts to prevent the occurrence of risk factors, while reactive primary prevention aims to improve coping responses following exposure to stressors. In our framework, proactive prevention would eliminate or modify the environmental stressor or the aspect of the built environment that is provoking stress. Reactive primary prevention would help people cope

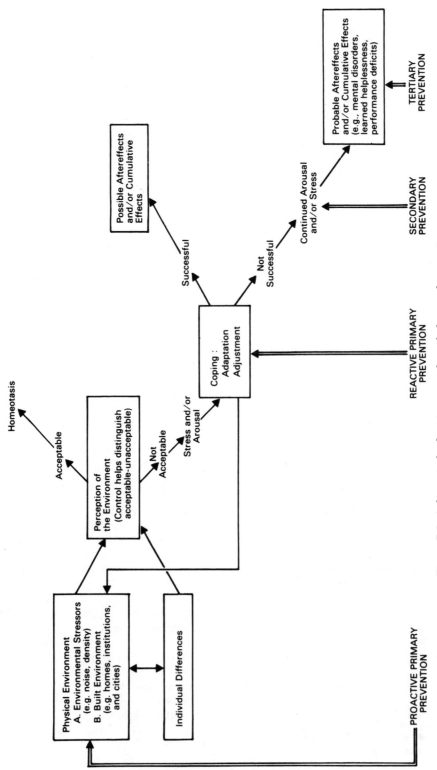

Figure 7.1. A framework of environmental psychology and prevention.

with the stress early in the process (before it is likely to produce harmful effects). *Secondary* prevention efforts would be targeted when initial coping attempts have not been successful and there is continued stress. *Tertiary* prevention would work to reduce the harmful effects.

This framework is broader than the traditional approaches in primary prevention taken by community psychologists. Catalano and Dooley (1980) note that the President's Commission on Mental Health aimed at *reactive prevention* (reducing the stressful consequences) and at *microlevel* interventions ("microlevel" refers to relatively small-scale foci such as small group and agency activities; "macrolevel" refers to large-scale foci such as state or federal policy). They argue that this emphasis is due to the greater familiarity mental health professionals have with microlevel and supportive interventions. We hope to broaden the perspectives and techniques of prevention activities, and propose that if environmental and community psychologists work together, they can work more effectively and efficiently on prevention activities on a broader array of issues and have more enduring effects.

We would like to emphasize that while our framework may appear to have a linear quality, we take a systems-oriented perspective in which the relationship between parts of the framework are dynamic, interactive, and often reciprocal. Feedback loops could be drawn into many parts of the framework to reflect this orientation. In order to facilitate the clarity of our discussion and the implications for preventive interventions, we have portrayed a framework that is simpler to follow and points out the major components and the general nature of the relationships.

## The Physical Environment

The air we breathe, the streets we walk on, and the environments we live and work in are generally inconspicuous. We tend to notice them only when something is wrong. Until recently, mental health professionals have paid relatively little attention to the role of environments in our lives. In this section we will review theory, conceptualization, and research on the roles that environmental stressors and the built environment can play in people's behavior and coping.

### Environmental Stressors

Low-quality environmental conditions such as high population density, air pollution, heat, noise, and toxic chemicals have received considerable attention from the public. Acute awareness of our environment

is brought about by crisis situations such as Love Canal or Three Mile Island. Daily conditions often do not draw special attention, although people do casually discuss the heat, the smelly air, or the noisy construction across the street. Environmental psychologists have been studying the effects of environmental stressors such as density, air pollution, noise, and toxic chemicals in the last ten years, and the topic of environmental stress was the focus of a recent special issue of the *Journal of Social Issues* (Evans, 1981). In this section, we will discuss these environmental stressors and their effects.

### DENSITY

The largest number of psychological studies on environmental stress has been performed on population density. A relationship between crowded conditions and urban riots in the late 1960s has been cited as one reason for this interest (Harries, 1980). Density has been distinguished from crowding in the following fashion: density is an objective measure of the number of people in a given space, while crowding is the negative psychological state which *may* result from high density.

The following studies illustrate some of the effects density can have on the social environment, performance, and health. One study investigated students who had been randomly assigned by the housing office to live in doubles or triples (that is, two people living in rooms designed for two people versus three people living in rooms designed for two people), due to a lack of dormitory space. Karlin, Epstein, and Aiello (1978) made assessments early in the first semester and at the end of the semester. The results showed that students living in triples had lower grades and lower performance on complex tasks. Tripled women had more physical and psychological problems than students living in doubles or tripled men, and all of the female triples dissolved by the end of the first semester.

In a study of the effects of density on social climate, interpersonal relations, and health in a juvenile correctional institution (Ray, Wandersman, Huntington, & Ellisor, in press), the social environment and treatment program deteriorated when density increased. The social climate of the dorm was disorganized, hostile, and disruptive under high-density conditions. For example, to the statement, "This unit is very well organized," 100 percent of the residents answered "false" during high density, while 42 percent answered "false" during low density. Additional studies on density in dormitories and prisons have found similar results (e.g., Baron, Mandel, Adams, & Griffen, 1976; Paulus, McCain, & Cox, 1978). Baum and Valins (1977) found that students living in high-density conditions were more likely to withdraw from social interaction.

The simple hypothesis that high density always leads to crowding and negative effects has not been supported by research (e.g., Baum & Valins, 1979; Freedman, 1975). A number of *mediating* conditions such as architectural features and feelings of control have been found to moderate the effects of high density (Baum & Valins, 1979). Baum and Valins propose that "crowding is experienced when high density inhibits individuals' ability to regulate the nature and frequency of their social interaction with others [p. 138]." Epstein (1981) concludes that the effects of density in laboratory and residential settings are ameliorated by control and the interpersonal orientation of the group (for example, competition versus cooperation) and thus group factors can moderate the effects of density.

## NOISE

Noise can be bothersome and can have important negative effects. The distinction between sound and noise is somewhat similar to the distinction between density and crowding. Noise is a psychological concept defined as "sound that is unwanted by the listener because it is unpleasant, bothersome, interferes with important activities, or is believed to be physiologically harmful [Cohen & Weinstein, 1981, p. 38]." Negative effects of noise have been demonstrated on cognitive abilities and social behavior.

Cohen, Glass, and Singer (1973) investigated the effects of highway noise on children living in high-rise apartments. Children on the lower (noisier) levels performed significantly more poorly on auditory discrimination and reading tests than children on higher floors. A similar pattern of difficulties was found in children whose classrooms were next to a railroad compared to those whose classes were on the other side of the building (Bronzaft & McCarthy, 1975). Cohen, Evans, Krantz, and Stokols (1980) investigated the effects of airplane noise on children in terms of feelings of personal control, attentional strategies, and physiological processes related to health. They compared children attending schools under the airport corridor of a busy metropolitan airport to children in quiet schools. The schools were matched for race and social class variables. Students from the noisier schools had higher blood pressure, were more likely to fail on a cognitive task, and were more likely to "give up" before the time to complete the task had elapsed than the children from quiet schools. Some expected

differences were not found (for example, reading scores).

Social behavior has also been affected by high noise levels (Glass & Singer, 1972; Page, 1977). Appleyard and Lintell (1972) studied streets which varied in the amount of traffic (and therefore traffic noise) they had. There was more casual social interaction on the light traffic street, while residents on the high traffic street reported that it was a more lonely place to live. Some of the coping behaviors used by adults to cope with residential noise include changing bedrooms, planting trees, and taking sleeping pills (Cohen & Weinstein, 1981).

Cohen and Weinstein (1981) note that several studies suggest relationships between noise and mental hospital admissions, although methodological problems exist with the studies. Similarly, studies have suggested relationships between noise and pregnancy complications and between noise and psychosomatic disorders, although methodological issues caution any conclusions at this point (Cohen & Weinstein, 1981).

## AIR POLLUTION

The hazy film hanging over the city, fumes from automobiles on the highways, billowing black smoke from industrial wastes, and even the unwanted cigarette smoke drifting your way—all constitute types of air pollution. The effects of air pollutants upon well-being have been pervasive enough to add another illness to medical terminology—APS, or air pollution syndrome, which is characterized by a number of complaints induced by overexposure to air pollutants and is essentially an allergic-type reaction (Bell et al., 1978). According to the President's Council on Environmental Quality, "in 1976, forty-three major cities comprising over half of the U.S. population had unhealthy air quality [Evans & Jacobs, 1981, p. 95]."

Air pollution, primarily carbon monoxide and sulfur dioxide, has been shown to affect scores on mental health and physical health indices. Strahilevitz, Strahilevitz, and Miller (1979), for example, found a relationship between air pollution and admissions to a psychiatric hospital. A recent study provides information that levels of pollutants in the air are predictive of crime rate and that cumulative effects (over a period of two days) are even more predictive—adding an 8.7% relative increase in predictive power (Lowensohn, 1977).

Evans and Jacobs (1981) indicate that performance under air pollution has not shown many significant interferences, when social stimulation is controlled for and when concentration is necessary. However, they do point out that many of these studies have been done with young, healthy adult males and have only been for short periods of exposure.

### TOXIC WASTES

The danger of toxic chemicals has been brought to public attention by national coverage of Three Mile Island and Love Canal and local coverage of numerous examples of toxic waste problems, from leaking barrels in recycling dumps to the derailing of railroad cars filled with dangerous substances. The psychological implications of toxic wastes provide a new area of investigation for environmental psychologists. A study of the aftereffects of the Three Mile Island (TMI) incident by Baum and his associates (1982) illustrates the role psychological research can play. The researchers compared residents living in four locations (living near TMI, living near an undamaged nuclear plant, living near a coal-fired plant, and not living near a power plant). They found that residents living near TMI reported more somatic and psychological problems (such as headache, nausea, depression, and anxiety) and showed poorer task performance and higher levels of catecholamines in the urine (a biochemical measure of stress) than the three comparison groups. The difference between the TMI and other residents still existed a year and a half after the incident.

In summary, environmental factors have been found to affect performance, physical and mental health, and interpersonal behavior. However, from previously reported studies on various environmental stressors it is readily apparent that psychological factors play an important role in people's perception of the environment and resulting behavior. The necessity for distinguishing between objective stimuli and the psychological state (density versus crowding, noise versus sound) provides evidence for this assertion. For example, it is not clear in the case of Three Mile Island discussed above whether the actual levels of radioactivity in the air were enough to be dangerous. Regardless of the radioactivity levels, the fear of what might happen, which was heightened by media coverage, added to the intensity of the stressor. There is clearly a need for more systematic psychological research on environmental stressors and more sophisticated longitudinal research designs which examine the role of mediating variables (Cohen & Weinstein, 1981; Evans & Jacobs, 1981).

## The Built Environment

In this section, we will focus on institutional environments, residential environments, and the urban environment to illustrate the relationship between the built environment, coping, and effects on behavior.

### *Institutional Environments: Mental Health Treatment Settings*

There has been a considerable amount of research relating environmental features to behavior in institutions such as mental hospitals and schools. While the studies described in this section generally do not focus on primary prevention, they illustrate applications of environmental psychology which may have implications for primary prevention in the future and they are pertinent to secondary and tertiary prevention. Social isolation and withdrawal are the characteristic behaviors a first-time visitor or a seasoned professional sees in a nonacute psychiatric mental hospital ward. Are these behaviors an inevitable concomitant of mental illness or is the design of the ward related to these and other important behaviors? Can changes in design lead to more positive behaviors?

Several studies suggest that seating arrangements can affect social interaction. Sommer and Ross (1958) found that women in a geriatric hospital room engaged in limited contact when chairs were in a row along dayroom walls. However, when seating was manipulated by the experimenters into small clusters of chairs, they discovered that conversation was facilitated. Similarly, Holahan (1972) found that quality and quantity of conversation were facilitated when small groups of male psychiatric patients were seated around a table, as opposed to being seated in rows around the wall.

While the preceding examples involve small-scale interventions into the problems of withdrawal, other research has focused on the effects of larger-scale redesign. Holahan and Saegert (1973) document the effects of a large-scale manipulation of the environment: ward redesign. Remodeling of a psychiatric admissions ward was based on the preferences and dissatisfactions of patients and staff who were interviewed, and consisted of repainting, refurnishing, and creating areas on the ward which "afforded a wide range of social options." Another admissions ward of the hospital did not undergo the redesign and served as a control. The hypothesis of the experiment, which was supported, was that after the remodeling, patients on the experimental ward would engage in more social behavior and would thus be less withdrawn than the patients on the control ward. In addition, it is important to note that the change in design effected a change in the ward social system. For example, new expectations and competencies developed among staff as they participated in the planning of the redesign, and the ward became a showplace for hospital administrators. Holahan notes that the increased feeling of competence and effectance learning during the process "generalized naturally to other role behaviors involving therapeutic planning, interpersonal staff relations, and more healthy contacts with patients [1979, p. 226]."

Whitehead, Polsky, Crookshank, and Fik (in press) also investigated the ward redesign of a 30-bed psychiatric unit in an aging federal hospital. In this project rooms were redesigned to provide a more flexible use of space, ranging from relatively private to relatively public use. In addition, several spaces were designed to encourage and focus social interaction around recreation, work, and other ward activities. As in the previous study, a similar ward which did not undergo redesign served as a control. Both subjective and objective measures indicated that "structural changes were accompanied by increased staff-patient contacts, . . . a redistribution of patients to areas for socializing, . . . and a significant reduction in the disabling psychopathology seen among the patients [Whitehead et al., in press]."

The preceding studies focused on the manipulation of furniture and physical space as a means of increasing the social interaction of psychiatric patients and thus preventing isolated, socially withdrawn behavior. Ittelson, Proshansky, and Rivlin (1970), however, approach the problem of passive, withdrawn behavior from another perspective by asserting that the issue underlying increased social interaction is the patient's freedom of choice. They discovered sharp behavioral differences between patients of single- and multiple-occupancy rooms. Those patients who occupied a single-occupancy room exhibited a wider range of behavior and less withdrawn behavior than those patients assigned to multiple-occupancy rooms. Residents who shared rooms were observed spending almost one-half of their time lying on their bed, either asleep or awake. Ittelson et al. account for this behavior by suggesting that the patient within the multiple-occupancy room sees his range of behavioral options as limited and is constrained to choose isolated, passive behavior over any other.

Knight, Zimring, Weitzer, and Wheeler (1978) found similar results in a project redesigning the living environment in a large state training facility for the developmentally disabled. Two types of renovations of large, open living quarters were performed: one renovation created single or double rooms with doors that could be locked, the second maintained the large sleeping room but 4½-foot partitions were built around the beds. The experiment consisted of sampling behaviors of residents both before and after renovation. In addition, residents' behaviors on the renovated wards were compared to the behaviors of residents from an unrenovated control ward. Preliminary reports indicated that residents recognized and used their

private spaces when such spaces were well defined. "Residents were more alert, interacted more with other residents, and used their own space more. These changes were seen despite the very low functional ability of the residents [Zimring, 1981, p. 154]." Zimring suggests that this was due to the environmental design allowing residents to control their social interaction and their ambient environment (heat, noise, light). Also, an increase in various socially valued activities such as appropriate use of space and respect for the privacy of others occurred both during and following renovation, especially for the occupants of one- and two-person bedrooms. However, the researchers note that respect for privacy of residents on the ward that had partitions was dependent upon staff behavior. When staff respected privacy in the partitioned areas, so did the residents. When the staff did not respect privacy, neither did the residents. Also, the staff were pressured by administrators and parents' organizations to perform supervisory and custodial roles. Therefore, staff were pressed to ignore some of the purposes of the new architectural design.

### Institutional Environments: Schools

Schools are one of the major institutional settings and cultural influences in our society. While most psychological aspects of schools have been studied extensively, relatively little research has been done on the effects of environmental factors on school children's behavior. Those involved in preventive efforts in the school need to consider a model of service delivery which is based on the child-environment relationship (Hiltonsmith & Keller, 1982). In this section we will briefly discuss several studies which suggest that physical environmental features in the school can affect behavior.

#### AMBIENT CONDITIONS

The Climate Group at the National Swedish Institute for Building Research has done extensive research on the effects of the thermal environment and, in particular, has looked at school children's performance under high temperatures. The researchers were able to exert a great deal of control over the exact ambient conditions and experimental design and found that students were less effective at arithmetic tasks and perform more poorly in language laboratories under hot conditions. Less able children were especially adversely affected, with many test results lowered under hot conditions (Lee, 1976). In comparing "model" to "marginal" thermal environments, one study found students performing more poorly on reasoning tasks and even on a clerical task (cf. Lee, 1976). They did not find learning from a film to be significantly affected, however. Weather outdoors has also been found to affect in-school behavior (Auliciems, 1972), with low outdoor temperatures, relatively low wind speeds, low relative humidity, and lack of sunshine significantly related to good performance.

Fluorescent lighting has been associated with hyperactive behavior which was reduced when lighting was changed to conventional full-spectrum lighting (Mayron, Ott, Nations, & Mayron, 1977). Learning disabled students seemed to be affected by the quality of the lighting, and this is proposed to be due to the radiation from the fluorescent lighting. Well-lit areas are considered to be pleasant and arousing, while contrast (or glare) is perceived as unpleasant (Mehrabian & Russell, 1974). Since full-spectrum lighting is less likely to result in glare or shadows, this is another possible explanation for Mayron et al.'s results.

### RESOURCES

The availability of play materials has been found to affect intellectual development, with disadvantaged children in particular (Wargo, Campeau, & Talmadge, in Jason, 1980). Availability affects social play, with the presence of social versus isolate play material dramatically increasing participation (Quilitch & Risley, 1973). Robson, Lipshutz, and Jason (in Jason, 1980) also looked at sharing behavior and the number of available toys. They found that elementary school children shared more when the number of play materials was restricted than when toys were available for all children.

Most schools have playground areas. "Adventure" playgrounds have grown in popularity in the past decade. These playgrounds look drastically different from their metal and plastic predecessors. The adventure playground is designed and created by children and is constructed of readily available materials, such as old tires and wood beams. These creative play areas are preferred over conventional playgrounds by school-age children and have materials (clubhouses and so on) which have been found to produce more peer interaction and verbal communication (Hayward, Rothenberg, & Beasley, 1974). Since children spend considerable time outdoors for recess periods, this aspect of the school's physical environment should not be ignored. Social behavior can also be affected by where play is occurring. Outdoors, more cooperative play occurs and boys participate in more dramatic social play. Indoors, children are more involved in individual solitary dramatic play—especially young children (Henninger, 1979).

### SEATING

Seating patterns can affect student performance. A horseshoe arrangement, seminar rooms, and informal-laboratory settings have been found to produce more discussion. Students in the front of traditional classrooms also participate more (Sommer, 1969). There is some evidence that mere seating affects performance. For example, in one study students were alphabetically assigned to seats in a large auditorium, and those in the middle (regardless of other characteristics) received higher test scores than those sitting on the sides (Stires, 1980). Simply sitting in a leadership position at a table also seems to automatically raise an individual's dominance or status as perceived by others (Arbarbanel, 1972; Hiers & Heckel, 1977).

### PHYSICAL DESIGN

The physical environment of the "open classroom" was originally conceptualized to have different learning "centers" in the room, so that the children could move from one to another as they completed their tasks. However, not all open classrooms employed this design. It has been observed that in some cases the only change from the traditional classroom was to make an entryway between same-grade classrooms (allowing students to change teachers for different classes) and then to call this an "open" classroom. It is not surprising that teachers sometimes found the noise from the adjacent classrooms disturbing! Due to difficulties in implementing open classroom concepts, mixed reviews of the use of this flexible model have caused the decline (and restructuring) of the open classroom concept (Gump, 1978). In general, it is the more creative, intelligent children who benefit from the unstructured classroom (O'Neill, 1976).

Little research has been done which controlled the physical and social environment of the classroom and other relevant variables to tell us exactly what effects the classroom has on children. In some instances researchers apparently did not use environmental research in investigating the physical environment. Several aspects of classroom ecology may need to be considered. In one study (Winnett, Battersby, & Edwards, 1975), elementary school students were moved from their one-piece chair-desks to smaller desks with movable chairs which had been arranged into groups of eight. Classroom behavior did not improve. Since children tend to consider their desks to be their territory and the space around it to be their personal space, it is not surprising that such an intervention did not improve classroom behavior (Freeman, 1978). More positive results have been obtained with college students. For example, providing school dorm residents with movable furniture rather than fixed furniture provides a wider range of options for interpersonal activities and results in more satisfied students (High & Sundstrom, 1977).

### SIZE

Barker and Gump's (1964) classic work demonstrated differences in student behavior when they are in small versus large schools. Even marginal students were encouraged to participate in activities in the small schools. Group size can affect children's behavior, with large, unstructured groups manifesting higher amounts of misbehavior than large structured or small structured groups (Jason, 1980). The problem inherent in these studies is that physical and social size factors have not been separated; thus it is unclear if it is the large school or the large number of students and the large classroom or the social size of the group which is affecting behavior.

In summary, while the quality of our schools is a major issue in society today, little attention has been paid to the physical environment of the schools as an influence on behavior. Those involved in preventive efforts in schools need to be aware of these research findings and to employ interventions appropriate to an environmental problem or potential problem.

### Residential Environments

The dwellings in which people live can serve as a physical and psychological shelter as well as a place for activities (e.g., Rainwater, 1966). In this section we will discuss how housing, including the individual living unit and the type of unit (for instance, high-rise or single family houses) is related to coping and outcomes.

Ruesch and Kees (1956) contend, from clinical observation, that arrangements of furniture in a home "designate and control the 'where' and 'how' of interaction [p. 128]." Also Behrens, Meyers, Goldfarb, Goldfarb, and Fieldsteel (1967) through similar observation note that the arrangement of furniture can reflect a family's disturbed pattern of interaction. However, in contrast to the number of studies investigating manipulation of furniture on behavior in institutions, no studies appear to exist which have investigated personal interaction when furniture is experimentally rearranged in the home. While the home is a very important environment for most people, relatively little environmental research has investigated behavior inside the dwelling, partly due to the difficulties involved in gaining access to the home. Significantly more research exists on the condition of

housing and type of housing (such as low-rise versus high-rise).

The condition of housing can influence health, behavior, and attitudes. Wilner, Walkley, Pinkerton, and Tayback (1962) compared 300 black families who recently moved from substandard private housing (that is, a slum) to new public housing with 300 families who continued to live in the slum. The researchers found some improvement in those who had moved to new housing, including better relations with neighbors and somewhat higher self-esteem. In addition, children's illnesses were less severe, resulting in better school attendance and better grades. As Michelson (1970) notes, however, the effect of a change in housing has its limits; it did not appreciably change social problems such as those involved in family life or the lack of aspiration for upward mobility. In addition, other studies have noted that moving from the slum to housing projects can increase satisfaction with the apartment but reduce satisfaction with the neighborhood (Hollingshead & Rogler, 1963; Yancey, 1971).

### HIGH-RISE HOUSING

Housing projects, especially high-rise apartments, have received considerable attention from environmental researchers. One feature of high-rise public housing which produces dissatisfaction is the height of the building. A height-related problem which is central to our framework involves the high-rise tenants' lack of control over their environment. Yancey (1971), in his interviews with residents of the Pruitt-Igoe complex in St. Louis, Missouri, found that the architectural design of the building was such that as soon as a child left the confines of the apartment unit, he was "out of mother's sight and direct control." Similarly, Heimstra and McFarling (1978) noted that mothers in high-rises are not able to supervise their children as well as mothers in ground-level row housing or single family units. Often the mother restricts her children's activity to the apartment, which reduces her opportunities for social interaction. This decrease in opportunity for social interaction is in sharp contrast to those mothers who live in single family dwellings or row housing and have an enclosed yard, and thus have increased opportunity for informal contact. These problems of height have led Cappon (1971) to conclude that high rises are poor environments for families due to the alienation, withdrawal, and psychosomatic symptoms they foster.

> Kids and parents are trapped with each other, they constantly get on each other's nerves. . . . The couple can't get out and away from each other to exercise, relax and replenish their

libido. . . . Inevitably their lovemaking is plagued by auditory invasion. They hear the screaming and jumping of the neighbors; the walls feel as if they are dissolving [cited in Middlebrook, 1980, p. 488].

An equally troubling control issue fostered by architectural design involves tenants' lack of ability to feel secure in their housing environment. The hallways as well as the open ground space of high-rise buildings often lack any semblance of symbolic or physical boundaries that can act as territorial markers. Based on the concept of territoriality and its importance, Newman (1972) developed the idea of "defensible space," and has examined the effects experienced by residents when spatially undefined conditions exist. Newman states that design "can make it possible for both inhabitant and stranger to perceive that an area is under the undisputed influence of a group, that they dictate the activity taking place within it, and who its users are to be [pp. 2–3]." This "strongly defined area of influence" is known as "defensible space." In many of his interviews with public housing tenants, Newman found that "expression of territorial feelings correspond strongly with a concern for maintenance of law [p. 51]." Since high-rises often lack territorial markers (and consequently areas considered defensible space), territorial feelings among the tenants often do not surface. This provides one explanation for why high-rise public housing is much more conducive to crime than public housing which is only three to six stories high and provides defensible space. Evidence for this hypothesis was found in a comparison of housing projects across the street from each other in New York City, that were matched in population characteristics. The high-rise Van Dyke project was "totally devoid of defensible space qualities," while the low-rise buildings of the Brownsville project had comparatively more defensible space qualities. The high-rise apartments were found to have 50 percent more total crime incidents, including over three and one-half times as many robberies and 64 percent more felonies and misdemeanors than the low-rise apartments. Because high-rises lack territorial markers and open space is not under surveillance, they are much more conducive to crime than public housing which is only two to three stories high. These conditions have led to the abandonment of facilities. The Pruitt-Igoe housing project in St. Louis, a "famous failure," has been completely abandoned and the government has begun systematic demolition of the buildings.

McCarthy and Saegart (1979) lend some support to Newman's findings. They found that people in low-rise structures expressed a willingness to prevent vandalism within their buildings, whereas those in high-rises indicated minimal willingness, even when the vandalism was on their floor. In addition, those in high-rise structures felt no one would help if they were attacked within their building, in contrast to the low-rise residents, who felt someone would respond.

The problems found in high-rise apartments are not limited to public housing projects for the poor. For example, Fanning (1967) studied the wives and children of army personnel who were randomly assigned to live in either an apartment or a house. Sickness was 57 percent higher for those living in apartments, especially psychoneurotic symptoms and respiratory infections. The differences are attributed to the cramped space and greater isolation of women who live in apartments removed from the ground. The psychoneurotic difficulties are attributed to the greater distance from outdoor spaces where the women can have social interaction with their neighbors. Fanning finds further support for his hypothesis when he shows that women who live in apartments and who don't have children (and are thus freer to come and go) had excellent mental health. While the data about children can be interpreted differently, the results are suggestive.

RESIDENTIAL DESIGN

Several studies indicate that architecture can influence friendship formation. The classic study by Festinger, Schachter, and Back (1950) found that friendships are influenced by physical and functional distance. Living close to somebody facilitates social interaction and friendship formation. However, this relationship is mediated by perceived homogeneity of residents and by their need for friendships (see Michelson, 1970, for a detailed discussion of the relationship of environments, social composition, and mutual assistance).

Baum and Valins (1977) note that the architectural design of a college dormitory can affect the residents' perception of crowding and consequently their patterns of interaction. Their hypothesis was that if the architectural design of the dormitory provided semiprivate spaces, small group formation would be facilitated and the individual's ability to control unwanted social interaction would be strengthened. The investigators compared students living in a suite design (six people, two in a room, shared bathroom and lounge) versus a hall or corridor design (17 double-occupancy rooms sharing a central bathroom and an end hall lounge). The research indicated that residents of suite-designed housing, a design which included more semiprivate space, experienced greater feelings of privacy, less sense of crowding, and less desire to avoid other hall residents. In contrast, the members of corridor design dormitories, which had little or no provision of semi-private space, experienced more feelings of lack of privacy, more sense of crowding, and an increased desire to avoid other hall residents. In addition to residents' self-reports, data from behavioral mapping provided evidence for social withdrawal by the corridor residents (Baum & Valins, 1977).

### The Urban Environment

Crowds of people walking quickly along a busy street, staring straight ahead, unsmiling, purposeful. Loud taxi horns blaring, jackhammers cracking streets, streets full of slow-moving cars, street vendors hawking novelties and hot dogs, tall buildings shading out the sun.

A quiet, tree-lined street, children bicycling up and down driveways, the houses are one- and two-story single and two-family units, a few cars are parked on a near-empty street, occasionally a car passes, two women are talking, a man is mowing his lawn.

Popular views of the city conclude that it fosters negative behavior; cities are places of stress, tension, fear, complexity, confusion, crime, pollution, and crowding (Fischer, 1976; Proshansky, 1978). Empirical evidence verifies that persons in cities are more likely to encounter environmental stressors (such as noise and density) which have been shown to have negative effects on individuals in certain situations. Proshansky (1978) suggests, however, that many urban researchers have assumed that the city is undesirable and thus have focused on negative effects. He proposes that the effects are more complex and more positive than the research has revealed.

Urban sociologist Claude Fischer has summarized these major sociological theories of urbanism:

1. DETERMINIST THEORY (also called *Wirthian theory* or *theory of urban anomie*) argues that urbanism increases social and personality disorders over those found in rural places.

2. COMPOSITIONAL (or *nonecological*) THEORY denies such effects of urbanism; it attributes differences between urban and rural behavior to the composition of the different populations.

3. SUBCULTURAL THEORY adopts the basic orientation of the compositional school but

holds that urbanism does have certain effects on the people of the city, with consequences much like the ones determinists see as evidence of social disorganization [1976, p. 27].

Fischer points out that the subcultural theory results in a model more fully consistent with empirical facts, although many research issues have yet to be resolved. He concludes that available psychological research on urban effects has produced "little evidence that the city alters people's basic psychological conditions—that it 'disorders' or isolates them [1976; p. 66]." Fischer (1978) further notes that the most popular current position in sociology is that there are no psychological consequences of urbanization per se. In fact, the second description above of a quiet, residential street is of an urban residential neighborhood.

The city is a blend of social, cultural, and economic environments as well as a diverse physical environment. Most studies of cities have correlated the sociocultural environment with indices of psychological health (such as crime, alcoholism, and mental health facility contact). One project (Brogan & James, 1980), which selected 104 indices of the physical environment to correlate with 21 indices of psychosocial behavior, indicated that characteristics of the physical environment are about as important as characteristics of the sociocultural environment in explaining variation in psychosocial health. Therefore, it is important to look at the physical environment of the city.

#### NEGATIVE EFFECTS

Many stimuli identified as potential environmental stressors are more prevalent in cities than in nonurban areas, such as noise, air pollution, and density. In addition, it has been found that high traffic in the street on which one lives is related to less social interaction among neighbors and more territorial withdrawal and concerns about safety (Appleyard & Lintell, 1972). Fear of crime is associated with emotional reactions (Lawton, Nahemow, Yaffe, & Feldman, 1976; Lewis, 1981). City dwellers are more likely to avoid affiliation with strangers (Milgram, 1978) and may be less willing to help others in need (Korte, 1978).

#### POSITIVE EFFECTS

Some theorists have emphasized the positive aspects of urbanism, although only minimal empirical research has been conducted. Proshansky (1978) implies that the structural diversity confronting the urban dweller promotes personal growth and ability. He argues that urbanites have the freedom and opportunity not only to expect environmental choices but also to make the choices. The urbanite may also learn more overlapping social roles and socially mediated coping techniques, which encourages the individual to respond positively to environmental change. Fischer (1976) proposes that the structural differentiation of cities results in highly supportive subcultures, which increases the likelihood that one will have friends like oneself, mutual assistance, and exposure to innovative ideas.

## URBAN-NONURBAN COMPARISONS

In the classic Midtown Manhattan study (Srole & Fischer, 1976), 23.7 percent of a representative sample of individuals living in Midtown Manhattan were considered psychiatrically impaired, perhaps supporting a stereotype that many city inhabitants have psychological problems. However, Srole (1976) compared this study to another classic epidemiological study which used a representative sample in a rural area, the Stirling County study in Nova Scotia. He suggests that there were significantly more individuals in the rural area who were psychiatrically impaired than in Manhattan.

Correlational research has provided inconsistent information. Urban areas, when compared to nonurban areas, reveal higher rates of crime (Harries, 1980), mental hospital admissions (Kirmeyer, 1978), and alcoholism (Fischer, 1976). But differences in rates may be attributable to more sophisticated reporting and/or service availability in urban areas. Fischer's (1976) review of the evidence suggests that (1) urbanites are increasingly reporting lower life satisfaction; (2) there is no consistent difference in the suicide rates between urban and rural areas; and (3) surveys reveal community size is not associated with stress symptoms or expressions of powerlessness.

Sadalla (1978) reviewed evidence that urban structural differentiation may promote anonymity, deindividuation, deviance, or differences in personality development which influences the individual's social behavior in various ways. For instance, certain styles of social interaction such as competitiveness, dominance, and dependence appear early among urban children, while rural environments tend to reinforce conflict avoidance, group orientation, and cooperation.

Franck (1980) compared the relationships formed by graduate student newcomers to New York City to those formed by graduate student newcomers to a town of 31,000. Franck found several surprising results. While the New York group had fewer friends two months after their move, by seven or eight months there were no differences in number of friends or frequency of contact with friends. However, in relationships with strangers, the urban group did report greater mistrust and fear. Urban newcomers also reported that they liked the variety of experiences and were more broad-minded. While there are limitations which qualify the findings (for example, the type of sample studied), the results suggest in a nutshell some of the strengths and weaknesses of urban life.

This brief review suggests that urban environments are complex and have a variety of effects, both positive and negative. Below we will use our framework to help organize how and why the urban environment has its effects. The urban environment presents an individual with objective physical conditions. How a physical condition, such as an environmental stressor, is perceived can be affected by individual differences. For example, urban newcomers from smaller communities are adversely affected by urban stressors. Newcomers report sensing higher levels of noise and crowding, and awareness of crime and fast pace of life (Wohlwill & Kohn, 1973). Differences between long-term urbanites and newcomers tend to disappear within the first year on most dimensions (Ittelson, 1978).

A number of psychological concepts have been proposed to explain how urban environments produce their effects. These concepts can be considered under the heading of "Perception of the Environment." Baldassare and Fischer (1977) review five different social psychological assumptions upon which urban sociological theory is based, noting the need to test these assumptions: (1) *psychic overload*, which assumes the city overstimulates and thus induces stress on individuals, requiring adaptation which may lead to pathology; (2) *territoriality*, which assumes the individual needs space and that frustration of this need leads to stress and perhaps pathology; (3) *structural differentiation*, which posits that higher densities create more numerous role opportunities for individuals, which may lead to identity problems and weakened social support; (4) *social-psychological theory*, which has focused on isolated factors such as density and crowding and subsequent effects; and (5) *nonecological theory*, which assumes that both urban and rural people conduct themselves in small groups, and that thus urbanism has no substantial impact on social life or personality.

Urban effects also vary by degree of *control* perceived by the individual (Cogen, 1978). Since certain subpopulations such as the elderly or the poor may have generalized low control, these groups may be at higher risk of disorder induced by environmental effects. Related to the framework, perception of the environment as unacceptable leads to attempts to *cope*. The attempts to cope can be successful or unsuccessful and can lead to the types of effects described earlier (for instance, affecting helping behavior and levels of social interaction).

The inconclusive results concerning the effects of the urban environment reflect the state of current psychological theory in this area. Generally studies of urban stressors and/or urban life have focused on isolated factors and assumed rather simplistic views of the person-environment interaction. Proshansky (1978) criticizes the dearth of theory and notes that researchers are intensely gathering data without making theoretical linkages.

In the following sections we will discuss in more detail factors and processes which mediate the relationship between the physical environment and its effects on mental health.

## Individual Differences

Environmental psychology has emphasized the influence of the physical environment on behavior. The influence of individual differences in affecting perception and coping with environmental conditions is an underdeveloped area. Craik (1976) and Wandersman and Florin (1981) discuss the conceptual importance of examining the interaction of the person and the situation and the important contributions that can be made by combining aspects of the personology and environmental psychology literatures. Below we provide several examples which point to the potential importance of this area. Weinstein (1978) found that college students who reported greater sensitivity to noise had lower intellectual ability and less confidence during interpersonal interactions. Leonard and Borsky (1973, in Baum et al., 1981) found high correlations of fear of nearby airplane crashes with individual annoyance with airport noise. Prior experience plays an important role in perception of the environment, as demonstrated in several studies such as Wohlwill and Kohn's study (discussed earlier) which related adaptation level to perception of the environment.

The relationship between the built environment and individual differences is further illustrated in studies with children and families. The age of a patient is an important factor in designing psychiatric facilities. Rivlin, Wolfe, and Beyda (1973) note the need children have for play space. Hospital wards are confining and children's play may bother the staff. Instead of recognizing that a normal child might behave similarly in a restricted physical space, children's active behaviors in the ward are often defined as part of the disorder. This suggests that design should attempt to facilitate the normal behaviors for a given population. Altman, Nelson, and Lett (cited in Altman, 1975) differentiate

two family types from which implications for design can be made. The "open" or informal type makes minimal use of the environment to control privacy. The family members' openness is evidenced by open bedroom doors and many common areas shared by all family members. On the other hand, the second family type uses environmental controls over privacy. Specifically, the family may designate rooms as the specific territories of certain members and may be more inclined to close doors to accomplish privacy. Clearly, differing design options would be needed for satisfactory family communication. Whereas the first family type would be less bothered by a design which provided for minimal privacy, the second family might experience interpersonal stress and tension because of such a design.

Environmental conditions vary in the extent to which perception and human behavior are influenced by individual differences. In other words, some environments have stronger and more uniform impacts (such as a nuclear meltdown) than others (a high-density room). The sparseness of research in this and other areas suggests an urgent need for research on the interaction of individual differences with the physical environment.

## Perception of the Environment: The Significance of Personal Control

Perception of the environment is influenced by objective physical conditions and individual differences. A judgment is made about whether the environment is in the acceptable or unacceptable range. (Some models refer to the judgment as optimal or nonoptimal; we find the term "optimal" too extreme.) Perception of the environment involves a number of processes and concepts, including risk, novelty and complexity, and territoriality and privacy (see Bell et al., 1978 for a review).

Privacy and social interaction are key concepts and concerns in the environments we have discussed—mental hospitals, schools, residential environments, and urban settings. In these settings people do not seem to want too much or too little social interaction. Altman (1975; Altman, Vinsel & Brown, 1981) has crystallized this issue by discussing privacy as a dialectic which involves *control* over social interactions with others. Sometimes people want to be with others. When they do not achieve their desired state of interaction (that is, too much privacy), feelings of social isolation result. When there is more interaction than the person wishes, then the person feels crowded. The key issue, then, is *control* over the amount of interaction itself. Now we can see the importance of control in the perception of the environment box in Figure 7.1. Control or lack of control influences whether one feels crowded, or one's territory is infringed, or overloaded with stimuli, and so forth. In this section we will focus on the role of control in perception of the environment.

The concept of control is being discussed as perhaps the most significant element in understanding the effects of stressful environments on human behavior (Cohen & Sherrod, 1978). A common theme underlying the discussion is that the person who can exercise control or believes that control is available is more likely to be mentally healthy since he or she can adjust an undesirable environment or adapt positively to environmental stressors. Although a need exists for the refinement of the control concept (Baum, Singer, & Valins, 1978), our focus will be to review selected evidence pertaining to control as a mediator of environmental stress effects.

An individual need only believe in his or her ability to control the environment in order for psychological benefits to occur (Geer & Maisel, 1972; Glass & Singer, 1972). Such *perceived control* does not imply the ability to implement actual control. Perceived control may result from actual control, from information suggesting potential control, or from any social or psychological interventions that make the environment appear more manageable (Sherrod & Cohen, 1978).

Cohen and Sherrod (1978) provide a concise overview of various psychological theories about why control affects human responses to crowding stress. At a general level, perceived control is theorized to affect a person's self-perceptions, expectancies, and motivation, so that the perception that a person can effectively manipulate the environment increases that person's sense of competence. Weak or low control leads to expectations of ineffectiveness, addressed in learned helplessness theory (Seligman, 1975). From a cognitive overload perspective, perceived control can be interpreted as relaxing a person's attentions to the environment for unpredictable and threatening inputs, which allows greater responsiveness to other attentional demands such as task performance or social behavior, thus promoting healthy functioning (Cohen, 1978).

### Empirical Evidence of Control as a Mediator of Stress

Empirical evidence that an individual's perception of control over aversive events significantly influences his or her stress reactions has been demonstrated for such environmental stressors as noise (Glass & Singer, 1972), crowding (Baron & Rodin, 1978; Cohen & Sherrod, 1978), traffic (Novaco, Stokols, Campbell, & Stokols, 1978), and train commuting (Singer, Lundberg, & Frankenhaeuser, 1978). Adverse effects of relatively low perceived control include aftereffects following cessation of the stressor (Cohen et al., 1980; Sherrod, 1974). Cohen and Sherrod (1978) have posited that the inconsistent findings in experimental research on density can be explained by the concept of control; that is, negative density effects on human behavior may be attributable to uncontrollability rather than to density per se. They also suggest that certain populations may be more susceptible to physical and mental distress because as a group their general expectancies for control over environments is low. Such groups include the very young, the old, the poor and uneducated, and persons living in institutions.

## Coping

In our framework, arousal and/or stress follows the perception of the physical environment as unacceptable. This leads to coping behaviors. It is useful to distinguish two types of behavioral coping responses to the environment: (1) adaptation (a quantitative shift in a response as a result of continued exposure to an environmental stimulus), and (2) adjustment (a change in behavior which modifies the environmental stimulus) (Wohlwill, 1972). Behavior which uses the environment in unintended ways can also be considered adjustment (Wandersman, Murday, & Wadsworth, 1979). Behaviorally, we may liken adaptation to a passive, acceptive response to the environmental stimuli or forces (that is, the person's behavior is modified to fit the environment). Adjustment may be considered a response which modifies or manipulates the environment to make the environment more congruent with the person's needs. For example, if a student is studying for finals in the dormitory and a group of people are talking loudly in the hall, the student can adjust his or her environment by closing the door or asking the noisemakers to move to the lounge, or adapt by stopping work and daydreaming. Bell, Fisher, and Loomis (1978) describe a number of findings and approaches in environmental psychology organized around the concepts of adaptation and adjustment. They discuss adaptation in terms of molding behavior to fit the environment—for example, becoming accustomed to the pollution level of a city. Adjustment is discussed in terms of molding the environment to fit behavior through environmental design.

## Implications for Prevention

In this section we discuss implications for prevention for several of the major sections in the framework.

## Environmental Stressors

The most obvious, but by no means the easiest, preventive programs involving environmental stressors involve primary proactive prevention which would remove the stressor. Building more dormitories so that high density does not exist, creating regulations limiting noise or not building schools and airports near each other, passing legislation reducing air pollutants, or not building nuclear reactors represent prevention examples at the macrolevel that would eliminate stress and the potential effects that can follow. These are difficult to implement and may be viewed as beyond the scope of many psychologists because they involve policy and legislation. But roles do exist for psychologists in helping to implement large-scale interventions or providing research information relevant to policy formulation (e.g., Stough & Wandersman, 1980).

Microproactive preventive programs may be easier for psychologists in traditional roles to be involved in (Catalano & Dooley, 1980). Several studies have found that high density and corridor architectural design in dormitories lead to crowding, negative affect, withdrawal, and behavior symptomatic of learned helplessness by affecting the degree to which an individual can control social contact. Baum and Davis (1980) experimentally investigated the effects of an architectural intervention which reduced the number of residents living on a long corridor from 40 to 20. The intervention converted three bedrooms in the middle of the corridor into a lounge, essentially bisecting the floor. They found that students living in the bisected dorm corridor had more positive interaction on the floor, more confidence in their ability to control events in the dormitory, and less withdrawal in both residential and nonresidential settings. This positive experience was equivalent to an unbisected control *short*-corridor dorm. The results show more symptoms of stress, withdrawal, and helplessness on the long corridor. The authors conclude, "Direct architectural intervention prevented crowding stress and post stressor effects. In the long run a preventive strategy of the kind taken in the present research may be more beneficial to residents of high-density settings than treatment programs instituted after the problem has been identified [p. 480]."

Several studies have investigated reactive interventions to reduce stress in high-density situations. Clinical strategies have been explored which aimed at coping skills. Karlin, Katz, Epstein, and Woolfolk (1979) used behavioral or perceptual cognitive techniques such as restructuring the situation, distraction, and relaxation. Other studies have used nonclinical strategies such as providing preparatory information about the upcoming situation (e.g., Langer & Saegert, 1977) or providing people with actual or perceived control over the situation (e.g., Rodin, Solomon, & Metcalf, 1978). Right now the research in this area is preliminary, but it is promising. Similar types of prevention interventions at the proactive and reactive level either have been or can be developed for other environmental stressors.

## Built Environment

There has not been much empirical evidence to show the preventive effects of interventions involving the built environment. Below we provide some examples which suggest preventive effects in the built environment, even though empirical evidence may not be available.

At the primary proactive level, design incorporating defensible space concepts may reduce alienation, fear, and crime, and increase control. Dingemans and Schinzel (1977) indicate that several cities and states have adopted policies requiring that plans for new public housing be examined by boards or police departments in light of security design principles. Noting, however, that the "vast majority of new housing being built today is neither high-rise, nor public housing," Dingemans and Schinzel (1977) indicate that preventive design principles must be applied to the design of the most rapidly increasing type of housing, low-rise garden apartments and suburban townhouses. Based on a survey of 75 townhouse developments in northern California, the authors make several recommendations to ensure "defensible space defects" will not be repeated. These recommendations could be applied to public housing as well:

> Subdivide the homes into small clusters of houses that are clearly labeled and share a definite area of open space and parking. . . . Provide better surveillance of the garage entrances and parking spaces. . . . Provide private space around the front and rear of each house, even if it requires subdividing part of the greenbelt. . . . Provide outdoor recreation areas for children that are within the view and territorial domain of individual homes. . . . Place the windows and home face to face with the greenbelts in such a way that residents will actually look out of their windows on a regular and casual basis without feeling that anyone's privacy is being invaded. . . . Establish and use a design bank of superior design ideas [pp. 35–36].

At a primary prevention reactive level, strategies to promote positive coping include the targeting of situations or populations for which risk of mental disorder is high. Levi and Andersson (1975) address the issue of high-risk urban situations by calling for a policy that creates an "early warning system" which would alert program administrators to the possibility that negative effects may result from impending changes in the population and/or environment. Such changes would be likely to expose many people to new physical or social structures and processes, requiring major adaptations. Crisis intervention could be offered as a means to prevent serious disorder. For instance, when a particular neighborhood is targeted for "redevelopment," which typically refers to physical renovations that subsequently affect the social environment, psychological and social interventions could be offered to the neighborhood residents prior to the physical interventions. High-risk populations would include those with high rates of generalized low control, such as the elderly, the young, the poor, or groups undergoing rapid change (for example, newcomers from rural or foreign areas). Planned interventions can enhance coping and increase sense of control. For example, educational programs to increase understanding of the urban environment have been offered for cultural groups such as Native Americans who leave reservations for jobs or training in the city and Indo-Chinese refugees newly arrived in American cities.

At a secondary prevention level, an example offered by Harshbarger (1976) in describing the psychological effects of a crisis suggests the need to consider the environment in planning treatment interventions. Harshbarger notes that following the Buffalo Creek flood, in which hundreds of families suddenly lost their homes, priorities among emergency personnel were to (1) clear the debris, and (2) locate quasi-permanent shelter for persons who lost their homes. The Department of Housing and Urban Development provided mobile homes to the survivors. However, when families were assigned to mobile homes, no attempt was made to cluster residents according to their former neighborhoods; thus, social groupings among the survivors were further splintered. Harshbarger notes such action probably negatively affected the individuals' adaptation to stress. By planning the environment to accommodate existing social networks, adaptation costs might have been prevented.

## Control

Available evidence supports the position that enhancing a person's opportunity to perceive or exercise control

when confronted with an environmental stressor will promote healthy coping and prevent negative effects such as decreased task performance, generalized helplessness, or more severe pathology. Strategies to maximize control can be regarded as preventive interventions. Recommendations for how to maximize control generally fall into three categories: (1) designing, constructing, and/or modifying environments so that they are "responsive," maximizing the user's ability to achieve his or her goals and to control social interactions (Carr & Lynch, 1978; Leff, 1978); (2) providing information and/or experiences to change the individual's attitudes toward the environment (Cohen & Sherrod, 1978) or skills and resources for coping with the environment (Baron & Rodin, 1978); and (3) increasing freedom of choice regarding selection (Korte, 1978) and/or periodic escapes from environments (Cohen & Sherrod, 1978). A number of advocates speak of redistributing societal power in order to enhance individual control (Leff, 1978; Rappaport, 1981; Turner, 1976). Interventions to maximize control must be directed at reducing barriers to the perception and exercise of control as well as creating new opportunities for control.

## Coping

The issue of coping and the processes of adaptation and adjustment are central to prevention. In our earlier prevention examples, environmental and community psychology experts played the major role in developing strategies to help people cope with the stressor. While self-help and informal support groups have been given attention by community psychologists and user participation has been acknowledged by environmental designers, the role of citizens in prevention, especially proactive prevention, seems to be an undeveloped resource. The story at the beginning of this chapter illustrates the active role one citizen took in attempting to deal with both the stressor and the stress it produced. Mrs. Dooley developed an organization to help people cope with pregnancy problems (reactive primary prevention and secondary prevention) and pressured state health officials to check pesticide levels (attempt at proactive prevention). Citizen participation and citizen involvement are appealing concepts for ideological and pragmatic reasons, yet they have not really been systematically included within the prevention area. Participation represents a form of adjustment. We feel that participation has a potentially useful role to play in prevention activities, and therefore would like to discuss it here.

Citizen participation (participation by the user, consumer, client, resident, and so on in decision-making) has been proposed as a major strategy for optimizing environments because it enables citizens to influence, plan, or otherwise affect the environment or program and thus increase the congruence of the environment with individual needs and values, and foster satisfaction, responsibility, positive self-concept, and positive behaviors. It can be a method for increasing control over an environment. Wandersman (1979a) found that participants who designed dormitory environments had greater liking of the environment (even though quality of the environment was constant), and felt more creative, responsible, and helpful and less anonymous than nonparticipants. Participation increased congruence between a person's own needs and values and the designed environment, and feelings of *control* over the environment.

Participation as a strategy incorporates a number of prevention principles, including (1) early intervention before symptoms of disorder appear; (2) the potential to affect and involve large numbers of people; (3) belief in the competence of people to help themselves and solve problems; (4) basis in a growth model which assumes (a) people can change, particularly in response to educative intervention, (b) environments are dynamic, and (c) person-environment interactions can be targeted for positive change; and (5) intervention into natural systems, since people are continuously interacting with their environments. Participation meets Caplan's (1964) criteria for social action as part of a prevention program by (1) attenuating hazardous circumstances, for example, removing the stress-inducing properties of environments through more satisfactory designs; and (2) providing services to foster healthy coping, for example, allowing citizens to develop competencies and positive feelings through the process of participation. These principles and criteria serve as a foundation for relating participation to prevention. There is a vast literature in the area of participation. Wandersman (1979b, 1981) has developed frameworks which attempt to systematize theory and research on participation in planning environments and participation in community organizations. Critical issues are addressed which need to be asked in regard to prevention as well; for example, which people participate and which do not, what techniques of participation can be used, what are the characteristics of successful organizations, and what are the effects of participation for the individual and the community?

Many examples of citizen participation exist, including block and neighborhood organizations. Increasingly, neighbors are joining together by participating in neighborhood organizations to enhance their neighborhood support systems, exercise their political skills to solve neighborhood problems, and,

as a consequence, better the quality of their living environment (Ahlbrandt & Cunningham, 1979; Boyte, 1980; Rich, 1979, 1980). Minimal estimates of the number of active neighborhood associations existing range from four to eight thousand groups. These neighborhood organizations have been successful in tackling such issues as neighborhood preservation, zoning and land use, and crime and safety (Perlman, 1976, 1978). Wandersman's (1978) longitudinal study of participation in block organizations investigates such issues as: (1) who participates and why (demographic, psychological and event variables related to participation in Wandersman, Jakubs, & Giamartino, 1981; cognitive social learning variables related to participation in Wandersman & Florin, 1981); (2) what are the effects of citizen participation on the individual, interpersonal relationships, and the group; and (3) what characteristics of the organization (for instance, cohesiveness, order, and organization) are related to satisfaction and involvement in the organization (Giamartino & Wandersman, in press). The study will aid in the evaluation of citizen participation as a strategy for optimizing environments.

In addition to the potential benefits of participation discussed above, participation may enable community and environmental psychologists to get beyond some of the problems that Rappaport (1981) argues are part of the prevention model, including dependency and the perpetuation of a professional-client relationship. Rappaport proposes a collaborative relationship in which citizens have control over their own lives. There are many citizen participation cases which can serve as examples of this type of relationship.

## The Potential for Collaboration between Environmental, Community, and Clinical Psychology

Cowen (1980) cites two major factors in mental health that have encouraged interest in prevention: (1) "The frustration and pessimism of trying to undo psychological damage once it had passed a certain critical point; (2) the costly, time-consuming, culture-bound nature of mental health's basic approaches, and their unavailability to, and ineffectiveness with, large segments of society in great need [p. 259]." The ultimate goal of primary prevention, according to Cowen, is "to engineer structures, processes, situations, events, and programs that maximally benefit, both in scope and temporal stability, the psychological adjustment, effectiveness, happiness, and coping skills of large numbers of individuals [p. 264]." The general thrust in the mental health field has been on reactive and microlevel (small-group) interventions, illustrated by the President's Commission on Mental Health and the vast majority of prevention programs undertaken by mental health workers (Catalano & Dooley, 1980). The reason for this seems to be that these approaches are more suited to the perspective and training of mental health professionals. Yet as this chapter attempts to demonstrate, utilization of knowledge about environments and behavior and interventions aimed at environments are among the more powerful approaches available for meeting Cowen's criteria of maximum benefit in scope and stability. The achievement of preventive interventions that involve the design and programming of built environments, the removal of environmental stressors, and the enhancement of people to cope with environments will benefit from a collaboration of environmental, community, and clinical psychologists. This collaboration is necessary because each has special knowledge and skills to contribute and because each has been limited in perspective and skills by "virtue" of their training. The collaboration can be enhanced by citizen input and activity, as was suggested in the earlier section on citizen participation.

A study by Holahan (1979) which instituted new ward designs in a psychiatric hospital illustrates the difficulties that can occur in environmental design interventions and the need for multiple skills and perspectives. Staff resistance was an important factor affecting the results. While some attempts were made to include staff input in the planning, there was still staff coldness toward the planners. For example, while all the parties had agreed to a plan to install partitions for privacy in advance, on the day the carpenters arrived the nursing staff decided against it, and the carpenters left. Then a compromise was reached and the partitions were installed. However, two weeks later the "evening staff had not assigned any patients to the new bedrooms, choosing instead to put patients in alcoves and hallways [Holahan, 1979, p. 253]." In addition to knowledge about environments, this situation required knowledge and skills about power, communication, and consultation, and an active willingness to get involved in social change. These are among the major skills that community psychologists develop. Environmental psychologists have tended to be objective researchers, carefully trained in research methods but generally not trained to take part in implementing interventions. Therefore, collaboration between environmental and community psychologists for planning better environments represents a natural marriage. (However, we do not believe the different approaches to training should remain fixed. There should be more communication and interchange in knowledge and skill areas for both community and environmental psychologists.)

In addition, community psychology has been concerned with aspects of the community that generally have not been part of environmental psychology. The framework in Figure 7.1 was primarily influenced by an environmental psychology approach (except for the prevention aspects). The framework portrays a sequence from environment to effects that primarily takes an *individual* perspective—how does the environment affect an individual's coping and behavior? However, the framework does not really take into account the group and community context of the individual. For example, the social characteristics of the group that an individual belongs to can influence the perception of an environmental stressor or the built environment, as illustrated in the following two examples.

If a plant is the primary employer for a town, then the community may perceive the sounds coming from the plant as not harmful. The town of Boron seems to welcome the aircraft noise from Edwards Air Force Base because of the base's economic contribution to the community.

> Despite the fact that, on an average, some four hundred flights a day take off from Edwards, and it is not unusual for a town to be rocked by twenty to thirty sonic booms between dawn and dusk, almost no one objects. On the contrary, the town makes a virtue of its affliction. "Air progress and history are made daily in the Boron area," proclaims a brochure put out by the Chamber of Commerce. Boron, it continues, ought to be called "The Boom Capital of the World" [Murray, 1972, cited in Ittelson, Proshansky, Rivlin, & Winkel, 1974, p. 307–308].

Merry (1981), in her discussion of the defensible space concept, notes that while architectural design is necessary to create spaces which can be defended, it is not always sufficient to ensure safety or prevention of crime. Using anthropological participant observations of a small inner-city housing project which conformed to defensible space design, she observed that several factors are essential for effective defense in addition to design. Within the project she investigated there was ethnic heterogeneity as well as a lack of interaction across these ethnic lines. Consequently, each group was unfamiliar and puzzled about the family structure and friendship patterns of the other groups, often resulting in inability to identify those who "belonged" and misinterpretation of interaction. In addition to the fragmented social organization and prevalence of stranger relationships among bystanders, the defensible space often remained undefended due to fear of retaliation and a sense of futility about calling the police.

The environmental psychology approach does not appear to have paid as much attention to factors affecting stress and coping as community and clinical psychologists have. Considerable research has been performed on the resources that can affect coping, including individual resources (such as skills, experiences), social networks and social support, and professional resources (consultation, advocacy, or therapy). The role of control and power has been extensively discussed (for example, community control issues). The effects cited in the environmental framework (Figure 7.1) have been individual effects. Group and community effects can also result from the process including changes in the environment itself, in social networks, and in the demographic makeup of the community. The new aspects outlined here (group context, resources, group and community effects) supplement the framework in Figure 7.1 and are presented in Figure 7.2 in the boxes with dotted lines.

Clinical psychologists can play an important role in this collaboration. Clinical psychologists have largely been responsible for developing the techniques that can be used and have been used in primary reactive, secondary, and tertiary prevention, including stress inoculation, cognitive restructuring, and behavioral training (see Catalano & Dooley, 1980). In addition, clinical psychologists can act as important advocates for primary proactive prevention.

A collaborative strategy should facilitate the identification of the most effective and efficient focus for an intervention. There would be greater flexibility in developing appropriate interventions with a broader array of skills. Below we outline several ways in which environmental knowledge can be used by collaborative interests to improve placement and care in mental-health-related environments such as psychiatric hospitals and group homes. These suggestions are presented in more detail in Wandersman and Moos (1981) and can be applied to many other types of environments as well.

### COMPARING AND CONTRASTING PROGRAMS

Environmental assessment procedures can provide more differentiated information upon which to compare programs than do current data, which are usually limited to staff-resident ratios and cost-per-resident figures. The data can be used by administrative personnel as a management tool to provide an up-to-date picture of ongoing resident care, to identify potential trouble spots, and to institute preventive action.

### FACILITATING ENVIRONMENTAL CHANGE

Feedback of information on social and physical environments can facilitate environmental change. Feedback can be provided about a program, about how different groups compare with each other (such as residents and caretakers), and about how the setting compares to what people consider ideal. Ways in which specific changes can be made can then be outlined.

### FORMULATING CLINICAL CASE DESCRIPTIONS

Information about people's environments can be used in case descriptions to help plan treatment and placement (see Moos & Fuhr, 1982).

### MAXIMIZING ENVIRONMENTAL INFORMATION

Environmental assessment procedures may be useful in compiling more accurate and complete descriptions of living environments. Giving residents and caretakers information about a program can enhance the accuracy of their perceptions and/or expectations and make it easier for them to adapt to a new environment. The information can also be used to select an appropriate placement for a particular person, and thereby may help to increase satisfaction and morale.

### ENHANCING ENVIRONMENTAL COMPETENCIES

Knowledge concerning the ways in which the environment relates to human functioning can be used to teach people how to create, select, and transcend environments, that is, to enhance environmental competence. People can be sensitized to the characteristics of varied behavior settings and taught what to expect and how to act in these settings. Or those responsible for selecting the environments of others, such as social workers who make decisions about community placements, can do so with a greater awareness of the traits or behaviors which alternative environments encourage. There is a need for environmental educators who can teach people about their environment—how to conceptualize its component parts and their interrelationships, and how to understand and control its potential impact in their everyday lives.

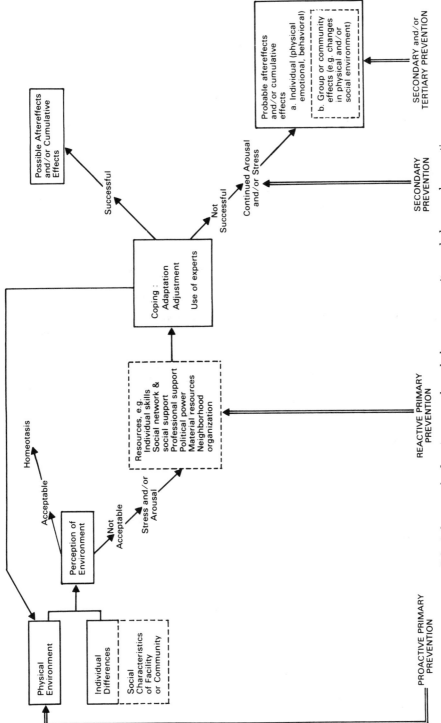

Figure 7.2. A framework of environmental psychology, community psychology, and prevention.

INFLUENCING THE DESIGN OF NEW
ENVIRONMENTS OR THE RENOVATION OF
OLD ENVIRONMENTS

Suggestions from previous research can be used to design environments that facilitate positive behaviors such as social interaction and client control over unwanted interaction. As experience dictates, consultation with important user groups is warranted.

Serious interest in optimizing environments requires a broad approach to conceptualizing, assessing, and evaluating environments and to utilizing knowledge about people and environments (Stough & Wandersman, 1980; Wandersman & Moos, 1981). This would be greatly enhanced by collaborative relationships which use the combined knowledge and skills of environmental, community and clinical psychologists.

## Concluding Comment

One of our major goals in this chapter has been to increase psychological interest in the relationship between the everyday physical environments in which people live and work, and adaptive and maladaptive behaviors. We have presented frameworks which help to organize these relationships and suggest places for prevention. They should be helpful in suggesting directions for future research and practice. They may also serve as a basis for the development of psychological impact assessments or community mental health impact assessments of environments. We encourage the development of collaborative relationships among environmental, community, and clinical psychologists and citizens which offer "real visions" for improving our environments and the quality of our lives.

## References

Ahlbrandt, R. S., & Cunningham, J. V. *A new public policy for neighborhood preservation.* New York: Praeger, 1979.

Altman, I. *The environment and social behavior: Privacy, personal space, territory and crowding.* Monterey: Brooks/Cole, 1975.

Altman, I., Vinsel, A., & Brown, B. B. Dialectic conceptions in social psychology: An application to social penetration and privacy regulation. In L. Berkowitz (Ed.), *Advances in experimental social psychology.* Vol. 14. New York: Academic Press, 1981.

Appleyard, D., & Lintell, M. The environmental quality of city streets: The residents' viewpoint. *Journal of the American Institute of Planners,* 1972, **38**(2), 84–101.

Arbarbanel, A. *Redefining the environment: Behavior and physical setting.* New York: School of Industrial Relations, 1972.

Auliciems, A. Some observed relationships between atmospheric environments and mental work. *Environmental Research,* 1972, **5**, 217–240.

Baldassare, M. & Fischer, C. The relevance of crowding experiments to urban studies. In Stokols, D. (Ed.), *Perspectives on environment and behavior: Theory, research, and applications.* New York: Plenum Press, 1977.

Barker, R. G., & Gump, P. V. *Big school, small school.* Stanford: Stanford University Press, 1964.

Baron, R. M., Mandel, D. R., Adams, C. A., & Griffen, L. M. Effects of social density in university residential environments. *Journal of Personality and Social Psychology,* 1976, **34**, 434–446.

Baron, R. M., & Rodin, J. Personal control as a mediator of crowding. In Baum, A., Singer, J., & Valins, S. (Eds.), *Advances in environmental psychology.* Vol. 1. *The urban environment.* Hillsdale, N.J.: Lawrence Erlbaum, 1978.

Baum, A., Collins, D. L., & Singer, J. E. Coping with chronic stress at Three Mile Island: Psychological and biochemical evidence unpublished manuscript, 1982.

Baum, A., & Davis, G. E. Reducing the stress of high density living: An architectural intervention. *Journal of Personality and Social Psychology,* 1980, **38**(3), 471–481.

Baum, A., Singer, J. E., & Baum, C. S. Stress and the environment. *Journal of Social Issues,* 1981, **37**(1), 4–35.

Baum, A., Singer, J., & Valins, S. (Eds.) *Advances in environmental psychology.* Vol. 1. *The urban environment.* Hillsdale, N.J.: Lawrence Erlbaum, 1978.

Baum, A., & Valins, S. *Architecture and social behavior.* Hillsdale, N.J.: Lawrence Erlbaum, 1977.

Baum, A., & Valins, S. Architectural mediation of residential density and control: Crowding and the regulation of social contact. In L. Berkowitz (Ed.), *Advances in experimental social psychology.* Vol. 12. New York: Academic Press, 1979.

Behrens, M. L., Meyers, D. I., Goldfarb, W., Goldfarb, N., & Fieldsteel, N. D. The Henry Ittelson Center Family Interaction Scales. *Genetic Psychology Monographs,* 1969, **80**, 203–295.

Bell, P. A., Fisher, J. D., & Loomis, R. J. *Environmental psychology.* Philadelphia: Saunders, 1978.

Boyte, H. C. *The backyard revolution.* Philadelphia: Temple University Press, 1980.

Brogan, D. R., & James, L. D. Physical environment correlates of psychosocial health among urban residents. *American Journal of Community Psychology,* 1980, **8**(5), 507–522.

Bronzaft, A. L., & McCarthy, D. P. The effect of elevated train noise on reading ability. *Environment and Behavior,* 1975, **7**, 517–528.

Caplan, G. *Principles of preventive psychiatry.* New York: Basic Books, 1964.

Cappon, D. Mental health in the high rise. *Canadian Journal of Public Health,* 1971, **62**, 426–431.

Carr, S., & Lynch, K. Where learning happens. *Daedalus,* 1968, 1281–1286.

Catalano, R., & Dooley, D. Economic change in primary prevention. In R. H. Price, R. F. Ketterer, B. C. Bader, & J. Monahan (Eds.), *Prevention in mental health: Research, policy, and practice.* Beverly Hills: Sage, 1980.

Cohen, S. Environmental load and the allocation of attention. In Baum, A., Singer, J., & Valins, S. (Eds.), *Advances in environmental psychology.* Vol. 1. *The urban environment.* Hillsdale, N.J.: Lawrence Erlbaum, 1978.

Cohen, S., Evans, G. W., Krantz, D. S., & Stokols, D. Physiological, motivational and cognitive effects of aircraft noise on children. *American Psychologist*, 1980, **35**, 231–243.

Cohen, S., Glass, D., & Singer, J. Apartment noise, auditory discrimination, and reading ability in children. *Journal of Experimental Social Psychology*, 1973, **9**, 407–422.

Cohen, S., & Sherrod, D. R. When density matters: Environmental control as a determinant of crowding effects in laboratory and residential settings. In L. Severy (Ed.), *Crowding: Theoretical and research implications for population-environment psychology*. New York: Human Sciences, 1978.

Cohen, S., & Weinstein, N. Nonauditory effects of noise on behavior and health. *Journal of Social Issues*, 1981, **37**(1), 36–70.

Cowen, E. L. The wooing of primary prevention. *American Journal of Community Psychology*, 1980, **8**(3), 253–284.

Craik, K. H. The personality research paradigm in environmental psychology. In S. Wapner, S. B. Cohen, & B. Kaplan (Eds.), *Experiencing the environment*. New York: Plenum Press, 1976.

Dingemans, D. J., & Schinzel, R. H. Defensible space design of housing for crime prevention. *Police Chief*, 1977, 34–36.

Epstein, Y. Crowding, stress and human behavior. *Journal of Social Issues*, 1981, **37**(1), 126–144.

Evans, G. W. (Ed.) *Journal of Social Issues*, 1981, **37**(1).

Evans, G. W., & Jacobs, S. V. Air pollution and human behavior. *Journal of Social Issues*, 1981, **37**(1), 95–125.

Fanning, D. M. Families in flats. *British Medical Journal*, 1967, **18**, 382–386.

Festinger, L., Schachter, S., & Back, K. *Social pressures in informal groups*. Stanford: Stanford University Press, 1950.

Fischer, C. S. *The urban experience*. New York: Harcourt Brace Jovanovich, 1976.

Fischer, C. S. Sociological comments on psychological approaches to urban life. In Baum, A., Singer, J., & Valins, S. (Eds.), *Advances in environmental psychology*. Vol. 1. *The urban environment*. Hillsdale, N.J.: Lawrence Erlbaum, 1978.

Franck, K. A. Friends and strangers: The social experience of living in urban and non-urban settings. *Journal of Social Issues*, 1980, **36**(3), 52–71.

Freeman, H. Mental health and the environment: A review. *British Journal of Psychiatry*, 1978, **132**, 113–124.

Freedman, J. L. *Crowding and behavior*. New York: Viking, 1975.

Geer, J. H., & Maisel, E. Evaluating the effects of the prediction-control confound. *Journal of Personality and Social Psychology*, 1972, **23**(3), 314–319.

Giamartino, G., & Wandersman, A. Organizational climate correlates of variable urban block organizations. *American Journal of Community Psychology*, in press.

Glass, D., & Singer, J. *Urban stress*. New York: Academic Press, 1972.

Gump, P. V. School environments. In I. Altman & J. F. Wohlwill (Eds.), *Children and the environment*. New York: Plenum Press, 1978.

Harries, K. D. *Crime and the environment*. Springfield, Ill.: C. Thomas, 1980.

Harshbarger, D. An ecological perspective on disaster intervention. In H. J. Parad, H. L. Resnick, & L. Parad (Eds.), *Emergency and disaster management: A mental health service book*. Bowie, Md., Charles Press, 1976.

Hayward, D. G., Rothenberg, M., & Beasley, R. R. Children's play and urban environments: A comparison of traditional, contemporary and adventure playground types. *Environmental and Behavior*, 1974, **6**(2), 131–168.

Heimstra, N. W., & McFarling, L. H. *Environmental psychology*. (2nd ed.) Monterey, Calif.: Brooks/Cole, 1978.

Henninger, M. Environmental classes. *Dissertation Abstracts International*, 1978, **38**(7a), 4030–4031.

Hiers, M., & Heckel, R. V. Seating choice, leadership, and locus of control. *Journal of Social Psychology*, 1977, **103**, 313–314.

High, T., & Sundstrom, E. Room flexibility and space use in a dormitory. *Environment and Behavior*, 1977, **9**(1), 81–90.

Hiltonsmith, R., & Keller, H. What happened to the setting in person-setting assessment? Current status and future directions in the assessment of settings. Unpublished manuscript, Syracuse University, 1982.

Holahan, C. Seating patterns and patient behavior in an experimental dayroom. *Journal of Abnormal Psychology*, 1972, **80**, 115–124.

Holahan, C. J. Environmental psychology in psychiatric hospital settings. In D. Canter & S. Canter (Eds.), *Designing for therapeutic environments: A review of research*. New York: Wiley, 1979.

Holahan, C., & Saegert, S. Behavioral and attitudinal effects of large-scale variation in the physical environment of psychiatric wards. *Journal of Abnormal Psychology*, 1973, **83**, 454–462.

Hollingshead, A. B., & Rogler, L. Attitudes towards public housing in Puerto Rico. In L. Duhl (Ed.), *The urban condition*. New York: Basic Books, 1963.

Ittelson, W. H. Environmental perception and urban experience. *Environment and Behavior*, 1978, **10**(2), 193–213.

Ittelson, W. H., Proshansky, H. M., & Rivlin, L. G. A study of bedroom use on two psychiatric wards. *Hospital and Community Psychology*, 1970, **21**(6), 25–28.

Ittelson, W. H., Proshansky, H. M., Rivlin, L. G., & Winkel, G. H. *An introduction to environmental psychology*. New York: Holt, Rinehart & Winston, 1974.

Jason, L. A. Prevention in the schools. In R. H. Price, R. F. Ketterer, B. C. Bader, & J. Monahan (Eds.), *Prevention in mental health: Research, policy and practice*. Beverly Hills: Sage, 1980.

Karlin, R. A., Epstein, Y. M., & Aiello, J. R. Strategies for the investigation of crowding. In A. Esser & B. Greenbie (Eds.), *Design for community and privacy*. New York: Plenum Press, 1978.

Karlin, R. A., Katz, S., Epstein, Y. M., & Woolfolk, R. L. The use of therapeutic interventions to reduce crowding related arousal: A preliminary investigation. *Environmental Psychology and Nonverbal Behavior*, 1979, **3**, 219–227.

Kirmeyer, S. Urban density and pathology: A review of research. *Environment and Behavior*, 1978, **10**(2), 247–269.

Klemesrud, J. Women take initiative in countering threats to unborn children. *Columbia Record*, 1980.

Knight, R. C., Zimring, C. M., Weitzer, W. H., & Wheeler, H. C. Effects of the living environment on the mentally retarded. In A. Friedman, C. Zimring, & E. Zube (Eds.), *Environmental design evaluation*. New York: Plenum Press, 1978.

Korte, C. Helpfulness in the urban environment. In A. Baum, J. Singer, & S. Valins (Eds.), *Advances in environmental psychology.* Vol. 1. *The urban environment.* Hillsdale, N.J.: Lawrence Erlbaum, 1978.

Langer, E., & Saegert, S. Crowding and cognitive control. *Journal of Personality and Social Psychology,* 1977, **35,** 175–182.

Lawton, M. P., Nahemow, L., Yaffe, S., & Feldman, S. Psychological aspects of crime and fear of crime. In Goldsmith, S. (Ed.), *Crime and the elderly.* Lexington, Mass.: D. C. Heath, 1976.

Lazarus, R. S. *Psychological stress and the coping process.* New York: McGraw-Hill, 1966.

Lee, T. *Psychology and the environment.* London: Methuen, 1976.

Leff, H. L. *Experience, environment, and human potentials.* New York: Oxford University Press, 1978.

Levi, L., & Andersson, L. *Psychological stress: Population, environment, and the quality of life.* New York: Spectrum, 1975.

Lewis, D. A. (Ed.) *Reactions to crime.* Beverly Hills: Sage, 1981.

Lowensohn, B. A. An investigation of the relation between atmospheric quality and crime rates in the greater Los Angeles area. *Dissertation Abstracts International,* 1977, **38**(5-B), 2432.

Mayron, L. W., Ott, J., Nations, R., & Mayron, E. Light, radiation and academic behavior: Initial studies on the effects of full-spectrum lighting and radiation shielding on behavior and academic performance in school children. *Academic Therapy,* 1974, **10,** 33–47.

McCarthy, D. P., & Saegert, S. Residential density, social overload, and social withdrawal. In J. R. Aiello & A. Baum (Eds.), *Residential crowding and design.* New York: Plenum Press, 1979.

Mehrabian, A., & Russell, J. *An Approach to environmental psychology.* Cambridge: MIT Press, 1974.

Merry, S. E. Defensible space undefended: Social factors in crime control through environmental design. *Urban Affairs Quarterly,* 1981, **16**(4), 397–422.

Michelson, W. *Man and his urban environment: A sociological approach.* Palo Alto, Calif.: Addison-Wesley, 1970.

Middlebrook, P. N. *Social psychology and modern life.* (2nd ed.) New York: Knopf, 1980.

Milgram, S. The experience of living in cities. *Science,* 1970, **13,** 1461–1464.

Moos, R., & Fuhr, R. The clinical use of ecological concepts: The case of an adolescent girl. *American Journal of Orthopsychiatry,* 1982, **52,** 111–122.

Newman, O. *Defensible space.* New York: Macmillan, 1972.

Novaco, R. W., Stokols, D., Campbell, J., & Stokols, J. Transportation, stress, and community psychology. *American Journal of Community Psychology,* 1979, 361–380.

O'Neill, P. Educating divergent thinkers: An ecological investigation. *American Journal of Community Psychology,* 1976, **4,** 99–107.

Page. R. Noise and helping behavior. *Environment and Behavior,* 1977, **9**(3), 311–340.

Paulus, P. B., McCain, G., & Cox, V. Death rates, psychiatric commitments, blood pressure and perceived crowding as a function of institutional crowding. *Environmental Psychology and Nonverbal Behavior,* 1978, **3,** 107–116.

Perlman, J. Grassrooting the system. *Social Policy,* 1976, **7,** 4–20.

Perlman, J. Grassroots participation from neighborhood to nation. In S. Langton (Ed.), *Citizen participation in America.* Lexington, Mass.: D. C. Heath, 1978.

Proshansky, H. M. The city and self-identity. *Environment and Behavior,* 1978, **10**(2), 147–169.

Quilitch, H. R., & Risley, T. R. The effects of play materials on social play. *Journal of Applied Behavior Analysis,* 1973, **6,** 573–578.

Rainwater, L. Fear and the house-as-haven in the lower class. *Journal of the American Institute of Planners,* 1966, **32,** 23–31.

Rappaport, J. In praise of paradox: A social policy of empowerment over prevention. *American Journal of Community Psychology,* 1981, **9**(1), 1–25.

Ray, D. W. Wandersman, A., Huntington, D. E., & Ellisor, J. The effects of high density in a juvenile correctional institution: A field test of spatial and social density. *Basic and Applied Social Psychology,* in press.

Rich, R. C. The roles of neighborhood organization in urban service delivery. *NASPAA Urban Affairs Papers,* 1979, **1,** 2–23.

Rich, R. C. The dynamics of leadership in neighborhood organizations. *Social Science Quarterly,* 1980, **60,** 570–587.

Rivlin, L. G., Wolfe, M., & Beyda, M. Age-related differences in the use of space. In W. F. E. Preiser (Ed.), *Environmental design research.* Philadelphia: Dowden, Hutchinson, & Ross, 1973.

Rodin, J., Solomon, S., & Metcalf, J. Role of control in mediating perceptions of density. *Journal of Personality and Social Psychology,* 1978, **36,** 988–999.

Ruesch, J., & Kees, W. *Nonverbal communication: Notes on the visual perception of human relations.* Berkeley: University of California Press, 1956.

Russell, J. A., & Ward, L. M. Environmental psychology. *Annual Reviews, Inc.,* 1981, **110,** 163–168.

Sadalla, E. K. Population size, structural differentiation, and human behavior. *Environment and Behavior,* 1978, **10,** 271–291.

Seligman, M. *Helplessness: On depression, development, and death.* San Francisco: Freeman, 1975.

Sherrod, D. R. Crowding, perceived control, and behavioral aftereffects. *Journal of Applied Social Psychology,* 1974, **4,** 171–186.

Sherrod, D. R., & Cohen, S. Density, personal control, and design. In J. R. Aiello & A. Baum (Eds.), *Residential crowding and design.* New York: Plenum Press, 1979.

Singer, J., Lundberg, U., & Frankenhaeuser, M. Stress on the train: A study of urban commuting. In Baum, A., Singer, J., & Valins, S. (Eds.), *Advances in environmental psychology.* Vol. 1. *The urban environment.* Hillsdale, N.J.: Lawrence Erlbaum, 1978.

Sommer, R. *Personal space: The behavioral basis of design.* Englewood Cliffs, N.J.: Prentice-Hall, 1969.

Sommer, R., & Ross, H. Social interaction on a geriatric ward. *International Journal of Social Psychiatry,* 1958, **4,** 128–133.

Srole, L. The city versus town and country: New evidence on an ancient bias. In L. Srole & A. K. Fischer (Eds.), *Mental health in the metropolis.* New York: Harper & Row, 1976.

Srole, L., & Fisher, A. K. The city versus town and country: New evidence on an ancient bias. In L. Srole & A. K. Fischer (Eds.), *Mental health in the metropolis.* New York: Harper & Row, 1976.

Stires, L. Classroom seating location, student grades, and attitudes: Environment or self selection? *Environment and Behavior*, 1980, 12(2), 241–254.

Stokols, D. Environmental psychology. *Annual Reviews, Inc.*, 1978, 29, 253–295.

Stough, R. & Wandersman, A. (Eds.) *Optimizing environments: Research practice, and policy*. Washington, D.C.: Environmental Design Research Association, 1980.

Strahilevitz, M., Strahilevitz, A., & Miller, J. Air pollutants and the admission rate of psychiatric patients. *American Journal of Psychiatry*, 1979, 136, 205–207.

Swift, C. Primary prevention. In R. H. Price, R. F. Ketterer, B. C. Bader, & J. Monahan (Eds.), *Prevention in mental health: Research, policy and practice*. Beverly Hills: Sage, 1980.

Turner, J. F. C. *Housing by people: Towards autonomy in building environments*. London: Calder & Boyers, 1976.

Wandersman, A. Participation in block organizations. National Science Foundation Grant #BNS-78-08827, 1978–82, 1978.

Wandersman, A. User participation: A study of types of participation, effects, mediators and individual differences. *Environment and Behavior*, 1979, 11(2), 185–208. (a)

Wandersman, A. User participation in planning environments: A conceptual framework. *Environment and Behavior*, 1979, 11(4), 465–482. (b)

Wandersman, A. A framework of participation in community organizations. *Journal of Applied Behavioral Science*, 1981, 17(1), 27–58.

Wandersman, A., & Florin, P. A cognitive social learning approach to the crossroads of cognition, social behavior and the environment. In J. Harvey (Ed.), *Cognition, social behavior and the environment*. Hillsdale, N.J.: Lawrence Erlbaum, 1981.

Wandersman, A., Jakubs, J., & Giamartino, G. Participation in block organizations. *Journal of Community Action*, 1981, 1(1), 40–47.

Wandersman, A., & Moos, R. H. Assessing and evaluating residential environments: A sheltered living environments example. *Environment and Behavior*, 1981, 13(4), 481–508.

Wandersman, A., Murday, D., & Wadsworth, J. C. The environment-behavior-person relationship: Implications for research. In A. Seidel & S. Danford (Eds.), *Environmental design: Research, theory, and application*. Washington, D.C.: Environmental Design Research Association, 1979.

Weinstein, N. D. Individual differences in reactions to noise: A longitudinal study in a college dormitory. *Journal of Applied Psychology*, 1978, 63, 458–466.

Whitehead, C., Polsky, R. H., Crookshank, C., & Fik, E. An ethological evaluation of psychoenvironmental design. In press.

Wilner, D. L., Walkley, R. D., Pinkerton, T. C., & Tayback, M. *The housing environment and family life*. Baltimore: Johns Hopkins University Press, 1962.

Winnett, R., Battersby, C., & Edwards, S. The effects of architectural changes, individualized instruction and group contingencies on academic performance and social behavior of 6th graders. *Journal of School Psychology*, 1975, 13, 28–40.

Wohlwill, J. Behavioral response and adaptation to environmental stimulation. In *NBN Publication Series: No. 72-1*, Pennsylvania State University, 1972.

Wohlwill, J., & Kohn, I. The environments experienced by the migrant: An adaptation-level view. *Representative Research in Social Psychology*, 1973, 4(1), 135–164.

Yancey, W. Architecture, interaction, and social control: The case of a large-scale public housing project. *Environment and Behavior*, 1971, 3, 3–21.

Zimring, C. M. Stress and the designed environment. *Journal of Social Issues*, 1981, 37(1), 145–171.

# 8 PREVENTIVE BEHAVIORAL INTERVENTIONS

## Leonard A. Jason and G. Anne Bogat

In the last two decades, increasing attention has been directed toward two independent movements: behavior modification, a model which presents an approach for understanding the etiology, treatment, and prognosis of behavioral problems; and preventive psychology, a model which provides alternative ways of extending the reach of mental health services. The present chapter is devoted to delineating behavioral approaches within a preventive paradigm. To understand better the synthesis of these two fields, it is first necessary to be somewhat familiar with the history and current status of both behavior modification and preventive psychology. The sections below will describe these independent content areas, the advantages in subscribing to these models, and alternative competing models. Finally, the rationale for adopting a synthesis of these two fields, a heuristic schema for conceptualizing this emerging area, and illustrative research will be presented.

### Behavior Modification

The behavioral model represents one of several conceptual approaches for treating psychological problems. Alternative competing models include the medical, psychoanalytic, statistical, phenomenological-existential, and sociological approaches. A central premise of the medical model is that abnormal behavior is similar to a disease; that is, psychological problems are caused by either infectious diseases (for instance, syphilis), systemic diseases (such as schizophrenia), or traumatic diseases (for example, a brain injury following an automobile accident). Treatment would involve first identifying and then possibly eradicating the precipitating disease irritants (Davison & Neale, 1974). In contrast, the psychoanalytic approach postulates that adult psychological disturbances are caused by unconscious traumatic childhood events. In order to remove the symptoms, the psychoanalyst helps the patient consciously remember these early traumatic events (Rychlak, 1973). Based on a statistical model, abnormality is defined as that which deviates from the average in specific behavioral or personality characteristics (for example, neuroticism, introversion-extroversion, and psychoticism; Eysenck, 1960). Successful treatment might involve helping clients attain levels of functioning which are within the normal range. Phenomenological-existential perspectives stress the importance of conscious experience in determining behavior (Mears & Gatchel, 1979). Clinicians adhering to this model help individuals take responsibility for developing self-acceptance and for finding meaning in life. Finally, a sociological model includes the following two assumptions: (a) economic deprivations and poor physical surroundings contribute to the development of psychological deviance (Srole, Langner, Michael, Opler, & Rennie, 1962); and (b) individuals labeled as deviant actively maintain their deviant roles (Tittle, 1975). Advocates of this model indicate the need to ameliorate debilitating conditions of poverty and eliminate the labeling process. These diverse models indicate that the etiology of, and treatment for, dysfunctional behavior can be viewed from many perspectives. In order to avoid confusion concerning goals and objectives of treatment efforts, it is incumbent on clinical community psychologists to articulate explicitly their theoretical models prior to initiating intervention programs.

The behavioral model, which relies on objective measurable data, has the strongest foundation in experimentally rooted clinical procedures (Mahoney, Kazdin, & Lesswing, 1974). This model initially was popularized in the United States in the early 1900s by John Watson, who suggested that psychology should be concerned with observable events, that is, the prediction and control of behavior. At a very early point, two different types of learning—classical and operant conditioning—became associated with this behavioral model.

Classical conditioning was discovered by Pavlov (1927) at the turn of the century. He found that when meat powder, which automatically elicits salivation, was preceded several times by a bell, this neutral stimulus began to elicit the salivary response. This experiment later provided a possible theoretical explanation of how strong emotional responses, such as fear, could be conditioned to many types of neutral stimuli.* If fearful responses can be learned, they also can be unlearned through counterconditioning, a procedure in which one response to a stimulus is substituted for another. For example, Wolpe (1958) developed a procedure called systematic desensitization, whereby clients visualize increasingly anxiety-provoking scenes while engaging in deep muscle relaxation. When formerly anxiety-arousing stimuli only elicit nonfearful responses, the client has been successfully counterconditioned.† Other types of counterconditioning include assertiveness training (providing expressions of assertiveness to individuals who have difficulties expressing positive or negative feelings; Salter, 1949), aversive conditioning (associating aversive feelings to stimuli—drugs and alcohol—considered

inappropriately attractive; Rachman & Teasdale, 1969), and organismic reorientation (increasing sexual arousal to stimuli having low levels of arousal; Davison & Neale, 1974).

The second type of learning was discovered by Edward Thorndike. He watched alley cats free themselves from a cage after they accidentally hit a latch. When recaged, the cats soon learned to touch the latch and escape. Based on these observations, Thorndike formulated the law of effect, which states that behavior which is followed by satisfying consequences will be repeated, whereas behavior followed by unpleasant consequences will be discouraged. This principle was later renamed operant conditioning and expanded upon by Skinner (1938). Operant conditioning has been used to explain how diverse normal and abnormal behaviors are learned and maintained. For example, Lovaas (1968) used these procedures to establish attending, motor, and vocal behaviors in psychotic children; Jason (1977a) employed operant techniques to establish social and academic repertoires in preschool disadvantaged children; Patterson (1974) systematically used operant strategies to decrease children's aggressive and antisocial behaviors; and Haring and Schiefelbusch (1976) reviewed operant procedures which successfully have enhanced learning in children with communication disorders, aberrant behavior, sensory handicaps, and neurological and health impairments.

In addition to counterconditioning and operant conditioning, two new types of behavioral approaches, modeling and cognitive restructuring, recently have emerged. Bandura (1969) has been principally responsible for popularizing the notion that children and adults can acquire complex behaviors merely through observing others perform the target behaviors. For example, after withdrawn children viewed a film of a child progressively increasing his participation in interactions having positive consequences, their social interactions increased considerably (O'Connor, 1969). Modeling has also been employed in reducing and eliminating anxieties and inhibitions. This is illustrated in an experiment by Bandura, Grusec, and Menlove (1967), which reported reduced dog phobias in young children after they watched a fearless peer exhibit progressively greater interactions with a dog.

The last approach, cognitive restructuring, has been receiving increasing attention among behavior therapists. Advocates of this approach argue that internal processes (thoughts, feelings, and so on) are subject to the same learning principles as are external behaviors (Kanfer & Phillips, 1970). As an example, Ellis (1962) maintains that maladaptive emotional reactions stem from irrational self-statements. In Ra-

---

* More recent explanations of the acquisition of phobic behavior have focused on Mowrer's two-factor theory, modeling, and operant conditioning (Davidson & Neale, 1974).

† Alternative viable explanations of desensitization include extinction, operant shaping, modeling, self-instruction training, and expectations of change (Kazdin, 1979).

tional Emotive Therapy, Ellis attempts to modify negative statements which clients make to themselves in order to avoid aversive emotional reactions. Beck (1976), another cognitive behavioral therapist, maintains that depressives draw illogical conclusions in evaluating themselves. Beck has reported success in altering thinking patterns and alleviating negative feelings in depressive clients. It should be mentioned that this is the most controversial approach, with some behavioral investigators adamantly rejecting cognitive restructuring techniques which often deal with cognitive, internal, and mediational concepts as opposed to overt, public behaviors (Ledwidge, 1978).

In recent years, several criticisms have been directed at the behavioral model. For example, London (1972) has stated that the theoretical bases for many behavioral techniques (such as systematic desensitization, covert conditioning, aversion therapy) are still unclear. Nevertheless, behavioral practitioners are committed to drawing upon basic experimental findings (such as positive reinforcement, problem solving, information processing) in supporting their programmatic treatment and research efforts. In regard to the differential effectiveness of behavior therapy, a recent meta-analysis of treatment effects involving hundreds of outcome studies indicated that behavior therapy is about as effective as psychotherapy (Smith & Glass, 1977). This large-scale analysis should caution behavioral practitioners from making global claims that the behavioral approach, which involves many different techniques applied to diverse problems, is unquestionably the most effective. However, there is evidence that behavioral techniques are more effective than traditional psychotherapeutic techniques in treating specific problems (for example, phobias, obsessive compulsive disorders, enhancing development in autistic and mentally retarded children; Kazdin, 1979).

Even when behavior modification programs have attained considerable success in altering behaviors by the end of an intervention, maintenance of gains often has not been achieved during follow-up periods (e.g., Davidson & Wolfred, 1977). In part, this difficulty in achieving enduring effects might be due to three factors: (a) reliance on a one-to-one, person-centered service delivery model; (b) an overreliance on deficit, endstate goals; and (c) a failure to modify organizational, community, and societal environmental factors. In support of the first contention, MacDonald, Hedberg, and Campbell (1974) reviewed four major behavioral journals and found 89 percent of the articles to be person-centered. Furthermore, Nietzel, Winett, MacDonald, and Davidson (1977) have claimed that a majority of these person-centered interventions have focused on remediating deficits.

To the extent that the vast majority of research time is invested in such traditional styles of service delivery, potentially more efficacious conceptual approaches are ignored. As an example of an alternative approach, Holland (1978) has argued cogently that instead of changing the behaviors of individual alcoholics and criminals, behaviorists need to begin analyzing and changing the societal contingencies which continue to produce alcoholics and criminals. In the next section, the traditional model of delivering mental health services will be explored, and its limitations will be delineated.

## Traditional Model

Salient characteristics of the more traditional service delivery model include: (a) a one-to-one format, with a psychotherapist treating a single patient or a group of patients at one time; (b) a late treatment focus, which is directed toward individuals with already identified and often entrenched disorders; and (c) a passive-receptive stance, where mental health professionals wait for patients to arrive at their clinics. Figure 8.1 depicts a heuristic scheme which aids in the identification of different models of service delivery (Jason, 1977b).

The traditional model is located in the cells intersecting the secondary and tertiary time point, and in individual and group target points (cells with diagonal lines through them). The vertical dimension of Figure 8.1 indicates that it is possible to intervene at three distinct time points (Caplan, 1964) in implementing an intervention. Primary preventive interventions attempt to prevent onset of disorders and/or strengthen areas of competence. Secondary preventive programs seek to identify incipient problems and formulate interventions to reverse them. Tertiary interventions focus on remediating or restoring areas of competence in those individuals with long-standing dysfunctions. The traditional model has exclusively targeted interventions to the secondary and tertiary time points.

The horizontal dimension of Figure 8.1 indicates that interventions can focus on individuals, groups, organizations, communities, and societies (Reiff, 1975). The traditional model has focused most of its attention on individuals experiencing problems. An example of this approach would be a psychotherapist providing services to a patient with a clearly identified problem. The traditional model also has directed attention to delivering services to groups, a typical example being group therapy. Organizational, community, and societal level interventions have not been subsumed within the purview of the traditional model.

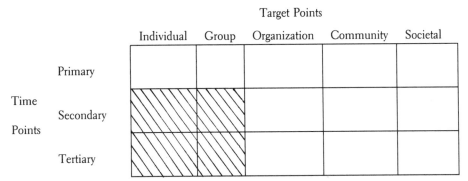

Figure 8.1. Time and target dimensions.

### Limitations in the Traditional Model

The traditional orientation has several serious limitations. For example, as long as the traditional model maintains center stage, with its one-to-one basis for extending services, there will never be enough professionals available to meet the ever-increasing demand for services (Albee, 1967). This growing demand is evidenced by the fact that whenever new facilities for extending mental health services are opened, waiting lists develop quickly (Zax & Cowen, 1976). The unmet need for mental health services clearly outstrips the identifiable demand for services, as is indicated by several epidemiological studies (Leighton, 1956; Srole et al., 1962). The need for services is also evident in Glidewell and Swallow's (1969) survey, which found that 30 percent of elementary school children have identifiable difficulties in school adjustment and 10 percent are sufficiently maladjusted to require professional assistance. Another area of unmet needs is the approximately 18 million children experiencing disruptions (divorce, separation) in parental relationships (Anthony, 1974). Extremely high rates of unwanted teenage pregnancy, in part due to the fact that less than 20 percent of those 15 to 19 use contraceptives regularly, represent another serious problem (Bloom, 1977). In addition, there are approximately 5 to 10 million alcoholics in this country. Furthermore, estimates of suicides each year range from 25,000 to 60,000 (Mears & Gatchel, 1979). Kiesler (1980) estimates that more than 50 percent of people treated by general practitioners are there for psychological problems. This means that up to 100 million people are receiving inappropriate treatment for problems which are largely psychological. In addition, at any one time 20 to 45 million people experience serious mental health problems. If all psychologists and psychiatrists adopted the traditional model, they would be able to extend services only to about 2 percent of those in need of mental health services. Given the waiting stance and one-to-one delivery mode of the traditional model, its professional personnel can never meet the demand and need for services (Cowen, 1973).

Another criticism leveled at the traditional model concerns the limited success in demonstrating the efficacy of psychotherapy. In the professional and research literature, the effectiveness of psychotherapy remains a heated topic (e.g., Rimland, 1979; Smith & Glass, 1977). Even in evaluating behavior therapy, numerous studies unfortunately have relied on case study reports, and few interventions adequately have assessed the long-term consequences of treatment (Callner, 1975; Eysenck & Beech, 1971; Willems, 1974). Shapiro (1971) has maintained that psychotherapy primarily relies on the placebo effect; that is, the therapist's favorable feelings reduce the patient's guilt and anxiety, and consequently enable the patient to mobilize hope and better utilize previously impaired assets. Even more discouraging is Garfield's (1971) finding that many clinics lose half their patients by the eighth interview, most of whom fail to return for scheduled appointments. For alcoholics in outpatient treatment, dropout rates rise to 52 to 75 percent by the fourth session (Baekeland & Lundwall, 1975). These limitations—failures in (a) retaining clients, (b) providing unequivocal theoretical models accounting for change, and (c) demonstrating effectiveness—are serious problems of the traditional model, which relies so heavily on psychotherapy as its modus operandi.

Another serious shortcoming of the traditional model is its limited success in treating schizophrenia. In 1973, more than 120,000 individuals with the diagnosis of schizophrenia resided at state and county hospitals. In addition, 72 percent of schizophrenics admitted to hospitals previously had received similar care (Keith, Gunderson, Buchsbaum, & Mosher, 1976). Even though behavioral investigators have succeeded in altering classic schizophrenic symptoms (Liberman, Wallace, Teigen, & Davis, 1974; Ullmann & Krasner, 1969), treatment variables within hospitals are not significantly related to how well patients function in the community following discharge from mental hospitals (Erickson, 1975). As long as treatment efforts focus on rehabilitating schizophrenics within hospitals, as opposed to enhancing their functioning in community settings, excessively high rates of recidivism will continue to exist. Various estimates suggest that from 43 to 75 percent of state hospital patients could be treated outside of these institutional settings (Kiesler, 1980). Often resources are not available to develop more community-based treatments because 70 percent of mental health dollars still are spent for institutional care of patients.

Traditional mental health services also have been delivered inadequately to the economically disadvantaged. Low-income individuals often are hesitant to seek out therapy. If they do apply for treatment, these clients are more likely to be seen by inexperienced therapists and to receive only supportive or somatic treatment (Lorion, 1978; Sauna, 1966). This is particularly unfortunate in light of consistent findings that the highest rates of psychopathology are found in the lowest socioeconomic strata (Dohrenwend & Dohrenwend, 1969; Hollingshead & Redlich, 1958). It is regrettable that traditional therapists have devoted a disproportionate amount of their time to treating those who are young, attractive, verbal, intelligent, and successful (that is, the Yavis syndrome; Savage, 1968) as opposed to disadvantaged, lower-income clients.

A final criticism of the traditional medical model is the emergence of theoretical perspectives which focus predominantly on the individual organism without consideration of the social/environmental texture of human life. This trend has resulted in the development of an asocial psychology (Sarason, 1981). Sarason argues that in pursuit of federal funds following World War II, clinical psychology forged an unhealthy alliance with psychiatry and its medical settings. This partnership was the beginning of psychology's link to a particular service delivery institution (first Veterans Administration hospitals, then community mental health centers) and a definition of personal problems in terms of individual psychology (influenced to a great extent by the medical model, as manifested in psychiatric facilities). "American psychology, invented in and by American society, went on to invent its subject matter: the self-contained individual [pp. 835–836]." The traditional model and its insistence on

ignoring the societal context of individual behaviors has led to problematic outcomes.

### The Community Mental Health Model

The above-mentioned shortcomings of the traditional model created conditions that stimulated the emergence of an alternative preventive paradigm consisting of two approaches: a community mental health movement and a preventive psychology orientation (Jason & Glenwick, 1980). Both approaches adopt an active stance, directly entering community settings to deliver services, and seek to extend the reach of mental health services via consultation and use of paraprofessionals. A key component of the active approach is that the mental health professional leaves an office or clinic to develop or evaluate programs within the community (Rappaport & Chinsky, 1974).

Through consultation, mental health professionals can strengthen the abilities of natural helpers. This can be accomplished by enhancing the help-givers' confidence and security, providing them with the knowledge needed to suggest meaningful alternatives to persons in crisis, and helping them develop greater sensitivity to psychological determinants of disorders (Zax & Cowen, 1976). Two categories of helpers include natural caregivers—professionals who are not mental health specialists, such as physicians, lawyers, clergymen, and educators (Caplan, 1964)—and urban agents, individuals without mental health backgrounds, such as policemen, welfare investigators, barbers, cabdrivers, and shop owners (Kelly, 1964). Because most individuals in distress do not seek out mental health professionals, natural caregivers and urban agents play important roles in ameliorating mental health-related problems in the community. The critical role played by natural caregivers was supported in a study by Gurin, Veroff, and Feld (1960), which found that among those individuals needing help, 42 percent took their emotional problems to clergymen, 29 percent to physicians, and only 18 percent to mental health professionals.

Another way to broaden the reach of services is to employ paraprofessionals to perform functions traditionally reserved for professionals (Truax & Mitchell, 1971). As an example of this approach, in the mid-1950s college undergraduates began to be used as paraprofessional volunteers working with patients in psychiatric hospitals (Umbarger, Dalsimer, Morrison, & Breggin, 1962). These enthusiastic paraprofessionals brought spirit, activity, engagement, and genuine caring to patients whose settings previously had fostered dependency, passivity, alienation, and despair. A rigorous early evaluation study by Poser (1966) compared the effectiveness of undergraduate paraprofessionals and experienced mental health professionals in leading groups of psychiatric patients over a five-month period. At the end of the program, the student-led groups achieved significantly greater improvement in perceptual, verbal, and psychomotor tasks.

A recent comprehensive survey of 42 studies comparing the effectiveness of paraprofessional and professional helpers yielded somewhat similar results (Durlak, 1979). This survey included interventions which focused on individual and group psychotherapy, academic counseling for college students, crisis intervention for adults, and specific target problems. In 28 investigations there were no significant differences between the paraprofessional and professional helpers, the paraprofessionals were more effective in 12 studies, and the professionals were more effective in 2 studies. These studies suggest that paraprofessionals can assume at least some roles traditionally assigned to professionals, thereby freeing professionals to engage in consultation, supervision, evaluation, and program development and dissemination.

While the community mental health orientation assumes an active stance and broadens the reach of services through use of consultation and paraprofessionals, this approach in practice has tended to focus on individuals and groups experiencing either incipient or entrenched problems. Both the traditional and community mental health approaches occupy the same intersecting cells in Figure 8.1, (that is, the individual or group target, and the secondary or tertiary time points). For example, using a traditional model, a third grade youngster experiencing school adjustment problems might be seen by a psychologist. Within a community mental health approach, the same child might be treated by a paraprofessional or the teacher might be offered consultation services. While the approaches differ in the way services are extended, they tend to focus on similar types of problems.

### Behavioral Community Mental Health Interventions

Most behavioral psychologists have operated out of a more traditional model for extending services. In contrast to the traditional approach, behavioral community mental health practitioners actively enter the community to develop, support, or evaluate interventions. In delivering services, community mental health adherents frequently employ consultation and the use of paraprofessionals, rather than a one-to-one delivery model.

As an example of behavioral community mental health intervention at the individual target point and

secondary time point, Jason and Ferone (1979) implemented a behavioral school consultation program. First graders evidencing high levels of acting-out behaviors were selected for the program. During weekly meetings with the behavioral consultant, individualized behavioral interventions were devised for each of the target youngsters. For example, one child received daily positive or negative teacher reports contingent upon the level of his disruptive behavior in class. At program end, significant reductions in problem behaviors were noted and these gains were maintained at a one-month follow-up. In this behavioral community mental health project, a teacher was provided the expertise to implement individualized interventions with several children evidencing incipient behavior problems.

Glenwick and LaGana Arata (in press) provide an example of a behavioral community mental health intervention at the individual target point and the tertiary time point. The rehabilitation clients in this project had been afflicted with long-standing behavioral, psychological, and physical disorders. The intervention program featured paraprofessional college students who attempted to strengthen social skills and assertiveness in their clients. In this program, the reach of professional services was broadened considerably by utilizing college undergraduates to deliver the treatment package.

Group-based behavioral community mental health interventions focus their efforts on groups of clients as opposed to individual members. An example of a group-focused intervention at the secondary preventive time point was provided by Durlak (1977). In this intervention, maladapting second graders were seen weekly for one hour in groups of five to seven. The college student paraprofessional group leaders provided token reinforcement and praise for pupils' performance of targeted desired behaviors. That is, shy children were rewarded for working with others, disruptive youngsters were rewarded for waiting their turns, and children with poor work habits were rewarded for working on tasks. At program end and a seven-month follow-up, children provided the group intervention improved significantly in classroom adjustment, in comparison to control children.

Finally, Koegel and Rincover (1974) provide an example of a behavioral community mental health intervention at the group target point and tertiary time point. In this project, a teacher and teacher aides were taught to prompt autistic children to imitate specific responses. As the children attained an 80 percent criterion level of imitation, they gradually were placed in larger group sizes. By program end, 88 percent of the autistic children were able to perform basic skills at a rate of 80 percent or higher in groups consisting of eight children.

As the above studies indicate, the community mental health approach exponentially extends the reach of mental health services by utilizing consultation and paraprofessionals. However, the emphasis still is focused on individuals or groups experiencing early or long-standing psychological disorders. Some critics of this approach have posited that no widespread human disease has ever been brought under control solely by treating afflicted individuals (Kessler & Albee, 1975). The community mental health approach has also been criticized for its focus on early detection of children with behavioral or social difficulties. If a child is labeled deviant, the stigma might function to confirm repeatedly the initial diagnosis (Rosenthal & Jacobson, 1966). As a suggestive example of this iatrogenic problem, a 30-year follow-up of a secondary preventive program aimed at delinquent youths found that the program children, when compared to nonprogram controls, were more likely to evidence signs of alcoholism, had more serious psychiatric problems, died at an earlier age, evidenced more stress in their circulatory systems, and were more likely to commit second crimes (McCord, 1978). While these findings should caution community mental health professionals who are implementing early secondary preventive programs, there still are patent needs to help children and youngsters with early signs of behavioral and social problems. Potential negative second order effects might be avoided if interventions are designed which avoid or minimize the labeling and stigmatizing process. For example, an intervention could be aimed at an entire classroom of youngsters, with none identified as the exclusive target of the project. At intervention end, if several youngsters who initially were evidencing academic lags in basic skills areas had progressed to performance within the normal range, the intervention would have succeeded in boosting their abilities without the concomitant possible negative effects of labeling.

## An Alternative Model

As was mentioned previously, there are two somewhat distinct variations in the alternative service delivery model, the community mental health and preventive psychology approaches. Both approaches adopt a seeking, proactive stance; utilize the services of paraprofessionals; and strengthen the abilities of natural helpers through consultation. The preventive approach, however, broadens the scope of interventions to incorporate time and target domains beyond those of traditional and community mental health ap-

proaches. In Figure 8.1, a preventive psychology approach involves primary prevention interventions at the individual and group level and those which focus on organizational, community and societal level targets. The organizational target point switches the emphasis from individuals and groups to the environments which influence them. Organizations include inanimate elements (physical design, resources, ambient conditions), characteristics of individuals inhabiting the setting (socioeconomic status, age, sex), interactions between individuals and environments, and the setting's social climate. Community level interventions influence many organizations and people within a community (mass transit, support systems throughout a community). Finally, societal level interventions involve attempts at influencing policy at a national level (executive actions, judicial decisions, legislative enactments).

While the traditional and community mental health approaches have a built-in preoccupation with delivering services to dysfunctional individuals and groups, the preventive model is invested in intercepting problems prior to their inception (Jason & Glenwick, 1980) and the creation of more effective and humane systems of socialization and support (Goodstein & Sandler, 1978). Both prevention and environmental modification have historical roots in a public health approach that focuses on physical as opposed to psychological problems. For example, in 1746 an inoculation against smallpox was discovered after it was observed that children who had had cowpox rarely developed smallpox. In other words, children who had been exposed to a mild version of the disease built up an immunization to smallpox (Catalano, 1979). This model might serve as a prototype for averting mental health problems; that is, individuals might be exposed to stress inoculation procedures to "immunize" them against psychological problems.

A concern for environmental issues first was noted by Hippocrates, who suggested that cities not be built near wet grounds and still water. When followed, this recommendation led to a reduction in malaria. Another public health intervention, implemented around A.D. 1000, was a quarantine which effectively combated the black plague and leprosy (Catalano, 1979). During the Middle Ages, cleanup efforts were mounted in many communities; the concerted attack on environmental pollution helped reduce the spread of many diseases (Bloom, 1977).

Switching from physical to psychological irritants, preventive psychologists have realized that social, political, and economic factors, such as poverty, unemployment, and inadequate schools and other institutions, can exert powerful detrimental effects on many individuals. An essential element of the preventive psychology ideology is that environmental irritants predisposing toward psychological pathologies can systematically be evaluated and modified.

The preventive movement makes a concerted effort to articulate explicitly those foundational values which serve as guideposts for implementing interventions. For example, Rappaport (1977) posits several core values, including (a) extending mental health services to local communities; (b) developing existing neighborhood resources and strengths; (c) supporting cultural diversity (that is, valuing differences between groups and enabling them to develop self-defined goals); and (d) maximizing person-environment fits (in other words, locating optimal matches between individuals with specific abilities and their settings). Another frequently mentioned value is Sarason's (1974) psychological sense of community; that is, interventions which serve to enhance a community's sense of responsibility, purpose, support, and connectiveness. Other key values discussed at the 1980 Community Psychology Conference at Tampa, Florida (Stenmark, 1980), include helping settings encourage rather than discourage growth; fostering citizen participation in the decision-making process; developing knowledge useful for improving people's lives; altering community and social irritants which establish and maintain maladaptive behaviors; developing mutually beneficial reciprocal relationships with clients; identifying and enhancing natural support systems in order to facilitate well-being, promoting health and competence in groups and organizations; and understanding cross-cultural diversity and its effects on psychological functioning. While there is some overlap between these values, what emerges is a core concern for respecting differences, enhancing competencies, and analyzing environmental factors influencing adaptation.

As previously mentioned, most behaviorally oriented psychologists have tended to deliver services through the traditional modality. Preventive-oriented psychologists, on the other hand, have tended to embrace nonbehavioral treatment approaches. Dialogue and collaborative investigations between behavioral- and preventive-oriented advocates recently have begun to occur. The visionary approach of the preventive model increasingly has been recognized as eminently compatible with the rigorous, empirical inductive approach of the behavioral paradigm. The preventive ideologists have offered alternative strategies for extending services and have identified neglected time and target points of interventions; behavioral investigators have supplied a potent technology for effecting behavioral change. In combination, the behavioral-preventive approach represents a conceptually attractive, alternative way of delivering mental health services. In the paragraphs below, examples of a behavioral preventive approach will be presented.

### Behavioral Primary Prevention Interventions

Behaviorists adopting a preventive model can focus on primary prevention and thus avoid several of the problems inherent within the community mental health approach. Primary prevention approaches are directed toward either (a) ensuring that children from high-risk populations (for example, children whose parents are schizophrenic) do not succumb to those disorders; (b) preventing the onset of specific maladaptive behaviors (such as cigarette smoking); (c) building in competencies and strengths (for instance, interpersonal problem-solving skills); or (d) helping individuals cope with milestone transitions (marriage, school entrance). Any of these primary preventive approaches can employ either classical conditioning, operant conditioning, modeling, or cognitive restructuring strategies (Jason, 1981). In Figure 8.2, a rectangular figure displays these two dimensions, the behavioral technology (classical, operant, and so on) on the horizontal axis and the type of preventive activity on the vertical axis. Any group-based, behavioral, primary preventive intervention can be placed in one of the cells in this top figure. In Table 8.1 there is a further subdivision, indicating it is possible to categorize interventions by subtype (for example, transitions can occur in the family, school, or work) and period (childhood, adolescence, and so on).

The first type of primary preventive intervention focuses on high-risk groups manifesting genetic, constitutional, or psychological vulnerabilities alone or in combination with environmental stressors. For example, one high-risk group consists of parents who have a Down syndrome child. These parents have a 33 percent risk of having a second child with this syndrome (Cytryn & Lourie, 1975). Actively identifying high-risk families and providing genetic counseling might be effective in discouraging conception or preventing the birth of genetically malformed infants. Another high-risk group consists of newly inducted soldiers who oversecrete pepsinogen in their stomachs. When these soldiers were exposed to the stress of basic training, 14 percent of them developed ulcers (Weiner, Thaler, Reiser, & Mirsky, 1957). A preventive intervention might involve screening such high-risk groups from basic training and active military service or teaching them stress reduction techniques. Poser and Hartman (1979) have devised behavioral preventive interventions for another type of high-risk group, high

Behavioral Technology

|  | Operant | Classical | Modeling | Cognitive |
|---|---|---|---|---|
| High risk | | | | |
| Prevent onset of behavior | | | | |
| Competency enhancement | | | | |
| Transitions | | | | |

Types

Figure 8.2. Types of primary prevention interventions.

school students whose test performance on a broad range of psychological tests indicates vulnerability even though their everyday behavior is within the normal range. Mednick and Wilkin-Lanoie (1977) focused upon nursery school children with extremely fast recovery skin conductance, which has been identified as a possible predictor of schizophrenia. These children were provided supportive nursery school experiences which effectively counterconditioned their previously high levels of fear and anxiety. The principal hazard with these latter high-risk projects is that normally functioning children might inadvertently be labeled or stigmatized as marginally adjusted.

The second type of primary prevention program attempts to prevent the onset of a maladaptive response. In contrast to the high-risk approach, where a select group of target youngsters is identified as having a particular vulnerability, this second type of primary prevention provides groups of normal, functioning children and adults with experiences designed to prevent establishment of maladaptive addictive responses. As an example, a school might provide an antismoking intervention to all nonsmoking youngsters, rather than solely a target group of youngsters considered highly vulnerable to developing this habit. Along these lines, a study by Spitzzeri and Jason (1979) involved ninth grade classes of children in weekly role-playing sketches depicting everyday encounters with smoking. The youngsters had an opportunity to practice assertive responses in resisting peer pressure to begin smoking. At program end and at a three-month follow-up, two-thirds of the smokers had quit smoking, and none of the youngsters who had never smoked before had begun this habit. In addition to addictive behaviors,

primary preventive programs can attempt to offset excessive, debilitating physiological arousal. For example, behavioral prevention interventions have been aimed at "immunizing" children to dental treatment (Melamed, Yurcheson, Fleece, Hutcherson, & Hawes, 1978), public speaking (Cradock, Cotler, & Jason, 1978), and snake phobias (Poser & King, 1975).

A third type of primary preventive intervention switches the emphasis from preventing maladaptive behaviors to promoting and enhancing adaptivity and healthy functioning. Building or strengthening low probability competencies in social, affective, cognitive, and health modalities typifies this approach. Examples of behavioral programs aimed at developing competencies include teaching child-rearing skills to parents of normal children (Sirbu, Cotler, & Jason, 1978); fostering creativity (Glover & Gary, 1976); enhancing problem-solving abilities (Allen, Chinsky, Larcen, Lochman & Selinger, 1976); and teaching peer-tutoring skills (Jason, Ferone, & Soucy, 1979) to elementary school children. A comprehensive project by Winett, Battersby, and Edwards (1975) effectively brought about positive changes in an entire classroom through the use of individualized instructions and group contingencies; if 90 percent of the children attained a target behavior, the work period was followed by recess. Their behavioral intervention led to increases in child social behaviors (increased smiling and laughing) and more positive teacher behaviors (increased smiling and praise). Attractive features of these types of primary prevention interventions include the focus on positive, salutary goals and the avoidance of potential harmful effects of labeling or stigmatizing target youngsters or adults.

Table 8.1.

| SUBTYPE | | | PERIOD | | | |
|---|---|---|---|---|---|---|
| | | | CHILDHOOD | ADOLESCENCE | ADULT | SENIOR CITIZEN |
| High Risk | Genetic vulnerability | | Close monitoring of children with possible genetic deficits | Special diets or stimulation for adolescents with genetic deficits | Genetic counseling prior to conception | Identifying elderly with genetic deficits, counseling their children |
| | Constitutional and psychological vulnerability | | Socialization experiences for high-risk infants | Identifying high-risk students through psychological batteries, formulating interventions | Screening vulnerable recruits prior to military service | Identifying high-risk elderly through psychological tests |
| Prevent Onset of Behavior | Addictive behaviors | | Training to help parents discourage children from smoking | School-based program to prevent onset: taking drugs | Company-sponsored incentive programs to discourage excessive drinking | Senior centers devising interventions to prevent onset: addictive behaviors |
| | Excessive physiological responding | | Test anxiety | Public speaking anxiety | Anger in interpersonal situations | Surgery anxiety |
| Competency Enhancement | Social | | Enhancing sharing in nursery school | Reducing prejudice in school | Fostering cooperation at work | Establishing social supports for elderly |
| | Affective | | Fostering positive physical contact among preschoolers | Teaching relaxation in school | Assertiveness training with family members | Groups encourage sharing feelings and experiences |
| | Cognitive | | Preschool problem-solving programs | Rational thinking | Cognitive restructuring programs | Teaching coping responses to senior citizens |
| | Health | | Encourage teeth-brushing | Nutrition education in school | Biofeedback for optimal blood pressures | Exercise program |
| Transitions | School | | Enter school | Graduate high school | Enter professional school | Return to college |
| | Work | | First part-time job | First summer full-time job | First full-time job | Retirement |
| | Family | | Birth of sibling | First intimate relationship | Marriage | Birth of grandchild |

The final approach attempts to build in strengths or inoculate individuals about to experience milestone transitional events. These transitional events occur in the following three areas: school, work, and family life. Most individuals regularly are exposed to milestone transitions, which sometimes are characterized as involving three phases: initial psychological turmoil, painful preoccupation with the past, and finally remobilization and adjustment (Cumming & Cumming, 1962). Mastery of transitional events can lead to enhancement of capabilities to cope successfully with future transitions, whereas inadequate attempts to deal with these milestone events can adversely prepare individuals for future transitions. Examples of transitional training in programs with a primary preventive focus have included behavioral child management skill programs for parents prior to the birth of their first child (Matese, Shorr, & Jason, 1982), behavioral orientation programs for students prior to their transfer to a new school (Bogat, Jones, & Jason, 1980), and transition groups for minority students entering college (Boyd, Shueman, McMullan, & Fretz, 1979). Strategic placement of specific skill-building experiences prior to transitional events represents an attractive, preventive approach for enhancing coping skills to deal with stressful experiences.

## Environmental Interventions

While the interventions described were focused on individuals or groups, behavioral preventive interventions also can focus on environmental change in organizations, communities, or societies (see Figure 8.1). Interventions at these levels have the potential for bringing about positive change in numerous individuals affected by particular settings. The organizational target point refers to characteristics of enclosed settings or institutions. At the organizational level, it is possible to bring about change in four dimensions: (a) the inanimate environment (available resources, ambient conditions, physical design), (b) characteristics of a setting's inhabitants (such as member density, stability); (c) transactions between the individuals and their environments; and (d) the setting's social climate (Jason, 1981). Organizational-level interventions illustrating several of these dimensions are provided below.

### Organizational Interventions

Interventions in this category having a primary preventive thrust focus on identifying and fostering environmental stimuli within organizations which enhance competencies or prevent maldevelopment in normal functioning individuals. Primary preventive interventions might attempt to alter the resources (play materials, curriculum, work apparatus, and so on) which exist within settings. For example, play behavior—which has been shown to be critically important for normal social development—is affected heavily by the types of available play materials. Quilitch and Risley (1973) found that seven-year-olds engaged in social play 85 percent of the time when social toys, toys designed for use by several youngsters at a time, were available, and only 10 percent of the time when isolate toys (toys designed for use by one child at a time) were used. More than likely, selection of appropriate play resources can function to encourage, support, and develop positive peer interactions in children. Another area ripe for primary preventive interventions involves the influence of characteristics of residents of a setting (age, ability levels, socioeconomic status, number of residents, staff-resident ratio, etc.). As an example, DeCoster (1966) found that when high-ability students were concentrated in certain residence halls, their academic achievements were higher than those of similar students assigned to halls with both low- and moderate-ability students. Interventions might be devised which place individuals into organizations having resident characteristics which have facilitating effects on rates of learning, adjustment, and mental health. Primary preventive interventions also might focus on analyzing and utilizing reinforcement contingencies within the settings themselves. Comprehensive interventions which alter organizational contingencies can help create more effective and supportive environments. For example, Turner and Goodson (1977) effectively employed behavioral principles to organize an entire community mental health center.

Organizational-level interventions at the secondary preventive time point have focused on environmental stimuli which affect inhabitants having early-identified problems. Ambient conditions (for example, noise, light, and temperature) represent an inanimate part of the environment which can have adverse affects on resident behavior. High sound level, for example, can interfere with studying and sleeping among undergraduates in college dormitories. A secondary preventive intervention by Meyers, Artz, and Craighead (1976) successfully reduced noise in a college dormitory by providing instructions for playing more quietly and by making rewards contingent on reduced noise. Secondary preventive interventions might also focus on overall organizational contingencies. In a classroom setting, behavioral community psychologists might first identify natural reinforcing contingencies and then systematically use these facilitating conditions to bring about behavioral change in children. For example, Jason, Robson, and Lipshutz (1980) identified first and third grade youngsters who evidenced low rates of sharing. When these children were placed in groups of high sharers, the low sharers evidenced significant increases in sharing behaviors. This finding suggests that strategic placement of children into behavior settings with natural facilitating contingencies can effectively bring about predictable behavior change.

Organizational interventions at the tertiary time point have focused on environmental stimuli impinging on residents or clients with long-standing, entrenched problems. An illustration of a physical design intervention at a tertiary time point involved geriatric clients in a nursing home. Peterson, Knapp, Rosen, and Pither (1977) noticed that residents of a geriatric ward rarely talked to each other when chairs on the ward were located against the walls. When the chairs were rearranged and placed around tables, considerable increases occurred in talking among residents. In other words, the arrangement of furniture on a ward can exert strong effects on the amount of residents' conversational behavior. As previously mentioned, an organizational intervention can focus on characteristics of a setting's inhabitants. For example, Skeels (1966) placed eleven retarded, understimulated infants into a new setting inhabited by older retarded girls. The retarded infants received considerable attention and affection from the older girls. After a period of time, all the infants were adopted. At a 21-year follow-up, each of the formerly retarded infants was self-supporting and none evidenced any antisocial or delinquent behaviors. This study indicates that profound, longterm improvements can be achieved when seriously impaired youngsters are placed in settings whose inhabitant characteristics facilitate salutary behavior change.

### Community Interventions

In working at the community level, behaviorists might develop interventions aimed at the natural environment (e.g., geography, resources), components of the built environment (e.g., quality of buildings), overall characteristics of inhabitants (e.g., density), and systems which interconnect throughout the community (e.g., transportation, media). (See the last chapter in this book for a more comprehensive description of this schema.) Primary preventive community interventions might involve supporting informal social support systems within communities (Caplan, 1974; Jeger, Slotnick & Schure, 1980). Informal social supports include the extended family, family physicians, clergy, teachers, hairdressers, and bartenders. Sometimes these people are sought out because they are recognized as having either knowledge about a community's care-giving system or effective coping strategies for adapting to personal misfortune. As an example of this approach, Sale (1973) developed a network of informal caregivers. Sale provided a supportive setting where mothers from both licensed and unlicensed family day care centers could meet and share skills and concerns. Through the project, a toy library system was established, the mothers developed a self-help organization, and they were provided a special program at a nearby university whereby they could earn a certificate in family day care. Evaluating the preventive potentials inherent in supporting natural systems of help-giving remains a high priority area for behaviorists interested in preventive psychology.

Community interventions at the secondary preventive level have focused on already existing environmental problems which are not deeply ingrained and intractable. For example, behaviorists have devised several effective strategies—reinforcing antilitter behavior, giving instructions, and designing attractive trash receptacles—for reducing litter in urban streets, campgrounds, parks, zoos, and highways (Geller, 1980). One of the most offensive types of litter involves dog droppings. Jason, McCoy, Blanco, and Zolik (1980) consulted with a community group in order to ameliorate this dog litter problem. In the actual intervention project, community residents were trained to prompt dog owners to use pooper scoopers in cleaning up after their dogs. At program end there were considerable reductions in dog litter, and at a 13-month follow-up there was overall an 85 percent reduction in dog litter in the four-by-two-block area surrounding the study site. The positive follow-up data suggest that an attractive way of maintaining change within a community might involve teaching skills to indigenous change agents, who then might continue to intervene after formal intervention ends.

Tertiary time point community interventions might focus on entrenched, long-term environmental problems such as crime, unemployment, dilapidated housing, and antiquated mass transit systems. As an example of this approach, Jones and Azrin (1973) placed ads in a newspaper soliciting job-opening information. Individuals offering job leads were paid $25.00 if an applicant was hired and three additional payments at the end of each of three weeks of employment. During the reward ad condition, 20 job openings were reported and eight formerly unemployed applicants eventually were hired. These findings are of added importance when considering the possibility that unemployment might be related causally to crime, mental illness, alcoholism, and family desertion.

## Societal Interventions

Societal-level interventions influence the functioning of communities, organizations, groups, and individuals. Primary preventive interventions are directed toward preventing the emergence of societal problems or enhancing strengths and competencies throughout many communities. Some societal-level programs designed by nonbehaviorists have incorporated behavioral procedures. For example, the World Bank has invested over $300 million in its training and visit system to improve agricultural productivity in several underdeveloped countries (Rowen, 1979). Behavioral components in this system include incentives (workers at the village level are given free housing), precise recording (of the number of insects per plant, to reduce the need for insecticide spraying), transmitting knowledge in small doses, and modeling (practices of successful farmers are demonstrated to neighbors). This program has resulted in gains such as doubling of grain production in India.

Secondary preventive societal interventions are directed at already existing problems which, if unchecked, could become alarmingly destructive. At the secondary preventive level, LoLordo and Shapiro (1980) have suggested potential societal-level strategies for birth control, including immediate cash payments for vasectomy and small payments for maintenance of a nonpregnant condition. Unfortunately, LoLordo and Shapiro suggest that most government policies are, in fact, pronatalist: they encourage more births through higher welfare payments and tax deductions for additional children. India is one exception to this situation. There innovative birth control policies have been implemented, including cash and vacations from work for sterilization, and higher rents in public housing following the birth of a family's fourth child. Behavioral psychologists have much to offer in evaluating positive and negative incentive plans directed toward limiting growth of populations throughout the world.

Tertiary time point interventions focus on long-standing, entrenched societal-level problems. For example, mental institutions frequently have failed to provide humane psychological and physical environments to patients. Fowler and Brodsky (1978) were involved directly in the development of the *Wyatt* vs. *Stickney* case, which ultimately found grossly deficient treatment at an institution. The court ordered minimum standards to be enacted, including individualized treatment plans, quality staff in sufficient numbers, rights to privacy and dignity, and the right to receive the least restrictive conditions necessary (Rosenhan & London, 1975). This court ruling subsequently has had direct implications for the rights of patients in mental institutions throughout the United States. Besides participating in judicial processes, behaviorists might also monitor stipulated behavior changes following judicial or legislative rulings and evaluate strategies to enhance compliance to new policies and laws.

## Conclusion

The earlier sections of this chapter were devoted to defining models for conceptualizing the etiology, treatment, and prognosis of psychological problems (humanistic, psychoanalytic, behavioral) and models for delivering mental health services (traditional, community mental health, preventive psychology). The behavioral paradigm was identified as an attractive approach for treating mental health problems, whereas the preventive psychology model was depicted as an innovative way of delivering mental health service, through primary prevention and environmental modification. While the preventive movement recognizes relatively unexplored targets of intervention, the behavioral approach provides a potent technology for monitoring and bringing about behavior change.

Illustrations of innovative behavioral preventive interventions were presented in the latter sections of this chapter. While this approach appears to be conceptually solid, the development of a firm foundation will require answers to several key, pressing questions. For example, Kazdin (1980) has speculated whether behavioral techniques can be administered on a large scale without significant loss in efficiency, and whether their technology can effectively be transferred to agencies which then would implement the programs. Fawcett, Mathews, and Fletcher (1980) have asked whether behavioral technology can be developed that is inexpensive, decentralized, flexible, sustainable, simple, and compatible. We hope questions such as these will guide the evolution of the entire behavioral preventive model.

## References

Albee, G. W. The relation of conceptual models to manpower needs. In E. L. Cowen, E. A. Gardner, & M. Zax (Eds.), *Emergent approaches to mental health problems.* New York: Appleton-Century-Crofts, 1967.

Allen, G. J., Chinsky, J. M., Larcen, S. W., Lochman, J. E., & Selinger, H. V. *Community psychology and the schools.* New York: Wiley, 1976.

Anthony, E. J. Children at risk from divorce: A review. In E. J. Anthony & C. Kopernik (Eds.), *The child in his family: Children at psychiatric risk.* New York: Wiley, 1974.

Baekeland, F., & Lundwall, L. Dropping out of treatment: A critical review. *Psychological Bulletin,* 1975, **82,** 738–783.

Bandura, A. *Principles of behavior modification.* New York: Holt, Rinehart & Winston, 1969.

Bandura, A., Grusec, J. E., & Menlove, F. L. Vicarious extinction of avoidance behavior. *Journal of Personality and Social Psychology*, 1967, **5**, 16–23.

Beck, A. T. *Cognitive therapy and the emotional disorders.* New York: International Universities Press, 1976.

Bloom, B. L. *Community mental health: A general introduction.* Monterey, Calif.: Brooks/Cole, 1977.

Bogat, G. A., Jones, J. W., & Jason, L. A. School transitions: Preventive intervention following an elementary school closing. *Journal of Community Psychology*, 1980, **8**, 343–352.

Boyd, V. S., Shueman, S., McMullan, Y. O., & Fretz, B. R. Transition groups for black freshmen: Integrated service and training. *Professional Psychology*, 1979, **10**, 42–48.

Callner, D. A. Behavioral treatment approaches to drug abuse: A critical review of the research. *Psychological Bulletin*, 1975, **82**, 143–164.

Caplan, G. *Principles of preventive psychiatry.* New York: Basic Books, 1964.

Caplan, G. *Support systems and community mental health.* New York: Behavioral Publications, 1974.

Catalano, R. *Health, behavior and the community.* New York: Pergamon Press, 1979.

Cowen, E. L. Social and community interventions. *Annual Review of Psychology*, 1973, **24**, 423–472.

Cradock, C., Cotler, S., & Jason, L. A. Primary prevention: Immunization of children for speech anxiety. *Cognitive Therapy and Research*, 1978, **2**, 389–396.

Cumming, J., & Cumming, E. *Ego and milieu: Theory and practice of environmental therapy.* New York: Atherton, 1962.

Cytryn, L., & Lourie, R. S. Mental retardation. In A. M. Freedman, H. I. Kaplan, & B. J. Sadock (Eds.), *Comprehensive textbook of psychiatry.* Vol. 2. Baltimore: Williams and Wilkins, 1975.

Davidson, W. S., & Wolfred, T. R. Evaluation of a community-based behavior modification program for prevention of delinquency: The failure of a success. *Community Mental Health Journal*, 1977, **13**, 295–305.

Davison, G. C., & Neale, J. M. *Abnormal psychology: An experimental clinical approach.* New York: Wiley, 1974.

DeCoster, D. Housing assignments for high ability students. *Journal of College Student Personnel*, 1966, **7**, 10–22.

Dohrenwend, B. P., & Dohrenwend, B. S. *Social status and psychological disorder.* New York: Wiley, 1969.

Durlak, J. A. Description and evaluation of a behaviorally oriented school based preventive mental health program. *Journal of Consulting and Clinical Psychology*, 1977, **45**, 27–33.

Durlak, J. A. Comparative effectiveness of paraprofessional and professional helpers. *Psychological Bulletin*, 1979, **86**, 80–92.

Ellis, A. *Reason and emotion in psychotherapy.* New York: Lyle Stuart, 1962.

Erickson, R. C. Outcome studies in mental hospitals: A review. *Psychological Bulletin*, 1975, **82**, 819–840.

Eysenck, H. J. Classification and the problem of diagnosis. In H. J. Eysenck (Ed.), *Handbook of abnormal psychology.* London: Pitman, 1960.

Eysenck, H. J., & Beech, H. R. Counter-conditioning and related methods. In A. E. Bergin & S. L. Garfield

(Eds.), *Handbook of psychotherapy and behavior change.* New York: Wiley, 1971.

Fawcett, S. B., Mathews, R. M., & Fletcher, R. K. Behavioral technology for community applications: Some promising directions. *Journal of Applied Behavior Analysis*, 1980, **13**, 505–518.

Fowler, R. D., & Brodsky, S. L. Development of a correctional-clinical psychology program. *Professional Psychology*, 1978, **9**, 440–447.

Garfield, S. L. Research on client variables in psychotherapy. In S. L. Garfield & A. E. Bergen (Eds.), *Handbook of psychotherapy and behavior change.* New York: Wiley, 1971.

Geller, E. S. Applications of behavioral analysis for litter control. In D. S. Glenwick & L. A. Jason (Eds.), *Behavioral community psychology: Progress and prospects.* New York: Praeger, 1980.

Glenwick, D. S. & LaGana Arata, C. Assertiveness training in a college companion program: Effects on student volunteers and rehabilitation center clients. *Rehabilitation Psychology*, in press.

Glidewell, J. C., & Swallow, C. S. *The prevalence of maladjustment in elementary schools: A report prepared for the Joint Commission on the Mental Health of Children.* Chicago: University of Chicago Press, 1969.

Glover, J., & Gary, A. L. Procedures to increase some aspects of creativity. *Journal of Applied Behavior Analysis*, 1976, **9**, 79–84.

Goodstein, L. D., & Sandler, I. Using psychology to promote human welfare. A conceptual analysis of the role of community psychology. *American Psychologist*, 1978, **33**, 882–892.

Gurin, G., Veroff, J., & Feld, S. *Americans view their mental health: A nationwide interview survey.* New York: Basic Books, 1960.

Haring, N. G., & Schiefelbusch, R. L. (Eds.), *Teaching special children.* New York: McGraw-Hill, 1976.

Holland, J. Behaviorism: Part of the problem or part of the solution? *Journal of Applied Behavior Analysis*, 1978, **11**, 163–174.

Hollingshead, A. B., & Redlich, F. C. *Social class and mental illness: A community study.* New York: Wiley, 1958.

Jason, L. A. A behavioral approach in enhancing disadvantaged children's academic abilities. *American Journal of Community Psychology*, 1977, **5**, 413–421.

Jason, L. A. Behavioral community psychology: Conceptualizations and applications. *Journal of Community Psychology*, 1977, **5**, 303–312. (b)

Jason, L. A. Prevention and environmental modification in a behavioral community model. *Behavioral Counseling Quarterly*, 1981, **1**, 91–107.

Jason, L. A., & Ferone, L. Behavioral versus process consultation interventions in school settings. In C. M. Franks & G. T. Wilson (Eds.), *Annual review of behavior therapy, theory and practice.* New York: Brunner/ Mazel, 1979.

Jason, L. A., Ferone, L., & Soucy, G. Teaching peer-tutoring behaviors in first and third grade classrooms. *Psychology in the Schools*, 1979, **16**, 261–269.

Jason, L. A., & Glenwick, D. S. Future directions: A critical look at the behavioral community approach. In D. S. Glenwick & L. A. Jason (Eds.), *Behavioral community psychology: Progress and prospects.* New York: Praeger, 1980.

Jason, L. A., McCoy, L., Blanco, D., & Zolik, E. S. Decreasing dog litter: Behavioral consultation to help a community group. *Evaluation Review*, 1980, **4**, 355–369.

Jason, L. A., Robson, S. D., & Lipshutz, S. A. Enhancing sharing behaviors through the use of naturalistic contingencies. *Journal of Community Psychology*, 1980, **8**, 237–244.

Jeger, A. M., Slotnick, R. S., & Schure, M. Towards a "self-help/professional model" of human service delivery. In D. E. Biegel & A. J. Naparstek (Eds.), *Community support systems and mental health: Building linkages*. New York: Springer, 1980.

Jones, R. J., & Azrin, N. H. An experimental application of a social reinforcement approach to the problem of job-finding. *Journal of Applied Behavior Analysis*, 1973, **6**, 345–353.

Kanfer, F. H., & Phillips, J. S. *Learning foundations of behavior therapy*. New York: Wiley, 1970.

Kazdin, A. E. Fictions, factions, and functions of behavior therapy. *Behavior Therapy*, 1979, **10**, 629–654.

Kazdin, A. E. Implications and obstacles for community extensions of behavioral techniques. In D. S. Glenwick & L. A. Jason (Eds.), *Behavioral community psychology: Progress and prospects*. New York: Praeger, 1980.

Keith, S. J., Gunderson, A. R., Buchsbaum, S., & Mosher, L. R. Special report: Schizophrenia 1976. *Schizophrenia Bulletin*, 1976, **2**, 510–565.

Kelly, J. G. The mental health agent in the urban community. In *Urban America and the planning of mental health services*. New York: Group for Advancement of Psychiatry, 1964.

Kessler, M., & Albee, G. W. Primary prevention. In M. R. Rosenzweig & L. W. Porter (Eds.), *Annual review of psychology*. Palo Alto, Calif.: Annual Reviews, 1975.

Kiesler, C. A. Mental health policy as a field of inquiry for psychology. *American Psychologist*, 1980, **35**, 1066–1080.

Koegel, R. L., & Rincover, A. Treatment of psychotic children in a classroom environment. *Journal of Applied Behavior Analysis*, 1974, **7**, 45–59.

Ledwidge, B. Cognitive behavior modification: A step in the wrong direction? *Psychological Bulletin*, 1978, **85**, 353–375.

Leighton, D. C. Distribution of psychiatric symptoms in a small town. *American Journal of Psychiatry*, 1956, **112**, 716–723.

Liberman, R. P., Wallace, C., Teigen, J., & Davis, J. Interventions with psychotic behaviors. In K. S. Calhoun, H. E. Adams, & K. M. Mitchell (Eds.), *Innovative treatment methods in psychopathology*. New York: Wiley, 1974.

LoLordo, V. M., & Shapiro, K. L. A behavioral approach to population control. In D. S. Glenwick & L. A. Jason (Eds.), *Behavioral community psychology: Progress and prospects*. New York: Praeger, 1980.

London, P. The end of ideology in behavior modification. *American Psychologist*, 1972, **27**, 913–920.

Lorion, R. P. Research on psychotherapy and behavior change with the disadvantaged: Past, present, and future directions. In S. L. Garfield & A. E. Bergin (Eds.), *Handbook of psychotherapy and behavior change*. New York: Wiley, 1978.

Lovaas, O. I. A program for the establishment of speech in psychotic children. In H. Y. Sloane, Jr., & B. B. MacAulay (Eds.), *Operant procedures in remedial speech in language training*. Boston: Houghton Mifflin, 1968.

MacDonald, K. R., Hedberg, A. D., & Campbell, L. M. A behavioral revolution in community mental health.

Community Mental Health Journal, 1974, **10**, 228–235.

Mahoney, M. J., Kazdin, A. E., & Lesswing, N. J. Behavior modification: Delusion or deliverance? In C. M. Franks & G. T. Wilson (Eds.), *Annual review of behavior therapy, theory and practice*. New York: Brunner/Mazel, 1974.

Matese, F., Shorr, S., & Jason, L. A. Behavioral and community interventions during transitions to parenthood. In A. Jeger & R. Slotnick (Eds.), *Community mental health: A behavioral-ecological perspective*. New York: Plenum Press, 1982.

McCord, J. A thirty-year follow-up of treatment effects. *American Psychologist*, 1978, **33**, 284–289.

Mears, F., & Gatchel, R. J. *Fundamentals of abnormal behavior*. Chicago: Rand McNally, 1979.

Mednick, S. A., & Wilkin-Lanoie, G. H. Intervention in children at high risk for schizophrenia. In G. W. Albee & J. M. Joffe (Eds.), *Primary prevention of psychopathology*. Vol. 1. *The issues*. Hanover, N.H.: University Press of New England, 1977.

Melamed, B. G., Yurcheson, R., Fleece, E. L., Hutcherson, S., & Hawes, R. Effects of film modeling on the reduction of anxiety-related behaviors in individuals varying in level of previous experience in the stress situation. *Journal of Consulting and Clinical Psychology*, 1978, **46**, 1357–1367.

Meyers, A. W., Artz, L. M., & Craighead, W. E. The effects of instructions, incentive, and feedback on a community problem: Dormitory noise. *Journal of Applied Behavior Analysis*, 1976, **9**, 445–457.

Nietzel, M. T., Winett, R. A., MacDonald, M. L., & Davidson, W. S. *Behavioral approaches to community psychology*. New York: Pergamon Press, 1977.

O'Connor, R. D. Modification of social withdrawal through symbolic modeling. *Journal of Applied Behavior Analysis*, 1969, **2**, 15–22.

Patterson, G. R. Interventions for boys with conduct problems: Multiple settings, treatments, and criteria. *Journal of Consulting and Clinical Psychology*, 1974, **42**, 471–481.

Pavlov, I. P. *Conditioned reflexes*. London: Oxford University Press, 1927.

Peterson, R. F., Knapp, T. J., Rosen, J. C., & Pither, B. F. The effects of furniture arrangement on the behavior of geriatric patients. *Behavior Therapy*, 1977, **8**, 464–467.

Poser, E. G. The effect of therapist training on group therapeutic outcome. *Journal of Consulting Psychology*, 1966, **30**, 283–289.

Poser, E. G., & Hartman, L. M. Issues in behavioral prevention: Empirical findings. *Advances in Behavior Research and Therapy*, 1979, **2**, 1–25.

Poser, E. G., & King, M. Strategies for the prevention of maladaptive fear responses. *Canadian Journal of Behavioral Sciences*, 1975, **7**, 279–294.

Quilitch, H. R., & Risley, T. R. The effects of play materials on social play. *Journal of Applied Behavior Analysis*, 1973, **6**, 573–578.

Rachman, S., & Teasdale, J. *Aversion therapy and behavior disorders: An analysis*. Coral Gables, Fla.: University of Miami Press, 1969.

Rappaport, J. *Community psychology: Values, research and action*. New York: Holt, Rinehart & Winston, 1977.

Rappaport, J., & Chinsky, J. M. Models for delivery of service from a historical and conceptual perspective. *Professional Psychology*, 1974, **5**, 42–50.

Reiff, R. Of cabbages and kings. *American Journal of Community Psychology*, 1975, **3**, 187–196.

Rimland, B. Death knell for psychotherapy? *American Psychologist*, 1979, **34**, 192.

Rosenhan, D. L., & London, P. (Eds.), *Theory and research in abnormal psychology*. New York: Holt, Rinehart & Winston, 1975.

Rosenthal, R., & Jacobson, L. Teachers' expectancies: Determinants of pupils' I.Q. gains. *Psychological Reports*, 1966, **19**, 115–118.

Rowen, H. Chutzpah and a hectare of land. *Cornell Alumni News*, 1979, **81**, 18–22.

Rychlak, J. F. *Introduction to personality theory*. Boston: Houghton Mifflin, 1973.

Sale, J. S. Family day care: One alternative in the delivery of developmental services in early childhood. *American Journal of Orthopsychiatry*, 1973, **43**, 37–45.

Salter, A. *Conditioned reflex therapy*. New York: Farrar, Straus, 1949.

Sarason, S. B. *The psychological sense of community*. San Francisco: Jossey-Bass, 1974.

Sarason, S. B. An asocial psychology and a misdirected clinical psychology. *American Psychologist*, 1981, **36**, 827–836.

Sauna, V. D. Sociocultural aspects of psychotherapy and treatment: A review of the literature. In L. E. Abt & L. Bellak (Eds.), *Progress in clinical psychology*. Vol. 3. New York: Grune & Stratton, 1966.

Savage, C. Psychedelic therapy. In J. M. Shlien (Ed.), *Research in psychotherapy*. Vol. 3. Washington, D.C.: American Psychological Association, 1968.

Shapiro, A. K. Placebo effects in medicine, psychotherapy, and psychoanalysis. In A. E. Bergin & S. L. Garfield (Eds.), *Handbook of psychotherapy and behavior change*. New York: Wiley, 1971.

Sirbu, W., Cotler, S., & Jason, L. A. Primary prevention: Teaching parents behavioral child rearing skills. *Family Therapy*, 1978, **5**, 163–170.

Skeels, H. M. Adult status of children with contrasting early life experiences: A follow-up study. *Monographs of the Society for Research in Child Development*, 1966, **31** (3).

Skinner, B. F. *The behavior of organisms: An experimental analysis*. New York: Appleton-Century, 1938.

Smith, M. L., & Glass, G. V. Meta-analysis of psychotherapy outcome studies. *American Psychologist*, 1977, **32**, 752–760.

Spitzzeri, A., & Jason, L. A. Prevention and treatment of smoking in school age children. *Journal of Drug Education*, 1979, **9**, 315–326.

Srole, L., Langner, T. S., Michael, S. T., Opler, M. K., & Rennie, T. A. C. *Mental health in the metropolis: The Midtown Manhattan study*. New York: McGraw-Hill, 1962.

Stenmark, D. Notes from the Community Psychology Conference. Unpublished manuscript, Tampa, Fla., 1980.

Tittle, C. R. Labelling and crime: An empirical evaluation. In W. R. Grove (Ed.), *The labeling of deviance*. New York: Halsted Press, 1975.

Truax, C. B., & Mitchell, K. M. Research in certain therapist interpersonal skills in relation to process and outcome. In A. E. Bergin & S. L. Garfield (Eds.), *Handbook of psychotherapy and behavior change*. New York: Wiley, 1971.

Turner, A. J., & Goodson, W. H. Behavioral technology applied to a community mental health center: A demonstration. *Journal of Community Psychology*, 1977, **5**, 209–224.

Ullmann, L. P., & Krasner, L. *A psychological approach to abnormal behavior*. Englewood Cliffs, N.J.: Prentice-Hall, 1969.

Umbarger, C. C., Dalsimer, J. S., Morrison, A. P., & Breggin, P. R. *College students in a mental hospital*. New York: Grune & Stratton, 1962.

Weiner, H., Thaler, M., Reiser, M. F., & Mirsky, I. A. Etiology of duodenal ulcer: I. Relation of specific psychological characteristics to rate of gastric secretion (serious pepsinogen). *Psychosomatic Medicine*, 1957, **19**, 1–10.

Willems, E. P. Behavioral technology and behavioral ecology. *Journal of Applied Behavior Analysis*, 1974, **7**, 151–165.

Winett, R. A., Battersby, C. D., & Edwards, S. M. The effects of architectural change, individualized instruction, and group contingencies on the academic performance and social behavior of sixth graders. *Journal of School Psychology*, 1975, **13**, 28–40.

Wolpe, J. *Psychotherapy by reciprocal inhibition*. Stanford: Stanford University Press, 1958.

Zax, M., & Cowen, E. L. *Abnormal psychology: Changing conceptions*. (2nd ed.) New York: Holt, Rinehart & Winston, 1976.

# PART IV
# PERSPECTIVES ON LIFE STRESS

# INTRODUCTION TO PART IV

A key concern for preventive psychology is the development of a greater understanding of factors which influence the vulnerability of individuals and populations to psychosocial and somatic dysfunction. The focus of this section is on environmental conditions that are associated with increased levels of stress and the processes that bear on the relative vulnerability of those who experience such circumstances. Drawing from the two preceding sections which focused on those personal and environmental variables that may facilitate adaptation, the conceptualizations of the stress process offered in this section offer suggestions for how these factors and others may be viewed as complimentary elements of the coping processes called for by both chronically stressful conditions as well as discrete life events or transitions.

In the first chapter Allen and Britt attempt an integration of the current research regarding social class and mental health. Their examination of the well established relationship between social class and dysfunction leads them to offer several suggestions for refinement of previously posed explanatory models which view stress as a key moderator of the link between social class and psychological disorder. The Dohrenwends' (1981) hypothesized feedback loop between stress and disorder is elaborated, and Allen and Britt seek to extend the feedback loop to include a reciprocal relationship between social class and stress. Beyond the reciprocity of their three-step social class-stress-disorder model, they discuss a feedback system to help explain the role of potential coping resources in the stress process. The accessibility and strength of an individual's economic, social, and personal resources are believed to serve as buffers of the inevitable stressful shifts in life circumstances that everyone faces. These three resources mutually influence each other in a feedback system. Since economic resources are, by definition, tied to social class, the implications of such a system on stress buffering becomes obvious. The reciprocal impacts of economic resources on social and personal resources and vice versa are also elaborated. The authors finally tie the two feedback loops together to aid in the interpretation of social class-disorder relationships.

A second population believed to be at high risk for disorder are those of minority status. While the term "minorities" usually connotes membership in a nondominant ethnic or cultural group, the definition is broadened by Moritsugu and Sue to include any group with numerical, social, cultural, or political minority status. The dimensions that may determine such status are seen to include any distinguishing characteristic of an individual in relation to his or her community.

A key element of both Allen and Britt's and Moritsugu and Sue's broader considerations of the relationship between social class or minority status and well-being is the role of economic resources. In their chapter Seidman and Rapkin focus more specifically on how economic resources relate to the experience of stress. These authors offer an ecological framework for understanding and classifying the association between economic conditions and dysfunction. Literature that examines the links between the economy and psychosocial dysfunction cross-sectionally, as well as over time, is reviewed briefly, as is that on the specific impact of job loss. The authors demonstrate that a position which views deprivation or gain as relative, rather than based on absolute income change or socioeconomic conditions, is of particular utility for explicating the association between dysfunction and economic resources.

The final chapter by Felner, Farber and Primavera considers the implications of life events and changes for prevention and for enhancement of functioning. Prior work on multiple and single life events is reviewed and the limitations of the findings and conceptual frameworks of this work for informing preventive efforts are discussed. The authors argue that the traditions in which much of this work is based have led to an overemphasis on the stress and adverse consequences associated with life events and, thus, to the development of conceptual frameworks which are ill suited to the more positive adaptive mastery goals of prevention. Further, Felner et al. argue that while much of the prior work purports to deal with life change, in fact, it overlooks the elements of such change to instead concentrate only on one aspect of that change, i.e., stress. They present a Life Transitions model that clarifies differences among life events and places greater emphasis on the mastery of the adaptive tasks that accompany major life changes. Within this framework, factors that have traditionally been viewed primarily as moderators of life stress, such as social support, are shown to not only "buffer" stress but be reflective of both the pre-event competence and coping abilities of the individual as well as the reflective of the degree to which they have successfully dealt with the adaptive tasks posed by the transitions.

Felner et al. point out that the amount of change and the degree of stress are not one and the same, though one may influence the other. They advocate a shift in the study of life events to search for better understanding of the change process so as to anticipate the skills necessary to facilitate growth from the inevitable turnings in life's course.

The four chapters all point to a need for a more complex model to understand the process of coping with stress and life change. All acknowledge the importance of both the individual and the environment in studying stress and its impact. Explicitly or implicitly they acknowledge the reciprocal nature of the variable interaction within this process. Each chapter sought not only to build models but also to specify action programs that these models prescribe. They are, in the words of Allen and Britt, "suggestive and provocative" for future work in this area.

# 9 SOCIAL CLASS, MENTAL HEALTH, AND MENTAL ILLNESS: THE IMPACT OF RESOURCES AND FEEDBACK

La Rue Allen and
David W. Britt

The correlation between social class and prevalence of symptoms of psychological disorder is one of the most thoroughly documented relationships in epidemiological research. So consistent are these findings, with so few exceptions, that we will assume this relationship as given and move on to questions of theory and practice which derive from this relationship. Our first objective will be to bring clarity to the selection-causation argument by showing the dependence of these processes on feedback as a driving force among the relevant variables. Second, we will show the significance of this argument for preventive interventions. The unifying theme for considering these questions is an examination of the substantial role of economic, social, and personal resources. In the first case, we will argue that differentiating among resources brings clarity regarding the dynamics of the causation-selection argument and permits exploitation of the role of feedback in this argument. In the second case, we will argue that resources and their vulnerabilities must be separated from the individual and his or her vulnerability if attention to the proper loci of intervention is to be attained.

## Causation or Selection: The Initial Relationships

Variation in the prevalence of types of psychological disorder by class has been reported with consistency over the last four decades (Faris & Dunham, 1939; Hollingshead & Redlich, 1958; Srole, Langner, Michael, Opler, & Rennie, 1962). Dohrenwend and Dohrenwend (1969) found that of 25 studies with relevant data, 20 showed the highest rates of pathology in the lowest economic strata. In a review including more than 20 new studies, this relationship was still evident (Dohrenwend & Dohrenwend, 1974). In this section we will review representative studies that tested this relationship and discuss theoretical rationales which may help us to understand its existence.

Two kinds of explanations are possible in a two-variable model—that A causes B or that B causes A. In the former instance A, social class, may cause B, psychological disorder, because class membership carries with it life conditions that expose one to whatever it is that produces disorder.[1] Theories such as this have been called social causation theories and have assumed that the sociocultural environment (which varies with social class) influences an individual's

149

functioning. An exemplar of research from this realm is Hollingshead and Redlich's seminal work on class structure and mental illness (1958). Using a psychiatric census of the New Haven metropolitan area, they tested hypotheses derived from a hierarchical view of the relationship between social class (as the causal force) and mental illness.

One of the study's central discoveries was that there was a systematic relationship between class and the prevalence of treated psychological disorder. With social class divided into five levels, disorder was underrepresented in the highest level (class I) and twice what might have been expected in class V (the lowest level), with projections based on the proportion of each class in the wider community. The second hypothesis, that status and diagnosis would overlap, was also confirmed. Across the five classes (from high to low) the proportion of psychotics increased and the proportion of neurotics decreased. Hypothesis three was also confirmed; Hollingshead and Redlich found "real differences in where, how, and how long, persons in the several classes have been cared for by psychiatrists." The bias was so evident that even where patients from different classes were seen at the same facility, there was an inverse relationship between class on the one hand and depth and duration of psychiatric intervention on the other.

Focusing on treatment populations can be misleading because social class position may affect the treatment received (as Hollingshead and Redlich found) quite apart from any effects of class on diagnosis or actual disorder (Dohrenwend & Dohrenwend, 1969, 1974). The Midtown Study (Srole et al., 1962; Srole, Langner, Michael, Kirkpatrick, Opler, & Rennie, 1978) addressed this possible confound with an early examination of rates of disorder in a nontreatment population. Around the same time, Leighton and others (Leighton, Harding, Macklin, Macmillan, & Leighton, 1963) reported on interview and questionnaire data from a random sample of residents of rural Stirling County, Nova Scotia. Both sets of studies found first, a large unmet need for treatment among the general population and second, the same inverse relationship between class and prevalence of disorder.

In contrast to the social causation position, other theorists have argued that the causal flow between social class and psychological disorder is indeed in one direction—but with psychological disorder causing social class placement. People with psychological disorders are said to select themselves (or are selected) into the lower social classes. For instance, Dunham originally ascribed the varying prevalence of psychological disorder to the effects of life in different ecological zones, a classic social causation argument (Faris & Dunham, 1939). But in 1965 he recanted in a report on admissions and readmissions to Detroit psychiatric hospitals. This study revealed that, when length of residence in the Detroit area was held constant, the pattern of highest admission rates from poverty areas held only for first admissions. Based on these findings, Dunham argued that disordered people drift into poverty areas rather than becoming disordered as a result of being there. Additional support for the social selection argument has come from studies of social mobility. If the family of origin is of a higher social class than the maladjusted offspring, then the disorders must have precipitated a decline in social class (Goldberg & Morrison, 1963; Turner & Wagenfeld, 1967).

Neither social selection nor social causation arguments are undisputed; nor is it necessary to cling to one or the other set of propositions tenaciously. It is quite likely that future research will show that some disorders are caused by the social environment, while in other cases disorder determines class position and concomitant social environment (Dohrenwend & Dohrenwend, 1981b). In still other cases the relationship is likely to be proven genuinely reciprocal.

Direct manipulation of the relationship between class and disorder would require sufficient understanding of what it is about social status and psychological disorder that sustains the relationship. A two-variable model leaves us with too few options for explanation and for prediction. For instance, if disorder can alter class placement, interventions derived from the two-variable model would have to be aimed at directly reducing disorder—but how? There are no clues. Clearly, knowing that the relationship between disorder and class placement might be reciprocal may partially resolve some roughly specified theoretical questions, but it does not substantially improve our ability to intervene. Our options at this point would be to call for a radical redistribution of income, occupational access, and so on, or wave a magic wand to reduce the incidence and prevalence of psychological disorder in the lower classes. Rather than resorting to either of these extremes—though the voodoo-economic magic wand approach does have some appeal—a more prudent course would be to respecify this two-variable model to better understand why the relationships exist, and improve our ability to effectively intervene (Hilliard, 1981).

## Stressful Life Events as a Mediator

Further specification is provided by expanding our discussion to the consideration of three-variable models, with stressful life events added to social class and psychological disorder. Stressful life events have been catalogued and rated on a number of dimensions relating to how great an impact they have on a person's life—whether a positive impact or a deleterious one (Dohrenwend & Dohrenwend, 1974; Holmes & Rahe, 1967). However, no single event has the same impact on all who are faced with it. In addition, it is unlikely that all who are confronted with a major stressor, such as the death of a spouse, will react similarly. Stressful life events (SLEs) have two common characteristics: (1) they involve change; and (2) the amount of change generated by an undesirable event is generally greater than the amount generated by a desirable one (Dohrenwend, 1978).

The most straightforward and best researched of the three-variable models is a simple recursive one which posits an inverse relationship between class position and stressful life events and then a positive relationship between stressful life events and psychological disorder as shown:

$$\text{Social Class} \rightarrow \text{Stressful Life Events} \rightarrow \text{Psychological Disorder}$$

The Dohrenwends (1969, 1981a) have argued that stressful life events are differentially distributed by class, so that those in the lower classes, exposed to more stressful life events and/or less able to manage them, are at greater risk for a high level of disorder.

In such a model, stressful life events may be said to interpret the negative consequences of lower-class membership. But does differential exposure to stressful life events account for all of the impact of social class position on psychological disorder? Several authors have argued that it does not, and that there is a sizable residual, direct effect which is not related to the distribution of stressful life events:

$$\left. \begin{array}{l} \text{Social} \\ \text{Class} \end{array} \right\} \begin{array}{l} \xrightarrow{\hspace{2cm}} \\ \rightarrow \text{Stressful} \rightarrow \\ \text{Life Events} \end{array} \left\{ \begin{array}{l} \text{Psychological} \\ \text{Disorder} \end{array} \right.$$

Several researchers have speculated about the factors involved in this residual effect (Dohrenwend, 1978; Kessler, 1979a; 1979b). Kessler (1979a), for example, speaks of differential vulnerability to stress: stressful life events may occur in the middle and upper classes, but their effects are partially offset by the relative invulnerability which these classes enjoy. In this model, it is still unclear to what such class-related invulnerability should be attributed, but there are some provocative possibilities involving access to resources which we will shortly discuss. Others have argued that it is not differential vulnerability to stressful life events which is involved, but rather a relative vulnerability to being labeled as unbalanced or mentally ill.[2] Scheff

(1975) and Szasz (1961) were early proponents of this position, which, if taken to its extreme, would mean that mental disorder is as likely in the middle and upper classes as in the lower classes: all that differs is the extent to which people can successfully challenge and defeat efforts to label them as mentally ill and ward off the negative consequences of being so labeled.

A variant of both of these differential vulnerability hypotheses proposes that the influence of upper-class position as a buffer against stressful life events and labeling is so strong that it goes farther than merely offsetting the negative impact of situational stress. The result is an interactive relationship in which people from the lower classes, exposed to frequent and severe stressors, are *especially* likely to manifest disordered behavior. The effect, in other words, is much greater than would be expected on the basis of the additive effects of class position and stressful life events. Alternatively, the middle and upper classes may be thought of as somehow insulated from the effects of frequent and severe stressful life events, so that when such events occur, they may be dealt with effectively before serious negative consequences ensue. Kessler's (1979b) analysis lends considerable support to such a differential vulnerability interpretation. Whichever of these interpretations is correct, it is at least clear that the reasons for the apparently large separate and interactive effects of social class must be better understood. Some of the more plausible reasons will be investigated as we introduce additional relevant variables into the model.

All of the three-variable models relating social class, stressful life events, and psychological disorder that have been discussed so far have been recursive in the sense that the direction of causality is assumed to be in one direction only, from social class, through (in some) stressful life events, to psychopathology (see Note 1). By introducing feedback into the model a more discrete examination of the social selection and social causation arguments may be developed.[3] Let us consider these in two stages:

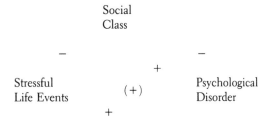

In this model we assume that the presence of dysfunctional symptoms may increase the chances that stressful life events will occur. Since increases

in stressful life events generate further symptoms, escalating stressors and symptoms is established— shown by the (+) inside the causal loop between stress and disorder. By assuming for the moment that such a feedback cycle exists, our understanding of the insulating role of upper- and middle-class placement is expanded. We need not infer only that being in the upper and middle classes reduces the chances of experiencing disturbing symptoms. We may stretch our conceptualization of that influence by noting how class position affects the speed with which the feedback between disorder and stressful life events takes place and how large an impact each variable has on the other. It appears that as class position increases, the magnitude of the stressful-life-event/ disorder reciprocal relationship decreases and may occur more slowly as well. Higher class position may then be said to dampen the stressful-life-events/disorder cycle; lower class position may be said, conversely, to exacerbate the stressful-life-event/disorder relationship. Such an understanding of the role of class is compatible with both the Dohrenwends' (1981b) interpretation in terms of differential exposure to stress and Kessler's (1979b) argument that differential vulnerability is at work. First, lower class membership increases the chances of exposure to severe and frequent stressful life events, and the risk of psychological disorder. Second, lower class membership increases the vulnerability of people to the negative consequences of both stressful life events and psychological disorder. Conversely, people at the top run somewhat less risk of stressful life events and psychological disorder and are more insulated when these conditions do occur.

The Dohrenwends (1981b) have labeled the reciprocal relationship between stressful life events and symptoms the "proneness" hypothesis. The central mechanism or driving force in our model, however, is not that people are differentially prone to experiencing symptoms (they may be, of course, for genetic, physiological, or other environmental reasons), but that feedback between the two variables leads to progressive worsening or perpetuation of both frequent and severe stressful life events and to indices of severe and frequent disorder. The power of feedback to create progressively worsening conditions—especially in the lower classes— must be recognized.

Complicating this model only slightly in our second stage, we include another feedback loop to provide a somewhat different perspective from which to consider the selection/causation problem discussed in our first section.

Social $\xrightarrow{\quad}$ Stressful $\xrightarrow{\quad +}$ Psychological
Class    (+)   Life Events   (+)   Disorder
       −                    +

Stressful life events here become critical for both the social selection and causation hypotheses, setting up mutually reinforcing positive feedback loops with both social class and psychological disorder. More frequent and/or severe stressors may, for example, reduce one's ability to generate income. If carried forward, driven as in this case by the relationship between stressful life events and disorder, they can lead to downward mobility. In this case, a person might be displaced either from his parents' or his own earlier class position (intergenerational versus intragenerational downward mobility). These may indeed be powerful dynamics, made more so when we recognize the great likelihood that most residual direct effects between social class and psychological disorder (not pictured here) would only serve to reinforce the impact of these two feedback loops.

The impression one is left with after examining these relationships is that secure class positions, normal and tolerable stress levels, and mild and infrequent symptoms are a fragile reality—especially for the lower classes. We know, however, that class position is relatively stable across time (Blau & Duncan, 1967; Coleman & Rainwater, 1978), that almost everyone experiences at least temporary periods of severe stress (Caplan, 1964), and that the prevalence of self-reported symptoms for at least short periods of time is relatively high (Srole et al., 1962). Consequently, it seems reasonable to assume that there are strong countervailing forces that can act on the pernicious dynamics which we have been discussing. Obvious nominees for such forces are those factors which are assumed to be so strongly related to social class that social class has traditionally served as their proxy: resources.

## Resources: Divide and Conquer

A frequently advanced alternative explanation for the effects of social class placement on differential rates of psychological disorder emphasizes access to resources. Upper- and middle-class persons are thought to have greater access to resources, and therefore to have their vulnerability to the development of disordered behavior directly reduced. Alternatively, the effect may be an indirect one, with resources having their effect through another variable that provides some buffer or insulation against the pernicious effects of stressful life events. Surprisingly, however, the discussion of resources in the relevant literature is almost invariably oversimplified. In some cases, resources—particularly economic and political ones—are assumed to be so obviously associated with social class as to require no explanation (Kessler, 1979b). Economic resources have been used to define social class (Eaton, 1981), though there are some (Liem & Liem, 1978) who have argued that economic resources should be considered as distinct from social class. Others have combined economic and social resources (Myers, Lindenthal & Pepper, 1975) to speak of that venerable but vague sociological construct, social integration. Still others have focused almost exclusively on one type of resource, whether social support systems (Cobb, 1976; Dean & Lin, 1977; Lin, Simeone, Ensel, & Kuo, 1979), individual invulnerability (Kessler, 1979a, 1979b; Liem & Liem, 1978), or economic resiliency (Brenner, 1973; Catalano & Dooley, 1980). But there has been little discussion of how these resources are definitionally discrete and conceptually interrelated, or of how they, in turn, affect (and are affected by) social class, stressful life events, and psychological disorder.

We would propose that differentiating among personal, economic, and social resources may provide a convenient wedge for disentangling and clarifying the interrelationships among class, disorder, and stressful life events. Through this clarification, we can focus attention on alternative and more effective ways of intervening as community psychologists. In this section we will establish some commonsense definitions of these resources and then discuss the implications of assuming that each of these (in turn) is the critical variable in understanding the relationships among social, economic, and personal resources and the relationships of those three resources to psychological disorder. We will follow this discussion by reintroducing social class and stressful life events to show how the dynamics involved in these relationships may be clarified by more careful specification of resources. There are instances where the distinctions among resources are more analytic than real. (For example, are you providing social or economic resources when you lend a friend some money?) So we are not aiming for completely independent definitions. Second, our definitions are intended to be suggestive and provocative, rather than exhaustive.

Economic resources have the greatest chance of being confounded with social class, since the latter is usually operationalized as some composite of education, occupation, and—most importantly here—income. Porter (1975) provides a starting place for an operationalizable definition in her discussion of the factors that lenders consider when judging an individual as a credit risk. The three Cs of credit are character (which we'll discuss later as a personal resource), capacity, and capital. Capacity refers to the financial ability to repay a loan, and is affected by such things as earnings, kind of job, length of time on the job, and prospects for advancement. More formally, capacity refers to how stable the applicant's income generation has been, the current level of income generation, and future prospects for generating income. Capital refers to assets which could serve as collateral, and would include such things as valuable paintings, cars, homes, stocks, bonds, and, of course, money in the bank. But in assessing the vulnerability of someone's economic resources, it is essential to also note how an individual's resources compare with those of his reference group. It is in this way that economic resources, as mediating factors, can tell us more than social class status alone would. Being unable to repay a $1 million loan might be more devastating in some circles than an inability to secure a $500 loan is in others. Less dramatically perhaps, not being able to afford the kind of vacation endorsed by one's social group can also constitute, or contribute to the creation of, a stressful life event. Such invidious comparisons may occur at any absolute level of economic resources.

Studies of social resources (many of which have been reviewed by Liem and Liem, 1978) have focused on primary and secondary interpersonal relationships (e.g., Brown, Birley, & Wing, 1972; Schwab, cited in Liem & Liem, 1978), and neighborhood and community attachment (e.g., Leighton et al., 1963; Lin et al., 1979), often organized under the rubric of social networks (Mitchell, 1974). These resources differ in, among other things, their components (Tolsdorf, 1976), and in the emotional support, informational value, and esteem provided to consumers of the resource (Cobb, 1976). Some of these clearly refer to structure, others to social resource content. Community psychologists consider building and strengthening social support systems important preventive tools (Dohrenwend, 1978) and assume that, by some still little-understood mechanism, support systems can be good for people.

Personal resources may refer to how you would perform as a borrower, that is, honesty, sense of responsibility, soundness of judgment—all the qualities which are attributed to good credit risks (Porter, 1975); your intelligence level (Yando, Seitz, & Zigler, 1979); the degree to which you are fatalistic (Wheaton, 1980); your self-esteem (Rosenberg, 1965); coping styles (Mechanic, 1974, 1975, 1977); political cynicism

(Greenberg, 1971); or communication skills (Dohrenwend & Dohrenwend, 1969). The list of personal resources could be extended, but these examples should serve to make the point; these are all attributes of individuals rather than of groups. They differ from economic resources in being characteristics which might *lead to* the generation of income rather than having immediate monetary value. We will assume that all of these resources may be placed on a continuum labeled "vulnerability to disruption." We consider relative vulnerability to be a property of each of these resources rather than an attribute of individuals only (unlike Monat & Lazarus, 1977, or Kessler, 1979a—though with Kessler, vulnerability in individuals is said to be both constitutionally and environmentally determined). Having defined these resources, let us consider a hypothetical closed system consisting of these three resources and psychological disorder. To simplify our discussion, we will divorce ourselves even further from the complexities of real life and imagine that we may elect each variable in turn as the primary catalyst or locus of causation while the rest react to hypothesized changes in the primary variable.

Let us begin our simulation by assigning causal primacy to social resources. If we imagine that social resources are becoming less vulnerable, what happens to the other variables in our hypothetical closed system? If social resources are functioning adequately (that is, remaining invulnerable to disruption), then they should be reducing the vulnerability of personal resources.[4] Having qualitative information (and role models) on effective coping styles should reinforce coping characteristics in individuals. For example, self-esteem levels are intimately associated with feedback from social groups (Cobb, 1976). Further, the subjective definition of events and situations as stressful or nonstressful is influenced by one's reference groups (Kessler, 1979a). All of these together speak to an indirect impact of social resources on psychological disorder, mediated by personal resources:

Social                Personal
Resource      →      Resource      →      Psychological
Vulnerability        Vulnerability         Disorder

Similarly, one could argue (as did Myers et al., 1975), that social resources may create economic resources, as in the proverbial "old boy" network, and thus have part of their overall impact on psychological disorder interpreted by economic resources. By this we mean that economic resources may be useful in further explaining the nature of the relationship between social resources and psychological disorder. The residual direct effects of social resources on disorder might

best be conceptualized as emotional support or a sense of belonging. Arguments regarding what is a genuine direct or indirect effect of social resources on psychological disorder could go on endlessly. The important points to remember here are that these resources are analytically discrete; one can imagine plausible effects of variation in social resources on the other two resources and on psychological disorder. A second point to remember is that networks may not always be positive in their impact—they may even be destructive, "schizophrenogenic" (Mishler & Wexler, 1965), more generally undermining of personal resources (Tolsdorf, 1976), or irrelevant to or undermining of the generation of economic resources.

There is a growing sense that social scientists have conceived of man as being too socialized (Wrong, 1961), too much the witless pawn of social forces. To the contrary, some have suggested that individuals may play a considerable role in the construction of the social resources upon which they call for support (Britt & Campbell, 1977). It is but a short step, then, to assigning causal primacy to personal resources in our hypothetical system. Various personal resources may facilitate the generation of economic resources or retard their development. Those with greater self-esteem, higher need for achievement, more intelligence, lower levels of fatalism, and more perseverance, and who display Porter's (1975) "character," should have a better chance of developing economic resources than those who do not. Hence even though fatalism, for example, may directly affect one's chances of developing symptoms (Wheaton, 1980), part of its total impact (and that of other personal resources) may be interpreted by its indirect effect through economic resources. Further, many of these personal attributes may facilitate surrounding oneself with invulnerable social resources. For example, a woman faced with trying to "make it in a man's world" (Pogrebin, 1970) may find discussions of what Johnny had for lunch on Thursday low in relevance. Over a period of time, she may shape her social network to generate more discussions of how Paul constructed a budget report or how Marlene found a new job. Here again, both direct and indirect effects of personal resource vulnerability could be advanced. Note, too, that all of these adjustments may not be beneficial; changes in the composition of social networks for short-term solutions may actually decrease the chances of long-term adjustment and accelerate the onset of psychological disorder. For instance, an adolescent, afraid of being unliked, may join a group of shoplifters to assure herself of companions. Adapting herself to this group's mores may mean that she has no time for self-confrontation, for discovering her own ideals and establishing a firm identity. Achieving this sense of identity is a primary task of adolescence which, left undone, can lead to role confusion (Erickson, 1963). Role confusion may lead to lowered self-esteem (among other things), which will make personal resources vulnerable in the future by way of this adolescent's choice of social resources for the present. Alternatively, surrounding oneself with really competent role models may backfire if they are given to invidious distinctions (compare Szasz's existential cannibalism) or if they create unrealistically high expectations for one's own performance.

Economic resources may also be made the root of all causation in our little system. Having a greater capacity to generate income may enable people to buy adequate external social support such as psychiatric services (Dohrenwend & Dohrenwend, 1969), if nothing else. But there is ample evidence that having more discretionary income creates the possibility for greater variation in lifestyle and friendship choice. In addition, having more "lendables" (cars, tools, boats, books, and so on) creates more possibilities for the sorts of exchange relationships that can solidify social networks. Suburbia, for example, is replete with exchanges of lawn spreaders for hammers, or sugar for eggs. But exchange relationships may not always lead to strengthened support networks. For instance, McAuliffe and Gordon (1974) have documented the dark side of these exchanges in their discussion of the social bankruptcy which may occur when one person (a heroin addict, in their study) constantly asks for more than he gives. And with regard to personal resource development, both greater capital and capacity may beneficially influence one's self-esteem and coping styles.

Finally, we will complete our modest simulation by imagining that we can manipulate psychological disorder and observe the effects ripple through the three resource variables. Hypothetically stimulating the level of psychological disorder in this way enables us to consider more closely the implications of the proneness hypothesis (Dohrenwend & Dohrenwend, 1981a), which, it will be recalled, focuses on the positive feedback loop between psychological disorder and stressful life events across time. Knowing that one's behavior signals psychological disorder may become immediately self-fulfilling (e.g., Storms & McCaul, 1976) if anxiety is an important index of psychological disorder, such as in the Midtown Study (Srole et al., 1962). The anxiety simply continues to feed on itself, acting as both cause and effect in this feedback loop. Were anxiety included as a personal resource characteristic rather than a part of the disorder variable, the result would be equally destructive, al-

though somewhat different conceptually. Just as plausibly, communication skills, self-esteem, and other personal resources may be undermined by the occurrence of marked symptoms of psychological disorder. In these cases the same strong sense of self-fulfillment, as stressors and severity of disorder cycle through time, continues to be present.

How fast a self-fulfilling prophecy of progressive illness occurs, what accelerates it, what dampens, stops, or even reverses it—these are in large measure empirical questions which are beyond the scope of this paper. Two preliminary observations should be noted. First, the proneness and vulnerability hypotheses can be seen to be conceptually identical once feedback is considered and personal resources are focused upon. (This should be no great surprise, as their dictionary definitions are quite similar.) In both cases, the essence of the argument appears to be the need for a threshold of adequacy for personal resources in dealing with stressful life events. Any self-esteem (communications skills and so on) in excess of that threshold (however intangible that point may be) could be said to reduce the pernicious effects of stressful life events and could dampen the vicious cycle between stressful life events and disorder. Correspondingly, those with barely adequate (or even less than adequate) personal resources may be said to have personal resource vulnerability, making the individual susceptible to the full impact of the viciousness of the feedback relationship between stressful life events and disorder.

That case where the stressful-life-events/disorder cycle appears to be moving along, unrestricted by adequate personal resources, brings us to the second observation, which may be introduced as a question: At what point do symptoms stabilize? One intriguing possibility which follows from our earlier discussion is that the cycle would stop at a point where stressful life events became manageable. Erickson (1963) has argued that adoption of the sick role (that is, coming to identify oneself as sick) has such an origin by virtue of being anxiety-reducing. [5] A full answer to the question of what dampens the stressful-life-events/disorder cycle, or what implications these processes have for the vulnerability hypothesis, cannot be attempted until economic and social resources are brought into the picture. Let us turn, then, to consideration of how increasing psychological disorder affects social resources. There is some research (Lemert, 1962; Mechanic, 1962) suggesting that the more isolated an individual is, the more likely he will be ostracized by the group. Members tend to close ranks *against* the bizarre-acting member, treating him as an outsider, defining his symptoms as internal ("Why is he so paranoid?"), and reducing the sufferer's chances of access to help in developing strategies for reducing the severity of his symptoms. The more fully the disordered member is integrated into the group, on the other hand, the greater the chance of its closing ranks *around* him, protecting him from outsiders, defining his symptoms as "only temporary," attributing the symptoms to external causes ("She's been under a lot of pressure lately"), and both generating and implementing coping strategies (Yarrow, Schwartz, Murphy, & Deasy, 1955). If these strategies are adaptive, or if the fact of being emotionally supported is itself anxiety-reducing, then the symptoms should stabilize or even become less pronounced as the cycle is dampened.

The vulnerability of a person's social resources depends on the adaptive utility and emotional support provided by these resources and the length of time (or frequency with which) a person may draw on these resources before becoming socially "bankrupt" (McAuliffe & Gordon, 1977). Defined as such, the vulnerability of personal and social resources may be combined according to some weighting scheme, to estimate the aggregate risk to the individual from both sources. Note again that vulnerability is thought of as a property of the resources rather than of the individual. This is more than a semantic difference, and has implications for how interventions are designed and implemented. Making vulnerability a property of individuals shapes efforts toward more clinical or individually based responses; viewing vulnerability as a property of resources biases our conceptualization of the intervention process toward community-based and social-policy-oriented solutions.

Economic resources, and the impact of more severe symptoms upon them, may be treated in the same way as social resources—perhaps even more easily, as the metaphor of bankruptcy is self-evident in such situations. More pronounced symptoms have been shown to reduce income-earning potential, presumably through a variety of mechanisms (Britt, 1976). Character (again, in the limited credit-institutional sense) and other personal resources (such as control of anxiety) would be affected, and would in turn diminish economic resources. There could also be an indirect effect through social resources, as networks break down, with predictable consequences for symptoms.

In sum, it would appear that psychological disorder and each of the variables in our hypothetical experiment, economic, social and personal resources, affect one another both directly and indirectly across time, yielding a rich but complicated pattern of relationships. But do we gain enough additional insight from distinguishing so finely among these types of resources to compensate for the additional complexity involved? Or are these resources so tightly interwoven that we

would do better to treat them as a block of mutually reinforcing variables (Blalock, 1970), and simply choose one resource as a proxy for the others? Might it be useful to simplify the resource variables by combining economic resources with personal (those economic resources available directly to the individual) and social resources (those economic resources available indirectly through one's social resources), or by weighting and summing all three for one resource score, rather than using one score as proxy for all three?

Trading increments of information for added complexity is a familiar problem for social scientists. We are confronted with a decision here that differs little from that made with respect to social class (consider class as an aggregate of income, education, and occupation, or measure each aspect separately?), psychological disorder (consider in the aggregate or distinguish types?), or even personal resources (consider self-esteem, mastery, and trustworthiness as discrete variables, or as an aggregate concept?). Generally, the more variables we try to consider, and the broader the thrust of the investigation, the greater the number of simplifying assumptions we must make in order to have an analysis that is both feasible and understandable. Adding three resource variables generates a great deal more complexity in a model that already has three variables in it—and whose relationships are nonrecursive and interactive. The information which we gain from the added complexity may not be sufficiently great to offset the added cumbersomeness of dealing with a six-variable model instead of a three- or four-variable model. Deciding conceptually among these alternatives requires our asking first how highly associated these resources are with one another.

Highly associated variables, from an empirical standpoint, may be treated as a block, and a proxy chosen for analytic purposes (Blalock, 1970). Arthur Stinchcombe once wrote a comment on a 27-variable model asking whether or not the whole effort in question was not like that of examining the extent to which a unicorn was like a horse, after controlling for the extent to which it shared characteristics with a rhino, a donkey, an eagle, and an ass. Our situation here is a bit less egregious, since conceptually at least the distinctions among the three resource types are fairly clear. The true test is whether we learn more—against cumbersomeness baseline—about the interrelationship of social class, stressful life events, and psychological disorder by adding all three resource variables, as opposed to treating them as an aggregate or merged pair with one resource combined with the other two. A second test is whether our understanding and ability to intervene are increased with respect to variables outside the model as it now stands, such as race and gender.

Although past empirical work has not anticipated all of our questions, there is sufficient evidence to suggest that transforming resources into a single block could seriously misrepresent real life. What we gain in convenience, we lose in accuracy. And more accurate specification of the sites of vulnerability in an individual's person-environment constellation may lead to better directed, and therefore more effective, preventive interventions.

Holmes and Rahe (1967), in constructing a scale of the relative impact of numerous stressful life events, based their selection of events on the implicit assumption that vulnerability in various resource realms is potentially harmful. Their questionnaire includes questions about events from the economic (e.g., fired at work), social (e.g., change in social activities) and personal (e.g., outstanding personal achievement) areas of an individual's life. Although it has frequently been assumed that the stressful life events scale is unidimensional, recent attempts have been made to apply multidimensional scaling techniques to the questionnaire data (Ruch, 1977). Current findings of multidimensionality in the life events scale reinforce our contention that resources may be correlated with one another and with social class but enjoy a sufficiently unique relationship with psychological disorder to warrant separate consideration.

Those who have preceded us in considering the role of resources in class/life-events/disorder relationships have often considered at least two dimensions to the resource variable. Dohrenwend (1978) discusses situational and psychological mediators of stress; Kohn (1972) divides resources into internal and external; Tolsdorf (1976) talks of individual mobilization and network mobilization as two kinds of coping responses; Liem and Liem (1978) propose that the extent to which the relationship between class and disorder is a function of differential access to material versus social resources is an empirical question.

We believe that the three-pronged resource model should be subjected to empirical testing. Resources are what explains why a person who has experienced few stressful life events collapses while another person who has been subjected to many emerges as tempered steel. Resources are differentially available to segments of the population. Group comparisons of disorder rates or response to stressors, as examples, could lead to erroneous conclusions if one group had a little of Resources 1 and 2 and a lot of Resource 3, while the other group had all three resources in abundance. And which of the three could be sacrificed if we thought that researching only two resources was the answer? Economic resources, we believe, would be a poor nominee. We have emphasized that this dimension measures access to material goods and is important in a relative-deprivation sense. It might drive you mad, for instance, if you had only 5 million in assets while your neighborhood average was 20 million. And personal resources such as self-esteem and social skills have been shown to turn those presumably at high risk into invulnerables (Albee, 1981), making personal resources unlikely candidates for exclusion from our model. The research on social resources such as social networks provides strong evidence that the usual domain of community psychology, the larger social systems surrounding an individual, are pivotal in understanding who, even within a social class, collapses under pressure and who resists, so social resources seem to have the potential to contribute to our understanding as well.

The implications of the three-resource model for understanding are clear; too much is lost if we assume that being smart is equal to knowing how to win and keep friends. The implications for preventive intervention will depend on one's outlook on how these things are done. If we believe that powerlessness and unequal distribution of income are the source of much psychopathology (Joffe & Albee, 1981), then political and large-scale social actions are the intervention of choice. At the same time, with mental health workers at the grassroots level concerned about how to translate theory into practice, we can suggest, perhaps counterintuitively, that if the three-pronged resource model were reduced for reasons of convenience, then merging personal resources into the other two might be a wise choice.

This untraditional suggestion is quickly redeemed if we consider that the model is constructed with the values and assumptions of community psychology as its foundation. Because the individual is rarely the focus of intervention in our discipline, an individual's personal resource vulnerability could be measured by the extent to which he or she is impaired in interactions with larger systems. Social skills training is an excellent example of a personal resource that would reduce the vulnerability of one's social resources. As another example, consider self-confidence. Self-confidence is nice to have, but to what end? As a factor in the class/disorder relationship, self-confidence assumes importance if it increases creditworthiness or other economic resources. Self-confidence might allow a working-class person to march into a bank and ask for a loan (so that a child's illness can be managed more easily, thus reducing its impact as a stressful life event), while an upper-middle-class person might be immobilized by doubts about the worthiness of his cause, or might incessantly calculate net worth, wondering if he could get a loan approved. So building self-confidence by way of specific attention to gaining access to or mobilizing one's economic resources would be another way that a personal resource could reduce vulnerability in an important area.

A prevention interventionist whose goal is improved quality of life or improved mental health for an entire community (Iscoe, 1981) would be likely to promote development of resources that could be described as social and as economic—for instance, making insurance companies come into the ghetto, or opening information centers for people who need to find a doctor, a lawyer, or a housekeeper for a sick relative. With three resources in our model, we might gain insight into why some people avail themselves of such community services and others do not. But at the same time, when we are concerned with community-wide psychological adjustment we can surely get "more bang for the buck" by subsuming the personal into the social and economic resource measures.

The model can also be tested by evaluating the extent to which it can accommodate important variables, such as race and gender, that are also known to influence the incidence of psychological disorder. Gender is readily adapted to the model when we note that females have access to different composite resources than do males (cf. Kessler, 1979b). For instance, females, who are recorded as depressed twice as often as are males (Boyd & Weissman, cited in Eaton, 1981), may be reporting more because their social support system fails them. Perhaps they need to be told to keep such things to themselves; or maybe men's networks manage depression for them (although the male suicide rate would suggest that such is not the case). Women might, alternatively, be reporting more because they have better networks—they get support for seeking help for their misery. To cite another example, anxiety in a female entrepreneur might become debilitating, while a male might manage his because of superior economic and social resources that are relevant to the causes of his anxiety. Relationships between social class and women's disorder rates can be illuminated by understanding how resource access differs among subgroups. For women, resources may be even more predictive than class, particularly if class membership is vicarious, that is, assigned because of her husband's or father's class position.

Finally, a brief look at how race would fare as an exogenous or immutable (following Eaton, 1981) variable in our model will complete our illustration. Blacks have more disorders than whites (to select two races for discussion), but the differences are minimal when class is considered. (Warheit, Holzer, & Arey,

1975). And much of the evidence on prevalence of disorder among blacks is contaminated by experimenter's failure to distinguish class and race adequately. But in studies that did control for race and class adequately, Dohrenwend and Dohrenwend (1969, 1981a) and Kessler (1979b) found that, within classes, blacks were subject to greater stressors than whites. They suggest that differential access to internal and external mediators means that stressors have a greater impact on blacks. While we agree with this argument as a whole, we suggest that personal and social resource development (for example, the church, the family, political savvy) play a large role in keeping some blacks safe despite a composite resource score that signals relative vulnerability.

This model, complex as it is, is meant to simulate the confounds and confusions of life. We do not imagine that anyone would ever test the whole six-variable version at once. But as a conceptual framework and a way of organizing thoughts, we hope that it will provide us with a foundation on which to build future work on the intricacies of resource interrelationships and the paths among resources and stressful life events, social class and social disorder, and other variables that may need to be evaluated.

## Summary and Conclusions

The two objectives with which we started this chapter were bringing some clarity to the causation/selection argument and providing an organizing scheme for community-oriented psychologists interested in reducing the rate of psychological disorder. Let us consider these in turn.

What is it that we know now about the causation/selection argument that we did not know before? A number of researchers have cited the relevance of stressful life events and social, economic, and personality variables to understanding the relationship between class and disorder. What has been missing, however, is a conceptual model relating all of these variables to one another in a fashion that highlights the immensely important role of feedback. Our discussion has been more suggestive than precise in this regard, but it has pointed to several specific places where considering feedback improves our sense of what drives the strong inverse correlation between social class and psychological disorder. Second, although the notion of differential vulnerability has been brought to bear on the class/disorder discussion in previous work, it has been discussed primarily as a property of individuals. We have suggested that additional mileage may be gained first by distinguishing among social, economic, and personal resources, and second by considering vulnerability to be a property of each of these resources rather than of individuals. By doing so, the effect of resource vulnerability on the interrelationships among stressful life events, class, and disorder is more easily explicated.

Looking just at stressful life events, social class, and psychological disorder, we get the sense of a system that must inevitably polarize, with the rates of psychological disorder and stressors becoming and remaining much higher in the lower classes than in the upper classes—through both causation and selection—as these feedback loops operate. Resources should moderate these relationships in several important ways. Statistically, although a plausible case may be made for social, economic, and personal resources being mutually reinforcing, both among themselves and with respect to their impact on psychological disorder, they need not be strongly associated with social class. In other words, resources may have independent effects on both stressful life events and psychological disorder, and the effects may differ for different social class levels.

It is the vulnerability of resources which appears to be the most critical element. Less vulnerable social, economic, and personal resources may serve to reduce the chances of encountering some kinds of stressors and psychological disorder *and* may withstand the impact of increases in frequency and severity of stressful life events on rates of psychological disorder to a greater extent than vulnerable resources. In this latter capacity, vulnerable resources may be said (for example) to *exacerbate* the impact of stressful life events on psychological disorder—*and* vice versa. Less vulnerable resources, on the other hand, may be said to *dampen* the impact of stressful life events and disorder on one another. The same dampening and exacerbating influences probably hold for all of the various elements of the causation and selection processes, though the exact nature of the impact of resources must await the development of empirical studies which can properly focus on the feedback relationships involved.

The implications of all of this for the practitioner, however, are more readily apparent. Policies which work toward expanding access, for all segments of the population, to the means for making resources less vulnerable will ultimately reduce rates of psychological disorder in our society. While it may be impractical to attempt change on a national policy level, we cannot shy away from macrosocietal levels of problem conception and problem-solving (Catalano & Dooley, 1980) because we are awed by the size of the intervention. The states will, more and more, serve as the locus for service delivery and will thus be ideally suited to serve as the headquarters for organizing change

in how intervention is conceived. The fact that as many as ten states are in the prevention business already (Tableman, 1980) makes this possibility appear all the more real.

We all expect that service delivery administrators can be pivotal in shifting the balance to full usage of the implications that invulnerable resource systems have for preventing psychological disorder. Tasks such as consulting to natural support systems and organizing community advocacy groups can increase administrators' impact, when guided by the two central conclusions of our work: that resource vulnerability exacerbates any relationships between stressful life events or social class and psychological disorder, and that interventions, even those that occur with one person at a time, must focus on the individual's resource systems rather than on the individual. And a final conclusion (that may be less useful on a daily basis in the trenches than it would be during moments of reflection upon what intervention means) is that recognizing a feedback loop for what it is can be valuable. Every point in our complex model has implications for relationships among all the other variables. So decisions about where to intervene have to face current economic, social, and political realities while incorporating means for handling whatever comes. We believe that long-term solutions will be proved more cost-effective in time, and are certain that resource systems are a significant part of any long-term solutions to the class/stressful-life-event/disorder quagmire.

## Notes

1. When the direction of causation flows one way (i.e., A causes B, or A→B), the variables are said to be arranged in hierarchical order, with those at the top of the hierarchy effecting change in those at the bottom, but not vice versa. A model (defined as a set of variables for which relationships have been explicitly specified) containing variables arranged in hierarchical order only is defined as being recursive, or a recursive system. When the direction of causation is assumed to flow both ways (i.e., A causes B and B causes A, or A⇄B), the relationships are said to be reciprocal, and a model containing such relationships is said to be nonrecursive. For convenience, we are using + to denote positive relationships (e.g., $A \xrightarrow{+} B$ means that as A increases, B increases), and − to denote negative relationships (e.g., $A \xrightarrow{-} B$ means that as A increases, B decreases).

2. This is not to suggest that being labeled "psychotic" or "mentally ill" is not a stressor. The emphasis, however, is on the extent to which one can ward off the consequences of being so labeled. This has typically referred to consequences deriving from contact with formal agencies of social control, where the focus is on incarceration or involuntary commitment. The argument may easily be extended to include less institutionalized consequences such as ostracism, rejection, and discrimination.

3. When changes in the value of a variable lead to later additional changes in value for that variable, a feedback loop exists. For example, if Psychological Disorder becomes more severe it will effect change in other variables with which it is related. These affected variables may then have a positive or negative effect on Psychological Disorder. If they do, they create the requisites for the existence of a feedback relationship. Feedback may be either direct, as when two variables are reciprocally related (e.g., $A \underset{+}{\overset{+}{\rightleftharpoons}} B$) or indirect, as when three or more variables are related in a closed loop (e.g., $A \overset{+}{\longrightarrow} B \overset{+}{\longrightarrow} C$). By convention loops are of two types, positive (+) and negative (−). Positive loops are made up of variables whose interrelationships are all positive (e.g., $A \underset{+}{\overset{+}{\rightleftharpoons}} B$), or which have an even number of negative relationships (e.g., $A \overset{-}{\longrightarrow} B \overset{-}{\longrightarrow} C$). The values of variables in positive feedback loops become progressively larger or smaller across time. Negative feedback loops (−) have an odd number of negative or inverse relationships (e.g., $A \underset{-}{\overset{+}{\rightleftharpoons}} B$) and are said to move toward equilibrium across time. As an example, consider that Psychological Disorder is involved in a negative feedback system with other variables. Over time, the levels of observed symptoms would tend to stabilize. On the other hand, if Psychological Disorder were involved in a positive feedback loop, the levels of symptoms would tend to get progressively worse or progressively better, depending on what the other variables were and how they were related to Psychological Disorder. It is the progressive escalating nature of feedback systems that makes them so potentially harmful or beneficial.

4. Examples of less vulnerable social support systems might be increased capacity and a willingness of the members of one's support system to provide emotional support or information, or serve as role models.

5. The stress which Erickson spoke of was multiple in origin, focusing mostly on the rather extraordinary anxiety generated both from self and from other uncertainty regarding how to define what is happening to the individual and how the individual should be reacted to.

# References

Albee, G. W. Politics, power, prevention, and social change. In J. M. Joffe & G. W. Albee (Eds.), *Prevention through political action and social change*. Hanover, N.H.: University Press of New England, 1981.

Blalock, H. M. *Introduction to social research*. Englewood Cliffs, N.J.: Prentice-Hall, 1970.

Blau, P. M., & Duncan, O. D. *The American occupational structure*. New York: Wiley, 1967.

Brenner, M. H. *Mental illness and the economy*. Cambridge: Harvard University Press, 1973.

Britt, D. W., & Campbell, E. Q. Assessing the linkage of norms, environments, and deviance. *Social Forces*, 1977, **56**, 532–550.

Britt, D. W. Social class and the sick role: Examining the issue of mutual influence. *Journal of Health and Social Behavior*, 1975, **16**, 178–182.

Brown, G., Birley, J., & Wing, J. Influence of family life on the course of schizophrenic disorder: A replication. *British Journal of Psychiatry*, 1972, **121**, 241–258.

Caplan, G. *Principles of preventive psychiatry*. New York: Basic Books, 1964.

Catalano, R., & Dooley, D. Economic change in primary prevention. In R. H. Price, R. F. Ketterer, C. Bader, & J. Monahan (Eds.), *Prevention in mental health*. Beverly Hills: Sage, 1980.

Cobb, S. Social support as a moderator of life stress. *Psychosomatic Medicine*, 1976, **38**, 300–314.

Coleman, R. P., & Rainwater, L. *Social standing in America*. New York: Basic Books, 1978.

Dean, A., & Lin, N. The stress-buffering role of social support. *Journal of Nervous and Mental Disease*, 1977, **165**, 403–417.

Dohrenwend, B. S. Social stress and community psychology. *American Journal of Community Psychology*, 1978, **6**, 1–14.

Dohrenwend, B. S., & Dohrenwend, B. P. Social and cultural influences on psychopathology. In M. R. Rosenzweig & L. W. Porter (Eds.), *Annual Review of Psychology*. Vol. 25. Palo Alto, Calif.: Annual Reviews, 1974.

Dohrenwend, B. S., & Dohrenwend, B. P. Life stress and psychopathology. In *Risk factor research in the major mental disorders*. DHHS Publication No. (ADM) 81-1068. Washington: Government Printing Office, 1981. (a)

Dohrenwend, B. S., & Dohrenwend, B. P. Socioenvironmental factors, stress, and psychopathology. *American Journal of Community Psychology*, 1981, **9**, 128–159. (b)

Dohrenwend, B. P., & Dohrenwend, B. S. *Social status and psychological disorder: A causal inquiry*. New York: Wiley-Interscience, 1969.

Dunham, H. W. *Community and schizophrenia: An epidemiological analysis*. Detroit: Wayne State University Press, 1965.

Eaton, W. W. Demographic and social ecologic risk factors for mental disorders. In *Risk factor research in the major mental disorders*. DHHS Publication No. (ADM) 81-1068. Washington: Government Printing Office, 1981.

Erickson, E. H. *Childhood and society*. (2nd ed.) New York: Norton, 1963.

Faris, R. E. L., & Dunham, H. W. *Mental disorders in urban areas: An ecological study of schizophrenia and other psychoses*. Chicago: Chicago University Press, 1939.

Goldberg, E. M., & Morrison, S. T. Schizophrenia and social class. *British Journal of Psychiatry*, 1963, **109**, 759–802.

Gove, W., & Tudor, J. Adult sex roles and mental illness. *American Journal of Sociology*, 1973, 78, 812–835.

Greenberg, E. S. Models of the political process: Implications for the black community. In E. S. Greenberg, N. Milner, & D. J. Olson (Eds.), *Black politics*. New York: Holt, Rinehart & Winston, 1971.

Hilliard, T. D. Political and social action in the prevention of psychopathology of blacks: A mental health strategy for oppressed people. In J. M. Jaffe & G. W. Albee (Eds.), *Prevention through political action and social change*. Hanover, N.H.: University Press of New England, 1981.

Hollingshead, A. B., & Redlich, F. C. *Social class and mental illness*. New York: Wiley, 1958.

Holmes, T. H., & Rahe, R. H. The social readjustment scale. *Journal of Psychosomatic Research*, 1967, **11**, 213–218.

Iscoe, I. Conceptual barriers to training for the primary prevention of psychopathology. In J. M. Jaffee & G. W. Albee (Eds.), *Prevention through political action and social change.* Hanover, N.H.: University Press of New England, 1981.

Joffe, J. M., & Albee, G. W. (Eds.) *Prevention through political action and social change.* Hanover, N.H.: University Press of New England, 1981.

Kessler, R. C. A strategy for studying differential vulnerability to the psychological consequences of stress. *Journal of Health and Social Behavior,* 1979, **20,** 100–108. (a)

Kessler, R. C. Stress, social status, and psychological distress. *Journal of Health and Social Behavior,* 1979, **20,** 259–272. (b)

Kohn, M. Social class and schizophrenia: A critical review and reformulation. *Schizophrenia Bulletin,* 1963, 7, 69–79.

Kohn, M. T. Class, family and schizophrenia. *Social Forces,* 1972, **50,** 295–302.

Leighton, D. C., Harding, J. S., Macklin, D. B., Macmillan, A. M., & Leighton, A. H. *The character of danger.* New York: Basic Books, 1963.

Lemert, E. M. Paranoia and the dynamics of exclusion. *Sociometry,* 1962, **25,** 2–20.

Lenski, G. *Power and privilege: A theory of social stratification.* New York: McGraw-Hill, 1966.

Liem, R., & Liem, J. Social class and mental illness reconsidered: The role of economic stress and social support. *Journal of Health and Social Behavior,* 1978, **19,** 139–156.

Lin, N., Simeone, R. S., Ensel, W. M., & Kuo, W. Social support, stressful life events, and illness: A model and an empirical test. *Journal of Health and Social Behavior,* 1979, **20,** 108–119.

McAuliffe, W., & Gordon, R. A test of Lindesmith's theory of addiction: The frequency of euphoria among long-term addicts. *American Journal of Sociology,* 1974, **79,** 795–840.

Mechanic, D. Some factors in identifying and defining mental illness. *Mental Hygiene,* 1962, **46,** 66–74.

Mechanic, D. Social structure and personal adaptation: Some neglected dimensions. In G. V. Coelho, D. A. Hamburg, & J. E. Adams (Eds.), *Coping and adaptation.* New York: Basic Books, 1974.

Mechanic, D. Sociocultural and socio-psychological factors affecting personal responses to psychological disorder. *Journal of Health and Social Behavior,* 1975, **16,** 393–404.

Mechanic, D. Some modes of adaptation: Defense. In A. Monat & R. S. Lazarus (Eds.), *Stress and coping.* New York: Columbia University Press, 1977.

Mishler, E., & Wexler, N. Family interaction patterns and schizophrenia: A review of current theories. *Merrill Palmer Quarterly,* 1965, **11,** 269–315.

Mitchell, J. C. Social networks. *Annual review of anthropology,* 1974, **3,** 279–300.

Monat, A., & Lazarus, R. S. *Stress and coping.* New York: Columbia University Press, 1977.

Myers, J., Lindenthal, J., & Pepper, M. Life events, social integration, and psychiatric symptomatology. *Journal of Health and Social Behavior,* 1975, **16,** 121–127.

Pogrebin, L. C. *How to make it in a man's world.* Garden City, N.Y.: Doubleday, 1970.

Porter, S. *Sylvia Porter's money book.* Garden City, N.Y.: Doubleday, 1975.

Rosenberg, M. *Society and the adolescent self-image.* Princeton: Princeton University Press, 1965.

Ross, C. E., & Mirowsky, J. A comparison of life-event-weighting schemes: change, undesirability, and effect-proportional indices. *Journal of Health and Social Behavior,* 1977, **20,** 166–177.

Ruch, L. O. A multidimensional analysis of the concept of life change. *Journal of Health and Social Behavior,* 1977, **18,** 71–83.

Scheff, T. *Labeling madness.* Englewood Cliffs, N.J.: Prentice-Hall, 1975.

Srole, L., Langner, T. S., Michael, S. T., Kirkpatrick, P., Opler, M. K., & Rennie, T. A. C. *Mental health in the metropolis: The Midtown Manhattan study.* New York: New York University Press, 1978.

Srole, L., Langner, T. S., Michael, S. T., Opler, M. K., & Rennie, T. A. C. *Mental health in the metropolis.* New York: McGraw-Hill, 1962.

Storms, M. D., & McCaul, K. D. Attribution processes and emotional exacerbation of dysfunctional behavior. In J. H. Harvey, W. J. Ickes, & R. F. Kidd (Eds.), *New directions in attribution research.* Vol. 1. Hillsdale, N.J.: Lawrence Erlbaum, 1976.

Szasz, T. S. *The myth of mental illness.* New York: Hoeber, 1961.

Tableman, B. Prevention activities at the state level. In R. H. Price, R. F. Ketterer, B. C. Bader, & J. Monahan (Eds.), *Prevention in mental health.* Beverly Hills: Sage, 1980.

Tolsdorf, C. C. Social networks, support, and coping: An exploratory study: *Family Process,* 1976, **15,** 407–417.

Turner, R. J., & Wagenfeld, M. O. Occupational mobility and schizophrenia: An assessment of the social causation and social selection hypotheses. *American Sociological Review,* 1967, **32,** 104–113.

Warheit, G. J., Holzer, C. E., III, & Arey, S. A. Race and mental illness: An epidemiological update. *Journal of Health and Social Behavior,* 1975, **16,** 243–256.

Wheaton, B. The sociogenesis of psychological disorder: An attributional theory. *Journal of Health and Social Behavior,* 1980, **21,** 100–124.

Wrong, D. H. The oversocialized conception of man in modern sociology. *American Sociological Review,* 1961, **26,** 183–193.

Yando, R., Seitz, V., & Zigler, E. *Intellectual and personality characteristics of children: Social-class and ethnic-group differences.* Hillsdale, N.J.: Lawrence Erlbaum, 1979.

Yarrow, M. R., Schwartz, C. G., Murphy, H. S., & Deasy, L. C. The psychological meaning of mental illness in the family. *Journal of Social Issues,* 1955, **11,** 12–24.

# 10 MINORITY STATUS AS A STRESSOR

## John Moritsugu and Stanley Sue

T he study of stressors, of systems-level causative factors for stress, and of the preventive interventions to deal with the ill effects of stress have been identified as key components of the community psychology movement (Bloom, 1979; Dohrenwend, 1978). Minority status as a specific stressor fits such a theoretical model of community processes and interventions. Individuals who are members of a minority group potentially face hostility, prejudice, the lack of effective support during times of crisis, and the development of a cognitive coping style that can be counterproductive. This chapter aims to discuss the work done on minority status as a stressor, the theories as to why it is a stressor, and the interventions directed at reducing the risk of dysfunction due to minority status. Our intent is to view minority status as a phenomenon that is embedded within the context of all community interventions. This review and discussion may be of help to social service providers in conceptualizing the social environments which they address. Rappaport (1977) believed community perspectives had to include a sensitivity to the cultural relativity and diversity found in our social settings. At the basis of minority status studies is the recognition of this relativity and diversity. An examination of the literature suggests that the topic of minority status as a stressor is important to an adequate conceptualization of any social environment and is not necessarily tied to the notion of ethnicity or social class. Any difference among peoples may potentially be interpreted as a signal for discrimination. It is believed, therefore, that this area of investigation has as its basic intention an examination of the substance of all social groupings, the glue that holds it together, and the forces that tear it apart.

## Minority Status and Life Stress

The study of environmental contributions to the development of mental illness has led to the delineation of several social and psychological stressors. Among these has been the notion that individuals who believe they are different or are believed to be different from the majority of society were at higher risk of displaying distress symptoms. The definition of minority or majority status could follow many criteria—social, cultural, occupational, sexual, or ethnic. Majority status is here defined as membership in the prevailing social group within a perceived community. Minority status is, therefore, the lack of membership in the prevailing group. This minority status might be statistically, politically, psychologically (that is, an individual's perception of him- or herself in comparison to others), or structurally determined, so long as the result is a common perception of the minority member as existing outside the dominant social structure. Durkheim (1951) believed anomie status, or rather the lack of social structure support, was associated with increased risk of suicide. Minority status could often lead to alienation and social isolation, heightened stress, and decreased social structure resources available to the stressed individual. Dohrenwend (1978) and Bloom (1979) saw increased stress resulting in increased rates of psychological dysfunction. Minority status, defined by racial-ethnic status or by other social or cultural status factors, could dispose individuals to feelings of isolation. The atypical characteristics of these individuals signal them and their neighbors as to their differences. Minority status within a community could thus increase the risk of mental disorder.

Several community studies have shown the rate of mental illness in ethnic groups increased as their proportionate size in the community decreased (Bloom, 1975; Faris & Dunham, 1939; Mintz & Schwartz, 1964; Rabkin, 1979; Schwartz & Mintz, 1963; Wechsler & Pugh, 1967). In Chicago, Faris and Dunham (1939) found the rate of hospitalization for schizophrenia was higher for whites and blacks in apartment communities in which they were minority members. The rates of hospitalization for foreign- and native-born whites were higher in comparison to the blacks' rates within black neighborhoods. Conversely, the rates of black hospitalization were higher than those of the native-born whites in the native-born white neighborhoods. The only exception to this rule was with the foreign-born whites' relatively high rates within their own communities. Reanalyzing some of the same data, Mintz and Schwartz (1964) showed whites residing in black areas had a rate of psychosis 313 percent higher than whites in white areas, while blacks in white areas had a 32 percent higher rate than blacks in black areas. Examination of Boston's Italian population (Mintz & Schwartz, 1964; Schwartz & Mintz, 1963) showed a similar pattern of increasing schizophrenia and manic depression as their overall presence in the community decreased. This relationship remained strong even after controlling for socioeconomic status. In a Pueblo, Colorado, study (Bloom, 1975), the 1970 hospitalization rates for Spanish-surnamed individuals were highest where they were in a minority. In turn, the same was found for the non-Spanish-surnamed when in a minority position. Rabkin (1979) analyzed ethnic group size within a community and psychiatric hospitalization in New York City. She consistently found that for whites, blacks, and Puerto Ricans, the smaller their group size was in an area, the higher their psychiatric hospitalization rate. This effect remained even after ac-

counting for poverty, family cohesiveness, and mobility. Ethnic minority status has consistently shown to be related to mental disorders. However, minority status may be defined by other than ethnic criteria.

Wechsler and Pugh (1967) found that a variety of social characteristics could serve to discriminate minority status. In their study of Massachusetts hospitalization, individuals possessing characteristics uncommon in their community were found to have higher rates of admission. Minority status based on age, marital status, place of birth, and occupation were related to these rate increases. Young people living in communities with few young people were at higher risk of hospitalization, as were middle-aged people living in communities with a low percentage of middle-aged individuals. Married persons had a higher rate of hospitalization when they lived in towns with few married persons. Massachusetts-born individuals were more prone to hospitalization when in towns with low proportions of other Massachusetts-born individuals. Professionals were at heightened risk of disturbance if they were in nonprofessional areas, and this also occurred for clerical workers, craftsmen, and laborers, along with other occupations.

Across many studies, spanning over 40 years of research, several minority groups, and several minority status criteria, the findings have been supportive of the proposition that minority status was associated with heightened risk of mental disorder. Considerable evidence, then, shows a relationship between minority status and psychopathology. In view of the correlational nature of the studies, cause and effect are difficult to establish. For example, already disturbed persons or those predisposed to emotional disorders may, for one reason or another, tend to reside in communities where they are in the minority. Another possibility is that minority group status and factors associated with it create stress. It is this possibility that we would like to explore, in view of the direct and indirect evidence that suggests minority status can act as a stressor.

## Factors Contributing to Stress

Working from Selye's (1956) concepts of stress, Dohrenwend and Dohrenwend (1979) defined three factors contributing to the levels of stress experienced. These factors were stressor stimuli, external mediating factors, and internal mediating factors. The stressor stimuli were described as any events that produce stress. This occurs by disruption or the threat of disruption of an individual's activities. The external mediators were those factors from the environment acting upon the individual. These include money, family, and overall social support and resources. The internal mediators were those psychological or physical dispositions carried within the individual, including values, expectations, and feelings. The severity of the stress was believed dependent on the duration and intensity of the stressor stimuli and the effects of the internal and external mediators. We will follow this line of thinking in examination of those factors believed to contribute to minority status as a stressor. Such a model for the stress process has found some support in Perlin, Menaghan, Lieberman, and Mullan's (1981) study of job disruption as a stressful event. In this instance, the stress resulted in negative effects on self-concept and sense of mastery (internal mediations), which they believed increased subjects' vulnerability to depression. As well, strong social support systems minimize the severity of depressive reactions to the stress.

Stressful stimuli are provided by the prejudice, discrimination, and attendant hostility from the social environment, as a function of minority status. This status also influences access to external mediators such as social support and material resources. Finally, because of interaction with the prevailing social groups, minority membership can result in internal-cognitive styles that exacerbate environmental events, increasing the stress experience for the individual.

### Stressor Stimuli

Minority status can be stressful. It is usually used to demarcate outside-of-group status and in this manner target the minority individual for discrimination and hostility (Harding, Proshansky, Kutner, & Chen, 1969; Sherif & Sherif, 1956). Research regarding the effects of prejudicial behavior on the victim suggests that he or she does indeed experience stress following the perception of victimization (Dion, Earn, & Lee, 1978).

Harding et al. (1969) argue that prejudicial activity presupposes an inside-of-group versus outside-of-group distinction. Any in-group/out-group formation can bring about prejudices. While Allport (1954) focused on ethnic and racial distinctions in his work on prejudice, he also acknowledged that a variety of dimensions could be used to discriminate in- and out-group membership. These included age, regional origin, religion, ideology, social class, and occupation. Notably, similar dimensions were included in the previously cited studies of minority status as a risk factor. Archibald MacLeish might have us believe that freckled versus nonfreckled facial qualities might be used to fractionate the world. Eagles or Rams football fans might come to blows, as Liverpool and Manchester Union soccer fans certainly do. Hence, there seems to be an almost infinite number of ways of dividing

up the world, which may potentially place one in a minority status. Nonetheless, within our culture certain characteristics (e.g., race, religion) appear to be far more salient as sources of such distinctions.

In a series of studies on group formation and competition, Sherif and Sherif (1956) found increased hostility following the creation of competing groups. Group members perceived the nongroup members as outside of their group and a potential threat to their well-being. The hostility to out-group members was manifested by negative stereotyping of the competing group's members, less favorable appraisal of out-group performance, a cutting off of initial friendships with outside-group members, overt aggression toward the out-group, and physical separation of the groups. This behavior was observed among a homogeneous subject population of 12-year-old white males who had not previously known each other. The in-group versus out-group distinction was created through the use of in-group activities and then group competition with an out-group. Given these experiences, the groups viewed members of competing groups as antagonists not only on the field of play, but also during meals and free time.

Allport (1954) detailed three rejection levels of out-group members: verbal rejection, discrimination, and physical attack. Verbal rejection was the expression of animosity. Discrimination was the unequal treatment of others. Physical attack described the various levels of violence leveled at the out-group. All three of these behaviors have obvious negative effects on the targeted out-group. The manifestations of such behavior may be economic and political as well as social. Discrimination over housing, job opportunity, educational opportunity, access to services, and access to both informal and formal power structures have all been discussed at length (Pettigrew, 1971; Steinfield, 1973). The impact of prejudice based on minority status can be multifaceted and insidious.

The actual experience of receiving the hostility, aggression, discrimination, and verbal rejection of majority in-group members is believed to be the stressor, but there are many and varied forms of these prejudicial behaviors. The perception of prejudice appears to be critical to the stress experience.

Dion et al. (1978) found that Jewish subjects who believed they were the victims of prejudice reported mood states indicative of stress. In this experimental study of prejudice, subjects assigned to the perceived prejudicial condition described feelings that closely paralleled the victims of stress as reported by Lazarus, Speisman, Mordkoff, and Davison (1962).

Minority status can lead to out-group status and prejudicial behavior directed at minority members.

Social psychological data illustrate the potential for hostility directed toward out-group members. The perception of this hostility and prejudice leads to stress. Notably, in discussing stressful stimuli Lazarus (1964) emphasized the cognitive mediators of the stress experience. The following sections on external and internal mediators to the stress process attempt to address some of the events that exacerbate or ameliorate the experience of stressful events.

### EXTERNAL MEDIATORS

The second factor determining the impact of stress on the individual is the external mediation found within an individual's environment. One such external mediator is the social support system available to individuals. Caplan (1974) pointed to three stress-mediating functions that support systems provide. They help the individual to organize their skills and resources for dealing with the stressful event. The system can help bear the burden of the stress. Finally, the system can supply material and emotional support.

Studies of social support and mental illness indicate its helpfulness in dealing with stress (Leighton, Harding, Macklin, MacMillan & Leighton, 1963; Lin, Simeone, Ensel, & Kuo, 1979; Myers, Lindenthal, & Pepper, 1975; Sandler, 1980). Lin et al. (1979) found among Chinese-Americans in Washington, D.C., that when social support, as defined by community involvement, was high, the impact of stressor stimuli was negligible. Even controlling for the influence of marital status and occupation, the importance of the social support factor remained significant. They concluded that social support served a mediating role between stressful life events and psychiatric symptomatology. Sandler's (1980) examination of a sample of inner-city elementary school children showed those without older siblings and those who were in the ethnic minority for their neighborhood had significantly more inhibition problems. He also argued for the positive effects of a support system.

Myers et al. (1975) found the level of "social integration" to mediate the influence of stressful events on psychiatric symptoms. This integration was defined by marriage, employment, higher income, and enjoyment of work. They believed such indices distinguished those "integrated" into society versus those who were isolated. Following our previous line of reasoning, the lack of integration for individuals might put them into minority status. This study followed the reasoning of Leighton et al. (1963), who believed social disintegration led to increased psychopathology. The indicators of this disintegration included "weak and fragmented communication networks; few and weak associations; and broken homes." These all suggested a lack of social support structures for these populations.

In Chapter 6 of this book, Heller and Swindle discuss at length the problems of envisioning social support as a panacea. They point out that the mere existence of such systems does not necessarily mean they are used. Perception of the system, skill in accessing the system, and knowledge about utilizing the system are all required before the full effect of support systems may be brought to bear on stressful situations. These are all related to personal-internal variables, and are the result of person-environment interactions that leave the individual with the capability to successfully utilize external resources. Minority status may not provide the most useful perceptual set, nor the appropriate cognitive mediators to set in motion the social skills necessary to access existent support systems.

Williams, Ware, and Donald (1981) have questioned the role of social support in the stress process. They found social support did not serve as a buffer against stress. Rather, increases in social support had a positive impact on mental health in a simple additive manner, regardless of stress levels experienced. Wilcox (1981), on the other hand, did find support for the buffering effects of social support. Such findings add substance to Heller and Swindle's cautionary note against too simplistic an interpretation of social support system effects.

A second external mediator is the minority individual's lack of access to economic resources. Several studies of economic status among the various ethnic minorities point to lower levels of income in these groups. It is widely believed that such discrepancies from their white majority counterparts are in part due to discrimination in educational opportunities, in job opportunities, and in opportunities for career advancement.

Among Asian-American groups, which at first glance appear better off than other ethnic minorities and at times the white majority, close examination of the data yields sobering findings (U.S. Commission on Civil Rights, 1980). While Asian-American groups have, on the average, superior education and income to the majority group, these differences disappear when looking at urban areas, where the concentration of Asians is highest in the United States. Here the Asian-American average for income is below the majority average, with one exception—Honolulu, where Asian-Americans are not in a minority. Looking at levels of education and its relation to income, it was found that Asian-Americans were usually paid less than white counterparts with similar education and experience.

This was so in government (Sowell, 1976) as well as academia (Freeman, 1978).

Similar cases might be made for blacks, Hispanics and native Americans (Kitano, 1980; Pinkney, 1975; Schiller, 1982; Simpson & Yinger, 1958) as well as women (U.S. Department of Labor, 1975). While discrimination has strong historical roots within American history (Steinfield, 1973), it can also be found globally in interactions between ethnic and nationalistic groupings (Hunt & Walker, 1974). The case of the Asian-American is especially telling, since it addresses the effects of discrimination on a "successful" minority's resources. While this may not be the case for all minorities within a community—for example, a professional in a nonprofessional neighborhood—the effect of minority status might be differential access to social as well as economic resources. The full gamut of possible minority status categories and the possible resources to which these minorities might have limited entry has not been explored.

Heller and Swindle's comments on social support systems in Chapter 6 might be recalled again. Does minority status limit the individual's perception of, access to, or ability to tap and utilize existent supports? The answer to this question may lie at both the social-external and the personal-internal levels, or possibly the interaction of the two levels. The challenge may be in defining the power of these effects. Pursuant to such a definition, let us proceed to an examination of possible internal factors influencing the impact of stress of a minority individual.

### INTERNAL MEDIATORS

The internal mediation factor relates to the cognitive or affective variables that influence the perception of external events and the ability to display adaptive behaviors. This further might also include any physiological dispositions to respond to stress stimuli. However, we have chosen not to address the issue of physiological dispositions, since discussions of Eysenck's (1967) neurological sensitivity, as manifested by the introversion-extroversion dimension, or of the dyathesis-stress theories regarding constitutional vulnerability to environmental stressors (Meehl, 1962; Rosenthal, 1971), are not germane to this chapter. The conceptualization of minority status as dependent on the characteristics of the individual's home community and not tied to ethnicity means that anyone may acquire minority status; physiological variables therefore do not apply to this consideration of minority status as a stressor.

Rather, in looking at the internal mediators, we will take some liberties and include those internal factors that are really the result of experiences with the external environment. These experiences have resulted in internal states mediating stressful life, through cognitive or perceptual sets and expectancies. Hinkle (1961) noted the importance of the individual's assessment of the environment. It was the evaluation of one's experience that seemed to affect the incidence of physical illness. Kobasa (1979) lent added support to the notion that the individual mediates the stress process. Her comparisons of executives who experience high stress but have low illness rates with those who have high stress and high illness rates indicated that personality variables mediated the effects of the stressors. Those who exhibited a sense of self-commitment, vigorousness, and meaningfulness and displayed an internal locus of control were less ill. They also perceived their lives as less stressful than the high illness group did.

Two internal factors have been researched and discussed in relation to their mediating effects: learned helplessness and poor self-concept. For minorities, learned helplessness may possibly be promoted by the lack of political power to bring about desired changes and to promote the minority member's own opinion within the community. Poor self-concept for minorities may be learned from experiences with the majority group. The following discussion focuses on the theoretical, survey, and experimental work in these two areas.

### LEARNED HELPLESSNESS

Seligman (1975) found that a subject would not attempt to escape an aversive situation if that subject had previously been unable to escape aversive stimulation. It was believed that the subject had learned that it was helpless in controlling the onset of negative experience. The belief that the experience was not predictable or controllable led to passive acceptance of the aversive stimulation, even when it could be terminated by some subject action. While this initial work was done on dogs, later research has supported the applicability of this paradigm to humans (Sue & Zane, 1980). With an increase in distance between individuals and their institutions (such as government, business, schools), the members of a community can feel disenfranchised and out of control of these institutions (Dunham, 1977; Sarason, 1974). These feelings lead to a loss of a "sense of community" and an increased sense of alienation from society. Seligman (1975), Sue (1977), and Sue and Zane (1980) regard this scenario as an especially appropriate description of the minority experience. In this case the outcomes of one's actions are often dependent upon one's minority status rather than on the actions themselves.

In a society where "the majority rules," the power of minorities to influence the direction of their communities and their own lives can be lost. The perception of helplessness or powerlessness may be an accurate one, but it negatively affects the individual's ability to deal with stressors (Glass, Singer, & Pennebaker, 1977; Kobasa, Maddi, & Courington, 1981; Seligman, 1975). From environmental experiences, the learning of helplessness leads to fewer efforts to adapt and to survive. The problems an individual faces may not be solved because there are few, if any, efforts to solve them. But beyond this is the *perception* of the world as uncontrollable and unpredictable; the individual is left helplessly floundering in the tide of societal and political movements.

Vance (1977) discussed the institutionalization of low status and helplessness roles for two minority groups, women and blacks. She emphasized the "perceptual-cognitive" results of these acquired roles as particularly harmful, in that they decrease the individual's adaptive abilities. However, it might be noted that these groups, in fact, might be highly adaptive to the institutional/environmental consequences for their behaviors. The conscious or unwitting intent of the institution and the society in developing these behaviors is debatable. Collier (1977) has argued that the cognitive sets which contribute to the majority's definition of failure and maladaptation may in fact be a deliberate action of the majority to cope with the economic, psychological, and cultural threats perceived to be coming from the minority. While Collier wrote this in regard to the white "majority" and the black "minority," it seems applicable to all majority-minority situations. In any case, both Vance (1977) and Collier (1977) would agree that the perceptual cognitive styles produced by the environmental experiences of minority members can be detrimental to their physical and psychological health.

These discussions have been notably at the theoretical level. Sue (1977) pointed to several research questions regarding the empirical validation of these ideas and the further elucidation of the minority experience. In particular, he called for examination of the areas which minorities feel important for them to control; minorities' beliefs concerning the controllability of their lives; the demographic variables that may relate to these beliefs; the relationship between feelings of control and psychological well-being; the differences in perception of control between majority and minority groups; and the effectiveness of intervention programs in dealing with this sense of helplessness. As is obvious from this list, there is still

much work to be done relating minority status to learned helplessness.

## SELF-CONCEPT

An internal mediator of stress with more empirical support is the minority member's self-concept. The basic hypothesis is that the minority group internalizes the values of the majority group—including the majority's disdain for the minority. The importance of self-concept as an internal mediating variable is related to personal constructs of reality. The interpretation of events as validating or invalidating self-expectations is dependent upon the individual's cognitive set. Stressor events may be interpreted as confirming negative self-images.

DeVos (1969) has examined the minority experience effect on self-identity among a minority group in Japan. This group is stereotyped as impoverished, undereducated, and criminal. He believed the minority group's identification was shaped for it through a series of social interactions with the majority, and that the minority individual then lives out the script written for him or her by the majority society. Eventually, the minority group became selective in its openness to experiences with the majority culture, as a way to protect itself from insult and influence. However, the group's selectivity was in reaction to the initial interactions with the majority, and its function was to perpetuate the group identity formed through these interactions.

Rosenberg's (1979) review of ethnic and religious group self-esteem studies did not show differences in self-concept among the minority and majority groups. However, no distinctions were made regarding the minority status of the subjects within their neighborhoods. In an earlier work on religious minority status, Rosenberg (1965) found a strong relationship between poor self-concept and religious minority status. In this study of adolescent self-esteem, he found that Catholics in non-Catholic neighborhoods had lower self-esteem and more psychosomatic symptoms than did Catholics in Catholic neighborhoods. The same held true for Protestants and Jews in comparisons of "consonant" and "dissonant" neighborhoods.

McCarthy and Yancoy (1971) have presented findings and arguments that black self-concept is indeed positive, since the reference group is not the white majority but rather other black comrades. They assumed an available group of colleagues from which comparisons could be made to provide the criteria for self-evaluations. However, such a criterion group may be unlikely for minorities within a community.

Experiments with prejudice performed by Dion et al. (1978) found self-esteem to be heightened immediately following the experience of prejudice. They offered a number of possible explanations for these reports. It was felt that the perception of prejudice could serve to increase feelings of solidarity with the minority member's own group, or might excuse negative experiences as the result of group hostilities and not personal qualities. Both of these reactions could serve to lessen the impact of the stressful events. However, in cases where these positive reactions could not be derived, the stress experience could be increased.

In a variation of the self-concept theme which incorporates external as well as internal actions, Parker and Kleiner (1966) believed that the acceptance of majority values and a majority reference group for determining success led to frustration and increased likelihood of mental disturbance for the black minority community. Mentally disturbed blacks, in comparison with normals, had greater discrepancies between how they thought of themselves and how they would like to be and between their occupational status and their aspiration levels. Similarly, Sewell and Haller (1959) found that high levels of psychopathology related to greater dissatisfaction over achievement and status. These studies fitted Merton's (1957) conception of anomie and alienation resulting from a discrepancy between socially valued goals and the means of attaining these goals. Again, the minority member's *perception* of this discrepancy was seen as the internal factor contributing to stress and the resultant mental disturbance. The impact of self-esteem can be negative, in that the reference group standards were attained. Or the impact can be positive, in that failure can be attributed to intergroup hostilities and not an individual's lack of qualifications. The choice of perception can greatly influence the impact of the stress associated with lack of goal attainment (Hinkle, 1961). The individual's positive self-image may help to attribute failure to minority group membership and not to personal responsibility. ("I am good and thus the failure is due to other factors.") A negative self-image might result in the attribution of failure to lack of personal capabilities. ("I am no good and this confirms my belief.") Kahn and French's (1970) research on self-evaluation indicated the impact of stressor stimuli to be greater when the subject's stress is associated with low status, less when the stress is associated with high status. The lowered self-concept which may result from minority status would appear to exacerbate the effects of stress on those holding such status.

There may be those who argue it is the "victim's fault" for these internal problems. It might be pointed out that it is the interaction with society that creates the victim's internal vulnerability. From a preventive perspective, the societal contributions to such vulnerability should be incorporated into any comprehensive approach to the problems of minority individuals and groups. Holahan and Spearly (1980) suggested the use of ecological models for defining coping strategies. These models highlight the effects of the environment, the effects of the individual, and the effects of the interaction and reciprocity of the environment and the individual. Such a conceptualization parallels the previous schemas describing the stress process—that is, there are external and internal variables influencing the stress syndrome. From our previous discussions of the factors influencing stress and with the Holahan and Spearly (1980) models in mind, let us now examine prevention programs— real and proposed—for dealing with minority status as a stressor.

## Prevention

Having reviewed the epidemiological literature on minority status and explored the possible stressor stimuli, external mediators to stress, and internal mediators to stress for those of minority status, we now address the question of preventive programs for these problems. We will first review some of the literature in this area, then offer some brief proposals for the future, and finally explore the implications of this discussion for all community interventions.

Kessler and Albee (1975) identified ten articles on prevention programs for low income and minority populations. However, only three of these articles are relevant to our discussion, since the others dealt with the economically disadvantaged or did not seek to address minority status as a stressor. The three relevant articles are by Christmas (1969), Peck, Kaplan, and Roman (1966), and Reissman and Hallowitz (1967). Christmas (1969) described a multiservice center based in Harlem in New York City. Family service, health services, and rehabilitation and community organization services were provided by a staff of professionals and paraprofessionals. Service, training, and research relevant to the community's interests were provided. Notably, the article was descriptive and did not present empirical data on effectiveness. The two other articles (Peck et al., 1966; Reissman & Hallowitz, 1967) described neighborhood service centers which were part of the Lincoln Hospital Mental Health Services. These centers tried to be accessible to the community by use of informal neighborhood locations and indigenous health aides. The program was seen as comprehensive, ranging from group therapy to community organization. Group work on social adjustment problems provided an effective form of intervention to members of the community experiencing stress. The issues raised come from community members, as did the solutions proposed. Educational offerings were also selected and presented. Community input on topic selection ensured the relevance of the material presented. The community organization component sought to aid the neighborhood in coming together and addressing immediate, concrete neighborhood problems. Following Alinsky's (1969, 1971) model of confrontation, project personnel helped to move a citizenry that felt powerless into effective action groups, helping to bond the members of that community and give them a new sense of self-determination and control. The targets of these actions were institutions and systems that impacted the neighborhood, such as schools, social agencies, and government bodies. Again, the problem with these reports is the lack of change measures for mental or community adjustment.

The described programs attempted prevention through community organization, early detection of social adjustment problems, and treatment of those problems individually and through groups. The emphasis was on basic, concrete issues that affected the livelihood of the individuals within the neighborhoods. The programs addressed the economic and social stressors of life in poor ethnic neighborhoods. They also provided experiences facilitative to the development of social organization and community cohesion. Finally, a demonstration of the power of collective action imbued district residents with a sense of control over their lives. Hopefully, such programs positively affected feelings of helplessness within the community.

These programs were but three of the many projects addressing ethnic minority communities through multiservice interventions. These attempts dealt with mental health problems from an ecological perspective, recognizing the interconnections between environment, economic and social structure, and behavior (Kelly, 1968). While these projects provided preventive interventions to populations primarily composed of ethnic minorities, it should be noted that they addressed high-risk neighborhoods and not minority status stress per se. Similar comments might be made about Head Start programs and the infant stimulation and school intervention programs. While exemplary, they deal with target groups identified not by minority status criteria but rather by early-detection measures of pathological risk. It is nonetheless interesting that ethnic minorities so often fall into these categories.

There are few programs that specifically attempt to prevent minority status stress. We have chosen to review two others here which we believe fit our model

of stress intervention. They are illustrative of preventive programs for this problem area.

The first program attempted to prevent the problems of value conflict among high school Asian-Americans (Yee & Lee, 1977). The authors organized weekly meetings of Asian students. Participants discussed topics related to ethnic identity and cultural integrity. They spoke of the conflicts arising between their own values and those of the majority high school peer group. These meetings served as a source of support and reference for the program members. Postprogram interviews indicated positive evaluations for this experience. The limitations of this study include the lack of a control group for comparisons and the lack of standardized adjustment measures to assess outcome. While aware of these problems, the authors reasoned that experimental research designs were not relevant to the intent of the community-based study and that there were not appropriately normed dependent variable measures for the target group. Notably, such concerns are typical for interventions with minority communities.

A second study dealing with minority stress was performed by Rooney-Rebeck and Jason (1980). They examined the effects of structured classroom exercises on interracial interactions. Cooperation across ethnic groups was reinforced in first and third grade classes. This resulted in an increased rate of interethnic playmate choices for the first graders. Notably, the first graders' academic performance also improved during this time. The programs positive intergroup friendship effects were not found for the third graders. In contrast, the control group youngsters showed a decline of interethnic friend choices during the study period. These results suggest that the encouragement and reinforcement of interethnic cooperation was useful in combating prejudice and social segregation when introduced early in the school experience, before prejudicial practices were firmly established. This program and its results paralleled other work on cooperative learning situations (DeVries, Edwards, & Slavin, 1978; Weigel, Wiser, & Cook, 1975). Gump's (1980) discussion of desegregation attempts supports the contention that interracial harmony did not occur spontaneously with the mixing of groups, but rather was the end product of a social milieu conducive to cross-race interdependence.

These studies address different levels of the stress process, but they all do so in a preventive fashion. The Rooney-Rebeck and Jason (1980) study attempted to intervene at the earliest time interval, before the onset of discrimination. By working on integration of ethnic groups, the in-group/out-group distinctions that lead to hostility directed at out-group minorities were not allowed to form. The Yee and Lee (1977) program provided a social support system to help mediate the stress of minority group value conflicts with the majority school culture. The Peck et al. (1966), Reissman and Hallowitz (1967), and Christmas (1969) programs were in reaction to the lack of community coherence resulting from the social and economic privations of the targeted neighborhoods—which might have been tied to their minority status within the larger community. Such programs demonstrate the practicality as well as the complexity and difficulty of preventive interventions within the community.

Others have underscored the problems of preventive programs for minority populations. Attempts at primary prevention may be resisted by institutional or governmental support sources (Kessler & Albee, 1975). Alinsky (1969, 1971) believed that the shift or redistribution of power within the community implicit in many minority programs led to resistance from the powerful majority. Suspicions as to intent are especially strong among minority groups, where historical and political factors are a part of the overall programmatic considerations (Montero & Levine, 1977). Morishima (1976) has pointed to the need for a redefinition of the roles played by all concerned with community research. The reciprocally beneficial nature of relationships among academia, community, and government should lead to more cooperation in research attempts. The community's needs for improved programs, the governmental needs for documentation, and academia's need for access to social groups are a starting point for these mutual efforts. There is hope for community research on prevention, but it will not be easy. For the willing, there are several directions for action that become apparent from our review of the literature.

The preventive prescription for future programs flowing from an examination of this area include interventions aimed at the three factors influencing the stress experience. The encouragement of the community's redefinition of in-group and out-group distinctions might deter hostility and prejudice that create stress for minority members. The creation of growth-enhancing support systems might give minorities the option of a stress-buffering external mediation group. The offering of structured experiences to foster the development of an individual's sense of control and predictability as well as of self-worth would strengthen the individual's ability to cope with the stress.

The definition of minority or majority status within a community is elastic. Criteria for membership can change over time to fit practical purposes. Rather than using a racial, ethnic, or social class basis for deriving in-group/out-group distinctions, the criteria for in-group membership might be expanded to include all of humanity, not excluding any peoples or groups (Harding et al., 1969). The focus could also be narrowed to all those who are contributing members of a community, regardless of arbitrary social or ethnic criteria (Sarason, 1974). This would reacknowledge the interdependency of the community, and reconfirm the worth of each individual for his or her part in that community. The need to belong and to sense a common bond among fellow human beings makes strong intuitive sense. The support system (Caplan, 1974), social integration (Leighton et al., 1968), and social structure (Durkheim, 1951; Merton, 1957) literature would support such a notion. Sherif and Sherif's (1956) work should help in such constructive redefinitions of group membership. One finding of particular note was the need for persistent and multiple attempts at bringing groups together to face common problems. As they learned from their research, efforts to consolidate and integrate communities require multifaceted programs, and patience. As a side note, there may also be developmental considerations to our efforts, that is, times at which the interventions are most effective, as suggested by Rooney-Rebeck and Jason's (1980) work.

Prevention programs addressing the external mediators of the stress process might focus on creating or strengthening social support networks for identifiable minority populations. In particular, the extended family may serve as a good basis for support system work. Smith, Burlew, Mosley, and Whitney (1978) pointed to the strength of the family system in ethnic minority groups. The family's importance has been demonstrated and discussed in regard to Chicanos (Keefe & Casas, 1980; Raymond, Rhoads, & Raymond, 1980), Japanese-Americans (Kitano, 1969), Indochinese (Moritsugu, Vo, & Meyada, 1980), and blacks (Jackson, 1973; Shimkin, Shimkin, & Frate, 1978). The familial ties appeared strong for all these groups. The importance of family support in dealing with adversity was also commonly emphasized. The natural caregivers in all instances were members of the nuclear or extended family, the former being defined as mother, father and siblings, the latter as uncles, aunts, cousins, nephews, grandparents, and any other relatives as defined by social or cultural practice. There were variations in the specific individuals sought or used for help, but the pattern of familial help agents was clear. If we are to address the needs of ethnic minorities, the family as a basic social unit may be most appropriate for intervention efforts, since this plays into a natural strength for these groups. The overall positive mediating effects of family membership are suggested by studies of health and illness in single and married populations (National Institute of Mental Health, 1971). Those living alone were found to fare worse than those who were married. The reestablishment or strengthening of family ties may be appropriate for any minority group, given this finding.

Alternatives to the family network may be to build the kinds of support groups Yee and Lee (1977) provided for Asian-American youth. The formation of formal or informal support systems within communities might aid individuals' ability to cope with the stress of minority status. These systems may be set up along the lines of interest or activity groups that create commonalities among their members.

A note of caution is needed in viewing social support systems as a panacea. Wilcox (1981) found the quality more than the quantity of social support to be a key factor in buffering the individual from stressful situations. Heller and Swindle, in Chapter 6, also point to the intricacies of these systems and their effects. Without the appropriate mix of individual and system qualities, the social support system may have negative effects on the individual's capabilities for coping with stress. It would be the responsibility of programs to discover and then provide this healthy mix. On the individual level, provision of such a mix might mean training in appropriate accessing skills, the ability to perceive the support, and the motivation to tap this support. On the systems level, social and material resources, appropriate social climate, willingness to help, and the skill to help the individual might make for a successful mix.

Beyond prevention programs focusing on external mediators of stress, the prevention programs for minorities might try to provide experiences that counter feelings of helplessness and poor self-concept. The strength of group membership and the provision of an affirmative reference group could help individuals to internalize healthy concepts about themselves and their ability to control their world.

Much as with clinical work in depression, following Seligman's model (Seligman, 1975), the community may be challenged with tasks directly affecting it. Community consultation and education would aid such efforts. Consultation could take the form of problem definition, referral to appropriate resources, motivation for action, and suggestions for concrete action. While community psychologists may be "Mr. Everyman" (Sarason, 1976), they carry not only the skills of research and evaluation, but also access to the "wisdom" of previous experiences in community work as described in the literature. Whether the community is trying to send letters to city hall, or to get a center funded, psychologists have information that

can increase the likelihood of success in measurable ways.

The challenge of the future lies not only in defining those factors that lead to higher risk of pathology in minority groups, but also in providing realistic, concrete alternatives to the modern medical-model Establishment solutions. "Native tradition"–based informal intervention strategies appear to have many advocates among those who have worked with ethnic minorities (Cohen, 1972; Padilla, Ruiz, & Alvarez, 1975; Sue, 1977).

The even larger challenge posed by this discussion is the reconceptualization of minority status categories. The definition of minority programs is usually established along the dimensions of race, sex, or age. However, our review of the literature points to the shortcomings of such definitions without consideration of the specific social ecology in which the targeted population is imbedded. Neglected considerations of numerical minority status within particular communities may have led to the contrary findings regarding ethnic minority incidence and prevalence rates in epidemiological studies reported by Dohrenwend (1969). He found half the studies of ethnic status indicated neighborhood risk and half indicated no risk for the groups. However, there is no report of the ethnic composition of the neighborhoods. While we assume that certain ethnic origins place people in a "minority status," this is not necessarily true. The stress comes from the psychologically defined sense of community or sense of alienation that individuals perceive from the environment. While the negative impact of racism, sexism, and agism is not to be ignored, the heightened risk of minority status in itself needs to be addressed in *any* considerations of communities and their programs.

The institutional and societal changes required for these alterations in perceptual sets are staggering to imagine. Yet preventive efforts to alleviate the stress of minority status should not be stopped by such reservations. Williams's (1977) review of staffing indices found marked improvements in institutional measures of discrimination and prejudice. There is still far to go in these efforts. For the less ambitious, or less patient, the potential for interventions at the levels of stressful event reduction, external mediation, or internal mediation remain viable and powerful. Work with social support systems and competency building has been effective in schools (Bogat, Jones, & Jason, 1980; Yee & Lee, 1977) and in colleges (Bloom, 1971). Work with increased sense of control and improved self-concept may show similar positive outcome possibilities. These approaches need to be expanded and applied to minority status populations in particular.

The potential usefulness of such programs is apparent from our discussion of the stress process.

As community psychologists, social workers, and helpers in the human social process, we need to be aware of the minority status factor's role in increasing risk of distress and psychopathology. These considerations should aid us all in future preventive efforts within the community, as well as helping us to conceptualize our role in systems and in interventions at the neighborhood or community level.

# References

Alinsky, S. D. *Reveille for radicals.* New York: Vintage, 1969.

Alinsky, S. D. *Rules for radicals.* New York: Random House, 1971.

Allport, G. *The nature of prejudice.* Cambridge, Mass.: Addison-Wesley, 1954.

Bloom, B. Prevention of mental disorders: Recent advances in theory and practice. *Community Mental Health Journal,* 1979, **15**, 179–191.

Bloom, B. A university freshman preventive intervention program: Report of a pilot project. *Journal of Consulting and Clinical Psychology,* 1971, **37**, 235–242.

Bloom, B. *Changing patterns of psychiatric care.* New York: Human Science Press, 1975.

Bogart, G. A., Jones, J., & Jason, L. School transitions: Preventive interventions following an elementary school closing. *Journal of Community Psychology,* 1980, **8**, 343–352.

Caplan, G. *Support systems and community mental health.* New York: Behavioral Publications, 1974.

Christmas, J. Sociopsychiatric rehabilitation in a black urban ghetto. 1. Conflicts, issues, and directions. *American Journal of Orthopsychiatry,* 1969, **39**, 651–661.

Cohen, R. Principles of preventive mental health programs for ethnic minority populations: The acculturation of Puerto Ricans to the United States. *American Journal of Psychiatry,* 1972, **128**, 1529–1533.

Collier, B. Economics, psychology, and racism: An analysis of oppression. *Journal of Black Psychology,* 1977, **3**, 50–60.

DeVos, G. Minority group identity. In J. Finney (Ed.), *Culture, change mental health and poverty,* New York: Simon & Schuster, 1969.

DeVries, D., Edwards, K., & Slavin, R. Biracial learning teams and race relations in the classroom; Four field experiments using Teams–Games–Tournaments. *Journal of Educational Psychology,* 1978, **70**, 356–362.

Dion, K. L., Earn, B., & Yee, P. H. The experience of being a victim of prejudice: An experimental approach. *International Journal of Psychology,* 1978, **13**, 197–214.

Dohrenwend, B. P. Social status and psychological disorder: An issue of substance and an issue of method. In L. Kolb, V. Bernard, & B. P. Dohrenwend (Eds.), *Urban challenges to psychiatry: The case history of a response.* Boston: Little, Brown, 1969.

Dohrenwend, B. Social stress and community psychology. *American Journal of Community Psychology,* 1978, **6**, 1–14.

Dohrenwend, B. S., & Dohrenwend, B. P. Class and race as status-related sources of stress. In S. Levine & N. Scotch (Eds.), *Social class.* Chicago: Aldine, 1979.

Dunham, H. Community as a process: Maintaining the delicate balance. *American Journal of Community Psychology,* 1977, **5**, 257–268.

Durkheim, E. *Suicide: A study in sociology.* Glencoe, Ill.: Free Press, 1951.

Eysenck, H. *The biological basis of personality.* Springfield, Ill.: Charles C. Thomas, 1967.

Faris, R. E., & Dunham, H. W. *Mental disorders in urban areas: An ecological study of schizophrenia and other psychoses.* Chicago: University of Chicago Press, 1939.

Freeman, R. Discrimination in the academic market place. In *Essays and data on American ethnic groups.* Washington, D.C.: Urban Institute, 1978.

Glass, D., Singer, J., & Pennebaker, J. Behavioral and physiological effects of uncontrollable environmental events. In D. Stokols (Ed.), *Perspective on environment and behavior: Theory, research, and applications.* New York: Plenum Press, 1977.

Gump, P. V. The school as a social situation. In L. Porter & M. Rosenzweig (Eds.), *Annual review of psychology.* Vol. 31. Palo Alto, Calif.: Annual Reviews, 1980.

Harding, J., Proshansky, H., Kutner, B., & Chen, I. Prejudice and ethnic relations. In G. Lindsey & E. Aronson, *The handbook of social psychology.* (2nd ed.) Vol. 5. Reading, Mass.: Addison-Wesley, 1969.

Hinkle, L. Ecological observations of the relation of physical illness, mental illness and the social environment. *Psychosomatic Medicine,* 1961, **23**, 289–296.

Holahan, C., & Spearly, J. L. Coping and ecology: An integrative model for community psychology. *American Journal of Community Psychology,* 1980, **8**, 671–685.

Hunt, C. L., & Walker, L. *Ethnic dynamics.* Homewood, Ill.: Dorsey, 1974.

Jackson, J. J. Family organization and ideology. In K. Miller & R. M. Dreger (Eds.), *Comparative studies of blacks and whites in the United States.* New York: Seminar Press, 1973.

Kahn, L., & French, J. Status and conflict: Two themes in the study of stress. In J. MacGrath (Ed.), *Social and psychological factors in stress.* New York: Holt, Rinehart & Winston, 1970.

Keefe, S., & Casas, J. Mexican-Americans and mental health: A selected review and recommendations for mental health service delivery. *American Journal of Community Psychology,* 1980, **8**, 303–326.

Kelly, J. Toward an ecological conception of preventive interventions. In J. Carter (Ed.), *Research contributions from psychology to community mental health.* New York: Behavioral Publications, 1968.

Kessler, M., & Albee, G. Primary prevention. In M. Rosenzweig & L. Poster (Eds.), *Annual review of psychology.* Vol. 26. Palo Alto, Calif.: Annual Reviews, 1975.

Kitano, H. *Japanese Americans: The evolution of a subculture.* Englewood Cliffs, N.J.: Prentice-Hall, 1969.

Kitano, H. *Race relations.* (2nd ed.) Englewood Cliffs, N. J.: Prentice-Hall, 1980.

Kobasa, S. Personality and resistance to illness. *American Journal of Community Psychology,* 1979, 7, 413–423.

Kobasa, S., Maddi, S., & Courington, S. Personality and constitution as mediators in the stress-illness relationship. *Journal of Health and Social Behavior,* 1981, **22**, 368–378.

Lazarus, R. A laboratory approach to the dynamics of psychological stress. *American Psychologist*, 1964, **19**, 400–411.

Lazarus, R., Speisman, J., Mordkoff, A., & Davison, L. A laboratory study of psychological stress produced by a motion picture film. *Psychological Monographs: General and Applied*, 1962, **76**, (34, Whole No. 553).

Leighton, D., Harding, J., Macklin, D., MacMillan, A., & Leighton, A. *The character of danger*. New York: Basic Books, 1968.

Lin, N., Simeone, R., Ensel, W., & Kuo, W. Social support, stressful life events, and illness: A model and an empirical test. *Journal of Health and Social Behavior*, 1979, **20**, 108–119.

McCarthy, J., & Yancoy, W. L. Uncle Tom and Mr. Charlie: Metaphysical pathos in the study of racism and personal disorganization. *American Journal of Sociology*, 1971, **76**, 648–672.

Meehl, P. E. Schizotaxia, schizotypy, schizophrenia. *American Psychologist*, 1962, **17**, 827–838.

Merton, R. K. *Social theory and social structure*. Glencoe, Ill.: Free Press, 1957.

Mintz, N., & Schwartz, D. Urban ecology and psychosis: Community factors in the incidence of schizophrenia and manic depression among Italians in greater Boston. *International Journal of Social Psychiatry*, 1964, **10**, 101–118.

Montero, D., & Levine, G. (Eds.) Research among racial and cultural minorities: Problems, prospects and pitfalls. *Journal of Social Issues*, 1977, **33**, 1–178.

Morishima, J. Community research in theory and in practice. Paper presented at Pacific Lutheran University, Summer 1976.

Moritsugu, J., Vo, J., & Meyada, L. Community support systems for Indochinese groups. Paper presented to the American Psychological Association, Montreal, 1980.

Myers, J., Lindenthal, J., & Pepper, M. Life events, social integration and psychiatric symptomatology. *Journal of Health and Social Behavior*, 1975, **16**, 421–429.

National Institute of Mental Health. *Socioeconomic characteristics of admissions to outpatient psychiatric services—1969*. DHEW Publication (HSM) 72-9045. Washington: Government Printing Office, 1971.

Padilla, A., Ruiz, R., & Alvarez, R. Community mental health services for the Spanish speaking/surnamed population. *American Psychologist*, 1975, **30**, 892–905.

Parker, S., & Kleiner, R. *Mental illness in the urban Negro community*. New York: Free Press, 1966.

Peck, H., Kaplan, S., & Roman, M. Prevention, treatment and social action: A strategy of intervention in a disadvantaged urban area. *American Journal of Orthopsychiatry*, 1966, **36**, 57–69.

Perlin, L., Menaghan, E., Lieberman, M., & Mullan, J. The stress process. *Journal of Health and Social Behavior*, 1981, **22**, 337–356.

Pettigrew, T. Race relations. In R. Merton & R. Nisbet (Eds.), *Contemporary social problems*. New York: Harcourt Brace Jovanovich, 1971.

Pinkney, A. *Black Americans*. Englewood Cliffs, N.J.: Prentice-Hall, 1975.

Rabkin, J. Ethnic density and psychiatric hospitalization: Hazards of minority status. *American Journal of Psychiatry*, 1979, **136**, 1562–1566.

Raymond, J., Rhoads, D., & Raymond, R. I. The relative impact of family and social involvement on Chicano mental health. *American Journal of Community Psychology*, 1980, **8**, 557–570.

Rappaport, J. *Community psychology: Values, research and action*. New York: Holt, Rinehart & Winston, 1977.

Reissman, F., & Hallowitz, E. The neighborhood service center: An innovation in preventive psychiatry. *American Journal of Psychiatry*, 1967, **123**, 1408–1412.

Rooney-Rebeck, P., & Jason, L. Prevention of prejudice in elementary school children. Paper presented to the Association for the Advancement of Behavior Therapy, New York, 1980.

Rosenberg, M. *Society and the adolescent self-image*. Princeton: Princeton University Press, 1965.

Rosenberg, M. Group rejection and self-rejection. *Research in Community and Mental Health*, 1979, **1**, 3–20.

Rosenthal, D. *Genetics of psychopathology*. New York: McGraw-Hill, 1971.

Sandler, I. Social support resources, stress and maladjust of poor children. *American Journal of Community Psychology*, 1980, **8**, 41–52.

Sarason, S. *The psychological sense of community: Prospects for a community psychology*. San Francisco: Jossey-Bass, 1974.

Sarason, S. Community psychology networks, and Mr. Everyman. *American Psychologist*, 1976, **31**, 317–328.

Schiller, J. Poverty, income and wealth distribution trends. In J. Schiller (Ed.), *The American poor*. Minneapolis: Augsburg, 1982.

Schwartz, D., & Mintz, N. Ecology and psychosis among Italians in 27 Boston communities. *Social Problems*, 1963, **10**, 371–374.

Seligman, M. *Helplessness: On depression, development, and death*. San Francisco: Freeman, 1975.

Selye, H. *The stress of life*. New York: McGraw-Hill, 1956.

Sewell, W., & Haller, A. Factors in the relationship between social status and the personality adjustment of the child. *American Sociological Review*, 1959, **24**, 511–520.

Sherif, M., & Sherif, C. *An outline of social psychology*. New York: Harper & Row, 1956.

Shimkin, D., Shimkin, E., & Frate, D. (Eds.) *The extended family in black societies*. The Hague: Mouton, 1978.

Simpson, G., & Yinger, J. *Racial and cultural minorities*. New York: Harper Bros., 1958.

Smith, W., Burlew, A., Mosely, M., & Whitney, N. M. *Minority issues in mental health*. Reading, Mass.: Addison-Wesley, 1978.

Sowell, T. (Ed.) State of California, State Personnel Board. *The status of Asian and Filipino employees in the California State Civil Service*. 1976.

Steinfield, M. *Cracks in the melting pot*. (2nd ed.) New York: Glencoe Press, 1973.

Sue, S. Psychological theory and implications for Asian-Americans. *Personnel and Guidance Journal*, 1977, **55**, 381–389.

Sue, S., & Zane, N. Learned helplessness theory and community psychology. In M. Gibbs, J. Lachenmeyer, & J. Sigal (Eds.), *Community psychology: Theoretical and empirical approaches*. New York: Gardner, 1980.

U.S. Commission on Civil Rights. *Success of Asian-Americans: Fact or fiction?* Clearinghouse Publication 64. 1980.

U.S. Department of Labor, Employment Standards Administration, Women's Bureau. *1975 Handbook on Women Workers*. Bulletin 297, 1975.

Vance, E. A typology of risk and the disabilities of low status. In G. Albee & J. Joffe (Eds.), *Primary prevention of psychopathology*. Vol. 1. *The issues*. Hanover, N.H.: University Press of New England, 1977.

Wechsler, H., & Pugh, T. Fit of individual and community characteristics and rates of psychiatric hospitalization. *American Journal of Sociology*, 1967, **73**, 331–338.

Weigel, R., Wiser, P., & Cook, S. The impact of cooperative learning experiences on cross-ethnic relations and attitudes. *Journal of Social Issues*, 1975, **31**, 219–244.

Wilcox, B. Social support, life stress, and psychological adjustment: A test of the buffering hypothesis. *American Journal of Community Psychology*, 1981, **9**, 371, 386.

Williams, A., Ware, J., & Donald, C. A model of mental health, life events, and social supports applicable to general populations. *Journal of Health and Social Behavior*, 1981, **22**, 324–336.

Williams, R. M. *Mutual accommodation: Ethnic conflict and cooperation*. Minneapolis: University of Minnesota Press, 1977.

Yee, T., & Lee, R. Based on cultural strengths: A school primary prevention program for Asian-American youth. *Community Mental Health Journal*, 1977, **13**, 239–248.

# 11 ECONOMICS AND PSYCHOSOCIAL DYSFUNCTION: TOWARD A CONCEPTUAL FRAMEWORK AND PREVENTION STRATEGIES*

Edward Seidman and
Bruce Rapkin

W hile in the folk wisdom of many cultures the relationship of economics and maladjustment has long been taken for granted, this topic has not received a great deal of systematic study in the social sciences, and particularly from psychology. This chapter provides an intensive exploration of the relationship between economics and psychosocial dysfunction.

Psychologists have long recognized the impact of various critical life events, including economic difficulties, on an individual's ongoing adaptation. Economic hardships, including job loss and poverty, have been related to the incidence of psychological disorders and criminal behaviors. Yet psychological research on economic stressors has lagged far behind research on the impact of other stressful life events, such as death, divorce, and illness. Nevertheless, in the current chapter we go beyond a search for person-centered psychological impacts of economic stressors in an attempt to discover high-risk populations, and more importantly, high-risk situations and events. Such an analysis of the relationship between economic stressors

* This chapter is an expansion and revision of an invited address delivered at the 28th Inter-American Congress of Psychology, Santo Domingo, Dominican Republic, June 1981.

and psychosocial dysfunctions anticipates and facilitates our closing discussion of prevention strategies.

Each construct of the economics/psychosocial-dysfunction linkage is interpreted rather broadly. Thus when discussing economics, a large set of variables including socioeconomic status, unemployment, business indices, and retirement are reviewed. Similarly, psychosocial dysfunctions refer to many diverse indices of maladjustment or social deviance, such as suicide, severe psychological disorder, unhappiness, and psychosomatic symptomatology, as well as delinquent and criminal behavior.

The chapter consists of five major sections. The first major section briefly considers the voluminous epidemiological and ecological literature on the relationship of social class status to psychosocial dysfunction, with an eye toward discerning the particular role of economic variables. In the second and most extensive section the role of economics is isolated by observing temporal changes in the economy and concomitant changes in rates of psychosocial dysfunctions. Third, a glimpse at the direct impact of job loss on an individual's psychological well-being is provided. In the fourth section a conceptual framework is developed that enables us to (1) more fully understand this body of literature and (2) highlight more fruitful research directions. Based on the foregoing extensive literature review and the conceptual framework, the final section explicates prevention strategies.

Throughout the first three review sections, a central theme will be highlighted in an effort to more fully anticipate the conceptual framework's development. This central theme centers on the question of whether or not absolute change in the economy or in a group or individual's economic status, while indeed quite predictive, is a sufficiently comprehensive construct by which to explain the dysfunctional psychosocial correlates and outcomes. It is postulated that a more adequate understanding can be achieved by first identifying the relevant referent, standard, or comparison level for the particular group or individual of interest. It may be that a group or individual's rate of dysfunction is better understood and indexed by assessing status in relation to salient referents in the social context. If so, a group or individual's discrepancy, gap, or relative as opposed to absolute economic status-change becomes central to a more adequate understanding of dysfunction. The resulting constructs or relational units of observation (Seidman & Rappaport, 1979), such as relative deprivation, grew out of the social psychological literature in the late 1940s and '50s (see Pettigrew, 1967, for an excellent review). However, these notions have been relatively dormant in recent years.

## Cross-Sectional Investigations of Economic Status

Historically, a direct linkage between economics and psychosocial adjustment has been inferred from the epidemiological and ecological literature on social class or socioeconomic status (SES). This, of course, is quite logical, since all indices of SES are some combination of education, occupation, and income. Separately or in combination, these variables are highly correlated with an individual's economic or financial status. While these studies are quite informative and compelling, they do not provide us with a comprehensive understanding of the transactional processes involved in the relationship between economics and psychosocial dysfunction. They simply inform us in static and global terms with regard to the existence of the relationship. In either case a brief summary of the SES research literature in several diverse areas of dysfunction provides us with an important backdrop for our subsequent journey.

Within each subsection we first look at analyses of global indices of social status as related to individual indices of psychosocial dysfunction, followed by ecological rates of dysfunction and SES, and lastly at the few cross-sectional investigations that isolate the as-sociation between specific indices of economic status and psychological dysfunction.

### Psychological Disorders

In this section we briefly summarize the data relating SES to disorders traditionally conceived of as being primarily psychological in nature, such as suicide and schizophrenia. Let us begin with suicide, which according to Menninger (1938) is the most profound and extreme of all disturbances; it is truly the most desperate and final act.

#### SUICIDE

The earliest theoretical conceptions (e.g., Durkheim, 1951) viewed suicide as far more characteristic of the highest social classes. Indeed, this conception was supported by early studies, most notably that of Henry and Short (1954), who examined suicides in the United States from 1920 to 1947. However, Henry and Short's examination of social status and suicide has been severely criticized by Maris (1969) for its methodological inadequacies—the gross indices of social status ("low status" was assigned to all women, the elderly, nonwhites, and those with low incomes) and the lack of control variables. Maris found that suicides were much more characteristic of lower social status occupations and SES scores in Cook County, Illinois, during the period 1959–63.

Powell (1958) found that unskilled labor manifested the highest suicide rate from 1937 to 1956 in Tulsa, Oklahoma. The professional-managerial occupations were close behind. However, the latter fact was primarily accounted for by an extremely high rate during the post-Depression period (1937–41). Perhaps most astounding is the 85.4 rate per 100,000 population for the retired and consequently totally unemployed; this is more than double the 38.7 rate for unskilled labor.

In examining 105 consecutive white male suicides in New Orleans during the period 1955–59, Breed (1963) found that the rates were disproportionately large for the lower occupational ranks. Furthermore, 75 percent of these suicides were found to manifest one or more indices of downward drift—intergenerational skidding, worklife mobility, and dwindling incomes. Only 50 percent of suicides were fully employed; the nonwork status for 25 percent of the partially and totally unemployed was of considerable duration (three weeks to several years).

Breed proposes an "adequacy standard." His interpretation is as follows:

> Measuring up to the standard gives the
> individual a feeling of achievement and self-

satisfaction; falling below it produces a painful sense of failure, or self-devaluation of shame. Using this criterion, many of our suicides were shown to lack competence on the job. And because in American society the work role is central for the man, work failure is not inadequacy in just one role among many, but spreads through other roles and the self-image to threaten a general collapse of the life organization [p. 188].

Hammermesh and Soss (1974) reanalyzed the three preceding investigations. They transformed the suicide rate into a relative index within each county/city by equating the professionals' rate of suicide with a base of 100. The index for each occupation group is related to it. This relative index dramatizes the high rates of suicide for service personnel and laborers: Cook County—service = 314; New Orleans—service = 502, laborers = 481; Tulsa—service = 68, laborers = 100. Further, they rank-ordered the mean family income and suicide index for each family income occupational group within county/city and correlated them. "The rank correlations of the suicide index with income are negative, although the sample size makes it difficult to claim a high degree of significance for them individually [p. 93]." Despite the latter caution, it seems that as the mean income per occupational group decreases, the relative index of suicide per occupational group increases.

The findings that suicides are more characteristic of low SES individuals are supported by several studies from other cultures, for example, those of Yap (1958) in Hong Kong and Sainsbury (1955) in London. More recently, Gibbons, Elliot, Urwin, and Gibbons (1978) reviewed three independent ecological studies of parasuicide rates in England, in Bristol (Morgan & Cheadle, 1975), Oxford (Bancroft, Skrimshire, Reynolds, Simkin, & Smith, 1975), and Edinburgh (Holding, Burglass, Duffy, & Kreitman, 1977), as well as their own in Southampton during the late 1960s to mid '70s. They consistently found that individuals attempting to poison themselves were characterized by their low SES occupations, that is, semi- and unskilled manual and personal service workers.

The early ecological studies of Cavan (1928) in Chicago and Schmid (1928) in Seattle and Minneapolis indicate that suicide tended to be concentrated in the central, poverty-laden, disorganized sections of large cities. In a more recent ecological portrayal of communities with high suicide rates Maris (1969) found that they were distinguished "by an older population, slightly more education and income, far more white-collar workers, fewer unemployed, far fewer Negroes,

more foreign stock, much lower population per household, more substandard housing, and slightly more residential mobility [pp. 154–155]." The higher rates of education, income, white-collar, and employed individuals characterizing these communities is somewhat discrepant with the epidemiological finding of this study that the casualties themselves were lower in social status. With the exception of the extreme hardships that characterized the Depression, a reasonable working hypothesis seems to be that suicides are most characteristic of low SES individuals and communities. Moreover, it seems that individuals of low social status living in communities that have considerable variability in their community characteristics and a relatively high mean level of social status are the most likely to take their own lives. Thus a reasonable speculation also seems to be that an individual or group's relative social status and relative employment status bears some relationship to suicide rates.

Let us turn now to a review of the empirical data with regard to other types of psychopathological entities. For brevity we rely heavily on the reviews of Dohrenwend and Dohrenwend (1974, 1981), who have assiduously recorded and interpreted this literature.

### MAJOR FUNCTIONAL DISORDERS

The Dohrenwends report the following epidemiological trends:

1. The highest overall rates of mental disorder were in the lowest social class in 28 of the 33 studies that reported data according to indicators of social class (Dohrenwend & Dohrenwend, 1974).
2. This relationship was strongest in the studies conducted in urban settings or mixed urban and rural settings (19 of 20 studies) (Dohrenwend & Dohrenwend, 1974).
3. The inverse relationship with class was consistent for schizophrenia (five of seven studies) (Dohrenwend & Dohrenwend, 1974), a finding further supported by most studies of relations between social class and treated rates of schizophrenia (Eaton, 1974).
4. It holds as well for personality disorder (11 of 14 studies) (Dohrenwend & Dohrenwend, 1974).
5. The two studies that provide the relevant data (Brown & Harris, 1978; Weissman & Myers, 1978) both indicate that the current prevalence of unipolar affective disorder is inversely related to social class, though perhaps only for women, who appear to show higher rates of affective disorder than males (Dohrenwend & Dohrenwend, 1981, p. 131; Weissman & Klerman, 1977).

These findings also receive corroboration in other cultures. For example, Katchadourian & Churchill (1969, 1973) replicate in urban Lebanon the classic findings of Hollingshead and Redlich (1958) that the prevalence of diagnostic psychiatric entities is inversely related to social class, and furthermore that psychoses characterize low SES individuals while neuroses characterize high SES individuals.

Ecological investigations of schizophrenia and other selected functional psychiatric disorders (e.g., Faris & Dunham, 1939), similar to suicide and other indices of the social breakdown syndrome, depict the low-SES, disorganized center-city areas as having the highest rates of hospital admissions. An important finding from the classic Faris and Dunham study was that "the schizophrenic rate is significantly higher for those races residing in areas not primarily populated by members of their own group [p. 56]." For example, the rate for blacks living in a primarily black apartment house district was extremely low in comparison to the rates for blacks living in other areas of Chicago, while the rates for whites who were either of native parentage or foreign-born were exceptionally high for this or for that matter any other area.

Levy and Rowitz (1973) followed up the Faris and Dunham study more than 30 years later with both confirmation and disconfirmation of the earlier findings. However, one of the most interesting findings was that areas characterized by the highest rates of admissions to public and private institutions were heterogeneous in social structure, while the lowest rates characterized homogeneous areas (Levy & Rowitz, 1973). Homogeneous areas had a labor force that was largely blue-collar, lower middle class, and almost exclusively white. The heterogeneous areas tended to be racially and ethnically mixed. Minority populations were characteristically black or native American and southern mountain white. Indices of poverty were large, with high rates of unemployment, yet they had a greater percentage of college graduates and more white-collar workers than did low rate areas.

The inverse relationship between SES and major functional disorders for individuals as well as communities is extremely strong. However, there are exceptions and contradictions which can conceptually be accounted for when considered in the light of an individual or group's standing vis-à-vis the nature of the referent community.

## DEMORALIZATION

Lastly, let us look at nonspecific psychological distress. Here we include psychophysiological symptoms, unhappiness, emotional distress, and so on. We shall adopt the concept of "demoralization" from Jerome Frank (1973) to refer to the symptoms and reactions that a person is likely to develop "when he finds that he cannot meet the demands placed on him by the environment, and cannot extricate himself from his predicament [p. 316]." Once again, for conciseness, we return to one of the Dohrenwends' (1981) conclusions: "rates of severe, nonspecific psychological distress are consistently highest in the lowest social class (8 of 8 studies) (Link & Dohrenwend, 1980)."

Sleep disturbances can also be conceived of as a manifestation of demoralization; it too has been related to SES. Karacan et al. (1976), in a health survey administered to residents of Aluchua County, Florida, found that the frequency of reported sleep disturbances was strongly and inversely related to SES.

Economic status and its association to demoralization and the nature of the community was directly assessed by Engelsmann et al. (1972). Income was grouped into low, medium, and high categories to directly assess economic status. The Langer Scale was used as a small part of an interview assessing symptoms of depression, anxiety and psychosomatic complaints. Individuals from three different types of Quebec communities were sampled: inner (central) city, outer (suburban) city, and rural area. Residents of the rural area reported extremely few symptoms and there is no difference between economic status. This is indeed a very homogeneous community in terms of income and education—both are low. No high economic class exists; 66 percent of the residents fall in the low and 34 percent in the middle economic class. The inner city is far more heterogeneous in ethnic status and education. Economically, the inner city does not have an upper class either (40 percent low economic status and 58 percent medium economic status). The low class reports far more symptoms than the middle class. The most heterogeneity in income and education characterized the outer city residents, and here the lowest economic class reports the largest number of symptoms of any class or community. They also make up 11 percent of the outer city, while the middle and upper class are 46 and 29 percent respectively.

Once again SES appears to be inversely related to indices of psychological disorder, that is, demoralization. The structure of the community and a group or individual's standing in it helps to further elucidate the specific nature of the SES-demoralization association.

## Delinquent and Criminal Behavior

We turn to a brief review of the relationship between social status and delinquent and criminal behavior.

Many theories are built upon the assumption that the association between social class and criminal and delinquent behavior is an inverse one. Indeed a strong inverse association characterized the earliest studies, but a recent provocative meta-analysis by Tittle et al. (1978) cast serious doubt upon this assumption. They reviewed all studies that assessed the social status of individuals and criminality. A wide array of variables were included, for example, type of data (self-report or official statistics), sex, race, age, sample size, sophistication of the SES assessment, type of offense, and the year data were gathered. For all studies taken collectively they found a very weak and practically meaningless inverse association between class and criminality. The relationship was a bit more substantial when only studies employing official statistics were utilized. Perhaps most intriguing was the finding that the inverse relationships across studies was quite high in data collected before the 1950s (gamma $= -.73$), but has progressively declined over time, with no relationship apparent across studies with data gathered during the 1970s. The decline accelerates dramatically after 1964. While Tittle and his colleagues provide several alternative explanations for these findings, they give most credence to the interpretation that the declining inverse association between class and official statistics of criminal and delinquent behavior is a function of changes in the criminality of the classes, or even more likely, changes in the classes differential treatment by criminal justice agencies and personnel. They infer that the latter changes may be a function of increased legal changes, media attention, concern, and self-consciousness about civil liberties, particularly for those of lower social status. These authors call for theories that "operate independently of supposed class differences" and the "need to identify more generic processes [p. 653]." As an example, they suggest a focus on discrepancies between aspiration and accomplishment.

Nevertheless, a salient addendum must accompany Tittle et al.'s conclusion. It has been clearly articulated by Daniel Glaser (1979): "homicide and other victimization data suggest that the most violent offenses still are perpetrated more often by poor than by affluent youths [p. 66]."

Investigations of the SES of ecological units and delinquency and criminal behavior rates demonstrate a consistent relationship. Shaw and McKay (1942) and Shaw, Zorbaugh, McKay, and Cottrell (1929) initially demonstrated that delinquency was concentrated in very poor and socially disorganized areas. Gordon (1967), in a thorough methodological critique, analysis, and review of the ecological literature, concludes: "Barring the appearance of surprising new data, there should no longer be any question about the ecological relations . . . between SES and official delinquency rates" [p. 943]." Glaser (1979) reaches a similar conclusion: "It has been shown that whether the units of ecological analysis are neighborhoods, cities, or states, there are impressive correlations between rates of delinquency or crime and extreme indices of poverty [p. 60]." For example, Loftin and Hill (1974) analyzed the average homicide rate (1959–61) for 48 states. A large variety of variables were included, along with an index of "structural poverty" (infant mortality rates, percent age 25 and over with less than five years of schooling, percent illiterate, percent of families with income under $1,000, Armed Forces Mental Test Failures, and percent of children living with one parent). The resulting equation accounted for 92 percent of the variance, with by far the largest regression coefficient being the structural poverty index. Thus the higher the rate of poverty per state the higher the number of murders.

One of these ecological investigations was conducted in Lexington, Kentucky, in 1960 by Quinney (1964). Besides finding that both crime and delinquency rates were inversely related to the predominant social status of the census tract, he found that offense rates were highest for blacks living in areas occupied predominantly by whites and vice versa. This association is clearest for the white delinquency rates: "The white delinquency rates generally increase with each racial area; that is, 12.2 for the 0–2% (nonwhite) racial area to 40.2 in the 50–85% (nonwhite) racial area [p. 152]." Thus it appears that crime and delinquency rates increase for members of a distinct minority group as the proportion constituting the majority group expands.

We turn to several ecological studies that directly examine specific economic variables in contrast to the more global indices of social status. The ecological unit of analysis is either the census tract or the Standard Metropolitan Statistical Area (SMSA).

Schmid (1960), using crime, economic, demographic, and social indices from the 1950 census for 93 census tracts in Seattle, finds the highest correlation between various specific offenses and percentage of males unemployed. These $r$'s are in the low to mid 80s, while the same offenses correlated with median income are substantially lower.

Using a sample of 57 large SMSAs, Danzinger and Wheeler (1975) regressed a variety of indices including punishment, expected sentence, racial status, education, population size, density, region, unemployment, and relative inequality separately on burglary, aggravated assault, and robbery rates for 1960 ($R^2 = .64, .73,$ and $.76$, respectively). The only component of SES was education; its only significant regression coefficient was for robbery. Unemployment did not bear any significant relationship to any of the regression equations. However, the measure of relative income inequality yielded significant regression coefficients in all three equations. In a subsequent study, Danzinger (1976) regressed income inequality, income level, deterrence level, and several socioeconomic characteristics on robbery and burglary rates for 222 SMSAs using 1970 data. The $R^2$ for robbery was .69, while it was .50 for burglary. Similar to the prior investigation the most noteworthy finding, for our purposes, is that the regression coefficients for an index of family income inequality (GINI coefficient) and the male unemployment rate were significant for both criterion variables. Thus the higher the male unemployment and income inequality in an SMSA, the higher the rates of robbery and burglary. In both studies relative inequality plays a major role.

The final study to be discussed in this section is particularly interesting on conceptual grounds. The basic postulate of the Eberts and Schwirian (1968) investigation was "Greater status disparities present in a social system, particularly those affecting lower class populations, will produce greater frustrations or relative deprivations in the lower class population, which will result in greater anti-social and criminal behavior [p. 44]." They anticipated that in economically heterogeneous communities with a high proportion of wealthy people the aspirations of the lower classes will be raised, not fulfilled, and consequently result in higher crime rates because of relative deprivation. Contrary to the relative deprivation hypothesis, they also anticipated high crime rates for the large lower-class SMSAs as a function of massive poverty. Using the 1960 census and 200 SMSAs they confirmed their expectations. They employed a ratio of the percentage of the population with incomes greater than $10,000 to those with incomes of less than $3,000. On the basis of this ratio they divided SMSAs into those labeled larger upper class, balanced, and larger lower class. The curvilinear relationship was apparent for all SMSAs, as well as for those with a large population, those with a high percentage of nonwhite residents, and those in the South. On the other hand, when considering SMSAs with a low percentage of nonwhite residents or those not in the South, only support for the relative deprivation hypothesis was evident; that is, the largest crime rates characterized the large upper classes.

While in general SES is related to the crime rates of individuals and communities, a much more refined understanding of the operative mechanisms is called from a consideration of an individual or group in relationship to their social context. This is most clearly evident in the studies employing relational indices like relative inequality.

## Macrolevel Effects of Economic Change

To this point the review has focused primarily upon global status indices of economic status, that is, social class. While economics is an important component of SES the prior review does not clearly isolate the specific contribution of economics to psychosocial dysfunction. In addition to the global nature of the assessment of social status, the studies have also been cross-sectional and static, that is, conducted at one specific point in time. Yet the economy is in constant flux. Observing the association between the economy and the aggregate level of psychosocial dysfunction over time is one method which might help to isolate and clarify the systemic contribution of the economy to psychosocial dysfunction.

Within each subsection we review studies that relate some economic index—unemployment, common stock prices, business indicators, industrial activity—to an index of psychosocial dysfunction—suicide rate, hospital admissions, outpatient treatment, life surveys, crime and delinquency rates. We examine where the study took place (nation, state, SMSA); the frequency and duration of observations (month, annually); and the magnitude and nature of the findings.

### Psychological Disorders

An outstanding review of longitudinal studies of economics and psychological disorders has recently been published by Dooley and Catalano (1980). Please refer to their paper for a thorough discussion of a number of salient methodological problems embodied in this literature. While we borrow heavily from their work, our orientation and presentation is somewhat different. Again we discuss the literature under the same headings as in the previous section—suicide, major functional disorders, and demoralization.

SUICIDE

In Table 11.1 a summary of the 10 independent studies relating macroeconomic change indices to suicide are displayed. They are in chronological order with regard to the period of data collection. As you can see, sociologists and economists have empirically observed this association since the early 1920s, with data going back to the middle of the 19th century. Many of these studies, particularly the earliest ones,

**Table 11.1. Summary of Studies Relating Macroeconomic Change to Suicide**

| STUDY | SITE | PERIOD | MACROECONOMIC INDICES | SUICIDE INDEX | FINDINGS |
|---|---|---|---|---|---|
| Thomas (1927) | U.K. | Annually, 1853–1913 | Business index composite | Suicide rate | $r = .50$<br>$r = -.47$ (lag = 1 year) |
| Ogburn & Thomas (1922) | U.S.A. | Annually, 1900–20 | Mean of nine detrended business indicators | Suicide rate for 100 cities | $r = -.74$ |
| Dublin & Bunzel (1933) | 1. U.S.A.<br>2. Mass.<br>3. 10 Eastern states | 1. Annually, 1911–31<br>2. Annually, 1910–31<br>a) annually ........<br><br>b) monthly ....... | General Busines Index (undefined) | Suicide rate | $r = -.55$<br><br>$r = -.47$<br>$(r = -.66$ (WM))<br>$(r = -.44$ (WF)) |
| Pierce (1967) | U.S.A. | Annually, 1919–40 | Absolute first differences in common stock prices | Age-adjusted white male suicide rate | $r = .74^d$ (lag = 1 year) |
| Henry & Short (1954) | U.S.A. | Annually, 1900–47 | Ayre's Index of Industrial Activity | Suicide rate | $r = -.76$ (WM)<br>$r = -.71$ (WF) |
| Swinscow (1951) | U.K. | Annually, 1923–47 | Unemployment (actual number of people) | Suicide (actual number) | $r = .93$ (M)<br>$r = .47$ (F) |
| MacMahon, Johnson, & Pugh (1963) | U.S.A. | Annually, 1929–59 | Unemployment (present) | Suicide rate | Graphic—quite high white males ages 45–54 |
| Vigderhous & Fishman (1978) | U.S.A. | 1. Annually, 1920–40<br><br><br><br>2. Annually, 1946–69 | First differences in unemployment rate | Age-standardized suicide rate | 1. $R^2 = .47^d$ (WM)<br>$R^2 = .28^d$ (NWM)<br>$R^2 = .03^d$ (WF)<br>$R^2 = .22^d$ (NWF)<br>2. $R^2 = .33^d$ (WM)<br>$R^2 = .15^d$ (NWM)<br>$R^2 = .02^d$ (WF)<br>$R^2 = .02^d$ (MWF) |
| Hammermesh & Soss (1974) | U.S.A. | Annually, 1947–67 | Unemployment rate plus several age and income predictors | Male suicide rate | $R^2 = .93^d$ |
| Brenner (1976) | 1. U.S.A.<br>2. N.Y.<br>3. Calif.<br>4. Mass. | Annually, 1940–73<br>Annually, 1937–70<br>Annually, 1937–70<br>Annually, 1937–70 | Per capita income, unemployment rate, inflation rate | Suicide rate | $R^2 = .91^d$<br>$R^2 = .96^d$<br>$R^2 = .90^d$<br>$R^2 = .95^d$ } lag = 0–5 years |

NOTE: If no lag is specified under the Findings column, it was synchronous. Superscript $d$ represents employment of the Durbin-Watson $d$ statistic; W = white; NW = Nonwhite; M = Males; F = Females.

were plagued with a major data analytic problem (see Dooley and Catalano, 1980, and Pierce, 1967, for a fuller discussion of this issue). That is, they failed to take account of the degree of autocorrelation of error terms in the time series designs. Such time series analytic techniques are based on the assumption that each error term is independent of, or unaffected by, the values of temporally prior error terms. Durbin and Watson (1950) presented a formula by which one could calculate the degree of autocorrelation and whether it falls within acceptable limits.

Only four of the ten studies employed the Durbin-Watson statistic, beginning with Pierce in 1967. Pierce criticized many of the earlier studies and questioned their findings. For example, he reanalyzed the Henry and Short (1954) investigation after deleting data primarily because the data was collected during the war years, in which it is known that suicides decrease. He was attempting to confirm Durkheim's theory that suicides rise in times of both economic decline and expansion. This partial reanalysis of Henry and Short indicated that the level of autocorrelation was unacceptable. The only finding that Pierce noted with an acceptable level of autocorrelation was between absolute first differences in common stock prices and the age-adjusted white male suicide rate with a lag of one year ($r = .74$). This corroborated Durkheim's theory that suicide rates were related to absolute changes in the economy.

Nevertheless, all other investigations report an inverse relationship between signed economic indices and suicide rates. This is true for those that report acceptable levels of autocorrelation as well as those that fail to take autocorrelation into account. The phenomenon appears to be quite robust! In general, it seems to hold from 1953 to 1970; in the United Kingdom as well as the United States; and across a variety of macroeconomic indices.

It seems that the relationship is substantially stronger for males than females. Historically, men have been more subject to the momentary fluctuations in employment or the business cycle. One should expect to see changes in this as women play an increasing role in the labor market. Full-time employment may soon become the collective as well as individual standard to which they compare themselves and, directly or indirectly, assess their well-being.

The suicide-employment association also appears to differ by age and race. The literature suggests that middle-aged workers and those around retirement may be more affected than more youthful individuals or those over 85 (Brenner, 1976; MacMahon, Johnson, & Pugh, 1963). Here, too, one can see that employment as a normative standard is much more critical

in middle age. It may even remain important in the early retirement years when one has not yet accommodated to a new standard. It is difficult to feel worthy in the early years of retirement, given that employment has been at the heart of Western man's definition of self-worth.

Another illustration of the importance of the standard of comparison in highlighting the strength of the employment-suicide association is manifested by the black-white differences. While the association for black males is much weaker it appears to increase in Northern black males. Again, the standard of comparison appears to change, and so do the consequences—for better and worse.

In general, the suicide rates seem to follow changes in employment quite rapidly, that is, either during the same year or within one year. However, the lag reported by Brenner (1976) appears to be a bit longer.

It should also be noted that in the regression studies that employ several macroeconomic indices (Brenner, 1976; Hammermesh & Soss, 1974), unemployment consistently plays the strongest role.

### MAJOR FUNCTIONAL DISORDERS

The major functional disorders are indexed by global hospital admission rates and inpatient usage. Occasionally the disorders are broken down into diagnostic categories (e.g., Brenner, 1973). A British study (Morgan & Cheadle, 1975) even looks at successful hospital discharges and level of employment and finds the association inversely related to regional unemployment. This is perhaps the only instance where females appear to be more sensitive to the association than males.

Table 11.2 summarizes the studies assessing the relationship between employment or unemployment and hospitalization. Brenner (1973) performed what has already become a classic study on the nature of this association. In *Mental illness and the economy* he presents a variety of thorough and complex analyses on this problem in the state of New York. Overall the relationship between the economy and hospital admissions is robust for 117 years. This study gave birth to recent interest in this area.

Brenner's analyses are far too extensive and complex to do justice to here; we shall only touch on several of the findings. We should add that his findings have not gone unchallenged. Brenner noted that the relationship was stronger for males than females from 1914 to 1960. He corroborated this for New York State with data from 1936 to 1970 and with U.S. data from 1940 to 1971 (Brenner, 1976). The Marshall and Funch (1979) reanalysis of his 1973 study only appears to contradict the greater sensitivity of males, since hospital capacity plays a much larger role in the rate of female admissions. Although the direction of the relationship is different in the Sclar and Hoffman (1978) investigation, males are still more sensitive to the unemployment/hospital-admission association. This is similar to the differential sex sensitivity found for suicide, and a similar interpretation seems reasonable.

Despite the fact that Marshall and Funch (1979) reanalyzed the major findings of Brenner's 1973 volume, they confirmed the fundamental finding. They also found that hospital capacity plays an important role in predicting hospital first admission rates. In fact, for the young and old, capacity is a better predictor of admission. Across studies working-age males appear to be the most sensitive to the economy-dysfunction association. Again, other groups in our society are less socialized to the standard necessity to be fully employed. Consequently, downturns in the economy are less likely to place them substantially below a standard that society has set for them as a group and that they have, as individuals, incorporated.

The findings of Sclar and Hoffman (1978) are the only ones that contradict the fundamental association noted by Brenner and others (see Table 11.2). Sclar and Hoffman find that inpatient use is inversely related to regional unemployment. These results are difficult to interpret, but the authors offer several speculations. The data are quite recent, 1950 to 1975. During the latter portion of this time the local CMHC began to pick up steam and may have reduced unnecessary admissions, funneling them into outpatient treatment. This is consistent with the finding that outpatient usage is directly related to unemployment in the same region. Sclar and Hoffman also employed a smaller ecological unit of analysis than a state or country. However, Catalano and Dooley (1979) and Barling and Handel (1980) employ smaller ecological units amd more recent data as well, and still confirm the fundamental finding of Brenner and others. Perhaps it is simply unique to this area, or a testimony to the efficacy of the local CMHC. In either case it is unclear why the relationship should be significant in the opposite direction.

Barling and Handel (1980) have shown that selected groups are most sensitive to the association: the unemployed; housewives, students and retired; and those with ony a partial high school education. Many of these are, at best, at the margin of poverty and are most effected by minor perturbations in the economy. Brenner (1973) presents several analyses consistent with this finding, although the meaning of a marginal education was grammar school at that time.

Brenner (1973) has also illustrated that for minority ethnic groups (for example, blacks), where the association is weak it gets stronger after World War II, when they become a more *bona fide* part of the work force. Individually and as a group their expectations have been raised; thus they are more subject to economic changes and associated effects.

Again, we see that other studies (all but one is confirmatory) demonstrate that it is the relationship or relative status vis-à-vis a socially imposed group standard and expectation that seems to play a strong role in determining a group's sensitivity to the unemployment/hospital-admission association. It appears that the more distant a group's status is from the standard, the more they will be negatively affected by downward trends in the economy.

## DEMORALIZATION

The studies reviewed in this section fairly consistently follow the recommendations of Dooley and Catalano (1980). First of all they employ a small ecological unit, such as a county, metropolitan or nonmetropolitan area, and frequently use a macroeconomic index based on economic as opposed to political entities, for instance, the SMSA. Third, the period of analysis, months and quarters, provides the opportunity for a more sensitive assessment. A wide variety of behavioral indices are included. Surveys of depressed mood and psychophysiological symptoms as well as outpatient usage are used to assess the relationship to the economy. Outpatient usage is conceived of as an index of demoralization; it seems much closer to life dissatisfaction than it is to major disorders. One would expect these demoralization indices to be affected prior to and more sensitively than hospital admission rates. All but the Barling and Handel (1980) study take account of autocorrelated errors. All of these studies have been reported recently.

The overall association between unemployment and demoralization characterizes only three of the five studies (Catalano & Dooley, 1977; Dooley & Catalano, 1979; Sclar & Hoffman, 1978). The association in the first two references is based on the same sample, but for different behavioral indices—depressed mood, psychophysiological symptoms, and economic life events. The remaining overall association is based on outpatient usage (Sclar & Hoffman, 1978).

Several studies disaggregate their data and illustrate that the economy-demoralization association lives on in a number of subgroups. Unfortunately, the nature of disaggregation differs for most studies; consequently it is difficult even to assert reasonable conjectures.

**Table 11.2. Summary of Studies Relating Macroeconomic Change to Major Functional Disorders**

| STUDY | SITE | PERIOD | MACROECONOMIC INDICES | FUNCTIONAL DISORDER | FINDINGS |
|---|---|---|---|---|---|
| Brenner (1973) | New York | Annually, 1914–60 | Manufacturing employment | First mental hospital admissions | Optimized lag<br>$R^2$ = .56[d] (M)<br>$R^2$ = .36[d] (F) |
| Marshall & Funch (1979) | New York | Annually, 1916–55 | Manufacturing employment & hospital capacity | First mental hospital admissions | Age-adjusted<br>$R^2$ = .91[d] (M)<br>$R^2$ = .96[d] (F) |
| Brenner (1976) | 1. U.S.A. | Annually, 1940–71 | Per capita income, unemployment rate, inflation rate | First mental hospital admissions | Lag = 0–5 years<br>1. $R^2$ = .97[d]<br>$R^2$ = .93[d] (M)<br>$R^2$ = .27[d] (F) |
| | 2. New York | Annually, 1936–70 | | | 2. $R^2$ = .78[d] (M)<br>$R^2$ = .46[d] (F) |
| Sclar & Hoffman (1978) | Mental health catchment area (Fitchburg-Leominster, MA) | 1. Monthly, 1950–75<br><br>2. Quarterly, 1950–75 | Regional unemployment, service availability, and trends | Inpatient use | $R^2$ = .69[d]*<br>$R^2$ = .65[d] (M)*<br>$R^2$ = .42[d] (F)*<br><br>$R^2$ = .83[d]*<br>$R^2$ = .83[d] (M)*<br>$R^2$ = .65[d] (F)* |
| Catalano & Dooley (1979) | Kansas City, MO | Monthly, October 1971-January, 1973 | Metropolitan unemployment | Mental hospitalization | Confirmation for most groups |

| Study | Location | Time period | Economic measure | Mental health measure | Findings |
|---|---|---|---|---|---|
| Barling & Handel (1980) | St. Louis, MO | Quarterly, 1970–75 | Metropolitan unemployment | Inpatient use | $r = .52$ (lag = 6 mos.)<br>$r = .43, .43$ (lag = 6 & 9 mos. for unemployed)<br>$r = .57$ (lag = 6 mos., for housewife, students & retired)<br>$r = .50, 48$ (lag = 6 & 9 mos. for partial high school education) |
| Morgan & Cheadle (1975) | West Midlands Region, England | Quarterly, 1964–73 | Regional unemployment rate | Hospital patient full-time open job placements | $r = -.36$ (M)<br>$r = -.53$ (F)<br>$r = -.49$ |
| Liem (1981) | Massachusetts | | Manufacturing employment | First admissions | Moderate confirmation for M only |

NOTE: If no lag is specified under the Findings column, it was synchronous. Superscript $d$ represents employment of the Durbin-Watson $d$ statistic; M = males; F = females.

* Inverse, not positive relationship.

185

**Table 11.3. Summary of Studies Relating Macroeconomic Change to Demoralization**

| STUDY | SITE | PERIOD | MACROECONOMIC INDICES | DEMORALIZATION | FINDINGS |
|---|---|---|---|---|---|
| Sclar & Hoffman (1978) | Mental health catchment area (Fitchbury-Leominster, MA) | 1. Monthly, 1958–75<br><br>2. Quarterly, 1958–75 | Regional unemployment, service availability, trends | Outpatient use | $R^2 = .81^d$<br>$R^2 = .74^d$ (M)<br>$R^2 = .80^d$ (F)<br><br>$R^2 = .89^d$<br>$R^2 = .83^d$ (M)<br>$R^2 = .90^d$ (F) |
| Barling & Handel (1980) | St. Louis, MO | Quarterly, 1970–75 | Metropolitan unemployment | Outpatient use | $r = .48$, skilled occupation<br>$r = -.40, -.42, -.31, \& -.41$, (9th grade educ., 0, 3, 6, 9 mos. lags respectively) |
| Catalano & Dooley (1977) | Kansas City, MO | Monthly, October 1971–January 1973 | Metropolitan & regional unemployment rate | 1. Surveyed depressed mood<br>2. Surveyed life change events | $R^2 = .68^d$ (lag 1–3 ADJ mos.)<br>$R^2 = .78^d$ (lag = 3 ADJ mos., absolute change) |
| Dooley & Catalano (1979) | Kansas City, MO | Monthly, October 1971–January 1973 | 1. Metropolitan unemployment<br>2. Regional unemployment | 1. Surveyed economic life events<br>2. Surveyed noneconomic life events<br>3. Surveyed psychophysiological symptoms | $r_{11} = .58^d$ (lag = 2 mos.)<br>$r_{21} = -.53^d \& .56^d$ (lag = 0 & 3 mos.)<br>$r_{21} = .59^d$ (lag = 3 mos.)<br>$r_{13} = .58^d$ (lag = 1 mo.) |
| Dooley, Catalano, Jackson, & Brownell (1981) | Washington County, Maryland | Monthly, December 1971–June 1974 | 1. Absolute change variables – total economy of basic sector<br>2. County unemployment<br>3. Total work force size<br>4. Basic sector work force size<br>5. Inflation | 1. Surveyed depressed mood<br>2. Surveyed psychophysiological symptoms<br>3. Surveyed life change events | Disconfirmation<br><br>Disconfirmation<br><br>Disconfirmation |

NOTE: If no lag is specified under the Findings column, it was synchronous. Superscript $d$ represents employment of the Durbin-Watson $d$ statistic; W = White; M = males; F = females.

However, Dooley et al. (1981) recently attempted to corroborate their Kansas City results in an almost identical study performed in a nonmetropolitan area of Maryland. They failed to confirm any of their prior findings (hypotheses).

Dooley et al. (1981) offer several potential explanations to account for the divergent findings. One compelling explanation has to do with differences in nonmetropolitan and rural versus metropolitan residents. The metropolitan areas seem to be far more heterogeneous in the demographic and educational characteristics of their residents. Rural and nonmetropolitan residents seem less concerned with economic opportunities and satisfaction and report greater satisfaction with their neighborhoods, friendships, and marriages; their social supports seem stronger. Consequently, the personal meaning of local economic fluctuations may be very different for groups and individuals in nonmetropolitan as opposed to metropolitan communities. However, the area of Massachusetts in which Sclar and Hoffman (1978) collected their data was also a nonmetropolitan area, and they found strong confirmation for the association, but with outpatient admissions as opposed to surveyed mood and symptoms.

Clearly more research is necessary to increase our understanding of the relationship between the economy and demoralization. Disaggregations on salient dimensions seem important. Furthermore, it is suggested that employing relational constructs and measures might bring greater clarity and specificity to the area.

Overall, the empirical data on the economy/psychological-disorder association is strong and compelling. This is particularly noteworthy given the miniscule exposure that most mental health practitioners have had to this body of literature. The implications for treatment and prevention are considerable.

### Crime and Delinquent Behavior

Social scientists have dramatically increased their interest in the association between economic change and mental health during the last 10 to 15 years. However, the interest in crime and the business cycle has a longer and more active history, as can be seen by scanning Tables 11.4, 11.5, and 11.6. We begin, however, with the two studies that focus upon homicide (see Table 11.4).

Using U.S. data from 1920 to 1940 Henry and Short (1954) noted a strong inverse relationship between the business index and the homicide rate for whites, but a weak positive association for nonwhites in the U.S. This time period was broken down into three

subperiods, over the course of which the inverse correlation for whites increased and the positive correlation for nonwhites decreased. The different signs of the correlations for white and nonwhite groups may be accounted for by each group's respective relative status in our society at the particular time.

Brenner (1976), using data from the U.S., New York State, California, and Massachusetts, confirmed the inverse association between the economy and homicide from prior to World War II through 1970. In disaggregations of the data by sex, males appeared to be more sensitive to the association, as in the studies on suicide and to some extent on hospital admissions.

We now turn to aggregate changes in the economy as they relate to imprisonment. We have uncovered four studies that assess this association (see Table 11.5). Two employ U.S. data (Brenner, 1976; Robinson, Smith, & Wolf, 1974) and span a recent period of 40 years with regard to state prison admissions and twelve years with regard to federal prisons. The association between unemployment and imprisonment is consistently positive and strong. Brenner does demonstrate that there is a small amount of differential sensitivity to the association by region of the country. A Canadian study during a portion of this time corroborates the U.S. association (Greenberg, 1977). A study around the turn of the century in New York State used the wholesale price index as the economic change indicator (Davies, 1922).

In Table 11.6 we present eight studies. They differ in the index of crime/delinquency employed. Five studies employ offense rates of some kind; one arrest rates; one prosecution rates; and one delinquent court cases. Unfortunately, few studies disaggregate the data by age, and age appears to have a major impact on not only the magnitude but the direction of the association as well.

First, we look closely at those studies attempting to assess the contribution of age to the unemployment-crime association. Wiers (1945) found that from 1921 to 1943 several indices of prosperity all related positively to delinquent court cases in Wayne County, Michigan. For 1932 to 1950 Glaser and Rice (1959) correlated U.S. offense rates with male unemployment by age grouping. The relationship is a strong inverse one for youth 17 and under. It is still inverse at 18, but nonsignificant. For 19- to 20-year-olds it becomes positive and continues to increase in strength with age until 34. The next age group again manifests an inverse relationship and it increases in magnitude with age. A similar pattern for age emerges when the crime-delinquency index is crimes against persons or misdemeanors. Glaser and Rice perform similar anal-

### Table 11.4. Summary of Studies Relating Macroeconomic Change to Homicide

| STUDY | SITE | PERIOD | MACROECONOMIC INDICES | HOMICIDE INDEX | FINDINGS |
|---|---|---|---|---|---|
| Henry & Short (1954) | U.S.A. | 1920–40 | Business index | Homicide rate | $r = -.80$ (W); $r = .26$ (NW) |
| Brenner (1976) | 1. U.S.A. | 1940–73 | Unemployment rate, per capita income, and inflation rate | Homicide rate | 1. $R^2 = .99^d$ |
| | 2. New York | 1937–70 | | | 2. $R^2 = .89^d$ |
| | 3. California | 1937–70 | | | 3. $R^2 = .73^d$; $R^2 = .76^d$ (M); $R^2 = .42^d$ (F) |
| | 4. Massachusetts | 1937–70 | | | 4. $R^2 = .82^d$; $R^2 = .83^d$ (M); $R^2 = .57^d$ (F) |

NOTE: If no lag is specified under the Findings column, it was synchronous. W = white; NW = nonwhite; M = males; F = females. Superscript $d$ represents employment of the Durbin-Watson $d$ statistic.

### Table 11.5. Summary of Studies Relating Macroeconomic Change to Imprisonment

| STUDY | SITE | PERIOD | MACROECONOMIC INDICES | IMPRISONMENT INDEX | FINDINGS |
|---|---|---|---|---|---|
| Davies (1922) | New York | 1896–1915 | Wholesale price index | Annual admissions to state prisons | $r = -.41$ |
| Brenner (1976) | U.S.A. | 1933–73 (excl. 1942–45) | Unemployment rate, per capita income, and inflation rate | State prison imprisonment rates | $R^2 = .79^d$ (lag = 0–2 yrs.) (sensitivity varies by region of the country) |
| Greenberg (1977) | Canada | 1945–59 | Unemployment rate | Per capita admissions to prisons | $r = .92$ |
| Robinson, Smith, & Wolf (1974) | U.S.A. | 1960–72 | Unemployment rate | 1. First admissions to federal prison | 1. $r = .91$ |
| | | | | 2. First admissions to state prison | 2. $r = .86$ |

NOTE: If no lag is specified under the Findings column, it was synchronous. Superscript $d$ represents employment of the Durbin-Watson $d$ statistic.

### Table 11.6. Summary of Studies Relating Macroeconomic Change to Criminal Delinquent Offenses

| STUDY | SITE | PERIOD | MACROECONOMIC INDICES | CRIME INDEX | FINDINGS |
|---|---|---|---|---|---|
| Von Mayr (reanalyzed by Woytinsky, 1929, cited in Sellin, 1937) | Bavaria | 1836–61 | Price of rye | Offenses against property | $r = .76$ |
| Ogburn & Thomas (1922) | New York | 1870–1920 | Mean of nine detrended business indicators | Criminal offenses (in the courts of record) | $r = -.35$ |
| Thomas (1927) | U.K. | 1857–1913 | Business index composite | 1. Prosecution for all indictable crimes | $r = -.25$ |
| | | | | 2. Prosecutions for crimes against property | $r = -.25$ |
| | | | | 3. Prosecutions for crimes against property with violence | $r = -.44$ |
| | | | | 4. Prosecutions for malicious injuries to properties | $r = .04$ |
| | | | | 5. Prosecutions for crimes of violence against a person | $r = .06$ |
| | | | | 6. Prosecutions for crimes against morals | $r = .05$ |
| Wiers (1945) | Wayne County (Detroit) Michigan | 1921–43 | 1. Nonagriculture employment | Delinquent court cases | $r = .70$ |
| | | | 2. Department store sales | | $r = .50$ |
| | | | 3. Gross national product (1939 prices) | | $r = .49$ |
| | | | 4. Industrial production | | $r = .48$ |
| Bogen (1944) | Los Angeles County | 1925–41 | Business activity | Juvenile court petitions | |
| Henry & Short (1954) | 1. 10 major U.S. cities | | Ayre's business index | 1. Burglaries | $r = -.74$ |
| | 2. 12 major U.S. cities | | | 2. Robberies | $r = -.65$ |

Table 11.6. (continued on p. 190)

**Table 11.6.** (*continued*)

| STUDY | SITE | PERIOD | MACROECONOMIC INDICES | CRIME INDEX | FINDINGS | | |
|---|---|---|---|---|---|---|---|
| | | | | | Age | *Property offense* | *Misdemeanors* |
| Glaser & Rice (1959) | 1. U.S.A. | 1932–50 | Male unemployment rate (age-specific) | Property offense & misdemeanors | 17 | $r = -.56$ | $r = +.02$ |
| | | | | | 18 | $r = -.34$ | $r = +.32$ |
| | | | | | 19–20 | $r = +.40$ | $r = +.61$ |
| | | | | | 21–24 | $r = +.48$ | $r = +.70$ |
| | | | | | 25–34 | $r = +.74$ | $r = +.96$ |
| | | | | | 35–44 | $r = -.26$ | $r = -.76$ |
| | | | | | ≥ 45 | $r = -.64$ | $r = -.84$ |
| | 2. Boston | 1930–56 | | Property theft, crimes against persons, & misdemeanors | Essential replication of U.S. data above | | |
| | 3. Chicago | 1930–56 | | Misdemeanors | Essential replication of U.S. data above | | |
| | 4. Cincinnati | 1935–56 | | Misdemeanors | Essential replication of U.S. data above | | |
| Fleisher (1966) | 1. U.S.A. | 1932–61 | Male unemployment rate (age-specific), war & trend | Arrest-offense ratio | $R^2 = .95$ (under age 24) | | |
| | 2. Boston, Cincinnati, & Chicago | 1935–56 | Male unemployment rate (age specific), war & trend | Property arrest rates | $R^2 = .91$ (age 21–24) | | |
| | 3. England & Wales | 1936–62 | Unemployment rate, war & trend | Property arrest rates | $R^2 = .70$ (under age 17) <br> $R^2 = .80$ (age 17–21) | | |
| Danzinger & Wheeler (1975) | U.S.A. | 1949–70 | Distribution of income and deterrence variables, unemployment, & percent of population 15–24 | Burglary <br> Aggravated assault <br> Robbery | $R^2 = .995$[d] <br> $R^2 = .990$[d] <br> $R^2 = .978$[d] | | |
| Singell (1967) | Detroit | Monthly, 1950–61 | Unemployment rate | Youth police contacts | $R^2 = .08$ (yet statistically significant) | | |

NOTE: Superscript *d* represents employment of the Durbin-Watson *d* statistic.

yses separately for arrest rates in Boston, Chicago,and Cincinnati. Again, in general the pattern, if not the magnitude, is similar. The age where the change between an inverse and positive relationship occurs is somewhat variable. For ages 45 and beyond the positive relationship attenuates some, but does not change direction. Chicago is somewhat more divergent from the dominant pattern manifested in the Boston, Cincinnati, and national analyses.

Fleisher (1966) also performed a set of time series analyses between the male age-specific unemployment rate and the U.S. arrest-offense ratio, separately at each age from under 15 to 24. The $R^2$ were consistently very high. An inverse regression coefficient for unemployment was evident for youth 15 and younger, but it decreases in magnitude with age, eventually becoming positive and statistically significant with increasing age (20 and over). He also regressed unemployment and other variables on property arrest rates for Boston, Chicago and Cincinnati taken together for the years 1936–56. One regression analysis was performed for youth under 21 and another for young men 21 to 24. The regression coefficients for unemployment in both equations were positively related to unemployment. The identical set of analyses was performed for data from Wales and England (1936–62). While both $R^2$ were statistically significant and small, the coefficient for unemployment was negative in the under-21 analysis.

Summarizing the studies on age, it seems that young adolescents evidence a negative correlation between unemployment and crime-delinquency rates, indicating that in times of prosperity youth seem to have larger arrest rates. What is most in doubt is the exact age at which this relationship decreases and eventually changes direction. Fleisher's three-city analysis is the only inconsistency with the prior generalization. However, he used all youth under 21, and from the other investigations it appears that the unemployment/arrest-rate relationship changes directions earlier in a young man's chronological development. Consequently, these results may be a function of summing across too many age groupings.

On the other hand, for men well into their 20s and 30s the unemployment-arrest relationship is strongly positive. Thus in times of economic decline criminal arrests go up. There is too little available age-disaggregated data on crime rates of older men to draw any inferences.

All but one of the remaining studies demonstrate to some degree that as the economy prospers, the rate of criminal offenses decreases and as the economy falters, the rate of criminal offenses rises. This is so

in Bavaria, the United Kingdom, and the U.S.A., as well as in a number of major U.S. urban centers.

The remaining investigation (Danzinger & Wheeler, 1975) demonstrates that income gap, "a measure of the distance between an individual's income and the average of his reference group [p. 115]," and relative inequality yield the strongest regression coefficients for equations predicting U.S. burglary, aggravated assault, and robbery rates from 1949 to 1970. There is a high degree of collinearity between the two measures; however, income gap appears to be the more potent. These results indicate that higher crime rates are associated with large income discrepancy or a relatively more unequal distribution of income.

In summary, the economy bears a powerful relationship to criminal and delinquent behavior. It is clear that relational constructs such as income gap and relative inequality offer a great deal of promise in improving our understanding of these phenomena.

## Microlevel Effects of Economic Change

In this section we review, in an extremely cursory fashion, several studies that bear on how unemployment per se impacts the psychosocial well-being of affected individuals. Most of these studies are not particularly rigorous. In fact, they are primarily retrospective, although a few prospective studies have been reported. Obviously, these studies do not clarify mechanisms involved in the association, but they do serve a heuristic function about individual processes.

### Psychological Disorders

In this section we rely almost exclusively upon the studies surveyed by Dooley and Catalano (1980).

#### SUICIDE AND MAJOR
#### FUNCTIONAL DISORDERS

Dooley and Catalano (1980) report several studies, mostly retrospective, indicating that unemployment characterized the recent history of individuals who committed suicide or attempted suicide (Breed, 1963; Lendrum, 1933; Sainsbury, 1956; Theorell, Lind, & Floderus, 1975; Tuckman & Lavell, 1953). Recent job change or unemployment was also related to psychiatric disability (Theorell et al., 1975).

#### DEMORALIZATION

Several prospective studies are reported by Dooley and Catalano (1980) demonstrating manifestations of demoralization related to unemployment (Cobb & Kasl, 1977; Cohn, 1978; Parnes & King, 1977). They are also supported by several prospective studies (Little, 1976; Schlozman & Verba, 1978).

### *Delinquent and Criminal Behavior*

Glaser (1979) reviews several retrospective interview studies that employ prisoners or individuals on parole and probation. From these studies he concludes that "offenders' circumstances . . . leave the impression that extreme failure at legitimate employment is high correlated with serious law violations [p. 74]."

## Toward a Conceptual Framework

Thus far in our discussion we have attempted to capture the flavor of the extant data relating economic phenomena to psychological and social dysfunction. At this point it will be useful to highlight certain trends in this knowledge base which we believe are essential underpinnings for future research efforts. Clearly, at both the macro- and microlevels absolute indices of economic conditions are correlated with rates of numerous psychosocial maladaptations, to a greater or lesser degree. These findings in their own right suggest both etiological hypotheses and interventive-preventive approaches. However, the numerous absolute indices have afforded only a "black box" look at the causal relationships which may exist between the two domains. Context for hypotheses about such linkages is generally found in the discussion sections of research articles, and is often based on informal observation or conjecture. Further, such absolute constructs are treated as unambiguously combinable and comparable, when such may not be true. For instance, is it reasonable to treat "male unemployment" in rural Kansas anything like the similarly labeled phenomena in New York City or Santo Domingo? To answer this question we need to know much more than the percent of the workforce jobless in each area; we may want to consider the income heterogeneity of the local community, differential sex or age role expectancies for full-time employment, and changes in unemployment over time, to name just a few relevant mediators. So-called absolute indices often ignore the complex nature of the economic phenomena of interest; thus scales which are defined and treated as unidimensional may, in fact, have hidden facets which can distort research findings.

From our review of the literature, it is evident that those studies which considered economic indices in context provided much richer and more satisfying portrayals of the phenomena of interest. Recall that while the general finding was that the crime rate rises in times of economic decline and falls in times of prosperity, this relationship seems to completely reverse itself for adolescents. It appears that the economic context for a working-age male has a very different meaning and subsequent impact than it does for a youth. This view necessarily leads to different explanatory considerations. Similarly Eberts and Schwirian's (1968) conclusions regarding crime rate in SMSAs with differing class structures demonstrate the utility of providing relative and contextualized indices of economic conditions.

It is our thesis that advancement in our understanding of the relationship of the economy to psychosocial dysfunction will require an understanding of the societal conditions which mediate the effects of economic phenomena on human behavior. To this end, we propose the use of indices which assess economic status relative to standards of comparison salient to the individual or group of interest. As such, attention would be drawn to relative deprivation or gain, rather than absolute income change, and socioeconomic conditions relative to normative expectancies that exist in the population. Hopefully, these relative indices will prove themselves superior to absolute measures in that they will enable researchers to better isolate the processes which are linked to dysfunctional outcomes. Indeed, it is reasonable to view the numerous correlational findings relating absolute indices to maladaptation as markers of processes which exist in a societal context. Below, we shall outline some considerations which are central to explicating and testing the nature of these processes with relational indices.

Pettigrew's (1967) seminal review and discussion of social evaluation theory provides ample theoretical precedent for framing societal conditions and events in relativistic terms in determining how these pertain to group and individual behavior. Pettigrew integrates such social psychological notions as social comparison and comparison levels with more sociological ideas, such as reference groups and relative deprivation, to suggest a comprehensive theory of motivation underlying social behavior. Fundamental to this theory is the premise that individual attitudes and source behaviors are necessarily a product of personal comparisons of present life experience to alternatives presented by salient reference groups and to societal norms and expectancies. Thus simply describing an individual as unemployed does not capture his experience as well as indicating that he is unemployed with a BA in accounting in a city where more accountants are employed.

From an entirely different perspective, economists Sheldon Danzinger and David Wheeler exemplify relativistic approach by providing and testing a model of relative economic status in accounting for personal and property crime rates. These authors discuss how reference groups play a role in determining criminal behavior, through income gap and relative economic inequality between zonal classes. The model they propose, which also includes criminal deterrence and acceptance of the social contract as predictors, is successful in predicting both personal and property crime in the aggregate as discussed in a prior section. Further, it lends insight into the differential importance of various factors which underlie the inverse relationship between income and crime by capturing forces which motivate criminal behavior.

Following Pettigrew's and Danziger and Wheeler's lead, the approach we are suggesting constitutes an ecological analysis of the economy/psychosocial-dysfunction linkage. As with any ecological analysis, attention to innumerable mediating phenomena and contextual concerns opens a Pandora's box of possible confounds and interactions that demand consideration. In an effort to systematize these factors, a conceptual framework may prove useful in operationalizing relative economic indices.

For our purposes absolute measures are defined as indices which capture one distinct phenomenon. Relative measures are indices which describe change in an absolute variable relative to change in one or more others. Comparisons entailed in relative indices may be achieved arithmetically (by subtraction or division), by computing standard scores, or by partial correlational or regression techniques. The particular method will depend on the variables being considered, but again, the purpose is to provide a contrast or comparison in the scale itself.

Keeping in mind our purpose of locating contrasts which reflect the contextual factors that influence adaptation, it will be useful to begin developing our framework by considering how an individual may represent and evaluate his or her economic condition. We shall concern ourselves with two major facets of contrast: the *comparative focus* and the *temporal dimension*.

A contrast can occur on either one of these two facets, or with regard to both simultaneously. The *comparative focus* centers upon contrasts between differing levels of social organization. For ease, let us borrow from Bronfenbrenner's (1979) ecological framework the following levels of social organization: the organism, the microsystem (situations with which the organism has face to face contact, for instance family, peer group, school, work), the exosystem (settings in which the organism does not directly participate, but which affect him or her nevertheless, such as local government, vitality of local business and

industry, the community's socioeconomic mix), and the macrosystem (the social construction of reality or ideology, culture). Contrasts can be drawn between any two levels of social organization, though it is simplest to envision a contrast drawn by an individual organism and an aspect of the micro-, eco-, or macrosystem. This is similar to the basic tenet of the theory of social evaluation (Pettigrew, 1967) that human beings understand themselves by comparing themselves to others. Thus the comparative focus or "referent" other of which Pettigrew speaks may be another individual, a specific group or category of individuals, or an idealized model based on personal expectancies or cultural norms. This is a psychological or social psychological mode of analysis. Consequently, intervention implications will most often be in a psychotherapeutic or secondary preventive vein.

Comparative contrasts can also be meaningfully drawn between levels excluding the organismic level. Contrasts can be drawn between a microsystem and an exosystem or macrosystem, or between an exosystem and the macrosystem. While such contrasts may help only minimally in understanding the behavior of a particular individual, they may help greatly in understanding an actual or ascribed group's behavior. Comparative contrasts of this nature, and with regard to the economy psychosocial-dysfunction linkage, are likely to lead to preventive and other policy-based implications.

Examples of contrasts made with varying comparative foci would include an individual's yearly income compared to the mean of his or her occupational group, the rate of unemployment among blacks versus that of whites in an SMSA, or the amount of salary increment an individual receives in a given time period minus the amount he or she expected upon entering a job. Note that contrasts of absolute indices to some comparative focus always juxtapose some index of the target individual's or group's economic status against some outside standard, to provide what Pettigrew refers to as a comparison level. A major research and assessment issue is the choice of the particular comparative focus. It is easier when trying to understand an individual's behavior because the individual organism can be asked/assessed at a psychological level. However, the problem is far more complex when the comparative focus being sought is that of a designated group, like unemployed Hispanics or adolescents of differing ages. Here some quantitative indices based on theoretical formulations of mediating conditions or prior descriptive studies of the ecology of the group(s) of interest might be employed.

Rather than refer to some external reference to establish a standard of comparison, individuals may also learn about themselves by drawing contrasts over time—the *temporal dimension*. The evaluation of relative economic success or failure over time may provide a powerful motivation for behavior of individuals and collectives. As Maris discusses, many suicides in low SES categories at time of death appear to have experienced a status change in the recent past. Although, as with the Dohrenwend's social drift hypothesis, there may be some difficulty in ascertaining the direction of a causal relationship from present data, it is clear that relative temporal change bears some relationship to numerous forms of maladaptation. Choice of the time frame for drawing such contrasts is problematic. As with the comparative focus discussed above, identifying salient temporal contrasts at levels beyond the individual is even more complex.

To summarize, the framework for defining different relative economic indices provides for contrasts along at least two distinct facets. Contrasts described thus far have been over single facets, with all others fixed. Of course, it is possible to develop indices which describe contrasts over multiple facets. Examples might include change in median income over time for two groups, or the class structure in a neighborhood compared to the class structure of a community as a whole. Although the possibilities are innumerable in the abstract, theoretical concerns and current social trends can guide researchers in developing such indices.

This framework has some utility in systematizing knowledge about the economy and psychosocial dysfunctions. Explicit attention to the score of different economic indices can safeguard against the "ecological fallacy" of generalizing across levels of analysis. Additionally, this framework implies relationships which have yet to be articulated and explored. Empirical examination of these contrasts may begin to shed light into the social and economic processes which affect individual and group dysfunction.

## Toward Prevention Strategies

The body of research reviewed in this chapter points to clear linkages between economic conditions and psychosocial dysfunction. Economic stressors function as precursors of preconditions contributing to the prevalence and incidence of any number of psychosocial maladaptations. Yet despite this impressive body of research, relatively few primary preventive efforts addressing economic conditions have been attempted. Catalano and Dooley (1980) attribute this to mental health professionals' tendency to accept socioenvironmental factors as given, and to frame solutions solely in terms of individual or small group change. Thus although the President's Commission on Mental Health (1978) sanctioned reactive primary preventive efforts to inoculate individuals against effects of various stressors, the commission was quite reluctant to endorse the types of proactive approaches necessary to prevent economic stressors themselves from occurring. We echo Catalano and Dooley's (1980) sentiment that proactive strategies addressing macrolevel economic phenomena are well within the purview of preventive psychology. Further, we also see considerable utility in various reactive approaches, especially those which attempt to reach large segments of a population. In this final section we shall briefly demonstrate how findings relating adjustment to absolute and especially relational indices of the economy might be used to plan and implement reactive and proactive changes at the macrolevel.

The basic formula for reactive primary prevention is to identify a population at risk for psychosocial dysfunction in order to provide an intervention which will reduce vulnerability to pathogenic factors. Research on the relationship of economic conditions to dysfunction is essential for identifying high-risk conditions for various groups. Conceptually, searching for person-situation combinations likely to lead to dysfunction implicitly leads one to frame this exploration in relational terms. That is to say, identifying a group "at risk" tacitly invites a contrast with other groups at less risk. Explicitly seeking those relative indices of economic conditions which most strongly predict prevalence and incidence of disorders will necessarily enable program planners to fine-tune their specification of who is at what degree of risk, and under what conditions. For example, the directional reversal of the relationship between unemployment and male criminal behavior in the age range from adolescence to young adulthood (Fleisher, 1966; Glaser & Rice, 1959) suggests that reactive crime-delinquency prevention would best be directed at different age groups, depending on economic conditions peculiar to the times. Similarly, given that in economic downturns greater rates of psychosocial disruption tend to be associated with lower-social-class neighborhoods nested in heterogeneous urban settings than with lower-class rural areas embedded in homogeneous districts (e.g., Levy & Rowitz, 1973; Quinney, 1964), resources for preventive programs might best be allocated to the former areas.

Selection of appropriate stress-inoculating strategies for populations at risk might also be informed by the research on the economic-psychosocial dysfunction linkage from a relational perspective. Returning to the example cited above, it may be instructive to consider the differences between homogeneous and heterogeneous settings; the latter may exacerbate the effects of economic stressors. One possibility may be that lower-income individuals in homogeneous settings are insulated from exposure to any large number of individuals who are significantly better off economically. On the other hand, lower-income individuals in heterogeneous settings observe and experience higher standards of living all around them on a daily basis, though they are personally not so fortunate, which may lead to self-attributions of failure or inadequacy. It is not difficult to imagine that for some these attributions and feelings may eventually lead to more significant forms of psychological disturbance.

Public education programs, perhaps employing the mass media, with the intention of demonstrating to these individuals that they are not alone and that many like them exposed to the threat or reality of unemployment become increasingly worried and anxious. Informing such groups of these systemic factors which lead to similar problems for many people in a similar plight may help to externalize this self-blame, and consequently inhibit or retard the further development of symptoms. Mutual support groups and resource-exchange networks might emerge following such education, as individuals experiencing similar stress become aware of common needs. (Considerable caution needs to be exercised in developing such public education programs because they run the unintended risk of becoming iatrogenic, alarming individuals and exacerbating the very problems they are intended to reduce and inhibit. An education program that emphasized examples of positive coping, like involvement in a mutual support group or resource-exchange network, is likely to maximize the beneficial and minimize the potential iatrogenic effects of this prevention strategy. Of course, this or any other program suggested here should be exposed to intensive assessment and rigorous examination prior to large-scale implementation.)

The reader will note that although these prevention strategies are reactive in nature, they are primarily educational and not "psychotherapeutic," and are also targeted toward relatively large portions of the community. Macrolevel reactive programs such as these are more in keeping with values of mass orientation (Cowen, 1980) and empowerment (Rappaport, 1981) than are the more symptom-oriented reactive programs described by Catalano and Dooley (1980). As such, these programs are less likely to lead to unintended "victim-blaming" consequences which characterize prevention programs based on a "needs" model (see Rappaport, 1981, for a fuller treatment of these distinctions). In any case, design of reactive programs for vulnerable groups should proceed from a clear, ecological understanding of why particular

population-setting combinations create a risk, while other combinations do not.

In essence, proactive approaches to primary prevention involve the identification of stressful or illness-causing conditions, in order to eliminate or reduce their effects. Beyond this basic principle, proactive interventions may be carried out in two distinct ways: by influencing economic policy decisions of governments or organizations themselves, or by working with groups to enable them to have impact upon the economic structures affecting them. Both modes of proactive prevention require detailed understanding of the linkage between economic conditions and adjustment. For example, Catalano and Dooley (1980) describe in detail the concept of "behavioral cost accounting" to analyze the relative costs and benefits of various alternative policies or procedures. In this three-step approach, the analyst must first forecast the outcomes of each alternative, then determine the costs and benefits associated with various outcomes from a particular frame of reference (for example, management's perspective versus labor's), and finally assign priority weights to each of the costs and benefits in order to combine and compare projected consequences. Clearly, forecasting behavioral outcomes would require information derived from research relating economic change to well-being, and the separation and weighting of costs and benefits for different groups once again points to the utility of referential indices of the economy-dysfunction linkage. For instance, if a corporation needed to lay off workers at one of many plants, and if prevalence of demoralization were the only consideration, then based on Dooley et al.'s (1981) findings it would be reasonable to cut back jobs at plants in nonmetropolitan as opposed to metropolitan regions. The assumption here is that certain (yet-to-be-identified) factors in the nonmetropolitan areas operate to reduce the impact of job loss. The policy decision takes advantage of this natural ecology to reduce the stressful nature of the change. Although this strategy is grossly oversimplified, it does make the point that focused, ecological research can play a central role in policy decisions to alleviate stressful conditions.

Other examples of "top-down" proactive interventions might include programs which expand the range of options for "adapting" to the economic system that are available to individuals. For instance, patterns in the literature suggest that working-age males have traditionally been more sensitive to economic downturns such as unemployment rates. As Breed (1963) discusses, our economic system promotes a "single standard of competence" against which individuals compare their performance. Those individuals who are most centrally connected to the workplace, and for whom this standard is particularly salient, also seem to be most sensitive to changes in employment and relative income. Proactive interventions might be targeted toward reducing the salience of this standard by influencing schools, business, and government to be more willing to support more diversity in career development. These institutions are generally constrained against such possible adaptations as midlife career change, job sharing, or taking from formal worklife to pursue other goals. Efforts to influence public and corporate policy toward these possibilities would provide opportunities for growth, development, and enhancement, in contrast to an increased likelihood of dysfunction.

The second mode of proactive prevention of economic stressors involves enabling groups or individuals to have impact on the economic forces affecting them. Note that this type of strategy is different from reactive approaches, which proceed from the premise that economic conditions are immutable. Rather, "bottom-up" proactive interventions provide information and skills necessary for individuals to gain greater control over stressful economic conditions. Although reduced vulnerability may be one consequence of this approach, the impetus for this sort of intervention would once again be change in the stressful conditions per se. Catalano and Dooley (1980) suggest community ownership of industry as one example of how individuals might gain control over economic stressors. Another example might include public education programs which would provide information about relevant policy issues and pending economic changes, and perhaps tips on citizen participation and lobbying for change as well. Additionally, resource exchange networks and consumer cooperatives might be implemented to reduce individuals' dependency on the larger system, thus placing them in a more secure position from which to bargain for change. As with reactive programs, implementation of "bottom-up" proactive programs might be targeted toward groups identified as being at risk, although broader applications of this sort of program may be empowering to the community at large. The specific nature of interventions might also follow from findings such as those presented here. Open discussion of the observed effects of economic downturn on various segments of the population may serve to motivate those groups to take action to change stressful conditions.

In summary, this section has identified and described several prevention strategies that logically follow from the research highlighting the robust relationship between the economy and psychosocial dysfunctions. It has also demonstrated how a relational perspective

can aid in the fine-tuning of these strategies, while emphasizing prevention programs aimed at large population groups in a reactive as well as proactive mode.

## References

Bancroft, J. H. J., Skrimshire, A. M., Reynolds, F., Simkin, S., & Smith, J. Self-poisoning and self-injury in the Oxford area. *British Journal of Preventive Social Medicine,* 1975, **29**, 170–177.

Barling, P., & Handel, P. Incidence of utilization of public mental health facilities as a function of short term economic decline. *American Journal of Community Psychology,* 1980, **8**, 31–40.

Bogen, D. Juvenile delinquency and economic trends. *American Sociological Review,* 1944, **9**, 178–184.

Breed, W. Occupational motility and suicide among white males. *American Sociological Review,* 1963, **28**, 179–188.

Brenner, M. H. *Mental illness and the economy.* Cambridge: Harvard University Press, 1973.

Brenner, M. H. *Estimating the social costs of economic policy: Implications for mental and physical health and criminal aggression.* Paper No. 5, Report to the Congressional Research Service of the Library of Congress and Joint Economic Committee of Congress. Washington: Government Printing Office, 1976.

Bronfenbrenner, U. *The ecology of human development.* Cambridge: Harvard University Press, 1979.

Brown, G. W., & Harris, T. *Social origins of depression.* New York: Free Press, 1978.

Catalano, R., & Dooley, D. Economic predictors of depressed mood and stressful life events in a metropolitan community. *Journal of Health and Social Behavior,* 1977, **18**, 292–307.

Catalano, R., & Dooley, D. Does economic change provoke or uncover behavior disorder: A preliminary test. In L. Ferman & J. Gordus (Eds.), *Mental health and the economy.* Kalamazoo, Mich.: Upjohn Foundation, 1979.

Catalano, R., & Dooley, D. Economic change in primary prevention. In R. H. Price, R. F. Ketterer, B. L. Bader, & J. Monohan (Eds.), *Prevention in mental health: Research, policy and practice.* Beverly Hills: Sage, 1980.'

Cavan, R. S. *Suicide.* Chicago: University of Chicago Press, 1928.

Cobb, S., & Kasl, S. V. *Termination: The consequences of job loss.* Report No. 76-1261. Cincinnati, Ohio: National Institute for Occupational Safety and Health, Behavioral and Motivational Factors Research, June 1977.

Cohn, R. M. The effect of employment status change on self attitudes. *Social Psychology,* 1978, **41**, 81–93.

Cowen, E. L. The wooing of primary prevention. *American Journal of Community Psychology,* 1980, **8**, 244–258.

Danzinger, S. Explaining urban crime rates. *Criminology,* 1976, **33**(2), 291–296.

Danzinger, S., & Wheeler, D. The economics of crime: Punishment or income redistribution? *Review of Social Economy,* 1975, **14**(1), 114–131.

Davies, G. R. Social aspects of the business cycle. *Quarterly Journal of the University of North Dakota,* 1922, **12**(2).

Dohrenwend, B. P. Problems in defining and sampling the relevant population of stressful life events. In B. S. Dohrenwend & B. P. Dohrenwend (Eds.), *Stressful life events: Their nature and effects.* New York: Wiley, 1974.

Dohrenwend, B. S., & Dohrenwend, B. P. (Eds.) *Stressful life events: Their nature and effects*. New York: Wiley, 1974.

Dohrenwend, B. P., & Dohrenwend, B. S. Socioenvironmental factors, stress and psychopathology. *American Journal of Community Psychology*, 1981, 9(2), 128–159.

Dooley, D., & Catalano, R. Economic, life, and disorder changes: Time-series analyses. *American Journal of Community Psychology*, 1979, 7, 381–396.

Dooley, D., & Catalano, R. Economic change as a cause of behavioral disorder. *Psychological Bulletin*, 1980, 87, 450–468.

Dooley, D., Catalano, R., Jackson, R., & Brownell, A. Economic, life, and symptom changes in a nonmetropolitan community. *Journal of Health and Social Behavior*, 1981, 22, 144–154.

Dublin, L. I., & Bunzel, B. *To be or not to be: A study of suicide*. New York: Smith and Haas, 1933.

Durbin, J., & Watson, G. S. Testing for serial correlation in least squares regression: Part I. *Biometrika*, 1950, 37, 409–423.

Durkheim, E. *Suicide: A study in sociology*. G. Simpson, Ed., J. A. Spaulding & G. Simpson, trans. New York: Free Press of Glencoe, 1951. (Originally published 1897.)

Eaton, W. W. Residence, social class, and schizophrenia. *Journal of Health and Social Behavior*, 1974, 15, 289–299.

Eberts, P., & Schwirian, K. P. Metropolitan crime rates and relative deprivation. *Criminologica*, 1968, 5, 43–52.

Engelsmann, F., Murphy, M. B. M., Price, R., Ledno, M., & Demers, H. Variation in responses to a symptom checklist by age, sex, income, residence, and ethnicity. *Social Psychiatry*, 1972, 7, 150–156.

Faris, R., & Dunham, H. *Mental disorders in urban areas*. New York: Hafner, 1939.

Fleisher, B. M. *The economics of delinquency*. Chicago: Quadrangle Books, 1966.

Frank, J. D. *Persuasion and healing*. Baltimore: Johns Hopkins University Press, 1973.

Gibbons, J. S., Elliot, J., Urwin, P., & Gibbons, J. L. The urban environment and deliberate self-poisoning: Trends in Southampton, 1972–1977. *Social Psychiatry*, 1978, 13, 159–166.

Glaser, D. Economic and sociocultural variables affecting rates of youth employment, delinquency, and crimes. *Youth and Society*, 1979, 11, 53–82.

Glaser, D., & Rice, K. Crime, age and employment. *American Sociological Review*, 1959, 24(1), 679–683.

Gordon, R. A. Issues in the ecological study of delinquency. *American Sociological Review*, 1967, 32, 927–944.

Greenberg, D. F. The dynamics of oscillatory punishment processes. *Journal of Criminal Law and Criminology*, 1977, 68.

Hammermesh, A. S., & Soss, N. M. An economic theory of suicide. *Journal of Political Economy*, 1974, 82, 83–98.

Henry, A. F., & Short, J. F., Jr. *Suicide and homicide*. New York: Free Press, 1954.

Holding, T. A., Burglass, D., Duffy, J. C. & Kreitman, N. Parasuicide in Edinburgh: A seven-year review, 1968–1974. *British Journal of Psychiatry*, 1977, 130, 534–543.

Hollingshead, A. B., & Redlich, F. L. *Social class and mental illness*. New York: Wiley, 1958.

Karacan, I., Thornby, J. I., Anch, M., Holzer, C. E., Warheit, G. J., Schwab, J. J., & Williams, R. L. Prevalence of sleep disturbance in a primarily urban Florida county. *Social Science and Medicine* (Oxford), 1976, 10(5), 239–244.

Katchadourian, H. A., & Churchill, C. W. Social class and mental illness in urban Lebanon. *Social Psychiatry*, 1969, 4(2), 49–55.

Katchadourian, H. A., & Churchill, C. W. Components of mental illness and social class in urban Lebanon. *Social Psychiatry*, 1973, 8, 145–151.

Lendrum, F. C. A thousand cases of attempted suicide. *American Journal of Psychiatry*, 1933, 13, 479–500.

Levy, L., & Rowitz, L. *The ecology of mental disorder*. New York: Behavioral Publications, 1973.

Liem, R. Economic change and unemployment: Contexts of illness. In *Social contexts of health, illness, and patient care*. Cambridge: Cambridge University Press, 1981.

Link, B., & Dohrenwend, B. P. Formulation of hypotheses about the true prevalence of demoralization in the United States. In B. P. Dohrenwend, B. S. Dohrenwend, M. S. Gould, B. Link, R. Neugebauer, & R. Wunsch-Hitzig, *Mental illness in the United States: Epidemiological estimates*. New York: Praeger, 1980.

Little, C. B. Technical-professional unemployment: Middle-class adaptability to personal crisis. *Sociological Quarterly*, 1976, 17, 262–274.

Loftin, C., & Hill, R. H. Regional subculture and homicide: An examination of the Gastil-Hackney thesis. *American Sociological Review*, 1974, 39, 714–724.

MacMahon, B., Johnson, S., & Pugh, T. F. Relation of suicide rates to social conditions: Evidence from U.S. vital statistics. *Public Health Reports*, 1963, 78, 285–293.

Maris, R. W. Major implications: A critical evaluation of Durkheim's theory of suicide. In R. Maris (Ed.), *Social forces in urban suicide*. Homewood, Ill.: Dorsey Press, 1969.

Marshall, J. P., & Funch, D. P. Mental illness and the economy: A critique and partial replication. *Journal of Health and Social Behavior*, 1979, 20, 282–289.

Menninger, K. *Man against himself*. New York: Harcourt Brace, 1938.

Morgan, R., & Cheadle, A. J. Unemployment impedes resettlement. *Social Psychiatry*, 1975, 10, 63–67.

Ogburn, W. F., & Thomas, D. S. The influence of the business cycle on certain social conditions. *Journal of the American Statistical Association*, 1922, 18, 324–340.

Parnes, H. S., & King, R. Middle-aged job losers. *Industrial Gerontology*, 1977, 4, 77–95.

Pettigrew, T. F. Social evaluation theory: Convergences and applications. *Nebraska Symposium on Motivation*, 1967, 241–311.

Pierce, A. The economic cycle and the social suicide rate. *American Sociological Review*, 1967, 32, 457–462.

Powell, E. Occupation, status and suicide. *American Sociological Review*, 1958, 23, 131–139.

Quinney, R. Crime, delinquency and social areas. *Journal of Research in Crime and Delinquency*, 1964, 1, 149–154.

Rappaport, J. In praise of paradox: A social policy of empowerment over prevention. *American Journal of Community Psychology*, 1981, 9(1), 1–25.

Robinson, N. H., Smith, P., & Wolf, J. Prison populations and costs-illustrative projections to 1980, 1974, cited in

D. F. Greenberg, The dynamics of oscillatory punishment processes. *Journal of Criminal Law and Criminology*, 1977, **68**.

Sainsbury, P. *Suicide in London: An ecological study.* New York: Basic Books, 1955.

Schlozman, K., & Verba, S. The new unemployment: Does it hurt? *Public Policy*, 1978, **26**, 333–357.

Schmid, C. *Suicide in Seattle, 1914–1925: An ecological and behavioristic study.* Seattle: University of Washington Press, 1928.

Schmid, C. F. Urban crime areas. *American Sociological Review*, 1960, **25**, 517–542.

Sclar, E. D., & Hoffman, V. J. *Planning mental health service for a declining economy.* Final Report to the National Health Services Research. Waltham, Mass.: Brandeis University, January 1978.

Seidman, E., & Rappaport, J. The search for alternative social change conceptions, methods, and interventions: A dialogue. Invited address in the Community and Social Change Public Lecture Series, University of Michigan, Ann Arbor, March 1979.

Shaw, C. R., & McKay, H. D. *Juvenile delinquency and urban areas.* Chicago: University of Chicago Press, 1942.

Shaw, C. R., Zorbaugh, F., McKay, H. D., & Cottrell, L. S. *Delinquency areas.* Chicago: University of Chicago Press, 1929.

Singell, L. D. An examination of the empirical relationship between unemployment and juvenile delinquency. *American Journal of Economics and Sociology*, 1967, **26**(4), 377–386.

Swinscow, D. Some suicide statistics. *British Medical Journal*, 1951, **1**, 1417–1422.

Theorell, T., Lind, E., & Floderus, B. The relationship of disturbing life-changes and emotions to the early development of myocardial infarctions and other serious illnesses. *International Journal of Epidemiology*, 1975, **4**, 281–293.

Thomas, D. S. *Social aspects of the business cycle.* New York: Knopf, 1927.

Tittle, C. R., Villence, W. J., & Smith, D. A. The myth of social class and criminality: An empirical assessment of the empirical evidence. *American Sociological Review*, 1978, **43**, 643–656.

Tuckman, J., & Lavell, M. Study of suicide in Philadelphia. *Public Health Reports*, 1958, **73**, 547–553.

Vigderhous, G., & Fishman, G. The impact of unemployment and social integration on changing suicide rates in the U.S.A., 1920–1969. *Social Psychiatry*, 1978, **13**, 239–248.

Von Mayr, G. Statistik der gerichtlichen Polizei in Konigreiche Bayern und in einigen anderen Ländern. Munich, 1867. Cited in T. Sellin, Research memorandum on crime in the depression. *Social Science Research Council Bulletin*, 1937, **27**, 23–24.

Weissman, M. M., & Klerman, G. L. Sex differences and the epidemiology of depression. *Archives of General Psychiatry*, 1977, **34**, 98–111.

Weissman, M. M., & Myers, J. K. Affective disorders in a U.S. urban community: The use of research diagnostic criteria in an epidemiological survey. *Archives of General Psychiatry*, 1978, **35**, 1304–1311.

Wiers, P. Wartime increase in Michigan delinquency. *American Sociological Review*, 1945, **10**, 515–523.

Yap, Pow-Meng. *Suicide in Hong Kong, with special reference to attempted suicide.* Hong Kong: Hong Kong University Press, 1958.

# 12 TRANSITIONS AND STRESSFUL LIFE EVENTS: A MODEL FOR PRIMARY PREVENTION

Robert D. Felner,
Stephanie S. Farber and
Judith Primavera

An almost inescapable part of modern life is the need to adapt to change. In addition to those changes in the individual which result from the unfolding of normal developmental processes, a rapidly shifting psychosocial environment forms part of the situational context to which individuals must adapt. Perhaps as never before in history, individuals are faced with the task of adapting to frequent and often abrupt life changes. Residential relocations and changes in jobs and occupational status, as well as entries and exits from important interpersonal relationships such as marriage, are but a few of the many life events which occur at a rate far beyond that experienced by previous generations.

As our appreciation of the importance of life events which precipitate change in the lives of individuals has grown, so too has the recognition that such events may play an important role in the etiology of somatic and psychiatric disorders (Dohrenwend & Dohrenwend, 1974). For primary prevention in particular, a focus on such life events has frequently been argued for as a cornerstone on which to build both a knowledge base and interventions (Bloom, 1979; Felner, Farber, & Primavera, 1980; Goldston, 1977). The present chapter will examine current conceptualizations of the process by which life events impact adaptation and examine the utility of these perspectives for primary

prevention. A major intent of this chapter is to offer a broader theoretical framework for understanding life events and life change that is more compatible with the goals of primary prevention than are current models. Toward this end, we will first present a brief discussion of primary prevention, with a particular focus on the issues of relevance for adaptation to life events. Following that, an overview of relevant work on life events to date will be provided. Here we will begin with an examination of theory and data on the relation between life events and well-being. This will be followed by a similar discussion of the salience of single life events or changes for adaptation and health. Finally, suggestions will be offered for additions to or modifications of such work which may enhance the "fit" between this work and the need for a broader heuristic model to more fully allow life events to be addressed from a preventive perspective.

## Life Events and Primary Prevention

Several arguments have been advanced emphasizing the need to target preventive efforts at life change events. One key set of assumptions underlying these arguments is that change in individuals' lives resulting from such events may be associated with heightened levels of psychosocial stress and, in turn, that such stress is an important etiological factor in physical and psychological disorder (B. P. Dohrenwend, 1979; B. S. Dohrenwend, 1978; Sandler, 1979). In further defining those events of particular salience Bloom (1979) has argued that preventive efforts should be organized around "a stressful life event that appears to have undesirable consequences in a significant proportion of the population [p. 183]" and that the goal of such efforts should be the reduction or elimination of negative consequences of the events. From this perspective, then, it is the pathogenic aspects of the stress associated with life change which is of central interest for prevention.

Before discussing these issues further, it may be helpful to briefly reiterate the goals and concerns of primary prevention. One important goal is to reduce the incidence of physical or psychological pathology. This is, however, just one of the primary major goals of prevention. Cowen (1980) has argued that the ultimate goals of primary prevention are "to engineer structures, processes, situations, events, and programs that maximally benefit, both in scope and temporal stability, the psychological adjustment, effectiveness, happiness, and coping skills of large members of individuals [p. 264]." Thus, it is not just the prevention of pathology with which we need be concerned from a preventive perspective, but equally important the building of competence, health, and well-being, as well as the facilitation of mastery and effectance (see Chapter 1 of the present volume). Despite these positively focused goals for prevention, Cowen (1980) and others (e.g., Felner, Aber, Primavera, & Cauce, 1983) have noted that within the area of prevention, as well as in psychology more generally, the amount of effort aimed at understanding conditions which produce positive adaptive outcomes has been relatively miniscule when compared to efforts focusing on pathology.

Consistent with this pattern of differential emphasis, much of the prior work linking prevention and life events has, as can be seen from the statements above, only paid passing attention to the competence- and health-enhancing goals of prevention. Indeed, the past emphasis of preventive work on reducing pathology is illustrated by the pervasive pairing of the terms "life events" and "stress," as in "stressful life events" (Dohrenwend, 1978; Felner et al., 1980) or "life stress events" (Sandler, 1979). As we shall see, such a stance has led to a focus on certain qualities of life events at the expense of others, but investigation of these latter qualities may be essential if we are to, as it has been argued we must, get beyond primarily seeking to contain or reduce the malevolent consequences of "damage-producing structures, processes and events"

toward the facilitation of mastery and well-being (Cowen, 1980).

## Theory and Research on Life Events

Two distinct though somewhat overlapping bodies of conceptual and empirical literature have served as the primary bases on which links between life events and primary prevention have been built. The first is rooted in epidemiology. The focus of work based on this tradition has been on the prediction and understanding of the rate of physical or psychological disorder in a population as a function of its association with the presence of single or multiple life events. The second line of work focuses more on the individual and seeks to understand the process by which individuals adapt to discrete "critical" life events. Although this latter approach owes some debt to epidemiology (Bloom, Asher, & White, 1978), it is also derived from crisis theory (Caplan, 1964) and conceptualizations for understanding the impact of specific environmental stressors on an individual's well-being (Felner et al., 1980; Goldston, 1977; Sandler, 1979).

It is important to note that while both of these approaches have been employed for the conceptualization and development of primary prevention efforts, neither had such development as its original goal or impetus. Thus in the presentation of representative work from each of these bodies of literature which follows, particular attention will be paid to how the core conceptual frameworks which guided the framing of questions for these studies may have led to paradigms which do not adequately address the concerns of primary prevention.

## Multiple Life Events

The association between multiple life events which occur in relatively close temporal proximity to one another and the presence of mental or physical disorder has been a major focus of efforts to clarify the role of life events in the etiology of such dysfunction. Much of the current work exploring the association between cumulative stress from life events and pathology builds on that of Holmes and Rahe (1967). In order to provide a context for a discussion of more recent studies in this area we will first briefly review Holmes and Rahe's seminal work.

In 1967 Holmes and Rahe published the Social Readjustment Rating Scale (SRRS). This measure consists of 43 events and asks individuals to indicate which of these events they have experienced in the recent past. The impetus for the development of the scale was an effort to identify antecedents or precipitants of disease onset (Holmes, 1979). In preliminary work on this issue (Hawkins, Davies, & Holmes, 1957; Rahe, Meyer, Smith, Kjaer, & Holmes, 1964) Holmes, Rahe, and their coworkers noted that one important factor which seemed to be associated with the onset of disease was the accumulation of life changes. A key goal in the development of the SRRS was to provide a way of not only identifying whether or not an individual had experienced an event but also to develop a quantitative way of defining the salience of the events for predicting disease onset (Holmes, 1979). Drawing from the methodology of psychophysics, a sample of 394 subjects was asked to rate the amount of social readjustment that each event required, with marriage assigned an arbitrary value of 500 to serve as a comparison point. Social readjustment was defined as "the intensity and length of time necessary to accommodate to a life event, regardless of the desirability of this event" (Holmes & Rahe, 1967). The LCUs when summed yield a total life stress score.

The SRRS is based on the assumption that life changes and consequent demands for readjustment are stressful regardless of the perceived desirability of the event (Sarason, Johnson, & Siegel, 1978) and that such changes and demands delineate the concept of stress in everyday life (Uhlenhuth, 1979). Further, the authors feel that the LCUs are accurate quantitative reflections of the amount of change engendered by each event. Holmes (1979) has stated, "What we are studying here is the amount of change required by these 43 life events. The relative importance of each item is determined not by the item's desirability, by the emotions associated with the item, nor by the meaning of the item for the individual; it is the amount of change that we are studying and the relationship of the amount of change to the onset of illness [p. 47]."

Holmes and his colleagues sought further validation of their quantification method by performing a series of cross-cultural studies involving such diverse populations as French- and Spanish-speaking people in Europe and Central America, Americans, Hawaiians, Japanese citizens, and American inner-city blacks and Chicanos, among others (Celdran, 1970; Harmon, Masuda, & Holmes, 1970; Janney, Masuda, & Holmes, 1977; Komaroff, Masuda, & Holmes, 1968; Masuda & Holmes, 1967; Ruch & Holmes, 1971; Seppa, 1972). Across these studies correlation coefficients ranged between .65 and .85, indicating what Holmes (1979) feels is a high degree of worldwide consistency in the assigning of change magnitudes to the events.

In addition to the SRRS, a number of similar scales have been developed for adults and children which attempt to assign life change or stress weights to various life events (e.g., Coddington, 1972; Hough, Fairbank, & Garcia, 1976; Monaghan, Robinson, & Dodge, 1979). Studies with these life event scales have found significant associations between the occurrence of life events in the recent past (generally within the past two years or less) and a wide array of physical and psychological disorders. Physical disorders associated with the experience of increased levels of life events include cardiac and respiratory problems, complications associated with surgery and/or pregnancy, overall illness rates and levels, and physical injuries (Bramwell, Masuda, Wagner, & Holmes, 1975; de Araujo, Van Arsdel, Holmes, & Dudley, 1973; McGrath & Burkhart, 1983; Nuckolls, Cassel, & Kaplan, 1972; Petrich & Holmes, 1977; Rahe, Mahan, & Arthur, 1979; Syler, Masuda, & Holmes, 1971). Similarly, significant relationships have been reported between the experience of multiple life events and psychological, academic, and occupational dysfunction and difficulties in both adults (Dohrenwend, 1973; Harris, 1972; Johnson & Sarason, 1978, 1979; Markush & Favero, 1974; McGrath & Burkhart, 1983; Myers et al., 1974; Paykel, 1974; Zautra & Reich, 1980) and children (Gersten, Langner, Eisenberg, & Simcha-Fagen, 1977; Heisel, Ream, Ratz, Rappaport & Coddington, 1973; Sandler & Block, 1979).

Despite the generally consistent significant associations between life events and psychological or physical disorder in the above studies and others like them, the absolute magnitude of the correlations between stress and illness are often modest at best, with many of the correlations in the .30 range (Dohrenwend, 1979; Rabkin & Streuning, 1976). These somewhat disappointing results have given rise to a number of criticisms as well as suggestions for improving life events scales. Many of the key issues involved in the assessment of life event stress may be subsumed into three broad areas. These include (a) specification of the properties and types of events that are of concern; (b) the content of the inventories; and (c) assessment of the magnitude of the life events and consequent scoring of stress levels (Dohrenwend & Dohrenwend, 1978; Hurst, 1979). Work in each of these spheres bears heavily on the other two. For the sake of clarity we will address each separately, but with attention to key points of interdependence.

### Properties of Life Events

Recent work focusing on the association between life events and their consequences has reflected the growing recognition that the adaptive impact of life events may be a function not only of the number of events and their magnitude, but of qualities of the events as well (Felner et al., 1980; Pearlin, Menaghan, Lieberman, & Mullen, 1981; Sandler, 1979). This is reflected in current efforts to distinguish among life events according to such properties as their common meanings (Hurst, 1979; Paykel, 1976; Uhlenhuth & Paykel, 1973), their desirability (Dohrenwend, 1979; Gersten et al., 1977; Johnson, 1982; Sarason et al., 1978; Zautra & Simons, 1979), the degree of control people have over their occurrence (Dohrenwend & Martin, 1979; Fairbank & Hough, 1979; Sandler, 1979); their degree of independence of other events (Fontana, Marcus, Noel, & Rakusin, 1972; Zautra & Reich, 1980), and their anticipability (Dohrenwend & Martin, 1979; Felner, Primavera, & Cauce, 1981).

Dohrenwend (1979) has argued that the most important evidence that "a particular or more usual stressful life event is important would be provided by verification of the hypothesis that the event produces pathology in previously normal persons [p. 5]." Among those qualities of events which have been identified as potentially linked to adverse consequences, studies of the association between the desirability of the event and such outcomes have yielded the most impressively consistent results. It should be noted that there are some issues which at present are still unresolved about how the valence of an event should be determined. We will return to these issues in some detail in our discussion of the scoring of life event inventories. However, for the moment what is important is that negative life changes, however determined, have been consistently found to correlate significantly with adverse physical or psychological conditions, while positive events often do not (Sarason et al., 1978; Zautra & Reich, 1980). Based on these findings, it has been argued that life stress may be more adequately conceptualized in terms of events that have a negative impact on the individual (Dohrenwend, 1979; Johnson, 1982; McGrath & Burkhart, 1983) than in terms of change per se, as suggested by Holmes and Rahe (Holmes, 1979; Holmes & Rahe, 1967).

Another key feature of life events which has emerged as central to understanding their association with disorder is whether they are antecedent to or a consequence of the disorder. Billings and Moos (1982) have noted that much of the research on life events has assumed that their occurrence is random. They argue, however, that individuals may have a propensity to experience increased numbers of negative life events due to preexisting emotional or physical dysfunction or adverse socioenvironmental factors. Similarly, Dohrenwend (1979) and others (Fontana et al., 1972;

Schless, Schwartz, Goetz & Mendels, 1974) have similarly noted that a number of the life events on scales such as that of Holmes and Rahe (1967) might just as easily be seen as manifestations of, rather than causes of, psychological difficulties. Such event items as sexual difficulties, divorce, being fired from work, and "increase in the number of arguments with spouse" may be viewed as potential consequences rather than causes of pathology. Fontana et al. (1972) refer to such events as contingent events to indicate the individual often has a hand in bringing them about. From this perspective, it is recognized that while stressful life events may lead to impaired functioning, so too may impaired functioning lead to the experience of stressful life events.

The view that an individual's level of functioning may influence his or her experience of life events may in part account for the consistent associations found between negative, but not positive, life events and dysfunction noted above. That is, one might expect precisely those events which are typically viewed as negative to be more frequently experienced by individuals who are functioning more poorly. Further, individuals with existing pathology would also be less likely to experience positive life events and changes such as job promotion or marriage. By contrast, it could be predicted that individuals with more adequate coping skills and adjustment would experience more positive events and fewer negative events. Thus, it may be that in actual fact negative events pose little more adaptive challenge to individuals than do positive events. Rather, their seeming greater significance may, at least in part, be more a reflection of their being a consequence of preexisting difficulties.

Hurst (1979) has argued that it may also be helpful to cluster life events into groups with common meanings when considering their relationship to dysfunction. The distinctions noted above of desirable versus undesirable or origin versus pawn events (Zautra & Reich, 1980) are examples of such clustering. Events may also be classified according to their locus in a particular area of an individual's life (Hurst, 1979). For example, in a study by Rose, Jenkins, and Hurst (1978) of stresses experienced by air traffic controllers, 13 distinct life event content clusters were identified, including marital, family, work, education, health, children, dating, and anticipated life events clusters. Rose et al. (1978) also present data which seem to indicate that stressors in different content areas may potentially be differentially related to various psychological and physical difficulties.

In a similar study with children, Sandler and Ramsey (1980) sought to identify qualitative properties of life events which were associated with child adjustment problems. Utilizing a cognitive dimensional model, seven meaningful factors were identified: events dealing with loss, entrance, family trouble, sibling problems, positive events, primary environment change, and physical harm. Further, scores on only two of the dimensions, family troubles and entrance event, were found to significantly differentiate between maladapting and control children. Both Hurst (1979) and Sandler (1979) conclude that studies such as these which focus on qualitative differences (e.g., Newcomb, Huba, & Bentler, 1981; Paykel, 1976; Uhlenhuth & Paykel, 1973) may be helpful in identifying events with common effects on individuals and thus lead to further understanding of those stresses which contribute to adjustment problems in specific samples of interest.

Two other properties of life events which have been identified as being of potential significance in determining their impact are the extent to which they may be anticipated and the individual's perception of control. Further, these properties may be interrelated. For example, Dohrenwend and Martin (1979) note that a wide variety of studies have found that stressful life events seem to be most pathogenic when they are perceived as uncontrollable. However, the authors questioned whether perceived control of an event was a function of the individual or some characteristic of the event, particularly the degree to which it could be anticipated by the individual. In an investigation of this issue they concluded that situational factors may influence an individual's perception of control over events to a greater extent than personal predisposition (Dohrenwend & Martin, 1979). While raising some caution about the failure of their work to identify specific situational determinates that may influence perception of control, they argue that preventive efforts should target situational factors to reduce feelings of lack of personal control over events and hence minimize their adverse consequences.

### The Content of Life Event Inventories

In assessing the amount of life stress experienced by an individual, which events are included in the inventory may play a critical role in shaping the results obtained. The need to identify a sample of events that is appropriate to the population has been underscored by a number of authors (Dohrenwend & Dohrenwend, 1978; Hurst, 1979; Masuda & Holmes, 1978; Sandler, 1979; Uhlenhuth, 1979). Hurst (1979) has suggested a general principle for the construction of life events inventories which reflects this issue. He argues that the events listed in an inventory must be ones that it is clearly reasonable to expect the individuals

in the sample of concern to experience in the given time span. Further, Uhlenhuth (1979) has noted that while certainly choosing events which yield an optimal response rate is important, there is another factor which is also of concern. If we are indeed interested in the stress placed on persons by events as defined by the demands for social readjustment they engender, then we need to choose events which fit such a model. Illustratively, he notes that certain day-to-day stressors, although they occur frequently, may after their first few occurrences cease to require the development of new behaviors or accommodations to the environment (Uhlenhuth, 1979).

The choice of what items to include in a life event inventory, then, depends on the focus of the research, both in terms of sample and outcome. As we shall see later in this chapter, the emphasis on the relationship between life events and disorder that is the focus of most work to date may lead to events being either included or omitted which are different than those we would select for inclusion or omission if our concern is prevention and positive adaptive outcomes.

### The Scoring of Life Events

Many of the issues raised thus far are reflected in the controversies which surround the question of how best to score life events inventories, particularly as this relates to their utility in predicting and understanding the consequences of life events. To date, the answers to this question have been quite clearly ones which reflect a primary view of life events as environmental stressors which are important because of their links to physical and psychological disorder (Dohrenwend, 1979). Several key issues and debates have evolved as investigators have begun to address this concern. What is to be scored, how items are to be scored, and what summary scores are to be used are among the central questions that have received attention (Felner et al., 1980; Hurst, 1979; Sandler, 1979; Sarason et al., 1978).

What is to be scored has varied to some extent as a function of the particular theoretical orientation of the investigators. In a recent review, Hurst (1979) noted that among response metrics employed, subjects may be asked to rate such concepts as stress, distress, or upset experienced, the degree of adjustment or readjustment required by an event, or some combination of these. Studies concerned with the predictive validity of alternative scoring metrics have yielded equivocal results. Some have found that alternative scoring metrics or the general rank order assigned to life events may make little difference with regard to the predictive validity of such scales (Hurst, Jenkins,

& Rose, 1978; McGrath and Burkhart, 1983). Others report ratings using different metrics to be predictive of highly divergent outcomes (Hurst, 1979). Thus what is rated may, at least in some cases, lead to quite different conclusions.

The lack of clear findings concerning the relationship between the specific characteristics of the event that are scored (for example, change, distress) and the utility of life events scales may, in part, be a function of the interaction of this issue with other scoring concerns. The question of how the weighted scores are obtained is central here. Felner et al. (1980) have argued that a major limitation of life stress scales such as those of Holmes and Rahe (1967) has been their failure to consider that individuals are not equally stressed by similar events. To allow for the consideration of the specific impact or meaning an event may have for an individual, several authors have emphasized the need for scales which allow for idiosyncratic weightings (Byrne & Whyte, 1980; Newcomb, et al., 1981; Sarason et al., 1978). Several recent studies have found that the use of individual weightings of the degree of stressfulness or change associated with life events on scales such as that of Sarason et al. (1978) may enhance their predictive validity for dysfunction (Hurst, 1979; Johnson, 1982; Sarason et al., 1978). However, other studies have failed to find any additional utility for idiosyncratic weightings over those yielded by "objective" unit weights derived from consensus among groups of raters (McGrath & Burkhart, 1983; Newcomb et al., 1981).

In addition to the equivocal empirical evidence on the utility of individual weightings, theoretical concerns have also been raised about their use. Dohrenwend (1979) has argued that the use of subjective ratings by individuals whose stress levels are being investigated as they relate to disorder confounds any findings obtained. She notes that individuals who have experienced an event which has been followed by some negative outcome are far more likely to rate such events as more stressful than those who do not experience such a follow-up event. Similarly, psychiatric patients tend to rate events as more stressful than nonpatients (Dohrenwend, 1979). That is not, however, to say that such subjective ratings may not be useful, but only that they should not be seen as an adequate measure of the stress engendered by the event per se. Rather, perhaps they are better viewed as reflecting an individual's personal vulnerability to such events (Dohrenwend, 1979; Uhlenhuth, 1979).

Another concern pertaining to the scoring of life event scales is that of what summary scores to use. While Holmes and Rahe (1967) argued that the desirability of the event should not be considered in summary scoring, more recent work disagrees sharply with this position (e.g., Dohrenwend & Dohrenwend, 1978, Johnson, 1982; Sandler, 1979; Sarason et al., 1978). Indeed, although there is some lack of consensus about many of the other issues in the assessment of stress from life events, this is one area where a high degree of concordance exists. Given the findings noted above on the strong positive relationship between negative or undesirable life events and dysfunction, it has been argued that combining positive and negative life events scores into one summary score may obscure the strength of this relationship (Johnson, 1982; Sandler, 1979; Sarason et al., 1978). Empirical evidence supports this contention. In studies where summary scores for negative and positive life events have been obtained separately, clear inverse relations between adjustment and negative life events have been found, while the associations between positive events and adaptation have been much less consistent (Dohrenwend, 1979; Johnson, 1982; McGrath & Burkhart, 1983; Newcomb et al., 1981; Sarason et. al., 1978; Zautra & Simons, 1979). Interestingly, in at least one of those studies in which no difference was found in the utility of subjectively or objectively assigned life change event stress weightings for predicting dysfunction, there were differences as a function of whether the event was objectively or subjectively defined as aversive. McGrath and Burkhart (1983) found that objective ratings of desirability proved inferior to idiographic labeling of the event in yielding desirability scores predictive of dysfunction. It should be noted that the superiority of summary distress scores over other scores containing positive events rests primarily on their ability to predict dysfunction and disease (Dohrenwend, 1979; Felner et al., 1980; Johnson, 1982; Sandler, 1979). Whether this is a goal which has served to yield data with the greatest utility for primary prevention is something we shall explore below.

Several other alternatives for obtaining summary scores on life event scales should be briefly mentioned. As noted above, various authors have sought information on the individual's feelings of control over the event, the length of time which has elapsed since the event, and the dimension of meaning among events. Studies to date which have employed separate summary scores based on these dimensions are not as yet plentiful, and few consistent patterns of results have emerged.

There is an essential point which must be kept in mind when evaluating the utility of the conclusions drawn from most of the above work for preventive efforts. That is, in the search for answers to the question of how best to score life events inventories the benchmarks against which predictive validity has most often been assessed are ones which reflect a primary view of life events as stressors which may have importance primarily because of their association with physical and emotional disorder. Rarely, if at all, have indices of positive adaptive outcomes been employed in evaluating the usefulness of various scoring procedures.

## Multiple Life Events and Prevention

It is not our intent in the foregoing to provide an exhaustive review of the issues involved in the assessment of stress resulting from the experience of multiple life events. Rather, we have endeavored to provide an overview of issues in this area which are important for providing a context for consideration of what such work has to offer us for focusing preventive efforts on life events. Before going on to a discussion of work on individual life events then, let us now consider how well current concerns and conceptualizations in the work on multiple life events fit with those of primary prevention, and underscore some issues which must be addressed if the fit is to be improved.

On a positive note, it is clear from much of the above that an examination of life events recently experienced by an individual may be helpful in identifying individuals who may be said to be at risk for the development of emotional or physical disorders prior to the beginnings of such difficulties actually being manifest. Given that one focus of primary prevention is on "before the fact" programs, which may reduce the incidence of new disorder, a careful assessment of the number and types (for example, positive or negative) of life events experienced by an individual or population may be important indicators of the need for such programs (Felner & Aber, 1983). Indeed, Felner and Aber (1983) have argued that the identification of conditions which consistently predispose individuals to developing physical or psychological difficulties, such as experiencing life events, may be critical to the success of efforts to justify the need for the allocation of scarce resources to preventive services. Without such evidence it may be difficult to convince those professionals trained in the more reactive, rather than proactive, human service delivery system tradition to address programs to individuals who "have no problems" (Felner, Norton, Cowen, & Farber, 1981). Thus the research to date on cumulative life events and their impact may serve to focus attention on one set of individuals at risk and substantiate the importance of addressing preventive programming efforts toward them.

A second contribution to a preventive approach of the research to date on cumulative life events has been its highlighting of the need to consider potential mediating factors which increase or decrease the impact of the stress associated with life events. Assuredly, all individuals are not equally stressed by similar events. While some may experience geographic relocation or a traffic ticket as highly stressful, others may adapt to these events with relative ease (Felner et al., 1980). The identification of specific variables, such as social support, perceived control, or an individual's personal appraisal of an event (for example, desirability, degrees of readjustment required), which facilitate the prediction of which individuals may be at particular risk for displaying inadequate levels of coping when experiencing life events, is of clear importance to the targeting of primary prevention programs. Moreover, knowledge of such factors may facilitate the design of more effective preventive efforts by helping program planners evaluate and address deficits in individuals or their environments which increase their vulnerability to the possible adverse consequences of life events. Examples of efforts of this type, such as seeking to increase the levels of social support available to individuals experiencing key life events (Felner, Ginter, & Primavera, 1982; Gottleib, 1981) or providing information which influences their appraisal of the event (Peterson & Shigetomi, 1981) abound, and demonstrate the utility of such knowledge in designing effective preventive efforts.

Despite the clear importance for primary prevention of research concerning stress which results from cumulative life events, the conceptualization, goals, and course of efforts in this area may also have had unintended limiting or adverse effects on the development of frameworks for organizing primary prevention programs around life events. Three aspects of the work on cumulative stressful life events which may be particularly problematic for primary prevention are (1) the primary emphasis on the potential pathological outcomes of life events; (2) a view of life events and changes which ascribes central importance to the "stressful" properties of such occurrences, rather than a concern with the nature of life change per se and individuals' efforts to adapt to change; and (3) the use of methodologies which by their nature and implicit or explicit assumptions ignore or obscure qualitative differences among items included as events.

To understand the problems of adapting current work on life events to the adaptive enhancement goals of primary prevention, we first need to consider the systematic imbalance in emphasis on pathology versus positive enhancement of adaptation in this work, as well as the reasons such an imbalance exists. Much of the past and present work on cumulative stress resulting from life events (e.g., Dohrenwend & Dohrenwend, 1978; Holmes & Rahe, 1967; Hurst, 1979) is rooted in an epidemiological, public health model of prevention, which does not fully share the concerns and goals of a definition of primary prevention which is more rooted in psychology. Rather, such work is most concerned with factors which impact the onset of physical and psychological disorder (Dohrenwend, 1979; Holmes, 1979), and pays at best only passing attention to enhancement of functioning.

Given this public health orientation, one cannot in any sense fault or criticize in an absolute sense the explicitly stated emphasis of work which focuses on the pathogenic consequences of life events at the expense of positive coping and adaptations (Bloom, 1979; B. P. Dohrenwend, 1979; B. S. Dohrenwend, 1978). However, one may question why this paradigmatic regularity has not been recognized as a factor which has impeded efforts to develop frameworks for viewing life events that facilitate the achieving of the full range of preventive psychology's goals. Here it is interesting to note that one of the frequent claims and arguments made for the adoption of a preventive stance in psychology is that it will free us from the traditional "medical model" and many of its pitfalls for mental health service delivery (Rappoport, 1977; Zax & Cowen, 1976; Zax & Spector, 1974). While this has certainly been the case to some extent, in the area of life events particularly, as well as prevention more generally, we may have merely exchanged the old medical model for a new one. That is, we have failed to pay sufficient attention to the fact that the public health model from which much of our thinking about prevention has been borrowed, particularly in the life events area (Bloom et al., 1978), is at its core also a medical model which is still fundamentally more concerned with disease reduction than with enhancement of functioning in individuals who are not yet showing problems. Indeed, to some extent the literature on life events discussed above seems to reflect a "health is the absence of disease" assumption— certainly one that is neither new nor consistent with the goals and assumptions of prevention (Cowen, 1980; see also Chapters 1 and 2 of the present volume). Let us now examine some of the ways the pathology orientation of most previous studies of life events may have led them to be less than optimally helpful for developing a theoretical framework for viewing life events which has heuristic and practical value for the full range of primary prevention's goals. The three aspects of such work we elaborated at the outset of this section will be of particular concern.

As noted above, with few exceptions (e.g., Finkel, 1975; Zautra and Reich, 1980; Zautra & Simmons, 1979) studies of cumulative life events have argued that we should be concerned with events that are associated with a clearly identifiable negative impact on the individual (Sandler, 1979; Sarason et al., 1978). This focus has led to an emphasis on undesirable events, either objectively or subjectively defined. Perhaps the key limitation of such an emphasis for primary prevention lies in the way it may lead us to overlook the adaptive significance of more positive events. Whether we are talking about an event which may be generally agreed to be positive (for instance, marriage, a long-sought promotion, or graduation) or only subjectively defined as positive (such as a divorce sought by both partners), it should be clear that such events post adaptive problems and tasks. Studies of cumulative life events have not found consistent associations between such positive events and serious physical and psychological dysfunction. However, what has been overlooked is that the ways in which individuals adapt to positive events may, nonetheless, have important implications for their well-being, life satisfaction, and happiness (Zautra & Reich, 1980). If primary prevention is truly concerned with enhancing these latter areas of functioning it seems that an approach which overlooks the significance of positive life events, particularly those which precipitate long-term life changes, may not allow us to fully address these goals.

Similarly, a focus confined solely to the pathological outcomes of negative events may also be too narrow. The adaptive challenges posed by such life events have the potential to influence areas of functioning as well. As Caplan (1964) pointed out, a key element of even serious negative life crises is the opportunities for positive growth they provide. Thus, for example, it behooves us to include in studies of negative events not only assessments of dysfunction but also of positive adaptation and well-being. Only then may we be able to assess the full significance of such events for primary prevention and health and adaptation.

A related issue is the emphasis prior work has placed on the "stressful" properties of life events at the expense of elaborating other characteristics of such events which may be equally important. For example, although studies have asked individuals to rate events on everything from their "stressfulness" to the "readjustment" or amount of life change they demand (Holmes & Rahe, 1967; Holmes, 1979; Hurst, 1979; Uhlenhuth, 1979), generally the concept of life change is used almost interchangeably with stress. A clear illustration of this is provided by Uhlenhuth (1979), who states that "the greatest contribution made by

Holmes and Rahe (1967) probably is their clear delineation of a concept of stress in everyday life—the demand for social readjustment placed on the person by events, regardless of their desirability or other properties [p. 55]." He goes on to note that Holmes and his colleagues see such changes as important due to their increasing susceptibility to illness.

Clearly, much of the reason the stressful properties of life events or changes are the primary concern of investigators stems from their central interest in the dysfunctional correlates of such events. However, if we broaden our view of the importance of life events to include both positive and negative adaptive consequences, then the stressful properties of such events and changes no longer have sufficient salience to merit virtually synonymous usage of the terms "life stress" and "change" or "readjustment." Rather, the degree of stress associated with life events and life change becomes but one of the factors individuals must cope with in adapting to such changes. From this perspective, then, coping with stress and the adaptive tasks posed for individuals by life changes are not one and the same. The former is but one of the set of adaptive tasks which must be mastered by the individual, and the degree to which these tasks are mastered may have both positive and negative implications for the individual's functioning. We shall return to and further elaborate the issue of adaptive tasks engendered by life events following our discussion of research on single events. For the moment, however, the key point is that a framework for understanding life events that seeks to fully inform primary prevention should not view the amount of change and the degree of stress engendered by a life event as one and the same. A corollary of this position is that studies interested in prevention may wish to unhook the term "stressful" from "life events," as this pairing may have unintended limiting and shaping consequences for thinking about such events.

A third difficulty with the work on cumulative stress from life events derives from an implicit assumption suggested by the use of life events inventories as they are usually constructed. That is, although additional information may be sought about the items, such as their valence or the individual's perceived responsibility, the items are nevertheless considered sufficiently similar in some overriding way that their mutual inclusion on the same basic inventory is justified. This assumption may be justified, in fact, when the focus is on the stressfulness of such experiences and their aversive consequences for individuals. Illustratively, after raising many of the issues we have discussed above about dimensions on which life events may be grouped, Dohrenwend and Dohrenwend (1978)

nonetheless conclude that "there is, nevertheless, a strong argument for the general procedure developed by Holmes and his colleagues [p. 11]." However, in light of our preceding concerns about primary prevention this position may be less viable. Of particular concern is the inability of the inventories as constructed to capture or illuminate the qualitative differences in adaptive challenges the "events" pose for individuals. A statement by Holmes (1979) may serve to illustrate the greatly misleading positions to which the use of life event inventories which seek to somehow quantify, on a similar metric, life change or stress may lead. After reviewing cross-cultural "validation" studies of the magnitude of life change units assigned to the items on the Social Readjustment Rating Scale, Holmes concludes, "Essentially, worldwide, death of a spouse requires twice as much change in adjustment as marriage and 10 times as much change and adjustment as a traffic ticket [1979, p. 47]."

The difficulties with such a statement are obvious. While in some rare instances ten traffic tickets may indeed require as much change as death of a spouse, or twice as much adjustment as marriage, one would be hard-pressed, to say the least, to argue for this as the general case. How then could so many investigators get themselves in the position of extensively using a procedure that can yield such statements? In part, this may be understood by examining the goals of the procedures. Although researchers utilizing such procedures continue to talk about life change or readjustment, it is not truly these qualities of the events that are of primary concern to them. Rather, they are in fact approaching the question from the point of view of a stress model. This has led to a shift in focus, as noted above, from change per se to the perceived or judged stressfulness of the event. It is somewhat easier, although perhaps still less than accurate, to defend a position that ten traffic tickets, if one were to get them all at once, might be perceived as equally stressful as the death of a spouse at the moment either event occurred. However, the amount of readjustment and change, and concomitant enduring stress which follows each set of events may be quite different.

This is for us a critical, previously overlooked way in which the events on life event inventories diverge. Some are truly circumscribed events; others, however, while also identifiable "events," are less important for the individual's long-term functioning as "stressful events" per se than they are precipitants or signs of major changes occurring in the organization and context of the individual's life and, as such, may require adaptive efforts for prolonged periods subsequent to the "event." Thus, although it was perhaps an original goal of the life events inventories to quantify life change (Holmes, 1979), the goals of research and theory in this area may have led us to overlook precisely this characteristic of life events as one on which life events are qualitatively different. While some events included on life event inventories in actual fact generally relate to little or no enduring change in individuals lives (for instance a traffic ticket, Christmas, vacation), others are the precipitants of large and enduring shifts in the nature of people's lives (marriage, the birth of a child, developing a chronic or serious illness, divorce). As we shall see in our discussion of single life events, a focus on differences in the types and extent of change these events precipitate may have important implications for both generative research in the area (Cowen, 1980) and for the design and implementation of programs.

## Single Life Events

Dohrenwend (1978) has offered a used model that has been widely used, particularly in the area of prevention, for understanding the impact of single life events. Life events are viewed as associated with psychosocial stress, and she proposes a framework for viewing life events which seeks to verify how psychosocial stress leads to psychopathology. In Dohrenwend's (1978) model there are several steps. The first focuses on the extent of the individual's responsibility for the event. Here, a prime concern is with the recognition that an individual may take part in causing events which later seem to be the cause of psychological difficulties. That is, it needs to be recognized that the event may be a consequence rather than a cause of at least some of the dysfunction identified. This model next postulates the occurrence of an immediate, time-limited stress reaction following the event, with the outcome of this reaction dependent upon the mediation of psychological and situational factors that serve to provide the context in which it occurs. Situational mediators include characteristics of the environment which impinge on the individual, such as social and material supports, as well as other environmental stressors (Lazarus & Cohen, 1977). Psychological mediators encompass specific characteristics of the individual. These include background and personality factors such as age, sex, cognitive and emotional development, the resolution of previous coping experiences, and coping abilities and competencies of the individual (Dohrenwend, 1978; Felner et al., 1980; Turk, 1979). Finally, there may be three alternative outcomes. The individual may develop some form and degree of psychopathology; there may be no discernible change in emotional or physical

functioning; or there may be substantial growth and adaptive changes. Dohrenwend (1978) argues that at the earliest, clinical interventions occur after a reaction to a stressful event has occurred. By contrast, preventive approaches are concerned with preexisting circumstances or characteristics of the person which tend to promote or inhibit the occurrence of the stressful event.

This model is one which is undeniably of help in clarifying the factors that influence adaptation to stress resulting from a life event. Moreover, the elaboration of a framework for considering mediation of an individual's efforts to cope with stress explicitly recognizes that all individuals do not respond to an event in the same fashion. This perspective on single life events thus goes well beyond some of the early cumulative life stress work and complements some of the current developments in that area. There are, however, still some difficulties and limitations to this view of the importance of single life events for preventive efforts.

Just as in the case for cumulative life events, the primary concern of research on single life events is the stressfulness and potential negative effects associated with them. Further evidence that this is the case is provided by Bloom (1979), who notes that a major step toward organizing preventive efforts around life events is to "identify a stressful life event that appears to have undesirable consequences in a significant proportion of the population" and to develop knowledge "related to how one might go about reducing or eliminating the negative consequences of the event [p. 183]." Clearly, while there may be some passing attention to positive adaptive outcomes, the overriding concern remains alleviating the pathogenic stressfulness of the event and reducing negative consequences. This stressful life event position still reflects the "new medical model" which, as discussed above, underlies the cumulative life stress area. While this model is preventive in its focus, it is not primarily concerned with the enhancement of an individual's sense of mastery, development, or life satisfaction, as suggested by Cowen (1980) or by Danish and his colleagues in Chapter 4 of this volume. In the following pages we will suggest a framework for viewing life events, building on that of Dohrenwend (1978) and others (Parkes, 1971; Tyhurst, 1958), which may move us closer to an approach to understanding and intervening with life events that more fully reflects the range of goals of prevention.

## Life Transitions

A starting point for us involves a key, often overlooked distinction among life events. That is, some of the events included on inventories are truly "events," in that they are limited both temporally and in their repercussions on individuals' lives. By contrast, other "events" are really better viewed as markers or precipitants of the unfolding of major changes in an individual's life which may engender new stresses and changes and demand adaptive effort for some time to come (Felner et al., 1980). Often it seems that referring to the occurrence of such major shifts in an individual's life as unraveling "events" tends to remove the focus from the change process per se to the variables which surround the changes. Thus, for example, in Dohrenwend's (1979) model much emphasis is placed on mediating factors but relatively little on the nature of the "event." Felner el al. (1980) have argued that rather than conceptualizing life changes such as divorce, marriage, geographic relocation, retirement, onset of chronic illness, and so on as unitary stressful events, a preventive focus would be better served by a view which focuses on the entire transitional period during which individuals are being called upon to engage in adaptive efforts by the change process they are experiencing.

Recent evidence has suggested that at least for some events, this life transition position may more fully reflect the adaptive process than do crises or stressful life event models. Hetherington (1978) has well documented that the process of adapting to divorce, by both adults and children, may extend over several years. Similarly, other studies focusing on individual efforts to cope with a serious illness or loss of a loved one have shown that adaptive tasks may take far longer to resolve than would be predicted from crisis theory or would allow one to reasonably speak of them as "events" (Felner et al., 1982; Gottesman & Lewis, 1982; Lewis, Gottesman, & Gutstein, 1979; Primavera, Farber, & Felner, 1982).

Recognition of the differences in duration necessary to resolve the adaptive tasks of a life transition versus what we are calling a stressful life event is a key first step in developing a model which is more useful for primary prevention. Another important element involves shifting the focus from stress and its pathogenic effects as the predominant concern, to the nature of the changes which characterize such transitions and the process of adapting to them. Here the stress involved in adapting to these changes is but one element of a larger process which includes mastery of the range of adaptive tasks engendered by the life change (Felner et al., 1980).

Before proceeding, a note of caution is in order. In previous discussion the term "transition" as it relates to life change and mental health has been employed in two somewhat distinct ways. Tyhurst (1958) has written of transition states with the intention of focusing on the state of change (that is, the individual's reaction to change) rather than the change itself. By contrast, Parkes (1971) notes that he prefers to view a transition as a process rather than a state. As our preceding comments suggest, it is with the position taken by Parkes that our own view is most consistent.

What does this view of life transitions, which emphasizes adapting to changes over reducing stress, offer to primary prevention? One obvious contribution is that it legitimizes concern with those positive changes in an individual's life which may have tremendous long-term impact on his or her functioning, yet do not result in high rates of dysfunction. That preventive efforts aimed at helping individuals understand and master the adaptive challenges posed by marriage, the birth of a child, completing school, and other such generally positive events may have enduring effects on the quality of their lives and personal competencies, as well as on those around them, is apparent. If our focus is on life change and positive adaptation to it, rather than on the avoidance of adverse consequences of stress, then we may also begin to develop preventive efforts aimed at the facilitation of positive outcomes and the enhancement of the ability of individuals to be resilient in the face of other potentially dysfunction-producing circumstances.

Once we shift our focus to the individual's efforts to adapt to change rather than merely reduce or contain stress, the questions remain: What is the nature of the changes which must be dealt with? What factors influence this process? In keeping our emphasis on the development of a framework that is consistent with primary prevention's emphasis on positive outcomes as well as the reduction of disorder, we would like to suggest that a key aspect of a transition perspective on life change must be an emphasis on identifying the specific types of changes which confront the individual during the transition as tasks which must be actively mastered by the individual. Such a perspective would serve to put the emphasis on the specific problems and issues which need to be resolved, rather than on coping with some vaguely defined level of stress. That is, we are no longer almost exclusively concerned with the individual's affective response to the change (that is, the experienced level of stress). Rather, from this perspective we are centrally concerned with what it is that people must do, cognitively and/ or behaviorally, to achieve satisfactory levels of adaptation to the new circumstances in their life resulting from events and the transitional tasks they precipitate. Further, it assumes that there may be tasks which are common across most transitions, regardless of the specific content or nature of the precipitating event.

An active task-mastery view of the way individuals deal with transitions also has some consequences for the way we view mediating factors. The individual's coping skills and problem-solving abilities assume a far more central role in determining the outcome of the adaptive process. Not only may these factors directly influence adaptive effects, as in Dohrenwend's (1978) model, but it becomes apparent that they may also act somewhat indirectly, through their influence on environmental forces. In stress-focused approaches to life events, situational mediators such as social support are viewed as factors which influence or "buffer" the individual's experienced stress by their presence or absence, with the individual essentially viewed as a passive recipient of their effects (Dohrenwend, 1978; Wilcox, 1981). Such a position may be true in part. However, if we recognize that individuals may be actively engaged in adapting to change, then it becomes evident that they may also actively employ their problem-solving abilities to either gain or reshape the environmental resources they draw upon to enhance their adaptive efforts. Thus the quality of an environmental mediator as a coping resource reflects, at least to some extent, the adequacy or relative success of the individual's coping efforts. As we will further elaborate, some of the tasks which confront individuals during transitions may be the active reorganization and modification of such potential environmental mediators of stress as the extent and level of social networks and supports available, or the level of predictability and organization in day-to-day life.

A life transition framework which recognizes that some life events are potential precipitants or markers of transitional processes rather than more limited events makes it possible, indeed critical, to attempt to identify common defining characteristics of transitions which may have greater levels of adaptive significance. While transitions such as retirement, geographic relocation, divorce, loss of a spouse, being disabled, marriage or remarriage, becoming a parent, and changing or completing school appear to involve divergent sets of issues to resolve, they may be quite similar in terms of the types of tasks or changes they engender for individuals. A transitional framework allows us to focus on such commonalities and to develop strategies for enhancing individuals' adaptive abilities across a wide array of life changes. Authors writing about life events and life transitions have already suggested a number of possible common tasks that confront individuals experiencing life changes.

Parkes (1971) has argued that individuals who are confronting lasting and major changes in their life space face the task of reordering their "assumptive worlds." The assumptive world includes an individual's

view of the world both as it is and as it might be. Areas which comprise an individual's assumptive world include interpersonal relationships, familiar environments, possessions, physical and mental capacities, and roles and status (Parkes, 1971). From this perspective, when individuals face major life changes the key task they are confronted with is to modify their existing set of expectations and assumptions about their world and develop others which more accurately reflect their new situation.

Parkes's (1971) view of the individual's assumptive world may also be helpful in reconsidering the way we think about the person's cognitive appraisal of a situation as a mediator of adaptation during life change. In Dohrenwend's (1978) model, an individual's appraisal of a life event is essentially static; that is, it does not seem to change during the coping process. Within this model as well as that of other authors who discuss the process by which individuals attempt to cope with stress (Kobasa, 1979; Lazarus & Cohen, 1977; Lazarus & Launier, 1978), the individual's cognitive appraisal of an event is viewed as central in determining the amount of stress the event generates for him or her. Given that we have shifted our view of life changes to emphasize the transition process rather than the "single point" event, we also need to modify our view of cognitive appraisal as a mediator. Parkes's view may be informative here. Rather than viewing cognitive appraisal as exclusively a mediator of the adaptive process, if we adopt a life transition framework one of the tasks individuals confront when coping with life change is modifying their views of their life situations (i.e., their appraisals) in such a way that their views come to reflect their changed circumstances and allow them to function effectively. Thus while an individual's cognitive appraisal of a situation may indirectly mediate other adaptive outcomes through moderating the level of stress they experience, so too may it be considered an indicator of adaptive success in its own right.

Another set of changes which may accompany most transitions are shifts in role definition. Pearlin et al. (1981) have proposed that life events may serve to alter the meaning of persistent, ongoing life stressors and that the increased stress accompanying life events results from adverse alterations in these meanings. As may be seen, this position closely resembles that of Parkes (1971). Further, however, Pearlin and his colleagues view role change or role strain as a central element which must be mastered and may shape the alterations in meaning of the ongoing stressors which occur. Similarly, Klein and Ross (1965) argue that during transitions the successful redefinition of roles may be critical to adaptation. For example, in discussing a child's entry to school they state that "inadequately resolved intrafamilial and parental role tensions generated by school entry may not only hamper a child's school adjustment, but may also block needed home-school collaboration [p. 148]."

The way events such as retirement, promotions, moves, or shifts in marital status change an individual's roles vis-à-vis his or her social networks is clearly a potentially key problem which must be solved by individuals experiencing such life changes.

Transitions, then, may dramatically change the roles of individuals and bring about concomitant shifts in the expectations of others. Moving from "child" to "spouse" following marriage, from student to responsible adult following graduation from high school or college, or from spouse to "dating single" following divorce are but a few of the dramatic role shifts which accompany life changes. The degree to which an individual is able to recognize and master changes in the way they view themselves and in the way they are perceived by others may significantly influence the level of success he or she has in coping with life transition.

Individuals experiencing life transitions may also be confronted with the reorganization or reconstruction of their social networks and social support systems. Studies of the experiences of individuals who have changed schools (Felner et al., 1982; Felner et al., 1981), who have been divorced (Hetherington, 1979) or whose spouse has died (Parkes, 1975) have all shown that a frequent consequence of these life changes is rapid and dramatic shifts in social and family networks. In general, studies of stressful life events and circumstances which are concerned with social support as a mediator of stress have tended to overlook this shifting quality of social support (Barrerra, Sandler, & Ramsey, 1981; Cauce, Felner, & Primavera, 1981; Sandler & Lakey, 1982; Wilcox, 1981). However, a life transition framework reflects a position which views the individual as taking a more active role in organizing, modifying, and utilizing his or her social supports following life changes.

A great deal of data indicate that the level of social support available to an individual experiencing stress or change may impact their subsequent adaptation (Cauce et al., 1981; Gottlieb, 1981). However, during a transition an individual's social supports and social networks do not, as noted above, remain static. Rather, they are changing, in their function, structure, and participants. The individual, if he or she is to adequately master the adaptive tasks posed by the transition, must be actively involved in shaping these changes. Adequate social supports may serve to buffer stress from life change and predict how well the individual may adapt

the changes which are occurring (Sandler & Lakey, 1982; Wilcox, 1981). However, the level of social support and its perceived adequacy by the individual may also, to some extent, serve as an indicator of "outcome" or as a gauge of the individual's mastery of one of the adaptive tasks of the transition. The presence of high levels of social support or satisfactory interactions with members of the social network may be indicative of the individual's successfully recognizing the need to reorganize these sources of support and satisfaction and developing appropriate strategies for doing so.

Thus, the consistent association found between higher levels of social support and more positive adjustment may be as much a function of the fact that individuals with good coping abilities are able to seek and maintain the support they need as it is a function of any stress-"buffering" effects of social support. Those individuals with better coping skills and higher levels of adaptive functioning should be better able to obtain and retain the levels of support they need than those who have poor skills or are less well adjusted. An individual's level of social support, then, may just as easily by viewed as a reflection of level of adaptation as it is a mediator of such adaptation. Developing and reorganizing social networks following life change, as well as more generally, demands that individuals bring their coping skills and social competencies to bear. From this perspective we see that while social support may facilitate more successful coping efforts, so too successful coping efforts may lead to more adequate and satisfactory levels of social support. It seems clear that future studies of the role of social support in adapting to life events need to recognize that this relationship may certainly be a bidirectional one, with greater emphasis placed on the relationship between the coping skills and personality of individuals and their levels and types of social support.

As we have noted, there are a number of other potential tasks, whose exact natures need further elaboration, which may be common to most life transitions. As an individual goes through a transition, life circumstances shift to disrupt old patterns of behaving and interacting. Certainly most people experiencing transitions or major life changes face the tasks of reestablishing the routines of daily life or interaction patterns within their family lives. For example, Felner et al. (1980) have argued that divorce may not only require that a family adapt to the change in marital circumstances per se, but also may pose other tasks precipitated by the divorce, such as reorganization of the family's daily routine, development of new skills, and restructuring of family interaction patterns. As Johnson (1982) notes, many of these same tasks may be required of individuals experiencing other major life changes, such as the death of a spouse or parent, pregnancy, a parent's incarceration, or major changes in the occupational status of a parent or in the financial status of the family.

## Stress in Life Transitions

The preceding section highlighted some of the potential adaptive tasks confronting individuals during and following life transitions. Such tasks appear to be key characteristics of transitions. Mastery of these tasks may facilitate more positive adaptation and individual happiness, while failure may result in increased stress and dysfunction. Further, exploration and identification of those changes and tasks contributing to the total life transition and elaboration of coping styles, problem-solving skills, and environmental resources which facilitate their mastery are necessary to progressing beyond what Cowen (1982) calls the "baby-steps" level that prevention efforts reflect currently.

If we are to fully understand the impact of life transitions, it will also be necessary to understand how the role of stress and its sources ought to be viewed from such a framework. DeLongis, Coyne, Dakof, Folkman, and Lazarus (1982) offer some suggestions which may be helpful here. They propose a distinction between major life events and the residual, day-to-day stressors they engender or exacerbate. Toward further clarifying this distinction, they propose that the former are "distal" stressors while the latter are "proximal" stressors. This distinction is based on what is termed the "conceptual proximity" of events or stressors. According to this view, life events are considered distal because they do not describe directly the life circumstances and demands that result from them or the adaptive processes they require. By contrast, proximal stressors are those daily person-environment transactions that the person sees as an adaptive challenge or threat. In a similar vein, Pearlin et al. (1981) have argued that life events do not necessarily exert their effects on people directly, but instead do so by intensifying or creating new life strains which lead to stress. As may be clear, a transitional framework accommodates these positions far better than does a life events model. From a life transitions perspective, with its focus on the processes of change as well as the precipitating event, it is relatively simple to incorporate a concern with the type and levels of day-to-day strain in an individual's life and how they are exacerbated or mitigated by the changes which are taking place. Clearly, the common major tasks we spoke of above, which characterize transitions, may be easily thought of as new sources of strain in an

individual's life. Indeed, not only is such a position easily accommodated, it is vital to understanding the nature and place of the stress experienced by individuals going through life changes. While the initial event may, of course, in itself produce some acute as well as lasting distress, it is the level and type of proximal stressors which follow the event which are at least equally important in determining the individual's experienced levels of distress or well-being subsequent to the precipitating event.

## Summary and Concluding Comments

In this chapter we have endeavored to highlight some of the contributions and limitations of a stressful life event approach both for primary prevention specifically, and for viewing adaptive functioning more generally. While providing a firm base upon which to build preventive efforts such an approach was seen to place an overemphasis on pathology and stressful occurrences at the expense of understanding life changes and the adaptive challenges confronted by the individuals experiencing them. A shift in focus to the adaptive tasks which follow the "event" rather than the time-limited affective reaction which is its immediate sequel also was seen to have implications for the types of life changes which may be considered particularly salient, as well as for the way in which we view a set of factors previously considered primarily for their role in mediating stress. The adaptive implications of positively valenced life changes are, from the transitional perspective proposed, brought much more sharply into focus than by the prior model, with its emphasis on pathogenic consequences. This shift is a key step for balancing the investment of prevention efforts with life events and life changes in health versus dysfunction. Similarly, the broader focus presented for viewing life changes and adaptation sees coping with the stress engendered by life events as only one of the range of adaptive challenges the individual confronts during transitions. Further, it may also serve to illuminate aspects of the interaction between personal coping skills and environmental coping resources that have been previously overlooked. Rather than exclusively perceiving such aspects of the coping process as the individual's cognitive appraisal of the event, social support, and/or family organization as factors which mediate adaptive outcome, we have seen that these variables may also, in fact, be reflective of adaptation in themselves. Hence the consistent association found between these factors and the individual's levels of psychological and somatic functioning may as much reflect the individual's overall level of coping efficacy as it does the enhancement of the latter by these mediators.

The identification of common transitional tasks engendered across precipitating events may also help us to discriminate between those events which are timely markers of life transitions and those which are merely stressful, circumscribed events. As our knowledge of the changes and tasks which typically follow certain events grows, qualitative differences in the nature of the items listed on life events will become clearer. That we develop such a knowledge base and set of clearly defining criteria for transitions is critical if we are to avoid the conceptual imprecision and multitude of uses that are associated with the terms stress and stressful life events. Disagreements with family members, non-life-threatening acute illness, or traffic tickets, while certainly stressful, give rise neither to long-term changes in the individual's world nor to shifts in their views of themselves, and thereby are excluded from the level of life transitions. One caveat must be kept in mind when deciding which events do or do not typically precipitate transitional states and processes: While we may define the set of events which usually are of the magnitude of major life transitions, the degree and extent of these changes will vary across individuals as a function of both personal resources and environmental circumstances. These individual variations in the level of adaptive tasks and challenges posed should not be overlooked. There is no need in the life transition area to repeat all the mistakes and achievements of the stressful life events work. Rather, as we have sought to do in this chapter we should use this work to provide a sound base by which we may be guided, but by which we should not be constrained.

In summary, we have suggested several possible elements of the structure of transitions which may be salient for adaptation. Others will no doubt be identified as we focus increased attention on the process of adaptation to change more generally, rather than simply on stress from life events. We feel that such a framework allows for a far more precise definition of what an individual is attempting to cope with than does a stressful event model when applied to occurrences which precipitate major shifts in people's lives. If so, this should facilitate our ability to develop programs which are more focused, proactive, and truly preventive. For example, to say we hope to develop a program for aiding individuals in coping with the stress of retirement or widowhood results in an amorphous and ill-defined task. However, if we can elaborate the tasks, adaptive challenges, and strains which are common to all life transitions, then we will have much clearer starting points for formulating program design and implementation.

# References

Barrerra, M., Sandler, I. N., & Ramsey, T. B. Preliminary development of a scale of social support: Studies on college students. *American Journal of Community Psychology*, 1981, **9**, 435–448.

Billings, A. C., & Moos, R. H. Stressful life events and symptoms: A longitudinal model. *Health Psychology*, 1982, **1**, 99–117.

Bloom, B. L. Prevention of mental disorders: Recent advances in theory and practice. *Community Mental Health Journal*, 1979, **15**, 179–191.

Bloom, B. L., Asher, S. J., & White, S. W. Marital disruption as a stressor: A review and analysis. *Psychological Bulletin*, 1978, **85**, 867–894.

Bramwell, S. T., Masuda, M., Wagner, N. N., & Holmes, T. H. Psychosocial factors in athletic injuries. *Journal of Human Stress*, 1975, **1**, 6–22.

Byrne, D. G., & Whyte, H. M. Life events and myocardial infarcation revisited: The role of measures of individual impact. *Psychosomatic Medicine*, 1980, **42**, 1–10.

Caplan, G. *Principles of preventive psychiatry*. New York: Basic Books, 1964.

Cauce, A. M., Felner, R. D., & Primavera, J. Social support systems in high risk adolescents: Structural components and adaptive impact. *American Journal of Community Psychology*, 1982, **10**(4), 417–428.

Celdran, H. H. The cross-cultural consistency of two social consensus scales: The Seriousness of Illness Rating Scale and the Social Readjustment Ratings Scale in Spain. Unpublished thesis, University of Washington, Seattle, 1970.

Coddington, R. D. The significance of life events as etiological factors in the diseases of children. A survey of professional workers. *Journal of Psychosomatic Research*, 1972, **16**, 7–18.

Cowen, E. L. The wooing of primary prevention. *American Journal of Community Psychology*, 1980, **8**, 258–284.

Cowen, E. L. The special number: A complete roadmap. *American Journal of Community Psychology*, 1982, **10**, 239–250.

de Araujo, G., Van Arsdel, P. P., Holmes, T. H., & Dudley, D. L. Life change, coping ability and chronic intrinsic asthma. *Journal of Psychosomatic Research*, 1973, **17**, 359–363.

DeLongis, A., Coyne, J. C., Dakof, G., Folkman, S., & Lazarus, R. S. Relationships of hassles, uplifts, and major life events to health status. *Health Psychology*, 1982, **1**, 119–136.

Dohrenwend, B. P. Stressful life events and psychopathology: Some issues of theory and method. In J. E. Barrett (Ed.), *Stress and mental disorder*. New York: Raven Press, 1979.

Dohrenwend, B. S. Life events as stressors: A methodological inquiry. *Journal of Health and Social Behavior*, 1973, **14**, 167–175.

Dohrenwend, B. S. Social stress and community psychology. *American Journal of Community Psychology*, 1978, **6**, 1–14.

Dohrenwend, B. S., & Dohrenwend, B. P. Overview and prospects for research on stressful life events. In B. S.

Dohrenwend & B. P. Dohrenwend (Eds.), *Stressful life events: Their nature and effects.* New York: Wiley, 1974.

Dohrenwend, B. S., & Dohrenwend, B. P. Some issues in research on stressful life events. *Journal of Nervous and Mental Disease*, 1978, **166**, 7–15.

Dohrenwend, B. S., & Martin, J. L. Personal versus situational determinants of anticipation and control of the occurrence of stressful life events. *American Journal of Community Psychology*, 1979, **7**, 453–468.

Fairbank, D. T., & Hough, R. L. Life event classifications and the event-illness relationship. *Journal of Human Stress*, 1979, **5**, 41–47.

Felner, R. D., & Aber, M. S. Primary prevention for children: A framework for the assessment of need. *Prevention in Human Services*, 1983, in press.

Felner, R. D., Aber, M. S., Primavera, J., & Cauce, A. M. Adaptation and vulnerability in high risk adolescents: An examination of environmental mediators. *Journal of Community Psychology*, 1983, in press.

Felner, R. D., Farber, S. S., & Primavera, J. Transitions and stressful life events: A model for primary prevention. In R. H. Price, R. F. Ketterer, B. C. Bader, & J. Monahan (Eds.), *Prevention in mental health: Research, policy and practice.* Beverly Hills: Sage, 1980.

Felner, R. D., Ginter, M. A., & Primavera, J. Primary prevention during school transitions: Social support and environmental structure. *American Journal of Community Psychology*, 1982, **10**(3), 227–290.

Felner, R. D., Norton, P. L., Cowen, E. L., & Farber, S. S. A prevention program for children experiencing life crisis. *Professional Psychology*, 1981, **12**, 446–452.

Felner, R. D., Primavera, J., & Cauce, A. M. The impact of school transitions: A focus for preventive efforts. *American Journal of Community Psychology*, 1981, **9**(4), 449–459.

Finkel, N. J. Stress, trauma and trauma resolution. *American Journal of Community Psychology*, 1975, **3**, 173–178.

Fontana, A. F., Marcus, J. L., Noel, B., & Rakusin, J. M. Prehospitalization coping styles of psychiatric patients: The goal-directedness of life events. *Journal of Nervous Mental Disorders*, 1972, **155**, 311–321.

Gersten, J. C., Langner, T. S., Eisenberg, J. G., & Simcha-Fagan, O. An evaluation of the etiological role of stressful life-change events in psychological disorders. *Journal of Health and Social Behavior*, 1977, **18**, 228–244.

Goldston, S. E. Defining primary prevention. In G. W. Albee & J. M. Joffe (Eds.), *Primary prevention of psychopathology.* Vol. 1. *The issues.* Hanover, N.H.: University Press of New England, 1977.

Gottesman, D., & Lewis, M. Differences in crisis reactions among cancer and surgery patients. *Journal of Consulting and Clinical Psychology*, 1982, **3**, 381–388.

Gottlieb, B. H. Social networks and social support in community mental health. In B. H. Gottlieb (Ed.), *Social networks and social support.* Beverly Hills: Sage, 1981.

Harmon, D. K., Masuda, M., & Holmes, T. H. The social readjustment rating scale: A cross-cultural study of Western Europeans and Americans. *Journal of Psychosomatic Research*, 1970, **14**, 391–400.

Harris, P. W. The relationship of life change to academic performance among selected college freshmen at varying levels of college readiness. Unpublished doctoral dissertation, East Texas State University, 1972.

Hawkins, N. G., Davies, R., & Holmes, T. H. Evidence of psychosocial factors in the development of pulmonary tuberculosis. *American Review of Tuberculosis and Pulmonary Disorders*, 1957, **75**, 768–780.

Heisel, J. S., Ream, S., Ratz, R., Rappaport, M., & Coddington, R. D. The significance of life events as contributing factors in the diseases of children. *Behavioral Pediatrics*, 1973, **83**, 119–123.

Hetherington, E. Divorce: A child's perspective. *American Psychologist*, 1979, **34**, 851–858.

Holmes, T. H. Development and application of a quantitative measure of life change magnitude. In J. E. Barrett (Ed.), *Stress and mental disorder.* New York: Raven Press, 1979.

Holmes, T. H., & Rahe, R. H. The social readjustment rating scale. *Journal of Psychosomatic Research*, 1967, **11**, 213–218.

Hough, R. L., Fairbank, D. T., & Garcia, A. M. Problems in the ratio measurement of life stress. *Journal of Health and Social Behavior*, 1976, **17**, 70–82.

Hurst, M. W. Life changes and psychiatric symptom development: Issues of content, scoring, and clustering. In J. E. Barrett (Ed.), *Stress and mental disorder.* New York: Raven Press, 1979.

Hurst, M., Jenkins, C., & Rose, R. The assessment of life change stress: A comparative and methodological inquiry. *Psychosomatic Medicine*, 1978, **40**, 127–142.

Janney, J. G., Masuda, M., & Holmes, T. H.: Impact of a natural catastrophe on life events. *Journal of Human Stress*, 1977, **3**, 22–34.

Johnson, J. H. Life events as stressors in childhood and adolescence. In B. B. Lahey & A. E. Kazdin (Eds.), *Advances in clinical child psychology.* New York: Plenum Press, 1982.

Johnson, J. H., & Sarason, I. G. Life stress, depression and anxiety: Internal-external control as a moderator variable. *Journal of Psychosomatic Research*, 1978, **22**, 205–208.

Johnson, J. H., & Sarason, I. G. Moderator variables in life stress research. In I. G. Sarason & C. D. Spielberger (Eds.), *Stress and anxiety.* Vol. 6. Washington, D.C.: Hemisphere, 1979.

Klein, D. C., & Ross, A. Kindergarten entry: A study of role transitions. In H. Parad (Ed.), *Crisis intervention: Selected readings.* New York: Family Service Association of America, 1965.

Kobasa, S. C. Personality and resistance to illness. *American Journal of Community Psychology*, 1979, **7**, 413–424.

Komaroff, A. L., Masuda, M., & Holmes, T. H. The social readjustment rating scale: A comparative study of Negro, Mexican, and White Americans. *Journal of Psychosomatic Research*, 1968, **12**, 121–128.

Lazarus, R. S., & Cohen, J. B. Environmental stress. In I. Altman & J. Wohlwill (Eds.), *Human behavior and environment.* Vol. 1. New York: Plenum Press, 1977.

Lazarus, R. D., & Launier, R. Stress-related transactions between person and environment. In L. A. Pervin & M. Lewis (Eds.), *Perspectives in interactional psychology.* New York: Plenum Press, 1978.

Lewis, M. S., Gottesman, D., & Gutstein, S. The course and duration of crisis. *Journal of Consulting and Clinical Psychology*, 1979, **47**, 128–134.

Markush, R. E., & Favero, R. V. Epidemiological assessment of stressful life events, depressed mood, and psychophysiological symptoms—A preliminary report. In B. S. Dohrenwend & B. P. Dohrenwend (Eds.), *Stressful life events: Their nature and effects.* New York: Wiley, 1974.

Masuda, M., & Holmes, T. H. The social readjustment rating scale: A cross-cultural study of Japanese and Americans. *Journal of Psychosomatic Research*, 1967, **11**, 221–237.

Masuda, M., & Holmes, T. H. Life events: Perceptions and frequencies. *Psychosomatic Medicine*, 1978, **40**, 236–261.

McGrath, R. E. V., & Burkhart, B. R. Measuring life stress: A comparison of different scoring systems for the Social Readjustment Rating Scale. *Journal of Clinical Psychology*, 1983, in press.

Monaghan, J. H., Robinson, J. O., & Dodge, J. A. The Children's Life Events Inventory. *Journal of Psychomatic Research*, 1979, **23**, 63–68.

Myers, J. R., Lindenthal, J. J., & Pepper, M. P. Social class, life events, and psychiatric symptoms: A longitudinal study. In B. S. Dohrenwend & B. P. Dohrenwend (Eds.), *Stressful life events: Their nature and effects*. New York: Wiley, 1974.

Newcomb, M. D., Huba, G. J., & Bentler, P. M. A multidimensional assessment of stressful life events among adolescents: Deviation and correlates. *Journal of Health and Social Behavior*, 1981, **22**, 400–415.

Nuckolls, K. B., Cassel, J., & Kaplan, B. H. Psychosocial assets, life crisis and the prognosis of pregnancy. *American Journal of Epidemiology*, 1972, **95**, 431–441.

Parkes, C. M. Psycho-social transactions: A field for study. *Social Science and Medicine*, 1971, **5**, 101–115.

Parkes, C. M. Unexpected and untimely bereavement: A statistical study of young Boston widows and widowers. In B. S. Schoenberg, I. Gerber, A. Weiner, A. H. Kutcher, D. Peretz, & A. C. Carr (Eds.), *Bereavement: Its psychosocial aspects*. New York: Columbia University Press, 1975.

Paykel, E. S. Life stress and psychiatric disorder: Applications of the clinical approach. In B. S. Dohrenwend & B. P. Dohrenwend (Eds.), *Stressful life events: Their nature and effects*. New York: Wiley, 1974.

Paykel, E. S. Life stress, depression, and suicide. *Journal of Human Stress*, 1976, **2**, 3–14.

Pearlin, L. I. Life strains and psychological distress among adults. In N. J. Smelser & E. H. Erickson (Eds.), *Themes of love and work in adulthood*. Cambridge: Harvard University Press, 1980.

Pearlin, L. I., Menaghan, E. G., Lieberman, M. A., & Mullen, J. T. The stress process. *Journal of Health and Social Behavior*, 1981, **22**, 337–356.

Peterson, L., Shigetomi, C. The use of coping techniques to minimize anxiety in hospitalized children. *Behavior Therapy*, 1981, **12**, 1–14.

Petrich, J., & Holmes, T. H. Life change and onset of illness. In A. Reading & T. N. Wise (Eds.), *The medical clinics of North America: Symposium on psychiatry in internal medicine*. Philadelphia: Saunders, 1977.

Primavera, J., Farber, S. S., & Felner, R. D. Parental death and adolescents: Factors mediating adaptation. Presentation to the 90th Annual Meeting of the American Psychological Association, Washington, D.C., August 1982.

Rabkin, J. G., & Struening, E. L. Life events, stress, and illness. *Science*, 1976, **194**, 1013–1020.

Rahe, R. H., Mahan, J. L., & Arthur, R. J. Prediction of near-future health changes from subjects preceding life changes. *Journal of Psychosomatic Research*, 1979, **14**, 401–406.

Rahe, R. H., Meyer, M., Smith, M., Kjaer, G., & Holmes, T. H. Social stress and illness onset. *Journal of Psychosomatic Research*, 1964, **8**, 35–44.

Rappaport, J. *Community psychology: Values, research and action*. New York: Holt, Rinehart & Winston, 1977.

Rose, R. M., Jenkins, C., & Hurst, M. Health change in air traffic controllers: A prospective study. I. Background and description. *Psychosomatic Medicine*, 1978, **40**, 143–165.

Ruch, L. L., & Holmes, T. H. Scaling of life change: Comparison of direct and indirect methods. *Journal of Psychosomatic Research*, 1971, **15**, 221–227.

Sandler, I. N. Life stress events and community psychology. In I. G. Sarason & C. Speilberger (Eds.), *Stress and anxiety*. Vol. 6. New York: Halstead Press, 1979.

Sandler, I. N., & Block, M. Life stress and maladaptation of children. *American Journal of Community Psychology*, 1979, **7**, 425–440.

Sandler, I. N., & Lakey, B. Locus of control as a stress moderator: The role of control perceptions and social support. *American Journal of Community Psychology*, 1982, **10**, 65–80.

Sandler, I. N., & Ramsey, T. B. Dimensional analysis of children's stressful life events. *American Journal of Community Psychology*, 1980, **8**, 285–302.

Sarason, I. G., Johnson, J. H., & Siegel, J. M. Assessing the impact of life changes: Development of the Life Experiences Survey. *Journal of Consulting and Clinical Psychology*, 1978, **46**, 932–46.

Schless, A. P., Schwartz, L., Goetz, C., & Mendels, J. How depressives view the significance of life events. *British Journal of Psychiatry*, 1974, **125**, 406–410.

Seppa, M. T. The Social Readjustment Rating Scale and the Seriousness of Illness Rating Scale: A comparison of Salvadorans, Spanish and Americans. Unpublished thesis, University of Washington, Seattle, 1972.

Syler, A. R., Masuda, M., & Holmes, T. H. Magnitude of life events and seriousness of illness. *Psychosomatic Medicine*, 1971, **33**, 115–122.

Turk, D. C. Factors influencing the adaptive process with chronic illness: Implications for intervention. In I. G. Sarason & C. D. Spielberger (Eds.), *Stress and anxiety*. Vol. 6. Washington, D.C.: Hemisphere Publishing, 1979.

Tyhurst, J. S. The role of transition states—including disasters—in mental illness. *Symposium on Preventive and Social Psychiatry*. Washington: Government Printing Office, 1958.

Uhlenhuth, E. H., Discussion, Part I. Life stress and illness: The search for significance. In J. E. Barrett (Ed.), *Stress and mental disorder*. New York: Raven Press, 1979.

Uhlenhuth, E. H., & Paykel, E. S. Symptom intensity and life events. *Archives of General Psychiatry*, 1973, **28**, 473–477.

Wilcox, B. L. Social support, life stress and psychological adjustments: A test of the buffering hypothesis. *American Journal of Community Psychology*, 1981, **9**, 371–386.

Zautra, A., & Reich, J. Positive life events and reports of well-being: Some useful distinctions. *American Journal of Community Psychology*, 1980, **8**, 657–670.

Zautra, A., & Simons, L. S. Some effects of positive life events on individual and community mental health. *American Journal of Community Psychology*, 1979.

Zax, M., & Cowen, E. L. *Abnormal psychology: Changing conceptions*. New York: Holt, Rinehart & Winston, 1976.

Zax, M., & Spector, G. A. *An introduction to community psychology*. New York: Wiley, 1974.

# PART V
# THE PRACTICE OF PREVENTION IN THE COMMUNITY

# INTRODUCTION TO PART V

In the preceding sections of this volume, our concern has been primarily with the conceptual and empirical underpinnings of preventive psychology. In this section of the volume, we now turn our attention to some of the central issues and concerns that must be engaged by the preventive psychologist in implementing preventive research and intervention efforts. We should start by noting that as psychologists have become increasingly invested in and committed to the development of preventive efforts, so have they increasingly recognized the need to venture into non-traditional and alien arenas, often with strange bedfellows, to accomplish this goal. With great regularity preventively-oriented psychologists have confronted the need to work with those in disciplines or settings who do not see their primary mission as the enhancement of the psychological well-being of their constituency. While schools, legal, and government institutions and officials, physicians, architects, and other professionals may be concerned about the mental health of the individuals they serve, it is generally not their central focus. In this section, focusing particularly on preventive efforts in health care settings and the social policy process as models, the contributors consider factors that bear on the preventive psychologist's involvements with other disciplines and settings, offer suggestions for ways to identify and understand problems of concern that take into account the context in which they are to be addressed, and elaborate on avenues for evaluating the adequacy of preventive efforts that ultimately enhance knowledge and improve future interventions.

In the first chapter, Albino points out the difficulty in considering prevention in mental health apart from health in the more general sense. The challenges to general health promotion are not seen to be greatly different from those that confront primary prevention in mental health. She notes that definitions of health by the World Health Organization and APA's Division of Health Psychology underscore the central role of psychological factors in physical as well as in mental health. The major concerns and efforts of health psychology vis-à-vis prevention, especially as they parallel and overlap with the interests of psychologists working in mental health settings, are carefully elaborated. The case is cogently made for psychology to understand that the knowledge base and concerns of one often parallel and complement the other. The psychologist's role in health care settings, as well as modifications both in roles and the settings themselves which may facilitate preventive efforts, are discussed. Albino suggests four areas that may serve as the central focus of preventively-oriented health psychologists' efforts. Particularly fruitful avenues for prevention specialists in health care settings are mentioned, including: the identification of risk factors and development of services for reducing risk; facilitating adherence to medical recommendations; reducing stress and enhancing the process of coping; and the development and implementation of health care programs. Far more exchange between preventive psychologists working in health settings and those involved in mental health is called for by Albino. This is seen as particularly useful in helping facilitate the movement of health psychologists from a stance that is primarily individual in its focus to one that is more community-oriented, both in its conceptualization and addressing of problems.

The problems and benefits of collaboration between preventive psychologists and those in other disciplines for developing viable preventive interventions are explored by Reppucci, Mulvey and Kastner. Using the example of teenage pregnancy, they illustrate how social, economic, political, moral, and psychological perspectives, among others, may combine to add to and shape the strategies employed to address a social problem. A case is presented for the need for a fully elaborated ecological model for approaching such problems. This is seen as key to the degree to which we can alleviate these problems while at the same time avoiding adverse unintended consequences.

While Reppucci et al. illustrate some of the benefits that may accrue for preventive psychology from interdisciplinary collaboration in social policy development, Sarason offers a view of the potential pitfalls that confront the psychologist in such endeavors. The public policy process is briefly elaborated and historical and disciplinary barriers to psychologists' successful involvement in the policy process are discussed. Sarason notes that psychology, generally, and preventive and community psychology, particularly, have generally been unrelated to and/or unsophisticated about public policy. The roots of community and preventive psychology in clinical psychology are noted, and the problems such ancestry pose for developing a genuine understanding of and focus on prevention, enhancement, and public policy, are discussed. More generally, the historical growth of community psychology is examined as a way of challenging accustomed perspectives and raising concerns that preventive psychology needs to recognize if it is to understand the larger social picture. Sarason feels it must, if it is to inform sound public policy decisions. He asserts that if psychologists want to understand the social world perhaps the best avenue for doing so continues to be an active effort to change it in some fashion. In so doing, he argues, our understanding of the phenomena with which we are concerned will be both broadened and deepened.

In the final chapter of this section, Lorion argues that insufficient attention to both the building of a careful empirical base for prevention and the use of systematic evaluation procedures for preventive interventions has impeded the development and implementation of effective preventive interventions. Prior work evaluating empirical strategies used for assessing intervention programs is reviewed, and reporting and design limitations of such assessments are discussed. A number of basic principles for research and scientific reporting are proposed in order to insure that the deficiencies found in previous evaluation studies are not repeated. It is argued that unless these "givens" are attended to in the evaluation of prevention efforts, opposition to and skepticism of prevention may be difficult to overcome.

The planning of prevention research is considered next. Here some factors are discussed that may help guide decisions as to the form prevention efforts should take. Key among these is the objective determination of the state of knowledge about the target population. A brief but careful review and extension of Cowen's (1980) model for distinguishing between executive and generative research is presented as a means of elucidating further relevant steps in the sequence of planning the research effort.

Particular concerns raised by Lorion that pertain to conducting successful field research relate to the politics which surround such efforts and factors which may bear on the validity of their findings. Cautions are raised about natural tensions between the needs of the research endeavor and those of the field setting in which it is carried out, and suggestions are made for enhancing the collaborative processes necessary for the research to go forward in a way that benefits both parties. In discussing the problems of ensuring that the data yielded are valid, Lorion considers, but goes beyond, the criteria for internal and external validity offered by Campbell and Stanley (1963). Particular attention is paid to the identification and selection of appropriate subject populations and outcome measures as well as to the ecological validity of the intervention.

Taken together, these chapters reinforce the promise of prevention, while simultaneously illuminating some of the persistent obstacles that have been encountered in fulfilling that promise. As Lorion notes, much remains to be done in developing the systematic and requisite knowledge base for prevention. Understanding the wrong turns in the road that has been thus far taken, elaborated in these and the other chapters in this volume, may be as valuable for building that base as the substantive conceptual and empirical advances which have also been presented.

# 13 HEALTH PSYCHOLOGY AND PRIMARY PREVENTION: NATURAL ALLIES

## Judith E. Albino

Although this volume focuses on primary prevention in mental health, it is difficult to consider mental health apart from health in the more general sense. It is becoming increasingly clear that both psychological and somatic factors contribute—probably in an interactive manner—to the state that we term "health." According to a definition adopted by the World Health Organization (WHO) in 1946, "Health is a state of complete physical, mental, and social well-being and is not merely the absence of disease and infirmity." Some more recently proposed definitions of the term "health" may be more explicit, but none captures better the essence of a new perspective that has been emerging in recent years among both providers and consumers of health care.

The potential contributions of psychology to the promotion of total health are reflected in the WHO definition. The scope of health issues and the specific problems that psychology addresses beyond those with clearly mental or emotional components may not be familiar to some readers, however. The new and changing roles of psychologists as health professionals also may need clarification. This chapter will describe some of the major concerns and efforts of health

psychology vis-à-vis prevention—especially as they parallel and overlap the interests of psychologists working in mental health settings. Also of particular interest will be those efforts that encompass a community perspective in reaching beyond the medical-clinical model of health care toward service models that acknowledge the social and environmental contexts of health and illness.

It should be noted at the outset that the term "health psychology" is a relatively new one. Until quite recently, in fact, health psychology could not be defined beyond a description of the activities of a particular psychologist in a specific health setting. In the 1970s the term "behavioral medicine" began to be heard. It soon became apparent, however, that this term did not adequately reflect the endeavors of a large number of those providing services or engaging in research, teaching, or consultation related to problems of physical health and illness. It seemed to many to be too strongly rooted in the traditional medical model that perceives health care as primarily a clinical, or treatment-oriented, response to presenting illness.

"Behavioral health" was suggested by Matarazzo (1980) as the description for a specialty in behavioral medicine that would include efforts focused primarily on prevention. It reflects also the movement of psychologists away from a stereotypical role as "medical psychologists" who provide individual psychotherapy as an adjunct to medical treatment. "Behavioral health" is by design a label that goes beyond any discipline, thereby reflecting the philosophy that any number of disciplines might contribute to the generation of knowledge and to service in this field.

The term "health psychology," on the other hand, came about as psychologists began to organize their thinking about health problems and to communicate about the issues that they were aproaching from a common background of psychological theories and methods. This description has gained broad acceptance within the discipline of psychology, and in 1978 the Division of Health Psychology, the 38th division of the American Psychological Association, was formed. Its membership has grown to about 1,500 or nearly 3 percent of all APA members, in just three years. In an effort to describe the common interests and goals of psychologists interested in health issues, that organization recently produced the following definition of health psychology, which was approved in a referendum of the membership:

> "Health Psychology is the aggregate of the specific educational, scientific and professional contributions of the discipline of psychology to the promotion and maintenance of health, the prevention and treatment of illness, the identification of etiologic and diagnostic correlates of health and illness and related dysfunction, and to the analysis and improvement of the health care system and health policy formation [APA Division 38, 1981].

This definition suggests that psychological approaches and methods have application in virtually all aspects of human health and illness. Yet some delineation of functions, or staking of territory, seems necessary— if only because our health care systems have traditionally created clearly defined and highly specialized areas of responsibility and authority.

George Stone (1979) has perceived the roles of psychologists in health as distinct from those of other health care providers primarily because of their ability to focus on behavior and on facilitating behavior change. This perspective encourages application of the psychologist's strong training in and understanding of human behavior and motivation. Stone has emphasized, moreover, that this role of change agentry can be applied to health care systems and to health professionals, as well as to individuals and their families.

Tefft and Simeonsson (1979) also described an emphasis on change, but they have focused more specifically on the setting creation process, as described by Sarason (1972). This approach suggests that both health and illness represent constantly changing situations that are fraught with psychosocial considerations and are subject to a variety of interpretations. Health care delivery systems, however, generally are too complex and rich in tradition, too wedded to the idea of medical experts dispensing finite solutions, to provide for the broad range of psychosocial needs that are presented. Meeting patients' needs in these areas appears to require changes in the roles of both health care professionals and patients, with the latter assuming greater responsibility. Tefft and Simeonsson seem to agree with Stone (1979) and Matarazzo (1980) that psychologists are best prepared to facilitate such changes. They point out, however, that historically the roles of psychologists in medical settings have tended to follow the medical care model, perhaps indicating again the resistance of a complex system to the creation of new settings. A variety of alternative roles and services for psychologists exist in the health care setting, however. Tefft and Simeonsson view these in terms of combinations of such components as level and geographical location of intervention, as well as primary goals for planned interventions. It is clear that they perceive the greatest potential contributions in terms of goals focused on health maintenance that are achieved through community-oriented and nontraditional service modes.

Matarazzo (1980) also viewed the area of behavioral health as perhaps the most important area in which health psychologists are now making contributions. While others, including public-health-oriented physicians and nurses, allied health professionals, and health educators, may have a longer-standing interest in the area of prevention, the lack of focus on human behavior in these disciplines and the secondary emphasis on primary prevention as opposed to disease control, have limited their success. Psychologists, on the other hand, have the skills and knowledge to move into these areas and, indeed, they have begun to do so.

There currently are pressures from both consumers and health professionals to increase this emphasis on prevention and health maintenance, as opposed to the treatment of acute and chronic diseases. This altered direction for health services, however, requires a number of changes within individuals, society, and our health care systems and institutions. Individuals are seeking and are being expected to take more active responsibility for understanding their health, the risk factors related to disease, and the self-help approaches that are important for health maintenance. The social changes that also must take place involve broad-based attitude and policy changes that will allow recognition and support for health-promoting lifestyles and for coping with risk factors. There is pressure to reflect in health policies the perception of health care as a right rather than a privilege. Our health care systems and health professionals, on the other hand, are in the process of trying to adapt to the more informed client who may question prescribed treatment, who engages in self-care, and who holds health care providers accountable for the quality of services provided. These changes touch the lives of virtually everyone, and because they involve such a basic life issue—health—they are stressful and, therefore, more difficult to attain.

Psychologists functioning as skilled facilitators of personal and social change fit into this transformation of health care perspectives in a variety of ways. The individual therapist helping a client develop behavioral approaches for lifestyle changes is acting as a health psychologist. The evaluation consultant working with a public health agency to assess program impact is also involved in health psychology.

In functioning to bring about positive behavior changes that promote health, psychologists are employed in a wide variety of settings and with diverse job descriptions. They act as direct service providers, or as administrators and supervisors in service settings, including newer health settings such as health maintenance organizations and wellness clinics. They also serve as educators and consultants whose work includes extensive consultation to health systems, as well as teaching health professions students and providing continuing education. Finally, they are extensively involved as researchers in universities and other research organizations. There they are working to provide the necessary information about the relationship of human behavior to health and to evaluate applications of this information.

## Issues in Primary Prevention

Of greater interest than general, job-related descriptions of the work of health psychologists are the issues of prevention toward which this group is directing its efforts. For purposes of this presentation, consideration generally will be focused on those areas that truly represent *primary* prevention. By this is meant those activities aimed at reducing the rate of occurrence of medical disorders—or, preferably, increasing or prolonging the maintenance of health. There appear to be four categories of problems or issues related to

primary prevention in which psychologists have been, and continue to be, heavily involved. These are:

1. Identification of risk factors in health maintenance and development of educational and support services for reducing risks;
2. Adherence to health recommendations, such as lifestyle changes, avoidance of environmental contributors to illness, and so on;
3. Coping with threats to health, including stressors of everyday life;
4. Development and evaluation of effective systems for health care delivery, including program planning and quality assurance evaluation.

It is not within the scope of this chapter to document the state of knowledge and applications in each of these areas. The intention is rather to provide an introduction to the types of work in which health psychologists are involved. It should also be understood that the four areas listed here are not perceived as mutually exclusive. Instead, they are considered to be inextricably related—particularly when viewed from a community perspective. For example, providing optimal support services for individuals coping with health-threatening stresses would, in all likelihood, involve both the development of effective health delivery systems and consideration of methods for maximizing adherence to health recommendations. The four areas of effort outlined, therefore, are general and only relatively discrete categories of interest toward which various health psychologists are directing their energies. As such, they provide a general taxonomy of the issues and problems subsumed as health psychology. Each clearly merits a more detailed consideration, and each will be discussed in terms of community approaches to primary prevention.

### Risk Factors

The major action thrust of health psychology is probably occurring through the community-oriented health outreach efforts that are conducted as public health programs. Public health as a field of research and service has always been prevention-oriented. The efforts of this movement, however, have more often focused on the biological aspects of health than the psychosocial. They have also focused more on infectious disease than on some of the other chronic health problems that now appear to have strong social and behavioral correlates. There is still a tremendous need to develop complete information about this latter group of problems and the related risk factors. Beyond that, there is a need for well-developed primary prevention programs that deal directly with such risk factors.

Prevention of illness, whether we are concerned with diseases of the physical body or problems of living, cannot take place without some understanding of etiological factors involved in the disorder. Unfortunately, the status of knowledge about precipitating or triggering factors in many diseases is limited, even among health professionals. With respect to some prevalent diseases and to good health in general, however, considerable knowledge and some standard recommendations are available. A clear example of this is essential hypertension.

Hypertension is of greatest concern because of its relationship to cardiovascular disease. Hypertension itself does not produce alarming symptoms in its early stages. Diagnosis, unless accomplished through routine screening, usually occurs only after there has been irreversible damage to vital organs. Thus wide participation in screening programs is a major factor in prevention. Knowledge of the risk factors involved in hypertension, however, can determine the need for more or less frequent examinations. In essential hypertension there are both unavoidable risks and avoidable risks. The former include such factors as family history, age, and sex, while avoidable risks include cigarette smoking, overweight, high sodium intake and possibly high cholesterol intake, lack of regular exercise, and probably stress and Type A behaviors, such as hostility and time urgency. These avoidable risks, it is quite apparent, represent or reflect behavior or lifestyle variables.

While public health professionals have documented some of the social and demographic correlates of hypertension, preventive methods generally have focused on screening for active disorders and their treatment, rather than on avoidable risks and their prevention. The fact that recent epidemiological studies have found the prevalence of hypertension among children and adolescents to be higher than expected simply underscores the need for work in this area. We do not yet know enough about psychosocial risk factors in young people to be confident in prescribing some of the lifestyle changes that are recommended for adult hypertensives. And in the case of many of these risk factors, it is not at all clear whether the same standards should be used in assessing adults and children or adolescents.

One area in which psychologists are making substantial contributions to the understanding of risk factors in hypertension and cardiovascular disease is in the investigation of the Type A, or coronary-prone, behavior pattern (Jenkins, Rosenman, & Zyzanski, 1974). Described generally as hard-driving and competitive personalities who are impatient and highly results-oriented in their approach to life as well as to work,

Type A individuals have been shown to have almost double the risk for cardiovascular disease as that evidenced by their Type B counterparts, who demonstrate more relaxed behaviors and work styles. This 1.97 risk factor is that obtained after adjustments for four other factors: age, cholesterol, systolic blood pressure, and smoking (Rosenman, Brand, Sholtz, & Friedman, 1976). Work in this area has involved exploration of the Type A construct itself and research aimed at identifying and explaining the ways in which Type A behaviors are learned. A program of research initiated by Matthews (1977) has focused on assessing and investigating Type A behaviors in children and exploring their relationship to the onset of hypertension and cardiovascular disease.

Having documented the role of various risk factors, it remains to develop methods of reducing these risks. Again, health psychology has a major role to play. In the case of essential hypertension, as for many other health problems, risk reduction must involve effective targeting. This means that the "at risk" population must be made aware of risks and then must be offered acceptable approaches to dealing with these risk factors.

Looking just at the unavoidable risk factors, we know that hypertension is more prevalent among males than females, more prevalent among blacks than whites, and, according to at least some studies, more prevalent among lower than higher socioeconomic groups (Coates, Perry, Killen, & Slinkard, 1981). In each of these comparisons, the group at risk is the same one that makes less use of the physicians and the formal medical care system. This information alone suggests that effective risk reduction efforts may need to use nontraditional methods of reaching clients.

Another consideration in reaching the at risk population for any health problem is the level of intervention. In the case of hypertension, where there are moderate to strong intrafamilial correlations for virtually all known risk factors, it is obvious that some attention needs to be given to the family as well as the individual. When programs are directed at children or adolescents, special consideration of social learning and peer pressure mechanisms is needed. This issue has been of particular concern in the antismoking programs that have been developed for use in schools. It is becoming increasingly apparent that reaching the at-risk individual and changing his or her awareness of a health issue necessitates consideration of factors in the individual's environment. Community approaches to risk reduction are now being designated that utilize every avenue available to reach the population at risk. The landmark North Karelia study of a Finnish community with one of the world's highest rates of cardiovascular disease has produced promising reports of significantly improved behaviors and clinical symptomatology as the result of a multiple-intervention approach (McAlister, Puska, Salinen, Tuomilehto, & Koskelak, 1982).

The tailoring of programs to meet the needs of particular groups requires an understanding of the interactions between individuals and their environment. Where is health information generally acquired (if it is), and in what ways must the individual interact with the environment to obtain health information and act on it? What support is available for acting on this information, and how can it be mobilized? The beliefs and behaviors of an inner-city adolescent school dropout who smokes, consumes a high-cholesterol diet, and has a hypertensive parent probably cannot be altered in the same way as those of a middle-aged executive with exactly the same risk profile.

Every possible medium and setting, from the corporation to schools, churches, or informal street organizations, television, newspapers, and subway posters, may need to be considered in the development of programs to increase awareness of hypertension risks. Screening clinics are not attracting many who are at risk or already hypertensive. Many dentists now check blood pressure routinely in their offices. It is entirely feasible that others might also perform this service. Individuals not even associated with health care, such as schoolteachers, and perhaps social workers, could be trained to perform initial screening for hypertension.

An analysis of each social setting is required in order to identify the most productive routes for reaching the population at risk within that group. If there is truly a deficit in the area of prevention research in hypertension, I believe that it is this. The research funded during the 1970s under the National High Blood Pressure Education Program of the National Heart, Lung, and Blood Institute has increased in exponential terms what was known about communicating with and changing the behaviors of individuals who are hypertensive. Most of this research focused, however, on specific techniques for increasing patient compliance with medical regimens and, therefore, constituted prevention efforts at the secondary or tertiary level. Again, what we have not seen enough of are efforts to analyze and identify methods of communicating about hypertension with individuals at risk through use of the natural settings that are most likely to support desired responses.

The example of hypertension and its risks has been used here merely to provide a substantive focus. It is also a particularly compelling example because of its prevalence and direct relationship to cardiovascular disease, which is responsible for just over half of the deaths recorded annually in the United States. The twofold task of identifying psychosocial risk factors and maximizing use of this information through analysis of social and communication networks applies to virtually any health problem. Diabetes mellitus has its own set of risk factors and its own social epidemiology to which these approaches can be applied. Periodontal disease affects about two-thirds of the adult population and is responsible for most tooth loss in this group, yet the risk factors are known and the disease is preventable in virtually every case. Sports injuries, certain forms of cancer, diseases of addiction, and any number of other health problems have their own risk patterns as well.

While considerable work has been directed at identifying risk factors, there remains a need to confront the basic issues of human and physical environments and their effects on health. Risk factors need to be viewed in terms of the individual's ability to understand and avoid these risks. The lack of information, of intellectual or emotional ability, or of social support systems for dealing with health problems and their solutions should themselves be viewed as risk factors in the etiology of many diseases. It is these social and psychological variables particularly that require more attention from psychologists interested in primary prevention.

### Adherence to Health Recommendations

Psychological work in the area of adherence to health recommendations could be considered an extension or subset of the activities described in the previous section. This area, however, has become quite sharply focused and merits separate discussion. Recent reviews by Haynes, Taylor, and Sackett (1979), by Kirscht and Rosenstock (1979), and by Masur (1981) will provide a more detailed overview than can be presented here.

As these recent reviews clearly indicate, psychological research in the area of compliance with or adherence to medical recommendations has increased dramatically in the past ten or so years. This growth reflects an acute awareness on the part of health professionals of the pivotal role of patient behavior in treatment outcomes. Many physicians speculate that in the majority of cases for which treatment outcomes are not successful, this failure is due not to inadequate treatment regimens nor to severity of the disease itself, but rather to inadequate adherence to the prescribed treatment. A 1970 review of compliance research (Marston, 1970) reported a median of 43 percent noncompliance, based on 33 studies. In some cases, the percentage of patients not adhering to recommendations was as high as 92 percent. Masur (1981) points out that these data, viewed across various health problems and treatments, represent a pattern of noncompliance in about one-third of the patients studied. Such data do, indeed, seem to indicate that the failures of treatment regimens are more often behavioral than biological or pharmacological.

The phenomenon of noncompliance is perhaps more apparent in the case of chronic health problems such as diabetes mellitus, where adherence to prescribed medications and diet is essential to control of the disease (Johnson, 1980). The diabetic who does not rigidly adhere to medical recommendations will almost certainly, and usually quite quickly, experience symptoms. These may range from fatigue to coma and even death. Another vivid example of the adherence problem is that of the glaucoma patient (Norrell, 1980). In most cases, the successful control of glaucoma requires that the patient use eye drops several times daily. Adhering to this treatment schedule is difficult for many patients, however. The fact that the drops themselves cloud vision after use does not provide reinforcement for their proper application. This situation is further complicated because the disease usually involves a progressive but gradual loss of vision, beginning with loss at the periphery of the visual field. Glaucoma patients, therefore, may notice no loss of vision at all in the early stages of the disease. Failure to properly and consistently use the prescribed medication, however, can lead to progressive and irreversible loss of vision, with eventual blindness a possibility.

These examples of the adherence problem are offered to provide some concrete examples of the issues involved and the stakes. Any number of other examples could be provided—ranging from such diverse regimens as medication and exercise programs for hypertensive patients to strict oral hygiene requirements for patients with advanced periodontal disease.

The issues that can be considered primary prevention in the strictest sense, however, are those that deal with lifestyle changes for the prevention of disease *prior* to the occurrence of any symptoms. These would include avoiding or stopping smoking, regular exercise programs, weight control, limiting or avoiding the use of drugs and alcohol, stress management, avoidance of carcinogens, development of healthy eating habits and maintenance of good nutrition, daily brushing and flossing of the teeth, practice of contraception, prenatal care, participation in a broad range of hygiene issues, disease-screening programs, obtaining rec-

ommended immunizations, and the general maintenance of a healthy lifestyle. Programs to promote the behaviors involved in the primary prevention of disease are clearly more difficult to implement than those that deal with the control or elimination of symptoms that are already present. In primary prevention, we are dealing with efforts to change behaviors for which the only observable effects will be the preventive behaviors themselves. Since there are no symptoms, there will be no relief of symptoms. To many people, unfortunately, this is the equivalent of fixing something that isn't broken.

From a community psychology perspective, it is important to recognize that, in general, problems of adherence to health recommendations are not consistently related to either patient personality or social variables. A possible exception are findings suggesting that lower socioeconomic status is associated with dropping out of treatment for patients with chronic health problems (Baekeland & Lundwall, 1975). In the previous section it was noted that certain groups, including lower socioeconomic groups, tend to make less use of health services than others, and that this may occur even when treatment is provided free of cost (Rosenstock & Kirscht, 1979).

Obviously, it is important to recognize the need to target such groups and to plan especially for their needs in developing approaches to increasing adherence. There is also a great need to investigate the reasons that such groups fail to use services. It is possible that the answer to these questions may reside not in the patients themselves but in responses to the patient by health care providers or the health care system. For example, we know that patients are more likely to follow health recommendations when they understand the specific behaviors required (Becker, Drachman, & Kirscht, 1972; Kirscht & Rosenstock, 1979), but we do not know to what extent different types of patients are provided with this type of information.

Answering questions about quality of care and patient-provider interactions with respect to primary prevention is particularly difficult because, as has already been alluded to, it is not clear whose responsibility this is. The increasing use of health educators and others with psychosocial training may provide a partial answer, but there is no evidence that this alone is the ideal solution. Artz, Cooke, Meyers, and Stalgaitis (1981) reported on the use of community volunteers to conduct hypertension screening among apartment-complex residents. They found this method far more effective and less expensive than clinic screening programs. This type of project especially needs to be considered now, since dwindling resources for public health programs are already limiting screening and other primary prevention projects.

Rather than considering the community as both patient and provider in the way that Artz and her colleagues did, most of the compliance research has utilized traditional health service settings. Within this context, it has focused on initiating and sustaining behavior at the individual level and has relied on principles of human learning and behavior change. In addition to information exchange efforts, these approaches have included behavior modification techniques, modeling, persuasive communications and fear arousal methods, cognitive restructuring, and specific adaptations of these and other techniques. The criteria in such studies have included more objective measures such as pill counts, drug levels in the blood or urine, and biochemical assessments of dietary components, as well as relatively subjective measures such as self-reports and home monitoring or charting.

The results of this work will not be discussed in detail here, although the reader is referred to the reviews already cited for more information. Most of these motivational techniques have proved successful in one or more situations. It is obvious that across health problems and across some patient variables, however, there are tremendous problems in replicating results. These inconsistencies often are explained by researchers in terms of the complexity of the behaviors or health problems involved. For example, we know that the more health recommendations interfere with established life patterns or personal lifestyles, the less likely they are to be followed (Davis & Eichhorn, 1963; McAlister, Farquhar, Thoreson, & Maccoby, 1976). If it is assumed that this holds true for primary as well as secondary preventive behaviors, the influence that social and cultural environment can have on health maintenance is immediately apparent. Epidemiological studies are already showing differential cardiovascular and other disease rates across countries where diet, smoking, work, and leisure patterns differ. Even within a country, we can find vast differences on such factors as social support for health-promoting lifestyles.

The support of family and friends has been found to be related to adherence to medical regimens among those with chronic health problems. Green's work with hypertensives (Green, Levine, Wolle, & Deeds, 1979) and with asthma patients (Green, Werlin, Schauffler, & Avery, 1977) clearly reflects the possibility of mobilizing the influence of group pressures toward positive health behavior. But the problem of providing a supportive environment for modifying the lifestyles of entire populations of generally well people presents a much greater challenge. Research on compliance as an individual response to health recommendations usually assumes that a decision has been made to obtain treatment. This assumption cannot be made with respect to general health recommendations of the primary prevention type, or "class regimens," as Gibson (1979) has called them. We know that health-maintaining regimens do become accepted and gain acceptance within entire groups of people, but there has been very little investigation of how this occurs.

Kelly (1979) has suggested that the communications media can contribute to work in this area, yet he reports that a well-designed study of the effects of television commercials aimed at increasing the use of seat belts in automobiles showed no results. Green (1979), on the other hand, has described a more complex approach to community primary prevention. It involves the coordination of efforts used in schools, clinics, pharmacies, and workplaces, and combinations of approaches using verbal, print, and visual media. He suggests that such efforts need to be directed at health and human service providers, as well as at individuals and communities at large. Furthermore, attention needs to be given to repetition of health messages and other mechanisms for supporting change once the initial linkage has been made. Such efforts clearly will require an analytic approach, not only to the health and adherence issues involved, but also to the features of the social and health care systems within which primary prevention programs will be implemented.

### Stress and Coping

Hans Selye (1956) was one of the first to both articulate and explain a relationship between stress and disease. He suggested that any noxious stimulus could result in a General Adaptation Syndrome, characterized by increased pituitary-adrenal cortical hormone secretions. This phenomenon produces extreme physiological reactions and lowered resistance that, if prolonged, can be expected to lead to disease.

Others have used a similar model, but without the biological constructs, to explain how stressful life events may lead to illness. In general, research on stressful life events has suggested that positive life events, as well as negative ones, can lead to illness. Rahe and his colleagues (Holmes & Rahe, 1967; Rahe, 1972; Rahe & Arthur, 1978) made this assumption in developing their Schedule of Recent Experiences (SRE), which is designed to survey life change events occurring within a two-year period. These events were weighted for the level of adjustment required, with weights based on normative assessments.

The investigators found that the sums of these weighted scores could be used to predict the occurrence of illness.

The life change approach has been widely investigated and refined somewhat (e.g., Dohrenwend & Dohrenwend, 1974; Holmes & Masuda, 1974; Horowitz, Schaefer, Hiroto, Wilner, & Levin, 1977). A major departure from the original approach has been the consideration of moderating variables that function along with life change events to predict health and illness. These variables include a wide array, such as hereditary factors, coping styles, formal and informal support systems, and the individual's subjective evaluation of the stressful nature of the event. This last factor has been discussed at length by Antonovsky (1979), a sociologist who takes the position that all of us live with stress throughout our lives. He believes that interpretations of the severity of stress induced by a single event will vary, but that it is the ease with which various people cope, not the objective amount or the perception of stress, that determines adaptation. Some will disagree with Antonovsky's view, but few deny that similar events are responded to differently by various individuals.

A recent development in the general area of stress and health has been the thesis advanced by Kanner, Coyne, Schaefer, and Lazarus (1981) that relatively minor events are better predictors of psychological symptoms than are events reflecting major changes in an individual's life. Their data indicate that, indeed, chronic daily hassles appear to account for the same symptoms that can be predicted by major life events and also for additional factors that are predicted independently. It remains to relate these predictors to physical symptoms or to identify variables that mediate this relationship. Nevertheless, this line of research suggests strongly that we should look more closely at the quality of everyday life if we are to understand and prevent health problems. Some of the disease-specific work appears to be consistent with this view. An example is Jenkins's (1976) data suggesting that coronary heart disease is related to work overload and chronic conflict situations.

Recognizing a relationship between stressful life events, whether major or minor, one could take either of two approaches to primary prevention. There is the option of eliminating the source of stress, and there is the possibility of enhancing the individual's ability to cope with stress. Interestingly—though perhaps not surprisingly—psychologists have more often chosen the latter approach. Comparatively little work has focused on the reduction of life stress through attempts to enhance the environment.

Moos (1979) has described the development and major components of a social-ecological perspective on health and illness. His conceptual model suggests that physical and organizational variables, as well as personal and social variables, influence a person's appraisal of the total environment, and that this appraisal, in turn, influences level of arousal and coping efforts which largely determine health behaviors. The model is perceived as a dynamic one in which coping and health behaviors and health status feed back into the environmental system as components of the individual's experience. Moos also has categorized the variables within the environmental and personal systems that he discusses. The former include: (1) elements of the physical setting, including climate and architecture; (2) organizational factors within work, educational, institutional, or other settings; (3) the human aggregate, referring to the entire range of variables describing a given population; and (4) the social climate, which includes group attitudes, needs, and goals.

While a few specific environmental factors, such as population density and crowding (Dean, Pugh, & Gunderson, 1975; McCain, Cox, & Paulus, 1976) and environmental noise (Cohen, Evans, Krantz, & Stokols, 1980) have been investigated in terms of their direct relationship to health status measures, this area is relatively unexplored. There has been some work in the role of social support in relation to specific health problems, however. For example, Levy (1980) described positive results obtained in a number of studies using peer group or spouse support for weight reduction and blood pressure control. We do not yet know enough about the reasons for these results, however. Primary prevention issues, furthermore, have not been analyzed in terms of environmental presses in spite of the fact that, logically, it appears these factors could have an even stronger influence than when there is an experienced health problem toward which behavior changes are directed.

Issues related to environmental stress and coping responses are gaining increased attention from community psychologists, who are becoming interested in physical health outcomes as well as those reflected by social and psychological adjustment. In specific areas such as chemical pollution of the environment, there is a need for careful study of the social-psychological processes involved in efforts to prevent the development of health hazards, as well as for studies of their effects. Coping with environmental stress means planning for biological, physical, and social environments that enhance health-promoting lifestyles. This is an area in which traditional health professionals have not been fully active or fully cognizant and to which community and environmental psychologists have a great deal to offer.

### Health Care Delivery

Both consumer-interest movements directed at making health care institutions more responsive to patients and the emergence of behavioral medicine and health psychology as distinct disciplines dealing with psychosocial aspects of health have been responsible for some of the recent innovations in health service delivery. Most medical as well as dental, nursing, pharmacy, and health-related professions' schools now provide at least some instruction in communicating with patients (Kahn, Cohen, & Jason, 1979). Courses in patient motivation and other psychosocial topics also are becoming more common. Many hospitals provide patients with a "bill of rights" describing what they are entitled to know and what they should expect from their health care. Large clinics sometimes appoint patient advocates to help troubleshoot as patients work their way through complex, highly specialized and departmentalized, and often confusing health care systems. There also has been an increasing focus on making health care more convenient, accessible, and cost-effective, particularly as a result of the Regional Medical Programs, Model Cities, and Comprehensive Health Planning and Public Health Services legislation begun in the 1960s. In primary prevention, too, there have been positive strides associated with these efforts. Nevertheless, our health care system has only begun to respond to the challenges of health promotion.

This chapter has already alluded to one of the major obstacles to the acceptance of primary prevention—that is, the fact that primary prevention programs have no clear outcomes in terms of symptom reduction. Primary prevention cannot be motivated by the desire to reduce symptoms because, by definition, symptoms do not exist. Many health care professionals, trained in a tradition where success means eliminating or reducing disease, have difficulty justifying time spent on keeping healthy people in that status. They also fear that patients are not willing to pay for prevention—as some are not.

For these reasons, primary prevention activities have been largely restricted to the public health sector and, more recently, to health maintenance organizations (HMOs). Many HMOs in operation today were begun under the 1972 legislation that provided seed money for building these prepaid health care organizations and that required them to provide a strong focus on preventive medicine. As a result, HMOs are typically in the forefront in terms of providing such preventive services as general health examinations and screening for specific diseases, as well as group programs aimed at weight control or smoking cessation. Where these organizations appear to experience more difficulty, however, is in providing ongoing support for a generally healthy lifestyle. Care tends to remain episodic—even preventive care. This is in part due to the medical model that still pervades virtually all health care and that is primarily treatment-oriented.

To some extent, it is for this same reason that public health departments and programs are more likely to emphasize immunizations than to promote regular exercise, more likely to provide prenatal care than education in planning nutritional meals. In addition, the programs emphasized by public health agencies tend to reflect that field's traditional concern with control of communicable diseases. The outcomes of this work, of course, can be measured within a relatively short time in terms of the reduced prevalence of those diseases.

Another major obstacle to the expansion of primary prevention efforts is that analysis of community primary prevention needs has generally been neglected. Yet any successful health program should be designed to meet the needs of those it serves. Community-oriented health psychologists have tremendous opportunities to influence health systems through activities related to needs assessment and planning. Once needs have been identified, programs should be developed that are both accessible *and* acceptable to the population they are intended to serve.

Gibson (1979) has described a sequence of organizational steps for insuring effective management of medical treatment involving compliance problems. These include detection, linkage, clinical evaluation, initiation of the regimen, compliance, and long-term follow-up and care. With respect to primary prevention, a similar model might involve most of these same steps, but in a different order and with a somewhat different emphasis.

Primary prevention appears to begin with linkage to a source of information and recommendations. The source need not be a health care agency per se, and in fact service utilization patterns suggest that formal service organizations may *not* be the best source for some socioeconomic groups (Rosenstock & Kirscht, 1979). Linkage should be followed by initiation of the preventive regimen and activities aimed at promoting compliance, with clinical evaluation that incorporates detection of risk factors as a part of the regimen. Long-term follow-up, in the case of primary prevention, will probably be most effective in the form of natural social and other environmental supports for maintenance of the regimen. In this model, then, the responsibilities of health care professionals and the service delivery system are primarily those of facilitating the involvement of clients in their own health maintenance.

The most important step in this system can probably be viewed as the linkage or contact with the primary prevention regimen. And again, this means that major emphasis needs to be placed on accessibility of the source. The literature on health care utilization contains a number of descriptions of barriers to care (e.g., Albino, 1980; Coe, 1978; Rosenstock & Kirscht, 1979), but in one form or another most take into account what can be descriptively labeled as practical, cognitive, and psychosocial obstacles (Albino, 1980). Practical barriers, of course, include all those factors such as location, cost, and time convenience of services that have the potential for making health services difficult to obtain. Cognitive barriers incorporate knowledge deficits that usually function as failures to motivate or enable the seeking of services, rather than as barriers per se. Thus if individuals or groups of people do not know that they are susceptible to a particular health problem, or that it is serious, or what they can do to avoid it, then they are unlikely to take action to prevent it. These factors have been described in terms of the health beliefs model (Becker & Maiman, 1975; Rosenstock, 1966, 1974). This model has been one of the most widely used for explaining when and why people take preventive actions relating to their health. Finally, psychosocial barriers include all those components of the health care system that communicate negatively to the client, that threaten rather than enhance his or her sense of self and belonging, or—as Tefft and Simeonsson (1979) would probably describe it—that hinder the creation of positive health settings.

Although this discussion of psychology's role in promoting effective health care services has focused on understanding and enhancing the individual's response to health care, psychologists are also involved at the organizational level with such issues as cost-effectiveness and the political processes related to provision of services. Expertise in applied research methodology and program evaluation skills are particularly in demand for consulting on a wide range of issues involving system change. We have just begun, for example, to obtain much needed data that allow comparison of service utilization and health outcomes between fee-for-service and prepaid models for medical care. A major issue in primary prevention programs, which are often treated as token efforts, lies in identifying the minimum level of resources that must be committed in order to effect change. The development of quality-assurance programs that provide meaningful

information to health care professionals about the effectiveness of services is another important area. Research aimed at the assessment of patient satisfaction with services represents a specific component of quality of care. This work also provides information for use in projects related to design facilities, including waiting rooms and specialized treatment areas, such as those used for kidney dialysis patients. With respect to primary prevention, the opportunities for psychologists are unlimited. The design and implementation of health education programs and the development of innovative approaches to providing support for compliance with these programs will require an understanding of human learning and motivation as they function in the health setting, as well as the ability to mobilize support networks for long-term maintenance of new health behaviors.

## Summary and Concluding Comments

In many respects the challenges of general health promotion are not greatly different from the challenges of primary prevention in mental health. The parallels are striking between what Price, Bader, and Ketterer (1980) have described as major conceptual issues for primary prevention in mental health and the important issues being identified by health psychologists.

Price et al. have described a basic problem with definition and measurement of primary prevention. Although they perceive these problems to be greater in mental health fields where "specific disease entities with known etiologies are the exception," the point has been made here that health psychologists share this difficulty. With a few exceptions, precisely defined etiologies and preventive regimens are also rare in the field of general physical health. Both fields also share the problem of measuring the absence of symptoms in a way that allows attribution of causality to preventive efforts. Similarly, in describing a health psychology approach to health promotion and maintenance, I have also discussed the interest in social and environmental variables as precipitating factors in disease experience. This orientation, along with the new interest in everyday stressors as well as major life changes, reflects the same shift in attention from "high risk populations" to "high risk situations" that Price et al. described. Finally, health psychologists face the same demand as do their colleagues in mental health settings to demonstrate that the activities or behaviors they promote do, in fact, have preventive effects.

This chapter has already described a number of substantive issues for which the interests of psychologists in health and mental health settings overlap. The area of life stresses represents just one of these in which it would be difficult to separate mental health from overall health concerns. In such areas there will no doubt continue to be both direct and indirect collaboration.

There are two areas in which I believe that there should be far more exchange between psychologists working in health settings and those involved in mental health. The first of these is the general issue of community-focused applications for primary prevention efforts. Because health psychology developed from *within* the medical and health care professions, it has had some difficulty in moving away from the individual patient treatment mode. While the community orientation is also relatively new within the discipline of psychology as a whole, there are models available and paradigms that will allow productive thinking about health promotion at the community level.

Health psychology has been a successful movement in part because the traditional health professions recognized that many of their treatment problems are not biological, but behavioral, in origin. The four areas of effort described in this chapter (risk factors, adherence, stress, and health delivery systems) have been recognized by the health professions as areas in which behavioral scientists have primary expertise. I think it will become equally clear to those of us involved in this work, as well as to the other health professions, that the area of health promotion belongs to psychologists with a community orientation. In the final analysis, our efforts to identify and educate people about risk factors or to induce adherence to recommended health regimen will not succeed if the structures to support and maintain them are not in place. This means building social and environmental support, as well as competence within individuals. Changes required in our delivery systems as we approach new perceptions of health care can only be brought about by informed and thorough analysis of all the needs and demands those institutions serve. Again, these are areas in which community-oriented psychologists are especially well qualified.

The second general issue that I believe will be best served through the collaboration of psychologists in varied settings is the fundamental question of values. There must be some concern with values and the extent to which they can and should influence our work and our approaches to problems of health. This question is particularly potent with respect to primary prevention or health promotion, because we are suggesting major changes in the way that people live their lives and the responsibilities that they will take in doing so. Particularly when we are working without adequate data on the effectiveness of some of these

efforts, it behooves us to take a cautious approach to promoting what we only *believe* will be desirable and worthwhile for someone else. This basic issue with all its ramifications has not been fully explored either by health psychologists or by their colleagues working toward improving quality of life with respect to mental health issues. An interesting aspect of this question, however, is that psychologists in health promotion often are not forced to examine the issue when acting as psychologists within the medical system. Medically oriented health care has a tradition of values that generally are perceived as unquestionable. This creates a temptation to hide behind the cloak of medicine and thus ignore our responsibility to prove ourselves and our approaches. Such a situation makes the issue of values that much more critical.

In concluding, it is perhaps worth stating that while health care professionals and much of the public as well have identified a need for efforts focused on prevention and enhancing health, and while "psychology" has been prescribed to treat this need, the prognosis remains unclear. Only if we are willing to rise to complex challenges in an area where still too little is known, and only if we do this by maintaining a scientific approach to problems that require, above all, humanitarian concern—only then can psychology as a discipline make significant contributions to the basic and very important issue of health maintenance and to the development of health-promoting environments and communities.

# References

Albino, J. E. Motivating underserved groups to use community dental services. In S. L. Silberman, A. F. Tryon, & A. F. Gardner (Eds.), *Community dentistry: A problem-oriented approach*. Littleton, Mass.: PSG Publishing, 1980.

Antonovsky, A. *Health, stress, and coping*. San Francisco: Jossey-Bass, 1979.

APA Division 38. *The Health Psychologist*, 1981, **3**(2), 6.

Artz, L., Cooke, C. J., Meyers, A., & Stalgaitis, S. Community change agents and health interventions: Hypertension screening. *American Journal of Community Psychology*, 1981, **9**(3), 361–370.

Baekeland, F., & Lundwall, L. Dropping out of treatment: A critical review. *Psychological Bulletin*, 1975, **82**, 738–783.

Becker, M. H., Drachman, R. H., & Kirscht, J. P. Motivation as predictors of health behavior. *Health Services Reports*, 1972, **87**, 852–862.

Becker, M. H., & Maiman, L. A. Sociobehavioral determinants of compliance with health and medical care recommendations. *Medical Care*, 1975, **13**, 10–24.

Coates, T. J., Perry, C., Killen, J., & Slinkard, L. A. Primary prevention of cardiovascular disease in children and adolescents. In C. K. Prokop & L. A. Bradley (Eds.), *Medical psychology*. New York: Academic Press, 1981.

Coe, R. M. Notes on the politics of health care delivery. In R. M. Coe (Ed.), *Sociology of medicine*. New York: McGraw-Hill, 1978.

Cohen, S., Evans, G. W., Krantz, D. S., & Stokols, D. Physiological, motivational, and cognitive effects of aircraft noise on children: Moving from the laboratory to the field. *American Psychologist*, 1980, **35**, 231–243.

Davis, M. S., & Eichhorn, R. Compliance with medical regimens: A panel study. *Journal of Health and Human Behavior*, 1963, **4**, 240–249.

Dean, L., Pugh, W., & Gunderson, E. Spatial and perceptual components of crowding effects on health and satisfaction. *Environment and Behavior*, 1975, **7**, 225–236.

Dohrenwend, B. S., & Dohrenwend, B. P. (Eds.), *Stressful life events: Their nature and effects*. New York: Wiley, 1974.

Gibson, E. S. Compliance and the organization of health services. In R. B. Haynes, D. W. Taylor, & W. L. Sackett (Eds.), *Compliance in health care*. Baltimore: Johns Hopkins University Press, 1979.

Green, L. W. Educational strategies to improve compliance with therapeutic and preventive regimens: The recent evidence. In R. B. Haynes, D. W. Taylor, & D. L. Sackett (Eds.), *Compliance in health care*. Baltimore: Johns Hopkins University Press, 1979.

Green, L. W., Levine, M. D., Wolle, J., & Deeds, S. Development of randomized patient education experiments with urban poor hypertensives. *Patient Counseling and Health Education*, 1979, **1**, 106–111.

Green, L. W., Werlin, S. H., Schauffler, H. H., & Avery, C. H. Research and demonstration issues in self-care: Measuring the decline of medicocentrisin. *Health Education Monographs*, 1977, **5**, 161–189.

Haynes, R. B., Taylor, D. W., & Sackett, D. L. (Eds.), *Compliance in health care*. Baltimore: Johns Hopkins University Press, 1979.

Holmes, T. H., & Masuda, M. Life change and illness susceptibility. In B. S. Dohrenwend & B. P. Dohrenwend (Eds.), *Stressful life events: Their nature and effects*. New York: Wiley, 1974.

Holmes, T. H., & Rahe, R. H. The Social Readjustment Rating Scale. *Journal of Psychosomatic Research*, 1967, **11**, 213–218.

Horowitz, M. J., Schaefer, C., Hiroto, D., Wilner, N., & Levin, B. Life event questionnaires for measuring presumptive stress. *Psychosomatic Medicine*, 1977, **39**, 413–431.

Jenkins, C. D. Recent evidence supporting psychologic and social risk factors for coronary disease. *New England Journal of Medicine*, 1976, **294**, 987–994.

Jenkins, C. D., Rosenman, R. H., & Zyzanski, S. J. Prediction of clinical coronary heart disease by a test for the coronary-prone behavior pattern. *New England Journal of Medicine*, 1974, **290**, 1271–1275.

Johnson, S. B. Psychosocial factors in juvenile diabetes. *Journal of Behavioral Medicine*, 1980, **3**, 95–116.

Kahn, G., Cohen, B., & Jason, H. The teaching of interpersonal skills in the United States medical schools. *Journal of Medical Education*, 1979, **54**, 29–35.

Kanner, A. D., Coyne, J. C., Schaefer, C., & Lazarus, R. S. Comparison of two modes of stress measurement: Daily hassles and uplifts versus major life events. *Journal of Behavioral Medicine*, 1981, **4**(1), 1–39.

Kelly, A. B. A media role for public health compliance? In R. B. Haynes, D. W. Taylor, & D. L. Sackett (Eds.), *Compliance in health care*. Baltimore: Johns Hopkins University Press, 1979.

Kirscht, J. P., & Rosenstock, I. M. Patients' problems in following recommendations of health experts. In G. C. Stone, F. Cohen, & N. E. Adler (Eds.), *Health psychology*. San Francisco: Jossey-Bass, 1979.

Levy, R. L. The role of social support in patient compliance: A selective review. In R. B. Haynes, M. E. Mattson, & T. O. Engebretson (Eds.), *Patient compliance to prescribed antihypertensive medication regimens: A report to the National, Heart, Lung, and Blood Institute*. NIH Publication No. 81-2102. Bethesda, Md.: U.S. Dept. of Health and Human Services, 1980.

Marston, W. V. Compliance with medical regimens: A review of the literature. *Nursing Research*, 1970, **19**, 312–323.

Masur, F. T. Adherence to health care regimens. In C. K. Prokop & L. A. Bradley (Eds.), *Medical psychology*. New York: Academic Press, 1981.

Matarazzo, J. D. Behavioral health and behavioral medicine: Frontiers for a new health psychology. *American Psychologist*, 1980, **35**, 807–817.

Matthews, K. Caregiver-child interactions and the Type A coronary-prone behavior pattern. *Child Development*, 1977, **48**, 1752–1756.

McAlister, A. L., Farquhar, J. W., Thoreson, C. E., & Maccoby, N. Behavioral science applied to cardiovascular health: Progress and research needs in the modification of risk-taking habits in adult populations. *Health Education Monographs*, 1976, **4**, 45–74.

McAlister, A., Puska, P., Salinen, J., Tuomilehto, J., & Koskelak. Theory and action for health promotion: Illustrations from the North Karelia Project. *American Journal of Public Health*, 1982, **72**, 43–50.

McCain, G., Cox, V., & Paulus, P. The relationship between illness complaints and degree of crowding in prison environments. *Environment and Behavior*, 1976, **8**, 283–290.

Moos, R. H. Social-ecological perspectives on health. In G. C. Stone, F. Cohen, & N. E. Adler (Eds.), *Health psychology*. San Francisco: Jossey-Bass, 1979.

Norrell, S. Medication behavior: A study of outpatients treated with pilocarpine eye drops for primary open-angle glaucoma. *Acta Opthalmologica*, 1980, Supplement 143.

Price, R. H., Bader, B. C., & Ketterer, R. F. Prevention in community mental health: The state of the art. In R. H. Price, R. F. Ketterer, B. Bader, & J. Monahan (Eds.), *Prevention in mental health: Research, policy, and practice*. Beverly Hills: Sage, 1980.

Rahe, R. H. Subjects' recent life changes and their near-future illness susceptibility. *Advances in Psychosomatic Medicine*, 1972, **8**, 2–19.

Rahe, R. H., & Arthur, R. H. Life change and illness studies. *Journal of Human Stress*, 1978, **4**(1), 3–15.

Rosenman, R. H., Brand, R. J., Sholtz, R. I., & Friedman, M. Multivariate predictions of coronary heart disease during 8.5 year follow-up in the Western Collaborative Group Study. *American Journal of Cardiology*, 1976, **37**, 902–910.

Rosenstock, I. M. Why people use health services. *Milbank Memorial Fund Quarterly*, 1966, **44**, 94–127.

Rosenstock, I. M. The health belief model and preventive health behavior. *Health Education Monographs*, 1974, **2**, 27–36.

Rosenstock, I. M., & Kirscht, J. P. Why people seek health care. In G. C. Stone, F. Cohen, & N. E. Adler (Eds.), *Health psychology*. San Francisco: Jossey-Bass, 1979.

Sarason, S. B. *The creation of settings and the future societies*. San Fancisco: Jossey-Bass, 1972.

Selye, H. *The stress of life*. New York: McGraw-Hill, 1956.

Stone, G. C. Psychology and the health system. In G. C. Stone, F. Cohen, & N. E. Adler (Eds.), *Health psychology*. San Francisco: Jossey-Bass, 1979.

Tefft, B. M., & Simeonsson, R. J. Psychology and the creation of health care settings. *Professional Psychology*, 1979, **10**, 4, 558–570.

# 14 PREVENTION AND INTERDISCIPLINARY PERSPECTIVES: A FRAMEWORK AND CASE ANALYSIS

N. Dickon Reppucci,
Edward P. Mulvey, and
Laura Kastner

Prevention has arrived in the parlor of mental health or, at the very least, is knocking at the front door. Inspired by advances in the prevention of physical disorders (e.g., Maccoby & Alexander, 1979) and fostered by a general shift toward interactionism in psychological theory (Goldfried, 1980; Mischel, 1977), mental health services have adopted prevention as an organizing principle (President's Commission, 1978). Since the Community Mental Health Act of 1963 and Caplan's (1964) adaptation of the public health concepts of primary, secondary, and tertiary prevention, a wide array of mental health services have been dubbed "preventive." Approaches as diverse as standard therapeutic treatment and social action have been considered under this same theoretical umbrella (Bloom, 1978; Cowen, 1977). Institutionalization is "prevented" by drug maintenance of patients in the community; crime is "prevented" by neighborhood watch programs; disruptive young children are "prevented" from having further school problems by tutoring programs.

To suppose that prevention is based on a solid set of theoretical principles and proven approaches would be an error. As Price, Bader, and Ketterer (1980) note, "the goal of prevention is now more broadly accepted

than ever. . . . However, the routes to that goal are far from clearly mapped [p. 10]." The general principle of prevention, short-circuiting the onset of disorders by early or global intervention, is difficult to argue against (President's Commission, 1978). On the other hand, the methods and theories of this approach are difficult to state clearly.

Fortunately, refinement of general prevention notions is presently occurring. Accounts of successful prevention efforts have been collected and critiqued (Monahan & Heller, 1977; Munoz, Snowden, & Kelly, 1979; President's Commission, 1978; Price, Ketterer, Bader, & Monahan, 1980; Rappaport, 1977), attempts at definitional boundaries for types of prevention have been offered (Albee & Joffe, 1977; Cowen, 1977, 1980, 1982; Forgays, 1978; Klein & Goldston, 1977), and spirited debate has begun about the overall value of a primary prevention approach (Albee, 1981; Eisenberg, 1975; Herbert, 1979; Lamb & Zusman, 1979; Rappaport, 1981). While summaries of this burgeoning literature can be found elsewhere in the present volume, the purpose of this chapter is to focus attention on the need for collaboration between psychology and other disciplines around prevention of social problems. In our opinion, multidisciplinary analysis and collaboration are necessary to mount effective prevention efforts.

Being primarily rooted in a public-health, epidemiological approach, the basic goal of prevention is not one of isolating the cure or ultimate solution of a problem, but is instead one of reducing the population-wide incidence of a specific problem (Heller & Monahan, 1977). Unfortunately, epidemiological analysis does not adequately confront the issue of problem selection, so important in addressing social problems. The determination of what incidence level of a social problem is required to warrant attention and how that problem is best framed for consideration are areas of considerable political and personal, rather than theoretical, judgment (Caplan & Nelson, 1973; Seidman, 1978). Indicators of social problems (for example, underachievement of black children) are sources of extensive debate. Also, reliance on a multifactorial causation model (Price, 1974), although theoretically sound, creates a vast pool of potentially causative constructs. Thus even if the selection of the problem reflects wide consensus, there is no guarantee that the constructs examined in relation to it will show any consistency. Although somewhat facetious, Kessler and Albee's (1975) comment that everything from titanium paint to venereal disease can be considered relevant to primary prevention captures the inherent difficulty. Namely, the sorting out and refinement of constructs related to prevention is a massive undertaking.

Reliance on convergent constructs, findings, and methodologies from disciplines other than psychology can provide some guidance for this large task. An interdisciplinary approach would appear especially helpful in conceptualizing prevention programs aimed at maximizing the benefits of a setting or altering social roles. Anthropological and sociological constructs regarding resource exchange, for instance, could provide frameworks for thinking about the potentials of social networks for distribution of resources or dissemination of information. Anthropological field methods could direct some of the early descriptive research necessary to formulate more specific prevention research designs (Rappaport, 1979). Similarly, knowledge and consideration of economic theory, aggregate data techniques, and urban development trends may help in regional planning with social benefits as a realizable goal (Catalano & Dooley, 1980; Catalano & Monahan, 1975). Obviously, a number of uses can be made of interdisciplinary knowledge in organizing and researching prevention strategies.

As a method of highlighting the necessity for interdisciplinary collaboration, we have chosen to examine a particular problem—adolescent pregnancy—

from multiple perspectives. The goal is to discuss social, economic, political, moral, psychological, and theoretical considerations that should be taken into account in order to begin to understand the issue in its ecological complexity. As Caplan and Nelson (1973) so convincingly demonstrate, disciplinary perspectives yield disciplinary solutions, which are usually narrow in scope and inadequate in conceptualization. One caution: by advocating an inter- or multidisciplinary approach to social problems, we are not naively suggesting that solutions will be readily apparent. Rather, we are suggesting that most social problems demand diverse perspectives in order to resist the tendency to adopt simplistic solutions to inherently complex issues. Moreover, once an issue, such as teenage pregnancy, becomes labeled a social problem, it inevitably becomes linked with public policy. This fact implies that any solutions will then be based on compromise regarding values and political constituencies as much as on scientific findings from any discipline. Thus the potential for multidisciplinary collaboration is critical for problem definition, solution generation, and program implementation.

## Adolescent Pregnancy

Adolescent pregnancy in the United States has been described as an "epidemic" since publication of the widely publicized the Alan Guttmacher Institute's *Eleven million teenagers: What can be done about the epidemic of adolescent pregnancies in the United States* (1976). Unfortunately, the word "epidemic" connotes a contagious disease plaguing teenage America. It is questionable whether this is an accurate or helpful metaphor. The institute's report did not state what the increase in pregnancy rate was, only that "each year, more than one million 15–19 year olds became pregnant [p. 10]." Obviously, each of these pregnancies did not result in a live birth, and a fuller understanding of teenage pregnancy can only be obtained by consideration of the rates of births, abortions, and miscarriages in the female population as a whole.

Contrary to a common impression, the overall rates of childbearing among teenagers actually decreased from the mid-1950s to the mid-1970s, from a high of 97.3 births per 1,000 females aged 15–19 in 1957 to 58.7 in 1974 (Baldwin, 1976). In 1976 the birthrate fell to 53.5, and projections for the 1980s estimate a continued decline in teenage fertility rates (Stickle & Ma, 1975). Although the total number of births among teenagers changed very little from 1960 to 1974 (609,000 and 608,000, respectively), the population of female teenagers had grown. Because childbearing rates among older women have declined, teenagers have been contributing a greater proportion of births to the national birthrate, increasing from 14 percent of the total rate in 1960 to 19 percent in 1974 (Baldwin, 1976). In addition, the level of premarital pregnancy among teenagers almost doubled between 1971 and 1979, increasing from 9 to 16 percent (Zelnik & Kantner, 1980). Abortion rates among this group also increased (Zelnik & Kantner, 1980). These are just a few of the reasons why adolescent fertility has been identified as a problem despite the decline in childbearing rates for this age group.

While use of the term "epidemic" has succeeded in alerting many to the prevalence of adolescent pregnancy, it is a misleading representation. This framing of the issues fails to recognize the *Zeitgeist* of social, political, economic, psychological, and moral forces connected with adolescent pregnancy. One of the consequences of this narrow focus on the so-called epidemic has been that efforts to prevent adolescent pregnancy have also been narrowly conceived. The two primary prevention approaches have been increasing dissemination of information through sex education and increasing access to contraceptive services among adolescents through the expansion, both in number and size, of family planning clinics. The limited impact of these strategies suggests that this oversimplified approach to problem definition and prevention requires rethinking.

### Medical and Social Costs to Adolescent Parents and Their Children

The least controversial reason for identifying adolescent pregnancy as a problem relates to the medical dangers for both the baby and mother. Compared to older mothers, adolescents have a greater number of obstetrical complications (Ballard & Gold, 1971; Stepto, Keith, & Keith, 1975), and their babies have higher risk of prematurity, prenatal mortality, anemia, toxemia, congenital defects, and mental and physical handicaps (Menken, 1975). Although these risks may be minimal if adolescents receive adequate prenatal care (Baldwin & Cain, 1980), the fact remains that they are less likely to receive the needed care.

Considerable attention also has been given to the negative social, educational, and vocational "consequences" of early childbearing on the lives of adolescent parents (Card & Wise, 1978; Moore, 1978; Trussell, 1976). Perhaps the most convincing evidence comes from Furstenberg's (1976) comprehensive study comparing 331 adolescent mothers, mainly low-income urban blacks, with matched, nonpregnant classmates over a five-year period. Adolescent mothers had greater problems with marriages, education, em-

ployment, and financial support. Other extreme circumstances that have been related to adolescent childbearing are child behavior problems (Oppel & Royston, 1971), child abuse (Gelles, 1973), and suicide among the young mothers (Braen, 1971; Gabrielson, Klerman, Curie, Tyler & Jekel, 1970).

The results from studies examining the social consequences of adolescent pregnancy suggest that negative life circumstances are direct "consequences" or "effects" of adolescent pregnancy. However, experimental designs or well-controlled prospective studies that would allow causal interpretations are sparse. The erroneous tendency to draw causal conclusions when a pregnancy coexists with other problems in an adolescent's life seems to preclude a full appreciation of the number of sociocultural and psychological factors which could actually be responsible for both the pregnancy and the myriad other observed problems. Prevention efforts usually make assumptions about the direction and strength of effects, but in this case the exact nature of these relationships is open to speculation.

Existing literature has discussed adolescent pregnancy as an adaptation to the culture of poverty (Cutwright, 1971; Connally, 1975; Presser, 1974). For disadvantaged adolescents who are lacking in educational resources, vocational opportunities, and alternative models to young motherhood, pregnancy can be an attractive goal. Adolescents have reported several positive incentives for having a baby: payments from Aid to Families with Dependent Children (AFDC); an excuse for leaving home; increased status in certain peer groups; a chance to have "something" of one's very own; a chance to be loved and have someone to love; coercion of a boyfriend into marriage; and an escape from boredom. Almost one-third of adolescent premarital pregnancies are estimated to be intended (Zelnik & Kantner, 1978a), but the extent to which the motivations listed above create the intention is unknown.

Regardless of the degree to which adolescent pregnancy is a cause or symptom of the negative conditions in some young mothers' lives, there is considerable support for Campbell's (1968) widely quoted remark that the teenage mother has "90 percent of her life script written for her." The burdens of child care lead to less time and energy for the achievement of other goals. Because of the numerous medical, social, and economic disadvantages for adolescent parents and their children, objections to adolescent pregnancy have been voiced and supported. However, concentration on this aspect of the problem has been only one reason for societal opposition—and probably the least controversial and easiest to identify.

## Economic Costs to Society

The staggering economic cost of adolescent pregnancy is another key factor that has moved the government to recognize this area as a major social problem. The Stanford Research Institute (1979) estimated that adolescent pregnancies cost American taxpayers about $8.3 billion a year in welfare and related outlays. This estimate included all cash support payments, food stamps, support services, free medical services, and related welfare outlays by the federal, state, and local governments to households containing teenaged mothers or women who first became pregnant in their teens. The calculated long-term welfare costs for females having their first child as a teenager in 1979 would amount to about $7.1 billion, with medical care adding the remaining $1.2 billion to the bill.

The Alan Guttmacher Institute (1976) describes how economic concerns are involved in almost every aspect of the social problem—for the adolescents themselves as well as the taxpayers who finance the costly programs needed to support them. Seventy-five percent of the mothers age 17 and younger have no health insurance. Only one-sixth of this group is covered for prenatal care, and less than one-fifth for hospital and medical bills. Also, it is unlikely that these mothers will be working. One study conducted in New York City found that 91 percent of women who first had babies when they were between the ages of 15 and 17 were unemployed 19 months after delivery (Presser, 1974). Moreover, using data from a national probability sample, Bacon (1974) found that pregnant adolescents were much more likely to be from families below the federal poverty line. One-third of the young mothers between the ages of 13 and 15 were from poverty situations, an incidence 2.6 times hgher than the women who had had their first babies after the age of 20. Young mothers at the ages of 16 and 17 were two times as likely to be poor, and 18- and 19-year-olds were 1.4 times as likely to fall into the poverty bracket.

Several researchers have noted that the increased drain of public funds to finance AFDC has accompanied escalating rates of childbirth among unmarried couples (Cutwright, 1971; Juhasz, 1974; Nye, 1977). Between 1961 and 1974, the rate of out-of-wedlock childbearing increased by about 33 percent among 18- to-19-year-olds and by 75 percent among 14-to-17-year-olds (Alan Guttmacher Institute, 1976). The Alan Guttmacher Institute reported that this increase resulted in teenagers accounting for more than half of all out-of-wedlock births in the U.S. What these data indicate is that although the actual increase in absolute numbers of childbirths is either illusory or minimal, the circumstances of childbearing by teenage youth have changed drastically. What happened in the past within the societal institution of marriage is now occurring without the marriage contract to condone it, and the economic costs to society have escalated concomitantly.

## Political and Moral Implications of Abortion

Abortion is one of the most volatile issues in American society. Negative societal attitudes about adolescent pregnancy are unavoidably entangled with sentiments regarding abortion. One-third of the 1.3 million abortions that occurred in 1978 were obtained by adolescents under 20 years of age (Forrest, Sullivan, & Tietze, 1979). Moreover, teenagers are the age group most likely to terminate their pregnancies by abortion (58 percent of pregnant girls under the age of 15 and 44 percent of those aged 15 to 18). While proabortion forces may perceive abortion as a positive alternative to unwanted and "premature" motherhood, opponents interpret these statistics as evidence that teenagers are the greatest abusers of this "unacceptable" procedure.

The abortion rate among adolescents increased by more than 75 percent between 1972, the year before the Supreme Court decision legalized abortions, and 1975, and the rate for those under 15 nearly doubled during this period (Alan Guttmacher Institute, 1976). Since the birthrate among adolescents was fairly stable and slightly declining over these years, the increased abortion rate evidently helped to limit the potential effects on the birthrate of the rising rates of adolescent pregnancy and sexual activity. Although improved contraceptive practices also helped to suppress the impact of wider sexual activity on the birthrate, abortion appears to be a common last resort for adolescents who choose not to deliver (Zelnick & Kantner, 1978b, 1980).

Although abortion has been interpreted as a prevention strategy, it is clearly not primary prevention since it occurs after a problem already exists. As an intervention, abortion succeeds in limiting a certain number of adolescent childbirths, but is a procedure which could be avoided if suitable precautions were taken to prevent its necessity. The practice of contraception represents such a preventive approach. However, while Zelnik and Kantner's (1980) most recent survey revealed that 34 percent of sexually active adolescents in 1979 used contraceptives consistently (an improvement over the 29 percent rate in 1976), it also noted a decline in the use of the most effective medical methods—the pill and the

IUD—with a concurrent rise in the use of the least effective methods, especially withdrawal. Paralleling this change was a reported increase in the abortion rate by unmarried teenagers from 33 percent in 1976 to 37 percent in 1979.

The subject of abortion has a long history of acrimonious debate among politicians and citizens alike. The anti-abortion movement, representing a passionate force of opposition to the practice at large, contributes some of the more emotional arguments of preventing pregnancy among adolescents. Their moral opposition to abortion is total. They view it as a "planned assault on life, a murder without extenuating circumstances [Hacker, 1979, p. 16]." Incensed by the 1973 Roe v. Wade Supreme Court decision,* their major political victory has been congressional passage of the Hyde Amendment in 1976. This amendment prohibits federal funding of abortions unless childbirth risked the mother's life or one of the subsequently added (1977 and 1978) congressional conditions of promptly reported rape or incest (Trussell, Menken, Lindheim, & Vaughn, 1980).** Unfortunately, many who endorse the "right to life" principle often view sexual abstinence rather than contraception as the answer to the teenage pregnancy problem. However, to many this goal seems unrealistic, and perhaps even counterproductive. Like the attempts to control the "vice" of alcoholic indulgence through Prohibition, efforts to encourage abstinence or sexual inhibition would seem to have little likelihood of decreasing sexual activity rates.

## Morality and Adolescent Sexuality

The moral dilemmas involved in the adolescent abortion issue are intimately tied to those which plague the broader area of adolescent sexuality itself. Although effective contraception techniques exist, it is unlikely that they will be promoted maximally through government action. Recognition of adolescent sexuality, in its own way, is almost as volatile a moral and

political issue as abortion. Witness the frequent controversies over the teaching of sex education in the schools. Yet the psychological acceptance of one's own sexuality is an essential precursor to adolescent contraceptive use (Byrne, 1977; Cvetkovich, 1980; Cvetkovich, Grote, Bjorseth, & Sarkissian, 1975; Fox, 1977; Fox & Inazu, 1980; Goldsmith, Gabrielson, Gabrielson, Mathews, & Potts, 1972; Lindemann, 1974; Mitchell, 1972; Needle, 1977; Reiss, Banwart, & Foreman, 1975; Sandberg & Jacobs, 1971; Wagner, Perthou, Fujita, & Pion, 1969).

The process of acquiring a sexual identity requires that the teenager rationally accept the reality of whatever sexual activity she or he may have engaged in, so that contraceptive needs can be faced when sexual intercourse occurs. Unfortunately, the realistic definition of oneself as a sexual person, who could get pregnant or cause a pregnancy, usually follows a period of coital activity. Therefore, acquiring and using contraceptives almost always follows a period of unprotected intercourse. This phenomenon helps explain why half of the premarital pregnancies among teenagers occur in the first six months of coital activity (Zabin, Kantner, & Zelnik, 1979). Although this implies that preventive programs need to precede sexual activity for young teenagers, it also suggests that the paradoxical situation may occur where efforts to prepare adolescents for their contraceptive needs by encouraging the acceptance of their sexuality may contradict efforts to encourage sexual abstinence. Prevention efforts rooted in awareness of psychological processes could be directly at odds with moral concerns.

Researchers who examine the developmental aspects of sexual identity (e.g., Cvetkovich, 1980; Fox, 1977) have described how adolescents internalize our societal moral values during socialization to the extent that guilt or at least mixed emotional reactions accompany the initiation of sexual intercourse, especially for females. Guilt often interferes with the rational acceptance of the fact that sexual intercourse has occurred, preventing adequate contraceptive planning. Using this conceptualization, prevention programs might be developed to help adolescents accept their sexuality. However, fear exists that such programs may communicate approval of sexual activity; this has therefore led to strong opposition. From this perspective, it can be argued that moral conflicts at the societal level restrict preventive interventions to resolve the moral conflicts among the adolescents themselves, and this may be partly responsible for contraceptive nonuse and adolescent pregnancy.

Keeping sexual education within the province of the family is one alternative, but most parents have difficulty discussing sexuality with their teenagers.

---

* Roe v. Wade, 410 U.S. 113, 93 S. CT. 705, 35 L. Ed. 2d 147 (1973).

** The Alan Guttmacher Institute (1979) reported that Medicaid abortions dropped from 295,000 to 2,000 the year after the amendment went into effect. Thus the amendment had a major impact. However, several states still accept the full cost of abortions among low-income women, so the actual reduction in the number of abortions was closer to 35 percent. It should also be noted that shift toward more restrictive abortion policies, such as the Hyde Amendment, reflects an increasingly conservative congressional membership rather than any broad change in public attitudes toward abortion (Trangott & Vinoviskis, 1980).

One expressed reason is that they will appear to be encouraging sexual activity. In the only empirical study regarding this matter, Kastner (1979) had 237 females (ages 15–19) complete an extensive questionnaire regarding all aspects of sexuality and contraceptive use. Of this group, 130 had experienced sexual intercourse and 107 had not. Within each of these two groups there were girls who had received information about sexuality and contraceptive use from their mothers. There were no statistically significant differences that indicated an increase in sexual activity as a result of this increased communication and information. However, the data strongly suggested that those girls who were sexually active, had openly discussed sex with their mothers, and had had it treated as a healthy and normal part of life, were more likely to use contraceptives. These data would suggest that a causal link between increased sexual activity and both open discussion of sexuality and the provision of contraceptive information may be more myth than reality.

Although acceptance of sexuality is only one of several possible precursors of contraceptive use (Luker, 1975), it is probably one of the least addressed areas in prevention models. Recommended goals, such as increasing the dissemination of information and access to contraceptive services, despite their limited utility, are obviously not as threatening or abstract as a focus on acceptance of sexuality. Moral objections to adolescent sexual activity constitute the most sensitive core of the societal outrage about adolescent pregnancy. Adolescent sexuality commonly evokes such uncomfortable and confusing feelings that both professionals and parents can lapse into what Monsour and Stewart (1973) called a "conspiracy of silence." Discomfort and various personal inhibitions may often render adults unprepared and unwilling to discuss human sexuality openly. Educational curricula focused on such concerns as adolescent pregnancy, abortion, and contraception conceal or avoid discussion of the behavior which makes these topics relevant in the first place—sexual intercourse.

The increasing prevalence of premarital coital experience among adolescents was documented in the 1960s (Chilman, 1968). Fears that the trend would continue into the 1970s were confirmed by Zelnik and Kantner's (1978a) extensive survey research conducted in 1971 and 1976. The 27 percent rate of coital experience found among 15-to-19-year-old females in the 1971 survey increased to a 35 percent rate in the 1976 survey. In their 1979 survey update Zelnik and Kantner (1980) suggest that 50 percent of 15-to-19-year-old women residing in metropolitan areas of the United States have engaged in premarital in-

tercourse. For this population, this represents an increase from 30 percent in 1971 and 43 percent in 1976. It should also be noted that virtually all of the growth in coitus between 1976 and 1979 is accounted for by increased sexual activity among never-married whites.

Consensus among parents and teenagers is that contraceptive information is a worthwhile approach to prevention (Yankelovich, Skelly, & White, 1979), but there is much greater opposition to specific target areas such as improving attitudes toward contraception or encouraging the acceptance of sexuality. The hypothesis that these areas may help teenagers initiate contraceptive use with advent of sexual activity is difficult to test when society's priority lies in preventing sexual activity rather than preventing pregnancy. Since more than half of our adolescent females are sexually active by the time they finish their teenage years, as are 70 percent of adolescent males (Zelnik & Kantner, 1980), perhaps we should question the utility and rationality of this goal. One way our society has traditionally attempted to keep teenage girls chaste is through the guilt-inducing tactic of the "nice girl construct," which dictates that "nice girls don't have sex" (Fox, 1977). How can we expect this guilt not to prohibit contraception also, when contraceptives are concrete evidence of sexual activity? Fox suggested that the reverse seems to be more often the case: that guilt does not prevent sexual intercourse but instead discourages contraception because it represents a double deviance—sexual intercourse with premeditation.

It is plausible that adolescent pregnancy has not been approached rationally at the societal level because of moral and emotional conflicts about sexuality which occur across the life span. Although governmental funds have been appropriated for services to already pregnant teenagers, funds are needed for comprehensive prospective studies, pilot demonstration projects, and innovative educational programs. Since research of this nature would involve teenagers not yet sexually active, it would inherently run the anticipated risk of stimulating sexual activity. Hence, regardless of its potential effects in preventing pregnancy, such research is likely to engender public opposition, and therefore unlikely to become a priority. In 1966, Reiss claimed that when a social problem continues to thrive over a long period of time, it is because, "man is only partly a rational creature and he will not use the most efficient means to his ends if he is afraid of those means or has moral objections . . . at times our moral values promote the very thing we morally condemn [p. 136]." Since little to nothing has been gained by society's "moral" stance on issues like alcohol, pornography, marijuana, and premarital sex, it seems that this 16-year-old warning might be worth heeding.

## Theoretical Issues

One of the most serious deficiencies in the research on adolescent pregnancy has been the lack of a coherently articulated theoretical base. The result has been a wide assortment of findings, interpretations, and case studies, but a paucity of empirical data that can help either to understand adolescent contraceptive behavior in its complexity or to plan prevention programs effectively. The vast majority of published studies speculate about the etiological bases of certain *individuals'* behavior and concentrate on the characteristics of the teenagers which place them at risk for pregnancy. Society's role in these pregnancies, or fertility "mistakes," is rarely addressed, since it is generally considered the responsibility of any sexual active individual to contracept competently. Yet this individually focused research has not adequately explained why contraceptive nonuse is so flagrant among teenagers who have adequate knowledge and access to contraceptives, nor has it generated adequate prevention methods.

Instead of viewing an adolescent's failure to acquire and use contraceptives as a deviance of the individual, a multidisciplinary, ecological focus should be considered. Bronfenbrenner (1977, 1979), Kelly (1966, 1968), and others (e.g., Catalano, 1979; Garbarino, 1980; Rosenberg & Reppucci, 1982) have argued an ecological approach to prevention, and the labyrinth of concerns around teenage pregnancy illustrates the necessity for such broad conceptualization. Much past research addressing etiological questions regarding adolescent pregnancy has been psychiatrically oriented and focused on deficits and personality problems of pregnant individuals (e.g., Babikian & Goldman, 1971; Harrison, 1969; Pohlman, 1965). Based on small samples, these studies represent an endogenous orientation on "abnormal" behavior, which is inappropriate given the prevalence of adolescent pregnancy and its many exogenous determinants. Just as the overly rationalistic perspective may be the expectation that prevention efforts simply need to expose adolescents to more information and provide greater access to contraceptives, the opposite and equally extreme view may be reflected in this psychiatric orientation relating adolescent pregnancy to unconscious motivations and psychopathology. Both perspectives have a myopic focus on isolated aspects of the individual or environment and neglect the social ecological and developmental context of adolescent sexual behavior.

While little empirical research has been initiated, the burgeoning awareness that adolescent contraceptive behavior should be considered within a developmental framework is becoming increasingly evident (Baizerman, 1977; Chilman, 1979; Cobliner, 1974; Cvetkovich et al., 1975; Presser, 1974). Recent studies have explored facets of the adolescent's social ecology that related to contraceptive use by investigating such areas as relationships with parents, peers, and sexual partners (Akpom, Akpom, & Davis, 1976; Cvetkovich, 1980; Fox & Inazu, 1980; Fischman, 1975; Furstenberg, 1976; Kantner & Zelnik, 1973; Kastner, 1979; Lindemann, 1974; Schinke, Gilchrist, & Small, 1979; Settlage, Fordney, Baroff, & Cooper, 1973). For the most part, these inquiries have been embedded in studies ranging from surveys to program evaluations and have lacked a coherent theoretical perspective. However, the value of their "ecological" focus is evidenced by results which indicate that communication and discussion about sex with parents, boyfriends, and friends facilitated adolescents' contraceptive use. An ecological approach to prevention appears promising because it suggests that ways of enhancing those "resources" that already exist in the adolescent's environment could be developed (Kastner, 1980).

A natural extension of examining the ecological roles of family and peer systems involves consideration of the impact of societal attitudes and values on contraceptive behavior among adolescents. Adolescents predominantly create their impressions about society's moral values on the basis of their experience with people in common settings like the home, school, church, and community. Although adults from these settings may convey a sense of disapproval of sexual activity for teenagers, mass media are a potent influence reflecting a confusing set of values. Witness the September 1980 *Newsweek* cover story entitled, "Teenage sex: The new morality hits home" (Gelman, Weathers, Whitman, Abramson, Maitland, & Copeland, 1980). Sexuality is flagrantly exploited in the very society which prohibits contraceptives from being advertised. Adolescents receive contradictory messages which inevitably contribute to their conflicts about sexual morality. Although this is obviously a difficult area of research, it is important to recognize the extent to which adolescents must process extremely complicated information in order to make decisions about their sexual behavior. Moreover, approaching the problem without a broader awareness of the many social and psychological pressures creating such a situation greatly limits our view of research and prevention potentials.

Indirect "advocacy" for adolescent contraceptive use has occurred through changes in social policy and legal decisions (*Griswold* v. *State*; *Eisenstadt* v.

*Baird)** which have helped both to increase the enrollment of adolescents in clinics and to enrich the sex education curriculum in many schools (Jaffe & Dryfoos, 1976). However, the limited effects of these changes are evident in the concomitant high rates of pregnancy, clinic dropouts, and contraceptive nonuse. This is not surprising, given the number of opposing forces which complicate the task of adolescent contraception. They exist at every level of our culture, ranging from the cognitive and emotional development of the individual to the moral attitudes and norms of our society.

With the use of new information about the unique needs of adolescents, the expansion and innovation of clinic services and sex education programs to prevent adolescent pregnancy should probably be continued as a matter of public policy. Special attention should be given to society's contribution to the moral dilemmas involved in contraceptive decision-making among adolescents. However, objections to prevention strategies undoubtedly would be even greater if action were taken to resolve some of the sexual identity conflicts which deter contraceptive use, because of the fear that it might also eliminate some of the moral barriers restraining sexual expression. The paradox is that given the high rates of adolescent sexual activity and relatively low rates of contraceptive use, it appears that moral guilt may not be strong enough to restrain premarital sex, but may indeed deter contraception.

Although adolescents often experience more liberal moral values among their peers than from their parents, the societal values internalized during childhood are not easily discarded. This ambiguous schism in sexual standards between parents and peers often leads to confusion in both the decision to initiate sexual activity and contraception. With the two so intimately bound, it is unrealistic to expect that enforcing the moral restraints on premarital sex will not also have mutual restraining effects on contraception. Over a decade ago, Wagner and his colleagues (Wagner et al., 1969) astutely observed, "Society has increasing difficulty in imposing moral willpower based on fear; it must develop this willpower on the basis of choice, which is a more difficult task [p. 70]." These authors implied that rather than being solely a function of choice, current sexual and contraceptive behavior is highly influenced by moral inhibitions that are more likely to lead to ambivalence and contraceptive nonuse than sexual abstinence.

* *Griswold* v. *State*, 381 U.S. 479, 85 S. CT. 1678, 14 L. Ed. 2d 510 (1965). *Eisenstadt* v. *Baird*, 405 U.S. 438, 92 S. CT. 1029, 31 L. Ed. 2d 349 (1972).

It is not known whether prevention programs designed to enhance sex education, teenage programs at clinics, and communication about adolescent sexuality will lead to a higher rate of adolescent sexual activity. However, a grave societal value judgment is whether it is more desirable to provide viable support for these efforts or to abandon them. Given the consequences of adolescent pregnancy and the moral fervor around the issues of abortion and premarital sex, the results of these alternative paths of action render this value judgment particularly vulnerable to moral quandary at the societal level. Hopefully, its critical implication for the future of prevention in this area will prohibit the kind of indecision, avoidance, denial, and inaction which seems to have contributed so much to the problem of contraceptive nonuse at the individual level.

The impetus for our societal focus on adolescent pregnancy has developed from a combination of sources, including our national concern about economic matters and the moral polemics involved in the issues of abortion, out-of-wedlock pregnancy, and the greater prevalence of sexual activity among teenagers. Perhaps even the upsurge of evangelism, the Moral Majority, and moral conservatism in the post–Nixon/Watergate era has helped fuel the fire. With the media and literature focusing on the "epidemic" of adolescent pregnancy rather than the ecological phenomena which are so integrally related to it, we might be distracted from some of the key issues which create and maintain this social problem.

## Conclusion

Prevention efforts are often caught in a paradox similar to that witnessed in the case of adolescent pregnancy. Full understanding of the ecological model should increase our awareness that forces beyond our specific disciplinary conceptualizations of social problems are necessary. Each discipline offers a refined approach to examining one aspect of a broad social problem. Our discussion of teenage pregnancy attempted to illuminate how multiple perspectives can provide increased insight into a particular issue. The example highlighted the web of forces which can maintain a problem and effectively subvert certain prevention efforts.

Teenage pregnancy is not unlike many other burning social issues which social scientists are called upon to deal with. The complexity of such issues is often frustrating and frequently avoided when searching for the most effective program to be mounted. A careful multidisciplinary examination has the potential to prevent myopic analogies from producing narrowly conceived prevention efforts. Moving primary prevention from a dream toward a reality requires that broad, multidisciplinary lens.

# References

Alan Guttmacher Institute. *Eleven million teenagers: What can be done about the epidemic of adolescent pregnancies in the United States.* New York: Planned Parenthood Federation of America, 1976.

Alan Guttmacher Institute. *Abortions and the poor: Private morality, public responsibility.* New York: Planned Parenthood Federation of America, 1979.

Akpom, C. C., Akpom, K. L., & Davis, M. Prior sexual behavior of teenagers attending rap sessions for the first time. *Family Planning Perspectives,* 1976, 8(4), 203–207.

Albee, G. W. Politics, power, prevention, and social change. In J. M. Joffe & G. W. Albee (Eds.), *Prevention through political action and social change.* Hanover, N.H.: University of New England Press, 1981.

Albee, G. W., & Joffe, J. M. (Eds.) *Primary prevention of psychopathology.* Vol. 1. *The issues.* Hanover, N.H.: University Press of New England, 1977.

Babikian, H. M., & Goldman, A. A study in teenage pregnancy. *American Journal of Psychiatry,* 1971, 128, 11–115.

Bacon, L. A. Early motherhood, accelerated role transition, and social pathology. *Social Forces,* 1974, 3, 333–341.

Baizerman, M. A critique of the research literature concerning pregnant adolescents, 1960–1970. *Journal of Youth and Adolescence,* 1977, 7, 343–351.

Baldwin, W. H. Adolescent pregnancy and childbearing—growing concerns for Americans. *Population Bulletin,* 1976, 31(2), 1–34.

Baldwin, W., & Cain, V. S. The children of teenage parents. *Family Planning Perspectives,* 1980, 12(1), 34–43.

Ballard, W. M., & Gold, E. M. Medical and health aspects of reproduction in the adolescent. *Clinical Obstetrics and Gynecology,* 1971, 14, 473–475.

Bloom, B. L. Community psychology: Midstream and mid-dream. *American Journal of Community Psychology,* 1978, 6(3), 205–214.

Braen, B. B. The school-age pregnant girl. *Clinical Child Psychology Journal,* 1971, 10, 17–20.

Bronfenbrenner, U. Toward an experimental ecology of human development. *American Psychologist,* 1977, 32, 513–531.

Bronfenbrenner, U. *The ecology of human development: Experiments by nature and design.* Cambridge: Harvard University Press, 1979.

Byrne, D. A pregnant pause in the sexual revolution. *Psychology Today,* 1977, 7, 67–68.

Campbell, A. The role of family planning in the reduction of poverty. *Journal of Marriage and the Family,* 1968, 30, 238–245.

Caplan, G. *Principles of preventive psychiatry.* New York: Basic Books, 1964.

Caplan, N., & Nelson, S. On being useful: The nature and consequences of psychological research in social problems. *American Psychologist,* 1973, 28, 199–211.

Card, J. J., & Wise, L. L. Teenage mothers and teenage fathers: The impact of early childbearing on the parents' personal and professional lives. *Family Planning Perspectives,* 1978, 10(4), 199–205.

Catalano, R. *Health, behavior and the community: An ecological perspective.* New York: Pergamon Press, 1979.

Catalano, R., & Dooley, D. Economic change in primary prevention. In R. H. Price, R. F. Ketterer, B. C. Bader, & J. Monahan (Eds.), *Prevention in mental health: Research, policy and practice.* Beverly Hills: Sage, 1980.

Catalano, R., & Monahan, J. The community psychologist as social planner: Designing optimal environments. *American Journal of Community Psychology,* 1975, 3, 327–334.

Chilman, C. S. Fertility and poverty in the U.S.: Some implications for family planning programs, evaluation, and research. *Journal of Marriage and the Family,* 1968, 30, 207–227.

Chilman, C. S. *Adolescent sexuality in a changing America: Social and psychological perspectives.* Publication No. (NIH) 79-1429. Washington: U.S. Department of Health, Education, and Welfare, 1979.

Cobliner, W. G. Pregnancy in the single adolescent girl: The role of the cognitive functions. *Journal of Youth and Adolescence,* 1974, 3, 17–29.

Connally, L. Little mothers. *Human Behavior,* June 1975, 17–23.

Cowen, E. L. Baby-steps toward primary prevention. *American Journal of Community Psychology,* 1977, 5, 1–22.

Cowen, E. L. The wooing of primary prevention. *American Journal of Community Psychology,* 1980, 8, 258–284.

Cowen, E. L. Primary prevention research: Barriers, needs and opportunities. *Journal of Primary Prevention,* 1982, 2, 131–137.

Cutwright, P. Illegitimacy: Myths, causes, and cures. *Family Planning Perspectives,* 1971, 3(1), 25–48.

Cvetkovich, G. Towards a theory of psychosocial development and fertility control. Paper presented at the Symposium on Developmental Approaches to Population Research: Issues, Methods, and Problems. Annual convention of the American Psychological Association, Montreal, September 1980.

Cvetkovich, G., Grote, B., Bjorseth, A., & Sarkissian, J. On the psychology of adolescents' use of contraceptives. *Journal of Sex Research,* 1975, 11(3), 256–270.

Eisenberg, L. Primary prevention and early detection in mental illness. *Bulletin of the New York Academy of Medicine,* 1975, 51, 118–129.

Fischman, S. The pregnancy-resolution decisions of unwed adolescents. *Nursing Clinic of North America,* 1975, 10, 217–227.

Forgays, D. G. (Ed.) *Primary prevention of psychopathology.* Vol. 2. *Environmental influences and strategies in primary prevention.* Hanover, N.H.: University Press of New England, 1978.

Forrest, J. D., Sullivan, E., & Tietze, C. Abortion in the United States, 1977–1978. *Family Planning Perspectives,* 1979, 11(6), 329–341.

Fox, G. L. "Nice girl": Social control of women through a value construct. *Signs: Journal of Women and Culture in Society,* 1977, 2(4), 805–817.

Fox, G. L., & Inazu, J. K. Patterns and outcomes of mother-daughter communication about sexuality. *Journal of Social Issues,* 1980, 36(1), 7–30.

Furstenberg, F. F. *Unplanned parenthood: The social consequences of teenage childbearing.* New York: Free Press, 1976.

Gabrielson, I. W., Klerman, L. V., Currie, J. B., Tyler, N. C., & Jekel, J. F. Suicide attempts in a population of pregnant teenagers. *American Journal of Public Health*, 1970, **60**, 2289–2301.

Garbarino, J. High risk neighborhoods and high risk families: The human ecology of child maltreatment. *Child Development*, 1980, **51**, 188–198.

Gelles, R. J. Child abuse as psychopathology: A sociological critique. *American Journal of Orthopsychiatry*, 1973, **43**, 611–621.

Gelman, D., Weathers, D., Whitman, L., Abramson, P., Maitland, T., & Copeland, J. Teenage sex: The new morality hits home. *Newsweek*, September 1, 1980, **96**, 48–53.

Goldfried, M. R. Toward the delineation of therapeutic change principles. *American Psychologist*, 1980, **35**(11), 991–999.

Goldsmith, S., Gabrielson, M., Gabrielson, A., Mathews, V., & Potts, L. Teenagers, sex, and contraception. *Family Planning Perspectives*, 1972, **4**(1), 32–38.

Hacker, A. Of two minds about abortion. *Harper's Magazine*, September 1979, 16–22.

Harrison, C. P. Teenage pregnancy—is abortion the answer? *Pediatric Clinics of North America*, 1969, **16**(20), 363–369.

Heller, K., & Monahan, J. *Psychology and community change*. Homewood, Ill.: Dorsey, 1977.

Herbert, W. The politics of prevention. *APA Monitor*, 1979, **10**, 5, 7, 8, 9.

Jaffe, F. S., & Dryfoos, J. G. Fertility control services for adolescents: Access and utilization. *Family Planning Perspectives*, 1976, **8**(4), 167–184.

Juhasz, A. The unmarried adolescent parent. *Adolescence*, 1974, **9**, 263–272.

Kane, F. J., & Lachenbruch, P. A. Adolescent pregnancy: A study of aborters and non-aborters. *American Journal of Orthopsychiatry*, 1973, **43**(10), 796–803.

Kantner, J. F., & Zelnik, M. Contraception and pregnancy: Experience of young unmarried women in the U.S. *Family Planning Perspectives*, 1973, **5**, 21–35.

Kastner, L. S. Adolescent perceptions of personal and ecological factors predicting contraceptive use: A multilevel, multivariable study. Unpublished doctoral dissertation, University of Virginia, 1979.

Kastner, L. S. On adolescent pregnancy prevention: An ecological study of factors predicting contraceptive use. Paper presented at the American Psychological Association Annual Meeting, Montreal, September 1980.

Kelly, J. G. Ecological constraints on mental health services. *American Psychologist*, 1966, **21**, 535–539.

Kelly, J. G. Toward an ecological conception of preventive interventions. In J. Carter (Ed.), *Research contributions from psychology to community mental health*. New York: Behavioral Publications, 1968.

Kessler, M., & Albee, G. W. Primary prevention. *Annual Review of Psychology*, 1975, **26**, 557–591.

Klein, D. C., & Goldston, S. E. (Eds.) *Primary prevention: An idea whose time has come*. Washington: Government Printing Office, 1977.

Lamb, H. R., & Zusman, J. Primary prevention in perspective. *American Journal of Psychiatry*, 1981, **9**, 1–26.

Lindemann, C. *Birth control and unmarried young women*. New York: Springer, 1974.

Luker, K. *Taking chances: Abortion and the decision not to contracept*. Berkeley: University of California Press, 1975.

Maccoby, N., & Alexander, J. Reducing heart rate disease risk using the mass media: Comparing the effects on

three communities. In R. F. Munoz, L. R. Snowden, & J. G. Kelly (Eds.), *Social and psychological research in community settings*. San Francisco: Jossey-Bass, 1979.

Menken, J. *The health and demographic consequences of adolescent pregnancy and childbearing*. Paper presented at the conference of research on the consequences of adolescent pregnancy and childbearing. Center for population research, National Institute of Health, 1975.

Mischel, W. On the future of personality assessment. *American Psychologist*, 1977, **32**(4), 246–254.

Mitchell, J. Some psychological dimensions of adolescent sexuality. *Adolescence*, 1972, **8**(28), 447–458.

Monsour, J. J., & Stewart, B. Abortion and sexual behavior in college women. *American Journal of Orthopsychiatry*, 1973, **43**, 804–814.

Moore, K. A. Teenage childbirth and welfare dependency. *Family Planning Perspectives*, 1978, **10**(4), 233–235.

Munoz, R. F., Snowden, L. R., & Kelly, J. G. (Eds.) *Social and psychological research in community settings*. San Francisco: Jossey-Bass, 1979.

Needle, R. H. Factors affecting contraceptive practices of high school and college-age students. *Journal of School Health*, 1977, **6**, 340–345.

Nye, I. *School-age parenthood*. Extension Bulletin 667. Pullman: Washington State University, 1977.

Oppel, W. C., & Royston, A. B. Teenage births: Some social, psychological, and physical sequelae. *American Journal of Public Health*, 1971, **61**, 751–756.

Pohlman, E. W. Wanted and unwanted pregnancy: Toward less ambiguous definitions. *Eugenics Quarterly*, 1965, **12**, 19–27.

President's Commission on Mental Health. *Report to the President from the President's Commission on Mental Health*, Vols. 1, 4. Washington: Government Printing Office, 1978.

Presser, H. P. Early motherhood: Ignorance or bliss? *Family Planning Perspectives*, 1974, **6**(1), 8–14.

Price, R. H. Etiology, the social environment, and the prevention of psychological dysfunction. In P. Insel & R. H. Moos (Eds.), *Health and the social environment*. Lexington, Mass.: Heath, 1974.

Price, R. H., Bader, B. C., & Ketterer, R. F. Prevention in community mental health: The state of the art. In R. H. Price, R. F. Ketterer, B. C. Bader, & J. Monahan (Eds.), *Prevention in mental health: Research, policy and practice*. Beverly Hills: Sage, 1980.

Price, R. H., Ketterer, R. F., Bader, B. C., & Monahan, J. (Eds.) *Prevention in mental health: Research policy and practice*. Beverly Hills: Sage, 1980.

Rappaport, J. *Community psychology: Values, research, and action*. New York: Holt, Rinehart & Winston, 1977.

Rappaport, J, Interview. In R. F. Munoz, L. R. Snowden, & J. G. Kelly (Eds.), *Social and psychological research in community settings*. San Francisco: Jossey-Bass, 1979.

Rappaport, J. In praise of paradox: A social policy of empowerment over prevention. *American Journal of Community Psychology*, 1981, **9**, 1–26.

Reiss, I. L. The sexual renaissance: A summary and analysis. *Journal of Social Issues*, 1966, **22**(2), 123–138.

Reiss, I. L., Banwart, A., & Foreman, H. Premarital contraceptive usage: A study and some theoretical explorations. *Journal of Marriage and the Family*, 1975, **37**, 617–630.

Rosenberg, M. S., & Reppucci, N. D. Child abuse: A review with special focus on an ecological approach in rural communities. In A. W. Childs & G. B. Melton, (Eds.), *Rural psychology*. New York: Plenum Press, 1982.

Sandberg, E., & Jacobs, R. Psychology of the misuse and rejection of contraception. *American Journal of Obstetrics and Gynecology*, 971, 110(2), 227–241.

Schinke, S. P., Gilchrist, L. D., & Small, R. W. Preventing unwanted adolescent pregnancy: A cognitive-behavioral approach. *American Journal of Orthopsychiatry*, 1979, 49(1), 81–88.

Seidman, E. Justice, values and social science: Unexamined premises. In R. J. Simon (Ed.), *Research in law and sociology*. Vol. 1. Greenwich, Conn.: JAI Press, 1978.

Settlage, D., Fordney, S., Baroff, S., & Cooper, D. Sexual experience of younger teenage girls seeking contraceptive assistance for the first time. *Family Planning Perspectives*, 1973, 5(4), 223–226.

Stanford Research Institute International. *An analysis of government expenditures consequent on teenage childbirth*. Prepared for Population Resource Center, New York, April 1979.

Stepto, R. C., Keith, L., & Keith, D. Obstetrical and medical problems of teenage pregnancy. In J. Zachler & W. Brandstadt (Eds.), *The teenage pregnant girl*. Springfield, Ill.: Charles C. Thomas, 1975.

Stickle, G., & Ma, P. Pregnancy in adolescents: Scope of the problem. *Contemporary Ob/Gyn*, June 1975.

Trangott, M. W., & Vinoviskis, M. A. Abortion and the 1978 congressional elections. *Family Planning Perspectives*, 1980, 12(5), 238–246.

Trussel, J. T. Economic consequences of teenage childbearing. *Family Planning Perspectives*, 1976, 8(4), 184–192.

Trussell, J., Menken, J., Lindheim, B. L., & Vaughn, B. The impact of restricting Medicaid financing for abortion. *Family Planning Perspectives*, 1980, 12(3), 130–136.

Wagner, N., Perthou, N., Fujita, B., & Pion, R. Sexual behavior of the adolescent. *Postgraduate Medicine*, 1969, 46(4), 68–72.

Yankelovich, S., Skelly, J., & White, B. Parents and teens agree: Teenagers should get birth control information from parents primarily. *Family Planning Perspectives Digest*, 1979, 11(3), 200–201.

Zabin, L. S., Kantner, J. F. & Zelnik, M. The risk of adolescent pregnancy in the first months of intercourse. *Family Planning Perspectives*, 1979, 11(4), 215–222.

Zelnik, M. & Kantner, J. F. Contraceptive patterns and premarital pregnancy among women aged 15–19 in 1976. *Family Planning Perspectives*, 1978, 10(3), 135–142. (a)

Zelnik, M. & Kantner, J. F. First pregnancies to women aged 15–19: 1976 and 1971. *Family Planning Perspectives*, 1978, 10(1), 11–20. (b)

Zelnik, M., & Kantner, J. F. Sexual activity, contraceptive use and pregnancy among metropolitan-area teenagers, 1971–1979. *Family Planning Perspectives*, 1980, 12(5), 230–237.

# 15 PSYCHOLOGY AND PUBLIC POLICY: MISSED OPPORTUNITY

## Seymour B. Sarason

By public policy I refer first to all those individuals who see their interests and purposes as being related to and affected by (positively or negatively) an issue that in some form is intended to be the basis for legislation or administrative actions. These participants may not know each other, but they know, and certainly come to know, *of* each other. They expend time, energy, and frequently money either to influence the formulation of a policy or to try to prevent the issues from becoming a policy. By public policy I also refer to a process that manifests itself in forums, utilizes different media for persuasive expression, and gives rise to constituency building. It is a process that by tradition or legislative or administrative precedent and regulations provides vehicles for presentation of information and positions. Public policy issues always give rise to coalitions and polarizations, if only because the participants see the issues as differentially affecting their self-interest. But these self-interests are never seen or described in crassly narrow terms, but rather in terms of conceptions of how life should be lived and organized in the society (that is, the larger society, the state, or the local community). So, for example, an agency will never say that it is for or against a particular policy because of its effects on the agency *qua* agency, but rather because that agency seeks to maintain, strengthen, and improve the social fabric, a fabric held together by certain values. That is to say, the agency is not an agent for its employees but for the community; the self-interests of the agency and the community are seen as identical. If differences of opinion make for horse races, so differences of view about what communities are and should be make public policy thrilling to the participants. It cannot be otherwise, when what is seen as at stake are conceptions of what society is and should be.

However the participants may differ in their view of and relation to public policy, they agree on several points. First, the outcome will be a difference that makes a difference. That prediction may turn out to be wrong or right, in whole or in part, but the participants are convinced (or act as if they are convinced) that the outcome will have discernible consequences. Second, the participants recognize that differences among them arise in part either because of differing values or, when there is agreement on values, because of differences on how to act on those values. Third, there is agreement that two groups will be affected by public policy: those who have to implement the policy and those whom the policy is supposed to serve; the former are usually formal agencies, the latter individuals. Fourth, and far less explicit than the others, is agreement that what happens in regard to *a* policy has impact on other policies, in place or proposed.

To take but one example: In 1975 Congress passed the Education for All Handicapped Children Act, referred to either as Public Law 94-142 or the "mainstreaming" law. Its passage signaled the intent to bring about dramatic changes in our public schools, affecting as it would all schools, all teachers, all children, parents, and finances (Sarason, 1982; Sarason and Doris, 1979). If one took a semester's sabbatical one might be able to read and digest the transcripts of the testimony given before congressional committees. At the very least, one would learn a good deal about the issues and myriad individuals, group, and agencies with an interest (pro and con, but mostly pro) in the legislation. This testimony reveals several important points about the issues involved:

1. Support for the legislation was based on countless experiences of individuals and groups in communities around the country. The drama was taking place in Washington, but a good deal of the substance of the script reflected what some people had experienced in their communities.

2. The importance of what was happening in local communities was illustrated by the fact that some states, notably Massachusetts, already had passed legislation that was being recommended as a model for what the national legislation should be. In short, whatever was taking place in Washington had already been "rehearsed" in some states.

3. Most of the participants who were for the legislation were highly critical of the ways in which schools and their personnel responded to the needs *and* rights of handicapped children *and* their parents. At the level of the local community there were serious polarizations between school personnel and parents of handicapped children.

4. Historically, the proposed legislation had its roots in the ways in which local and state agencies (such as public schools and state institutions) did and did not provide educational programs for handicapped children. More specifically, the legislation was, morally and constitutionally, a direct descendant of the 1954 desegregation decision.

5. The proposed legislation, based as it was on the recognition that parents of handicapped children had little or no power in educational decision-making, was intended to alter that distribution of power.

In short, Public Law 94-142 brought to the fore as never before long-standing conflicts in our communities. In this connection it has to be noted (and emphasized) that although the legislation is popularly known as the mainstreaming law, the word "mainstreaming" never appears in it. And that, as some

who helped write that legislation have told me, was not fortuitous. As one of these individuals said to me (paraphrased): "The guts of the legislation are in its due process clauses. We wanted to make sure that school personnel would no longer be able to make unilateral decisions about handicapped children." Public law 94-142 *arose from local conflicts* and anticipated that its *implementation would be marked by conflict.*

Public policy is defined and experienced in different ways by its diverse participants. To describe and understand any public policy in its current and social historical context is a formidable task if only because in our contemporary world public policy always has local, state, and national significances. Public policy is transactional in nature: it is shaped by different forces and shapes those very forces. There are no beginning and end points, and our traditional cause-and-effect (stimulus-and-response) way of thinking is inadequate, indeed inappropriate.

## The Origins of Community Psychology

The previous section was a necessary prologue to an assertion and a question. The assertion is that any individual or field that purports to be interested in understanding and/or influencing the dynamics of our communities has to become sophisticated about public policy. Public policy reflects and exposes community organization, relationships, and dynamics. For a community psychologist whose explicit goal is to understand and influence community functioning, the area of public policy has to be part of his or her sphere of interest and participation. This is not a matter of choice, unless the label and concept of "community" are so superficial, so devoid of meaning, that they are at best slogans and at worst an intellectual travesty. I am not suggesting that the community psychologist should drop whatever he or she is doing and plunge into the arena of public policy. What I am asserting is that whichever problem, issue, or group a community psychologist is studying or attempting to influence has to be seen, at some point, in terms of existing or proposed public policy. And on the level of understanding and action, that is no easy task. But more about that later.

The question for which the previous section was prologue is: Why has community psychology been so unrelated to public policy? From its formal beginnings as a field in the early 1960s until today, community psychology has hardly been related to the arena of public policy. With increasing frequency since the 1960s the literature in community psychology contains the words "public policy," but rarely do they refer to the unbounded, complex arena I have briefly described. The use of these words is testimony to the recognition that public policy reflects and in turn gives rise to community dynamics and problems of interest to community psychology. But this recognition has neither depth nor scope. Neither on a theoretical level nor on the level of practice and research has community psychology made illuminating contributions to our understanding of public policy. So, for example, in regard to Public Law 94-142 one would be hard put to find community psychologists who were sensitive to and involved with the federal, state, and local manifestations of the public policy issues.

The unrelatedness of community psychology to the policy arena is in part a function of the historical fact that the field emerged from and was symbiotically related to clinical psychology. Put in another way, community psychology was an expression by some clinical psychologists of their dissatisfaction with clinical psychology. Those dissatisfactions had four major aspects:

1. It was a revolt, long simmering, against psychiatric domination of the mental health professions (Sarason, 1981a,b). In terms of professional worth, scope of theoretical and research orientation, and sites of practice, clinical psychologists felt hemmed in and wasted.

2. There was a growing awareness that there were large segments of the population for whom mental health services did not exist or, if they did exist, were either beyond their financial means or inappropriate in a cultural sense. It was not only that mental health services were inequitably distributed in the society, but that the mental health professions were dependent on a very narrow band of treatment possibilities that were not sensitive to cultural and racial variations.

3. These clinical psychologists, aware as they were in the early sixties of the forces that were leading to destructive community conflicts and polarizations, recognized that the nature of these forces had to be understood and means to influence them found. Traditional clinical psychology had little or nothing to contribute to such understanding and intervention.

4. Clinical psychology (like all other clinical endeavors) focuses on behavior and events *after* they have become problematic. The virtues of such a focus aside, clinical psychologists began to see a limitation of the clinical approach: the failure or inability to think in terms of prevention (Cowen, 1980).

These dissatisfactions posed for the infant field of community psychology a dilemma that was hardly formulated: How could people trained and steeped in the clinical tradition free themselves from those parts of the tradition that had led them down such narrow paths? For example, how could such professionals used to thinking in terms of an individual psychology alter their world view consistent with the goal of conceptualizing and describing communities or significant parts of them? Could this be done at the same time that they remained institutionally and programmatically in their familiar settings? Would not being in such familiar settings be a barrier to identifying bodies of knowledge and practice relevant to overcoming the dissatisfactions of these clinical psychologists?

Socialization into a professional field aims to provide a picture of what that part of the world is and should be (Sarason, 1981a,b). That picture, if the socialization "takes," has both articulated and unarticulated features and it is the latter far more than the former that have fateful consequences precisely because of their silent, axiomatic nature. One does not become aware of these silent axioms until the cumulative impact of forces from within and without exposes the fact that one has been taking things for granted that one should not have. That is what happened to some clinical psychologists in the late 1950s and early '60s. However clear they were about what they were rebelling against, they understandably underestimated what would be required to give substance to the new field into which they wanted to move. They not only had to *unlearn* ways of thinking and acting, but they also had to learn new ways of thinking and unfamiliar bodies of knowledge. I say "understandably" because at best one can only partially free one's self from one's socialization into the society and one's field. If one has spent one's professional life in clinical and related settings devoted to helping individuals, restricting as that inevitably is about how one sees and understands the larger society, there is the obvious danger that when one tries to move out of those settings (behaviorally and conceptually), those silent axioms continue to be an obstacle. This is well illustrated by the fact that in its period of origin community psychology was for all practical and conceptual purposes formulated into the context of "mental health." And that insured several consequences. First, community psychology would continue to see communities and the larger society from a very parochial experience and viewpoint. Second, this parochialism would reinforce the orientation to "repair" and the nonnurturing of the preventive orientation. Third, the opportunity conceptually to relate community psychology to other fields (such as economics, political science, public health, demography, education) would be glossed over. Fourth, the new field, like that of clinical psychology, would have primarily an emphasis on the deficits of individuals and communities and not on assets, actual and potential. Fifth, the arena of public policy—unrivaled for the ways it reflects the phenotypic and genotypic characteristics of a community—would remain foreign territory for community psychology, if only because that arena cannot be comprehended through the lens of mental health concerns.

The reader would be wrong if he or she interpreted what I have said as criticism, as if I were deriding the motivations, capabilities, and imaginativeness of the clinical psychologists who were trying to shape a new field. They were on average a courageous and pioneering group who truly wanted to alter and enlarge their perspectives, to try to see things more "whole" than their clinical training and experience had allowed them. If that was not the case, then why did they put the adjective "community" before the noun "psychology"? That label said a lot about the degree to which they wanted to shift their focus from what went on in clinical settings to what went on in communities. But if their too-global vision far exceeded their conceptual grasp, that was not explainable simply in psychological terms—for example, the force of tradition demonstrating its strength in individual psyches. There were potent institutional obstacles as well. One obstacle, for example, was political-economic. Precisely because community psychology emerged from and usually remained a subsidiary part of clinical psychology programs, the new field lacked clout and constituency. Furthermore, because a significant portion of support for clinical programs came from government sources, one could not expect that these programs would be enthusiastic about allocating resources to the new field. In this connection, one should not underestimate the role of the fact that the new field was based on an explicit criticism of the narrowness of clinical programs. Community psychology was intended to reflect a break with a tradition, not a bolstering of it. One could argue that community psychology represented an extension of clinical theory and practice, or an effort to move it in new directions, but that argument concedes the point that the new field represented a challenge and threat to the established order of things. What would have required explanation is if the new field had been otherwise perceived. These political-economic obstacles tended to have the effect of exerting pressure on the new field to emphasize its continuity with rather than differences from clinical psychology. And that kind of pressure, subtle but powerful, does not nurture radical thinking and actions. But there was an even more significant pressure that came from the broader field of psychology. I refer to that part of the ideology of American psychology that defined what was "good and bad" research, that is, the criteria

by which a scholarly or research effort was deemed worthy or unworthy. Briefly and oversimplified, it was a "scientific" view that worshipped experimentation (the manipulation of variables) and "hard data." It was a view that prevented recognition of the complexity of the task of conceptually bringing together ideas, observations, and hard data from fields long concerned with the macro- and microfunctioning of communities, the state, and the federal apparatus. If that task had been seriously undertaken, community psychology might have been stimulated and sobered by the failures of the policy fields to live up to *their* proclaimed promise. They might have been stimulated both by the intrinsic social implications of public policy and the vast gulf between intended and unintended consequences. They might have been sobered by the fact that this gulf had less to do with facts and data than with competing views about what our society is and should be and with the sources and distribution of power (e.g., Nelson, 1977; Rappaport, 1977).

There is no point in faulting history, but there is a point to examining history as a way of challenging our accustomed perspectives. In the case of community psychology, its historical origins within psychology generally and clinical psychology in particular had and continue to have fateful consequences, not the least of which is limited scope. This is not to say that what has been done and written under the rubric of community psychology has been without value (although much of it is trivial), but that these contributions do not seem to be informed by overarching conceptions of what our society has been and is and the ways it works. That is to say, when I read the literature I find myself asking several questions. Why does the problem on which the study focused exist? Did it always exist in this form, with this frequency? If it did not exist in this form, how does one account for the change? Is this a problem that can be ameliorated by individual professionals or agencies; that is, are there sufficient professionals, acting as individuals or collectivities, to impact on the causes and consequences of the problem? Is this a problem that will require marked community-institutional changes, and if so, how can they be brought about? What are the predictable obstacles that such efforts will encounter from what parts of the community? Why do these obstacles exist and what do they tell us about our communities and society? Is the problem being defined in terms of an individual psychology or as a community-social one (the two definitions having enormously different consequences for action)? Should one not expect that a community psychologist would always define the problems of individuals in terms of the community-societal context? These and other questions occur to me not because I expect community psychologists (at least those who publish) to develop grand theories, but because I expect them to see any problem (for example, stress, divorce, deviance, support structures) in relation to the nature of our society and its communities. Put in another way, any problem is an instance of a broader set of problems which in turn reflect dynamics of our society. This expectation was built into the very basis of community psychology's criticism of clinical psychology. Explicit in that criticism was the point that by fixating on individuals or on this or that group of individuals clinical psychology was coming up with practices and recommendations that were as socially self-defeating as they were parochial. There was, the criticism said, a larger social picture that clinical psychology could not recognize. It is that criticism I am now directing at community psychology.

Let me illustrate my position by discussing briefly Dr. Adelaide Levine's (1982) recent book, *The Love Canal: Science, politics, and people.* Many books have been written on the horrors of the Love Canal, but this is the first that attempts to describe in detail how and why myriad individuals, groups, and agencies (local, state, and federal) became part of a larger picture reflecting characteristics of our societal structures and dynamics. One could read this book and come away with the judgment that Dr. Levine has given us a model of investigative reporting. That valid judgment, however, completely obscures the fact that Dr. Levine came to the problem with a sophisticated conception of "how things work," leading her to look for and pursue interconnections that ordinarily escape examination. The Love Canal was a crisis and catastrophe, but what Dr. Levine dwells on are the processes of public policy that were set in motion. The Love Canal was a consequence of public policies (or their absence) but it was also the cause of new and changing policies on the local, state, and federal levels. The impact of the book is precisely because of its poignant and comprehensive description of the policy process. Dr. Levine never loses sight of that larger picture and her readers, therefore, are not likely to commit the error of misplaced emphasis. She gives us a drama with a large and extremely varied cast of characters but no actor is *the* star, there is no beginning and there is no ending, there is no author or director, and it is a drama that takes place concomitantly on many different stages. The most egregious mistake Dr. Levine's readers could make would be to conclude that the genotypic processes, conflicts, interconnections, and individual and group behavior illustrated in her book were peculiar or idiosyncratic to the Love Canal story. What she illustrates, far from being

unique, is what happens whenever there is a challenge to or the pursuit of a public policy. The fact that the Love Canal was about life, death, illness, and human misery compels our interest and sympathy, but it should not distract us from the fact that what Dr. Levine describes is in no basic way unusual when a social issue becomes the magnet to which competing interests and group are drawn.

> At Love Canal, many of the most important events could be understood as the consequence of well-known social processes. In the slowly developing, multifaceted situation, the various groups viewed and defined the situation from their own perspectives, adding to the persistent conflict. Moreover, each group formed opinions and acted in terms of its self-interest—whether financial, political, professional, moral, or survival. Other social processes were going on as well. Nothing occurred at Love Canal, however, that was theoretically surprising or even theoretically new to a social scientist. What is important, rather is the fact that what happened was so broadly predictable, for it means that the same processes will be present at other Love Canals [p. 219].

Dr. Levine is right in saying that what happened at Love Canal was neither surprising nor unpredictable to social scientists. But it is also correct to add that social scientists, including community psychologists, have been inept or irresponsible in taking their theories seriously when it comes to public policy. They are ept and responsible when it comes to evaluating the consequences of public policy that are already in place, but their track record in regard to appropriately informing and influencing the development of policy is very poor. That is the major point that Nelson (1977) has made and it is the basis for Moynihan's position that social scientists should be kept at arm's length from public policy. It is as if when social scientists actively participate in public policy, their theories about how the ways things work and get done in our society are forgotten.

For many of the participants, lay and professional, in the Love Canal story their experience was an eye-opener, a transforming life experience. Why? A large part of the answer lies in our inability to comprehend the myriad ways in which we are actually or potentially interconnected, synergistically or adversarially, with other individuals, groups, or agencies. It takes an issue that affects our interests to teach us about how things work and how things get done or not done. The uses of power, the role of self-interest, the dilemmas of limited resources, the need for constituency, the fear of change and fear of status, access to the communications media, the federal-state-local complex of interconnections, greed and lying, and courage and heroism—the education is not about any one of these but about how they all are contained in a picture to which our eyes are opened as we become partisans. Courage and heroism: in Dr. Levine's story these became characteristics of people *after* their eyes were opened to how things work and how things get done.

As I defined it earlier, public policy is an unrivaled arena for understanding our communities and society. This point was vaguely sensed by those who struggled to give shape and direction to community psychology. Let us not forget that community psychology was born during the sixties, when all kinds of challenges were directed to what our society was and how it seemed to work. Those challenges are, for all practical purposes, no longer a part of community psychology's *Weltanschauung*.

If anything has been demonstrated in the history of science, it is that an understanding of phenomena widens and deepens as the investigator attempts to influence or alter them. The process of changing the substance, shape, and direction of phenomena is an eye-opener, regardless of whether it confirms or disconfirms our conceptions. The scientist who is experimenting is not only studying but trying to *change* something. In that sense he or she is an activist. So when I suggest that the community psychologist should at some point become an activist, it is because in that role the community psychologist will have his or her eyes opened to what our society is and how it works. It is a strange and difficult role because one walks a tightrope between partisanship on the one side and the desire to learn on the other, and to make that learning public in a way that allows others to examine critically what one thinks one has learned. Activism, in this sense, is not an immediately practical and applied endeavor but a way of furthering one's development and contributing to knowledge. I subscribe fully to the maxim that if you want to understand the social world, you should experience trying to change it in some way. That is why I believe that community psychology will be viable to the extent that public policy becomes more central to its concerns.

## References

Cowen, E. L. The wooing of primary prevention. *American Journal of Community Psychology*, 1980, **8**, 258–284.

Levine, A. *The Love Canal: Science, politics, and people.* New York: Lexington Books, 1982.

Nelson, R. *The moon and the ghetto.* New York: Norton, 1977.

Rappaport, J. *Community psychology.* Holt, Rinehart & Winston, 1977.

Sarason, S. B. An asocial psychology and a misdirected clinical psychology. *American Psychologist*, 1981, **36**, 827–836.(a)

Sarason, S. B. *Psychology misdirected.* New York: Free Press, 1981.(b)

Sarason, S. B. *The culture of the school and the problem of change.* (2nd ed.) Boston: Allyn and Bacon, 1982.

Sarason, S. B., & Doris, J. *Educational handicap, public policy, and social history.* New York: Free Press, 1979.

# 16 EVALUATING PREVENTIVE INTERVENTIONS: GUIDELINES FOR THE SERIOUS SOCIAL CHANGE AGENT

## Raymond P. Lorion

## Overview

The title of this chapter is intended to reflect frustration rather than arrogance. For more than a decade, the mental health professions have discussed the *potential* benefits of developing and implementing preventive interventions. Policymakers have been urged to shift their emphasis and resources from interventions which respond to established disorder to those which avoid or interrupt incipient or potential disorder. The hypothesized consequence of such a policy shift will be a reduction in the number of individuals who experience any level of disorder or its observable diagnosable manifestations. Incipient forms of disorder which do appear within preventive systems are presumed to require less intense treatment for shorter periods of time than their advanced counterparts. Economically, therefore, it is argued that an initial investment in the development of *effective* (therein lies the rub!) preventive interventions will return a handsome dividend by reducing the nation's increasing mental health costs. Moreover, significant human dividends are also presumably attached to preventive strategies. By removing psychosocial pathogens from the environment, or by minimizing their impact, preventive interventions also protect individuals from both the primary and secondary consequences of disorder. The basis is thereby established for the initiation of positive rather than negative cycles. The combined payoffs of preventive strategies represent a true pot of gold which, it is argued, justifies a costly trip to the end of that rainbow.

The journey is still not over, yet the pot of gold seems no less elusive than a decade ago. The frustration alluded to earlier may relate to a seed of doubt planted many years ago. Early in his career, the author was introduced to the lofty goals of prevention by way of the oft-repeated parable of the mental health professionals who stood on the banks of the river and retrieved bodies as they floated downstream. Alarmed at the mixed and sometimes limited impact of their efforts, some rescuers headed upstream to discover, according to the parable, "who or what was pushing these people in the water." The merit of their journey was assured, since at the very least they would have an opportunity to rescue the river's victims early, and ideally would keep them out of the water entirely. The logic of the parable's message seemed irrefutable, the primacy of the need to discover preventive efforts unquestionable.

Like any convert, the author sought to share the message with the unenlightened. An early target was a leading psychoanalyst who had previously been one of the author's psychotherapy supervisors.* He listened intently and asked if the rescuers who were heading upstream were certain that keeping people out of the river was a genuine benefit. Were there no advantages to being in the river? Did individuals need to struggle somewhat with the emotional consequences of such experiences if they were to gain control over their lives? Did everyone enter the river at some time? Did not, in fact, most of us leave and reenter numerous times in our lives? If so, at what point along the river should entering it (he rarely spoke of falling in or being pushed) be "prevented"? In his view, without answers to such questions, those who preached about prevention were blindly involving themselves in the lives of others with unpredictable consequences.

Needless to say, the author had few answers to such questions. In his haste to catch up with those already heading upstream, he saw little need to pause and respond to them. He has not, however, forgotten the questions. Their relevance becomes increasingly apparent as the journey continues. In an earlier article on this topic (Lorion & Lounsbury, 1981), the author discussed obstacles to reaching that goal and suggested a number of relevant research strategies which might contribute to progress toward that end. The intent of this chapter is to consider further these issues and to propose additional investigatory strategies. In spite of his frustration (impatience?) in response to the limited progress to date in reaching the sought-after goal, the author remains convinced of its legitimacy.

Attainment of that end, however, will necessitate, in the author's view, a shift from immediate program development toward the cautious analysis of the target problem and its effected population. Based on those data, systematic evaluation procedures must be used at all stages of the program development with continuous monitoring throughout the program's life. In the absence of rigorous and continuous evaluation, it is unlikely that preventive interventions will or should become integral to the nation's mental health system. If introduced at all, they may be harmful, will likely be short-lived, or may be gradually transformed into impotent *modi operandi*. Preventive interventions should encounter the same resistance from the proponents of the status quo as have other innovative strategies (interested readers are referred to Fairweather & Tornatzky, 1977; Levine, 1981; and Munoz, Snowden, & Kelly, 1979, for detailed discussions of obstacles to the effective dissemination of new ideas and approaches). Such challenges presented by de-

fenders of the status quo represent, in part, their legitimate concern for the welfare of those served by existing programs. However limited and inadequate existing solutions may be, at least they are known entities with foreseeable consequences. Typically, the long-range impacts of proposed alternatives are less clear and, therefore, suspect.

To *assume* (as opposed to demonstrate) that preventive strategies will have only positive or, at worse, neutral consequences represents a naive and irresponsible position. It is inconceivable that an intervention which is designed to avoid or limit the impact of a pathological process or to generate heretofore absent inter- or intrapersonal competencies could not be recognized as also able to cause negative outcomes. Those who doubt this should recall the as yet unanswered questions posed by my psychoanalytic colleague. They should also review the surprisingly underemphasized findings reported in McCord's (1978) long-term follow-up study of the Cambridge-Somerville project (Powers & Witmer, 1951), a classic early example of the preventive approach.

Based on official records and information obtained from personal contacts, McCord assessed the differential life experiences of 506 individuals who as adolescents were judged to be delinquency-prone. These people were assigned randomly to a preventively oriented counseling program (208 of the original 253 subjects were followed) or a no-treatment control group (202 of the original 253 were followed). McCord compared both groups on 57 variables relevant to their experiences with marriage, occupation, children, drinking, health, criminal behavior, and attitudes toward the treatment program. *None* of these comparisons favored the treatment group; *all* seven significant differences favored those *excluded* from the preventive intervention. Specifically, McCord reports:

> The objective evidence presents a disturbing picture. The program seems not only to have failed to prevent its clients from committing crimes—but also to have provided negative side effects. As compared with the control group:
>
> 1. Men who had been in the treatment program were more likely to commit (at least) a second crime.
> 2. Men who had been in the treatment program were more likely to evidence signs of alcoholism.
> 3. Men from the treatment group more commonly manifested signs of serious mental illness.

---

* Dr. Sidney Rubin's unequaled capacity to stimulate long-term thought about issues relevant to the complexity of human behavior is gratefully acknowledged.

4. Among men who had died, those from the treatment group died younger.
5. Men from the treatment group were more likely to report having had at least one stress-related disease; in particular, they were more likely to have experienced high blood pressure or heart trouble.
6. Men from the treatment group tended to have occupations with lower prestige.
7. Men from the treatment group tended more often to report their work as not satisfying [p. 288].

McCord's findings serve as a stark reminder of the need to examine in detail preventive interventions in order to identify their potential positive and negative consequences.

Support for McCord's caution is provided by Gersten, Langner, and Simcha-Fagan (1979), who report that their secondary prevention program increased rather than decreased dysfunctional risk. These investigators argue that the fault lies not with the concept of prevention per se but with their failure to appreciate the natural ontogenetic sequence of functional and dysfunctional processes. Specifically, the observed increase in dysfunctional risk related to the premature determination that observed behaviors reflected evidence of pathological risk. According to Gersten et al., early detection and remediation efforts must be carefully timed so as not to interrupt that point in the development of a dysfunctional condition when risk-related behaviors typically disappear from non-dysfunctional individuals. Prior to that time, the targeted behaviors are found in both risk and nonrisk populations. Premature identification labels some nonrisk individuals as false positives. Consequently, they may manifest disorder later as a result of stigma or a related self-fulfilling mechanism. Although their exact cause is unknown, Gersten et al.'s findings underscore the need for caution in introducing preventive strategies.

Not only must timing considerations be appreciated but, as demonstrated by Lorion, Cowen, and Caldwell (1974), the specificity of the target population must be carefully defined in order not to dilute the efficacy of the preventive intervention. Moreover, the complexity of delineating long-term predictors of health and dysfunction must be appreciated and systematically resolved (Lorion, 1979; Lorion, Barker, Cahill, Gallagher, Passons, & Kaufki, 1981; Sameroff, 1977; White, 1975; White, 1977). Overall, it should be apparent that however important and desirable it might be for preventive efforts to get underway, considerable preparatory work is necessary before that goal becomes

a reality. Integral to that preparation is the application of rigorous evaluation methods to all phases of problem definition, program development, implementation, assessment, and, if appropriate, disssemination.

## The Limits of Community Research

It has often been stated that those who are ignorant of history are condemned to repeat it. That admonition seems particularly relevant to the mental health professions, which appear to have a fondness for old wine in new bottles (Cowen, 1973; Levine, 1981; Levine & Levine, 1970). Knowledge of history alone, however, does not protect one from taking the circuitous route back to the status quo. In discussing his experiences in developing innovative human service strategies, Sarason (1976, 1978, 1981) underlines the difficulties inherent in preserving the innovativeness of programmatic alternatives. For that reason, readers are encouraged to delay devising preventive interventions until they are thoroughly familiar with their historical antecedents. Among the references which should be considered are Bloom (1977), Levine (1981), Levine and Levine (1970), Zax and Cowen (1973), Sarason (1972, 1981), and the reports of the two presidential commissions on mental health: *Action for Mental Health* (Joint Commission, 1961) and the *Report to the President* of the President's Commission on Mental Health (1978), volumes one through four. Specific reviews of the substantive area of prevention are available in Albee and Joffe (1977); Bloom (1979); Cowen (1973, 1977, 1980), Forgays (1978); Kent and Rolf (1979): Kessler and Albee (1975); and Munoz, Snowden, and Kelly (1979). Familiarity with these sources will not insure complete avoidance of prior errors. It will, however, decrease the likelihood of their occurring due to sheer ignorance. Furthermore, it will sensitize the would-be program developer to the nature and intensity of individual and institutional forces to preserve the status quo (readers are urged to consider seriously the "anarchist insight" described by Sarason, 1976).

Of specific relevance to this chapter's focus are the empirical strategies used to date in assessing such programs. Although not limited to research on prevention, three analyses of the methodological procedures used by community psychologists have recently been published (Lounsbury, Leader, Meares, & Cook, 1980; McClure, Cannon, Allen, Belton, Connor, D'Ascoli, Stone, Sullivan, & McClure, 1980; Novaco & Monahan, 1980). Consideration of the findings presented in these reports provides insights into the nature of our methodological practices and suggestions for their improvement.

In their review, McClure et al. analyzed a sample of 26 percent of the articles in the *American Journal of Community Psychology* (AJCP), the *Journal of Community Psychology* (JCP), the *Community Mental Health Journal* (CMHJ), and the *Journal of Applied Social Psychology* (JASP) published between 1975 and the end of 1978. While the topics addressed by this sample of articles were consistent with the conceptual emphases of community psychology, McClure et al. concluded that "the data indicate virtually no growth of an interpretable, empirical, intervention research base clarifying the relationships between individual functioning and higher ecological variables [p. 1007]." Fully 43.1 percent of the articles reviewed either presented no data or "reported designs judged as too weak to permit reasonable causal inferences [p. 1004]." An additional 34.7 percent relied on correlational procedures to analyze their findings. Only 12.5 percent of the articles reviewed involved research designs (experimental or quasi-experimental) which permitted inferential consideration of causality.

Novaco and Monahan (1980) examined the 235 articles published in *AJCP* from 1973 through 1978. Dimensions considered in analyzing each article included its procedural focus, experimental design, dependent and independent measures, and focus on prevention. Their findings are quite discouraging. Although three-fourths of the articles were classified as "empirical" (that is, quantified data were collected to answer a question posed by the investigator), their methodological rigor makes use of that term suspect. Only 29.8 percent of the studies reported were directly linked to a conceptual framework; fully 27.3 percent made no attempt to relate their research to any theoretical base. Even more disconcerting, however, is the fact that more than three-fifths of the "empirical" articles reviewed failed to specify their experimental hypotheses in any form. Programmatic research, particularly of existing programs, was significantly underrepresented in the articles reviewed.

Novaco and Monahan commented on the lack of experimental sophistication of the articles reviewed. Approximately half relied on "one-shot assessments or correlational analyses with no control or comparison group and without connection to an intervention program [p. 140]." In more than three-fifths of the studies, self-report measures were used; nearly one-third of the studies employed a single measurement strategy. Variables of interest more often related to the deficits (31.7 percent) than to the competencies (19.8 percent) of subjects; nearly one-third (29.9 percent) of the articles focused on neither. In contrast to the field's defining objectives, only 12.6 percent of the articles were characterized by their authors as related to primary or secondary prevention. Not surprisingly, Novaco and Monahan concluded that "an unduly large portion of the research on community psychology consists of methodologically inadequate answers to questions devoid of theoretical content [p. 144]."

Lounsbury et al. (1980) provide the most comprehensive analysis of experimental procedures used in community psychology research. These authors examined carefully all 478 articles published in *JCP* and *AJCP* from 1973 through 1978. On dimensions common to both reviews, Lounsbury et al.'s conclusions support those reported by Novaco and Monahan. Thus, hypotheses were rarely stated; multiple procedures to assess a dependent variable were rarely used; paper and pencil measures were typical; and the longitudinal assessment of experimental effects was infrequent.

Lounsbury et al. provide additional information about the methodological nature of community psychology's research base. Specifically, they documented how basic principles of experimentation and scientific reporting have been ignored. In less than one-half of the studies were subjects adequately identified in terms of demographic characteristics such as gender, ethnicity, and religious affiliation. Even less information was provided about subjects' socioeconomic and marital status, in the case of adults, or with respect to children, their birth order and parenting circumstances (one versus both parents present in the home), in spite of the relevance of such information to interpreting and generalizing from reported findings.

Subject selection and measurement procedures are equally inadequate. Acceptable sampling procedures were employed in less than one-fifth of the studies. Although control subjects were used nearly 60 percent of the time, random assignment and/or matching procedures were used in only one-fifth of these cases. Although not reluctant to design measures specifically for a given study, experimenters rarely documented the psychometric acceptability of their instruments. Detailed analyses of a measure's reliability from multiple perspectives (for example, test-retest *and* interrater) were rare; systematic demonstrations of its construct validity were virtually nonexistent. Overall, Lounsbury et al. confess their disappointment at

> several factors of most research designs which reduced their statistical power and lowered the confidence with which we could draw meaningful conclusions from them. Among these were unrepresentative sampling of subjects, small sample sizes, and frequent use of nonequivalent comparison groups. The ability

of many studies to faithfully model a complex reality was also impaired by measurement narrowness, both in terms of a narrow range of types of variables examined and a near absence of using different methods to measure variables [p. 440].

It is interesting to note that the reviews just summarized were conducted independently. Unaware that the other reviews were in process, the authors examined the research from multiple, somewhat overlapping perspectives. At least one review (Lounsbury et al., 1980) was motivated by the reviewers' general impression that flaws existed in community psychology's research base. The extent and nature of these flaws, however, exceeded their initial expectations. Given the consistency of the findings, it is reasonable to assume the reliability of the reviewers' conclusions. Might we not, however, cry foul? After all, it is always possible to second-guess another's research and to suggest this or that alteration in the design and/or statistical techniques.

## Basic Research Principles

Were the three reviews limited to Monday-morning quarterbacking, it would be reasonable to dismiss their conclusions as unfair critiques which should be perceived as future guidelines rather than indictments of past practices. To do so, however, would be a disservice to the reviewers who, like Pogo, have found that the enemy—the quality of our research threatens the very integrity of our discipline—it is us! Remediation of the gross inadequacies in experimentation and scientific reporting uncovered in the three reviews is an essential prerequisite for community psychology's and prevention's future. The complexities of investigating issues in the field are well known (Cowen, 1978) and very real. These complexities explain but do not justify ignoring basic scientific principles in the conduct of research. Data which are uninterpretable, nongeneralizable, and nonreplicable will contribute little if anything to the advancement of our knowledge about prevention. Moreover, poor research obfuscates rather than elucidates our attempts to understand these within the "real world." In addition, it generates disregard for our efforts.

Ideally, this chapter will contribute somewhat to the reversal of identified trends. In the sections which follow, methodological considerations for evaluating preventive interventions will be discussed. Preliminary to those comments, however, the following principles of research and scientific reporting are presented in order to underline the findings of the three research surveys. These principles are as follows:

1. The purpose(s) of research should be clearly specified. Hypotheses should be stated so that their acceptance or rejection can be determined easily by the reader. In studies which examine the nature of relationships among variables, directional expectations should be specified if warranted by the existing literature. Observational research, needs assessments, and so on should be accompanied by a detailed statement of the rationale underlying the focal questions. Evaluation studies should include statements which describe expected outcomes.

2. All aspects of the research methodology should be presented in sufficient detail such that the naive reader could replicate the study in an appropriate independent setting. Such information should be available on request if its length exceeds standard journal space limitations.

3. Subject selection procedures should adhere to accepted scientific standards. Sampling procedures should be described in detail and the representativeness of the sample to the relevant population demonstrated. When representative sampling is impossible, the investigator should justify the selection procedures used and describe the resulting limits to generalizing the study's findings.

4. Sufficient demographic information should be provided about subjects to enable readers to determine the limits of generalizability from the resulting data. Adult subjects should be described minimally in terms of age, sex, ethnicity, marital status, religious affiliation, occupation, education, and socioeconomic background. Children used as subjects should be described minimally in terms of age, sex, ethnicity, birth order, parenting status (one or both parents present in the home; foster/adopted child) and parents' educational, occupational, and socioeconomic characteristics. Children enrolled in schools should be described in terms of their academic achievement, grade level, and, if relevant, years within a particular class. In all instances, the criteria by which subjects were assigned to diagnostic or special education categories should be presented in detail. Participants in a treatment program should be described in terms of admission criteria, treatment duration, and prior treatment experience.

5. Comparison groups should be used whenever possible. Random assignment to experimental conditions should not be rejected a priori. Instead, it should be considered in the initial design and replaced only if necessary. Systematic matching procedures should represent the first option when random assignment cannot be used. Selected matching variables

should be operationally defined and examined statistically. Rigorous standards should be established for defining a group as matched. Merely avoiding a significant difference between comparison groups (in some instances at a $p \leq .07$ level) is inadequate. Exact probability levels should be reported for all comparisons of matching variables. Finally, if neither of the above procedures can be used to establish a control group, carefully selected multiple nonequivalent comparison groups should be used, with the parameters of (non)equivalency reported in detail. By systematically contrasting the experimental and comparison groups, important insights can be obtained into the limitations of the experimental condition. Needless to say, findings obtained using nonequivalent comparison groups should be considered tentative until replicated using controlled comparison procedures.

6. The independent variable(s) should be operationally defined and replicable in an independent setting. If assignment to experimental conditions is based on a measurement procedure, the psychometric characteristics of that procedure should be reported, including information on scale development, standardization sample, reliability, validity, structural integrity (that is, is the measure uni- or multidimensional?), scoring, and interpretation. Involvement in a treatment/intervention must be operationally defined in terms of setting, personnel, admission criteria, programmatic procedures, and client and staff expectations.

7. The dependent measure(s) must similarly be operationalized with detailed information about their psychometric characteristics. Archival data should be described in terms of the procedures employed in its collection, reduction, and storage. Reliance on a single dependent variable is rarely justified. Multiple dependent variables should be selected to reflect the multidimensional impact of the independent variable. Insofar as possible, paper and pencil measures should be balanced by complementary behavioral indices and/or ratings by those who are indirectly effected by programs (for instance, spouses, children, coworkers). Ideally, multiple procedures should be used to assess each of multiple dependent variables. In all cases, readers should be informed of the potential and actual range of scores for each measurement procedure. Exact scoring procedures used should be described. If raters are used, their qualifications, training, and agreement level should be presented.

8. Experimental findings should always include appropriate descriptive statistics. Statistical procedures should be clearly identified, including information about specific commercially available statistical packages which were used. Criteria for reporting factor analytic results are presented in detail in Comrey (1978). Statistical procedures, parametric and nonparametric, should be selected for their power and clarity rather than their current popularity. When appropriate, multivariate procedures should be used in conjunction with or in place of univariate procedures. The former are essential in those instances in which multiple measurement techniques are employed to assess one or more (ideally) dependent variables. Significance levels should be determined by the nature of the experimental question rather than by convention (readers are referred to Skipper, Guenther, and Nass, 1967, for an extended discussion of this issue). Finally, careful consideration should be given to the determination of the significance and power of findings. Cohen (1977) provides a detailed analysis of power analyses for interested readers.

The foregoing principles are assumed to be "givens" throughout this chapter. Undoubtedly they represent additional burdens for those of us involved in field-based applied research. Yet unless prevention's evaluation procedures are incorporated within scientifically sound research designs, their heuristic value will be extremely limited. Unless considered sacrosanct, the principles of generalizability and replicability will be sacrificed to convenience and pragmatism. Consequently, evaluative results will be limited in their application to specific programs in specific settings and, in extreme instances, to specific program recipients. Under such conditions, skeptical policymakers and service providers can justify their opposition to prevention by pointing out the limits of our data and our inability to determine a priori the positive and negative consequences of our efforts.

## Planning Prevention Research

Thus far the term "prevention" has been used to refer to a generic category of interventions which share a common goal—reducing the amount of mental illness in society. The concept of prevention within mental health has its historic roots in the public health movement, which justifiably argues that its biggest victories over major illnesses have been in prevention rather than treatment (President's Commission on Mental Health, 1978, Vol. 1). Within the public health model, preventive efforts are categorized as primary, secondary, and tertiary. Differences among these categories relate to the point in the disorder's development at which intervention is begun.

*Tertiary* efforts are initiated once disorder is established and its manifestations are differentially diagnosible. The intent of tertiary efforts is to minimize the disorder's duration and contribute to the rehabilitative effort. If successful, such efforts will enable the victims of disorder to approximate their premorbid status. Tertiary efforts do not, however, in any way "prevent" the disorder or its secondary consequences (Bloom, 1979; Cowen, 1973, 1977; Kessler & Albee, 1975).

*Secondary* efforts, by contrast, are targeted so as to interrupt the pathological sequence as early as possible following its onset. Although underway, the evolving dysfunction is prevented from achieving full symptomatic status through the effective application of early detection and remediation procedures. If successful, such efforts protect the individual from the full direct and indirect consequences of the established disorder. In order for such a program to be effective, the investigator must rely on the products of extensive preliminary research to identify accurately the early behavioral manifestations which differentiate pathological from normal premorbid states. As noted, the timing of secondary interventions is of critical importance (Gersten et al., 1979). All secondary efforts— for example, a program for school children—have the *potential* (as yet only minimally investigated) for negatively influencing developmental processes. The experimenter must appreciate the need to monitor children involved in such programs so as to identify as early as possible negative consequences associated with being labeled "at risk" and with the expectations generated in the target children and their peers, family, teachers, and so forth following referral to a remedial program. It is possible that a second-level secondary effort may be necessary to counter the iatrogenic influences resulting from screening. In spite of their potentially negative side effects, secondary efforts, such as the example given, represent viable strategies which use diagnostic and treatment skills already available and incorporated within existing human service delivery system concepts.

Increasingly, proponents of preventive efforts argue that *primary* efforts represent the only true form of prevention (Cowen 1977, 1980; Kessler & Albee, 1975). Their point is well taken! Primary efforts are designed to avoid completely the onset of disorder and seek "to engineer structures, processes, situations, events, and programs that maximally benefit, both in scope and temporal stability, the psychological adjustment, effectiveness, happiness, and coping skills of large numbers of individuals [Cowen, 1980, p. 264]." Danish, Smyer, and Nowak (1980) propose distinguishing between primary prevention efforts which aim to eliminate the causes of dysfunction and those which intend to promote health through the development of positive competencies. The latter ef

forts, according to Danish et al., should be referred to as "enhancement" and appreciated as qualitatively distinct, in terms both of target and procedures, from pathology reduction efforts. Enhancement efforts seek to create positive increments in skills which improve the quality of life in participating individuals. For example, teaching individuals about assertiveness, expectant parents about child development and parenting strategies, or engaged couples about marital adjustment and sexuality represent a sample of potential enhancement programs. Obviously, the discrepancy between primary prevention and enhancement efforts often reflects relative emphases and, as noted below, distinctions in targeting specificity, rather than absolute differences.

Presently, primary prevention enhancement efforts appear to be valued above all other forms of prevention. As Cowen (1977) so colorfully explains:

> Primary prevention is a glittering, diffuse, thoroughly abstract term. Its aura is so exalted that some put it on the same plane as the Nobel prize. It holds the mysterious, exciting promise of "breakthrough." It offers a sharp contrast to all that mental health had done, a shadowy, but nevertheless grand, alternative. It is terribly "major"—in the lingo of childhood games I have known, something to be approached with massive "great steps" [p. 1].

Yet in spite of the "aura" attributed to primary prevention, in the final analysis the form of prevention attempted should reflect two related factors: (1) the nature of the disorder to be addressed, and (2) the state of knowledge about its ontogenesis, including causative factors, developmental manifestations, and direct and indirect consequences. In the absence of knowledge of a disorder's causes and/or of the individual, familial, and environmental conditions for its manifestations, the initiation of a primary prevention effort appears premature. Similarly, if one is ignorant of the preliminary manifestations of a target disorder, unable to systematically detect their presence, or incapable of altering their evolution, one is unprepared to attack a problem at the secondary level. Finally if we are unaware of how a specific skill develops and is maintained in the everyday environment, enhancement efforts may need to be deferred.

Thus the first step in planning a prevention program is the objective determination of our state of knowledge about the target problem. All three forms of prevention (primary, secondary, and enhancement) assume the availability of considerable background information. Cowen (1980) underscores the importance of this fact in differentiating "prevention" or "executive" from "preventive" or "generative" research. The former terms refer to programs which reduce the rates, duration or development of specific targeted behaviors. As noted elsewhere (Lorion & Lounsbury, 1981), the bottom line for evaluating such programs is demonstrated evidence of reductions in the *incidence* (the number of new cases observed during a specified time period) and *prevalence* (the total number of affected individuals within a specified population) of the target disorder. Effective primary prevention should decrease both the disorder's incidence and prevalence rates. Effective secondary prevention programs should reduce the disorder's prevalence (by reducing the duration of individual cases) but not, in the absolute sense, its incidence (since early manifestations may continue to be counted). Thus the term "prevention" should be used to refer to an active involvement with disorder, in Kelly's (1977) terms, to "deeds and actions that work."

By contrast, *preventive* or *generative* research involves the accumulation and analysis of information necessary for the subsequent development of prevention programs. Findings from such research should serve as guides which define, direct, and/or correct the implementation and evaluation of the intervention. In many instances, a portion of the requisite generative base can be found in the general psychological literature (in the author's opinion, the literature on early childhood development is the most promising vein to mine for this material). In those cases in which an inadequate foundation exists for immediate program development, priority should be given to the generation of solid information about targeted phenomena. Bypassing this step leaves the investigator vulnerable to the situation described in the oft-televised oil filter commercial—"You can pay me now [for the filter] or you can pay me later [for the engine]." As Kuhn (1970) so clearly explains in his description of the work of natural science, apparent scientific leaps actually represent the end product of scores of little steps. In all likelihood, the "giant step" of primary prevention described by Cowen (1980) will have a similar genesis!

Elsewhere (Lorion & Lounsbury, 1981) the author has presented an expanded version of Cowen's (1980) mini-framework for generating preventive and prevention knowledge. The components of this expanded model will not be discussed in detail here; interested readers are referred to the original sources for that information (Cowen, 1980; Lorion & Lounsbury, 1981). The identified dimensions of this model, however, will be reviewed briefly as relevant steps in the decision-making sequence of planning the research effort. These dimensions relate to the researcher's selection of objectives, anticipation of obstacles, identification of methodological alternatives, and determination of the cost-benefit ratios of selected investigatory procedures. The suggested decision steps are as follows:

### 1. FOCUS

Is the proposed research to involve the development, implementation, and evaluation of an intervention—that is, an executive/prevention effort—or is it to represent preliminary knowledge gathering—a generative/preventive effort?

### 2. CONTENT DIRECTION

Is the planned research to be involved with the interruption of an already initiated dysfunctional process (with the early detection/intervention components of secondary prevention), with the avoidance of the onset of the targeted disorder (primary prevention), or with the development of skills/competencies related to healthy functioning (enhancement)?

### 3. TARGET SPECIFICITY

Can the direct and indirect targets of the proposed research be identified such that, for example, the direct impact of a secondary prevention program upon the identified person can be assessed and, simultaneously, the concomitant indirect impact of the program on peers, teachers, parents, and significant others?

### 4. KNOWLEDGE-GATHERING MODE

Will the direct and/or indirect impacts of the proposed research be assessed via systematic observation, self-report, behavioral ratings, objective indices, or archival records? Will the procedure(s) (the aforementioned alternatives should not be considered mutually exclusive) used be collected as part of a field study, natural experiment, or quasi-experimental or experimental design?

### 5. RESEARCH TYPE

Will the proposed research focus on delineating the nature and extent of interrelationships among variables of interest through the application of correlational procedures (that is, *relational*) or attempt to infer the magnitude of an intervention (*programmatic*)? Will dependent and/or independent variables be considered in terms of their unique or interactive (univariate versus multivariate analyses) contributions to knowledge?

### 6. TEMPORAL PERSPECTIVE

Does the proposed research consider the variable(s) of interest and/or the impact(s) of the intervention to reflect state or process entities? Are measurements to be made immediately prior to and/or following the intervention, or on multiple occasions preceding and following the event(s) under investigation?

As noted, the foregoing dimensions are intended to serve as global guidelines for planning a priori the basic components of prevention research. For the most part, such research is field based and must adapt to the idiosyncratic demands of applied settings. The following section will briefly address issues centrally related to the conduct of applied research. It is obviously not intended as a detailed review of a topic in which interest has grown exponentially during the past decade. Interested readers are referred to the following sources for detailed consideration of the area: Cook and Campbell (1979); Cowen (1978); Fairweather and Tornatzky (1977); Guttentag and Struening (1975): Posavac and Carey (1980); Rossi, Freeman and Wright (1979); Struening and Guttentag (1975); and Weiss (1972).

## The "Politics" of Field Research

Having exhaustively considered all of the parameters of the proposed research, planned every detail, operationalized every variable beyond reproach, the experimenter now enters the field in which it is assumed Murphy's law reigns supreme—"If anything can go wrong, it will"! Armed with this admonition, the researcher ventures forth to meet and, hopefully, conquer the enemy. The neophyte field researcher has been alerted to adopt a paranoid stance, give little faith to assurances for access and cooperation, and appreciate the negative valence attached to research by "practitioners" of any sort. Although the author knows of no such study, it would seem reasonable to assess systematically the self-fulfilling potential of such expectations. Could it possibly be that we have, in part, contributed to the problems "out there" and that, once again, Pogo is right—"it is us"? Described as "perhaps the only proposition in social science that approaches the status of an immutable law" Thomas's dictum seems applicable in this situation: "if men define situations as real, they are real in their consequences [Bronfenbrenner, 1977, p. 516]."

Equally negative and counterproductive expectations of the "real" motives of researchers may be held by field personnel. Behind the rhetoric of scientific gains and benefits for those in need are presumed to exist the researcher's personal desire for recognition within the university and scientific community, for the benefits associated with grants and publications, and for the autonomy which often accompanies an active research program. The researcher is perceived as insensitive to the "real" demands of providing services and as unlikely to provide tangible benefits to the host agency or program. Feedback, if provided at all, often is limited to a copy of a technical report or scientific paper. Additional services, resources, and university involvement will, of course, cease upon attainment of the researcher's objectives or termination of funding. Consequently, the field setting will be accused of irresponsibility and/or insensitivity if it fails to continue with the "project" once the researcher leaves. Field personnel may then wonder why they should bother, since it is a guaranteed "no win" situation.

Yet in spite of the mutual suspiciousness, applied research occurs. It does so because those involved appreciate its most important principle—collaboration. Open communication among all parties from the outset can be a very powerful weapon against the aforementioned negative self-fulfilling expectations. Prior to entering the field the researcher should prepare a written description of the study's purposes, anticipated timelines, expectations about the involvement of field personnel, and procedures for data collection, anonymity, and feedback. This document should be viewed by all concerned as a starting point for negotiation. The knowledgeable researcher will determine beforehand the approximate administrative level at which to make entry and have the individual responsible for the level identify who should engage in preliminary negotiations. Many a field project has been seriously undermined (if not terminated) because the negotiating process occurred at the wrong level. For example, the author has learned (the hard way, of course!) that research in the schools should not be approved by a principal without prior approval from the superintendent's office. Moreover, all approvals should represent an enlightened decision (informed consent, if you will). Approval given in haste by field personnel without a detailed description of the study's aims and procedures and accepted gleefully by the researcher can be just as quickly rescinded when the administrator must answer the questions of an inquisitive principal, irate parent, or angry school board member. Careful steps taken early can prevent considerable backtracking later. Put another way, if you don't look the gift horse in the mouth, it may bite you later!

Throughout the negotiating process, the researcher should make every effort to balance immediate costs and direct benefits to the setting. In many instances the research effort, if slightly modified, can simultaneously obtain information helpful to the setting. In other instances, the researcher can provide an "in-kind match" for the setting's cooperation by conducting in-service training sessions, analyzing data of interest to the setting, or agreeing to assist in grant preparation. If only limited funds are available for reimbursing field personnel, the option to allow these individuals to use the entire amount at their discretion (for example, for a new coffee pot, classroom plants, a special lunch) is typically well received. A primary key to successful negotiation is the development, within field setting personnel, of a sense of proprietorship about the research—that it is *their* research. Demonstrations of the researcher's respect for their expertise and openness to their suggestions and insights about the proposed research can both increase the likelihood of the project's acceptance and significantly improve its final products.

By way of illustration, the author's current research involves the development of a multilevel (primary and secondary) prevention program whose focal component is a comprehensive developmental assessment of children entering kindergarten. Information obtained from this evaluation is made available to the kindergarten teacher for individualized instruction; consultation with parents, special educators, and the school psychologists, and curriculum planning. Ideally, children in need of special education services will be identified and remediated early. In some instances, alterations of the instructional program are expected to obviate the need for special education involvement. It is assumed that most children will benefit from the increased individualism in their curriculum. The ultimate decision to involve all children represents a positive suggestion of field setting personnel to mitigate the negative stigma of involvement in a "special program." Moreover, by doing so the program replaces the state-mandated screening for kindergarten children, thereby relieving the classroom teacher of a burdensome responsibility. The evaluative procedures, selected in conjunction with local special educators and school psychologists, are useful for case consultations and provide diagnostically relevant baseline information should a comprehensive assessment be subsequently necessary. An important measure of the project's long-term, system-level impact is expected to be documented shifts in the timing and nature of pupil personnel services in the target schools. Specifically, it is hypothesized that children in these schools will be referred earlier and require different and fewer services than children in control schools. Negotiation with school personnel resulted in the development of a computerized management information system which monitors all pupil personnel services provided in the schools. This system involves daily record-keeping in a format which line personnel find efficient and simple. In fact, the record-keeping procedures double as their daily calendar. The researchers benefit from this record-keeping system by obtaining more information than originally anticipated from all of the schools. Line personnel benefit because they are relieved of the demanding task of preparing quarterly and annual reports. The school system benefits by gaining improved accountability procedures for state and federally supported special education services and by obtaining base rate information on service utilization patterns which can be used in personnel planning. Thus extensive preliminary negotiations have resulted in a set of dependent variables which exceed the initial data requirements of the researcher and provide multiple benefits to personnel throughout the school system.

## Validity Issues

It has often been stated that politics is the art of compromise. Throughout the negotiation process, however, it is essential that the researcher recognize and preserve nonnegotiable aspects of the research program. If proposed changes in subject selection, data collection procedures, or research measures invalidate the information gained, they must be rejected. Campbell and Stanley's (1963) oft-cited criteria for internal and external validity represent useful guidelines for determining the negotiability of aspects of the research design. Given the pervasiveness of discussion of these criteria throughout the evaluation literature, a brief review of them will be sufficient for most readers. Those who are unfamiliar with these criteria are urged to review Campbell and Stanley (1963).

*Internal* validity refers to the absence of experimental confounds from the research design. In other words, observed changes in the dependent measures are influenced exclusively by the level of the independent variable(s). Factors which influence a study's internal validity include:

- *history*: the occurrence of uncontrolled events between pre- and posttesting or during the follow-up period which may influence the measured level of the dependent measure(s)
- *testing*: the impact of prior experience with the dependent measure between pre- and post-follow-up testing
- *statistical regression*: tendency of groups selected on basis of extreme scores to have less extreme scores in subsequent testing
- *selection*: differential biases in selection of comparison groups
- *experimental mortality*: differential loss of subjects (due to attrition or imcomplete data) from comparison groups.

*External* validity refers to the generalizability of research findings to other populations and settings. Specifically at issue is the applicability of the research findings outside of the research context. Factors which relate to external validity include:

- *reactive effects of testing*: influence of pretesting on the impact of the independent variable
- *interaction of selection biases and experimental variable*
- *reactive effects of experimental conditions*: influence on the dependent measure(s) of the research context and fact that subjects are, in effect, subjects in a research effort
- *multiple treatment interference*: influence on dependent measure(s) of subject's involvement in ongoing or prior intervention strategies.

Bronfenbrenner's (1977) consideration of *ecological* validity represents an important additional criterion for insuring the validity of research findings. Rejecting the assumption that conducting the research in a naturalistic setting assures that its findings will be ecologically valid, Bronfenbrenner proposes the following definition: "Ecological validity refers to the extent to which the environment experienced by the subjects in a scientific investigation has the properties it is supposed or assumed to have by the investigator [p. 516]." This definition assumes that careful consideration be given to the objective and subjective aspects of the research setting. Thomas's dictum on the link between perceptions of reality and consequences, discussed earlier, is appropriate in this context. Moreover, Bronfenbrenner emphasizes the fact that it is erroneous to presume a priori the validity of any setting. Depending on the specific experimental question, a school may or may not be the appropriate setting for conducting research on the early identification of learning disabilities, for example. It is essential, according to Bronfenbrenner, that the researcher recognize that ecological validity, unlike face validity, is not to be established through logic and appearance. Rather, the ecological validity of any experimental context must be demonstrated systematically using the experimental procedures typically associated with construct validity (Cronbach & Meehl, 1955). Thus, the generalizability of research findings from the original research setting to other settings is determined

by testing the ecological theory underlying the research operation—that is, the assumptions being made about the nature and generalizability of the environment in which the research is being conducted. For example,

when a laboratory study is regarded as representative of behaviors elsewhere, evidence must be provided of an empirical relation to similar activities in the other setting—in other words, validation against an external *ecological* criterion *with the possibility of systematic divergence explicitly taken into account*. It should be recognized, moreover, that such divergence may take the form not merely of differences in average response, but in the *total pattern of relationships, and in the underlying processes that they are presumed to reflect* [Bronfenbrenner, 1977, p. 319].

Thus the demonstration of ecological validity requires the application of rigorous experimental procedures in assessing the influence of environmental variables upon the dependent measures. It is apparent that this process involves multilevel replications in which setting conditions are systematically altered and their effects measured. In so doing, the researcher becomes capable of identifying and ultimately controlling the setting characteristics which are necessary to support the prevention effort under study. Accumulation of this information may circumvent significantly obstacles typically encountered in attempts to disseminate innovative programs (Fairweather & Tornatzky, 1977; Munoz, Snowden, & Kelly, 1979). At the very least, integration of Bronfenbrenner's concept of ecological validity into prevention research promises to increase its methodological rigor and scientific precision.

Apart from environmental factors which may influence the generalizability of observed findings, it should be apparent to the reader that the major threats to the validity of applied research involve subject and measurement factors. Two of the most demanding challenges encountered by the applied researcher involve selecting experimental and control subjects and maintaining their relative integrity over time. From the outset, biases are inherent in determining who participates in most field-based interventions. Differences between receptive and nonreceptive sites have yet to be systematically investigated, although Fairweather and Tornatzky's (1977) work on program dissemination provides some clues as to their nature. It appears that staff composition in terms of variables such as age, sex, and professional status is involved, as well as the organizational flexibility of the setting. For example, in many instances cooperative schools tend to be either in the inner city or in upper-middle-class neighborhoods in which parents actively support innovation. Thus the generalizability of a program's assessed impact to initially nonreceptive settings which may differ in multiple ways from the actual experimental schools must be carefully assessed.

Ideally, the experimenter will have available a sufficient number of potential sites so that they can be randomly assigned as experimental and control settings. Frequently, however, what opportunities exist for random assignment occur at the subject level. The likelihood of resistance to random assignment of subjects, however, depends in part on the type of prevention attempted. Population-focused efforts, such as primary prevention and enhancement, may encounter less resistance to random assignment to nontreatment groups than secondary efforts. In the latter instances, setting personnel are typically reluctant to deny individuals with identifiable dysfunctions access to a program which might help them. As a consequence, the definition of "risk" may be broadened and increasingly more established "early signs" included in selection criteria. In such cases, the secondary prevention program becomes de facto a treatment resource for individuals with established disorders. Statements such as "There is nothing wrong with Jimmy" or "Mary is so far behind," if translated into action, can result in the misapplication of secondary prevention procedures to subjects in need of tertiary prevention. A possible resolution of this dilemma is to admit such individuals into a special group whose data will be analyzed independently. Inclusion of such individuals in the regular experimental groups can have two negative consequences. First, their presence dilutes the intervention's perceived prevention focus and increases the likelihood of additional "special" referrals. Second, and more problematic, the need to respond simultaneously to incipient and established disorders alters in unpredictable ways the application of the intervention's procedures. Thus the researcher must monitor continuously the actual criteria used to select and assign subjects to experimental and control groups.

Two other subject-related issues must be considered. First, the researcher should insure that well-meaning field setting personnel and the control subjects themselves do not alter the nontreatment condition by making available or obtaining additional services, attention, or privileges. This confound occurs, for example, in school-based interventions as teachers resolve their discomfort about withholding services from children in need of help by providing tutoring, additional attention, and so on to control children. If not monitored or controlled, the differential history of experimental and control children can severely limit the interpretability of observed findings.

A frequent problem in longitudinal research is maintaining contact with subjects throughout the study period. With children as subjects, it is often helpful to obtain school codes as early as possible so that the children can easily be located if they change schools. For inner-city populations this is an important step. The author has also found it very useful to send birthday cards and holiday greetings to research subjects. In this way, both adults and children appreciate the personal contact and up-to-date mailing lists can be maintained. Moreover, in fact, presumably because of the ongoing contact, the collection of follow-up data appears to be facilitated. If funds are available, reimbursement of subjects with a bonus for completion of all data is, of course, useful. If the researcher anticipates major difficulties with subject attrition, it is essential that initial samples be sufficiently large at the outset to insure acceptable sample sizes at the project's conclusion. One way in which this may be achieved is to identify a large sample of potential subjects and randomly select a subsample as the initial experimental group. Once the initial sample has been served and posttesting begins, a second random sample is selected for the intervention. Then the initial experimental sample is assessed at follow-up as the second sample is posttested, and the remainder of the original sample continues to be monitored. If possible, additional experimental samples can be selected. This procedure allows for multiple replications and maintains the interest of control subjects who are assured of receiving services.

As noted, measurement limitations are the second major threat to the validity of prevention research findings. The methodological and statistical parameters of these limitations are discussed at length in Lorion and Lounsbury (1981). To avoid redundancy and conserve space, only the major principles detailed in that exposition shall be presented here. In general, the overarching guidelines are rather obvious—the researcher must avoid the temptation to short-circuit the demanding steps necessary to demonstrate that the measurement procedures are adequately reliable, valid, powerful, and sensitive. The reader who is tempted to dismiss this admonition as out of touch with reality of applied research is urged to reconsider the findings provided by the three reviews discussed earlier. Too often investments of time, money, professional reputation, community resources, and, most importantly, faith in the concept of prevention are jeopardized because inadequate measures produce nonreplicable and uninterpretable findings. Perhaps so much attention is paid to the political and fiscal demands associated with applied prevention research that basic empirical matters become secondary. Regardless of its causes, inadequate measurement jeopardizes the identification of effective prevention strategies and must be replaced by rigorous psychometric procedures.

An initial step in sound measurement involves identifying the range of possible programmatic impacts, direct and indirect, which can result from or relate to the preventive intervention. Each potential measure should be examined in terms of its capacity to reflect sensitively the intervention's impacts, its measurability, and its fit within the overall evaluative design. For example, the school-based prevention program described earlier can impact at a number of potential levels, including:

- direct individual effects on children (e.g., improved reading)
- direct individual effects on teachers (e.g., improved attitudes toward teaching)
- direct individual effects on parents (e.g., fewer school-related confrontations with children)
- interactional effects among the dyadic and triadic pairs of these individuals (e.g., parents and teachers, children and parents and teachers)
- indirect effects on the interpersonal contacts of the children, parents, and teachers (e.g., family impacts for teachers; effects of parent impacts on siblings of target child)
- direct system effects (e.g., changes in teacher assignment pattern, demand for special education services, policy considerations relevant to the link between service demand, reduced need, and special education personnel utilization)
- indirect system effects (e.g., the program's impact on curriculum planning in subsequent grades, requisite shifts in special education personnel at upper grades, alterations in the timing and success potential of mainstreaming decisions).

The preceding list represents a tempting invitation to "shotgun" the program's effects. To do so would be foolhardy. Measurement of that range of dependent measures exceeds the capability of even the most well-funded researcher. Moreover, the simultaneous assessment of so many levels of impact can create highly complex reactive effects which will confound the interpretability of observed results and seriously limit their external validity. For example, the simultaneous assessment of teacher attitudes toward teaching and parent-teacher interactional styles can be reciprocally reactive. Teachers may be sensitized to their attitudes toward teaching as a function of the assessment of their interactional style with parents or vice versa. Similarly, assessment of the parent/target-child interaction may effect reactively the assessment of the parent/other-child interaction.

The solution to this problem is to select carefully a set of dependent variables which can be optimally assessed in relation to resources available and measurement clarity. In the school-based prevention project described above, the decision was made to focus initial attention on direct individual child variables and direct and indirect system variables. It was assumed that this set of outcome measures would be minimally interreactive and provide a reasonable sample of the range of potential program impacts. As the number of experimental schools increases, monitoring of impacts on individual children will be continued in a sample of settings. Other sets of child, teacher, parent, or system variables will be assessed in independent samples of schools. Thus the overall project impact will be assessed systematically yet in a piecemeal fashion which minimizes the invalidating influences of the measurement process itself.

In general, prevention researchers should consider the following principles for selecting program criteria (Lorion & Lounsbury, 1981).

1. If possible, established measures should be used. The development of a measure for a specific study should be based solely on the absence of an acceptable alternative.

2. Regardless of the number or type of measures used, each should have demonstrated evidence of its psychometric goodness—reliability and validity.

3. Reliability estimates should be selected based on the purpose of measurement and the trait/state nature of the construct of interest. Although relatively easy to demonstrate, an index of internal consistency (for example, the Kudar-Richardson Formula—20) is insufficient evidence of reliability if the measure is to be used to predict over time or to reflect observer perceptions. Longitudinal and/or trait measures should be assessed in terms of their test-retest consistency. State measures should be assessed in terms of interrater agreement.

4. Evidence of a measure's concurrent validity should represent a minimal criterion for its use. In the absence of acceptable alternative indices against which to assess the focal measure, the first stage of the research effort should be focused on their development. Cronbach and Meehl's (1955) classic work on construct validity should be familiar to all who work in prevention, and its principles implemented.

5. The unit of analysis refers to the level at which behavior is to be studied. Once a unit is selected, it should be reflected throughout the measurement and statistical procedures. Thus, for example, if the decision were made to examine parent-child interaction, dyadic measurement procedures should be used throughout and represent the unit of statistical analysis.

6. Whenever possible, program procedures should be assessed simultaneously with outcome. Thus every prevention project should include a formative evaluation design in order to verify that the formal program description reflects actual procedures, and more importantly, to ascertain the (in)effective components of the program.

7. As noted above, an important consideration for field setting personnel in determining the acceptability of an applied research program is its direct relevance for their immediate and/or short-term needs. Thus, the measurement battery should include indices relevant to the setting's ongoing operations and/or policy review procedures.

8. If possible, dependent variables should be assessed using multiple criteria. Thus each outcome criterion, for example, should be assessed using a combination of behavioral, self-report, and rating measures. In this way, the *convergent validity* (Campbell & Fiske, 1959) of the program's reported outcome can be demonstrated.

9. Estimates of program impact should allow for a direct response to the question posed within a summative evaluation design, that is, "Does the program work?" If multiple outcome criteria are involved, the researcher should report outcome in terms of individual criteria and a composite index of overall program effectiveness. Clearly, any attempt to combine disparate measures into an overall index creates measurement difficulties. Rarely is it possible simply to sum separate outcome scores. In many instances, weighting of scores will be necessary in order to reflect the differential relevance of criteria to policy considerations as well as to control for redundancy among measures. Readers attempting to create a composite outcome measure are encouraged to refer to the literature on operations research (e.g., Nagel & Neef, 1976), decision theory (e.g., Raiffa, 1968), and psychometrics (e.g., Cohen, 1977; Ghiselli, 1964) for helpful guidelines in tackling this issue.

## The Measurement of Outcome

Cowen (1977, 1980) and others (Kelly, 1977; Kessler & Albee, 1975) describe prevention as a multiply beneficial shift in the conceptualization and remediation of psychosocial disorders. Their enthusiasm is well founded! Recall Cowen's (1980) distinction between generative and executive research. As noted earlier, the latter refers to the direct evaluation using both formative and summative procedures, of the processes and outcomes associated with strategies to reduce disorder and/or increase competencies. Issues relevant to executive research shall be addressed in

this section. Before addressing those issues, however, the author wishes to underline the extraordinary potential contributions of generative research for prevention's future. Just as the nation's space program produced increments in knowledge far beyond the relatively narrow problem of round-trip travel to and from the moon, so generative research informs us not only about possible steps for primary and secondary strategies but, perhaps of equal importance, about the very processes whereby functional and dysfunctional states develop and are maintained. Preventive research can increase our understanding of the environmental parameters which engender, maintain, and modify human behavior. If nothing else, increased emphasis on the preventability of disorder and the enhancement of competencies has served as an essential catalyst for investigating external behavioral influences and their interaction with individual difference variables. Consequently, the impact of architectural, interpersonal, systemic, and regulatory processes on behavior is now under scrutiny, which is likely to result in significant paradigmatic shifts in existing theories of human behavior.

Ideally, generative gains will be complemented by demonstrations of program effectiveness. In the final analysis, scientifically valid evidence must be produced to support the claimed benefits of preventive interventions. In the author's view, such evidence must meet certain minimal criteria. First, it must include demonstrated *reductions* in the incidence and/or prevalence of targeted disorders following participation in a primary or secondary intervention. Enhancement programs must demonstrate *both* acquisition of the target skill and the positive influence of that skill upon the enhanced individual's quality of life. Second, appropriate comparison groups (ideally, established through random assignment) must be part of any attempts at summative evaluations of prevention and enhancement programs. In their absence, demonstrated outcomes must be suspect. Third, both prevention and enhancement, by definition, postulate temporal outcomes. Therefore, their impacts must be assessed longitudinally with attention paid to both short- and long-term consequences. Finally, dependent measures must allow for the monitoring of both positive and negative consequences. In that way the negative outcomes potentially associated with prevention programs can be examined and, hopefully, themselves prevented.

As noted, the author views the objective demonstration of reductions in the incidence/prevalence of the targeted disorder as the *sine qua non* of prevention research. Reports of the actual procedures followed in the intervention, of the number of individuals serviced, and of the number of contact hours provided are important data. They do not, however, answer the critical question—has the disorder's onset been avoided or its development discontinued? Without evidence to that effect, prevention cannot be claimed!

An essential ingredient of this evaluation must be information relevant to the occurrence of the disorder prior to, during, and following implementation of the prevention program for served and unserved populations. Gathering such information is possible through the systematic application of epidemiological procedures (for example, as employed by Dohrenwend and Dohrenwend, 1974), especially those related to needs assessment (Lorion, 1978). Careful analysis of archival records represents an efficient and often objective strategy for establishing necessary base rates of the target disorder's occurrence (Siegel, Atkinson, & Cohn, 1977). The specific source of such records is of course determined by the intervention's focus. Potential sources include:

- fiscal and service delivery reports of federal, state, and local health and mental health planning and service delivery agencies
- the ongoing monitoring efforts of federal and state clearinghouses such as the biometry division of NIMH, the National Clearinghouse for Drug Abuse Information, the National Clearinghouse for Mental Health Information, the National Clearinghouse for Alcohol Information, and the National Center for Health Statistics
- records which reflect the consequences of the targeted disorder, such as arrests and/or convictions for driving while intoxicated and public drunkenness; the number of investigations of child abuse or domestic violence; industrial absenteeism and accident rates; adolescent pregnancies, abortions, and marriages; foster care placements; and a range of social indicators (Blum, 1974; Kilpatrick, 1973).

For example, the aforementioned school-based prevention program based its estimate of the incidence of emotional and learning disorders on the following data obtained from experimental and control schools during the two years prior to program onset:

- special education records of the number of primary grade children categorized in each of the handicapping categories
- records of the number of special education referrals and contacts and scheduled multidisciplinary team meetings
- records of the initial psychological evaluation referrals occurring at all elementary grade levels

- records of the duration of special education placement and the latency to resumption of mainstream placement.

The program's defining secondary preventive objectives will be evaluated in terms of these variables. In order to argue that secondary prevention has occurred, reductions favoring the experimental schools must be observed in:

- the number of primary grade children diagnosed as handicapped
- the duration of special education placements (i.e., earlier mainstreaming)
- the grade level at which initial psychological referrals are made (i.e., earlier recognition of deficits).

Evidence of the program's primary prevention and enhancement objectives must be documented in terms of evidence favoring the experimental schools relevant to such archival data as:

- the total number of handicapped children
- academic achievement scores for all kindergarten children (i.e., an improved learning environment)
- maintenance of observed decreases in handicapping conditions throughout subsequent grades
- maintenance of observed improvements in academic achievement throughout subsequent grades
- ultimate reductions in grade retentions and high-school dropout rates.

Thus archival data can provide important objective estimates of the incidence/prevalence of the target disorder and serve as a basis for continuously monitoring their levels. In conjunction with other dependent measures designed to monitor the program's unique effects, archival data can serve as a central component of a multifaceted outcome evaluation. In their absence the investigator may have to resort to more demanding alternatives. The most demanding of these is the community survey, examples of which are described by Hollingshead and Redlich (1958); Srole, Langner, Michael, Opler, and Rennie (1962); and Gersten et al. (1979). Such surveys are very time-consuming and costly, and their development represents a major research effort. In the absence of other data, however, they may be a necessary preliminary step to any prevention effort.

Indirect (and therefore less accurate) estimates of the extent of a problem's impact on a population can be obtained using three needs assessment procedures: the key informant technique, the community focus, and the nominal group approach (Hagedorn, Beck, Neubert, & Werlin, 1976). The first of these involves the administration of a survey questionnaire to a group of individuals selected on the basis of their knowledge of existing community needs. The nominal groups approach represents an extended version of this approach. At best, key informants and members of the nominal group provide a global index of the extent of the target problem. If subsequently involved in the development or implementation of the prevention program, however, the estimates of these individuals thereafter must be suspect.

The community forum involves the use of structured large-group strategies to enable residents of a target area or representatives of an "at risk" population to respond to structured questions about the occurrence or impact of a disorder. Comments obtained in such meetings are typically tape-recorded and content analyzed in order to obtain an index of disorder. Following the intervention, these forums can be repeated in order to obtain an equally indirect estimate of reduced need. Once again, however, the investigator must recognize the limitations of such feedback in assessing the impact of any intervention.

Yet another alternative for demonstrating preventive consequences is the development of a system to monitor demands for and allocations of service delivery procedures. Referred to generically as management information systems (MIS), these procedural analyses can provide objective evidence of changes in service needs which parallel the delivery of the prevention program. A number of MIS strategies are described in Hagedorn et al. (1976), Hargreaves and Atkinson (1977), and Atkinson, Hargreaves, Horowitz, and Sorenson (1978). As noted above, the school-based prevention program described throughout this chapter includes an MIS as a central evaluation component. A brief description of this procedure, the Educational Services Log (ESL—Hightower, Work, & Lorion, 1982) will serve to illustrate the evaluative potential of such indices.

The ESL is designed in a daily calendar format, enabling pupil personnel staff (school psychologists, educational diagnosticians, speech therapists, and so on) to record scheduled professional contacts and maintain an ongoing, up-to-date record of all services delivered. Collected monthly, ESL records are computer-compatible for efficient analysis. They provide current information about the location, nature, and length of services actually provided, the relevant handicapping conditions served, the integration of services, the history of prior services for individual children, and mainstreaming decisions. Thus ESL data serve as a continuous index of the intervention's secondary and primary preventive consequences. Moreover, ESL data provide ongoing information

about the relative costs of preventive rather than reactive responses to school-related disorders.

In addition to monitoring the prevalence/incidence indices of the target disorder and the utilization and nature of service delivery procedures, the investigator interested in documenting preventive outcome can assess numerous program specific evaluative questions using the design and measurement principles described throughout this chapter. In all cases, the researcher must avoid the temptation to seek immediate short-term answers to what theoretically and practically are long-term questions. The limitations of research to date, described in detail in the reviews presented earlier, must be appreciated and avoided. Their continuation will accomplish little beyond clouding our understanding of our actual capacity to prevent human dysfunction at any level. Without systematic and long-term evaluation, the positive and negative consequences of efforts to avoid, disrupt, or replace dysfunctional processes will remain suspect and, potentially, as risky as the conditions they are designed to influence.

## Conclusion

This chapter's title alludes to the relationship between prevention and social change. By now the nature of that link should be apparent to readers of this volume. Prevention represents a marked shift in our efforts to understand the processes involved with behavioral change and the procedures and systems required to effect that change. If the claims made by the proponents of preventive efforts can be substantiated, then significant social policy decisions will be necessary. The assumptions underlying special education, for example, will be seriously challenged. Diagnostic and rehabilitative procedures will require significant revision. Service deliverers will need to gain new skills and new perspectives on whom to serve, when to serve them, and how to serve them. Similar changes of equal or greater impact will be necessary in the mental health and public health fields if promised impacts in these areas hold true. Yet the "iffiness" of prevention's potential must be recognized and removed bit by bit before significant social policy considerations can be seriously addressed. The route to the development of the requisite knowledge base is charted in this chapter, in the previously discussed reviews of community psychology research, and in the original conceptual calls to arms (Cowen, 1973, 1980; Kelly, 1977; Kessler & Albee, 1975). In spite of the temptation to traverse that route via "giant steps" (Cowen, 1980), the field will benefit in direct proportion to our cautiousness and precision as we tiptoe to the end of the rainbow.

# References

Albee, G. W., & Joffe, J. M. (Eds.) *Primary prevention of psychopathology.* Vol. 1. *The issues.* Hanover, N.H.: University Press of New England, 1977.

Atkinson, C. C., Hargreaves, W. A., Horowitz, M. J., & Sorenson, J. E. (Eds.) *Evaluation of human service programs.* New York: Academic Press, 1978.

Bloom, B. L. Strategies for the prevention of mental disorders. In Task Force on Community Mental Health Division, Division 27 of the American Psychological Association, *Issues in community psychology and preventive mental health.* New York: Behavioral Publications, 1977.

Bloom, B. L. Prevention of mental disorder. *Community Mental Health Journal,* 1979, **15**(3), 179–191.

Blum, H. L. *Planning for health.* New York: Human Science Press, 1974.

Bronfenbrenner, U. Toward an experimental ecology of human development. *American Psychologist,* 1977, **32**, 513–531.

Campbell, D. T., & Fiske, D. W. Convergent and discriminant validation by the multitrait-multimethod matrix. *Psychological Bulletin,* 1959, **56**(2), 81–105.

Campbell, D. T., & Stanley, J. C. *Experimental and quasi-experimental designs for research.* Chicago: Rand McNally, 1963.

Cohen, J. *Statistical power analysis for the behavioral sciences.* New York: Academic Press, 1977.

Comrey, A. L. Common methodological problems in factor analytic studies. *Journal of Consulting and Clinical Psychology,* 1978, **46**, 648–659.

Cook, T. D., & Campbell, D. T. *Quasi-experimentation design and analysis issues for field settings.* New York: Rand McNally, 1979.

Cowen, E. L. Social and community interventions. *Annual Review of Psychology,* 1973, **24**, 423–472.

Cowen, E. L. Baby-steps toward primary prevention. *American Journal of Community Psychology,* 1977, **5**, 1–22.

Cowen, E. L. Some problems in community program evaluation research. *Journal of Consulting and Clinical Psychology,* 1978, **46**, 792–805.

Cowen, E. L. The wooing of primary prevention. *American Journal of Community Psychology,* 1980, **8**(3), 258–284.

Cronbach, L. J., & Meehl, P. E. Construct validity in psychological tests. *Psychological Bulletin,* 1955, **52**, 281–302.

Danish, S. J., Smyer, M. A., & Nowak, C. A. Developmental intervention: Enhancing life-event processes. In P. B. Baltes & O. G. Brim, Jr. (Eds.), *Life-span development and behavior.* Vol. 3. New York: Academic Press, 1980.

Dohrenwend, B. P., & Dohrenwend, B. S. Social and cultural influences on psychopathology. *Annual Review of Psychology,* 1974, **25**, 417–452.

Fairweather, G. W., & Tornatzky, L. G. *Experimental methods for social policy research.* New York: Pergamon Press, 1977.

Forgays, D. G. (Ed.) *Primary prevention of psychopathology.* Vol. 2. *Environmental influences.* Hanover, N.H.: University Press of New England, 1978.

Gersten, J. C., Langner, T. S., & Simcha-Fagan, O. Developmental patterns of types of behavioral disturbance and secondary prevention. *International Journal of Mental Health,* 1979, **7**(3–4), 132–149.

Ghiselli, E. E. *Theory of psychological measurement.* New York: McGraw-Hill, 1964.

Guttentag, M., & Struening, E. L. *Handbook of evaluation research.* Vol. 2. Beverly Hills: Sage, 1975.

Hagedorn, H. J., Beck, K. L., Neubert, S. F., & Werlin, S. H. *A working manual of simple program evaluation techniques for community mental health centers.* Washington: Government Printing Office, 1976.

Hargreaves, W. A., & Atkinson, C. C. *Resource materials for community mental health program evaluation.* Washington: Government Printing Office, 1977.

Hightower, A. D., Work, W. C., & Lorion, R. P. The Educational Services Log: A management information system for monitoring service delivery procedures. Unpublished manuscript, University of Tennessee, 1982.

Hollinghead, A. B., & Redlich, F. C. *Social class and mental illness.* New York: Wiley, 1958.

Joint Commission on Mental Illness and Health. *Action for mental health.* New York: Basic Books, 1961.

Kelly, J. G. The search for ideas and deeds that work. In G. W. Albee & J. M. Joffe (Eds.), *Primary prevention of psychopathology.* Vol. 1. *The issues.* Hanover, N.H.: University Press of New England, 1977.

Kent, M. W., & Rolf, J. E. (Eds.) *Primary prevention of psychopathology.* Vol. 3. *Social competence in children.* Hanover, N.H.: University Press of New England, 1979.

Kessler, M., and Albee, G. W. Primary prevention. *Annual Review of Psychology,* 1975, **26**, 557–591.

Kilpatrick, S. T. *Statistical principles in health care information.* Baltimore: University Park Press, 1973.

Kuhn, T. S. *The structure of scientific revolutions.* Chicago: University of Chicago Press, 1970.

Levine, M. *The history of politics of community mental health.* New York: Oxford University Press, 1981.

Levine, M., & Levine, A. *A social history of helping services.* New York: Appleton-Century-Crofts, 1970.

Lorion, R. P. Strategies for the assessment of productivity in health care. *Social Policy,* 1978, **9**, 35–41.

Lorion, R. P. Prevention of mental disorder. A developmental perspective. *Proceedings of the Silver Jubilee Psychiatric Research Meeting,* Psychiatric Research Division University Hospital, Saskatoon, Saskatchewan, 1979.

Lorion, R. P., Barker, W. F., Cahill, J., Gallagher, R., Passons, W. A., & Kaufki, M. Scale development, normative, and parametric analyses of a preschool screening measure. *American Journal of Community Psychology,* 1981, 193–208.

Lorion, R. P., Cowen, E. L., & Caldwell, R. A. Problem types of children referred to a school-based mental health program: Identification and outcome. *Journal of Consulting and Clinical Psychology,* 1974, **42**(4), 491–496.

Lorion, R. P., & Lounsbury, J. Conceptual and methodological considerations in evaluating preventive interventions. In W. R. Tash & G. Stahler (Eds.), *Innovative approaches to mental health evaluation.* New York: Academic Press, 1981.

Lounsbury, J. W., Leader, D. S., Meares, E. P., & Cook, M. An analytic review of research in community psychology. *American Journal of Community Psychology,* 1980, **8**(4), 415–441.

McClure, L., Cannon, D., Allen, S., Belton, E., Connor, P., D'Ascoli, C., Stone, P., Sullivan, B., & McClure, G. Community psychology concepts and research base: Promise and product. *American Psychologist,* 1980, **35**, 1000–1011.

McCord, J. A thirty-year follow-up of treatment effects. *American Psychologist,* 1978, **33**, 284–289.

Munoz, R. F., Snowden, L. R., & Kelly, J. G. *Social and psychological research in community settings.* San Francisco: Jossey-Bass, 1979.

Nagel, S. S., & Neef, M. *Policy analysis in social science research.* Beverly Hills: Sage, 1979.

Novaco, R. W., & Monahan, J. Research in community psychology: An analysis of work published in the first six years of the *American Journal of Community Psychology. American Journal of Community Psychology,* 1980, **8,** 131–146.

Posavac, E. M., & Carey, R. G. *Program evaluation: Methods and case studies.* Englewood Cliffs, N.J.: Prentice-Hall, 1980.

Powers, E., & Witmer, H. *An experiment in the prevention of delinquency: The Cambridge-Somerville youth study.* New York: Columbia University Press, 1951.

President's Commission on Mental Health. *Report to the President.* Vols. 1–4. Washington: Government Printing Office, 1978.

Raiffa, H. *Decision analysis: Introductory lectures on choices under uncertainty.* Reading, Mass.: Addison-Wesley, 1968.

Rossi, P. H., Freeman, H. E., & Wright, S. R. *Evaluation: A systematic approach.* Beverly Hills: Sage, 1979.

Sameroff, A. J. Concepts of humanity in primary prevention. In G. W. Albee & J. M. Joffe (Eds.), *Primary prevention of psychopathology.* Vol. 1. *The issues.* Hanover, N.H.: University Press of New England, 1977.

Sarason, S. B. *The creation of settings and the future societies.* San Francisco: Jossey-Bass, 1972.

Sarason, S. B. Community psychology and the anarchist insight. *American Journal of Community Psychology,* 1976, **4,** 246–261.

Sarason, S. B. The nature of problem-solving in social action. *American Psychologist,* 1978, **33,** 370–380.

Sarason, S. B. *Psychology misdirected.* New York: Free Press, 1981.

Skipper, J. K., Guenther, A. L., & Nass, G. The sacredness of .05: A note concerning the uses of statistical levels of significance in social science. *American Sociologist,* 1967, **2,** 16–18.

Siegel, L. M., Atkinson, C. C., & Cohn, A. H. Mental health needs assessment: Strategies and techniques. In W. A. Hargreaves & C. C. Atkinson (Eds.), *Resource materials for community mental health program evaluation.* Washington: Government Printing Office, 1977.

Srole, L., Langner, T. S., Michael, S. T., Opler, M. K., & Rennie, T. A. C. *Mental Health in the metropolis: The midtown Manhattan study.* New York: McGraw-Hill, 1962.

Struening, M., & Guttentag, E. L. *Handbook of evaluation research.* Vol. 1. Beverly Hills: Sage, 1975.

Weiss, C. H. (Ed.) *Evaluating action programs: Readings in social action and education.* Boston: Allyn and Bacon, 1972.

White, B. L. What we know about infants and what we need to know. Paper presented at the Texas Conference on Infancy, Thompson Conference Center, Austin, 1975.

White, R. W. Competence as an aspect of personal growth. In M. W. Kent & J. E. Rolf (Eds.), *Primary prevention of psychopathology.* Vol. 3. *Social competence in children.* Hanover, N.H.: University Press of New England, 1977.

Zax, M., & Cowen, E. L. *Abnormal psychology: Changing conceptions.* New York: Holt, Rinehart & Winston, 1976.

# PART VI:

# PERSPECTIVES ON TRAINING IN PREVENTIVE PSYCHOLOGY AND THE FUTURE

# INTRODUCTION TO PART VI

In this final section of the volume, the contributors focus on issues vital to the future growth and development of primary prevention. Where we are going from here and how we are to best educate future preventive psychologists to get us there guide much of the discussion that follows. Themes that have been interwoven throughout the preceding chapters, particularly those that concern the difference between the promise and fact of preventive efforts, the sense of having built a solid foundation to serve preventive psychology's growth, and the need for prevention to broaden its base within psychology, are reflected and built upon in the chapters that follow on training and future directions.

In Chapter 17, Edwin Zolik provides us with a thorough and critical appraisal of the current status of training in primary prevention that is taking place in doctoral psychology programs and applied settings. As is reflected in Dr. Zolik's discussion, the fortunes of prevention in psychology have been heavily tied to those of community psychology and community mental health, at least to date. Differences between a rhetoric that implies an emerging emphasis on prevention and the actual degree and types of training opportunities afforded in academic and applied settings are discussed. Increased faculty resources and greater emphasis on systems, rather than person-centered ap-

proaches to prevention, are seen as particularly critical to strengthening prevention's place in academic training. The departmental context and the unique place of training for prevention in this context are also seen as in need of reappraisal.

In applied settings, Zolik notes that although training staff indicate they feel prevention is of great importance, less than half of the students surveyed indicated that field training or practicum experience in prevention was available to them in these settings. Moreover, in those internship settings where such opportunities were present, the mean number of hours per week allocated to prevention was only four. Given these not so subtle behavioral cues from the training environment, it is not surprising that the demand for training in prevention by students in applied settings is generally seen by staff to be relatively low. If we hope to infuse students with enthusiasm for prevention, it seems clear that we must do more than talk about its importance: we must model our commitment.

When Zolik explores further, he finds additional illustrations that the commitment of the internship staff to prevention may not match its initial statements. Other more direct services are seen as even more valuable by training personnel. Further, demands for such services, allocations of funds within agencies, inadequate intern preparation, and lack of perceived need for prevention by the community are among the "major hurdles" noted by agency staff to developing greater prevention efforts. One can only ask how professionals who were truly committed to prevention training and intervention would react to these "hurdles," particularly the latter two. Certainly, one might hope that instead of seeing these issues as hurdles they would view both increasing community awareness of the needs for such services and intern education as parts of the mission of prevention training professionals.

As to the future, Zolik echoes what is a pervasive theme in both the chapters that have preceded his and those that follow. That is, if prevention is to continue to grow and develop, greater attention must be paid to building a substantive knowledge base and developing efficient ways of information dissemination, particularly for applied settings.

Price also considers prevention to be a worthwhile but not yet accomplished fact. Rather than seeing training in prevention as continuing to be solely linked to community psychology, he builds on a theme reflected throughout this volume in calling for prevention to be pursued within the context of a wide variety of specialties in psychology. The central importance for the future of prevention of the next generation of psychologists to be trained is underscored, and some suggestions are offered for developing effective training efforts. Within the broader context of the general process of knowledge development, Price considers the factors that need to be attended to in the design of an educational program for preventive psychology. The roles that preventive psychologists are to occupy are seen as particularly key in shaping this process.

Price next explores the issue of how best to fit training for prevention into psychology departments as they currently exist. Changes in the thrust of specialties that have previously had basic research as their focus are discussed and the implications of these changes for developing a broad training base for prevention elaborated. Subspecialties such as developmental, social, organizational, and health psychology

are seen as being both salient and critical contributors to the future growth and development of adequate training in prevention.

A proposal is offered for fitting training in prevention into the organizational context of psychology departments, which will allow for the contributions of multiple specialties. Although this multispecialty base is seen as important, Price notes that any such proposal must also allow preventive psychology to develop a recognizable and clearly articulated place in the organizational structure of the department. A particular concern to be kept in mind in the implementation of any such effort is the avoidance of the "isolation" that may accompany development of separate tracks in prevention.

Finally, Price explores the nature of the relationship between preventive psychologists and the populations they serve. He notes that the value position taken on this question may shape both what is done and how it is carried out. After considering alternative positions, he argues that a position that views vulnerable populations as prevention's constituency is well suited to prevention's goals. It is also congruent with a stance that allows our efforts to empower, rather than oppress.

In their concluding remarks, Jason, Felner, Moritsugu and Farber consider future directions preventive research and intervention may follow at both the person- and systems-centered levels. They underscore the need to develop preventive activities in settings that may easily accommodate them as natural and integrated components of ongoing processes. Health and pediatric settings are discussed as examples of situations offering such opportunities. At the social system level, roles and competencies are identified for psychologists interested in competency-building in the population at large. A framework for conceptualizing communities and social systems that may facilitate such efforts is presented, representative work to-date in each area is examined, and suggestions for future work are elaborated. Finally, potential obstacles to prevention's future growth are discussed, and prospects for the future are weighed.

# 17 TRAINING FOR PREVENTIVE PSYCHOLOGY IN COMMUNITY AND ACADEMIC SETTINGS*

Edwin S. Zolik

For primary prevention to become a significant dimension in our approach to mental health, it is necessary that training in prevention be an integral component of academic training programs as well as in the service delivery system. Further, the interdigitation of both these sectors is required if we are to develop the critical mass of professionals necessary for undertaking the requisite basic research, the development and evaluation of preventive programs in the crucible of practice, and the development and expansion of opportunities for training in prevention for mental health and non-mental-health personnel at all levels. All areas of human endeavor ultimately are dependent on training for their growth and development. Growth and development, in turn, are dependent on the interest and enthusiasm which an area stimulates. If one surveys professional journals and convention programs over the last half decade, it is very evident that primary prevention is an area of intense interest. In fact, it has become a glamour area, and a manifestation of interest or concern about primary prevention is a sign of membership in the avant-garde. This fervor is captured in the book entitled *Primary prevention: An idea whose time has come* (Klein & Goldston, 1977).

Training in prevention occurs at many levels—from the level of volunteers and paraprofessionals to the post-graduate level. This chapter will focus on training at the graduate level because of the importance of training at this level for the continued development of the field of preventive psychology. In addition, since prevention was designated part of the mission of the consultation and education programs of community mental health centers (CMHCs), this chapter is limited to an analysis of applied training and programming in preventive psychology in CMHCs. The chapter will present the current status, successes and problems, issues and needs in academic training and applied training in prevention. However, to appreciate and understand the current status of training, it is necessary to have an awareness of the process of legitimation that an emerging area undergoes, the status of consultation and education programs in CMHCs, and the relation between consultation and education and primary prevention. An overview of each of these will be presented.

The taproot of the current fervor for primary prevention is located in President Kennedy's 1963 historic message to Congress, which resulted in the passage of the Community Mental Health Centers Act. This legitimation of prevention in 1963, at the highest national level, did not result in immediate major innovations in practice and training. It was, however, the necessary agent and provided the authoritative

* The author wishes to acknowledge and extend his appreciation and thanks to Mary Connors for her assistance in the preparation of this chapter.

sanction for beginning the engagement in the required political and ideological confrontations, for stimulating concern about research in prevention, and for developing preventatively oriented programs—all of which were required if prevention eventually was to become a significant component in the mental health armamentarium.

In 1978 the President's Commission on Mental Health (1978), established by President Carter, reaffirmed the need for prevention by including primary prevention as one of the eight major areas recommended for federal action. In the area of physical health the Report of the Surgeon General (U.S. Department of Health, Education, & Welfare, 1979) highlighted the need for prevention if significant improvements in the health status of the nation were to be obtained.

Such legitimation and relegitimation of any activity or approach is the first step in a complex process which potentially involves scientific, social, economic, and political consequences. When the process threatens to disrupt the status quo, the process becomes more complex. As preventive psychology involves a Kuhnian paradigm shift (Kuhn, 1970; Rappaport, 1977), all of these factors impinge on the establishment of prevention as an alternate paradigm and consequently impact on the development of training in prevention.

## Consultation and Education in Primary Prevention

The Community Mental Health Centers Act of 1963 broke with past tradition. This shift was based on establishing a link between mental health practices and public health theory by requiring that one of the essential five services of CMHCs be consultation and education (C&E), of which primary prevention was one component (National Institute of Mental Health, 1966). As a consequence, the fate of preventive psychology has, until the recent past, been intertwined with the fate of C&E services.

The implication for training was the obvious need to develop training and research opportunities in C&E and prevention. Although a wide variety of C&E programs have been initiated over the last two decades, C&E services have remained underdeveloped and marginal—suffering from problems in conceptualization, deficiencies in research supporting theoretical formulations (National Institute of Mental Health, 1978), and ideological conflicts (Snow & Newton, 1976). In hindsight, the designation of C&E and prevention as indirect services and clinical services as direct was an unfortunate designation. This classification generates a polarity which contains dimensions of value and priority. *Webster's Dictionary* (1977) defines "indirect" as "deviating from a direct course, circuitous, equivocal," and "indirect evidence in law" as "inferential or circumstantial evidence." Consequently, for clinicians trained in the medical model C&E could easily be, and was, denigrated to an ancillary level in terms of programming, funding, and commitment.

The marginal "low man on the CMHC totem pole" status of C&E is indicated by the fact that only 4 to 5 percent of total CMHC staff time was devoted to C&E activities (Bass, 1974; NIMH Survey Reports Branch, 1978; Silverman, 1978; Snow & Newton, 1976), with only about one-half of this small effort being classifiable as primary prevention (Vayda & Perlmutter, 1977). In spite of this small involvement in C&E and prevention, 76 percent of C&E programs have been evaluated as being at least moderately effective (Silverman, 1978).

In view of the problems of funding for C&E and prevention, concern about their fate has been raised when the federal support received by centers terminated after eight years. Initial findings (Naierman et al., 1978) revealed that C&E programs sustained major reductions, with the ideology of community mental health being compromised, after the termination of federal funding. A subsequent study (Weiner, Woy, Sharfstein, & Bass, 1979) indicated that there were two distinct groups of graduate centers, "true graduates" and "quasi-graduates," and that C&E programs were not uniformly reduced. Unlike "true graduates," "quasi-graduates" were primarily dependent on federal, state, and local funding.

Differences in the programs of these two groups of centers, in retrospect, were evident as early as in their fifth year of operation. In the "true graduate" group, C&E services decreased by 60 percent, in contrast to a 20 percent decrease in the "quasi-graduate" group, as the funding from third party payers for clinical services increased over a five-year period (Woy, Wasserman, & Weiner-Pomerantz, 1981). The data, unfortunately, do not indicate whether the early movement away from C&E was the result of inadequate financial support for C&E or whether the lack of such support was the pretext for moving away from a commitment to prevention which originally was, at best, only minimally accepted by the staff and administration of the centers in the "true graduate" group. A major implication of these changes for applied training and prevention is the potential decrease in available training settings and the need to give consideration to the development of alternate settings—an issue which will be discussed in the section on needs in applied training.

In spite of the fact that the immediate future for the broad spectrum of C&E programs is not optimistic, those centers which have had a strong commitment to C&E and have arranged for alternate sources of C&E funding will be able to maintain preventive and mental health education programs. The existence of a core group of such centers presents an opportunity for the development of tested models which at a future time could be deployed on a larger scale. Descriptions of several such centers are presented in the section on applied training.

## The Rise of Primary Prevention

While the fortunes of C&E programs in CMHCs appear to be descending, those of primary prevention in its own right have been ascending, in both health and mental health. In addition to the focus on prevention by the surgeon general's report (U.S. Dept. of HEW, 1979) and the President's Commission on Mental Health (1978), the Alcohol, Drug Abuse and Mental Health Administration in 1977 designated prevention to be one of the agency's missions, and in 1979 the National Institute of Mental Health established the Office of Prevention. The Health Services and Centers Amendment of 1978 (Public Law 95-636) stipulated that a report be submitted to the president and Congress on the state of disease prevention and health promotion and, in compliance with this requirement, the 1980 report included for the first time a "Prevention profile" section (U.S. Department of Health & Human Services, 1980).

As a result of these laws and actions by various agencies, prevention has been incorporated incrementally during the 1970s as part of national policy. However, the current situation occasioned by the repeal of the Mental Health Systems Act through the inauguration of block grants to states contains many unknowns with regard to the funding of prevention. In the new block grant program, which consolidates 19 health programs into four blocks, the federal initiative in prevention is distributed through the various blocks. In the Alcohol, Drug Abuse, and Mental Health Block, the definition of services in a CMHC includes C&E and prevention as one of the required elements. This provides some degree of protection for C&E and prevention programs. However, on the whole the approach of state authorities to C&E programs has been at best, one of benign neglect and sufferance. Only a small number of states, among which Michigan and California are outstanding, have established prevention programs. Others, like Illinois, have no mechanism for funding C&E or prevention in state funding programs for mental health agencies.

As the block grant mechanism gives states more latitude in how to spend federal funds, psychologists and others concerned with prevention will have to monitor closely how funds are allocated in their state and be prepared to establish coalitions to combat the more limited resources allocated for prevention from being politically used, even partially, as electoral insurance premiums—an experience which various health and social programs have encountered in the past.

Concomitant with the rise of prevention at the policy level, there has been a similar increasing interest in prevention at the consumer level—an interest that can benefit training, research, and programming. More than 50 percent of Americans are more concerned about preventive health than they were a few years ago (Harris & Associates, 1978) and almost half of American adults have made changes in the recent past in their lifestyle in the interests of health (Yankelovich, Skelly, & White, 1979). Enhancing mental health has also caught the interest of the public. In a nine-city survey, stress reduction and the prevention of home accidents were rated the highest as the types of programs of most interest (American Hospital Association, 1978).

The American public increasingly recognizes that many aspects of both physical and mental health are under individuals' control and involve lifestyle and ecological changes. The growing skepticism toward the health care system and its escalating costs, the turning of the war against cancer into a biomedical Vietnam (Kennedy, 1981) which has required continually greater funding, and the scientific-political-legal donnybrook over Love Canal (Levine, 1982) have contributed to the growing public disillusionment with the business-as-usual approach to health. The recent decision of the U.S. Court of Appeals for the District of Columbia requiring that the Nuclear Regulatory Commission conduct an assessment of the psychological impact of restarting the undamaged nuclear generator at Three Mile Island is a recognition of the role of environmental factors in causing psychological stress (Marshall, 1982a). This is a landmark decision, since if it is upheld, psychological health becomes covered by the National Environmental Policy Act, and future environmental impact studies will have to take psychological well-being into consideration. As for training, the broad public interests in prevention indicate that training in ecological and social systems change should be given at least equal weight with training in person-oriented approaches to prevention which, as we shall see in the following sections, is the predominant approach to prevention at the present time.

## Academic Training in Primary Prevention

The emergence of the community mental health ideology was not accompanied by either a state of preparedness or a high degree of willingness on the part of the majority of academic departments in the mental health professions to initiate new training models or to undertake significant modifications in existing training programs. Academicians, although politically liberal and often in the vanguard of social change, become conservative with respect to changes in departmental programs. Vassily Leontieff (1982), the Nobelist in economics, in criticizing the dominating commitment to mathematical models by academic economics, agreed with Reder (1982) that the methods employed to maintain this orientation through control of training and research by the senior faculty of some of the most influential departments in the country "occasionally reminds one of those [methods] employed by the Marines to maintain discipline on Parris Island."

The introduction of alternate paradigms generates insecurity which often becomes rationalized as the need for more scientific evidence, the paucity of interest among students, and the lack of sufficient funding. In this process, proponents of change often become labeled as radicals. In addition, the proponents of change typically are younger faculty who lack the security of tenure and do not have the necessary power base to initiate other than incremental changes.

In those departments where community psychology/community mental health (CP/CMH) was sponsored by senior faculty, the introduction of CP/CMH was facilitated. In other departments the pragmatic need to provide some orientation to students who were to go on internship or obtain positions in community mental health centers served as the initial vehicle for including community topics in clinical programs. Further contributing to the slow introduction of CP/CMH into training programs was the lethargy of the Training Branch of the National Institute of Mental Health displayed in failing to use its power to bring about necessary changes in training through its funding of training programs. A major issue underlying the slow incorporation of CP/CMH by training programs was, and continues to be, the ideological conflict posed for many between a preventive orientation and the palliative-salvage approach underlying the deficit reparative orientation of traditional training programs.

### Growth of Training in CP/CMH and Prevention

The last decade has witnessed a steady, consistent growth in the number of academic departments offering course work or specialization in community psychology and community mental health (Barton, Andrulis, Grove, & Aponte, 1977; Golann, 1970; Zolik, Sirbu, & Hopkinson, 1977). The number of departments that offer a distinguishable sequence has grown from 1 to 62, 45 of which offer a doctorate (Meyer & Gerrard, 1977). The majority of community course work or sequences is located in clinical or clinical-community programs, followed by counseling, school psychology, and finally social psychology programs. Autonomous community psychology programs are still relatively small in number—a factor which is involved in the continuing identity crisis of community psychology.

With respect to training in prevention-oriented areas, a survey revealed that prevention is represented in the course content of 67 percent of the responding programs (N = 141), the relation between social milieu and emotional disorders in 49 percent of the programs, intervention programs for high-risk groups in 48 percent of the programs, identification of etiological factors in emotional disorders in 35 percent, and epidemiology of emotional disorders in 35 percent of the programs (Barton et al., 1977). On the basis of these data it is evident that preventive psychology and community mental health topics are receiving attention in a number of programs. The thrust of the coverage, however, is more toward applied programming and less toward the theoretical foundations of prevention and research.

### Student Evaluation of Training

A series of studies (Zolik, Hopkinson, Sirbu, & Pozzi, 1976; Zolik & Philipp, 1980, 1981) were directed at an assessment by advanced graduate students, representing between 76 and 80 percent of the doctoral-level programs in clinical, counseling and school psychology, of their academic and field training in CP/CMH. Whereas two-thirds of these students believed that there should be separate graduate curriculum in the theory and practice of CP/CMH, less than 45 percent considered their overall training in CP/CMH as having been adequate or more than adequate. The high degree of consensus about the need for a separate curriculum in CP/CMH among the three groups indicates the permeation of the three major applied specialty areas by the ideology of CP/CMH and preventive psychology. The low evaluation of the overall adequacy of their training in relation to their perceived needs indicates a receptivity for additional training. As advanced students sufficiently trained in the palliative and ameliorative procedures of their specialty areas, they recognized the need for training that would balance this orientation and enable them to function more broadly as professionals.

Table 17.1 presents an analysis of the academic coverage of the topic of primary prevention and other closely related areas, and the adequacy of the coverage in relation to the student's perceived needs. The majority of clinical (70 percent) and school psychology (76 percent) students and close to half of counseling students (47 percent) reported coverage or person-oriented approaches to primary prevention in course work. The majority in each group uniformly considered the coverage to be adequate for their needs. On the other hand, less than a majority, as indicated in Table 17.1, were exposed to social-system- and action-oriented approaches to primary prevention. Among the 30 areas related to CP/CMH covered in the survey, primary prevention ranked first in terms of academic coverage in clinical and school psychology programs and second in counseling programs. The results indicate that in relation to the various component areas of CP/CMH, person-centered or small-group-centered approaches are presented to a much higher degree in academic training. This orientation to the person-centered approach in contrast to a systems orientation is not surprising, since it is more compatible with the traditional treatment orientation in clinical, counseling, and school psychology. The much smaller emphasis on epidemiology and prevention-oriented research suggests that the content with respect to prevention is directed toward practice and application in many programs.

### Perceived Importance of Prevention

The development of an area within a discipline is related in part to the importance placed on the area by members in a discipline and especially by those who are about to embark on their professional careers. In a study of the importance of 30 topical areas related to the field of CP/CMH, advanced graduate students rated primary prevention to be among the most important areas—being ranked first by clinical and school psychology students and third most important by interns, counseling, and social psychology students (Zolik & Bogat, 1981). On the other hand, other areas related to prevention fared less well. The average rank of the five student groups combined for system consultation to service deliverers was 19.7, 16.4 for social system analysis and change, 18.8 for advocacy and social change, and 24.9 for mental health epidemiology. Overall, with the exception of person-oriented approaches to primary prevention, advanced graduate students regarded traditional community mental health areas as more important than the more untraditional

areas related to community and preventive psychology. The importance placed on person-centered approaches to primary prevention can be related to its greater coverage academically in relation to other areas. Nevertheless, the fact that it receives a high degree of attention academically and is viewed as an area of greater importance than other areas augurs well for the future of primary prevention.

A factor analysis indicated that the 30 CP/CMH areas can be accounted for by six factors: (1) community and social systems; (2) community research methodology; (3) child mental health programming; (4) direct clinical services; (5) consultation; and (6) primary prevention (Zolik, Soucy, & Bogat, 1982). Although there was no difference among the student groups' ratings of primary prevention, differences on other factors indicated that each student group rated the factors related to its area of specialization as being more important. The factor structure of the areas of CP/CMH indicates that although the area of specialization provides the focus for a person's main activities, a simultaneous orientation to other approaches can be maintained. The importance of direct clinical services, for example, can be coequal with the importance of primary prevention. On the basis of these various studies, it is thus evident that prevention, in terms of its values and potential, has an appreciable number of adherents who, upon entering their professional life, will devote a portion of their energies to some facet of prevention.

### Undergraduate Training in Prevention

A discussion of training in primary prevention would not be complete without some reference to the training of undergraduates. A review of journals and convention programs indicates that in many of these studies and reports, undergraduates have participated via undergraduate internships (Jason, 1981), experiential research courses, and independent study. In this manner undergraduates have received an introductory conceptual understanding of primary prevention and often gained experience in research and in conducting preventative projects. With the continued growth in the knowledge base of prevention, it would behoove community psychologists to consider introducing courses in primary prevention at the undergraduate level. For graduate-school-bound students, such courses might stimulate an interest in preventive psychology, and for other students such courses would contribute to the development of an informed and active citizenry.

## Needs in Academic Training

Although needs can vary from program to program, the results of the studies in the preceding section

Table 17.1. Academic Coverage and Field Experience: Availability and Adequacy

PERCENT OF RESPONDENTS INDICATING

| AREA | ACADEMIC COVERAGE AND ADEQUACY[a] | | | FIELD EXPERIENCE AVAILABILITY AND ADEQUACY[b] | | |
|---|---|---|---|---|---|---|
| | CLINICAL[c] (N = 385) | COUNSELING (N = 100) | SCHOOL (N = 63) | CLINICAL (N = 385) | COUNSELING (N = 100) | SCHOOL (N = 63) |
| Primary prevention | 70(60) | 47(68) | 76(65) | 44(78) | 35(85) | 62(72) |
| System consultation to non-mental-health systems | 38(52) | 30(70) | 48(63) | 40(77) | 28(67) | 41(74) |
| Advocacy and social action | 33(51) | 26(46) | 33(43) | 19(71) | 11(100) | 22(67) |
| Social system analysis and modification | 40(49) | 35(54) | 46(41) | 21(71) | 11(100) | 24(89) |
| Mental health epidemiology | 41(65) | 28(46) | 16(30) | 15(83) | 11(25) | 6(0) |

a Adequacy is designated in parentheses and is based on the number of respondents reporting that the topic coverage was adequate for their perceived needs.

b Adequacy is designated in parentheses and is based on the number who had field experience.

c This category includes clinical-community programs and the small number of community psychology programs that are not classified as applied social psychology programs.

278

indicate three major areas to which attention should be devoted. These are manpower needs related to the improvement of training opportunities, needs for improving training in systems approaches to prevention, and needs for increasing training in mental health epidemiology and its related areas.

### Manpower Needs

If training in preventive psychology in academic settings is to be enhanced and expanded, one of the major needs involves projections of future increases in faculty resources. Although there has been a significant increase in the number of programs offering some course work in community psychology, the mean number of faculty involved in such training is 3.75 (range 1 to 13) (Meyer & Gerrard, 1977). Many departments, however, only have a token community psychologist, and in some instances that person has been hired in the recent past. If faculty strength in community psychology is analyzed in terms of full-time equivalents (the number of faculty whose total academic load is devoted to community psychology), the picture becomes less optimistic with respect to continued expansion of training opportunities without additional faculty resources. The increasingly greater fiscal constraints being experienced by universities, coupled with the decreasing amount of both federal and state support, indicate that the remainder of the 1980s can be envisioned at best as a period in which growth will be severely constricted. As preventive psychology is one of the few growth areas in psychology, community psychologists can justify the need for additional faculty to develop the necessary critical mass of preventive psychologists required for training. However, in the increasingly competitive environment within and between disciplines for maintaining or increasing faculty strength, justification of need will have to be accompanied by the necessary academic politics. Otherwise it is not difficult to foresee that the concern about the emancipation of community psychology from community mental health and clinical psychology voiced at the Austin Conference on Training in Community Psychology (Bloom, 1977) will still be extant at the end of this decade.

### Approaches to Improving Training in Prevention

Most individuals who become engaged in some aspect of prevention have a specialty in areas other than community psychology. Students, independent of their specialty areas, must have access to adequate training in prevention if they are to function preventively in their professional career. To provide access to adequate training, attention might be directed at possible modifications in applied training programs. Clinical psychology can be used as an example, since the majority of students who take course work or a concentration in community psychology are in clinical programs. If community psychology is organized as a separate track within the clinical program, it is possible to introduce greater flexibility than that typically found in clinical-community programs. The question is whether this is sufficient to provide in-depth training in community psychology and prevention. The answer depends on the particular program.

Another option is to improve the relevance of training by enabling the student's academic program to approximate his career goals more closely. For example, do all clinical students need the intensity of training in psychodiagnostics currently mandated? Is it not possible to have an effective professional who is trained in prevention and in methods of psychotherapeutic interventions with a lesser degree of training in assessment than currently required? Implementing a proposal such as this will encounter the survival issues described by Tornatsky (1976). In addition, issues of accreditation, which unfortunately are impacted by the issues in clinical psychology concerning parity with psychiatry for third party reimbursement for services, would have to be resolved. Another approach would be structuring programs to enable students to pursue a dual specialization.

Postdoctoral programs in prevention would provide another option. The problems in this approach are those involved in funding and extending the academic training period, among others. However, for the immediate future postdoctoral training is the most promising avenue, especially for training those individuals interested in a full-time career in preventive research and programming. A concentrated postdoctoral program can overcome much of the current fragmentation in training, and facilitate the overcoming of existing manpower problems.

Other options can be proposed, but the basic point is that community psychologists interested in prevention need to examine the nature of current academic programs, assess the various options, and engage in the necessary academic dialogue with a view to increasing both the overall quantity and quality of preparation in prevention. The fact that the knowledge base for prevention is not identical with that for treatment should be a guiding principle in the development of preventive training programs.

### Systems Approaches, Advocacy, and Social Action

Training in prevention is largely focused on person-centered approaches (Table 17.1). Students obtain considerably less exposure to system approaches to prevention and to the area of advocacy and social action. However, if we are concerned in maximizing our preventive efforts, training in systems approaches needs to be enhanced through fostering interdisciplinary training, as voiced at the Austin Conference (Iscoe, Bloom, & Spielberger, 1977), and through other vehicles.

One such approach would be through the inauguration of case seminars. Case study seminars with the goal of formulating an action goal can provide rich learning experiences. For example, a seminar could be given disseminating the following three sets of information. First, although the elimination of lead form paints has been much heralded, the U.S. Department of Housing and Urban Development is not fully complying with its own regulations and has not given lead-based paint poisoning a high priority (U.S. General Accounting Office, 1980). Second, the Environmental Protection Agency proposed raising the lead content in gasoline by 10 percent, benefiting primarily the increasing number of small gasoline blenders that mix low-grade fuel with large quantities of lead (Marshall, 1982b), but after public protests reversed itself and proposed a 31 percent reduction of lead in the air over an eight-year period (Shabecoff, 1982), only to have this countered by the Office of Management and Budget. Third, it is estimated that about half of the lead in diets probably can be traced to food from lead-soldered cans (Settle & Patterson, 1980). Yet no publicity has been given to action by the Food and Drug Administration in this regard.

Given these facts and a goal of developing an action program, a case seminar approach would expose students to the effects of lead poisoning, systems approaches to prevention, the analysis of risk in regulatory decision-making, the fact that economic and political considerations often take precedence over scientific findings, some aspects of epidemiological analysis, and the frequently multidimensional nature of prevention. To develop a viable action program, it would be necessary for the students to analyze each proposed option in depth. In the absence of sufficient training in systems consultation, systems modification, advocacy, and social action, the rhetoric and concern about empowerment (Albee, 1980) will remain rhetorical.

### Mental Health Epidemiology

A final area of need pertains to the low exposure to mental health epidemiology and principles of epidemiology. This is not surprising, since the palliative-ameliorative model underlying traditional applied training makes little reference to epidemiology. However, as epidemiology is the basic science of prevention, it is vital that training programs provide adequate coverage of this area.

Students should have an understanding of the "web of causation" model (MacMahon, Pugh, & Ipsen, 1960) and its implication that the degree or level of prevention achieved is related to the importance of the linkage which is broken in the causal chain. This model is based on a multifactorial approach to etiology. Underlying this model is the well-known fact that prevention is possible without a complete understanding of etiology and that the control of factors correlated with a disorder can reduce the incidence of disorder. Major approaches to the prevention of cardiovascular disorders, whose etiology is poorly understood, is based on this principle (Levy & Moskowitz, 1982; McAlister, Puska, Salonen, Tuomilehto, & Kosela, 1982; Meyer, Nash, McAlister, Maccoby, & Farquhar, 1980).

The multifactorial model stands in contrast to the monoetiological model, which typically focuses on biological, physical or genetic factors and tends toward reductionism. The monoetiological model is an important approach in the area of infectious diseases, where there is a precise system of classification and diagnostic precision which often makes specific preventive measures, like immunization, possible. The reductionism in the monoetiological approach is reflected in the position of Eisenberg (1981), who raises concern that successful treatment of schizophrenics can result in increasing the genetic pool of schizophrenia, and proposes genetic counseling, in spite of the low penetrance of schizophrenia, for families with a schizophrenic member. In a similar vein, Lamb and Zusman (1982) proclaim the advent of "the 'new' prevention" based on increasing genetic evidence for the etiology of schizophrenia. The imagery which this " 'new' prevention" generates is one in which genetic counseling will be superseded by the genetic surgeon mating a nonschizophrenic sperm with a nonschizophrenic ovum and later, with the advance of medical high technology, excising the schizophrenia-producing genetic material and inserting non-pathology-inducing genetic material. These positions accept the assumption that major mental illnesses "are genetically determined and therefore probably not preventable [Lamb & Zusman, 1979]." The major fallacy is that genetics is equated with determinism. If we accept this position of genetic determinism, we should advocate, to be consistent, the disbanding of the successful programs for preventing cardiovascular disorders and hypertension, since genetic factors, although poorly understood, are involved (Smith, 1977).

If schizophrenia is the result of a dynamic interaction of genetic and environmental factors, the prediction of all schizophrenics is not possible, no matter how accurate an indicator of the genotypes is developed, as long as the contribution of environmental components is unpredictable (Hanson, Gottesman, & Meehl, 1977). As a consequence, genetic counseling can result in an unwarranted and ethically questionable alarmingly high rate of false positives being aborted. The appropriate use of genetic counseling, as a person-centered approach, for disorders such as Down's syndrome cannot be extrapolated at the present time to schizophrenia. A genetic factor in schizophrenia would be classified as a necessary precondition. But we have learned, as in the case of tuberculosis (MacMahon, Pugh, & Ipsen, 1960; Rosen, 1977), that prevention programs can be successful even when a necessary precondition is present. The approach is one of controlling the precondition from becoming manifest.

Parenthetically, it should be noted that genetic counseling needs to be based on diagnostic precision. The precision and elegance of the psychiatric diagnostic system was illustrated in the trial of John Hinckley, the young man who attempted to assassinate President Reagan. Stone (1982), a former president of the American Psychiatric Association, described the trial as a "psychiatric three-ring circus" in which the "main performers were trained psychiatric clowns."

Finally, training in epidemiology needs to provide an exposure to the competing philosophies of eradication versus control in prevention. Contemporary approaches to the prevention of major disorders, such as malaria (Harrison, 1978) and smallpox (Henderson, 1980), are based on integrated control or surveillance-containment. Eradication is a possible approach when the benefits justify the costs and when eradication does not create more hazards and problems than the disorder itself (for example, the unsuccessful war on malaria waged by eradicating the mosquito by DDT). In Britain the policy toward rubella is one of containment through the vaccination of persons most at risk (females between 11 and 15 years of age and selective postpartum females), whereas in the United States since rubella appears to be a good candidate for eradication the policy is one of mass vaccination of preschool males and females (Anderson & May, 1982). These contrasting approaches are based on different underlying philosophical orientations and complicated analyses of potential benefits. In contrast to rubella, however, it is debatable whether the costs of eradicating mumps and chicken pox are justified by the benefits (Anderson & May, 1982). The approach to prevention proposed by the President's Commission on Mental Health (1978), although this is not explicitly stated, is based on a philosophy of integrated control.

## Applied Training in Primary Prevention

Applied training in primary prevention takes place in a wide variety of settings—universities, CMHCs, and a broad array of health and social agencies. Such training may be obtained through fieldwork or practicum training, internship training, workshops, and in-service training programs. Training in primary prevention extends from the volunteer level, where interested individuals are trained in conducting various preventively oriented programs (Allen, Chinsky, Larsen, Lockman, & Sellinger, 1976; Bard & Berkowitz, 1967; Guerney, 1969; Silverman, 1976; Spivack & Shure, 1974; Zolik, DesLauriers, Graybill, & Hollon, 1962), through training at the postdoctoral level. The main focus in this section again is applied training at the graduate level, as it is this group of individuals who will assume the continuation of training and programming in primary prevention in the future.

### Adequacy of Field Training

Analyses of the data in Table 17.1 pertaining to the availability of prevention-related field experience and its perceived adequacy for clinical, counseling, and school psychology students present several interesting comparisons. Other than school psychologists, less than half of the doctoral students indicated that field or practicum experience in primary prevention was available as part of their academic program. This deficiency applied to both person-oriented and systems-oriented approaches. However, in spite of problems in the availability of training, in all but one area, mental health epidemiology, the majority of students considered the field experience which they obtained to be adequate for their needs. The reported adequacy of field experience in each of the areas was consistently higher than the adequacy of academic coverage of the same area, again with the exception of mental health epidemiology. These data suggest that there is a considerable need for the development of training in both person-centered and systems-centered prevention in graduate training programs. However, with respect to systems-oriented prevention, there is a need to improve both the quantity of academic training and the availability of applied training. Also, since the 1975 federal CMHC amendments specifically barred the use of community organization methods by C&E programs in CMHCs, field training in social action approaches and strategies would typically have to be obtained in other field settings.

Despite the lack of formal linkages between many academic programs and field settings, many students in these studies (Zolik et al., 1977; Zolik & Philipp, 1980; Zolik & Philipp, 1981) were ingenious in seeking out and obtaining the desired training on their own. Although the results of these studies indicate that applied training in prevention is still in a developmental stage, the results also indicate that primary prevention has captured the attention and enthusiasm of an important segment of students in clinical, counseling, and school psychology programs.

### Training at CMHCs Versus Other Settings

Since federally funded CMHCs with a philosophy of community mental health might be expected to be a source of innovative applied training, it is important to compare community related training at CMHCs with that provided by other internship facilities. A study (Zolik et al., 1976) based on responses of 220 interns in a nationally drawn sample of 135 internship facilities found that the amount and availability of training in C&E and prevention was greater at CMHCs than at other facilities. The rank order of the internship sites in terms of the amount of such training was CMHCs, state hospitals, psychiatric services in medical settings, and Veterans Administration hospitals. State hospitals and medical settings were generally equivalent in providing an atmosphere conducive to training in C&E and prevention. However, although such training and experience in medical settings was less frequent than in state hospitals, it was of a higher quality, in that interns in medical settings were more likely to receive special preparation and more supervision in their preventive work. At Veterans Administration internship sites, C&E prevention training was very infrequent and usually obtained through special external placements. However, good supervision, for which the VA is noted, generally accompanied this experience. Across internship sites, out of the total sample of 220 interns, 59 percent received some training related to the ideologies of community psychology and community mental health. More specifically, slightly less than half of the total group of interns had some experience in C&E and prevention. If these internship facilities are representative of the more than 200 such settings across the nation, a reasonable projection would be that slightly more than 200 interns a year are receiving some degree of training in C&E and primary prevention. Further, more than twice as many training directors consider that the preparation of students for community consultation has improved over the last three years than

the number reporting better preparation in psychotherapy and in psychodiagnostics (Shemberg & Leventhal, 1981).

These results dramatically show that the clinical psychology internship can be for many a fertile ground for innovative approaches to the provision of services to the community. In assessing their internship the majority of these students indicated that the opportunity for involvement in nontraditional activities through C&E and prevention was very important to their overall training. They decried, however, a lack of integration, such as poor linkages between the training facility and the community, and the heavy emphasis on direct clinical services.

### Training in Prevention at CMHCs

A study of training specifically focused on CMHCs found that 137 out of 389 CMHCs provided internship level training and 240 provided pre-internship level training (Zolik, Bogat, & Jason, 1980). The percentage of internship-level CMHCs reporting that interns typically were involved in various prevention-oriented training was 53 percent for primary prevention, 59 percent for consultee-centered consultation, 47 percent for early screening and identification, 36 percent for system consultation, 14 percent for social action and advocacy, 27 percent for program evaluation, and 4 percent for mental health epidemiology. With respect to opportunities for consultation, the mean was 6.8 hours per week (range 1–20 hours) devoted to consultation. The four consultation settings utilized by the largest percentage of CMHCs were schools (72 percent of the centers), courts (43 percent), welfare agencies (39 percent), and preschool settings (39 percent). The data, however, do not provide information about the extent of traditional clinical case consultation versus other types of consultation efforts in these settings.

The small amount of time provided for consultation is related in part to diversities in staff opinions of the importance of community-related experiences for interns. From the viewpoint of the training staff, community-related experiences for interns were considered to be of "great importance" at 36 percent of the centers, of "considerable importance" at 25 percent, of "some importance" at 30 percent, and of "minimal importance" at 9 percent. A further indication of the weight given to traditional clinical training is that the five top areas in which training at these 137 CMHCs were considered by training directors to be outstanding or exceptional were adult outpatient, child outpatient, crisis intervention, adolescent outpatient, and adult day hospital.

A follow-up survey two years later of a random sample (N = 23) of those internship-level CMHCs that had indicated intern involvement in primary prevention gives cause for both optimism and pessimism (Zolik, Philipp, & Jason, 1981). Training directors reported that the mean amount of time specifically devoted by interns to primary prevention was 4 hours per week (range 1.5–10 hours). However, they reported that the demand or request for training specifically in primary prevention was low and considerably lower than requests for training in C&E. Whereas 26 percent rated the demand for training in C&E as low or very low, 57 percent rated the demand for training in primary prevention as either low or very low. This low demand for training in prevention appears to be related to the orientation which students bring to their internship, their interest in further developing those clinical skills which are viewed as the *sine qua non* for future employment and, in the words of one training director, "the lack of awareness that primary prevention activities and training are possible." In contrast to the orientation of interns, 57 percent of the directors rated the training staff as being either positive or very positive toward intern involvement in primary prevention activities.

All but two CMHC training directors reported that training in primary prevention was confronted by both internal and external hurdles. The two major internal hurdles cited were the demand for direct services and the lack of adequate funding for prevention. Other constraints focused on the adequacy of preparation of interns by university training programs for primary prevention, the lack of sufficient staff with an adequate level of preparation for undertaking supervision in primary prevention, and finally the low priority for training in primary prevention in some centers. The training directors were equally divided in predicting an increase, no change, or a decrease in prevention activities at their CMHCs. The pessimism underlying no change or a decrease was related to the lack of administrative support and the need "to go where the bucks are." External hurdles focused on difficulties related to entry into the community, the lack of perceived need by the community for prevention programs, and the lack of community financial support for prevention.

The internal hurdles, apart from the lack of administrative and financial support, potentially contain the seeds of a vicious circle. If students are perceived as trained below the desired level for prevention activities, the possibility exists of their receiving limited exposure to prevention during internship. Unless this is subsequently remedied, when they later become employed at CMHCs they have less than adequate training for undertaking supervision in prevention. Such staff typically would not become involved in prevention programs, and as a consequence training in prevention becomes devalued.

As a group these studies indicate that applied training in preventive psychology is in a developmental stage characterized by varying degrees of commitment in different settings and confronted with various obstacles. In spite of these difficulties, a manpower pool with varying degrees of training is emerging, most of whom, it is hoped, will devote part of their energies to prevention. The richness of experience which this group has obtained, even though they are "baby-steps" (Cowen, 1977), can serve in the development of more effective programs. Confronted with the hurdles to program development previously described, a number of centers have developed innovative approaches which can serve as models in developing viable programs.

## Innovative Applied Programs

The programs discussed here are not the only ones that can serve as models, but were selected to illustrate a number of features. All are marked by strong administrative support for C&E and prevention; all have a strong commitment to training; all are characterized by a great effort toward fiscal self-sufficiency; all have strong community linkages and have developed programs focused on community needs.

### Northside Community Mental Health Center

The C&E program of the Northside Community Mental Health Center in Tampa, Florida, is directed toward the development of prevention and health promotion programs that can be delivered to a large extent by volunteers and self-help efforts. Erhlich (1982) has stated that training is a primary component in our prevention program. Training is provided at all levels, from the level of the lay volunteer and paraprofessional, who then become involved in conducting programs in various settings, through the postgraduate level. The programs are organized into four groups: a Primary Prevention Program directed at adult and community residents, a Health Promotion Program which offers stress management programs to a wide variety of public and private organizations, an Employee Assistance Program which serves the business sector and large public organizations, and a Marital and Family Disruption Project. Aggressive marketing of these C&E programs (Erhlich, 1981, 1982) in packages that meet community needs has enabled the C&E program to keep growing over the past several years.

A very innovative and wide-reaching mass media prevention program was developed by interesting media and advertising representatives and undertaking the development of a program for TV, radio, newspaper and billboard spots. This "Peace Yourself Together" campaign essentially became a community development program involving hundreds of individuals. Through the development of the necessary linkages with the creative talents in the community, interest in prevention has been stimulated far beyond what a CMHC could achieve on its own. For a $6,300 investment the center and the community obtained a program valued at more than $300,000. The program has won two national awards and several regional awards and has drawn the attention and interest of CMHCs in other parts of the country.

### Good Samaritan Mental Health Center

The Good Samaritan Community Mental Health Center in Dayton, Ohio, has developed an umbrella organization, the Life Management Institute, for its C&E and prevention programs. The prevention programs are packaged in forms acceptable to the targeted populations, without a connotation of mental illness. Gilligan (1982) states that the fiscal viability of their program in part stems from the staff becoming familiar with approaches to marketing by nonprofit organizations suggested by Kotler (1975), Kotler and Levy (1971), and Rados (1980). Training is an important dimension of the program, with the trainees representing a number of disciplines from the associate through the postgraduate level. The program exposes the trainees to the development, marketing, and implementation of various prevention packages in a variety of community settings. The C&E program has programs for a wide number of different target groups, including business and industry. Several programs targeted at children illustrate the center's active reaching out to the community.

A preschool program, serving urban and suburban schools on a contract basis, starts with the preregistration of the child. Home visits and parent-teacher get-togethers during the summer are directed at facilitating the home-school transition, followed by a heavy focus of effort at the beginning of the school year on children and parents. Parents and teachers receive considerable consultation during the year, with a preventive workshop in effective education provided for teachers. An after-school program for children of different ages, focused on social skill development, is offered through different recreational centers.

Through a contract with the park system, a series of summer preventive programs have been developed for children. These programs employ a fun-and-games format to make them attractive and appealing to children and parents. The progressive park system, recognizing the need, has underwritten the cost of the development of the programs. In the suburbs these programs are marketed on a fee-for-service basis. Gilligan (1982) states that once the real "wants" in the community are known, the ways to meet them are investigated. The process of determining "wants" results in establishing mutual beneficial relationships with community organizations and groups and the communication network that is necessary for subsequent program dissemination on a broad scale. The wide dissemination of well-developed programs makes it possible to spread the developmental costs and bring the per program cost down to a level easily affordable by small groups.

### Ravenswood Community Mental Health Center

At the Ravenswood Community Mental Health Center in Chicago, the fiscal deficit of the C&E and preventive program is covered by the hospital, which recognizes that the preventive programs significantly contribute to the image of the hospital as a wellness-oriented facility, along with developing good will in the community (Chutis, 1982). One major preventive focus is on the development of numerous self-help groups, meeting throughout the catchment area, devoted to potential problem areas spanning the life cycle. Another focus is on workshops, with over 18 workshops being offered in the spring of 1982. The preventive programs are directed at the development of social skills and problem-solving skills related to stresses in a variety of problem or potentially crisis-inducing areas experienced by children, adolescents, parents, single and step-families, and the elderly. In 1975 the center won a state award as the best overall community mental health program in Illinois, and in 1977 the preventive program for widows and widowers won a similar state award for its excellence. Training is provided for students from psychology, social work, guidance and counseling, urban affairs, and nursing. These students participate in conducting many of the programs as well as becoming familiar with the problems of program development, implementation, and evaluation.

### Katherine Hamilton Mental Health Center

At the Katherine Hamilton Mental Health Center in Terre Haute, Indiana, the initial federal support was utilized to develop a preventive orientation and programs were directed toward the ability of the center to sustain a broad preventive initiative upon termination of federal funding (Truitt, 1982). Again, the development, packaging, and marketing of relevant programs in meeting community needs has been a key factor in the ability of the center to offer programs from infant stimulation and developmental screening, at one end of the age continuum, to a number of skill development and self-enhancement programs for senior citizens, at the other end. The emphasis is on the development of competencies and skills of people in the community to cope at an early stage with problems that may develop. A strong commitment to training students at all levels from a variety of disciplines not only provides manpower for the programs offered to the community but more importantly provides students with a knowledge base in innovative program development. Emphasis also is placed on the training of paraprofessionals. Programs for business and industry are organized under a subsidiary, Hamilton Associates, which offers an employee assistance program, a health and wellness program, and a management training and development program, among others. Such a subsidiary, organized on a business basis, frequently finds greater receptivity in the business world, since its focus is on growth, development, and prevention, as contrasted to the deficit and casualty-impairment image characteristic of many CMHCs.

Brief descriptions cannot do justice to these programs. They can serve, however, as illustrations that a firm commitment to prevention, although buffeted by fiscal storms, can lead to effective programs that meet community needs. All these centers have a concern about the need for effective marketing. But for successful marketing they have had to develop an effective product that meets the needs of consumers. In each instance the training of students and others was a key program component—not only for internal manpower purposes but for the promotion of preventive programs in other settings by graduate trainees.

### State of Michigan

No description of innovative approaches to prevention would be complete without mention of the integrated program at the state level in Michigan—considered by many to be the best. The mission of the program at the state level is to develop pilot prevention demonstration projects which are carefully designed and evaluated. Upon subsequent replication and validation, program packages are to be made available to interested CMHCs and agencies. The overall thrust is to maximize the coping skills and support systems of pop-

ulations at risk to sustained stress (Tableman, 1980). Among the projects under way are an infant stimulation project, an adolescent parent project, a children-of-disordered-parents project, stress management training for women on public assistance, and a parent-training-for-low-income-families project, with the latter three projects being at the replication state (Tableman, 1981). The development and dissemination of such thoroughly validated prevention programs will do much to fill an existing void.

### Needs in Applied Training

The obvious need in the near future is one of survival. The extent to which CMHCs will be forced, or will volunteer, to significantly decrease their C&E and prevention effort is yet unknown. However, the lack of dedication to prevention on the part of many CMHCs suggests the need for possible alternate settings. Swift (1980) comments on the separation of services in the health area, with public health clinics functioning as the preventive component. Public health departments with their traditional orientation to prevention might be one alternative, especially with the increased focus on prevention in general health. The modification of lifestyles and behavior patterns for purposes of general or mental health could be organized under a single umbrella where community psychologists and health psychologists would find a common home with health planners, epidemiologists, and other specialties with whom they need to interact. Under the block grant program, states with strong health departments and a weak commitment to prevention on the part of the mental health department might make some movement in this direction. Another source of competition to CMHCs will come from hospitals and the for-profit health care corporations, which are rapidly moving into the wellness and prevention area. Some degree of competition for prevention funds might help advance the cause of prevention, but to the detriment of the community mental health ideology.

The fact that most applied training is person-oriented, with students receiving considerably less exposure to systems approaches, is not surprising. The technology of the former is not only more advanced but more compatible with the direct service orientation. However, applied programs in systems, social action, and change are more compatible with the programs of organizations other than CMHCs. As a result there is a need for improved linkages between academic programs and organizations other than CMHCs to facilitate the availability of training for students interested in these areas.

In view of the conceptual problems, funding difficulties, and initial lack of sufficient trained manpower, the fact that there has been as much development in applied prevention programs as has occurred can be viewed very positively and taken as a sign of an underlying momentum. Typically, there is a 20- to 30-year period between innovations in basic science and their utilization in medical therapies or weapon systems (Mosteller, 1981). For prevention the preceding two decades would be more appropriately considered the initial phase in a much longer interval. The need for a longer interval is based on the current limitations in our knowledge base, stemming from the complexity of the variables involved and the need for the competing paradigm to become firmly established.

## Future Directions

The battle over the feasibility of the prevention of emotional and mental disorders, although manifested in differences in theoretical orientations and value systems, ultimately is rooted in control and power (Albee, 1982; President's Commission, 1978; Zolik, 1981). The roots of the current crisis in health and mental illness care are embedded in the perverse and ungovernable economic incentives attained by the health care industry through its acquiescence in the 1960s to the proposed federal health policy for the provision of care to the elderly, the poor, and others who were unable to meet the rising costs of health care. Although millions of the poor and aged have received care through Medicare and Medicaid, physicians and hospitals also were major beneficiaries of government-sponsored programs. The domination of health care policy by the health industry, however, is being seriously challenged—notwithstanding the victory of the industry in having Congress stall the efforts of the Carter administration toward cost containment of health expenditures. Similar efforts by the Reagan administration also are being opposed. Cost containment will affect prevention, but the underlying issue is one of prevention being controlled by the health industry to offset in part the loss of other funds. If controlled by the health industry, prevention can thereby be interpreted in a manner consistent with the palliative-ameliorative function of traditional clinical practice; for example, coronary bypass surgery to prevent death rather than a truly effective national program directed at reducing risk factors, and abortion rather than a true preventive program to reduce the incidence of unwanted teenage pregnancies.

Preventionists are confronted with a need to rank order their various programs on a number of dimensions. One of these is cost-effectiveness. The faith in

human services, ability to improve the life situation of most segments of society, and especially that of the disadvantaged, is being replaced with skepticism and jaundiced scrutiny. The increasing demand for accountability and evidence of effectiveness is requiring more sophisticated evaluations of programs to justify their funding. It is not difficult to envision these demands as increasing, regardless of the future state of the economy or the predominant political persuasion of Congress.

Related to cost-effectiveness is the dimension of investment costs in relation to the degree of risk reduction. Most Americans are interested in improving the quality of life, but they also are middle-of-the-roaders. The degree of personal risk they are willing to undertake is related to the extent to which the costs involved do not jeopardize economic growth. Americans, as Etzioni (1979) stated, "are not willing to undermine the gilded machine which produces our affluent way of life." Proponents of systems approaches and empowerment need to take this into account in developing their programs.

Chesterton once said that there are no architectural rules for building clouds in the sky. Preventive programs based on rhetoric and face-validity rather than a substantive knowledge base are susceptible to becoming our clouds in the sky, subject to the prevailing winds of pseudoscientific fashion. Without a substantive knowledge base derived from basic research and program evaluation, prevention will become the golden calf worshipped by those for whom prevention has become a mystical religious belief system. The research base is beginning to develop in areas such as competency development and a few areas in social system modification to make it feasible to undertake pilot preventive projects. However, the complexity and interaction between the variables is poorly understood. Although the social problem-solving skills approach is being widely implemented in applied programs, the failure to replicate many findings reveals the complexities involved and cautions against large scale implementation of this technology (Gesten et al., 1982; Gillespie, Durlak, & Sherman, 1982; McKim et al., 1982). The research in this area illustrates the "operation bootstrap" process with which we are confronted.

For prevention to become firmly established, psychology has to overcome its prejudice against research directed toward replication and long-term studies. The linkage between any preventive program and enhanced or sustained adjustment or tolerance for stress has to be demonstrated on both a short-term and a long-term basis. Due to the long latency period frequently involved in emotional disorders—a period often greater than the interest or life span of researchers—there is a need for a number of prevention research centers which can serve as data depositories with a mission of long-term follow-up research. In addition there is a need for an efficient communication network in prevention programming. Gilligan (1982), in relation to the costs involved in developing effective preventive projects, voiced the need to avoid "the wheel being reinvented" at different centers.

Preventive programs need to be highly sensitive to untoward effects and prepared to introduce any necessary modifications or changes. As an example, research has indicated that in 27 states there was a higher number of fatal crashes among 16- and 17-year-olds who obtained licenses earlier after completing a driver's education course (Robertson & Zador, 1978), and that in nine school systems which discontinued driver education courses the crash rate among 16- and 17-year-olds declined 63 percent from 1975 to 1978, with no corresponding change in communities which continued these courses (Robertson, 1980). Whether the social-political process involved in prevention predominates over the scientific in the area remains to be seen.

All of these dimensions need to be included as part of training. In spite of Iscoe's (1981) contention that the predoctoral level is not the place where students interested in prevention are receiving such training, both academic and applied training are being obtained at the predoctoral level. However, as the knowledge required for prevention is not always the same as that required for treatment, the need for modification in training programs is a paramount concern if training is to be improved. Even though the rhetoric directed toward clinical psychology often is accompanied by underlying strains of an Oedipal symphony, accommodations in training have to be sought. New training formats must be explored; interdisciplinary dimensions must be introduced; current guidelines for accreditation must be challenged. Otherwise training obtained at the predoctoral level will by necessity have to be completed at the postdoctoral level into the indefinite future. In the applied training sector, Reiff's question (1967) as to whether prevention services can survive in CMHCs with their orientation toward traditional services is still open.

## Summary and Conclusions

Rosen (1977) considers that the state of prevention with respect to the major contemporary health problems "is analogous to the state of affairs around 1870 in terms of understanding and preventing the communicable diseases." No one would disagree with this. The advances in academic and applied training in prevention over the last decade have begun the process of laying a foundation whose structure is still incomplete. Its incompleteness constitutes a challenge. In this I am reminded of a friend who is a political scientist and a Jesuit and who, combining the lore from both, once impressed on me that if you are involved in something that you believe in and to which you are committed, focus on the gains achieved, no matter how small, to avoid the pain and frustration involved in not having achieved more distant goals. At the same time, remember that if the cause is important, others will follow and carry on with the task. Only by a concern for training will the development of a critical mass of psychologists committed to prevention ensure the achievement of the distant goal. The need for preventive interventions is so loud that only a deaf ear can ignore it.

## References

Albee, G. W. The fourth mental health revolution. *Journal of Prevention*, 1980, **1**, 67–70.

Albee, G. W. The politics of nature and nurture. *American Journal of Community Psychology*, 1982, **10**, 1–36.

Allen, G. J., Chinsky, J. M., Larsen, S. W., Lochman, J. E., & Sellinger, H. E. *Community psychology and the schools: A behaviorally oriented multi-level preventive approach.* Potomac, Md.: Lawrence Erlbaum, 1976.

American Hospital Association. A *national survey of consumers and business.* Chicago: American Hospital Association, 1978.

Anderson, R. M., & May, R. M. Directly transmitted infectious diseases: Control by vaccination. *Science*, 1982, **215**, 1053–1060.

Bard, M., & Berkowitz, B. Training police as specialists in family crisis intervention: A community psychology action program. *Community Mental Health Journal*, 1967, **3**, 315–317.

Barton, A. K., Andrulis, D. P., Grove, W. P., & Aponte, J. F. Training programs in the mid '70s. In I. Iscoe, B. L. Bloom, & C. D. Spielberger (Eds.), *Community psychology in transition.* Washington, D.C.: Hemisphere Publishing, 1977.

Bass, R. D. *Consultation and education services: Federally funded community mental health centers, 1973.* DHEW Publication ADM. 75-108. Washington: Government Printing Office, 1974.

Bloom, B. The rhetoric and some views of reality. In I. Iscoe, B. L. Bloom, & C. D. Spielberger (Eds.), *Community psychology in transition.* Washington, D.C.: Hemisphere Publishing, 1977.

Chutis, L. Personal communication. February 18, 1982.

Cowen, E. L. Baby-steps toward primary prevention. *American Journal of Community Psychology*, 1977, **5**, 1–22.

Eisenberg, L. A research framework for evaluating the promotion of mental health and prevention of mental illness. *Public Health Reports*, 1981, **96**, 3–19.

Erhlich, R. B. Alternatives for action. APA *Division of Community Psychology Newsletter*, 1981, **15**, 22.

Erhlich, R. B. Personal communication. June 15, 1982.

Etzioni, A. How much is life worth? *Social Policy,* 1979, **9,** 4–8.

Gesten, E. L., Rains, M. H., Rapkin, B. D., Weissberg, R. P., de Apodaca, R. F., Cowen, E. L., & Bowen, R. Training children in social-problem solving competencies: A first and second look. *American Journal of Community Psychology,* 1982, **10,** 95–115.

Gillespie, J., Durlak, J. A., & Sherman, D. Relationship between kindergarten children's interpersonal problem-solving skills and other indices of school adjustment: A cautionary note. *American Journal of Community Psychology,* 1982, **10,** 149–154.

Gilligan, T. Personal communication. June 9, 1982.

Golann, S. E. Community psychology and mental health: An analysis of strategies and a survey of training. In I. Iscoe & C. D. Spielberger (Eds.), *Community psychology: Perspectives in training and research.* New York: Appleton-Century-Crofts, 1970.

Guerney, B. G., Jr. *Psychotherapeutic agents: New roles for non-professionals, parents, and teachers.* New York: Holt, Rinehart & Winston, 1969.

Hanson, D. R., Gottesman, I. I., & Meehl, P. E. Genetic theories and the validation of psychiatric diagnoses: Implications for the study of children of schizophrenics. *Journal of Abnormal Psychology,* 1977, **86,** 575–588.

Harris, L., & Associates, Inc. *Health maintenance.* Newport Beach: Pacific Mutual Life Insurance Company, 1978.

Harrison, G. *Mosquitoes, malaria and man: A history of hostilities since 1880.* New York: Dutton, 1978.

Henderson, D. A. Smallpox eradication. *Public Health Reports,* 1980, **95,** 422–426.

Iscoe, I. Conceptual barriers to training for the primary prevention of psychopathology. In J. M. Joffe & G. W. Albee (Eds.), *Prevention through political action and social change.* Hanover, N.H.: University Press of New England, 1981.

Iscoe, I., Bloom, B. L., & Spielberger, C. D. (Eds.) *Community psychology in transition.* Washington, D.C.: Hemisphere Publishing, 1977.

Jason, L. A. Training undergraduates in behavior therapy and behavioral community psychology. *Behaviorists for Social Action Journal,* 1981, **3,** 1–8.

Kennedy, D. The politics of preventive health. *Technology Review,* 1981, **84,** 58–60.

Klein, D. C., & Goldston, S. E. (Eds.) *Primary prevention: An idea whose time has come.* Washington: National Institute of Mental Health, 1977.

Kotler, P. *Marketing for non-profit organizations.* Englewood Cliffs, N.J.: Prentice-Hall, 1975.

Kotler, P., & Levy, S. J. "Demarketing, yes, demarketing." *Harvard Business Review,* 1971, **26,** 3–12.

Kuhn, T. S. *The structure of scientific revolutions* (2nd ed.) Chicago: University of Chicago Press, 1970.

Lamb, H. R., & Zusman, J. Primary prevention in perspective. *American Journal of Psychiatry,* 1979, **136,** 12–17.

Lamb, H. R., & Zusman, J. The seductiveness of primary prevention. In F. D. Perlmutter (Ed.), *Mental health promotion and primary prevention.* San Francisco: Jossey-Bass, 1982.

Leontieff, V. Academic economics. *Science,* 1982, **127,** 104–106.

Levine, A. G. *Love Canal: Science, politics and people.* New York: Lexington Books, 1982.

Levitt, E. E. Internship versus campus: 1964 and 1971. *Professional Psychology,* 1973, **4,** 129–132.

Levy, R. I., & Moskowitz, J. Cardiovascular research: Decades of progress, a decade of promise. *Science,* 1982, **217,** 121–129.

MacMahon, B., Pugh, T. F., & Ipsen, J. *Epidemiological methods.* Boston: Little, Brown, 1960.

McAlister, A., Puska, P., Salonen, J., Tuomilehto, J., & Kosela, K. Theory and action for health promotion: Illustrations from the North Karelia project. *American Journal of Public Health,* 1982, **72,** 43–50.

McKim, B. J., Weissberg, R. P., Cowen, E. L., Geston, E. L., & Rapkin, B. D. A comparison of problem solving ability and adjustment of suburban and urban third grade children. *American Journal of Community Psychology,* 1982, **10,** 155–170.

Marshall, E. NRC must weigh psychic costs. *Science,* 1982, **216,** 1203–1204. (a)

Marshall, E. EPA may allow more lead in gasoline. *Science,* 1982, **215,** 1375–1378. (b)

Meyer, A. J., Nash, J. D., McAlister, A. L., Maccoby, N., & Farquhar, J. W. Skill training in a cardiovascular health education campaign. *Journal of Consulting and Clinical Psychology,* 1980, **48,** 129–142.

Meyer, M. L., & Gerrard, M. Graduate training in community psychology. *American Journal of Community Psychology,* 1977, **5,** 155–164.

Mosteller, F. Innovation and evaluation. *Science,* 1981, **211,** 881–886.

Naierman, N., Haskins, B., Robinson, G., Zook, C., & Wilson, D. *Community mental health centers: A decade later.* Cambridge, Mass.: Abt Books, 1978.

National Institute of Mental Health, Survey Reports Branch. *Provisional data on federally funded community mental health centers, 1976–77.* Washington: Division of Biometry and Epidemiology, National Institute of Mental Health, May 1978.

President's Commission on Mental Health. *Report to the President.* Vols. 1–4. Washington: Government Printing Office, 1978.

Rados, D. *Non-profit marketing: Text and cases.* Reading, Mass.: Addison-Wesley, 1980.

Rappaport, J. *Community psychology: Values, research, and action.* New York: Holt, Rinehart & Winston, 1977.

Reder, M. W. Chicago economics: Permanence and change. *Journal of Economic Literature,* 1982, **20,** 1–38.

Reiff, R. Mental health manpower and institutional change. In E. L. Cowen, E. A. Gardner, & M. Zaxs (Eds.), *Emergent approaches to mental health problems.* New York: Appleton-Century-Crofts, 1967.

Robertson, L. S. Crash involvement of teenaged drivers when driver education is eliminated from high school. *American Journal of Public Health,* 1980, **70,** 599–603.

Robertson, L. S., & Zador, P. L. Driver education and crash involvement of teenaged drivers. *American Journal of Public Health,* 1978, **63,** 959–965.

Rosen, G. *Preventive medicine in the United States, 1900–1975: Trends and interpretation.* New York: Prodist, 1977.

Settle, D., & Patterson, C. Lead in albacore: Guide to lead pollution in Americans. *Science,* 1980, **207,** 1167–1176.

Shabecoff, P. Rules to reduce the lead in gas reported ready. *New York Times,* August 1, 1982, 1.

Shemberg, K. M., & Leventhal, D. Attitudes of internship directors toward preinternship training and clinical training models. *Professional Psychology,* 1981, **12,** 639–646.

Silverman, M. Factors associated with effective implementation of policy goals of the CMHC Act of 1963. Unpublished doctoral dissertation, Northern Illinois University, 1978.

Silverman, P. The widow as a caregiver in a program of preventive intervention with other widows. In G. Caplan & M. Killilea (Eds.), *Support systems and mutual help: Multidisciplinary explorations.* New York: Grune & Stratton, 1976.

Smith, W. M. Epidemiology of hypertension. *Medical Clinics of North America,* 1977, **61**, 1467–1486.

Snow, D. L., & Newton, P. M. Task, social structure, and social progress in the community mental health center movement. *American Psychologist,* 1976, **31**, 582–594.

Spivack, G., & Schure, M. B. *Social adjustment of young children.* San Francisco: Jossey-Bass, 1974.

Stone, A. Interview on Sunday morning television program, Columbia Broadcasting System, July 4, 1982.

Swift, C. F. Primary prevention: Policy and practice. In R. H. Price, R. F. Ketterer, B. C. Bader, & J. Monahan (Eds.), *Prevention in mental health: Research, policy and practice.* Beverly Hills: Sage, 1980.

Tableman, B. Prevention activities at the state level. In R. H. Price, R. F. Ketterer, B. C. Bader, & J. Monahan (Eds.), *Prevention in mental health: Research, policy and practice.* Beverly Hills: Sage, 1980.

Tableman, B. *Progress report on prevention and indirect services.* Ann Arbor, Mich.: Department of Mental Health (mimeo), 1981.

Tornatsky, L. How a Ph.D. program aimed at survival issues survived. *American Psychologist,* 1976, **31**, 189–192.

Truitt, J. Personal communication. July 15, 1982.

U.S. Department of Health, Education & Welfare. *Healthy people: The Surgeon General's report on health promotion and disease prevention.* Washington: Government Printing Office, 1979.

U.S. Department of Health and Human Services. *Health, United States, 1980, with prevention profile.* Washington: Government Printing Office, 1980.

U.S. General Accounting Office. *Report by the Comptroller General of the United States: HUD not fulfilling responsibility to eliminate lead-based paint hazard in federal housing.* Gaithersburg, Md.: General Accounting Office, 1980.

Vayda, A., & Perlmutter, F. Primary prevention in community mental health centers: A survey of current activities. *Community Mental Health Journal,* 1977, **4**, 343–351.

Weiner, R. S., Woy, J. R., Sharfstein, S. S., & Bass, R. D. Community mental health centers and the "seed money" concept: Effects of terminating federal funds. *Community Mental Health Journal,* 1979, **15**, 129–138.

Woy, J. R., Wasserman, D. B., & Weiner-Pomerantz, R. Community mental health centers: Movement away from the model? *Community Mental Health Journal,* 1981, **17**, 265–276.

Yankelovich, D., Skelly, H., & White, R. *The General Mills American family report, 1978–79: Family health in an era of stress.* Minneapolis, Minn.: General Mills, 1979.

Zolik, E. S. Primary prevention. In W. Silverman (Ed.) *Community mental health: A source book for professionals and advisor board members.* New York: Praeger, 1981.

Zolik, E. S., & Bogat, A. G. Perceived importance of areas in community psychology–community mental health. Paper presented at the meeting of the American Psychological Association, 1981.

Zolik, E. S., Bogat, A. G., & Jason, L. A. Community training for interns and practicum students. Paper presented at the meeting of the American Psychological Association, 1980.

Zolik, E. S., DesLauriers, A., Graybill, J., & Hollon, T. Fulfilling the needs of "forgotten families." *American Journal of Orthopsychiatry,* 1962, **22**, 176–185.

Zolik, E. S., Hopkinson, D., Sirbu, W., & Pozzi, M. Intern perspectives on training in community psychology–community mental health. In E. Zolik (Chair), Community psychology–community mental health components in internship training. Symposium presented at the meeting of the American Psychological Association, 1976.

Zolik, E. S., & Philipp, M. Training in community psychology-community mental health in counseling programs. Paper presented at the meeting of the American Psychological Association, 1980.

Zolik, E. S., & Philipp, M. Training in community psychology-community mental health in school psychology programs. Paper presented at the meeting of the American Psychological Association, 1981.

Zolik, E. S., Philipp, M., & Jason, L. A. Status of training in primary prevention in CMHCs. Paper presented at the meeting of the American Psychological Association, 1981.

Zolik, E. S., Sirbu, W., & Hopkinson, D. Training programs from the perspective of graduate students. In I. Iscoe, B. L. Bloom, & C. D. Spielberger (Eds.), *Community psychology in transition.* Washington: Hemisphere Publishing, 1977.

Zolik, E. S., Soucy, G. J., & Bogat, G. A. Domains of community psychology/community mental health: A factor analytic study. Paper presented at the 20th International Congress of Applied Psychology, Edinburgh, Scotland, 1982.

# 18 THE EDUCATION OF A PREVENTION PSYCHOLOGIST

## Richard H. Price

Let us begin with some working assumptions. First, prevention psychology, while a worthwhile aspiration, is not an accomplished fact. It is, instead, a goal to be pursued by psychologists in a wide variety of disciplinary specialties, a number of which are represented in this volume.

Second, nothing in principle presents insurmountable barriers to reaching the goal of a working prevention psychology. Iscoe (1981) has observed, however, that there is a formidable array of practical and political barriers that this emerging field faces.

But there is an even more fundamental barrier that needs to be considered. It is that the current state of knowledge in the field is very incomplete. We are now only beginning to understand how to formulate problems in ways that suggest promising preventive innovations. The design of preventive innovations still relies more heavily on the individual skills of a few adventurous researchers than it does on a set of standard scientific principles and criteria for the development of effective innovations. Despite the explosion of publications in the field we need new prevention-relevant knowledge in psychology. Furthermore, we need to develop a cadre of researchers committed to creating that knowledge and using it.

From where will the knowledge come for a prevention psychology? Certainly, some useful knowledge is being developed now and published in a variety of forms (Cowen, 1982; Price, Ketterer, Bader, & Mon-

ahan, 1980). However, I am inclined to believe that the most important knowledge for a prevention psychology will come from the next generation of prevention researchers. They are, in some cases, people who have not yet entered graduate work. We must ask ourselves, How will they be educated? More specifically, what are the substantive disciplines that they should learn? What are the specific research skills that are appropriate? Once trained, who will be the audience for their research?

I also assume that prevention psychology is too complex to be accommodated by a single research role. Prevention research is actually a chain of linked activities. These activities are very different from one another. They are also interdependent, sequential, goal-directed, and presently isolated from one another. And they require that we create an educational and social structure in which they can flourish. Centers for prevention research that both carry out specific analytic skills and teach them to prevention researchers while providing them with the vision to understand where their work fits in the larger scheme do not yet exist. Thus prevention psychology as an idea is really a promissory note. Whether the field will be in a position to collect on that note in a decade or a generation remains to be seen.

To think creatively about the question of the education of prevention psychologists, we must first think about the process of knowledge development and knowledge use. For it is in the context of that process that the prevention researchers of the next generation will work. Once we have conceptualized that process, we can begin to imagine a variety of different but interdependent roles that prevention psychologists could play in the process of inquiry. Let us consider four interconnected research domains in the research process (Price, 1982) and then address the question of the research roles and skills that would be required to make this process come to life. These four domains and their relationships are shown in Figure 18.1.

This scheme suggests that the prevention research process begins in the domain of problem analysis. One product of that analysis is a set of modifiable risk factors and a problem definition that becomes the raw material for the next domain, that of innovation design. In turn, the product of innovation design may be subjected to field trials which, if successful, will provide innovation prototypes that can be diffused through various user populations or networks. And if they achieve widespread adoption, they may ultimately reduce the incidence of a problem or disorder in the community.

I have no illusions about this process unfolding in an unerring and mechanical fashion, producing preventive innovations from some scientific conveyor belt. We know far too little about each stage of this process, and how these stages can be interconnected. Nevertheless, in its broad outline I find this scheme helpful.

## Roles for Prevention Researchers

Havelock and Havelock (1973) have observed that a useful way to begin thinking about designing new educational programs is to try to envision the role that a graduate of the program might occupy. If we accept the assumptions and the framework outlined above, we can begin to sketch some of the implications for the education of prevention researchers. In addition, we can begin to identify some of the possible roles that prevention researchers might adopt. The roles that are described below are in some ways quite different from one another, though they interlock at various points. As I suggested earlier, I do not believe that any single role is capable of encompassing the enormous complexity and diversity of the research to be undertaken in the name of prevention.

Let us now briefly sketch each of these roles. What should a person in each of these role configurations

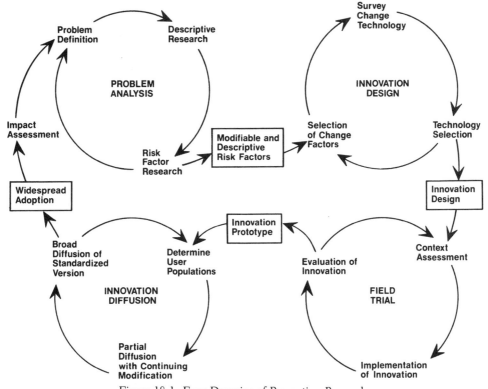

Figure 18.1. Four Domains of Prevention Research.

know? What should he or she be able to do? It is to those issues that we now turn.

## THE PROBLEM ANALYST

The first type of prevention researcher I can imagine is someone whose primary skill is in problem definition. Regardless of the substantive field under consideration, a problem analyst is someone who can identify those who are stakeholders in current definitions of the problem. Problems have a remarkable way of getting defined in terms that are consistent with the interests of the definer. A problem analyst also can try to see the problem from the point of view of the sufferer and those at risk rather than exclusively from an external point of view.

In addition, a problem analyst is someone who can count. Analysts are concerned to define the distribution of the problem, both demographically and geographically. In this sense, they share some of the characteristics of epidemiologists and are comfortable doing what Gruenberg (1981) calls "risk factor research."

On the other hand, the sort of problem analyst I am thinking of is not narrowly tied to a single methodological tradition. He or she is equally comfortable conducting and learning from ethnographic research (Spradley, 1979), involving participant observation, and interviewing people presumed to be at risk for a particular problem or disorder. Not content with survey results alone, the analyst will want to see the problem from the cultural perspective of the population thought to be at risk. Problem analyses that do not have this critical sensitivity are not only incomplete, but lead to formulations that are insensitive to the needs and circumstances of the people in whose name we are conducting our research. Problem analysts must also be able to communicate what they have learned about modifiable risk factors associated with a particular problem or condition. For it is these modifiable risk factors that become the working material of the second major group of researchers in our scheme, the innovation designers.

## INNOVATION DESIGNER

Innovation designers must be able to use the information produced by problem analysts in formulating the design of an innovation directed at the problem. Our innovation designer is someone who recognizes that, as Gregg, Preston, Geist, and Caplan (1979) have observed, social problems have been formulated almost exclusively at the individual level, and too often innovations have followed suit.

Innovation designers are people with a broad knowledge of change methods. One of their unique capacities should be to be able to make informed choices about the appropriateness, cost, potential effectiveness, and impact of a particular change technology. They also must be able to assess the impact of that technology from the point of view of those who will be affected by it. Finally, of course, the innovation designer must be able to communicate the design he or she has developed to field researchers whose role it is to transform the design into a reality.

## FIELD RESEARCHER

Perhaps one of the most familiar roles for psychologists is that of field researcher. In order to transform a design for a preventive innovation into a reality, field researchers must not only possess research design skills, but also be able to collaborate with administrators and local community groups that will serve as host for preventive innovations. While the skills of the field researcher may be most familiar to us, they are seldom described in ways which allow us to appreciate the subtle blend of political sensitivity and scientific hardheadedness that is needed to enact this role successfully. The ultimate product of a field researcher's work is not just an evaluation report, but a description of the successful innovation in sufficient detail to allow it to be adopted by other users in communities dispersed widely from the original field testing site.

## DIFFUSION RESEARCHER

Still another critical role in the prevention research process is that of diffusion researcher. We have recognized only recently that to "give psychology away," as Miller (1969) suggested, is not as easy as it sounds. Even low-cost, effective, culturally sensitive preventive innovations focused on an important problem will not necessarily be spontaneously adopted by potential user groups in the community. A diffusion researcher must be able to assess the adoption potential of various user groups and to involve potential users in examining the innovation and modifying it to some degree to suit local concerns, needs, and interests. Diffusion researchers will be able to draw upon the literature of knowledge utilization and communication (e.g., Rogers & Shoemaker, 1971) if preventive innovations are to be effectively disseminated to communities where they can be of use.

## LINKING THE ROLES

One can find activities resembling each of those I have just described in a variety of different research

contexts. Because they are isolated rather than interconnected, little communication occurs between
these various research domains. Consequently even
promising prevention research seldom is carried to
the next step in the process. It is possible that still
another fifth role, that of "linker," to use Havelock
and Havelock's (1973) term, is also desirable. Such
a role could be imagined between any two of the
research domains or roles I just described. But, as
they note:

> Creating a new role is an active social
> engineering in the truest sense. The diagrams
> below [reproduced here as Figure 18.2] may
> suggest some of the problems. We will never be
> introducing a new role into a social vacuum;
> there will always be a pre-existing structure or
> network of relationships between pre-existing
> roles, sometimes protected by considerable
> power, prestige, and thousands of years of
> tradition. In deciding that a new role is needed,
> we are presuming that a real gap exists in this
> network, not in terms of social relationships,
> but in terms of functional relationships to serve
> the system's goal. Hence, even though we may
> be filling a functional gap, we are at the same
> time disrupting an existing set of relationships
> and forcing on the system a new set of
> relationships.
>
> Role theorists have used the term "role set"
> to define the group of individuals with whom a

particular role holder must relate most closely
in his everyday work. The role set is very
important to a role holder because through their
perception and behavior they convey to the role
holder an image of himself. If they deny his
existence or refuse to treat him as a distinct
entity, he is powerless to act and will ultimately
fail in the role. For this reason, any good role
training design must (a) define the probable role
set for the trainee, and (b) indicate the ways in
which the role set will be led to accept the role
[pp. 63–65].

Figure 18.2 portrays the problem of creating a
new role and the new role set in schematic terms.
The notion of role set, taken in combination with
the prevention research process that has been described,
offers some useful conceptual tools for imagining what
would be required in the education of a prevention
psychologist.

## Prevention and the Subfields of Psychology

Having considered some of the roles for which prevention psychologists could be educated, let us turn
to the field itself to ask whether it could be hospitable
to this idea. There seems little question that the most
substantial historical precedents for prevention in psychology have emerged in the mental health clinical-
related fields (Albee, 1967; Bloom, 1979; Cowen,

**The Problem of Creating a New Role**

**The New Role and the Role Set**

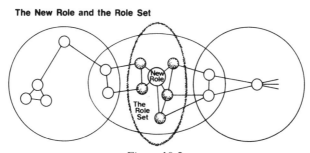

Figure 18.2
SOURCE: Havelock & Havelock, 1973.

1977; Price et al., 1980). As community psychology and community mental health began to capture the imagination of psychologists in the late 1960s and early '70s, increasing attention began to be devoted to prevention in mental health. Clinicians began to ask how preventively oriented programs could be developed to supplement the already existing focus on clinical intervention for chronic and acute psychological disorders. Thus it is safe to say that the fields of clinical and community psychology were pioneers in the development of a preventive orientation in the field of psychology.

Now a number of different influences are beginning to operate on the field of psychology. Specialties which previously maintained primarily a basic research focus have begun to concern themselves with mission-oriented research and practice. Notable among these is developmental psychology. What was once almost exclusively a laboratory-oriented basic research perspective on knowledge development and use has broadened considerably in recent years (Bronfenbrenner, 1977; Shure, 1979). In the field of developmental psychology, researchers such as Masterpasqua (1981) have called for an orientation to competence enhancement in real-life settings for children and have suggested than an applied-developmental psychologist can provide a knowledge base for advocacy of "developmental rights" in community settings. In addition, some researchers such as Garbarino (1980) have begun to ask what it is about some community contexts that increases potential risk for child maltreatment in some families. His research on culturally based attitudes and expectations about child-rearing identifies social variables that may undermine parental competence. In addition, recently several graduate programs have been initiated at the University of Michigan, University of California–Los Angeles, the University of North Carolina, and Yale University that are concerned primarily with the relationship between social policy and child development (*Networker*, 1982). These programs, while not exclusively oriented to preventive activities, provide developmental psychologists with an opportunity to consider extraindividual variables that have impact on the psychological and physical welfare of children.

Organizational and social psychologists have recently become increasingly concerned with the impact of various organizational arrangements on stress experienced by workers and on the quality of work life (Kahn, 1979). House (1981) has been concerned with the impact of work-related stress on psychological and physical well-being and the degree to which it can be buffered by various sources of social support. In industrial psychology, Foote and Erfurt (1980) have been concerned with the development of employee assistance programs to provide a prevention context to deal with emerging alcohol problems in industrial settings. Silver and Wortman's (1980) work on the impact of undesirable life events is a particularly evocative basis for developing a social psychology of prevention and early intervention.

Community psychologists have been concerned with ways in which preventive interventions can be established in various community settings and agencies. Cooper (1980) has surveyed the prospects in community mental health. Jason (1981) has demonstrated that behavioral interventions can be introduced for preventive purposes in schools, neighborhoods, and other community settings. Gottlieb (1981) and his colleagues have explored the preventive potential of social networks and social support in both health and mental health.

Finally, health psychology, now a rapidly growing field of interest in the field of psychology, has much to contribute to a prevention psychology (Stone, 1979). This potential contribution is explored in detail by Albino in Chapter 13 of this volume.

This cursory look at the prevention-relevant research in various areas of psychology is neither representative or complete. It does suggest that there is genuine interest and capacity in the field for the further development of a prevention psychology and, perhaps, for the education of prevention researchers.

## Organizational Context and the Education of Prevention Psychologists

In order to consider how we might organize ourselves to educate prevention psychologists, we have to ask both about the current state of psychology and about the nature of prevention research. Conventionally, departments of psychology are organized along lines of substantive content ranging over a number of different specialties within the field, including clinical, organizational, social, developmental, community, physiological, and learning. Indeed, the American Psychological Association has now more than 35 divisions representing more or less distinctive specialty areas within the field of psychology. We have said that the emergent character of prevention psychology is no less diverse and complex. Prevention research involves multiple, interconnected domains of inquiry and practice. This complexity and diversity, both in the field of psychology and in prevention research, has clear implications for how we might organize the education of prevention psychologists.

First, given the enormous diversity of substantive specialties within the field of psychology, the development of separate programs of prevention psychology within departments of psychology would be a serious strategic and intellectual error. Such programs could not (and should not) lay claim to a single substantive subdiscipline within the field of psychology. Furthermore, attempting such an arrangement would lose the intellectual contribution that various specialty areas within the field of psychology could provide to the mission-oriented research enterprise of prevention psychology.

A second organizational arrangement for prevention psychology within departments of psychology is to establish a track for prevention psychology within a particular subdiscipline. For example, prevention research training could be conducted within clinical or organizational or community psychology programs. While this arrangement might be more easily established initially, it has serious drawbacks. For example, it isolates prevention training not only within one specialty area, but also within one track in the specialty area. Such an organizationally and intellectually isolated effort is unlikely to flourish.

However, there are alternatives that we can consider that would both preserve the contributions of the multiple specialty areas of psychology to the emerging field of prevention psychology and, at the same time, allow preventive psychology to take an appropriate place in the organizational structure of psychology departments. An organizational arrangement well suited to this purpose is a matrix organization scheme in which substantive areas within the field of psychology are cross-hatched by mission-oriented concerns. Under such an arrangement a faculty member could be identified with a particular substantive area within the field, such as, for example, social or developmental psychology, and at the same time have a second primary identification with a mission-oriented thrust such as assessment, clinical applications, or prevention. Such an arrangement would allow a team of faculty members from diverse content areas to focus their energies on preventive research. It would legitimize collaboration across areas, it would provide a context for preventive research, and it would allow a continuity in preventive research efforts that otherwise may not be available. This organization design could provide postdoctoral training and research opportunities as well as predoctoral educational and research training roles for students.

The idea of matrix organizations is not new and has been suggested as a useful device for mission-oriented activities in the context of larger organizational structures (Galbraith, 1972). Furthermore, a model for such an arrangement already exists in the department of psychology at the University of Illinois at Chicago Circle, where, in recent years, prevention psychology has existed as a mission-oriented training program cutting across several substantive areas of the field.

## Vulnerable Populations as Constituencies

Up to this point our discussion has focused on education for prevention research roles, the organizational arrangements that might support prevention research training in psychology departments, and recent promising developments in various specialty fields of psychology. But there is a last element to be considered in the training of prevention researchers, and it is perhaps the most crucial element of all.

The question has to do with the nature of the relationship between the prevention researcher and the populations on behalf of whom he or she conducts research. The value position taken by the prevention researcher on this issue is of critical importance in how he or she views the subject matter of research and how that research is carried out. Rappaport (1981) argues that a prevention perspective toward high-risk populations will inevitably maintain a hierarchical "expert/helper" relationship in which members of the high-risk population will, by definition, be "one down." He recommends instead what he describes as a policy of "empowerment" in place of a policy of prevention. While Rappaport describes a very real concern for all researchers, I believe this perspective forecloses important options to us that need not be lost.

It is perfectly possible to ask members of a vulnerable population to be our teachers about their own condition and life circumstances, rather than to be students of our own way of doing things. It is perfectly possible to regard members of a vulnerable population as collaborators in our research, rather than as "subjects" for our scrutiny. It is also perfectly possible to view a vulnerable population as our constituency rather than as a dependent group. As researchers, we can recognize that our science can help to empower rather than oppress. I am optimistic about the role that prevention research can play in this process, rather than fatalistic about its potential negative impact on vulnerable populations.

Numerous studies of professional socialization have shown us that psychological distancing in attitudes toward client populations is established early in the education of professionals and becomes hardened as time goes on. Vulnerable people soon become "patients" or "subjects." Therefore, if there is a last critical ingredient in the education of prevention psychologists, it must be one that strives toward a relationship between the researcher and his constituency population that regards their view of the world, their hopes and needs, as the data of prime importance in prevention research.

# References

Albee, G. W. The relation of conceptual models to manpower needs. In E. L. Cowen, E. A. Gardener, & M. Zax (Eds.), *Emergent approaches to mental health problems.* New York: Appleton-Century-Crofts, 1967.

Bloom, B. L. Prevention of mental disorders: Recent advances in theory and practice. *Community Mental Health Journal*, 1979, **15**, 179–191.

Bronfenbrenner, U. Toward an experimental ecology of human development. *American Psychologist*, July 1977, **32**(7), 513–531.

Cooper, S. Implementing prevention programs: A community mental health center director's point of view. In R. H. Price, R. F. Ketterer, B. C. Bader, & J. Monahan (Eds.), *Prevention in community mental health: Research, policy and practice.* Beverly Hills: Sage, 1980.

Cowen, E. L. Baby-steps toward primary prevention. *American Journal of Community Psychology*, 1977, **5**, 1–22.

Cowen, E. L. The special number: A complete roadmap. *American Journal of Community Psychology: Special Issue on Prevention*, 1982, **10**, 239–250.

Foote, A., & Erfurt, J. C. Prevention in industrial settings: The employee assistance program. In R. H. Price, R. F. Ketterer, B. C. Bader, & J. Monahan (Eds.), *Prevention in community mental health: Research, policy and practice.* Beverly Hills: Sage, 1980.

Galbraith, J. R. *Designing complex organizations.* Reading, Mass.: Addison-Wesley, 1972.

Garbarino, J. Preventing child maltreatment. In R. H. Price, R. F. Ketterer, B. C. Bader, & J. Monahan (Eds.), *Prevention in community mental health: Research, policy and practice.* Beverly Hills: Sage, 1980.

Gottlieb, B. H. (Ed.) *Social networks and social support.* Beverly Hills: Sage, 1981.

Gregg, G., Preston, T., Geist, A., & Caplan, N. The caravan rolls on: 40 years of social problem research. *Knowledge: Creation, Diffusion, Utilization*, 1979, **1**, 31–61.

Gruenberg, E. M. Risk factor research methods. In D. A. Regier & G. Allen (Eds.), *Risk factor research in the major mental disorders.* National Institute of Mental Health, DHHS# (ADM) 81-1068. Washington: Government Printing Office, 1981.

Havelock, R. G., & Havelock, M. C. *Training for change*

*agents: A guide to the design of training programs in education and other fields.* Ann Arbor: Center for Research on the Utilization of Scientific Knowledge, Institute for Social Research, University of Michigan, 1973.

House, J. S. *Work stress and social support.* Reading, Mass.: Addison-Wesley, 1981.

Iscoe, I. Conceptual barriers to training for the primary prevention of psychopathology. In J. M. Joffe & G. W. Albee (Eds.), *Prevention through political action and social change.* Hanover, N.H.: The University Press of New England, 1981.

Jason, L. A. Prevention and environmental modification in a behavioral community model. *Behavioral Counseling Quarterly*, 1981, **1**, 91–107.

Kahn, R. L. *Work and mental health.* Washington: National Institute of Mental Health, 1979.

Masterpasqua, F. Toward a synergism of developmental and community psychology. *American Psychologist*, 1981, **36**, 782–786.

Miller, G. A. Psychology as a means of promoting human welfare. *American Psychologist*, 1969, **24**, 1063–1075.

*The Networker: The Newsletter of the Bush Program in Child Development and Social Policy.* P.O. Box 11-A, Yale Station, Yale University, New Haven, Conn. 06520, 1982.

Price, R. H. Four domains of prevention research. Paper presented to the NIMH Conference on Prevention Research, Austin, Texas, February 22–24, 1982.

Price, R. H., Ketterer, R. F., Bader, B. C., & Monahan, J. (Eds.) *Prevention in community mental health: Research, policy and practice.* Beverly Hills: Sage, 1980.

Rappaport, J. In praise of paradox: A social policy of empowerment over prevention. *American Journal of Community Psychology*, February 1981, **9**(1), 1–26.

Rogers, E., & Shoemaker, F. F. *The communication of innovations.* New York: Free Press, 1971.

Shure, M. B. Training children to solve interpersonal problems: A preventive mental health program. In R. E. Munoz, L. R. Snowden, & J. G. Kelly (Eds.), *Social and psychological research in community settings.* San Francisco: Jossey-Bass, 1979.

Silver, R. L., & Wortman, C. B. Coping with undesirable life events. In J. Garber & M. E. P. Seligman (Eds.), *Human helplessness.* New York: Academic Press, 1980.

Spradley, J. P. *The ethnographic interview.* New York: Holt, Rinehart & Winston, 1979.

Stone, G. C. *Health psychology.* San Francisco: Jossey-Bass, 1979.

# 19 FUTURE DIRECTIONS FOR PREVENTIVE PSYCHOLOGY

Leonard A. Jason,
Robert D. Felner,
John Moritsugu, and
Stephanie S. Farber

An analysis of the contents of this volume presents a picture of preventive psychology as an area in which we have made great strides in identifying significant conceptual, empirical, and practical bases to guide its future development. Certainly it now seems possible to move beyond the first generation of empirical studies toward greater elaboration of a broadly informed and integrated knowledge base. The first two-thirds of the volume presented an overview of both the strengths and limitations of some of the conceptual frameworks and lines of inquiry which have emerged as particularly salient for the development of prevention efforts. What seems clear from these chapters is that, while we may have a long way yet to go, prevention now seems sufficiently evolved to have a set of traditions and a knowledge base which may enable studies which comprise the current generation of work to be truly fruitful for furthering the development of viable preventive efforts. Next, the contributors to the fifth section of the volume elaborated some of the problems, issues, and pitfalls of attempting to implement and evaluate primary prevention efforts, as well as some of the challenges which confront prevention professionals as they move into the policy area. Finally, discussions have been presented of some of the issues involved in the education of psychologists

for prevention and the degree to which efforts toward this end may successfully be integrated into existing training programs and settings.

Certainly it seems preventive psychology has now moved far from the Swampscott Conference and an almost exclusive home in community psychology. A broad emerging base of conceptual, empirical, and practical knowledge exists for prevention which may provide a context out of which the next evolutionary steps—if they are as large as those initial ones from clinical interventions to secondary prevention—may bring us to a level where the successful implementation of true prevention efforts becomes the norm rather than the exception. Further, the increased involvement by psychologists in prevention activities from such diverse roots as clinical, developmental, social, and organizational psychology should lead to preventive efforts becoming commonplace in a far broader range of settings than is now the case. Indeed, as the theoretical frameworks and empirical evidence to guide preventive efforts become more clearly established, another set of challenges which face preventive psychologists, particularly those concerned with particular target populations, is the further identification of settings and systems where effective preventive efforts may be easily accommodated as a natural and integrated component of their ongoing processes.

An example of where this may already be occurring is provided in Chapter 13 by Judith Albino. Health settings may provide ideal opportunities for reaching individuals whose typical behavior increases their level of risk for physical health difficulties. Similarly, Felner (1982) has argued that health care settings may be particularly well suited to be host settings for programs aimed at individuals who are at high risk for emotional disturbance. Illustratively, in pediatric or other health settings the psychologist may enjoy certain unique advantages in attempting to develop preventive interventions which are organized around life change, due to the opportunities these settings afford for access to and contact with individuals experiencing such changes. Children or adults experiencing life changes such as divorce, bereavement, or geographic relocation often may not come to the attention of a mental health professional unless and until psychological distress is clearly recognizable. However, in the case of health/pediatric psychologists, and the events they are concerned with, this is not true. Thus it may be easier for psychologists in these settings to engage in programs which are more truly preventive, that is, before the fact, in their timing. Other settings may be identified which, due to the nature of contacts individuals may ordinarily have with them, afford similar advantages for the timing and implementation of programs for individuals at risk due to major life changes (for instance, industrial settings where workers are transferred, fired, and so forth) or opportunities for enhancing competencies and facilitating optimal development (social problem-solving programs in the schools, or parent training in pediatric settings). If preventive efforts are to be truly viable for targeted populations, it is important that mounted interventions be readily assimilable into the host setting or system. Otherwise, as has happened all too frequently in the past, when the involved mental health professional leaves, resources are shifted, or time constraints become salient, such programming will have all too brief a life span.

At the broader level of enhancing the health, adaptation, and well-being of the population at large, underexplored potentials exist for preventive psychologists to work within interdisciplinary teams and systems to affect the characteristics of communities. Preventive psychologists have suggested that an overarching metagoal in collaborating with communities on preventive and social-system-level interventions should be the development of competencies, broadly defined. Fostering competencies may be accomplished by valuing human diversity and promoting adaptive person-environment fit (Rappaport, 1977), providing personal and community resources which alleviate feelings of noncontrol (Sue & Zane, 1980), and helping

communities make decisions about issues confronting them (Iscoe, 1974). Roles and activities for psychologists interested in competency-building in the population at large may include but are not limited to: (a) focusing on the mental health implications of social system policies and practices; (b) mounting efforts particularly geared toward the analysis and modification of behaviors and attitudes; (c) helping design and evaluate community-initiated prevention interventions; and (d) serving as catalysts mobilizing interdisciplinary teams of investigators to work with communities in comprehensively analyzing and ameliorating unmet community needs. These core concerns and activities serve to enable prevention-oriented practitioners to play a unique role in working with communities to foster and promote competencies.

## Differentiating Community-Level Interventions

The above competency-building features have been employed in various community-based prevention efforts. One way in which communities may be conceptualized is along four dimensions: the natural environment (such as geography, resources), components of the built environment (quality of buildings, for example), overall characteristics of inhabitants (for example, density), and systems which inter-connect throughout the community (transportation, media). Table 19.1 presents a more detailed schema of this four-part categorization. In the sections below, preventive competency-enhancing projects implemented under each of these areas will be reviewed and potential directions elaborated.

### Natural Environment

The natural environment consists of topographical features of the land, climate, available resources, and parklands available for public recreation. While it certainly seems clear that the climate and geographical features of a community may affect the culture and activities of a society (Moos, 1974) successful direct attempts to influence these variables might be extremely difficult, if not impossible to carry out. Still, psychologists might participate in planning the creation of new towns and communities and the growth of existing ones in ways which take advantage of optimal geographic characteristics, or help to sensitize new residents to ways of adapting their lifestyles or interests to climatic conditions in order to enhance life satisfaction, or participate in dealing effectively with residues of natural catastrophes. For example, blizzards and snowstorms which deposit excessive amounts of

**Table 19.1. A Schema for Categorizing Components of Communities**

I. Natural Environment
   A. Geography and climate
   B. Resources: Energy, soil, water, vegetation, wildlife
   C. Parks
II. Built Environment
   A. Quality and nature of buildings and other structures
   B. Pollution: Noise, vibrations, odors, litter, radiation, thermal, chemicals
III. Aggregate Inhabitant Characteristics
   A. Density, income, age, sex, marital status, ethnicity, health status
   B. Person-environment fit
   C. Sense of community
   D. Social networks
IV. Systems
   A. Political processes: Legislative, executive, judicial
   B. Economic conditions: Available employment, percent unemployed
   C. Media: Newspapers, journals, television, radio
   D. Social service: CMHCs, settlement houses
   E. Educational settings
   F. Transportation
   G. Medical care agencies
   H. Correctional facilities
   I. Religious institutions
   J. Recreational facilities

snow on sidewalks and paths cause 200 deaths and 40,000 injuries annually. Preventive psychologists have worked effectively with neighborhood groups to develop strategies to remove excessive accumulations of snow following devastating blizzards (Mollica & Jason, 1981) and, as a consequence, reduce levels of isolation and stress in the community which accompany such environmental hazards.

Natural resources are another frequently overlooked but potentially important part of the environment for prevention efforts. Preventive psychologists can assume critical roles in conserving energy (Winett, 1980), safeguarding soil and vegetation (Eckholm, 1975), and preserving wildlife. As an example of the potential of such efforts, Rothstein (1980) implemented a large-scale energy conservation program in a Southern city. Each evening on the television news, the number of gallons of gas consumed during the previous day was graphed and conservation tips were offered. This relatively simple intervention, which consisted of feedback and information, led to an overall 32 percent reduction in gasoline usage for an entire city, and thus not only decreased pollutants but also reduced a stress-producing shortage of a critical natural resource.

Parks are open natural spaces within communities which contain pastures, woods, or lakes for public recreation and add to the life satisfaction of individuals. Areas for possible collaborative ventures might include helping to design parks to meet the needs of communities, advocating more parks in congested urban areas, and working with community groups to improve the functioning of parks. In a recent study, Bogat (1982) evaluated an intervention program whereby Scout troops throughout a city adopted small, one-acre parks. The project succeeded in providing younger members of the community an opportunity to take active responsibility for public areas, and led to considerable improvements in the overall aesthetic condition of parks in a major metropolitan area.

### Built Environment

The built environment consists of all manufactured structures which are superimposed upon the natural environment. As we have seen in Chapter 7, by Abraham Wandersman and his colleagues, the built environment may be of great salience either as a source of stress or for facilitating adaptation. When working in this area, preventive psychologists might collaborate with citizen groups in designing housing complexes which are functional, attractive, and safe from crime. High crime rates have been found in public housing which was isolated and stigmatized (Kalt & Zalkind, 1976). By contrast, low crime rates were found when outsiders perceived public space as part of tenants' personal territory. In addition to designing buildings and housing projects which deter crime and increase the security of residents by promoting territoriality, another strategy for prevention that psychologists might utilize to achieve these goals is the conducting of environmental impact studies to determine optimal sites for construction of housing projects and other buildings. An example of this latter strategy is provided in a study by Cohen, Evans, Krantz and Stokols (1980), who were concerned with the appropriate location of schools. They found that children in schools built under the air corridor of an airport manifested higher blood pressure and were more likely not to persist on test items than youngsters in quieter learning environments. Attention to such factors in the future will allow us to locate facilities and residences in ways which minimize hazards to optimal development and well-being.

Regrettably, activities which occur in the built environment frequently generate a host of pollutants as an unintentional by-product, including noise, vibrations, odors, litter, radiation, heat, and chemicals. In Chapter 7 Wandersman and his colleagues discussed some of those irritants which have been shown to have behavioral significance. Additional work has shown the viability of psychologists' involvement in the reduction of such health hazards. For example, in the area of litter control, several authors (Geller, 1980; Tuso & Geller, 1976) have investigated a variety of preventive strategies aimed at discouraging littering in communities (for example, placing attractive litter cans on streets). In a particularly effective study, Stokes and Fawcett (1977) studied a serious litter problem involving high levels of inadequately packaged refuse. They noted that garbage which overflows from trash cans represents a health hazard, since disease-carrying rodents and insects may feed on this food and transmit infection to individuals living or working in the area. In addition to the increased risk of physical disorder created by such conditions, there are also potentially associated detriments to the adaptive functioning of individuals, particularly children. In collaboration with community groups, an intervention to alleviate these conditions was planned and carried out. Refuse packaging violations were reduced from 59 to 10 percent when delinquent home residents were given a checklist of violations daily and told that refuse would be collected only if its packaging met specified standards. The results of the project were presented to city legislators and the procedures subsequently were enacted into a city ordinance. The continued collaboration of psychologists and public health professionals in the identification of environmental hazards to health which may be reduced through systematic behavioral intervention certainly appears to hold promise for preventive efforts (Susser, 1975).

### Aggregate Inhabitant Characteristics

While the previous categories have focused on inanimate qualities of the natural and built environment, the inhabitant dimension refers to characteristics of the people who reside in the communities. Some of these aggregate inhabitant characteristics include socioeconomic status, density, ethnicity, age, and coping styles. Density is a critical inhabitant dimension which potently effects the functioning of community residents. For example, when a community setting is undermanned, that is, when the number of participants is less than the minimum for adequate maintenance or for fulfilling needed social roles, then new or deviant members are more readily assimilated into the setting's activities (Wicker, 1976). This finding may be of significance for psychologists in working with citizen groups to involve residents meaningfully in community affairs, establishing a sense of belonging, and reducing alienation. Public policy-oriented psychologists might also wish to keep such factors in mind when attempting to understand conditions influencing the population

growth of a community or region. For instance, while government policies are frequently pronatalist (for example, sales of contraceptives are discouraged, higher income tax deductions are given for more children), several regions have achieved some success in attempting to directly control population density by offering positive or negative incentives (for example, the highest priority for subsidized housing given to those with two or fewer children; income tax deductions only for the first three children) (LoLordo & Shapiro, 1980; Wiest & Squier, 1974).

Another dimension of aggregate inhabitant characteristics is the person-environment fit, that is, the extent to which groups of individuals fit into a particular community. Zautra and Goodhart (1979) and Chapter 10 of this volume, by John Moritsugu and Stanley Sue, review studies indicating that problems arise when groups live in social environments where they constitute minorities on one or more dimensions. For example, higher rates of hospitalization have been found for groups which are younger, older, or of lower or higher occupational status than the majority-norm with the community. These findings suggest that community psychologists might further emphasize investigations to determine social system stressors on minority groups, with the ultimate intention of working with community groups to ameliorate deleterious influences. More broadly, psychologists might examine ongoing flows of individuals into communities with the hope of documenting factors which influence optimal levels of person-environment fit ultimately achieved by new residents, as well as the course of such development.

A third category consists of the aggregate perceptions of inhabitants of the quality of such environmental dimensions and characteristics as responsiveness of community agencies (Jason & Loitta, 1982a), quality of community services (Murrell & Schulte, 1980), community satisfaction (Mitchell, Barbarin, & Hurley, 1981), the psychological sense of community (Glynn, 1978; Sarason, 1974), neighborhood cohesion (Smith, 1975), physical safety (Saegert, 1976), quality of life (Flanagan, 1980), and sense of control (Chapter 7). In the process of collaboration with a community group on the design, evaluation, or implementation of competency-enhancing interventions, the assessment of perceptions of inhabitants concerning one or more of the above dimensions may provide valuable information when employed either as a direct outcome measure or to examine possible second-order ripple effects of the community project. Assessment of community perceptions can also aid in the prediction of neighborhoods' responsiveness to particular community interventions and, ultimately, enable community psychologists and neighborhood groups to tailor projects to communities' special needs (Wandersman & Giamartino, 1980).

The final construct within the aggregate inhabitation section involves social networks. Social networks include the extended family, informal helpers (individuals recognized as knowledgeable and helpful), neighborhood groups (such as block clubs, activity groups, parent-teacher associations), self-help groups (groups where individuals share common needs and problems), and social action groups (for instance, the National Organization for Women). These clusterings of individuals provide opportunities for socializing and emotional support (Hirsh, 1980), moderate the effects of various types of life stress (Cauce, Felner, & Primavera, 1982; Cobb, 1976; Felner, Ginter, & Primavera, 1982), enable relatively unimpeded access to information (Mitchell & Trickett, 1980), and can instigate social change processes (Davis, 1977). Several reasons might account for the recent upsurge of interest in neighborhood-based social networks, including professional failure to alleviate many psychological problems (Jeger, Slotnick, & Shure, 1981), frustration with traditional ways of delivering services (Buhler & McKay, 1977), and widespread disillusionment with government agencies and private social service organizations (Perlman, 1976).

Preventive psychologists can work with these social networks in several capacities, including evaluating the effects of participating in these neighborhood groups (Gottlieb & Schroter, 1978), organizing new social networks (Bronfenbrenner, 1975), consulting with already organized support groups (Caplan, 1974), encouraging professional groups to make referrals to these social networks (Gottlieb, in press), and identifying at-risk groups with severly truncated networks marked by low degrees of permanence and durability (Mitchell & Trickett, 1980).

While promising preliminary studies have been conducted in the area of social networks, it is important to consider the following caveats. First, many unanswered questions remain concerning the overall efficacy of various types of social networks (Lieberman & Mullan, 1978). Heller and Swindle, in Chapter 6 in this book, suggest that the literature on social support has been marred by conceptual and methodological errors; for example, scales measuring social support have had questionable psychometric properties, and support has often been confounded with measures of personal characteristics. In addition, some social networks might facilitate adjustment, but others might interfere with normal recovery processes or have negative buffering effects. Hirsch (1980), for example, found that multidimensional friendships (those having

several types of activities associated with them) were related significantly in a positive direction to self-esteem for women undergoing major life changes, whereas women experienced less satisfaction and emotional support from denser support systems (that is, where many relationships exist among members of an individual's support system). Similarly, Cauce, Felner, and Primavera (1982) found that for high-risk inner-city adolescents higher levels of family support, while associated with better academic performance, were also associated with decreased levels of self-esteem. When considering social support from peers the opposite pattern of results held true. That is, better self-concepts were associated with increased levels of peer support, but academic performance was negatively related to such support. Finally, it is important to note that communication patterns between members of social networks might be qualitatively different from traditional therapeutic relationships, often intentionally. Evidence in support of this (Reisman & Yamokoski, 1974) has suggested that within informal helping relationships, friends markedly prefer expository (giving expert analysis or explanations of problems and courses of action) as opposed to more traditionally therapeutic empathic styles of communication.

### Systems

The fourth major category in the schema for categorizing components of communities consists of the following systems: the political process, economic conditions, the media, social service agencies, educational settings, transportation systems, medical care agencies, correctional facilities, religious institutions, and recreational facilities. These systems form a complicated web of community-wide networks whose overall vitality directly influences the functioning of neighborhoods and individuals. Illustrations of several of these systems are described below.

#### POLITICAL PROCESSES

In Chapter 15 by Seymour Sarason the need for preventively oriented psychologists to become more sophisticated regarding public policy issues is articulated cogently. In part, this need exists because decisions at the executive, legislative, and judicial levels exert potent influences on communities. When institutional failures aggravate individual problems, corrective efforts can be initiated through the political process. Community psychologists have worked effectively with government, for example, in bringing to the attention of public officials attitudes of community residents toward upcoming policy decisions (Murrell & Schulte, 1980). In addition, psychologists can work directly toward change by employing several types of class advocacy (Knitzer, 1980). Accountability and administrative advocacy refer to efforts directed toward either making systems more accountable or influencing regulations and guidelines which may have implications for health and well-being. As an example of this approach, investigators in seven states are collecting data on the use of child safety restraints in automobiles in order to determine which types of legislation are most effective in ensuring that children are restrained securely (Fawcett, Seekins, Cohen, Elder, Geller, Jason, Schnelle, & Winett, 1982). Data from this investigation will be disseminated to 30 states that are in the process of introducing child passenger safety legislation in the hope of helping them set up guidelines for optimal legislation. Another approach, legislative advocacy, involves lobbying efforts designed to enact new or alter existing legislation. As an example, Jung and Jason (1982) collaborated with a self-help activist group to identify cost-effective methods of prompting members to participate in a letter-writing campaign aimed at motivating the executive branch to consider a particular antipollution ordinance. Finally, legal advocacy focuses on inducing change through the judicial process. Over the past ten years, psychologists at the University of Alabama's Center for Correctional Psychology (Brodsky & Miller, 1981; Fowler & Brodsky, 1978) have been particularly effective in presenting expert testimony at key court cases (e.g., *Wyatt* v. *Stickney, Donaldson* v. *O'Connor*) which have had pervasive effects on improving the psychological and physical environments of mental patients throughout the United States.

### ECONOMIC CONDITIONS

A community's economic base is determined at least in part by the types of business and industry, the available employment, the opportunities for advancement, and the percent of unemployed and underemployed. As Edward Seidman and Bruce Rapkin discuss in Chapter 11, the health of a community's economy has a direct link to indices of mental health. Brenner, Mandell, Blackman and Silberstein (1967) report that variations in economic indicators may account for more than 72 percent of the total variations in first admissions to public hospitals for functional psychoses. Preventive psychologists might participate in planning, implementing, and evaluating social programs geared toward directly affecting income levels among members of communities. As an example, a series of studies has evaluated the effects of a negative income tax, which sets a guaranteed level of support below which a participant's income cannot fall. Fam-

ilies receiving the negative income tax, in comparison to controls, have evidenced significant increases in elementary school children's reading achievement scores (Maynard & Murnane, 1980) and more often have been able to purchase their own houses (Kaluzny, 1980). These families have also evidenced roughly double the marital dissolution rates (Tuma, Hannan, & Groeneveld, 1980), and have manifested work disincentives of 3 to 6 percent for husbands and 26 to 30 percent for female-headed households (Moffitt, 1980). These studies point to the complexity of predicting and interpreting second-order effects of policy-level interventions generally, as well as in the case of poverty specifically. Other high-priority areas for research involving economic and work-related variables include assessing the effects of supported work programs (Masters & Maynard, 1980), the impact of maternal employment on children's development (Wallston, 1973), and changes in family functioning due to members' ability to participate in "flexitime" at work (Winett, Stefanek & Riley, 1982).

### MEDIA

A community's media sources, which include television, radio, newspapers, and magazines, transmit information and images which have important influences on the promotion of healthy as well as unhealthy life patterns. The media consume an appreciable amount of people's time: The average American spends four hours a day watching television, two-and-one-half hours listening to the radio, 30 minutes reading newspapers, and 15 minutes reading magazines (White, 1981). Since the media reach practically all members of a community for a significant amount of time, psychologists interested in prevention and enhancement would be well advised to develop strategies which might extend mental health services effectively through this medium. Talkback radio, for example, has been used to help distressed individuals solve problems (Monaghan, Shun Wah, Stewart, & Smith, 1978; Wolkon & Moriwaki, 1977). The media have also been used innovatively by mental health professionals to increase communities' ability to cognitively restructure problem situations (Schanie & Sundel, 1978) and reduce maladaptive smoking patterns (Best, 1980; Dubren, 1977). Innovative efforts have also been developed by mental health professionals to teach parents to help children watch television in ways that facilitate effectiveness and problem-solving development (Singer & Singer, 1981). One of the most ambitious projects to date involved a mass media effort to transmit information concerning cardiovascular disease, and as a result of the intervention, significant reductions were brought about in risk factors for residents of an entire town (Maccoby & Alexander, 1980).

Ageism, racism, sexism, and cigarette and alcohol advertisements are negative media images which might predispose individuals to unhealthy lifestyles, damage self-esteem, and restrict the number of viable occupational and social roles. Psychologists might attempt to alter these media images by either providing gathered information to activist groups or sending the data directly to the media sources. Since the media play a critical role in inculcating values, facilitating adoption of adaptive and maladaptive behaviors, and validating social roles, an important role for preventive psychologists might involve actively participating in the process of accentuating salutary features and altering harmful influences in the mass media (Jason & Klich, 1982).

### SOCIAL SERVICES

Social service agencies within a community consist of the network of community mental health centers, settlement houses, drug abuse agencies, alcohol treatment facilities, parent-child centers, and other organizations designed to provide resources, information, and services to community residents. Unfortunately, many of these agencies allocate few resources to preventive programs. Kaplan and Bohr (1976) found that community mental health centers, for example, spend less than one-tenth of staff hours in preventive activities. Psychologists might work within a preventive format by helping to establish service centers which are staffed by personnel sensitive to the needs, culture, and traditions of the client, and where policy formulation and allocation of funds is firmly controlled by community residents (e.g., Kahn, Williams, Galvez, Lejero, Conrad, & Goldstein, 1975). In addition, psychologists might collaborate in establishing preventive social service programs which provide supportive community resources (Weisbrod & Helming, 1980) and network-building interventions for elderly community residents (Bogat & Jason, in press). Professionals within social service agencies also might function as catalysts for identifying unmet community needs and coordinating multidisciplinary efforts to resolve target problems (Basker, Meir & Kleinhauz, 1981; Cardoza, Ackerly, & Leighton, 1975). Further, they might utilize efforts of natural caregivers to enhance access to the system by consulting with them to increase their capacities to make referrals (Leutz, 1976) or by placing impaired individuals in facilitative settings where indigenous change agents can provide naturalistic support (Skeels, 1966).

### EDUCATION

A community's educational system consists of the aggregate of settings where formal and informal instruction occurs (Fawcett, Fletcher & Mathews, 1980). In developing preventive programs, psychologists can develop means for educational systems to ensure that children from high-risk populations do not succumb to disorders, or to prevent onset of maladaptive behaviors and to help youngsters navigate milestone developmental transitions (Felner et al., 1982; Felner, Norton, Cowen, & Farber, 1981). Similar efforts aimed at building competencies in such areas as goal planning, decision-making, value clarification, assertiveness, relationship development, or self-control (Danish, 1977) may also be implemented. Regardless of the particular type of preventive program, a fundamental issue for psychologists is the need to bring enthusiasm, relevance, creativity, and innovation into school systems. These goals might be approached under an educational philosophy which characterized the Dewey School; that is, school was part of life, rather than a preparation for life (Sarason, 1972). As an example, curricula for caring could be implemented throughout a school system where students provide substitute care for working mothers, visit elderly citizens, and assist families in emergencies (Bronfenbrenner, 1977). The beneficial consequences of building bridges between the educational system and experimental opportunities in the community have been amply documented. For example, Epstein (1973) found that practically all minority high school students who participated in a work-study program graduated from high school, whereas one-third of those in the control groups dropped out of school.

Learning within school settings would be more relevant and meaningful if acquired knowledge and skills could be used to ameliorate current personal and environmental problems. In one university-based applied course, students were given the opportunity to design and implement projects aimed toward correcting a variety of environmental and community-based problems, including vandalism in a parking lot, theft in a department store, uncharged fire extinguishers in college dorms, garbage cans which were not regularly emptied in a housing complex, cigarette smoke in public settings, lights left on following the end of classes, cars which were parked in spaces reserved for handicapped drivers, high levels of disruptive conversation in a library, excessive car horn blowing on a residential block, and rude phone calls received by switchboard operators (Jason, 1981a,b). Evaluation by students showed high levels of involvement with the project specifically, and with school more generally.

TRANSPORTATION

In recent years, psychologists have devoted increasing attention to issues involving transportation systems (Everett, 1980). For example, studies have been directed toward reducing speeding by posting signs with feedback (Houten, Nau, & Marini, 1980), exploring conditions facilitating seat belt usage (Geller, Casali, & Johnson, 1980), reducing police vehicle accidents through use of feedback from a tachograph plus inspections (Larson, Schnelle, Kirchner, Carr, Domash, & Risley, 1980), and assessing the effects of different light-turning sequences on pedestrian jaywalking at a busy intersection (Jason & Liotta, 1982). Regarding mass transit, Everett, Hayward, and Meyers (1974) effectively increased bus ridership, whereas Lavelli, Lavelli, and Jason (1981) successfully reduced rider exposure to aversive noise levels in underground subways. The benefits accrued by making mass transit systems more attractive are numerous, and include savings in energy, less work on road repairs, less pollution and noise, and reductions in building facade decay. In addition, the mobility and consequent life satisfaction of a large proportion of the population which, for a variety of reasons, may have limited access to an automobile or driving privileges (for example, the elderly, inner-city poor, handicapped) may be directly related to the quality of public transportation. Individuals in these circumstances depend heavily on public transportation both to accomplish the basic tasks of life (such as shopping for food) and for access to social contacts and recreational activities. In general, the studies cited above indicate that psychologists can have considerable impact on transportation systems by promoting safety programs, reducing speeding, preventing accidents, prompting energy conservation and, more generally, otherwise encouraging the use of mass transit. Preventive psychologists might also work actively with public officials and neighborhood groups in planning changes as well as designing new transportation systems which increase the access of residents to such services and which insure that the needs of the population most in need of such service are not overlooked.

## Identifying Community Collaborators

These illustrations indicate how preventive oriented psychologists can achieve some of the goals of preventive psychology—more competent communities and more effective and humane systems of socialization and support (Goodstein & Sandler, 1978)—and expand ways of making social, economic, and personal resources more available to all segments of the population (see Chapter 9), thus providing conditions where haz-

ards to optimal development are minimized and enhanced health and well-being promoted. Throughout these interventions basic value decisions were made, either explicitly or implicitly, regarding the identification of community collaborators. However, in identifying community groups to work with, several potentially problematic issues might arise. Psychologists might inadvertently collaborate with local leaders who do not adequately represent or work toward the resolution of community needs (Levine, 1974). Also, for a particular problem area there might exist two community groups that propose radically contrasting solutions. Collaborating with one activist group would more than likely alienate the psychologist from the other group. A neighborhood association might fear property devaluations if a halfway house were located in its neighborhood; working on this issue might force the community psychologist to represent either the needs of the neighborhood association or the interests of clients being deinstitutionalized. In addition, a community's mainstream majority might support parochial policies which perniciously denigrate the rights of minority groups (for example, segregationist policies). In this case the community psychologist must decide which needs of which groups to support actively. Competence development and opportunities for full equality should guide collaborative activities with community groups and in working with neighborhood groups and public and private organizations. Psychologists may need to assume mediators' roles to reduce or clarify the difficult choices they may confront concerning which groups to help. Other issues involved in the relationship between the researcher and the host community were reviewed in Chapter 5 by Trudy Vincent and Edison Trickett, particularly in the section describing Kelly's ecological analogy, which illustrated how researchers can help a setting develop a sense of community and plan its own future.

A particular cautionary concern of preventive psychologists in the mounting of community or policy level interventions are the unintended consequences of such efforts. As we have seen above, for example when discussing economic programs, they may not lead to consequences which are uniformly perceived as positive by all segments of the community. Given the lack of precision which may be inherent in such efforts, we must be particularly careful to anticipate and assess unintended consequences. As a way of achieving the former goal, it has been suggested that it is particularly important, given preventive psychology's interdisciplinary emphasis and focus on developing programs in settings and systems which are not traditionally identified with mental health, that we pay careful attention to understanding the assumptions, values, and paradigms of the disciplines, settings, and systems involved (Felner & Farber, 1980). Such understanding may enable us to anticipate how the involvement of these disciplinary differences may shape the final implementation of the intervention or its usage and thus lead to consequences different than those the mental health professional intended.

## Evaluation

Preventive psychologists adopt a social system conceptual orientation and strive to bring methodological order into social change efforts (Reiff, 1977). Sarason (1976) aptly describes the community-oriented preventive psychologist as a Mr. Everyman, but "more consciously and expertly applied." In collaborating with community groups to initiate change, preventive psychologists can aid in the construction of a firm empirical foundation for the change process by utilizing reliable and valid measures (Nunnally, 1975), employing multimethod indices to evaluate change at postpoint and follow-up periods (Cowen, 1978), replicating successful efforts at different sites (Heller, Price, & Sher, 1980), and disseminating effective interventions (Tornatzky & Fergus, 1982). Other basic research principles are reviewed by Raymond Lorion in Chapter 16.

Approaching these methodological goals might take considerable time; therefore psychologists need to remain critical but be less harsh, and more tolerant of preliminary accrued data within the emerging field of preventive psychology. In evaluating the efforts of preventive psychologists, it is important to recognize serious limitations in other, even more established fields. For example, the White House Office on Science and Technology recently estimated that no more than 15 percent of generally accepted medical technology has been evaluated fully and found effective (Plaut, 1980). In mental health fields, those adhering to the traditional model of service delivery still are committed to having therapy primarily delivered by professionals, even though accumulating evidence indicates that less expensively trained paraprofessionals may be at least as effective in producing positive therapeutic outcomes as professionals (Durlak, 1979). Preventive psychology can prosper even though empirical ambiguity, similar to that which characterizes other fields, is evident; however, excessive demands by either professional groups or the public for immediate results will place an unreasonable burden on this emerging paradigm.

## Conclusion

The contents of much of this volume make clear that much of the progress to date toward the development of effective preventive efforts has been at the level of the individual or specific "at-risk" target populations. The thrust of this chapter in discussing future directions has been to underscore the need for additional attention to understanding and optimizing social structures which impact the development, health, and well-being of the population more generally. Certainly, convincing justification for this approach can be found in the field of public health. In the 20th century, the extension of the average life span by 15 years was accomplished primarily through environmental changes, including advances in the control of infectious disease through inoculation, improved water and milk supplies, and improved living conditions and sewage disposal systems (Cormier, Prefontaine, MacDonald, & Stuart, 1980). The potential financial benefits of successful preventive efforts are staggering. While research to develop polio vaccines cost less than $40 million, since mass vaccinations have been introduced the savings in hospital costs and income have been about $1 billion a year, and 2,000 deaths and 2,500 permanently crippling cases have been prevented yearly (Eisenberg, 1979).

The preceding is not in any sense to underemphasize the importance of preventive approaches which stress the developmental enhancement of the individual and the facilitation of social competence. The range of involvements of psychologists in such intervention efforts extends well beyond the topics covered in this volume (see, for example, Bond & Rosen, 1980; and Kent & Rolf, 1979) and encompasses populations from infancy to old age. The continued development and expansion of these efforts into such evolving areas as pediatric psychology is a key, integral part of preventive psychology's future. Our choice of emphasis in this chapter, then, was based not on any sense of relative valuing of individual versus social system level approaches, but on a wish to add weight to a position that may have been relatively less attended to in the rest of this volume than it merits.

In the field of mental health, the preventive approach still faces formidable obstacles. Albee (1978) has mentioned several of these barriers, including (1) the lack of a constituency to pressure public officials for preventive services; (2) the paucity of trained professionals involved in preventive activities; (3) the dearth of financial support for research in this area; and (4) the fear engendered by the raising of potentially threatening issues of social and environmental change. While these factors will function to impede the growth of the preventive movement, there is an emerging and growing core group of professionals committed to this field (see Chapter 17 by Edwin Zolik). As Richard Price (Chapter 18) and others (the authors, in Chapter 1) have indicated, some members of specialty areas (such as developmental, organizational, social, and health psychology) which previously maintained a basic research focus have begun to orient themselves to preventive, mission-oriented research, further expanding prevention's base. As we noted at the outset of this volume, the efforts of these professionals should contribute to the construction of a solid foundation of well-documented preventive strategies and principles which will promote the well-being of a larger segment of the population than has been served within the traditional model of service delivery. In addition, professionals in other disciplines, including anthropology, sociology, economics, and political science, are using creative research methodologies to gather information which is suggesting new approaches for reducing the population-wide incidence of different problems (see Chapter 14). We hope the efforts of these diverse groups ultimately will promote the well-being of a larger segment of the population than has been served within the traditional model of service delivery.

These then are the problems and the prospects for preventive psychology. Prevention has traveled a long and often obstacle-filled road since the initial call for a reevaluation of the mental health field by Congress in the 1950s. At long last it seems to have established itself as a legitimate and viable field of specialization. Although what has been accomplished is miniscule when compared to what remains to be done, the foundation for growth is in place and directions for fruitful preventive efforts are clearly delineated. It is our hope that the diverse groups of psychologists and professionals from other disciplines concerned with prevention will build on the theory and data reflected in the pages of this volume to raise the level of the well-being of the population well beyond what it is currently and further reduce the incidence of psychological and somatic dysfunction.

# References

Albee, G. W. Report of the task panel on prevention. In D. G. Forgays (Ed.), *Primary prevention of psychopathology*. Vol. 2. Hanover, N.H.: University Press of New England, 1978.

Basker, E., Meir, A. Z., & Kleinhauz, M. Community intervention and mental health: A case study of a neighborhood in Jaffa. *Community Mental Health Journal*, 1981, **17**, 123–131.

Best, J. A. Mass media, self-management, and smoking modification. In P. O. Davidson & S. M. Davidson (Eds.), *Behavioral medicine: Changing health lifestyles*. New York: Brunner/Mazel, 1980.

Bogat, G. A. Working with Scouts in improving urban parks. Unpublished doctoral dissertation, DePaul University, 1982.

Bogat, G. A., & Jason, L. A. An evaluation of two visiting programs for elderly community residents. *International Journal of Aging and Human Development*, in press.

Bond, L. A., Rosen, J. C. (Ed.), *Competence & coping during adulthood*. Hanover, N.H.: University Press of New England, 1980.

Brenner, M. H., Mandell, W., Blackman, S., & Silberstein, R. M. Economic conditions and mental hospitalization for functional psychosis. *Journal of Nervous and Mental Disease*, 1967, **145**, 371–384.

Brodsky, S. L., & Miller, K. S. Coercing changes in prisons and mental hospitals. In J. M. Joffe & G. W. Albee (Eds.), *Prevention through political action and social change*. Hanover, N.H.: University Press of New England, 1981.

Bronfenbrenner, U. Is early intervention effective? In M. Guttentag & E. L. Struening (Eds.), *Handbook of evaluation research*. Beverly Hills: Sage, 1975.

Bronfenbrenner, U. Toward an experimental ecology of human development. *American Psychologist*, 1977, **32**, 513–531.

Buhler, L., & McKay, R. Development of women's self-help clinic. In R. B. Stuart (Eds.), *Behavioral self-management*. New York: Brunner/Mazel, 1977.

Caplan, G. *Support systems and community mental health*. New York: Behavioral Publications, 1974.

Cardoza, V. G., Ackerly, W. C., & Leighton, A. H. Improving mental health through community action. *Community Mental Health Journal*, 1975, **11**, 215–227.

Cauce, A. M., Felner, R. D., & Primavera, J. Social support systems in high risk adolescents: Social support and environmental structure. *American Jounral of Community Psychology*, 1982, **10**(4), 417–428.

Cobb, S. Social supports as a moderator of life stress. *Psychosomatic Medicine*, 1976, **38**, 300–314.

Cohen, S., Evans, G. W., Krantz, D. S., & Stokols, D. Physiological, motivational, and cognitive effects of aircraft noise on children. *American Psychologist*, 1980, **35**, 231–243.

Cormier, A., Prefontaine, M., MacDonald, H., & Stuart, R. B. Lifestyle change on the campus: Pilot test of a program to improve student health practices. In P. O. Davidson & S. M. Davidson (Eds.), *Behavioral medicine: Changing health lifestyles*. New York: Brunner/Mazel, 1980.

Cowen, E. L. Some problems in community evaluation research. *Journal of Consulting and Clinical Psychology*, 1978, **46**, 792–805.

Danish, S. Human development and human services: A marriage proposal. In I. Iscoe, B. L. Bloom, & C. D. Spielberger (Eds.), *Community psychology in transition*. Washington: Halsted Press, 1977.

Davis, M. S. Women's liberation groups as a primary preventive mental health strategy. *Community Mental Health Journal*, 1977, **13**, 219–228.

Dubren, R. Self-reinforcement by recorded telephone messages to maintain nonsmoking behavior. *Journal of Consulting and Clinical Psychology*, 1977, **45**, 358–360.

Durlak, J. A. Comparative effectiveness of paraprofessional and professional helpers. *Psychological Bulletin*, 1979, **86**, 80–92.

Eckholm, E. P. The deterioration of mountain environments. *Science*, 1975, **189**, 764–770.

Eisenberg, L. Introduction. Preventive methods in psychiatry: Definitions, principles, and social policy. In I. N. Berlin

& L. A. Stone (Eds.), *Basic handbook of child psychiatry: Prevention and current issues.* Vol. 4. New York: Basic Books, 1979.

Epstein, Y. M. Work-study programs: Do they work? *American Journal of Community Psychology*, 1973, **1**, 159–172.

Everett, P. B. A behavioral approach to transportation systems management. In D. S. Glenwick & L. A. Jason (Eds.), *Behavioral community psychology: Progress and prospects.* New York: Praeger, 1980.

Everett, P. B., Hayward, S. C., & Meyers, A. W. The effect of a token reinforcement procedure in bus ridership. *Journal of Applied Behavior Analysis*, 1974, **7**, 1–9.

Fawcett, S. B., Fletcher, R. K., & Mathews, R. M. Applications of behavior analysis in community education. In D. S. Glenwick & L. A. Jason (Eds.), *Behavioral community psychology: Progress and prospects.* New York: Praeger, 1980.

Fawcett, S. B., Seekins, T., Cohen, S., Elder, J., Geller, S., Jason, L. A., Schnelle, J., & Winett, D. Personal communication, 1982.

Felner, R. D. Primary prevention in pediatric settings: Enhancing coping in vulnerable children. Invited presentation to the 90th Annual Meeting of the American Psychological Association, Washington, D.C., August 1982.

Felner, R. D., & Farber, S. S. Social policy for child custody: A multidisciplinary framework. *American Journal of Orthopsychiatry*, 1980, **50**, 341–347.

Felner, R. D., Ginter, M. A., & Primavera, J. Primary prevention during school transitions: Social support and environmental structure. *American Journal of Community Psychology*, 1982, **10**, 227–290.

Felner, R. D., Norton, P., Cowen, E. L., & Farber, S. S. A prevention program for children experiencing life crisis. *Professional Psychology*, 1981, **12**, 446–452.

Flanagan, J. C. Quality of life. In L. A. Bond & J. C. Rosen (Eds.), *Competence and coping during adulthood.* Hanover, N.H.: University Press of New England, 1980.

Fowler, R. D., & Brodsky, S. L. Development of a correctional-clinical psychology program. *Professional Psychology*, 1978, **9**, 440–447.

Geller, E. S. Applications of behavioral analysis for litter control. In D. S. Glenwick & L. A. Jason (Eds.), *Behavioral community psychology: Progress and prospects.* New York: Praeger, 1980.

Geller, E. S., Casali, J. G., & Johnson, R. P. Seat belt usage: A potential target for applied behavior analysis. *Journal of Applied Behavior Analysis*, 1980, **13**, 669–675.

Glynn, T. J. Community psychology and psychological sense of community: Measurement and application. Paper presented at the American Psychological Association, Toronto, August 1978.

Goodstein, L. D., & Sandler, I. Using psychology to promote human welfare: A conceptual analysis of the role of community psychology. *American Psychologist*, 1978, **33**, 882–892.

Gottlieb, B. H. Opportunities for collaboration with informal support systems. In S. Cooper & W. F. Hodges (Eds.), *The field of mental health consultation*, in press.

Gottlieb, B. H., & Schroter, C. Collaboration and resource exchange between professionals and natural support systems. *Professional Psychology*, 1978, **9**, 614–622.

Heller, K., Price, R. H., & Sher, K. J. Research and evaluation in primary prevention: Issues and guidelines. In

R. H. Price, R. F. Ketterer, B. C. Bader, & J. Monahan (Eds.), *Prevention in mental health. Research, policy, and practice.* Beverly Hills: Sage, 1980.

Hirsch, B. J. Natural support systems and coping with major life changes. *American Journal of Community Psychology*, 1980, **8**, 159–172.

Houton, R. V., Nau, P., & Marini, Z. An analysis of public posting in reducing speeding behavior on an urban highway. *Journal of Applied Behavior Analysis*, 1980, **13**, 393–395.

Iscoe, I. Community psychology and the competent community. *American Psychologist*, 1974, **29**, 607–613.

Jason, L. A. Developing behavioral skills in preventive psychology. Paper presented at the annual meeting of the Association for the Advancement of Behavior Therapy, Toronto, 1981.(a)

Jason, L. A. Training undergraduates in behavior therapy and behavioral community psychology. *Behaviorists for Social Action*, 1981 **3**, 1–8.(b)

Jason, L. A., & Klich, M. Intervening to alter inappropriate advertising in the mass media. *Behavioral Community Newsletter*, 1982, **1**, 9–16.

Jason, L. A., & Liotta, R. Assessing community responsiveness in a metropolitan area. *Evaluation Review*, 1982, **6**, 703–712. (a)

Jason, L. A., & Liotta, R. Pedestrian jaywalking under facilitating and nonfacilitating conditions. *Journal of Applied Behavior Analysis*, 1982, **15**, 469–473. (b)

Jeger, A. M., Slotnick, R. S., & Schure, M. Towards a "self-help/professional collaborative model" of human service delivery. In D. E. Biegel & A. J. Naparstek (Eds.), *Community support systems and mental health: Building linkages.* New York: Springer, 1981.

Jung, R., & Jason, L. A. An attempt to affect the political process. *Division 27 Newsletter*, 1982, **15**, 10.

Kahn, M. W., Williams, C., Galvez, E., Lejero, L., Conrad, R., & Goldstein, G. The Papago psychology service: A community mental health program on an American Indian reservation. *American Journal of Community Psychology*, 1975, **3**, 81–97.

Kalt, N. C., & Zalkind, S. S. Effects of some publicly financed housing programs for the urban poor. *Journal of Community Psychology*, 1976, **4**, 298–302.

Kaluzny, R. L. Evaluation of experimental effects on housing consumption: The Gary income maintenance experiment. In E. W. Stromsdorfer & G. Farkas (Eds.), *Evaluation studies review annual.* Vol. 5. Beverly Hills: Sage, 1980.

Kaplan, H. M., & Bohr, R. H. Change in the mental health field? *Community Mental Health Journal*, 1976, **12**, 244–251.

Kent, M. W. & Rolf, J. E. (Eds.), *Social competence in children.* Hanover, N.H.: University Press of New England; 1979.

Knitzer, J. Advocacy and community psychology. In M. S. Gibbs, J. R. Lachenmeyer, & J. Sigal (Eds.), *Community psychology: Theoretical and empirical approaches.* New York: Gardner Press, 1980.

Larson, L. D., Schnelle, J. F., Kirchner, R., Jr., Carr, A., Domash, M., & Risley, T. R. Reduction of police vehicle accidents through mechanically aided supervision. *Journal of Applied Behavior Analysis*, 1980, **13**, 571–581.

Lavelli, M., Lavelli, S., & Jason, L. A. Preventing hearing loss in underground subways. *Man-Environment Systems*, 1981, **11**, 247–248.

Leutz, W. N. The informal community caregiver: A link between the health care system and local residents.

American Journal of Orthopsychiatry, 1976, 46, 678–688.

Levine, D. The dangers of social action. In D. Harshbarger & R. F. Maley (Eds.), Behavior analysis and systems analysis: An integrative approach to mental health programs. Kalamazoo, Mich.: Behaviordelia, 1974.

Lieberman, M. A., & Mullan, J. T. Does help help? The adaptive consequences of obtaining help from professionals and social networks. American Journal of Community Psychology, 1978, 6, 499–517.

LoLordo, V. M., & Shapiro, K. L. A behavioral approach to population control. In D. S. Glenwick & L. A. Jason (Eds.), Behavioral community psychology: Progress and prospects. New York: Praeger, 1980.

Maccoby, N., & Alexander, J. Use of media in lifestyle programs. In P. O. Davidson & S. M. Davidson (Eds.), Behavioral medicine: Changing health lifestyles. New York: Brunner/Mazel, 1980.

Masters, S. L., & Maynard, R. A. Supported work: A demonstration of subsidized employment. In E. W. Stromsdorfer & G. Farkas (Eds.), Evaluation studies review annual. Vol. 5. Beverly Hills: Sage, 1980.

Maynard, R. A., & Murnane, R. J. The effects of a negative income tax on school performance. In E. W. Stromsdorfer & G. Farkas (Eds.), Evaluation studies review annual. Vol. 5. Beverly Hills: Sage, 1980.

Mitchell, R. E., Barbarin, O. A., & Hurley, D. J., Jr. Problem-solving, resource utilization, and community involvement in a black and a white community. American Journal of Community Psychology, 1981, 9, 233–246.

Mitchell, R. E., & Trickett, E. J. Task force report: Social networks as mediators of social support. An analysis of the effects and determinants of social networks. Community Mental Health Journal, 1980, 16, 27–44.

Moffitt, R. A. The labor supply response in the Gary experiment. In E. W. Stromsdorfer & G. Farkas (Eds.), Evaluation studies review annual. Vol. 5. Beverly Hills: Sage, 1980.

Mollica, M., & Jason, L. A. Modifying snow shoveling behaviors in an urban area. American Journal of Public Health, 1981, 71, 861.

Monaghan, J., Shun Wah, A., Stewart, I., & Smith, L. The role of talkback radio: A study. Journal of Community Psychology, 1978, 6, 351–356.

Moos, R. H. The social climate scales: An overview. Palo Alto, Calif.: Consulting Press, 1974.

Murrell, S. A., & Schulte, P. A procedure for systematic citizen input to community decision-making. American Journal of Community Psychology, 1980, 8(19), 30.

Nunnally, J. C. The study of change in evaluation research: Principles concerning measurements, experimental design, and analysis. In E. L. Struening & M. Guttentag (Eds.), Handbook of evaluation research. Beverly Hills: Sage, 1975.

Perlman, J. E. Grassrooting the system. Social Policy, 1976, 12, 4–20.

Plaut, T.F.A. Preventive policy: The federal perspective. In R. H. Price. R. F. Ketterer, B. C. Bader, & J. Monahan (Eds.), Prevention in mental health: Research, policy, and practice. Beverly Hills: Sage, 1980.

Rappaport, J. Community psychology: Values, research and action. New York: Holt, Rinehart & Winston, 1977.

Reiff, R. Ya gotta believe. In I. Iscoe, B. Bloom, & C. D. Spielberger (Eds.), Community psychology in transition. Washington, D.C.: Halsted Press, 1977.

Reisman, J. M. & Yamokoski, T. Psychotherapy and friend-

ship: An analysis of the communications of friends. Journal of Counseling Psychology, 1974, 21, 269–273.

Rothstein, R. N. Television feedback used to modify gasoline consumption. Behavior Therapy, 1980, 11, 683–688.

Saegert, S. Stress-inducing and -reducing qualities of environments. In H. M. Proshansky, W. H. Ittelson, & L. G. Rivlin (Eds.), Environmental psychology. New York: Holt, Rinehart & Winston, 1976.

Sarason, S. B. The culture of the school and the problem of change. Boston: Allyn and Bacon, 1972.

Sarason, S. B. The psychological sense of community. San Francisco: Jossey-Bass, 1974.

Sarason, S. B. Community psychology, networks, and Mr. Everyman. American Psychologist, 1976, 31, 317–328.

Schanie, C. F., & Sundel, M. A community mental health innovation in mass media preventive education: The alternative project. American Journal of Community Psychology, 1978, 6, 573–581.

Singer, D. G., Singer, J. L., & Zuckerman, D. M. Getting the most out of T.V. Santa Monica, Calif.: Goodyear, 1981.

Skeels, H. M. Adult status of children with contrasting early life experiences: A follow-up study. Monographs of the Society for Research in Child Development, 1966, 31 (No. 3).

Smith, R. A. Measuring neighborhood cohesion: A review and some suggestions. Human Ecology, 1975, 3, 143–160.

Stokes, T. F., & Fawcett, S. B. Evaluating municipal policy: An analysis of a refuse packaging program. Journal of Applied Behavior Analysis, 1977, 10, 391–398.

Sue, S., & Zane, N. Learned helplessness theory and community psychology. In M. S. Gibbs, J. R. Lachenmeyer, & J. Sigal (Eds.), Community psychology: Theoretical and empirical approaches. New York: Gardner Press, 1980.

Susser, M. Epidemiological models. In E. L. Struening & M. Guttentag (Eds.), Handbook of evaluation research. Beverly Hills: Sage, 1975.

Tornatzky, L. G., & Fergus, E. O. Innovation and diffusion in mental health: The community lodge. In A. M. Jeger & R. Slotnick (Eds.), Community mental health: A behavioral-ecological perspective. New York: Plenum Press, 1982.

Tuma, N. B., Hannan, M. T., & Groeneveld, L. P. Dynamic analysis of event histories. In E. W. Stromsdorfer & G. Farkas (Eds.), Evaluation studies review annual. Vol. 5. Beverly Hills: Sage, 1980.

Tuso, M. A., & Geller, E. S. Behavior analysis applied to environmental/ecological problems: A review. Journal of Applied Behavior Analysis, 1976, 9, 526.

Wallston, B. The effects of maternal employment on children. Journal of Child Psychology and Psychiatry, 1973, 14, 81–95.

Wandersman, A., & Gimartino, G. A. Community and individual difference characteristics as influences on initial participation. American Journal of Community Psychology, 1980, 8, 217–228.

Weisbrod, B. A., & Helming, M. What benefit-cost analysis can and cannot do: The case of treating the mentally ill. In E. W. Stromsdorfer & G. Farkas (Eds.), Evaluation studies review annual. Vol. 5. Beverly Hills: Sage, 1980.

White, D. M. "Mediacracy": Mass media and psychopathology. In J. M. Joffe & G. W. Albee (Eds.), Prevention through political action and social change. Hanover, N.H.: University Press of New England, 1981.

Wicker, A. W. Undermanning theory and research: Implications for the study of psychological and behavioral effects of excess human populations. In H. M. Proshansky, W. H. Ittelson, & L. G. Rivlin (Eds.), *Environmental psychology*. New York: Holt, Rinehart & Winston, 1976.

Wiest, W. M., & Squier, L. H. Incentives and reinforcement: A behavioral approach to fertility. *Journal of Social Issues*, 1974, **30**, 235–264.

Winett, R. A. An emerging approach to energy conservation. In D. S. Glenwick & L. A. Jason (Eds.), *Behavioral community psychology: Progress and prospects*. New York: Praeger, 1980.

Winett, R. A., Stefanek, M., & Riley, A. W. Preventive strategies with children and families: Small groups, organizations, communities. In T. H. Ollendick & M. Hersen (Eds.), *Handbook of child psychopathology*. New York: Plenum Press, 1982.

Wolkon, G. H. & Moriwaki, S. The ombudsman: A serendipitous mental health intervention. *Community Mental Health Journal*, 1977, **13**, 229–238.

Zautra, A., & Goodhart, D. Quality of life indicators: A review of the literature. *Community Mental Health Review*, 1979, **4**, 1–10.

# AFTERWORD: PREVENTION—
# THE THREAT AND THE PROMISE

## John C. Glidewell

I read the chapters of this book with some hope. Hope is based on estimates of the future—in a word, prospects. Probably all incentives are prospects; they don't work unless there is some promise of something. For prevention to work, the promise, it seems to me, is relief from a threat, relief from the fear of a likely and painful event, clear and close at hand.

After 30 years of trying to prevent the occurrence of a variety of threatening events—illnesses, accidents, floods, bankruptcy, riots, lying, stealing, and death itself—I still ponder about why people would rather buy insurance to pay for treatment than take preventive actions to ward off such threats. This book made me ponder again, and here are the notes on my pondering.

## On Public and Professional Support

### URGENCY

Preventive actions are rarely urgent. Pain and distress, illness and injury, here and now, demand urgent action. Under such urgent, emergency conditions the sufferers will act quickly, will accept great costs, will follow the advice of an expert, will allow even aides and orderlies to boss them around. On the other hand, the more distant *prospect* of pain and distress, illness and injury allows for time, delay, and more careful consideration. Persons can postpone the costs and shop around; can seek advice from many experts, and simply will not allow aides and orderlies to boss them around. Further, the expertise about prevention is less consistent and convincing than the expertise about surgery. Will cutting down on saturated fats *really* keep you from having a heart attack? Nobody *really* knows.

The great power of the healer (prevention's toughest competitor) is the arcane ability to bring blessed relief from pain and distress, or even from death. The most dramatic and heartfelt expression of escape from dire consequence is, "You saved my life!" As long as healers carry this kind of weight, they are going to stimulate support from the public and from other professional practitioners—ever so much more support than preventers can stimulate.

The great impotence of the preventer is that the people to be influenced feel fine, have no pain, and are in no hurry to find relief from feeling fine. A much esteemed former colleague had the task of improving the diet of pregnant teenagers. "How," she asked me constantly, "can I keep them sick longer? Once they feel great, I don't have a chance."

But people who feel fine do often get immunizations and physical exams, and even wear hard hats. Why? They see clear and dramatic examples of distress and

310

likely pain. When there were polio epidemics, and then immunization became available, community immunization levels climbed readily. Once the vaccine had time to work and there were no more polio epidemics, community immunization levels dropped. I remember vividly an interview with a hard-working mother of three who was going it alone. I asked why she had not taken advantage of free shots for her children. She explained that she'd lose a day from work. (The free clinics did require very long waiting times.) I asked if her children's protection from polio was worth a day's pay. She looked at me closely and answered, "If I don't get them shot, what are the chances my children will get polio?"

I tried everything I could think of to avoid that question, and after a long painful pause, I said, "About one in a hundred thousand."

She gave me a look of the most intense disgust I ever experienced; then she gave voice to her feelings: "Shit, man, get out of here."

The trouble with prevention is that the threat is so rarely urgent and likely.

### VISIBILITY

If prevention is successful only few people know it happened; even fewer know who did it. Did you ever notice the prevention of behavior disorders in schoolchildren, or see a TV special about a thriving, healthy child who *might* have been injured, confused, or hobbled by a severe anxiety? Healthy, thriving children, strangely, are seldom newsworthy, unless they excell in some remarkable way, and their excellence is never attributed to successful prevention.

If *primary* prevention is done really well, nobody much knows that it was done at all. To be really good, prevention should be unnoticed, because one never knows which individuals in a population at risk would have gotten sick had there been no prevention.

### APPRECIATION

As long as the preventive process is imperceptible, nobody knows whom to thank. Did you ever feel deeply appreciative for the fact that you don't have cholera? For effective sewage disposal? For competent restaurant inspection? The most brilliant preventive interventionist simply cannot expect a bequest from a deeply grateful rich family.

### ARCANE KNOWLEDGE

In the prevention of pain and distress, there has always been a gap between knowledge and practice. Snow took the handle off the Broad Street pump to stop the London cholera epidemic long before a germ theory of disease was thought of. In the prevention of psychological pain and distress, the gap is even wider. But prevention of behavior disorders in schoolchildren *is* possible—just as the prevention of cholera was—prior to a full understanding of the linkage between stressors in the environment and distress in the person. The trouble is that preventive actions are often very convincing. Giving up steak really won't assure you a strong heart. Developing or activating a social support system won't assure you self-confidence or self-esteem or psychological well-being. An active social support system *can* prevent anxiety or depression after the loss of a spouse, but it won't assure you contentment after your grief.

The moral of this story is that prevention lacks urgency, visibility, appreciation, and demonstrated arcane knowledge, and those inherent limitations make public and professional support of preventive programs rather lukewarm. To gain public and professional support, try to prevent some problem that:

1. Is specific and visible
2. Is likely and painful
3. Has a plausible rationale
4. Can be attributed to some community agency
5. Doesn't cause something worse.

## On Strategies

### MODIFY THE ENVIRONMENT

Wandersman and his colleagues articulate in this volume the essence of the idea: "The most obvious but by no means the easiest prevention programs . . . involve primary proactive prevention which would remove the stressor." More enabling building designs, more flexible barriers, more defensible and controllable space arrangements—all these strategies hold promise. But if they were politically and biosocially successful, they would be unnoticed by citizens, they would be unappreciated by the "clients," and important innovations would not be readily selected and retained in the culture in the process of social evolution.

### DEVELOP COPING SKILLS

Ecology is more than environment; it is organism-environment interaction. Vincent and Trickett articulate *the* ecological analogy and they make clear the variety of coping skills entailed in such interaction in the two high schools Kelly and company studied so thoroughly. Environmental changes come slowly; coping skills are more immediate.

In studying a thousand accounts of coping, I have found one thing I'm confident of: the people tell a story of hanging in there, hurting, hammering, staying alive, surviving, struggling. And also searching, exploring, even in frightening territories, discovering new facts, new ideas, new talents, new ways of living, and doing it all in such an unobtrusive and very private way that few people notice. Nowhere is this private process more vital than in the health psychology that Albino explicates or in the discussion of the tasks people face in going through transitions elaborated by Felner et al. Also, stress intensifies a person's identity by changing that identity, and people discover more clearly who they really are and who they are becoming and who they could be.

The remarkable resourcefulness of the human cognitive apparatus always astounds me. The remarkable fact to me is not that there is so much maladaptation; it is that there is so much sustaining coping. I marvel at the changes in the perception of the world, the use of the classical psychological defenses, and the reformulation of problems—all these in the service of maintaining and sharpening the self-image and managing the exchange of resources with the world. We humans use not only our heads to meditate, ruminate, read, pray, figure, puzzle, and mull over, but also our hearts to grieve, cry, sit and brood, take heart, sing the blues, muster courage, and keep us trying. We often do it rather awkwardly. The coping is often—not always—inefficient, dawdling, confusing, scary, and bumbling, but when you see so many successes in survival, in hanging in there, the whole thing could be a great store of truly creative acts, usually accomplished in private, so unobtrusively that nobody notices.

#### ACTIVATE SOCIAL SUPPORT SYSTEMS

Economic, social, and personal resources are linked in a series of deviation amplifying loops that Allen and Britt and Seidman and Rapkin have diagrammed so clearly. To activate a social support system is to activate economic and personal systems, too. But support systems are also control systems, and to some degree the need for autonomy conflicts with the need for support, in a deviation-correcting loop. The activation of the amplifying and correcting cycles in the ecology of social support and social control has often been shown to buffer stress, but the buffering processes are yet to be clearly explained. Indeed, as

we can see from Felner et al., there are times when the individual's level of social support is as much an indication of adaptive abilities and coping skills as it is a buffer of stress. As always in prevention, we need not wait for full explanation to take preventive action. But don't believe that the public will accept that friends and relatives are uniformly supportive.

Training a community psychologist to activate, extend, or modify social support systems is a sobering task. Price's guidelines certainly apply, but in this approach to prevention one could reduce the effectiveness of a natural, spontaneous process. Perhaps the most enabling point of intervention is the point at which social norms conflict: abortion, single parenthood, changed roles for women and men, divorce, widowhood.

#### INDUCE HARDINESS

Economic and social resources are linked to personal resources. Is the stress seen as a challenge or a hassle? Is the situation amenable to personal control or just environmental control? Does coping provide a flexible means to a firmly held goal? If the stress is a challenge, to be met by flexible means of reaching a firmly held goal, all under some personal control, it seems likely that the stress will cause less illness. But can a preventive interventionist train people to be hardy? It hasn't really been tried. If one could, one would get more attention, gratitude, plausibility, and thus support.

#### CREATE NEW SOCIAL SETTINGS

I need not belabor all the ideas for the creation of new settings, but the legacy of Seymour Sarason is alive in most of the papers in this book. And the creation of new social settings will also get you attention, appreciation, plausibility, and support.

#### TRACK AND FEEDBACK

Lorion's guidelines for evaluation are essential. If an enterprise such as prevention is to maintain or gain any public and professional support at all, it is vital to track its results as carefully and as clearly as technique allows. It is even more vital to communicate these results to the public and the professions who must provide the support.

Prevention has so little going for it that it needs all the help it can get.

# AUTHOR INDEX

# SUBJECT INDEX

# ABOUT THE EDITORS AND CONTRIBUTORS

**Robert D. Felner,** Ph.D., is Director of Clinical/Community Training and Associate Professor at Auburn University in Auburn, Alabama. Prior to his present position, he was Assistant Professor of Psychology at Yale University. He received his B.A. in Psychology from the University of Connecticut and his Ph.D. from the University of Rochester in 1977. He is a member of the National Institute of Mental Health Review Committee and Editorial Board of the *American Journal of Community Psychology*, the *Journal of Divorce*, the *Journal of Social and Clinical Psychology*, *Professional Psychology*, and the *Journal of Clinical Child Psychology*. He has served as a Regional Coordinator for the Division of Community Psychology and Chair of that Division's Task Force on Internships and Field Training and is currently its Membership Chair. Dr. Felner has authored over 60 articles, chapters, and papers, primarily in the areas of stress, coping, and vulnerability in children and families, primary prevention, and child custody.

**Leonard A. Jason** is the Director of Clinical Training at DePaul University. He has served as National Coordinator of Division 27 (Community Psychology) of the American Psychological Association and Coordinator of the Community Research Special Interest Group of the Association for the Advancement of Behavior Therapy. He is on the Editorial Board of the *American Journal of Community Psychology* and *Professional Psychology* and co-editor with David Glenwick the book entitled *Behavioral Community Psychology: Progress and Prospects*. Dr. Jason has published over 90 articles on varied topics including: behavioral community psychology, behavioral assessment, program evaluation, and preventive approaches in schools.

**John N. Moritsugu** is an Associate Professor of Psychology at Pacific Lutheran University, Tacoma, Washington. He has also held the position of Visiting Lecturer and Co-Director of the Community Psychology Program at the University of Waikato, Hamilton, New Zealand. Presently he is National Coordinator for the Division of Community Psychology of the American Psychological Association. His area of research and writing have included: minority mental health issues, community organization, and the adaptation problems of Eurasians in America. He received a B.A. in Psychology at the University of Hawaii. His M.A. and Ph.D. in Clinical Psychology were awarded by the University of Rochester.

**Stephanie S. Farber** is an Associate in Research at Yale University and is also a Psychology Associate at the West Haven Veterans Administration Medical Center. She received her B.S. from Barnard College and her Ph.D. from the Union Graduate School under Seymour B. Sarason. From 1978–1981 she served as Co-Director of the Families in Transition Project at Yale University. Her scholarly and research activities have focused on life transitions and inter-disciplinary collaborations for the development of social policy for children.

**George W. Albee** is Professor of Psychology at the University of Vermont. He and Justine M. Joffe are General Editors of a series of volumes on the primary prevention of psychopathology. In 1977–78 Albee was Chair of the Task Panel on Primary Prevention for President Carter's Commission on Mental Health and 20 years ago he was Director of the Task Force on Manpower for the Joint Commission on Mental Illness and Health. His research and scholarly activities have been in the area of primary prevention, the psychopathology of prejudice, and human resources affecting the delivery of psychological services. He has been President of the American Psychological Association (1970), The New England Psychological Association (1980), and Division 12 (Clinical) of APA. In 1975 he received the Distinguished Professional Contribution Award from APA and in 1981 a similar award from Division 27 (Community) of APA.

**Dr. Judith E. Albino** is Professor of Behavioral Sciences at the State University of New York at Buffalo where she is involved in research in health behavior and patient compliance with therapeutic recommendations. Her research on psychosocial response to dental-facial aesthetics has been funded by the National Institute for Dental Research. Dr. Albino teaches in the areas of dental behavioral sciences and health program evaluation. She is President-elect of Behavioral Scientists in Dental Research and is a member of the Executive Committee of the Division of Community Psychology of the American Psychological Association.

**LaRue Allen**, Ph.D., is an Assistant Professor of Clinical/Community Psychology at the University of Maryland in College Park, and a faculty affiliate at Yale University's Bush Center for Child Development and Social Policy. Her research focuses on the pro-

motion of competence and management of stress among children, women, and minorities.

**Arlene Andrews** is a doctoral student at the University of South Carolina in Clinical/Community Psychology. In addition, she is currently director of Sister Care, a service for battered women.

**G. Anne Bogat** received her doctoral degree in Clinical-Community Psychology at DePaul University. She is now an Assistant Professor of Psychology at Michigan State University.

**David W. Britt**, Ph.D., is a Clinical/Research Sociologist from the University of North Carolina at Chapel Hill. Before becoming a principal with Allen and Britt Associates, Dr. Britt has been on the faculties of Vanderbilt, Florida Atlantic and Nova Universities. Most recently he has held the position of Professor of Public Administration and Director of the Doctoral Program in Public Administration at Nova University. Dr. Britt's current research and clinical interests focus on economic, social, and personal resource development as focal points for intervention with both individuals and organizations.

**Emory L. Cowen** is Professor of Psychology (Psychiatry and Education) and Director of the Center for Community Study and the Primary Mental Health Project at the University of Rochester. He is a past president of American Psychological Association (APA) Division 27 (Community Psychology) a recipient of the Distinguished Contributions Award from that Division, and an associate editor of the *American Journal of Community Psychology*. He was a member of the Primary Prevention Task Panel of the President's Commission on Mental Health and has authored some 150 plus articles, chapters, and books in the field of Clinical and Community Psychology.

**Steven J. Danish** is Professor of Human Development at The Pennsylvania State University. He received his Ph.D. in Counseling Psychology from Michigan State University. Dr. Danish is a Fellow of APA and has his ABPP in Counseling Psychology. In 1981–82 he served as President of the Division of Community Psychology. His current research interests are designing and evaluating interventions for primary prevention and enhancement as well as sport psychology.

**Joseph A. Durlak**, Ph.D., received his final degree from Vanderbilt University in 1971. He served in the U.S. Army as a clinical psychologist for five years and then joined the faculty at Southern Illinois University in Carbondale. Currently he is an Associate Professor in Psychology at Loyola University of Chicago. His major interests in Community Psychology are preventive services and the use of paraprofessionals.

**Carrie Fancett** is a doctoral student in the School of Psychology at the University of South Carolina. Her research interests are in the areas of Environmental Psychology and the schools as well as stepfamilies.

**Nancy L. Galambos** is a doctoral candidate in the Department of Human Development and Family Studies at The Pennsylvania State University. Her main research interests are in child and adolescent development, with a focus on the social and academic adjustment of children affected by social trends of maternal employment and divorce.

**John C. Glidewell**, Ph.D., is Professor of Psychology at Peabody College of Vanderbilt University. Prior to joining the faculty there he served on the faculties of Washington University in St. Louis and the University of Chicago. In 1979 he received a Distinguished Contributions Award from Division 27 (Community) of the American Psychological Association. Currently he is Editor of the *American Journal of Community Psychology*.

**Kenneth Heller** is Professor of Psychology at Indiana University. A Ph.D. of Pennsylvania State University, he has been Visiting Scholar at the University of Michigan Institute for Social Research, Visiting Professor at the University of California (Irvine), and Special Research Fellow and Visiting Lecturer at the Laboratory of Community Psychiatry at Harvard Medical School. He is an APA Fellow, and from 1974–1978 served on the Board of Consulting Editors of the *Journal of Consulting and Clinical Psychology*. He served on the Panel of Advisory Editors for the Special Issue on Prevention published by the *American Journal of Community Psychology* in 1982. He is a co-author with John Monahan of *Psychology and Community Change* and with A. P. Goldstein and L. B. Sechrest of *Psychotherapy and the Psychology of Behavior Change*. His current research interests are in prevention, social support, coping with stress, and the factors involved in individual, organizational, and community change.

**Laura Kastner**, Ph.D., received her degree in Psychology in 1980 from the University of Virginia. She is currently on the faculty of the Medical Center of the University of Washington in Seattle. Her major research interests are in the area of teenage pregnancy.

**Idamarie Laquatra** received her Ph.D. in Applied Nutrition from The Pennsylvania State University. She is currently a postdoctoral fellow at the University of Medicine and Dentistry of New Jersey in Newark. Her major research interests are counseling skills of nutrition practitioners and preventive and therapeutic behavior change strategies.

**Raymond P. Lorion** is Professor of Psychology and Director of Graduate Programs in School and Community Psychology at the University of Tennessee, Knoxville. He received his B.S. degree in Psychology and French from Tufts University and his Ph.D. in Clinical Psychology from the University of Rochester in 1972. Prior to joining the University of Tennessee faculty, Dr. Lorion was on the faculties of the University of Rochester and Temple University. He is spending the 1982–83 year as a Visiting Scientist to the Center for Studies of Prevention at NIMH. Dr. Lorion's current research interests include the design and evaluation of strategies for identifying and preventing at a primary and/or secondary level educational, emotional, and behavioral dysfunctions in preschool and primary grade children. Dr. Lorion's research includes the design and assessment of alternative methodologies for evaluating preventive outcomes.

**Edward Mulvey** received his Ph.D. in Psychology in 1982 from the University of Virginia. He is currently a Post-Doctoral Fellow at Carnegie-Mellon University and an Assistant Professor at Western Psychiatric Institute in Pittsburgh. His major research interests include law and psychology, especially in relation to children and families, and community interventions in the criminal justice system.

**Richard H. Price** is Professor and Chairman of the Community Psychology Program at the University of Michigan. He received his Ph.D. from the University of Illinois in 1966. He served as Assistant and Associate Professor at Indiana University and Visiting Associate Professor at Stanford University. He is currently President-Elect of the Division of Community Psychology (27) of the American Psychological Association. He is the author and editor of a number of books in the area of mental health and prevention, including *Abnormal Behavior: Perspectives in Conflict, Community Mental Health: Social Action and Reaction,* and *Abnormal Behavior in the Human Context.* Most recently, he has coedited with Richard F. Ketterer, Barbara C. Bader and John Monahan, *Prevention in Mental Health: Research, Policy and Practice*. He has served on the Editorial Review Board for the *Journal of Abnormal Psychology* and for the *American Journal of Community Psychology*. His research interests include primary prevention and coping and adaptation in the social environment.

**Judith Primavera** is a doctoral candidate at Yale University, having received her B.A. from Mt. Holyoke College and her M.A. from Yale University. From 1981–1982 she was a clinical intern at the Yale Child Study Center. Her research interests include the development of prevention programs in the schools for high-risk students and adolescents and the impact of family disruption on family members.

**Bruce Rapkin** is a graduate student in Community and Clinical Psychology at the University of Illinois at Urbana-Champaign. He has also worked at the Center for Community Study in Rochester, New York. Rapkin's interests include the study of the social ecology of aging, economic factors, and psychological adjustment, and the analysis of interpersonal networks.

**N. Dickon Reppucci** received his Ph.D. in Clinical Psychology in 1968 from Harvard University. He has taught at Yale (1968–1976) and became Professor of Psychology at the University of Virginia in 1976, where he is currently Director of Graduate Training in Community Psychology and Preventive Intervention, and in Social Ecology and Development. Professor Reppucci is the author of more than 50 professional articles and book chapters. His current research interests include law, psychology and children, youth sports, and community and preventive interventions.

**David Riddle** is a graduate student in Clinical/Community Psychology at the University of South Carolina. His research interests are in the areas of Health Psychology and Clinical Psychology.

**Seymour B. Sarason**, Ph.D., has been at Yale since 1945. He is Professor of Psychology and a faculty member of the School of Organization and Management and the Institution for Social and Policy Studies. In 1978–79, Sarason was President of the Division of Clinical Psychology of the American Psychological Association. He has received the Distinguished Contributions Awards from Division 12 (Clinical) of APA in 1969, and Division 27 (Community) of APA in 1975. A similar award was presented to Dr. Sarason from the Divisions of Education and Psychology of the American Association of Mental

Deficiency in 1973 and he received a Special Award in the Field of Mental Retardation from AAMD in 1974. He is the author or co-author of 19 books and over 50 articles and chapters. His most recent books are *Psychology Misdirected, The Culture of the School and the Problem of Change* (second edition), and *Psychology and Social Action*.

**Edward Seidman** is Professor of Psychology and Director of Clinical and Community Psychology Training at the University of Illinois at Urbana-Champaign. At the national level he is chairperson of the Council of Community Psychology Program Directors and a member of the American Psychological Association's Task Force on Public Policy. Professor Seidman has done extensive research in the area of psychotherapy as well as the development, implementation, and evaluation of a wide array of innovations in the areas of mental health, juvenile justice, and education. His current research and scholarship include the study of mutual help groups, economics and psychosocial dysfunction, primary prevention and social policy. He is editor of the forthcoming, *Handbook of Social Intervention*.

**Stanley Sue** is Professor of Psychology at the University of California, Los Angeles. He previously served on the faculty at the University of Washington and was the Director of Clinical-Community Psychology Training at the National Asian American Psychology Training Center in San Francisco. His research interests include mental health service delivery systems and Asian American mental health. He has coauthored the *Mental Health of Asian Americans* with James K. Morishima.

**Ralph Swindle** is a Community Clinical Psychologist who has been employed for the past four years as a Research Associate in the Evaluation Research Department of the South Central CMHC in Bloomington, Indiana. He received his B.A. in Social Ecology at the University of California at Irvine, and his Ph.D. in Community-Clinical Psychology at Indiana University. He is currently interested in clarifying the inter-relationship between concepts of social competencies, social support processes, and stressful life events.

**Dr. Edison J. Trickett** is Professor and Director of Clinical/Community Training at the University of Maryland, College Park. He received his Ph.D. from Ohio State University, did post-doctoral work in the Social Ecology Laboratory at Stanford University, and was on the faculty at Yale. His research has focused on the metaphor of ecology as a framework for studying mental health consultation, the assessment of social environments, and the design of preventive interventions. He is currently (1982–83) serving as President of the Division of Community Psychology of the American Psychological Association.

**Trudy A. Vincent**, M.A., is a graduate student in the Clinical/Community Psychology Program at the University of Maryland. Most recently, she has coauthored (with Edison Trickett and James Kelly) a book chapter entitled "The Spirit of Ecological Inquiry in Community Psychology." She is currently working as a staff psychologist at Chelternham Center, a psychoeducational treatment center for emotionally disturbed children and adolescents, while completing her dissertation in the area of social support and adaptation.

**Abraham Wandersman** received his Ph.D. in 1976 from Cornell University in the areas of Social and Environmental Psychology, Child and Family Psychopathology and Sociology. He is currently Associate Professor of Psychology at the University of South Carolina. His major interests are in the areas of citizen participation in neighborhoods and prevention. He is Associate Editor of the *Journal of Voluntary Action Research* and serves on the editorial board of *Population and Environment*.

**Edwin S. Zolik** is Professor of Psychology and Director of the Community Psychology Program at DePaul University in Chicago, Illinois. For 1977–78 he received a Fullbright Fellowship to study Mental Health Service Delivery in Poland. His current interests are in the development and evaluation of training in Community Psychology and the area of prevention, particulary through systems change, consultations and social policy.

# Pergamon General Psychology Series

Editors: Arnold P. Goldstein, Syracuse University
Leonard Krasner, SUNY at Stony Brook